Routledge Revivals

England in the Nineteenth Century
Volume 2

Originally published in 1930, this volume is a continuation of the excellently received *England in the Nineteenth Century, 1801-1805* and covers literature, art and science as well as military, political and legal history in England, Scotland, and India, Canada and Australia.

England in the Nineteenth Century
1806-1810

A.F. Fremantle

First published in 1930 by George Allen & Unwin Ltd.

This edition first published in 2024 by Routledge
4 Park Square, Milton Park, Abingdon, Oxon, OX14 4RN

and by Routledge
605 Third Avenue, New York, NY 10158.

Routledge is an imprint of the Taylor & Francis Group, an informa business

© 1930 A.F. Fremantle.

The right of A.F. Fremantle to be identified as the author of this work has been asserted by him in accordance with sections 77 and 78 of the Copyright, Designs and Patents Act 1988.

All rights reserved. No part of this book may be reprinted or reproduced or utilised in any form or by any electronic, mechanical, or other means, now known or hereafter invented, including photocopying and recording, or in any information storage or retrieval system, without permission in writing from the publishers.

ISBN 13: 978-1-032-90164-0 (hbk)
ISBN 13: 978-1-003-54640-5 (ebk)
ISBN 13: 978-1-032-90165-7 (pbk)
Book DOI 10.4324/9781003546405

ENGLAND

IN THE NINETEENTH CENTURY
1806—1810

By

A. F. FREMANTLE

*La puissance d'un peuple se compose
de son histoire.*   NAPOLEON

LONDON
GEORGE ALLEN & UNWIN LTD
MUSEUM STREET

FIRST PUBLISHED IN 1930

All rights reserved
PRINTED IN GREAT BRITAIN BY
UNWIN BROTHERS LTD., WOKING

The solemn fraternity which a great nation composes—gathered together, in a stormy season, under the shade of ancestral feeling.
WORDSWORTH—*The Convention of Cintra*

AUTHOR'S NOTE

THIS volume is a continuation of England in the Nineteenth Century, 1801–1806. Chapter II belongs properly to the earlier period; while most of Chapters I and VI are introductory to the history of the century as a whole.

CONTENTS

Chapter I

LITERATURE, ART, AND SCIENCE

	PAGE
THE REVIVAL OF LETTERS AND ART	17
BLAKE	18
CRABBE	19
CAMPBELL	21
OTHER POETS	22
THE POETIC REVIVAL	23
WORDSWORTH, COLERIDGE, AND SOUTHEY	24
SCOTT	35
BYRON	37
MOORE	39
HOGG	40
DIBDIN	40
MUSIC	41
THE STAGE	44
PAINTING	49
SCULPTURE	54
ARCHITECTURE	54
PROSE	57
GODWIN	58
MALTHUS	60
PALEY	63
BENTHAM	63
NOVELS	66
MARIA EDGEWORTH	67
LIGHTER PROSE	69
THE REVIEWS	71
THE UNIVERSITIES	75
PORSON	76
EDUCATION	76
ASTRONOMY	79
GEOLOGY	80
PHYSICS AND CHEMISTRY	81
BOTANY	86

12 ENGLAND IN THE NINETEENTH CENTURY

	PAGE
BIOLOGY AND MEDICINE	86
INVENTIONS	90
ENGINEERING	92

CHAPTER II

INDIA AND THE EAST
(1801—1806)

THE GOVERNMENT OF INDIA	96
LORD WELLESLEY AS GOVERNOR-GENERAL	99
ANNEXATIONS FROM OUDH	102
THE INDIAN TRADE	104
THE CIVIL SERVICE	106
THE CALCUTTA COLLEGE	108
WELLESLEY AND ANGLO-INDIAN SOCIETY	109
WELLESLEY AND THE DIRECTORS	110
THE MARATHA CONFEDERACY	111
TREATY OF BASSEIN	112
ARTHUR WELLESLEY'S EARLY CAREER	114
THE ARMY IN INDIA	115
OUTBREAK OF THE MARATHA WAR	118
CAMPAIGNS OF 1803	122
CAMPAIGNS OF 1804–1805	128
CLOSE OF LORD WELLESLEY'S GOVERNOR-GENERALSHIP	133
GOVERNOR-GENERALSHIP OF CORNWALLIS	136
BARLOW'S SUCCESSION AS GOVERNOR-GENERAL	137
OTHER INTERESTS OF THE EAST INDIA COMPANY	140
CEYLON	141

CHAPTER III

THE MINISTRY OF ALL THE TALENTS
(JANUARY 1806—MARCH 1807)

OPENING OF PARLIAMENT	144
HONOURS PAID TO PITT	146
THE NEW MINISTRY	147
DEBATE ON ELLENBOROUGH'S POSITION	151
BUDGET OF 1806	152

CONTENTS

	PAGE
WINDHAM'S MILITARY REFORMS	153
HOSTILITIES WITH PRUSSIA	154
NAVAL OPERATIONS	156
NEGOTIATIONS WITH FRANCE	158
RESTORATION OF PEACE WITH PRUSSIA	161
MEASURES FOR THE ABOLITION OF THE SLAVE TRADE	162
IMPEACHMENT OF MELVILLE	164
EXPEDITION TO SOUTH AMERICA	166
BATTLE OF MAIDA	169
RUPTURE OF THE NEGOTIATIONS WITH FRANCE	172
DEATH OF FOX	174
THE YEAR 1806 AS A TURNING POINT	175
RECONSTITUTION OF THE MINISTRY	179
MEETING OF A NEW PARLIAMENT	180
THE BERLIN DECREE	181
PARLIAMENTARY AFFAIRS	183
FALL OF THE MINISTRY	184
THE DARDANELLES EXPEDITION	189
THE EGYPTIAN EXPEDITION	194

CHAPTER IV
THE DUKE OF PORTLAND'S ADMINISTRATION
(MARCH 1807—SEPTEMBER 1809)

PORTLAND'S ADMINISTRATION	196
GENERAL ELECTION	199
THE EGYPTIAN EXPEDITION	200
THE BRAZIL EXPEDITION	203
ARMY REORGANIZATION	204
PARLIAMENTARY AFFAIRS	206
TREATY OF TILSIT	208
THE DANISH EXPEDITION	209
HOSTILITIES WITH DENMARK	214
RESULTS OF THE EXPEDITION	216
RELATIONS WITH PORTUGAL	222
THE ORDERS IN COUNCIL AND THE CONTINENTAL SYSTEM	224
RELATIONS WITH THE UNITED STATES	228
EFFECT OF THE ORDERS	229
LANCASHIRE UNREST	231
BUDGET OF 1808	232

	PAGE
PARLIAMENTARY AFFAIRS	232
THE WAR ON THE CONTINENT AND IN THE MEDITERRANEAN	234
OUTBREAK OF THE PENINSULAR WAR	237
BATTLE OF VIMEIRO	240
ARMISTICE	242
CONVENTION OF CINTRA	243
MILITARY SITUATION IN SPAIN	245
MOORE'S CHARACTER	249
MOORE'S ADVANCE TO SAHAGUN	250
RETREAT TO CORUÑA	254
BATTLE OF CORUÑA	257
RETURN OF THE ARMY	260
INQUIRY REGARDING THE DUKE OF YORK	261
OTHER PARLIAMENTARY INQUIRIES	262
PARLIAMENTARY REFORM	264
OTHER MEASURES IN PARLIAMENT	266
FOREIGN RELATIONS	267
PROGRESS OF THE WAR	269
THE WAR IN THE PENINSULA	272
BATTLE OF TALAVERA	275
WELLESLEY'S RETIREMENT	281
OPERATIONS IN THE MEDITERRANEAN	284
THE WALCHEREN EXPEDITION	285
DISSOLUTION OF THE PORTLAND MINISTRY	289
DUEL BETWEEN CASTLEREAGH AND CANNING	292

CHAPTER V

PERCEVAL'S ADMINISTRATION TO THE ESTABLISHMENT
OF THE REGENCY
(OCTOBER 1809—DECEMBER 1810)

THE NEW ADMINISTRATION	294
THE O.P. RIOTS	297
AFFAIRS IN PARLIAMENT, 1810—THE WALCHEREN EXPEDITION	298
THE HONOUR TO WELLINGTON	300
CHATHAM'S RESIGNATION	301
NAVAL AFFAIRS	302
COMMITMENT OF JONES TO NEWGATE	305
COMMITMENT OF BURDETT TO THE TOWER	306

CONTENTS

	PAGE
THE BURDETT RIOTS	308
IMPRISONMENT OF COBBETT	313
POSITION OF PARLIAMENTARY PARTIES	314
THE BULLION COMMITTEE	316
THE CONTINENTAL SYSTEM AND THE WAR	320
RELATIONS WITH THE UNITED STATES	325
WELLINGTON'S DIFFICULTIES IN THE PENINSULA	331
THE PORTUGUESE ARMY	339
MASSÉNA'S INVASION OF PORTUGAL	343
OPERATIONS OF THE LIGHT DIVISION	344
MASSÉNA'S ADVANCE TO BUSSACO	347
BATTLE OF BUSSACO	348
THE RETREAT TO THE LINES	352
MASSÉNA'S RETIREMENT TO SANTAREM	357
MENTAL DERANGEMENT OF GEORGE III	359
ESTRANGEMENT BETWEEN NAPOLEON AND ALEXANDER	360

Chapter VI

INDIA (1807–1810), OTHER POSSESSIONS, SCOTLAND, SOCIAL ENGLAND AT THE CLOSE OF THE DECADE

MINTO'S GOVERNOR-GENERALSHIP OF INDIA	363
MADRAS MUTINY	367
OVERSEAS EXPEDITIONS FROM INDIA—MACAO	376
MAURITIUS	377
THE MOLUCCAS	379
NEW SOUTH WALES	380
BLIGH'S GOVERNORSHIP AND DEPOSITION	383
THE CAPE OF GOOD HOPE	386
OTHER AFRICAN POSSESSIONS	388
THE WEST INDIES	388
CANADA	389
SCOTLAND—THE HIGHLANDS	394
THE LOWLANDS	398
THE POOR LAW	399
EDUCATION	400
THE CHURCH	400
MATERIAL ADVANCE	402
GLASGOW	402

	PAGE
EDINBURGH	405
THE SCOTTISH LAW COURTS	407
SCOTTISH TORYISM	411
CLOSE OF THE DECADE IN ENGLAND—RELIGIOUS MOVEMENTS	412
SOCIAL MOVEMENTS	415
ECONOMIC MOVEMENTS	417
REFERENCES	419
BIBLIOGRAPHY	447
INDEX	463

ENGLAND IN THE NINETEENTH CENTURY

1806–1810

CHAPTER I

LITERATURE, ART, AND SCIENCE

THE French Revolution, if its full meaning is to be appreciated, must be treated as something much larger than a violent political change or series of changes. A vast movement which led men to examine the first principles of their existence can scarcely be comprised in a few years, or even confined to a single country. From this point of view, the day of the destruction of the Bastille, or the day of the execution of Louis XIV, is not more important than the day when Beaumarchais in his *Figaro* asked the applauding nobility of France what they had done to deserve so many good things, and answered his own question: "You have given yourselves the trouble of being born." To estimate the share of the French Revolution in bringing about the great revival in letters and art which took place in Great Britain at the end of the eighteenth century, it is necessary to go back to countless thoughts like this one of Beaumarchais which preceded the summoning of the States General by many years, like the scattered shafts of light which in the East come before the true dawn, and then die away into darkness once more. They were not confined to France alone. Both there and in other countries the effect of the movement, as regards literature and art, was to lead the nations back to the fountains of their being. In France this took the form of a classical revival. In Britain it led back to nature or to the ideals and forms of a gothic or a Tudor past.

One of the first streaks of dawn on the British side of the Channel appeared in 1783 in a note of discontent struck in a book of poems published by a boy only born in 1768. It was William Blake. An Irish hosier's son apprenticed to an engraver in London, he could not have read much or known much of what went on in the world. But a new spirit was in the air, and he already felt it when he addressed the Muses:

> "How have you left the ancient love
> That bards of old enjoyed in you!
> The languid streams do scarcely move!
> The sound is forc'd, the notes are few!"

True to his own appeal, he was quick to throw off the old conventional forms, and to give poetry a new dress. The poems, The Lamb and On another's Sorrow, in Songs of Innocence, first published in what is usually regarded as the first year of the French Revolution—1789, were a great change in style from the typical poetry of the age. They found few readers; and although Blake continued to write until far on in the nineteenth century, and did not die till 1827, he failed to impress his contemporaries as a poet. By a few who were able to judge he was, of course, appreciated. One of them was a head master of a grammar school by the name of Malkin, himself a writer. He had the misfortune to lose a very clever child at the age of six. It was a period when such instances of precocity were in fashion, and attracted attention, and a long notice of the boy duly appeared in the Monthly Review under the heading, "Memoirs of Eminent Persons". Thus encouraged, the Father published in 1806 the Memoirs of his Child. The book had a frontispiece by Blake, which gave Malkin the opportunity to eke out the work with a valuable account of him both as artist and poet—which has rescued father and son alike from oblivion—and a few selections of his poems—among them the magnificent "Tiger! Tiger!" But even when introduced to the world in such august fellowship the poet was not a success. The Father's Memoirs of his Child was welcomed; but it was observed that the poems did not rise above mediocrity. Such was the fate of Blake. Concerned as the general historian is, not with the ultimate value of authors and artists but with their share in the development of the thought of their age, he is obliged to pass regretfully by the great mystical genius, and to find space for many of lesser note.

Two of these were—each in their different way—forerunners of the romantic movement in poetry, George Crabbe and Thomas Campbell. The former occupies an interesting place in the history of letters. Crabbe was England's great realistic poet. Born in 1754, he succeeded at the age of twenty-six in convincing Edmund Burke of his literary talents, and, introduced through him to the world, took orders, and spent most of the remainder of his life as the incumbent of one country living after another. Most of his poems describe the Suffolk fishing town of Aldborough where he had been successively parish doctor and curate. He occupied himself with the realities of the very sordid lives lived in a part of the world which by his own account had nothing to recommend it. He wrote almost all his works in the time-honoured verse of ten syllables. But in other ways he broke with the eighteenth-century tradition. He scorned poetic diction, and addressed his productions, as he afterwards expressed himself in the preface to the Tales published in 1812, to the plain sense and sober judgement of his readers. From the first he attacked the pastoral convention of the superior happiness and virtue to be found in rural life. Yet, even in the crude realism with which he depicted men and women as he knew them, he opened a new world of romance of his own—lives which were almost as far removed from the lives of most of his readers as were the southern seas. Although, like many others, he fell under the false imputation of Jacobinism, he was singularly free of all theories of every kind. He merely represented what he took to be the truth. He was no pessimist. He cheerfully faced the plain facts of life. Deeply underlying his poetry is a conviction that after all these plain facts were not the things which mattered. The wise man, secluded among his books, may be right while the practical man is moving about in a world of unrealities. "Go on then, Son of Vision!" he hails him in The Library,

> "still pursue
> Thy airy dreams; the world is dreaming too".

Such lines, sounding a little strange coming from Crabbe, go some way to explain why he, although a poet of common life, did not treat it with any great depth of realism, and show besides that he too was touched by the growing idealistic spirit. The warmth of his religious nature is evinced by prayers which he composed for his own private use long before he took orders. He certainly had no mere conventional reverence for sacred things. It was characteristic of him, when tithe day was coming round, to say as he stepped down from the pulpit after his sermon: "I must have some money, gentlemen."

The opening of the new century ushered in the period of his greatest poetical activity. He had for some time attempted to throw his ideas into the form of novels, but he was dissatisfied, and burnt what he had written. The short story in prose does not seem to have occurred to him. The Parish Register, published in 1807, contained several short stories in verse as well as descriptions of life and reflections in the discursive manner of the time. By the time he wrote The Borough, three years later, he had come to the conclusion that there was more amusement to be got out of the middle classes than any other. The lower had no leisure or means for originality, while the higher was kept in order by the dread of observation. "Describe the Borough", he commands himself; and so he does. He plunges into a complete account of its churches, professions, trades, prisons, schools, alms-houses, and a great deal more. But intense realism somehow defeats its own object. After several thousand lines of description, the reader finds himself obliged to admit that he does not know very much about the Borough after all. Crabbe's poetry was, as he said himself, poetry without atmosphere; and in so flat a picture, where the hard dull light admits of no suggestion and no tone, there is very little which stands out and is seen in its proper relation to what surrounds it. Yet Crabbe hit the taste of the public. He was admired by the great men of the day, by Fox, Grey, and Canning, and deservedly so. The crudity of his work does not seem to have repelled them, while they could not fail to be touched by its sincerity. What is in reality an artistic fault probably seemed a merit —a certain tripping jauntiness of style, thoroughly in keeping with an age which had almost discarded the ponderous wigs of Doctor Johnson's time, stepped lightly about in knee-breeches and buckled shoes, and had not yet donned the surcoat and tight trousers of a later period. Hence the love of that day for the undignified anapæstic metre, one in which it is almost impossible to write great English poetry. Yet almost all who then wrote verse tried it, and some few succeeded—Canning in the song composed for the celebrated dinner in honour of Pitt in 1802, Scott in O, young Lochinvar is come out of the West, Byron in The Destruction of Senaccherib, and—strangest of all—Charles Wolfe in the Burial of Sir John Moore.

Thomas Campbell enjoyed even greater popularity. Born in 1777, a scion of one of those Argyllshire families which had left the land and turned to business, he drew little of his inspiration from the historical or legendary lore of his country, or from rural life or scenery. He wore a wig and made his home in Sydenham. Yet the romantic movement of the day carried him some distance in spite of himself. The Pleasures of Hope, published in 1799, preserved the conventional metre, and was quite in the cold classical style. But it drew some fire from the spark struck by the conflicts between religion and science and between liberty and oppression. For political liberty Campbell always had a passion, united in him with that love of country which produced that most popular of British patriotic poems, Ye Mariners of England. The war saw him break new ground in metre with Hohenlinden and The Battle of the Baltic, and here he won success in the very difficult task in the performance of which Homer and Virgil themselves cannot be said to have excelled—the description of a battle. He wrote nothing equal to these three poems. In 1809 he conceded to the romantic movement so far as to write a poem in the Spenserian stanza, in a much less formal style than The Pleasures of Hope. That work, Gertrude of Wyoming, was a failure. But it was not thought to be so at the time. Though too fastidious and too idle to write much, Campbell enjoyed during the first years of the century a great and ever-growing authority as poet and man of letters, and in 1806 received a pension of a gross £200 a year from the Ministry of the Talents. He and Crabbe are the two last poets of note of each of whom it may be said that he depended—though it was only for a small part of his life—upon patronage, and even lived as a member of the household of a great nobleman.

Another successful poet of the conventional school was Samuel Rogers. Fastidious like Campbell, but without his fire, he was now resting on his reputation, and more of an entertainer of poets than a poet. He selected a house overlooking Green Park in what Fox thought the best situation in London. He filled it with masterpieces of art and with the best editions of the best authors, "and moreover", adds Doctor Burney the musician, "he gives the best dinners to the best company of men of talents and genius I know". Meanwhile his fame did not suffer. His Pleasures of Memory ran through eighteen editions of over twenty thousand copies from 1792, the year of its first publication, to 1815.

It was the day of the discursive poem. Erasmus Darwin's studies of natural history in verse were still being published. Another poet of nature was Robert Blomfield, the author of The Farmer's Boy—and he had been one himself. It was to his happy idea of writing at all, being what he was, that he owed his extraordinary popularity; and certainly not to any revelation which he was able to give of the soul of the peasant and the countryside. Disquisitions in verse were indeed popular, and the title-pages of lesser books of this kind were sometimes almost as discursive as their contents. That of one short poem which ran through three editions combined the characters of a commercial advertisement and a religious tract. It was The Distress'd Village Poem, representing the distressing Effects of Fire, the happy Consequences of Insurance, the Excellence of Public Charity, and the great Enormity of wilfully destroying or attempting to destroy the Handy Works of God in his Providence. In such a time the elevation by Pitt of Henry Pye, the cause of wit in other men, to the office of Poet Laureate, almost stands excused. His blameless verses were tolerated by his contemporaries. A typical social novel, A Winter in London, makes a duchess who is describing the music at a Court birthday function add: "I really think the fire of the laureat, Pye, increases with his years." The ladies of that day were easily warmed. But there was need of something more and the time had now come.

There was, however, no cataclysmal change. The removal of the fetters which classical convention had placed upon English literature was announced by no such picturesque and sensational incidents as attended Victor Hugo's liberation of the French drama in 1830, nor can any such exact date be assigned for England. Nor were the factions which divided literary society in such sharp opposition as they were in Paris when he threw down his challenge. Irresistible as it was in reality everywhere, there were places where the tide of change seemed to be making little way, and others where it seemed to have overwhelmed every obstacle. Here a rock which appeared to be firm in its resistance all at once found itself surrounded. There, long after some part which appeared to have welcomed the whole of the flood was thought to have been covered, it was found that there were still some few patches which had escaped. Byron had to confess that he was a romantic in spite of himself. Wordsworth, long after opening his campaign against the idea that a special language existed for poetry, fell back under the influence of Virgil, most literary of all great poets, and —particularly in such classical poems as Laodamia—used many a phrase of a formal and antique cut. In 1791 the rebel Blake illustrated a book by the rebel Mary Wollstonecraft. Even at that early date it is somewhat startling to find that such a combination produced nothing more original, under the title Original Stories from Real Life, than a set of very prim tales indeed for the schoolroom with prints in the most stilted style of the eighteenth century. When protagonists like Wordsworth and Byron were themselves divided in their own minds, periodical literature reflected a similar variety. The selection of poetry of the day which the Annual Register for 1806, for example, offered to its readers began as in duty bound with two odes of the Laureate's, followed by some extracts from Scott's Lay of the Last Minstrel and his Minstrelsy of the Scottish Border. Later on, three of Wordsworth's sonnets and two of his Lyrical Ballads peep out from the dull flats of the older school.

The year in which the romantic revival at last showed itself clearly above the horizon was 1800. It was in that year that Lyrical Ballads was published in London with a Preface which sounded a challenge to the old ways in the world of poetry. Though his father was an attorney and his mother a tradesman's daughter, there was much in the early life and character of its author satisfactory to the common conception of what a poet should be, and it was appropriate that he should arise in that part of England the beauty of whose wilderness was already attracting tourists. Born in Cockermouth in Cumberland on the 7th of April, 1770, Wordsworth's childhood and schooldays were passed in that mountainous country. Here he grew hardy and adventurous; yet a constitution strong on the whole admitted weaknesses which gave him the excuse to be an idler at Cambridge university and moody and unsettled afterwards. He wandered to the Continent and to Wales in search of the picturesque. He was attracted by the cause of the poor and oppressed; became a violent republican, and finding himself in France in 1792 was tempted to place himself at the head of a revolutionary party. But he was driven home by want of money, after which more wanderings followed. He still pursued his popular fancies and, instead of entering the Church, as had been intended, ran a tilt against a bishop, Doctor Watson. He could live on very little, and was fortunate in the friends whom he managed to pick up. One of these left him £900 in 1795, which was almost all that he and his devoted sister Dorothy had to live upon for nearly eight years. Other friends procured him in succession at a low rent or no rent at all large and comfortable houses in the West of England, where the brother and sister lived a frugal life on bread and cheese and vegetables. Here they met one with whose name Wordsworth's became inseparably connected as a pioneer of the revival.

Samuel Taylor Coleridge, born at Ottery St. Mary in Devonshire in 1772, was the son of a clergyman. Like Pitt, he was never a boy, and yet he was a perpetual child. Learned even as a schoolboy, still more as an undergraduate, he was soon famous—in a limited circle—as an Unitarian preacher. In 1798 his friend Wedgwood's timely allowance of £150 a year enabled him to leave the ministry and devote his life to philosophy and poetry. He had already become notorious as the writer of violent political sonnets against Government. He soon became intimate with the Wordsworths. The two poets were neighbours. They walked and admired nature together; they discussed poetry, and helped to write one another's poems. Hitherto Wordsworth had been in the habit, like other young poets, of making up for lack of ideas by refinements upon the traditional language of verse. One of the poems which he had published in 1793, Descriptive Sketches, showed this in a striking manner. Coleridge told afterwards in his Biographia Literaria how such absurdities used to be rebuked by his own master at Christ's Hospital, the Reverend James Bowyer. "*Lute, harp*, and *lyre*, *Muse*, *Muses*, and *inspirations*, *Pegasus*, *Parnassus*, and *Hippocrene* were all an abomination to him. In fancy I can almost hear him now, exclaiming, 'Harp? Harp? Lyre? Pen and ink, boy, you mean!'" The idea soon found its way into the mind of Wordsworth, who embraced it with all the zeal of a novice, and went very much further than Coleridge. He drew the conclusion that poems should be written in a selection of the language ordinarily used by men. In the onslaught which he made in his Preface to Lyrical Ballads on the prevailing taste for what was known as poetic diction, he almost seemed to be attacking his own former self. One example of vicious taste which he gave was a sonnet of Gray's containing the lines:

> "In vain to me the smiling mornings shine,
> And reddening Phœbus lifts his golden fire."

His own Descriptive Sketches had contained an echo of these very lines:

> "He views the sun uplift his golden fire."

In the notice which that poem received in the Monthly Review at the time, the critic had commented on it on much the same lines, if with more disrespect, than Wordsworth himself had shown to Gray: "Must eternal changes be rung on uplands and lowlands, and nodding forests, and brooding clouds, and cells, and dells, and dingles?"

Wordsworth was, as he said of himself, averse from taking advice. He would not formally surrender his own judgement. But this undisturbed north-countryman's self-confidence made it all the easier for him to weigh quietly what others said and wrote. He gathered together and made his own the ideas which he found floating about in the brains of an old schoolmaster, of a critical reviewer, of a young poet, and—no doubt—elsewhere. That genius which in some respects appears so lonely was well said by Hazlitt to be a pure emanation of the Spirit of the Age.

The Preface sounded a challenge to the established conventions as regards the content of poetry as well as its form. Discouraged by the failure of the French revolutionaries to create a new world, he had taken refuge for a time in such abstract theories as he found in William Godwin's Political Justice, published at the moment of his disillusionment. Here he seemed to find firm ground. Here the ideal state existed, in theory if not in practice. But there was a touch of the practical man about him which still refused to be satisfied. Though all the world should read Political Justice, the world would be no better. And even that book seemed—in spite of its professed object—to throw the burden of making the world better on the individual man working out his own destiny and character. At this point in the growth of his mind he had become reunited with his sister, a Child of Nature in no ordinary sense.

> "She whispered still that brightness would return,
> She in the midst of all preserved me still
> A Poet, made me seek beneath that name,
> And that alone, my office upon earth."

In an age of Utopias, he decided to have his own, and he found it in the last place where he might have been expected to look for it:

> "In the very world, which is the world
> Of all of us—the place where in the end
> We find our happiness or not at all!"

It was his mission to show mankind an abiding source of happiness in Nature, and the love of Nature, and God who is revealed in Nature, to show how all-pervading these blessings are, how they are of far greater value than they are known to be even by those who are conscious of them, how too they are unconsciously possessed not by children only and the half-witted but by the coarsest and rudest of mankind. This comprehensive view of present happiness satisfied his republicanism. Mere political change seemed needless when he could thus assert the majesty of man. Like all those whose childhood meant anything for them, there had come a time for Wordsworth when he desired to teach others what he had himself learnt in childhood, the awe felt as a rambling schoolboy on his native mountains for the solitary shepherd appearing by a natural delusion

> "In size a giant, stalking through thick fog,
> His sheep like Greenland bears . . ."

and the respect which he thus learnt to feel for man as man. The Old Cumberland Beggar, for instance, was so far from being for him an object of sentimental commiseration, that he almost reverenced him as an honoured benefactor who bound together a whole countryside in offices of love.

Wordsworth always wrote of the poor with the same sense of their true dignity. Earlier poets like Goldsmith had loved them with something not very unlike a patronizing touch. Others there were—and there were more to come—who made a not much more pardonable mistake. They respected them indeed, but not in themselves, and only in some sort as those who should, if they had their own rights, be rich—children of misfortune like Oliver Twist, unlawfully cheated out of an inheritance which poetic justice or an actual revolution might give them. Against such materialism Wordsworth set his face. It was not because he was not bold to look on painful things. Few books contain such keen descriptions of human anguish as his earlier poems.

But he reserved his more profound pity for the wealthy—pity, not envy or contempt. He had never a doubt that what they had was dross in comparison with spiritual riches. His attitude to them was much that of Blake as he appears in such passages in Alexander Gilchrist's biography as the following: "A lady tells a pretty and very characteristic story of her first and only interview with the spiritual man, which illustrates, in another way, how he came by this happiness. The lady was thought extremely beautiful when a child, and was taken to an evening party and there presented to Blake. He looked at her very kindly for a long while, without speaking, and then, stroking her hair and long ringlets, said: 'May God make this world to you, my child, as beautiful as it has been to me!' She thought it strange, at the time—vain little darling of Fortune!—that such a poor old man, dressed in shabby clothes, could imagine that the world had ever been so beautiful to him as it must be to her, nursed in all the elegancies and luxuries of wealth. But, in after years, she understood plainly enough what he meant."

It was in much the same spirit that Wordsworth threw open a new world to the admiration of mankind, chose the subjects of his poems, as he said, from low and rustic life, and proposed to himself to write them in a selection of language really used by men. There was no notion in his mind of having recourse to dialect for examples of the vigour with which the primary passions and ideas of the sons of the soil find expression. He had no gift for this. Nor indeed had he sufficient dramatic talent to find for those of whom he wrote the kind of language which they might have used, divested of provincialisms. In his eagerness to show that simple stories of simple life can be made the objects of poetry, he chose such very simple ones indeed that they often want point, and when they have point too much is made of it. This type of poem had overweighted the first edition of Lyrical Ballads, of 1798, and it was not until that of 1800, which had been expanded to two volumes by the addition of the preface and many of his best poems, that the book began to be popular. He said himself that he made a hundred pounds in the first few years by it, and two more editions appeared in 1802 and 1805.

Whether it was because here again he was willing to weigh adverse criticism, or from the uninfluenced development of his own mind, he gradually after 1800 ceased to produce poems like Goody Blake and Harry Gill. The longest of this kind, Peter Bell, he laid aside, unpublished, for years. Intercourse with Coleridge, a visit with him to Germany in 1799, later visits to London, France, and Scotland, and finally a settlement which began in December 1799 in Dove cottage, near Grasmere, among his native lakes and mountains, followed by marriage but without a separation from Dorothy, had broadened and humanized him, as did his grief at the loss of a beloved sailor brother in 1805. By 1807, when his Sonnets dedicated to Liberty, the finest body of English patriotic poetry existing, his Scottish poems and his great Odes to Duty and on the Intimations, were published, he was already a force to be reckoned. The Edinburgh Review attacked him, nor did this prevent Byron from attacking him as well. On the other hand young men like William Hazlitt and Thomas de Quincey, who could see for themselves what good poetry was, had long admired him and eagerly sought him out. He was the friend of Rogers, at whose house he might have met almost everyone who counted. He did meet Fox, who greeted him as the head of a literary party: "I am glad to see you, Mr. Wordsworth, though I am not of your faction." Certainly he had a band of admirers, many of them humble men, who either did not read the critics or did not mind what they said.

But his fame did not increase. Not to speak of his Odes, which the world was not yet able to understand, his patriotic sonnets, perhaps because they came from an unexpected source, awoke no enthusiasm. He waited. He knew that he

LITERATURE, ART, AND SCIENCE

had a mission to make the world better and happier by his poems. It might have been thought wonderful that a man with so intense a love for his country should have been content to exist in a remote corner in such a time of stress, and to be nothing more than a home volunteer. He himself had some such feelings in 1800, when he wrote the lines:

> "Yea to this hour I cannot read a tale
> Of two brave vessels matched in deadly fight,
> And fighting to the death, but I am pleased
> More than a wise man ought to be. I wish,
> Fret, burn, and struggle, and in soul am there."

He felt that there were for him other duties—other palms to be won.

Lyrical Ballads had contained among other things of Coleridge, the Ancient Mariner. Among the numerous forms in which the romantic movement found its first dawn was an admiration (in translation) for German ballad poetry. Entirely ignorant of the fact that they were the contemporaries of the greatest genius of modern times in Goethe, men regarded that country as—in many ways, at least—two or three centuries behind civilized Europe; and the same kind of interest was taken in Bürger, who had only recently died, as was taken in Percy's Reliques of old English Ballads. No less than five translations of his Lenore were published in 1796, and it was even republished in London in the original. William Taylor's version in the Monthly Magazine, which Coleridge saw, full of archaic words and spelling as it was, evidently suggested the style of the Ancient Mariner. Such was the typical stanza:

> "Look up, look up, an airy crewe
> In roundel daunces reele:
> The moone is bryghte, and blue the nyghte,
> Mayst dimlie see them wheele."

Coleridge followed the antique style and sometimes the old spelling. But the public had now had enough of the forgeries of Chatterton; they did not want a revival of Percy's

Reliques; they had already begun to weary of translations from the German. They saw something of all these in the Rime of the Ancyent Marinere; they knew its woof and texture—or they thought they did; and the finest ballad in the English language fell nearly flat upon the world.

Coleridge's other great poem, Christabel, remained in manuscript; and not many poems can have obtained so large a circle of admirers when in that state since the discovery of printing. He did not write much verse. His vagaries were a jest to himself and his friends. Nervous ailments, with their disastrous remedy, opium, and the study of German which set him about translating Schiller and plunging into German philosophy, impaired his imagination; and the pathetic Ode to Dejection, of 1802, was almost his swan song as a poet. From his return from Germany in 1799 to 1810 he led many different lives. For a time he wrote excellent leading articles for the Morning Post, later on he was ordered south, and filled with credit the post of Secretary to the Governor of Malta, Sir Alexander Ball, who had been one of Nelson's captains. He also set up for some months a periodical of his own, the Friend, one of the most abstruse ever published. He gave lectures on literature at the Royal Institution, which were attended by the learned and the fashionable.

Coleridge had been tempted by Wordsworth to seek a home in Cumberland, and he in turn recommended it to Robert Southey, a College friend whose sister he had married. The three poets formed what was miscalled the Lake School. Southey's direct and limited mind had very little affinity with those of Coleridge and Wordsworth. But for that very reason he was more of a figure in his own time than either of them. His numerous short poems, and even the four long poems which he wrote up to 1810, had many of the merits of the best sort of verse which is devoid of genius. They were easy to read and found many readers. But the very mild Muse whom Southey courted did not grant him her favours as often as he wished, and in his beautiful home at Keswick he produced a prodigious number of prose books, translations, and criticisms. Through a friend whom he had made when at school at Westminster, Charles Wynn, a relative and political supporter of the Grenvilles, he obtained a pension of a nominal two hundred pounds like Campbell's in 1806.

The change of opinion on political and religious subjects which took place in the minds of the three poets in the twenty years which followed the outbreak of the war with France, offers a unique and almost insoluble problem in literary history. Southey's was the most remarkable. He was not only the more prominent figure to his contemporaries, but he was a plain downright man with a great facility in expression, which he was very ready to indulge, particularly in his letters to his sailor brother. He was a thoroughgoing republican in his youth. In advanced years he wrote that he was no more ashamed of having been one than of having been a boy. He and Wordsworth were still republicans in 1806; but De Quincey, who records their conversation, was more impressed by their jocular treatment of the subject of the Royal Family than by the earnestness of their convictions. Southey was, in truth, never much interested in constitutional questions. He was, above all, a friend of liberty. He could not understand, he said in 1809, how those who had like him turned their faces to the East to worship, in France, the rising sun of liberty, could, unlike him, persist after the sun had moved, in keeping their faces turned towards the same quarter, which had become that of darkness and oppression. This was why he threw in his lot with the new Tory Quarterly Review, which championed the cause of England and Spain and Portugal against the tyrant Bonaparte. In a letter written in justification of this decision to his brother he gave his whole profession of faith. He was a friend to reform as the one thing which could prevent revolution. It is obvious that anyone who believes in reform on these imperfect grounds is liable to be shaken in his faith when years pass by, reform is not given, and still there is no revolution. This was what happened to Southey. He was an enemy to Catholic emancipation, a personal view due principally to his own travels in Catholic countries. He was a friend to the Church establishment, not by any means as an orthodox member of it, but because it had been a practical blessing and its history appealed to his imagination.

Coleridge's political views underwent a change from the moment when France attacked Switzerland, and the liberator of Europe became an oppressor in her turn. Converted to deism while at Cambridge by the non-conformist don Freund, he had not been very long in reconverting himself and in trying to convert others to the creed of his father. The high Tory views which he came gradually to adopt in matters both of Church and State must be explained as partly due to the desire which the physically and morally weak always feel for a rock of refuge, and partly to reaction from views now held to be mischievous. He also, as well as his two friends, gradually discovered, as he came to know them better, that the great ones of the earth were not so evil as the fervid imagination of youthful republicanism had supposed them. With Wordsworth it was not Switzerland which turned the scale. He would not give France up for a single crime committed by their rulers. It was the republican idea which appealed to him. When he saw that idea itself superseded in France by a military despotism, he turned to his own native home. Here he had never seen differences of rank among the people with whom he had lived as a boy. The statesmen or small farmers of Cumberland and Westmorland had lived from time immemorial lives of independent brotherhood with which nothing that he had seen in France could be compared. His very republicanism threw him, with these northern associations and temperament, back upon conservatism. In his religious views, Wordsworth was for many years completely indifferent so far as Christianity went. The deep power of thought drew him to it in the midst of his indifference. He had spiritual affinity with evangelical Christianity such as that of Wilberforce. There are passages in his earlier poems, written when he was no churchgoer or reader of religious books or of the Bible, where he speaks of the blessings with which he is surrounded or the duty of patient resignation under suffering, which unconsciously breathe the spirit of the prevailing christianity of his day. The higher pantheism which he professed already contained its essence; and it became natural for him, living in domestic retirement near the place of his childhood, to accept its forms and dogmas.

The leader of the romantic revival on its national or gothic side was the most prominent literary figure of this, as of the two succeeding decades—Walter Scott. He was born in 1771, the son of middle-class Lowland Scottish parents; yet the social surroundings of his childhood and youth were far from narrow. As a Writer to the Signet, his father was legal man of business to a large circle of clients, while his mother's father, Doctor John Rutherford, was Professor of Medicine in the University of Edinburgh, and a man of some literary pretensions. Nor, in a country where pedigrees were so well remembered, was it forgotten that Walter Scott could claim his descent from a celebrated chieftain of the same name, or that his great-grandfather had suffered loss of property and almost life for the House of Stuart. An illness in infancy left him lame. This led to a somewhat chequered childhood; and partly owing to the interrupted course of his education, and partly to the strongly individual bent of his mind, he was largely self-taught. Like many another author, he has delighted to portray in one of his novels, Waverley, the desultory readings of his own childhood and early youth. His mind very soon took its permanent stamp, that of a literary antiquarian. He never had any real taste for music or any of the fine arts, or, in the highest sense, for literature itself. He looked on nature, on pictures and on objects of vertu through the medium of books; he looked on books in turn through the medium of man; that is to say he valued an old ballad not as a work of art, but as something which lent dignity to or threw a light upon human nature or history. His father's calling was attractive to his turn of mind, as he always loved the pedantries of the law. But he did not care for the dependent position which his father's branch of it entailed. He was, however, apprenticed to him in his fifteenth year; and now duty and inclination alike sent him frequently on riding or walking excursions into both Highlands and Lowlands. He mixed freely with the people of all classes, and studied every object of the slightest legendary or historic interest. He was himself a signal example of a circumstance to which he afterwards alluded in a striking simile. Just as the most interesting districts of the world are where the wild mountains meet at their base with the fertile plains, so the most interesting period is just where barbarism and feudalism is passing into civilization. Though he did not hail from the age of chivalry, he was a sort of link between two ages. In his early manhood he had seen many a dame whose talk was of Bonnie Prince Charlie and the '45, and he was just of age when Charles Leslie, the last of the Scottish minstrels, died in Aberdeenshire. While in Edinburgh, his taste for folklore was reinforced from a different quarter. In 1792 he was called to the bar, and later on, along with other advocates who had time on their hands, he joined a class which had been formed in Edinburgh for the purpose of studying Goethe and Schiller in the original. He was one of those who translated Lenore in 1796. Meanwhile he carried on his profession. He had none of the incisiveness or taste for disputation which is required in a good advocate, and was glad in 1799 to obtain the appointment of Sheriff of Selkirkshire.

LITERATURE, ART, AND SCIENCE 37

This short sketch of his youth and early manhood suggests the line which his first literary activities would probably take. Though fond even as a boy of telling stories, it hardly seems to have occured to him to take himself seriously as a romancer till well past thirty years of age; and his first serious work, which took him some years, was his collection of old border poems under the title of the Minstrelsy of the Scottish Border, the publication of which was completed in 1803. It was a great success. It gave their character to the original works of Scott's pen till he found that he had exhausted this particular species of literature, and had been eclipsed in poetry by Byron. Before it was finished, he had begun to be busy with the Lay of the Last Minstrel. In his choice of metre he owned a debt to Coleridge's Christabel. The poem was published in 1805, and attracted at once the pronounced admiration of Pitt. "He can't remain as he is", said the Minister, but it was reserved for the Ministry of All the Talents to give him the post of Clerk of Sessions in the following year. The poem brought him £769 6s. and fixed him in a literary career. Over 40,000 copies were sold up to 1830. The Lay was followed in 1808 by the equally popular Marmion. Two thousand copies of this were fixed at the high price of a guinea and a half, but the edition was at once sold out, and was followed up to 1815 by eight octavo editions numbering 26,000 copies. The Lady of the Lake followed in 1810, "a nail", in the author's words, "fixed in the proverbially inconstant wheel of Fortune".

The last years of the decade were signalized by the appearance in the world of one who was destined to stand for Europe at least as his country's greatest contemporary contribution to letters, George Gordon Noel Lord Byron. Born in 1788, he passed through an unenviable childhood with a poor, irritable, and injudicious mother, to enjoy the ordinary education of a nobleman at Harrow School and Trinity College, Cambridge. Very early in life he discovered that he hated the world, although, except for a lameness from birth which prevented him from putting his heels to the ground, and for the miscarriage of certain boyish—even childish—love affairs, he had little ground for complaint against fortune. In 1807 he published his first poems, Hours of Idleness, written while still at school. In his preface the boy announced his intention that his first poems should be his last. But in the middle of the strenuous idleness of his university career, he felt himself called upon to correct the literary taste of the day. Poets were, he found, beginning to refuse to take Pope for their model. He composed an attack upon them in the metre and style of that master, and while so engaged he was stirred by an unnecessarily harsh criticism of his published poems to make the change from "British Bards" to "English Bards and Scotch Reviewers". It was an odd combination, for the Edinburgh Review, whose attack he was now returning with considerable interest, was on his side in combating that very romantic tendency in poetry which he disliked. Byron and the reviewers were in agreement in their preference for Rogers, Campbell, and Crabbe, their dislike of Wordsworth, Coleridge, and, generally speaking, Southey, and their complaints against Scott. But the result was perfectly successful. Byron's poem, published in the spring of 1808, was the best piece of literary satire since Pope's, and—in one way—of much more abiding interest. As a rule the poets who are mocked live only in the line which mocks them. But Byron had the double advantage of having attacked men who had a better right to live than ever he proved himself to have; while on the other hand the judgement of contemporaries was, in the main, with him. He has the credit of being one of the forces which arrested the growing popularity of Wordsworth. While his poem was going through the Press he had made another addition to his victims. Typical aristocrat as he was, Byron lived in that exalted circle where everyone knew everyone else's affairs. As for the world outside, it was not worth while having any secrets from it, any more than it was necessary to lower the voice when talking family affairs to prevent the flunkeys from hearing. When the poem was already in print he had added two lines in praise of his cousin and guardian, the Earl of Carlisle, to whom he had dedicated his earlier book. Suddenly, on account of some petty half-imagined slights, he struck these out and had the execrable bad taste to insert several lines of virulent invective. There was no doubt that Byron was in the wrong, as he afterwards admitted in a famous stanza in Childe Harold; but in any case the general public can have had no interest in this small family quarrel, and it is no inconsiderable indication of how much the age still retained of eighteenth-century grossness of feeling that this indecent parade did not raise an universal cry of reprobation from the reading public throughout the country.

Three minor poets provide a link with music and the drama. The first of these was Thomas Moore, born in Dublin in 1779, one of the earliest Catholics admitted to Trinity College. An Irish patriot, and a self-indulgent one, he did not stay in his own country, but made use of his talents as player and singer to regain in English drawing-rooms the cause which his countrymen had lost on the battlefields of 1798. His nationalism did not go much further than that of Grattan or of Maria Edgeworth. Like them, he rested Irish claims not as was done later on their being a people misunderstood and whom Englishmen never could be expected to understand, but on their sharing with them an intelligible humanity. He made no attempt to convey that fanciful melancholy which is the peculiar note of the Celtic genius. But he succeeded in what he did undertake. Cultivated English men and women could no longer regard Irish Catholics as barbarians beyond the pale, when they had learnt from one of them to admire and to sing and unconsciously to appropriate the charming sentiment of The Harp that once through Tara's Halls and She is Far from the Land. For each of these Irish Melodies which

Moore collected and set to words of his own making he received a hundred guineas. It was a success to be placed not far behind that of Scott himself.

The second of these lesser poets was a Scotsman, James Hogg, the Ettrick Shepherd, called so from his home in the Scottish Lowlands and his occupation for the first thirty years of his life. Such a shepherd boy, living with the score or so of excellent books which helped to furnish even a humble Scottish home, might easily turn out a poet, like Burns. He first appeared in print in 1800 with the patriotic song, Donald M'Donald, which he had written while tending his sheep, and set to the well-known air of "Woo'd and married an' a' ". It was popular in concert rooms and barracks and messes. Most of the great clans were mentioned, but by a fortunate chance the leading name was also that of the General Commanding the Northern Army, who took the words to himself:

> "An' I their gude-brither, M'Donald,
> Shall ne'er be the last in the fray!
> Brogues an' brocken an a',
> Brocken an' brogues an a',
> An' up with the bonnie blue bonnet,
> The kilt an' the feather an' a'."

For the next ten years Hogg tried to farm and compose poetry together, but in neither did he as yet have much success.

The English poet was Charles Dibdin, unless the man who best celebrated in verse the gallantry and the joys and cares of those to whom Britain then owed her existence does not deserve to rank as one. Born in 1745, he had written Tom Bowling and most of his famous sea songs before the century ended, but he still entertained the world. He had a little theatre of his own. Here, and on his tours through the kingdom, he sang or recited his own compositions; his operas and dramatic pieces were performed at the regular theatres. Dibdin, and not Wordsworth or Scott or Campbell or even Hogg, was the true patriotic poet of the days when men armed against Napoleon. Nothing was too humble for his popular Muse. He gives the people a little history of what the Navy had done in the war: he takes them to a volunteer camp; he puffs the government lottery from the stage; he celebrates the generosity of the contributors to the patriotic fund at Lloyd's.

In music the country had reached a very low ebb. It was from no want of patronage. The King himself was a great supporter, and gave a ball and concert in 1805 at Windsor Castle entirely under his own direction, the joint expenses of which were put at £50,000. The Prince of Wales encouraged the art and was himself an excellent musician. The Academy of Ancient Music, where no pieces less than twenty years old might be performed, was the resort of the fashionable and the great. But there was little original talent, and the level of taste was low. Fiévée, visiting England during the Peace of Amiens, found that, apart of course from Handel, German music was unknown in that age of great composers—a contrast to France. The old fashion of chamber music had dropped out; the conduct of massed choirs and orchestras was not well understood; and the one form of music which flourished was the song for three or four parts allowing free scope for each individual voice, known as a glee. The common type was for male voices only, including the alto where possible; and men were able to meet in the evening in clubs and rooms like the Cave of Harmony where they could meet untroubled by the other sex, and combine glee-singing with other forms of jollity in which the audience shared. There was not much hope for composers so long as the verse for which they composed was merely formal and insipid. The poets of the day were not usually music lovers and did not write songs, so the romantic movement stopped short at the portals of harmony. The vapidity of the words did not matter so much when a song was in parts, as it did in a solo, but even here it had its effect. The frigid verses which Samuel Webbe, the great glee composer of the day, used for his music, left their mark on it; and it must have been partly due to this that even his Glorious Apollo, which was specially composed for the Glee Club and always opened its programme, was so stiff and lacking in vitality. One composer found a resource in Shakespeare; John Samuel Stevens' Ye Spotted Snakes and Sigh no more, Ladies, were worthy of him. The dearth of good words affected songs for single voices even more, as the time had not yet fully come when men like Lamb were to disclose to the world the riches of sixteenth- and seventeenth-century literature which lay hid in the volumes of old libraries. Hence the popularity of Dibdin's compositions and of individual airs such as the Bay of Biscay, which were set to words which really meant something, although no doubt these were seldom sung in drawing-rooms; of Tom Moore's Melodies, which frequently were; and of real or spurious Scottish songs, usually of a rather melancholy caste. Possibly these, and a few other English songs such as those which the ballad operas provided were enough for the tradesmen's daughters whose aspirations after accomplishments were so common a subject of complaint; but for the higher culture the Italian was necessary. It was not, after all, very ridiculous, as those who preferred English songs were very often singing Italian tunes without knowing it. Great as was the respect of foreign visitors for the general education of the middle-class Englishwoman, they had little to say in admiration of those accomplishments of voice and pianoforte which Jane Austen's Mr. Bennet dismissed so contemptuously in the case of his own and other people's daughters. Such talent as there was among pianists was rather curiously exotic. While Muzio Clementi, the great manufacturer as well as player of the new instrument, and his pupil, John Baptist Cramer, were foreigners who spent most of their lives in England; another pupil, John Field, a composer as well as a player of genius, was an Irishman who spent most of his life on the Continent. In vocal music the great success of the first year of the century, Mrs. Billington, a German, made £4,000 by singing alternately at the two great theatres for a season. Afterwards England owned the sway of the yet more wonderful Catarini, while the voice of the great male singer of the time, Braham, a German Jew by descent, was vitiated by mannerisms which he had learnt in Italy.

In an age of oratorios the most eminent of composers of religious music, Samuel Wesley, born in 1766, had ceased to compose them after the age of eleven. The son of the celebrated hymn writer, he had been a child of extraordinary precocity, and hardly fulfilled expectations. His best work was done for the Roman Church. The best composers of Anglican church music were Thomas Attwood and William Crotch, both generally stilted, neither of them rising much above the commonplace. In an age of weak religious imagination, where most of such inspiration as there was was echoed from Handel, oratorios were only remarkable for their number. But there was an unmistakeable tendency to demand something better both in cathedrals and in parish churches. Improvements were being introduced into the cathedral organs, which were now first provided with pedals. The rural equivalent, the odd mountebank band of village musicians, was now beginning to fill the galleries of the country churches, though they had little more to expend their art upon than the tunes set to Tate and Brady's metrical versions of the Psalms. Ambitious secular music, such as the ballad operas, had all the flatness of the wretched words and ideas which they had to express. A few composers like William Shield, Charles Dibdin, and even his son Thomas, deserved some of their success. But the dominating figure was the Irishman, Michael Kelly, singer, composer, musical director at Drury Lane, and manager of the Haymarket. Here were produced the sixty-two dramatic pieces for which he composed his miserable music—produced, as the covers were wont to assure that portion of the world which did not already know, with universal and unbounded applause, and published by him at his Musical Saloon in Pall Mall.

The theatre was under the most direct patronage of Royalty, and on the other hand enjoyed the services of one of the principal leaders of the Opposition, Sheridan, as both an author and a proprietor. The social position of the actors and actresses was high compared with that in other countries. Nor were they as yet known familiarly to the town by their Christian names. In 1796 one of them, Miss Farren, had become Countess of Derby. There were several small places of entertainment in London. In the West End the Haymarket had two theatres, the King's or Opera House, and the Little Theatre which was allowed to have a season of its own after that of the two large central theatres had closed. These, Covent Garden and Drury Lane, were the only two places which really counted; they were the only two regular licensed theatres. Drury Lane was Sheridan's, and had John Kemble as actor manager till 1802, after which he became actor manager of Covent Garden, having purchased a one-sixth share in the rights for £23,000. Both theatres were, however, so large that those on the stage had to strain their voices in order to be heard. The peculiar manners of a London audience offered them another difficulty. On one occasion, when Kemble, whose praiseworthy efforts to educate the public up to heavy tragedy were not always successful, was acting in a more than usually dull piece, he had to interrupt himself to entreat the attention of the gods in the gallery in a regular speech. Frequently these gentry —in default of anything better—provided their own entertainment, pelting those in the pit and even on the stage with orange peel and nutshells, or more rarely with some such concrete missile as a bottle, which would admit of a more unerring aim. One French visitor suggested that such acts were done owing to an exuberance of liberty; it was necessary to have a little too much in order to be certain of having enough. A German gentleman wrote that he had been on a battlefield and in a storm at sea, but had experienced nothing like the noise made by the gods when they insisted on a song. Those who exhibited such unmistakable tokens of their authority did not fail to exact their due. An actor, when entering, always made his bow, and there were other odd little traditional affectations. The fashionables were—in their own way—not much better than the vulgar. Many of the men went to quarrel and the women to talk.

Nor was the stage well served by authors. England never had a better master of comedy than Sheridan. But he had written nothing for the stage for years except his one musical tragedy, Pizarro, a bombastic adaptation from the German. This was an immense success. But the many other literary people who attempted to write for the stage at this time were remarkably unsuccessful. One authoress of stately blank verse tragedies, Joanna Baillie, got her De Montford put on the stage by Kemble in 1800, and obtained only a short run for it. She was consoled by the general opinion that her works, however unsuited for the stage, would never cease to be read. Of the rest, Scott felt himself so far her inferior that he gave up trying; Leigh Hunt was another who drew back; Wordsworth's work could not even get taken on the boards, nor for the present could that of Coleridge; Godwin's was tried and failed; the pit and gods made merry over poor Fanny Burney's tragedy; and Charles Lamb joined heartily with everyone else in damning his own Mr. H. on its first night. It is much to the credit of the age that Shakespeare was appreciated. It was possible to see a round dozen of his plays at the two great theatres in the season. But it was a Shakespeare converted. Following the stage tradition, Kemble gave King Lear a happy ending; and in order that Miranda in the Tempest might not be lonely on her Enchanted Isle—and that the lady who played her might not be the only one of the company—she was provided with a pretty sister, Dorina, for whom Prospero kept a lover, Hippolyto, in pickle. But alterations of this kind were not due to a shrinking on the part of the audiences from grand declamatory passages. They revelled in them. No bombast was too hard to swallow. An effect, unexampled in its generation, was produced by the climax of a patriotic epilogue by George Colman.

> "God! must this mushroom despot of the hour
> The spacious World encircle with his power?
> Forbid it Heaven; and forbid it man;
> Can man forbid it! YES—the ENGLISH CAN."

In the comic drama the stage was even less fortunate. There was a tendency, due partly to the large size of the theatres, to substitute broad farce for genuine comedy. The plays were racy enough and, where not adapted from the German, completely healthy, and, except for their tendency to run on money, there is little to object to about their tone. One popular play deserves more than a passing notice. Thomas Martin's Speed the Plough opens with a reference to a character behind the scenes which became one of the most famous through the next century. Farmer Ashfield and his Dame are talking over their success at market, and the latter draws an envious comparison with the price obtained by a neighbour for her butter. The farmer turns on his wife with, "Be quiet, woolye? always ding, dinging Dame Grundy into my ears—what will Mrs. Grundy say? What will Mrs. Grundy think?—Canst thee be quiet, let ur alone, and behave thyzel pratty?" The references through the play were all of this kind—a satire on the widespread fear of what our neighbours will say. It was not that Mrs. Grundy had set up a high standard of virtue. It was for the nineteenth century to erect her into a censor of morals; the eighteenth was quite innocent and unashamed.

But though such plays were fresh and easy to enjoy, the plots were silly, and the characterization generally poor. No one could approach the standard which Sheridan had set more than twenty years before. As Kelly told him, he was himself afraid to write—afraid of the author of The School For Scandal. Leigh Hunt, who about 1805 set a new standard in honest dramatic criticism, gave a curious explanation. He said that the age showed a dearth of dramatic character from which to draw, a strange complaint at a time when, apart from the eccentricities to be found in Yorkshire manors, midland meeting-houses, and Devonshire vicarages, one might in Bond Street come across such oddities as Old Quin ogling the girls, Beau Brummell with his coxcombical pretensions, "Citizen" Stanhope advertising his socialism, Lord Barrymore arm in arm with his unwashed butt Pasquin, the grand Lord Abercorn strutting in his order of the garter, and, great as he was, a great buffoon when he chose to be, Charley Fox. Lamb himself was so fortunate as to be able to discover a "character" in almost everyone of his relations and friends, from "S.T.C."—which was not difficult, seeing that by his own account Coleridge had become one by the time he emerged from childhood—down to his own father and, almost, his sister Mary. Had he possessed dramatic talent, he would have had no lack of material. It was this which was generally wanting, perhaps through the idea firmly fixed in the minds of most Englishmen that talking has very little to do with action. It is at least significant that, as Leigh Hunt pointed out, the three most amusing dramatists of the eighteenth century had been all Irishmen—Sheridan, Goldsmith, and O'Keefe.

How bad theatrical taste was, is instanced by the surprising success of Master Betty. His very brief career seemed to have been an expressly ordained exception to the rule that in vain is the net spread in the sight of the bird. It is perfectly obvious that a child must be incapable of expressing great passions. Yet the appearance on the London boards in 1804 of the Young Roscius, as he was called, at the age of thirteen, caused the most riotous excitement. The ill-dressed crowd surpassed themselves in violence, and the well-dressed were not behind them in disregard of order. His Douglas was admired by Pitt, who was seen to weep, by Fox who certainly should have known better, and by almost all the great people of the day. At Drury Lane he brought in over seventeen thousand pounds in twenty-eight nights, and received a salary himself of a hundred guineas a night. All of a sudden, after a few months, the town awoke to the fact that after all this was a boy without much more stock-in-trade than his consummate assurance, and sent him back to his books. The appearance of a female in the field—a young Roscia—crowned the absurdity, and completed the disillusionment on the subject of infant phenomena.

Yet these were the days of the great glory of the English stage, Kemble's sister, Sarah Siddons. The brother was the typical heavy tragedian. His sepulchral tones and unearthly dignity were well suited to the weightier passages of British drama, but he lacked life, he was monotonous, and his movements were pompous and even awkward. The sister had some kindred faults, which foreign visitors, though they were not wanting in admiration, did not fail to note. Baert found that her action wanted freedom and that she exaggerated the pathetic, Niebuhr that there was a false declamation of the serious passages. But all agreed that she was a Queen upon the stage. Her dignity was such that, as Madame de Staël wrote, she sacrificed nothing of it when she prostrated herself on the ground. Her power when she represented the great passions was extraordinary, and many stories are told of its wonderful effect. In one play she used to reach a climax with the cry, "Oh, my Biron! my Biron!" One night in Edinburgh a passionate girl was so moved by it that she had to be carried out of the theatre hysterically repeating the fatal words. It was the name with which a mysterious destiny was to connect her own unhappy lot. In an evil hour in the following year Catherine Gordon became the wife of the mad Jack Byron, who ruined her fortune and rendered her life miserable, and made her the mother of the child who immortalized his own heritage of woe. In audiences prepared to receive the contagion of emotion and to communicate it by that strange power which men and women crowded together have over one another, the effect was occasionally still more extraordinary. A young lawyer, afterwards well known as the friend of poets and philosophers, Henry Crabbe Robinson, one night interrupted one of the most pathetic scenes of the favourite with a loud laugh, and his outraged neighbours were just about to show their exasperation in a very summary way, when it was found that the youth was only suffering from a hysterical outburst. It was in parts where she could sweep the souls of her audience like a whirlwind that Mrs. Siddons excelled. Such was Lady Macbeth—a character in which her individuality had the fullest play. She improved upon stage tradition in her conception of the human and natural element in the part, on which she left her ideas on record, besides living once more in it in picture on the canvas of Richard Westall. A very different portrait of her is given, not by the painter's brush but by the pen of a visitor, as he once found her. She is in an attic—one babe taking nature's nourishment at her breast; she rocks the cradle in which another child is lying, while with her disengaged hand she holds the part which she is conning for the next performance. It is in such a homely moment that it is most delightful to picture the great Siddons.

Painting in England in the eighteenth century owed much to the institution of the Royal Academy, a happy mean between the direct patronage of the State in vogue on the Continent, and in England itself in Tudor and Stuart times, and the complete surrender of the art to the general public for encouragement. Opposition squibs made fun of Benjamin

West, the President, who had succeeded Sir Joshua Reynolds in 1792, as a mere nonentity conjured into artistic existence by George III, and posterity is disinclined to revoke the verdict. Yet, born in the American colonies, he had obtained a high reputation in Italy before he was introduced to the British court. Far from being a mere formalist, he had been an innovator in his day—another pioneer of romantic realism. He thought that scenes of contemporary life should be painted in the dress which the actors actually wore. He refused to portray General Wolfe and his men in the dress of ancient Rome, as James Barry persisted in doing, in spite of his example. He had done a great service, too, in advocating the original institution of the Academy in 1768. Several members of the original forty Academicians were still alive in 1801; the list contains some distinguished names of foreign origin, testifying to the extent to which England had become a home for artists. Among the original members were Angelica Kauffmann, the once gay and beautiful, and Francesco Bartolozzi, famed as an engraver, but unable under the Academy rules to have risen even to the degree of an Associate, had he not been a painter as well. Another foreigner was Henry Fuseli, noted rather as the Academy Professor of Painting and the friend and guide of other artists, than as an artist himself. Other Academicians were Thomas Stothard, prince of illustrators, and the rival successors to Reynolds as portrait painters, John Hoppner and Thomas Lawrence. The time was not far distant when the latter was to obtain the undisputed mastery, and a prescriptive right to the portraiture of all public men. Already in 1802 his price was 120 guineas for a whole length portrait, and it rose to 400 in 1810. The grace of the old days was indeed gone—lost with George Romney, who died a broken man in 1802. Something of the charm of those pictures of children, of a graciousness which brings moisture into the eyes of those who look at them, survived in Lawrence, but it was a faint echo only. It was in landscape, not in portraits, nor—as the age itself fondly believed—in historical pictures in the grand style, that the new century was to distinguish itself.

Joseph Mallord William Turner was born in London in 1775. There is something grandiloquent about such names for a barber's son as he was, and they lend some colour to the suggestion that the child was named after his mother's brother; for his father had married into a family of a rather higher social standing than his own. Whether he inherited his taste from this source or not, there is no doubt that to his mother Turner owed much of his eccentricity and uncertainty of temper. But on the father's side he was not far removed from the country. The barber had only migrated to London from Devon, that county of artists, a short while before the painter was born. Yet Turner was to derive his chief early inspiration not from the sunny west but from the scarred limestone hills of Yorkshire. In 1790 he exhibited his first drawing in the Academy, where he was now a student, though he learnt little either here or in the schools where he was taught to read and write. He was all his life something of an unlettered savage, though he could, when necessary, write a very tolerable letter. This most atmospheric of painters even composed strange poetry in which great ideas stand out sharply side by side like irregular blocks of marble piled one upon another. Perhaps it was owing to this very irregularity and imperfection in his education that, though eventually the most original of painters, it was so long before he felt himself able to stand alone. He was admitted as an Academician in 1802, when he had already for five years been exhibiting oil paintings at the Academy; but he went on imitating for many years, and it was long before his genius was to burst forth upwards into the sky and sunlight, its natural home. In his boyhood he had imitated Reynolds, in whose studio he studied for a while; in his early manhood the naval glories of his country inspired his brush, as well as that of many others, and set him about imitating the Dutch sea-painters; he had his periods too when, although he painted greatly, he painted after Claude, Poussin, and Wilson, and—rather more strangely—after far less eminent contemporaries such as Alexander Nasmyth and David Wilkie. At intervals, as during his tour to the Alps in 1802, and in his Yorkshire subjects, he was himself, but hardly yet even feeling his way to what he afterwards become.

It was fitting that the last generation of eminent Scotsmen who were still proud to be recognized by their speech to belong to the north of the Tweed, should have included Scotland's great portrait painter, Henry Raeburn. Born in 1756, a miller's son, he made a provident early marriage with a wealthy widow, which enabled him to complete his studies in Rome. A remarkable union of Scottish temperament with artistic talent, he refused to be drawn into any school, kept to the practical side of art, and painted exactly what he saw; and that was almost every eminent fellow countryman of his day. Painting at once with the brush, he lost no time over outlines, and finished his portraits in four or five sittings of an hour and a half each. His hard, strong lines were suited to the vigorous lineaments of his countrymen; after middle age he gained softness enough to do successful pictures of women, preferably strong-minded old ladies of the type for which the Auld Toun was famous. But he was always at his best in men; and it was in them that he excelled in revealing the dignity of human nature. He wisely remained in Edinburgh to honour his own people. David Wilkie, a son of a minister of the Kirk, did not. Like many a Scot before him, he came up to London by the Leith packet, as a mere boy, to seek his fortune. At a time when the general preference was for either the grand historical style, or sea-fights, or portraits of men or at least animals, this youth struck out a line of his own and painted the Village Politicians. He followed it up next year in the 1807 Exhibition with the Blind Fiddler, when he was still only just twenty-one. These homely scenes won universal popularity, and the young artist was hailed as second to no Dutchman who ever bore a palette on his thumb.

Southey made his usually rather uncomplimentary Spaniard write that the English excelled all other nations in water-colours. England had indeed the honour, through Thomas Girtin, of the discovery of water-colour painting as a distinct art. He was a companion and contemporary of Turner, who was greatly influenced by him. He died in 1802. Turner could hardly have made a living had he confined himself to his water-colours, excellent as they were; and the same has to be said of the struggling originators of the Norwich School, John Crome and John Cotman. "Old Crome", as he was called, founded in that town the first provincial art club in 1803. They had to teach in order to live, and they painted in oil as well as water-colour the fields and waterways of their native East Anglia and the barges sailing among them.

It was natural that only a few shillings could be obtained for the best water-colours. It was a time when the taste for the picturesque in nature was still very imperfectly developed. The average man's distrust of his own judgement in the case of an original work was heightened by the circumstance of his having to exercise it on a new class of artistic object altogether. Moreover, there already existed a mass of beautiful reproductions in colour and in black and white of pictures by established artists which he might himself have seen, and which in any case it was safe to admire. No paintings lent themselves better to reproduction in colour than those of George Morland, who brought a life shortened by drunkenness to an unhappy end in 1804, and whose charming pictures of country life and animals appealed to much that was characteristic of the British people. Among those who popularized him, the outstanding name is that of his brother-in-law, James Ward, pupil of John Raphael Smith, the great portrait engraver; but there were many others. The new arts of stipple engraving, of which Bartolozzi was such an exponent, and lithography, very soon found a home in the country where Prince Rupert had so successfully introduced the art of mezzotinting nearly a century and a half earlier. But some were not without invention even here. One was William Blake, a true pre-Raphaelite, the primitive reverence of whose conceptions as in his Procession from Calvary, recalls the qualities of the dawn of art, one, too, who owed as little as a man can owe to any predecessor. Few designs are more original than his own wonderful illustrations to his poem, Milton, published in 1804. Turner yielded to the prevailing taste for engravings in 1807, when he started the splendid series of mezzotinted etchings which he named the Liber Studiorum, the first group being etched by himself and engraved by his namesake Charles Turner.

It was the great day of British sculpture, even if it produced none who could, even distantly, be mentioned with the contemporary Canova. The strange miserly uncultivated Londoner of Dutch descent, Joseph Nollekens, was born as early as 1737. Almost till his death in 1823 he continued to exhibit at the Academy. His busts and monuments were everywhere throughout the country. He left £200,000. His great rival was John Flaxman, Blake's "Dear Sculptor of Eternity", a poor lad born in York in 1755. In his youth he designed for Wedgwood's cameo wares, later on he spent seven years in Rome and showed his instinct for classical art in his designs for Homer's poems, which Blake engraved. After his return from Rome in 1794 he became a sculptor principally of monuments, which he executed for many cathedrals and churches throughout England. He was represented at St. Paul's Cathedral by the monument to Sir Joshua Reynolds for which he designed the model. In 1810 he was appointed to the new post of Professor of Sculpture in the Academy.

Architecture was one of the first of the arts to receive the impulse of the romantic movement. In its early emancipation it took the form of gothic eccentricity in Horace Walpole's buildings on Strawberry Hill, precisely as literature did in his Castle of Otranto. Such mediaeval fancies of the sixties of the eighteenth century were not much more than indications of the genuine love of history, and admiration of what was good in the Middle Ages, which were to follow. The leading architect of the day was James Wyatt, born in 1746, a Royal Academician who filled the presidential chair in 1805 during a temporary retirement of West. He signalized himself by buildings of an absurdity, which surpassed the fantastic conceptions of the gothic romancer because they were designed upon a larger scale. At Fonthill, in Wiltshire, for example, he must share with its eccentric owner, William Beckford, the author of the Eastern Tale, Vathek, the responsibility for a preposterous mixture of an abbey and a castle which was described in the Gentleman's Magazine of the time as a building of wonderful grandeur and utility. Its main feature was a tower nearly three hundred feet high. In executing an order for a work in the classical style, as in the case of Doddington Park, in Gloucestershire, built about the same time, and in his London buildings, he was more successful; he seemed to have more confidence in himself. His younger contemporary, John Soane, born in 1753, although a man of deeper originality, adhered more generally to that style. His great work, the rebuilding of most of the Bank of England, which occupied the last years of the century, was a masterpiece in the adaptation of the classical style to modern requirements. He became Professor of Architecture at the Academy in 1806. A still younger man, Robert Smirke, born in 1781, architect to the Board of Trade and designer in 1809 of the Mint on on Tower Hill, was, like Wyatt, affectedly mediaeval in the noblemen's mansions which he constructed in the country, and classical in his public buildings.

There were some champions of another and an older

style of classical architecture. In the first years of the century a new world of art had been disclosed to the cultured classes of Europe, when the chief of the sculptures of the Parthenon temple at Athens which the seventh Earl of Elgin, Ambassador at Constantinople, had obtained leave from the Porte to remove, had been successfully conveyed to London. The merits of the finest sculptures in the world were not immediately recognized. But the best judges of the day were agreed, and few passages in the biographies of art are more inspiring than Benjamin Haydon's own account of the enthusiasm with which that young painter set about copying and studying them, working through the livelong day with scarcely a thought for food or rest. About the same time a Greek school in architecture was led by William Wilkins. Born in 1778, he had obtained in 1801 a travelling bachelorship from Cambridge University, and on his return from a tour in Greece, Asia Minor, and Italy, became the architect of Downing College. Like others, he designed in gothic for country residences. His design for Grange Park, in Hampshire, was an exception and a failure of a characteristic type. Gothic would have been unsuitable, as parts of the old Inigo Jones building were retained. But the slavish copy of the Parthenon which he put up was entirely unadapted to the surroundings and to the requirements of an Englishman's house.

The admirable proportions of the London houses and blocks of houses built about this time attest the influence of Wyatt and Soane as well as older architects. But the homes of the middle classes throughout the kingdom were little affected by them. Those charming houses, in which a desire for "elegance" was happily reconciled with both dignity and comfort, were the joint work of builder and owner. In the case of the poor, unfortunately, utility was the one consideration; but in the country, as cheapness of materials was essential, and the cheapest were those nearest to hand, a cottage usually produced the effect of having naturally grown out of its surroundings. The idea of utility governed the subject of furniture in the case of poor and rich alike. The last of the great eighteenth-century designers, Thomas Sheraton, was still alive, although his cabinets and beds were now beginning to lose their characteristic lightness of shape, influenced as he was by the heavy and at the same time somewhat fantastic style of the first French Empire. But in any case those who bought the furniture did not take much interest in the subject. They cared much more for their cornices, their mantelpieces, their chandeliers, their wines, and their books. They had also to attend to their shrubberies and parks. One Prime Minister of the day, Lord Grenville, is perhaps better remembered in the plantations which he laid out at his home, Dropmore, in Buckinghamshire, than in anything else. The passion for making nature suburban had by now disappeared. Writing in 1771, Arthur Young only expressed the feeling of the day in giving vent to his disgust at the miniature Versailles which a Duke of Devonshire had introduced among the hills of Derbyshire. The same traveller had admired Lord Rockingham for cutting off a part of a hill to let in the landscape. At least such an interference with nature was the effect of a desire for an extended view, not the work of a man content within a walled garden. As that century drew on to its close nature was trusted more and more; and where grounds had to be laid out, the owners of great places took her for their teacher. When the painter baronet, Sir George Beaumont, wished to lay out his grounds, he felt that he could go to no one better for a landscape gardener than his friend the poet Wordsworth.

In prose literature the time was singularly poor. The great historians of the eighteenth century seemed to have left no followers. Metaphysics were not studied. There were very few who, like Coleridge and Robinson, had the patience to learn the language of Immanuel Kant, and realized the privilege which they enjoyed in being his contemporaries.

Most of those Britons who regarded themselves as philosophers resembled Sir James Mackintosh who first avoided him as unintelligible, and, later on, about the time of his death in 1805, observing that German studies had grown deeper still, passed him over with relief as now disdainfully rejected even by his countrymen as a superficial and popular writer. Sermons were published and reviewed in larger numbers than any other class of book. This does not imply that the public was theologically inclined, much less the existence of searching inquiries into the nature of the Supreme Being or the sacred books of Christianity. At a time when a large proportion of the best writers on secular subjects were in orders it was natural for sermons to deal with a considerable range outside theology. Many of the clergy were indolent enough to be glad to borrow from the sermons published by others. The growing class of leisured female readers demanded more than the mere novelist or other composer of light literature was able to supply. Finally a volume of sermons formed pre-eminently a class of book usually bought for other people to read. All this, combined with the interest which under the impulse of the evangelical movement was beginning to be displayed in practical Christianity, explains the number of sermons issued from the press.

The four prose writers of the period who left some mark on contemporaries and on posterity, Paley, Bentham, Godwin, and Malthus, occupied that border country of which the Englishman is particularly fond, existing between philosophy proper and the inquiry into practical problems of politics and economics. It is impossible to think of the two divines among these four without recalling Shelley's bitter denunciation. "For my part, I had rather be damned with Plato and Lord Bacon, than go to Heaven with Paley and Malthus." There is little, however, to warm the heart about any of the four. Shelley's own father-in-law, William Godwin, cuts a very drab figure beside other composers of Utopias who have lived at different times in the world. Born in 1756, the son of a dry dissenting minister, he followed at first the same vocation. He soon lost his religious beliefs, but continued to retain the harsher qualities of the nonconformist temperament. At forty years of age he was at the height of his fame. Political Justice was the book of the day. His abstractions had power for a while to enchain the flight of Wordsworth. Coleridge was his passionate admirer. He wrote in 1800 a poor play, Antonio, and it was put on the boards by Kemble—unsuccessfully. Three years later he came before the public with a Life of Chaucer, and in 1805 with the third of his published novels, Fleetwood, or The New Man of Feeling. Both were read because they were by the author of Political Justice and of the novel Caleb Williams, though Godwin was a bookworm who knew little of mankind, and, in particular, was ill qualified as a biographer of one of the most human of poets.

A reformer of the world has a heavy task before him. He is bound—if he is to carry out his task faithfully—to study human nature in all its infinite variety. But Godwin had had no time for this. He found a shorter way. He took mankind in the mass. In the opening of his Enquiry concerning Political Justice and its influence on Morals and Happiness he wrote: "May it not be found, that the attempt to alter the morals of mankind singly and in detail is an erroneous and futile undertaking; and that it will then only be effectually and decisively performed, when, by regenerating their political institutions, we shall change their motives and produce a revolution in the influences that act upon them!" Godwin dealt in abstractions, like a German. His work appeared precisely at the one moment in their country's history when such a work was likely to appeal to a large class of Englishmen. It was February of the year 1793. Most thinking men had welcomed the French Revolution at the commencement. But some had been staggered by the writings of Burke; some had been shocked to discover in the past six months that the new order of things could only be inaugurated in France by appalling bloodshed; some had begun to see in that country's conduct of her foreign relations, which had just thrown her into a state of war with Great Britain, that she would prove the enemy of the time-honoured rights and liberties of mankind. Those who desired some better ground for the faith which was in them than the doings across the Channel, found Political Justice a book made to their purpose. But although Godwin treated of abstractions, he did not examine such ideas as justice and happiness in the manner of a true philosopher. He would not have been so popular with the English public if he had done so. While appearing to base his theory on abstract principles, he actually took the French Revolution and the authors whose works had led to it as his starting-point. He held that all men should be equal, and that human institutions and contracts were generally bad. He ridiculed family affection. He advocated free love. It is scarcely a coincidence that the decline in his literary authority set in with the close of the century, at just about the same time as that of the immoral German drama which was so effectually ridiculed in Canning's Anti-Jacobin. With the transformation of France from a power struggling to be free herself to one which destroyed the freedom of other countries, Godwin's works lost weight on the political side. But he was still perhaps the leading writer of the day.

It was interest in Political Justice which first brought a new writer into the field. The Reverend Thomas Malthus's Essay on the Principle of Population was first published in 1798, and, after a controversy with Godwin himself, it reached its final form in 1803. It was intended to show that there was another difficulty in the way of the perfectibility of mankind besides the evil character of political institutions, namely, the difficulty of obtaining enough to eat—as a biological age afterwards put it, the struggle for existence—

or, as the rationalizing eighteenth century preferred, the principle of population. As early as 1753, Robert Wallace, a Scottish minister, had shadowed forth the idea in his Dissertation on the Numbers of Mankind. Divested of its arithmetic form, Malthus's principle, which Coleridge and Southey derided as self-evident, was that population tended to increase at a much faster rate than the means of subsistence, and had to be kept down by certain checks. These —in the existing state of mankind—he found in vice and misery. His motives in writing were high. Born in 1766, he was young enough to improve his mind deeply by foreign travel between 1798 and 1803, and modest enough to recast a great part of the work before publishing the second edition. He was now much more than what he had been hitherto—a fellow of a Cambridge college. The new edition was, as he himself wrote in the preface, a new work. He admitted another check to population besides vice and misery. He notices only to disapprove the prudential checks mentioned by the Roman satirist Juvenal as existing in the Rome of the day. The only prudential checks approved by him—practically all that were known to the England of his time—were those of continence and late marriage. This destroyed much of the value of his book regarded as an answer to Godwin. For if mankind are to improve at all, it is not too much to expect that they will eventually reach that point of prudence and restraint already attained, according to Malthus himself, by clerks in counting-houses, and the sons of tradesmen and farmers, among whom it was not the practice to marry early. "And of course you wholely confute your former pamphlet", wrote Coleridge triumphantly in the margin of the preface in his copy. It was a just criticism. His numerous opponents were able to attack the admitted harshness of the conclusions of his first essay, and when they were confronted with the second, to point out its inconsistency.

Malthus was a typical Whig. He was naturally attracted

by Godwin's idea. But he found it impracticable, as it hanged too much on reason and too little on nature. Meanwhile he turned towards such obvious matters as the poor law, and the attitude usually taken up in society towards the institution of marriage. There was, he thought, quite a wrong way of thinking in vogue upon this matter. "If the subject be fairly considered", he wrote, "and the respected matron weighed in the scales of justice against the neglected old maid, it is possible that the matron might kick the beam". For the maid—so Malthus supposed—might almost certainly have married if she had been determined on doing so, and, as it was, her self-denial had made room for another marriage. Nor does he blame the poor man for having a large family. "He has always been told that to raise up subjects for his king and country is a very meritorious act. He has done this act, and yet is suffering for it." Or if not, it was only because he had been rescued from the natural consequences of his act by the poor law, which had also encouraged him to commit it, and this law Malthus, as a practical reformer, desired to abolish. Instead of continuing a vicious remedy for a vicious state of things, he wished to get rid of the evil at the source, to explain to the poor their true situation, and to prevent the market from being overstocked with labour. Writing as a lover of freedom, he regretted to observe another result of the pressure of population upon the means of subsistence, the tendency, which had been so particularly evident in 1800 and 1801, of the mob to get out of hand. The effect had been that the country gentlemen of England had given up a part of their birthright of liberty. "They appeared", he thought, "to surrender themselves to government on condition of being protected from the mob." And, as himself one of that same stock, he stood up for agriculture. He did not desire to see a surplus population filling the manufacturing towns. He was left cold by all that was said about England's growing wealth. It was its distribution and not its increase which mattered; and, to show what a price the manhood of the country had to pay for such improvements, he transcribed from Doctor Aikin's Description of the country round Manchester, the most complete account then published of the social evils of the factory system. The regrettable thing is, not as Malthus's numerous adversaries contended, that his views obtained so much influence, but that they did not obtain more.

The other Cambridge fellow who left a mark on the era was Archdeacon Paley. Born in 1743, he had written most of his works before the century closed. His Natural Theology, however, was published in 1802, only three years before his own death. The outstanding merit of both Godwin and Malthus was lucidity, and in this they did not surpass Paley. By this gift he was enabled to convey a sort of distinction to observations which had not much other merit. Malthus was one of those men of his time who had some glimmerings of the idea of evolution. But Paley had no notion of God fulfilling Himself by the process of developing higher out of lower forms of existence. To him the world was a wonderful mechanism, full of adjustments and contrivances suggesting an Almighty Contriver. One of the most attractive parts of Natural Theology was that in which he deduced the goodness of God from the happiness of His creatures; and with this he brought to a conclusion a work which had often been interrupted by the severe sufferings of the disorder from which he died, and in bearing which he showed a most exemplary fortitude. The quiet cheerfulness of his writings, which were like his life, was one cause of their popularity.

In his Principles of Moral and Political Philosophy, published in 1785, Paley had to some extent anticipated Jeremy Bentham, usually regarded as the founder of the Utilitarian philosophy. Virtue he defined as "the doing good to mankind, in obedience to the will of God, and for the sake of everlasting happiness". "Actions", he wrote in his chapter on Utility, "are to be estimated by their tendency. Whatever is expedient is right. It is the utility of any moral rule alone, which constitutes the obligation of it." This was treated as the basis of morality—in contrast to the idea of a moral sense—not merely by Paley, but by almost everyone at this time who thought anything at all about the matter. Not only did such men as Malthus believe in it, but it was accepted by idealists such as Godwin, and, after him, Wordsworth and Coleridge. It had long been in the air. As early as 1776, Bentham himself, in the preface to his Fragments on Government, casually observed that the basis of morals was the fundamental axiom: "It is the greatest happiness of the greatest number that is the measure of right and wrong." He did not claim originality for the formula. Born in 1748, the son of a London attorney he was himself educated for the bar, and was well qualified to spend a lifetime in exposing legal absurdities. He first brought himself into notice by the Fragment on Government, which was a trenchant attack on the standard legal work on the law and constitution, Blackstone's Commentaries. It brought him the friendship of Lord Shelburne, afterwards Lansdowne, and several other leading men of the day. About this time he flattered himself with the idea of becoming a philosopher. His Introduction to the Principles of Morals and Legislation was printed in 1780, but was not published till 1789. The foundation of Utilitarianism may be dated from this year. It hardly deserves to be called a philosophy; indeed, it would be scarcely too much to say that the founder of it did not trouble himself to inquire what philosophy was. As a young man, he believed it to be one of the functions of education to inspire a contempt for ancient philosophy, as being the philosophy of words; and by the position which he arrogated he inspired a disgust for modern philosophy himself. His own was the philosophy of lists. By some curious, possibly atavistic, strain in his nature, he was drawn to make the most bewildering and complicated lists of every kind of thing connected with his subject, much as his great-grandfather, who was a pawnbroker, might have done for the various articles in his shop. The result was a well elaborated system, which was, however, of no use to anyone. To explain it in the case of a part only of his Table of the Springs of Action would, Bentham wrote, have required a volume; and that volume he has not vouchsafed.

There are some commodities which, by a mysterious economic law, are increased in value by being exported to foreign countries and back again. The writings of Bentham belong to this class. He made presents of codes and constitutions to potentates in distant parts of the world, and, although they were not actually adopted, a widespread admiration was displayed for this genius who had so little honour in his own country. In 1802, while the British public was still wondering when he was going to publish something intelligible, a Swiss admirer, Etienne Dumont, took the "Introduction", cut out as much as possible of the useless morals, and produced a short treatise on the General Principles of Legislation in admirable French. The three slim volumes which he published in that lucid language were composed partly on the basis of the work of 1789, partly on that of the Sibylline leaves which were to be found scattered in the recess where the master worked. It was natural that Bentham should have been better known abroad than at home. At the same time he kept up a voluminous correspondence with men in power in England, mostly on some practical question of the day. His criticisms of Pitt's Poor Law Bill of 1797 helped to induce its withdrawal. He proposed to him in 1792 a plan for a circular prison, in which the inspector was to live in the centre and see everything which went on. He made him a definite offer to take charge of the building himself, to reside there, to take upon himself the control of a thousand convicts, and to defray most of the cost, which he could afford to do. At first all was favourable. But presently he found himself involved in one of those baffling mysteries which exasperate those who have to do with Government offices. First it was a Cabinet Minister, Lord Spencer, who would not sell Bentham his land. When the land had been purchased, it was the King himself who was the obstacle. This went on for twenty years. "Never was anyone worse used than Bentham", wrote Wilberforce on the subject. At last, in 1813, the Government escaped with a payment of £23,000 as compensation for him for his expenses, agreeably to an Act of Parliament "for the non-performance of an agreement between the said Jeremy Bentham and the Commissioners of His Majesty's Treasury". This was the chief practical matter in which he interested himself in those years. Others were the convict settlement in New South Wales, which he attacked as useless, the reform of the Scottish law-courts, for which he proposed a scheme to Lord Grenville, and the packing of special juries. It was in such comparatively small works that he was seen at his best. Some, such as The Elements of the Art of Packing, were not published for years afterwards, for fear of bringing trouble upon the author. The best, Truth versus Ashurst, is as amusing a bit of satire as one of Sydney Smith's. It is unfortunate alike for his contemporaries and for posterity that Bentham did not explore this vein more frequently, instead of trying his hand at being a philosopher.

In prose of a less serious kind the time was not rich. The art of novel writing was not yet understood by the generality of those who undertook to be purveyors of this kind of literature to the public. The output was small; it would have been easy for a determined female novel reader to peruse every one of the seventy or eighty published in the country in the year. Short stories in prose were not thought of; even a short novel such as Castle Rackrent was an exception. The public required a book of a certain length, and the average novel writer had little idea of how the reciprocal effect of character upon incident can be so treated as to sustain interest through the requisite three volumes. The commonest class was that popularized by Mrs. Radcliffe, whose Mysteries of Udolpho, published in 1794, was still being widely read and widely imitated ten years later. She had a limitation common to almost all the novelists of the day, of being unable to write at all except at long intervals; and published nothing between 1800 and 1810. Her school might be described by the title of a play of the same class written by Matthew Lewis, as the Castle Spectre school. Grim castles, mouldering abbeys, hidden doors, secret crimes, midnight ghosts, and clanking chains made up the staple of about half the new fiction read up to 1810. They were sometimes dignified with the title of romances to distinguish them from the mere novel. They satisfied and contributed to a growing taste for the gothic and mediaeval, which was soon to be turned to such splendid account by Walter Scott. The other class of novels proper described the contemporary life of the upper and upper middle classes. German sentimental influences were now weakening, and the taste for the immoral, though still strong, was on the decline. The age was losing its grossness, and the art of pandering to the lower passions without being coarse was always rare in Britain. The most successful novel of the decade was Surr's A Winter in London, which ran into its fifth edition in 1806, the year of its first publication. Weakness of plot and psychology was supplied by descriptions of some of the ordinary experiences of a fashionable Londoner, which insured its success with country readers. Hannah More took advantage of the popular taste, to publish Coelebs in Search of a Wife in 1807. It was, of course, a veiled religious tract, but it showed some folk how fashionable people lived, and was very popular.

Whether theological or not, the female novelist's tendency was to inculcate morality. This was exhibited in the principal woman writer of the day, Maria Edgeworth.

Born in 1767, the eldest daughter of a gentleman of many matrimonial adventures, who had a bewildering family of nineteen children by one or other of his four successive wives, she was early led to interest herself in the subject of the education of children. She wrote stories for children, and collaborated with her father in a work on education. All these were deservedly successful. In 1800 she turned aside to produce a masterpiece—Castle Rackrent. Spending, as she did, most of her time on her father's estate of Edgeworthstown in Ireland, she was a warm lover of the Irish. She belonged for the most part to that class of writers which is inclined to minimize the distinctions of race. Her mother and grandmother were English, and her father was far from being a typical Irishman. As a rule the distinctive oddities of the Irish character did not attract her; she was more anxious to show that they were a perfectly intelligible people which was misunderstood and oppressed. But the terrible events of 1798 shook her and inspired her. In Castle Rackrent she described a typical worthless spendthrift lovable Irish landlord from the point of view of a typical faithful humorous slovenly Irish retainer. Novel though the idea and the subject were, and in spite of the first edition being published anonymously, it was a complete success. But she never followed it up. It had long struck her father and her that education did not stop in childhood. She set herself to write society novels in which naughtiness brings a grown-up person to a bad end, the good are ultimately rewarded, and indulged with their fill of moral admonition during their pilgrimage, just as inevitably as occurs with children in a well-ordered nursery. In Belinda and in Leonora—the latter a crushing exposure of the sentimental female humbug whose character has been perverted by German novels, and what was then called metaphysics, but was no more than a muddleheaded casuistry—Maria behaved somewhat warily. But by 1809 when she began her Tales of Fashionable Life, she threw off all disguise, and appeared as a moral teacher to old and young alike. Meanwhile, she had already written Popular Tales for the sake of a poorer class of readers than those for whom novels were generally written. She wrote of the poor not as they appeared from the carriage windows, but as they actually were in their homes. She also showed that something much shorter than the ordinary novel was possible. Her style was admirably easy and popular. Except in Leonora, in which the old fashion of a series of letters is adopted, there is little in the style which recalls the peculiar characteristics of the eighteenth century. But there is in the general treatment of life. There is little real elevation of thought, and scarcely a mention of so much as the existence of religion in volume after volume of her works. It is significant that this side of life is completely left out of her book on Practical Education.

There was as yet little else that was good in the lighter side of prose literature. Two essayists who were afterwards celebrated had not yet found their vein. Charles Lamb, who was born in 1775, had early come forward as a writer. In 1798 he had the honour of being pilloried in the Anti-Jacobin along with Coleridge and others as a dangerous incendiary. His name was therefore known in the world. But his duties as a clerk in the India House kept him usually in London, and he had little time for intimacy with those who were, at this time, the vagabonds of literature. For many years he was not doing much besides journalist's hack work and unsuccessful efforts for the stage, until at last he succeeded, in collaboration with his sister Mary, with two books of stories for children, Mrs. Leicester's School, and the more celebrated Tales from Shakespear, published in 1807. These works show very clearly how far the romantic movement had gone on what may be called its realistic side. The Tales from Shakespear recognized that the child is something better than an undeveloped grown-up person. But they are not really written in a child's language. In the preface to Mrs. Leicester's School the confession is made that the children do not tell their stories altogether in their own words, and it is suggested that this defect is inevitable. The return to nature could not yet be complete, any more than in the conversations of children and village people in Maria Edgeworth's Tales. In the following year Lamb exhibited another aspect of the romantic movement. The cult of the greatest of English dramatists had been steadily growing for generations, and the Tales had rapidly become an immense success. The time now seemed to be ripe to call the attention of the world to the excellence of some of his contemporaries, of whom Lamb complained that only Fletcher and Massinger were then read. The attempt was made; the British Museum was largely put into requisition; and some fine specimens of the Elizabethan drama were successfully reintroduced to the world.

A fiercer spirit than Coleridge's gentle-hearted Charles was William Hazlitt, born in 1778, like Godwin a Nonconformist minister's son, who retained a theologian's bitterness long after he had lost his religion. At present he was amusing himself with philosophical and political tracts of little interest in themselves, but showing a foretaste of that splendid style which combines all the clarity of the eighteenth century with the chaste wealth of a mind which has drunk deeply of the best English literature of the past. The most popular and perhaps the purest prose published at this time was Southey's. His Letters from England by Don Manuel Alvarez Espriella, published in 1807, formed a delightful picture of England from the point of view of an imaginary Spanish traveller. Like Castle Rackrent it was an example of an author successfully attempting a new flight without the aid of a name which had already won popularity. The wittiest production of the decade, and that which produced incomparably the greatest sensation, was the Reverend Sydney Smith's Letters of Peter Plymley.

Such a mass of new literature required a new order of criticism, and this was provided in the Edinburgh Review, the first issue of which appeared in October 1802. The idea was due to Sydney Smith. Books were of course noticed in the magazines, such as the Monthly Magazine and the rather colourless Gentleman's Magazine, which filled much of its space and derived much of its interest from the English practice of permitting those who had anything to say to communicate it in the form of letters to the Editor. There were also reviews such as the Monthly Review in which an occasional attempt was made to enter rather more widely into the subject of the book under notice than is required for the purpose of mere passing criticism. But there was nothing of the sort in Edinburgh, and there were a number of young Whig lawyers and others who had great brains and energy, and not enough employment. One of these, Francis Jeffrey, became the editor of the new review, and among his coadjutors, besides Smith himself, were Henry Brougham and Francis Horner. At first the editorial "we" was a reality; the friends all met in a dingy room in the Old Town and discussed one another's proofs. But Jeffrey was soon established as regular editor. All the articles retained a certain common impress. The contributors, as behoved the natives of a country which was supposed to derive its prosperity from popular education, were enthusiasts for the advancement of knowledge. "The violence of the multitude is indeed to be dreaded, but it will not be violent unless it be uninformed. It is superfluous to add, that a people who are enlightened are likely to be in the same proportion contented; and that the diffusion of knowledge is yet more essential, perhaps, to their tranquillity than it is to their freedom." These words, with much more on the immunity of the wise man from the artifices of sophistry, might have formed part of an article by almost any one of the contributors to the Review for the next fifty years, even of Macaulay himself. They were as a matter of fact the mature judgement of Jeffrey in 1793, then a youth just getting out of his teens.

The ability of the staff at once established the Edinburgh Review in the estimation of the public. Most other reviews were the organs of publishers, or booksellers—which still meant much the same thing, and they could not afford to be independent. The writers in them could not review unfavourably the works published by their own firms, while to do so to works published elsewhere would have drawn on them the invidious charge of being moved by commercial prejudice. Smith proposed to the publisher, Constable, to allow the editor to be independent, and to pay ten guineas a sheet. This was done, the minimum being afterwards raised to sixteen guineas. The Review was free to strike out a new path. It was issued quarterly. It disclaimed any intention to cover the whole field of literature. The number of articles fell rapidly from twenty-nine in the first number to less than half. It amused by a freedom of speech which was devoid of malice. Almost entirely written by Scotsmen, it possessed several other Scottish characteristics. While in reality actuated by great caution it appeared downright and uncompromising. The Edinburgh Reviewer thus obtained an air of originality while merely expressing in clear well-chosen language what his readers were already thinking, or on the point of thinking. There was some affectation of omniscience. In all probability Jeffrey and Brougham would have been ready to undertake to review a work on any subject. But this too was done in such a manner as to offend few. The omniscience was passed on, so to speak, to the reader, as in the celebrated "every schoolboy knows" of Macaulay a generation later. It was an advantage that, with notable exceptions, the contributors to the Review were not specialists, unless it was in law. Science was treated by them as men of the world who assumed that other men of the world would like to know what the scientists had to tell it.

Many of these characteristics appear in Jeffrey's review of Wordsworth's Poems in 1807. He admits the popularity of the Lyrical Ballads, and says that it has been deserved. From the book before him he quotes some of Wordsworth's great patriotic sonnets with unstinted praise. But the defects of the new School alarm him. Actuated by a sense of public duty he feels himself compelled to interpose his peremptory veto on any further advance of the tide of such alarming innovation. An excellent exposure of some of the more obvious faults of Wordsworth's style and choice of subjects is marred by instances of a complete want of taste which makes this article one of the curiosities of literary criticism. Like a true Scotsman, where he finds something which he does not altogether understand, he will give no quarter. It must be nonsense, and his readers must think the same. He actually quotes the two finest stanzas in the Ode to Duty, and the magnificent ninth stanza in that on the Intimations, for no other purpose than to point out to his readers how unintelligible Wordsworth can be. But his praise is even more remarkable. He admires the poem on the restoration of Lord Clifford the Shepherd, and quotes the opening and the end. He merely omits four lines which are notoriously worth all the rest put together, and which, if they were all that Wordsworth had ever written, would alone have sufficed to set him among the poets.

> "Love had he found in huts where poor men lie;
> His daily teachers had been woods and rills,
> The silence that is in the starry sky,
> The sleep that is among the lonely hills."

The reason of the omission is obvious. They were, like the passages in the other two poems, utterly unintelligible, and he did not wish to disturb the tenor of his praise by any jarring interruption. He would have been under the necessity of stopping to ask himself and his readers how a wood or a rill could *teach*, and how anyone could learn anything anyway from *silence* and *sleep*. He would not risk being told that he admired nonsense. While he led the crowd he was careful to watch which way it wished to go. Occasionally he took an independent line, although, when he did so, he was not fortunate. An unfavourable criticism of Marmion brought about not indeed a termination of his friendship with Scott, but that writer's refusal to go on contributing prose articles to the Review as he had hitherto done; with the exception of one many years later. In the autumn the poet took a further step. Jeffrey, in whom Scottish caution had taken the form of pessimism, had collaborated with Brougham in an article which was lamentable from every point of view. Already in January of 1807 he had accused the people of the country of blindness because they had not given up hope of victory. In the following year it might have been expected that the spectacle of his country at last united with a people engaged in a national struggle for independent existence, would have joined every friend of liberty with Sheridan in zeal for the prosecution of the war. But in an article published in October 1808, "Don Cevallos on the usurpation of Spain", Jeffrey and Brougham went still further in pusillanimity as regards foreign affairs, and in prognostications of revolution at home. Many of the readers of the nine thousand copies which formed the Review's regular output, only did so because they could get no good literary criticism elsewhere. Canning saw the need for some counterpoise. He had himself been the soul of a brilliant effort in journalism on the Government side ten years earlier—the Anti-Jacobin. The editor had been William Gifford, a little man like Jeffrey. A weekly venture like this, depending on talents which were needed by Government for its own immediate service, could not last, and the Anti-Jacobin had been succeeded by a Review which had nothing of the earlier journal but its name and its principles. Something much better was required. Canning had recourse to Scott, and with his help Gifford was obtained as editor, and John

Murray of Fleet Street as publisher, described in his letter to the new editor as "a young bookseller of capital and enterprise". The result was the Quarterly Review, which first appeared in February 1809. Scott and Southey regularly contributed. A worthy rival of the Edinburgh, it could not surpass a periodical which commanded the peculiar talents of Jeffrey and his friends. Nor did it fulfil the expectation, with which it set out, of enjoying the special assistance of Ministers.

About the time when a Scottish author and a Scottish publisher were inviting Englishmen to throw off Scotland's yoke in matters relating to literary and political criticism, the English universities, which had been so woefully behind that of Edinburgh, were beginning to rouse themselves from a century of lethargy. An English university career was still considered as something of no great importance, and was completed at an early age. Byron, for example, took his Master of Arts degree at Cambridge at twenty. The education of a slightly older Harrovian, Palmerston was even briefer. He ascribed the most valuable part of his mental training to the philosopher Dugald Stuart, whose lectures he attended in Edinburgh at the age of sixteen. At eighteen he was admitted to St. John's College, Cambridge, but, studious though he was, attached little importance to what he could learn in the place. He took a nobleman's privilege of matriculating and becoming Master of Arts without examination on the same day a few months later. The total number of matriculations at Cambridge rarely rose above two hundred in the first years of the century. In the sister university, which had a greater prestige, it was about two hundred and thirty. Such education as was to be had at Oxford was of a broader type. Though much behind Cambridge in the institution of examinations for degrees, which did not exist even voluntarily till 1800, it recognized the existence of humane letters as well as mathematics. The Cantabs had only a mathematical, and no classical, tripos. Their standard of examination was low for the actual degree, two books of Euclid, simple and quadratic equations, and the early parts of Paley's moral philosophy, being all that was required. But this insistence on mathematics probably helped to account for some parts of the intellectual equipment of some of its greatest sons—Pitt's dexterous command of financial figures, and Wordsworth's early attachment to abstract ideas. Poor indeed as England then was in all the higher branches of mathematical research, the mere fact that Cambridge owned Newton kept alive a lofty and inspiring tradition. But the greatest living academical force belonged to the drunken son of an East country worsted weaver, Richard Porson.

Born in 1759, his talents were early recognized by a neighbouring squire, and he was sent to Eton as a scholar on the foundation. He then went to Trinity College, Cambridge, where he was irregularly admitted a fellow in 1782 while still a junior Bachelor of Arts. Ten years later he became Regius Professor of Greek. He did not reside at the University, but it could not escape his inspiration. Slovenly in most things, his beautiful Greek handwriting was chosen as a model for Greek type. Their love of books did not desert the Grenville brothers at one of the most critical hours of their country's history, and in 1801 they brought out a superb edition of Homer. It was Porson who prepared the text. His fine scholarship, which has seldom been surpassed, owed much to a wonderful memory, amounting almost to a painful incapacity to forget anything which he had ever read. It was a common thing at Cambridge or elsewhere to provoke him to perform some of his extraordinary feats. Drink ruined his health, and he died in 1808.

In 1806 Patrick Colquhoun, to whose statistics it is so constantly necessary to have recourse in default of better, estimated the total population of the United Kingdom, between the ages of six and thirteen, at 3,750,000. A third of this he believed to be children of the upper and middle classes receiving education. This very rough and certainly exaggerated figure must have included the clever sons of artisans who were occasionally educated in the public or grammar schools. These schools, with the exception of the select few which gradually acquired for themselves the exclusive name of public schools, had, as a class, deteriorated. Originally instituted for the purpose of teaching Latin and Greek, they had found a difficulty in meeting the growing demand for modern subjects. Some were completely empty. But this was because other means of education had come into existence. There were for example the schools established partly or entirely for the benefit of some special sect. Such was the school for boys and girls at Kendal in Westmorland in 1785, carried on by John Dalton, afterwards the celebrated chemist, and his elder brother, the announcement of which gives a lively picture of north country range in matters of instruction. Youth was to be taught English, Latin, Greek, French, mathematics, merchants' accounts, navigation, astronomy, mechanics, and other subjects connected with engineering. Besides these there were the schools of private venture. One county in the north was famous for them—Yorkshire. Southey introduced into his paper The Flagellant, for which he was expelled from Westminster school, a letter from a gentleman of moderate fortune who had been sent to one at the age of twelve, and not noticed by his relatives for five years. Later on, in Espriella, he enlarged on the subject. London tradesmen got rid of their sons in this way; the usual fees were sixteen pounds a year, clothing included; the curriculum consisted of the "three r's", and a practical knowledge of farming in which they were made to help their masters, often poor clergy with a glebe. All over England private schools were often due to the enterprise of clergy who wished to eke out the income of their benefices, or who had no benefices at all. In Scotland the system was satisfactory. There were burgh council schools maintained partly out of the rates. The existence of such scandals as the Yorkshire schools suggests that in the minds of large classes of Englishmen the desire to get rid of a boy predominated over the desire to have him taught. But those who did desire their children's good wished them to learn something. They did not yet send their boys to school to be made gentlemen.

The figure given by Colquhoun for lower class children receiving instruction, three quarters of a million, is most probably another exaggeration. A number of charity schools had sprung up in the eighteenth century, and their existence, as well as that of the excellent parish schools established in his own country of Scotland by a law which was strictly enforced throughout the lowlands, probably led him to make an over-estimate. He probably did not include the hedge-schools of Ireland or the Sunday schools. In any case the immediate success of two new movements in elementary education showed how large was the void which they were intended to fill—even in the capital itself. One was the scheme of Sunday schools, inaugurated by Robert Raikes. The other was the general expansion of elementary education connected with the names of Bell and Lancaster.

The difficulty which faced educationalists was that of shortage of teachers. Doctor Andrew Bell, born in 1753, physician as well as clergyman, had in the course of his work as chaplain in India rediscovered the method by which a school might, with the least possible help from a master, teach itself. In a climate which stimulates an often unwholesome precocity he could easily have found examples of bright boys apt at explaining what they had just learnt. On his return to England in 1797, he published his account of this experiment in education, and he put it in practice in one or two places. But it was reserved for the Quaker Joseph Lancaster to take it up vigorously. Born in 1778, he had early taken to teaching, but had found progress difficult until he became acquainted with Bell's method. He now moved rapidly forward. By 1808 he had in his school in the Borough Road in South London, nine hundred boys being educated under a single master for £156 yearly. Here he received a visit from the King. Lest his enjoyment of the Royal favour might be overlooked he made use of a seal with His Majesty's portrait surrounded by the motto "The Patron of Education". Indeed, the King gave more than his name, for the subscriptions of the Royal Family alone amounted to £300. But the Church party in education had already become alarmed, as Lancaster's system was undemoninational. Mrs. Sarah Trimmer, a great enthusiast for elementary education, objected to this, and to the military character of the Quaker's institution. From 1806 onwards a definite movement in favour of Church national schools was started by Bell on her instigation.

It was more owing to native vigour than to the educational system that considerable progress was being made at this time in several branches of science. No foreigner's visit to England was complete until after seeing the Royal Castle and the premier school of England at its foot, he had turned aside to the Slough Observatory, where William Herschel, tended and helped by his devoted sister Caroline, was engaged for livelong nights at his almost superhuman task of mapping the heavens. Born in Hanover in 1738, the discoverer of Uranus was now entering upon a vigorous and useful old age in his adopted country. He received £200 a year from George III, who had also paid £4,000 for the construction of his great forty-foot telescope. During the first years of the century, besides the strenuous labour of cataloguing nebulae, Herschel was remarkable for his writings on the newly discovered asteroids, his own discovery of the rotary motion of the double stars, and his theory of the connection between sunspots and the weather. While the German at Slough was winning his splendid triumphs, the Greenwich Observatory still continued its humbler labours for the perfecting the Art of Navigation—in the words of Charles II's original warrant to the Astronomer Royal—labours never more necessary than when England's vessels covered every sea.

The opening of the century found the science of geology under a cloud, a circumstance of which the nation made a characteristic use. It found the geological world divided between the followers of Werner, who ascribed the present formation of the globe to the agency of water, and those of Hutton who put it down mainly to fire. Doctor Paris, the biographer of Sir Humphry Davy, has made mention of the controversy as it was at its height. Abandoning their usual predilection in favour of their own people, even Scotsmen formed themselves into two camps, a part ranging themselves against their own countryman under the banner of the Freiburg professor. "I shall not easily forget", wrote Paris, "the din and fury of the elemental war, as it raged in Edinburgh when I was a student in that University; even the mineral dealers, who, like the artizans of a neutral city, sold arms and ammunition to both sides, still defended their own opinions with party fury." Their warfare had quite a different frontier from those which separated nations, but it equally extended over the continent, and when a discovery was made which was regarded by one side as a powerful argument, its author applied to Government for a flag of truce to convey his armaments for the discomfort of his spiritual foes. After a time geology came to be one of the subjects which—like theology in certain circles—is avoided as far as possible for fear of exciting evil passions. There was, for example, no article under this head in the English Encyclopaedia of 1802, although intended to include the complete circle of the arts and sciences. All observations came before the world already coloured with the prejudice of the observer. In meeting the difficulty Englishmen found a golden opportunity for giving free rein to their love of crude fact for its own sake. The Geological Society of

London was founded to enable chemists, mineralogists, and geologists to meet and exchange the results of their observations in an atmosphere in which controversy was left in the background. Meanwhile, William Smith had already discovered that the fossil contents of any particular formation of the earth supplied the key to the order in which it came into existence, and was preparing his monumental geological map of Great Britain.

In physics and chemistry these were great times for a nation which could show at once, from opposite quarters of the country, John Dalton born near Cockermouth in 1766, and Humphry Davy born in 1778 at Penzance. During the last thirty years of the century considerable progress had been made in the laboratory, but how small a distance had been really travelled appears from the article on Chemistry in the English Encyclopaedia for 1802. Here the writer, Doctor Thomas Thomson, remarkable for having afterwards had the honour of being the first to give Dalton's great discovery to the world in the 1807 edition of his System of Chemistry, actually places light and heat at the head of a list of original substances—a list which bears above it among others the honoured name of Lavoisier. Indeed, the notion that heat was a fluid, in spite of the opinions of Bacon and Newton, seemed rather to gain than lose ground during these years. In 1804 Davy gave as the accepted list of 43 elements a catalogue consisting of 6 simple earths, 6 alkaline substances, 22 metals, 3 acids, 3 inflammable solids, and 3 simple gases. Two years earlier he had said in London that chemistry consisted of a number of collections of facts not furnished as yet with a precise theory. That theory was being provided in Manchester almost while he was speaking.

A native and a lover of the mountains, Dalton's first interests naturally turned to meteorology. He was thus led to the study of the atmospheric moisture and the way in which gases penetrate into one another. This led him to formulate, in 1803, his atomic theory. Accepting Newton's view of the atomic constitution of matter, he found it necessary to ascribe different weights to the ultimate particles or atoms of the different elements, everything which was the result of chemical combination being composed of fixed multiples of each of the two or more combining elements. Until his time, while the composition of some compounds was known, it was cumbrously, though not accurately, expressed in percentages. The atomic theory made it possible for Berzelius, the Swedish chemist, to give chemistry a few years later its own simple nomenclature.

Most of his life Dalton lived at Manchester, where he worked from 1793, first as a teacher in the College which the Presbyterians had established there, and afterwards independently. He was in his element as member, and afterwards President of the Literary and Philosophic Society of that town. He was without gifts of expression to make up for his rough north-country manner, and in London he was not a great success, although he had no fault to find with his audience when he first lectured at the Royal Institution in 1803. "I was", he wrote, "agreeably disappointed to find so learned and attentive an audience, though many of them of rank." It was in that very year that the atomic theory was first elaborated, though it was not given to the world in his own words until 1808. He had friends and associates in the world of science who were also discoverers, such as Doctor William Henry. But Davy, though a personal friend, was long in accepting the atomic theory; and Dalton preferred his laboratory to the society even of scientific men and did not even become a member of the Royal Society until 1822.

The Cornishman was a contrast to the Cumbrian. Davy was very soon discovered, and he was only twenty-two when, in the first month of 1801, he delivered his introductory lecture at the Royal Institution. It had come into existence aptly for his purpose. The Royal Society, then under the presidency of Sir Joseph Banks, a practical botanist who had studied in many parts of the world, and the friend of every hopeful young scientist visiting London, was a steady-going learned body which listened to papers by Herschel and other leading men, usually on matters of pure science. The younger Society of Arts was also engaged in scientific work, and the Italian traveller Ferri de San Constant was particularly struck not only with its value, but with the proof which it afforded of the democratic attitude of England towards science. He observed that peers competed for its rewards, and that the Duke of Beaufort had obtained one. But there appeared to be room for yet another society, and Thomas Bernard the philanthropist who, in concert with Shute Barrington, Bishop of Durham, and Wilberforce, had established the Society for Bettering the Conditions of the Poor, wished to see something still more fertile in practical results. The outcome of their combined efforts and those of Count von Rumford was the Royal Institution, which had hardly been brought into active existence when the Count, who was the Superintendent and the soul of the movement, invited Davy to London.

All came to his lectures prepared to admire. The beaming "Thing of Hope", as his friend Coleridge called him, with his Cornishman's attractive clear-cut features and charming simplicity of manner, speedily became the darling of London drawing-rooms. It is easy to imagine the enthusiasm with which ingenuous youth of both sexes must have listened to the youthful teacher's assurance that they might look not to distant ages, but to the near future for the annihilation of labour, disease, and even death. These were indeed, what Davy denied that they were, brilliant though delusive dreams. But he worthily filled the post of Director of the Laboratory of the Institution and Professor of Chemistry. In a few years he had given valuable lectures on tanning and on agriculture on the scientific side; the recent discovery that compound bodies could be decomposed by electrical action had enabled him to isolate the two important elements of sodium and potassium; and he had, on the other hand found that what had been believed to be a compound was another element to which he gave its name—chlorine. No great electrical inventions are connected with his name; it was the great contemporary Italian discoverers, Galvani and Volta, and not Davy, who left their names as part of the vocabulary of that science; but the Englishman was at least able to claim for his countrymen—and, he might have added for himself—the credit of being foremost in applying galvanism, as it continued to be called, for the purpose of making chemical changes. As early as 1803 he was elected to the Royal Society. He was, besides, a notable example of the capacity possessed by the French from the Emperor downwards of putting aside national animosity where scientific eminence is concerned. In 1808 he was offered, and accepted, the three thousand franc medal for the best experiment of the year on the galvanic fluid.

Another brilliant contributor to the papers of the Royal Society was Doctor William Wollaston, who was remarkable for the minuteness with which he worked. At a time when laboratory appliances were generally large and clumsy, he was able to carry the materials for a curious experiment in his waistcoat pocket. He was equally remarkable for the secretiveness and regard for his own interests which enabled him to make a considerable fortune by the isolation of platinum and his discovery of its malleability. A noteworthy paper among the earliest proceedings of the Royal Institution contains Wollaston's spectroscopic observations. By using a narrow slit instead of a round hole to let in the light, he was able to analyse the solar rays much more completely than Newton had. But this line of enquiry was not expected to prove likely to lead to anything, and it was dropped. Much about the same time Doctor Thomas Young, another thinker who pursued and improved upon Newtonian conceptions, was making useful observations on the mechanism of the eye, and developing the undulatory theory of light.

It is somewhat strange that the theory of heat should have suffered even greater neglect than that of light; for no subject was dearer to the heart of the originator of the Institution. Born in Massachusetts before it had ceased to be a part of the British Empire, Benjamin Thompson had remained a loyal British subject and had obtained a knighthood from George III, and from the Elector of Bavaria the title of Count for his invaluable services there as principal officer of State. He was thus an Englishman enjoying a German title taken from a village in a republic; for Rumford, from which he took his new name, was in what was now the United States. Returning from Munich to England this many-sided man interested himself as a scientist in a similar class of philanthropic questions to those which had made him beloved as an administrator in Bavaria. Men like Bernard and Wilberforce found in him exactly what they wanted; and he gave a practical turn to the proceedings of the new institution from the outset. The first paper in the proceedings was one by him on economizing fuel, and the second, also by him, was on what has since been known as central heating. A "Rumford" became a household word, and his ovens and other practical contrivances for the kitchen continued to be studied long after his death. Fire, he pointed out, was required for almost every purpose; and he calculated that fuel cost the country ten millions annually. He directed attention to the deplorable waste which took place. But he did not succeed in interesting even the scientific world in the question what heat was. He himself believed it to be a mode of motion. Davy thought the same. He had been able as early as 1799 to produce heat by making two pieces of ice rub against one another in a vacuum. As nothing could have got into the receiver, and a substance could not have been produced inside the receiver out of nothing, it should seem to have been obvious that heat was not in itself a substance, but a condition of other substances. Young took up Davy's experiment and pointed these facts out, but the notion that heat, or "caloric", was a substance of itself continued to be entertained for almost half a century longer.

Organic chemistry did not exist as a separate science, until well on in the century. But Davy was showing the way in the lectures on Agricultural Chemistry which he delivered for the Board of Agriculture; and on the other hand progress was being made in the classification of plants and animals, and—rather incidentally than directly—in the scientific study of their nature. Britain's principal contribution to botany came from a Scotsman, Robert Brown, who was born in 1773. Sir Joseph Banks was no longer himself a collector. Earlier in life he had travelled and made extensive collections. He was now in control of the Botanical Gardens at Kew, and he employed his position, and that which he enjoyed as a baronet and President of the Royal Society to organize that connection between the Gardens and the colonies to which both owed a very great debt. He induced Brown to join an expedition which set sail for Australia in 1801 as one of the botanists of the party. The outcome was an accumulation of nearly 4,000 plants, and a work published in Latin, as scientific books then still frequently were. It was principally an account of the botanical results of the expedition, but he had already begun to display that originality of analysis which afterwards distinguished him.

Classification tended to dominate the study of forms in the domains of zoology and even medicine, as well as botany. The studies in the eighteenth century of Doctor John Hunter in comparative anatomy, and of Doctor Erasmus Darwin in what was beginning in the new century to be known as biology, are exceptions. Popular as this last writer was, it was unfortunate for science that his Zoonomia, which was not like his better-known works on botany in verse, should not have attracted more attention. For it was in that book that he laid down that one and the same kind of living filament is and has been the cause of all organic life, and that the differences between organisms were due to impulses, to reaction to external stimulants, and to contrivances for the purpose of security. The line of inquiry so suggested was left to be followed out by his illustrious— grandson. The article in the British Encyclopedia for 1809 on Medicine, written by Doctor John Good, a recognized medical authority, serves as an example of the unscientific treatment of scientific subjects which prevailed. It gives its readers their choice between five different lists of diseases, after five systems of classification. Here differentiation ceases. In causation and treatment there is not much variety. A state of disease was generally supposed to be due to some redundancy; and blood-letting, emetics, and cathartics follow one another in dreary uniformity. Most of the cruelties with which lunatics were then treated were not intended to be curative. But one was certainly so. For a maniac the cold bath was strongly recommended by the same authority; he was to be thrown in headlong, and this was to be done again and again until he became rational, or, in the alternative, very much debilitated. As regards the lancet a Peninsula veteran, Captain Dobbs, has left a characteristic description of an army doctor's way of treating the troops for ophthalmia, with which his regiment was attacked on the way to Portugal. It was thus that it lost first blood, and he estimated that it lost more on this voyage than throughout the war. It has to be owned that doctors were as unkind to themselves in this respect as to their patients. Erasmus Darwin's own death was an example. He had had an attack of fever, and 25 ounces of blood was let. A week later he seemed well, but the system was evidently much weakened, and the next day he suddenly felt faint and expired. His son, also a doctor, was with him, and described accurately what took place, without any remark on the debilitating effect of the treatment.

The use of drugs in the treatment of disease was largely empirical, and they were still most commonly taken in their natural form. Important alkaloids, such as morphine and quinine, were only first isolated during the early years of the nineteenth century. A famous doctor, Sir Benjamin Brodie, relates how he was taught his work at this time. He was sent to an apothecary who prescribed himself, and had so many patients that he eventually set up for a physician in a large house in Leicester Square. This man kept five large bottles out of which he dispensed in nearly every case. The practical bent of Englishmen was shown in the nature of such works of medical science as were produced in the period, which were rather of the style of compilations from the physician's note book. Such were John Abernethy's Surgical Observations on the Constitutional Origin and Treatment of Local Diseases, and Baillie's Morbid Anatomy of some of the most important Parts of the Human Body. The practical side of medicine was almost exclusively studied, and doctor's fees were so high that considerable resort was had not merely to apothecaries, who were called in to patients' houses to advise as well as consulted in their shops, but to quacks, of whom England was notoriously full. This did not prevent large fortunes being made by regular physicians. The largest practitioner at the beginning of the century was Matthew Baillie, brother of Joanna Baillie, and one of many successful Scottish doctors and scientists. He was reputed to be making ten thousand a year, but he was passed by an Englishman, Doctor Vaughan. That celebrated physician, born in 1766, one of the last of an old school, kept a regular account of what he received up to 1809, when the amount was close on five figures. After that year, and for another quarter of a century, Sir Henry Halford, as Vaughan now became, a family baronetcy being revived in his interest, was receiving well over his ten thousand a year.

The practical bias of British medical science was justified by the results. The French traveller Baert recognized the general superiority of British physicians. One great discovery in particular seemed to justify rule of thumb methods. "Vaccine inoculation"—so ran Public Characters, a New York publication of 1805—"is, beyond all comparison, the most valuable, and the most important discovery, ever made." The author of an article in the Danish Nyeste Skilderie for the 20th of October, 1807, breathing lasting hatred towards the nation which had just bombarded his capital, turned aside to mention Edward Jenner as one whose memory all mankind would ever bless. Born in 1749, he had been long acquainted with the prevalent belief in a part of his own county of Gloucestershire that the cow-pox conferred an immunity from small-pox. He adopted the practice of deliberately inoculating persons with the former disease as a preventive. In 1798 he formally published the result of his experiences, and the practice of vaccination spread like wildfire, and rapidly superseded the older ineffectual inoculation. It found many opponents. One champion of the old school, Benjamin Moseley, had written a well-known treatise on Tropical Diseases, in which his own practical experiences as a medical officer with troops in the West Indies were strangely mixed up with such phrases as "Galen justly observes", and appeals to the authority of Hippocrates and Aristotle. He had held many high medical posts, and it is difficult without the experience of reading the actual words to credit that he went so far in his support of the popular prejudice that the cow-pox would turn men into cattle, as to state in a professional controversial treatise that he had himself seen ox-faces growing on human beings after vaccination. But he did so, and described the phenomena in some detail. There was some justice, however, in his complaint that the new treatment was adopted by well-meaning but ignorant people everywhere with untoward results. The practical effects were so good on the whole that the Royal College of Physicians had to its honour taken the common-sense view of the case, and accorded its approval. But, as Moseley complained, no medical rationale had been either demanded or given. Indeed, the subject was not at all thoroughly understood even by its great promoter. He unscientifically traced the cow-pox to a disease in the feet of horses. He did not understand that vaccination conferred only temporary immunity. On one occasion he had been persuaded by a mother, Lady Grosvenor, to make only a single puncture in vaccinating her child, and then apparently made no protest when the pustule was rubbed by the nurse. Ten years later the boy had a serious attack of smallpox, which caused a considerable sensation and brought vaccination into some discredit; but happily this was only for a short time.

The first ten years of the nineteenth century formed part of an interlude in a period of great inventions. On the last day of the old century Boulton and Watt's patents expired, their partnership was dissolved, and the two great pioneers in the world of steam entered upon an honoured and deserved retirement, the famous firm at Soho, Birmingham, being continued in the names of their sons.

James Watt's native caution was actually inimical to further development. He had left off active life, but his brain was still clear, and he remained an industrial Nestor, consulted by young inventors who received from him courtesy rather than encouragement. In 1782 he had written to his partner: "There is now no doubt that fire-engines will drive mills, but I entertain some doubts whether anything is to be got by them." It is hardly astonishing, when the discoverer of the steam-condenser himself displayed so little warmth, that the firm's engines should by 1800 have aggregated no more than fourteen hundred horse power in London, Manchester, and Leeds taken together. The number of steam engines in use in England now rapidly increased, but the first years of the century were chiefly devoted, so far as they were concerned, to rendering them more compact and less clumsy machines than the venerable monstrosities which had issued from the brain of Watt. But they continued to be associated chiefly with mines and factories.

Early in life Watt had taken up the idea of the locomotive, but dropped it as a toy, and, when William Murdoch, who was in his employ, ran a tiny engine on the Cornish roads, he made him do the same. There had been several steamboats before 1800, and one invented a year later very nearly started the new era. A Lord Dundas employed William Symington, one of those concerned in a previous successful experiment, to make one for the Forth—Clyde Canal. The "Charlotte Dundas" was the result. A clumsy one-cylinder vessel with a stern wheel, she gave an exhibition in 1803, when she towed two vessels of 70 tons each $19\frac{1}{2}$ miles in 6 hours against a strong wind. It was enough for the Duke of Bridgewater, who at once gave an order for eight boats for his canal. But the Committee of the Forth—Clyde Canal condemned the vessel on account of the damage done by the wash to the banks, and the intimation of this reached Symington at the same time as that of the Duke's death. England's chance of leading the way was now lost. No one was enterprising enough to try the new invention on a river on this side of the Atlantic, and in 1807 the first regular steamship service was started in the United States. The engines were, however, Watt's engines, and the Birmingham firm's engineers came over to put them in.

Watt had a poor opinion of Scotsmen as mechanics, as he found that his countrymen did not care much about working with their hands. Perhaps this is what made some of them such good inventors. William Murdoch was one. Like many another promising mechanic and engineer from the north, he made his way south. He found employment in the Soho works, where he was successful in lighting a building from coal gas in 1798. Seven years later several mills were fitted with it. The young poet Byron derided it in 1809 as one of the four latest follies of science.

> "What varied wonders tempt us as they pass!
> The cow-pox, tractors, galvanism, and gas,
> In turns appear to make the vulgar stare,
> Till the swoln bubble bursts—and all is air!"

But of these four, only tractors—a quack cure for rheumatic disorders—failed to outlive him. Doubts as to the efficiency of illumination by gas began to be removed for Londoners in 1807, when Pall Mall was lit up as an experiment; and in spite of the opposition of those statesmen who objected to the public being tempted to waste their money on so volatile a substance, the Gas Light and Coke Company's Bill became law in 1810.

Two more great Scottish engineers were Thomas Telford born in 1757, and John Rennie born four years later. It has been claimed for Great Britain by those who admire her for her rule-of-thumb methods that her inventors were ignorant workmen. Olinthus Gregory of the Royal Military Academy, Woolwich, complained of the prevalence of this belief in 1809, when he wrote his Treatise on Mechanics. At the same time nothing of the sort could be said of Rennie, the son of a Lowland farmer. He had been both at the Dunbar burgh school and at the University of Edinburgh, and had distinguished himself as a mathematician. After some years preliminary work for Boulton and Watt, he became known as a canal engineer. In 1804 he completed the Rochdale Canal, carried over and through the mountain ridge which separates South Lancashire from Yorkshire. But his great work at this time was the draining of the Lincolnshire fens. To do justice to all his labours even during the first ten years of the century, would be to write an account of very many works made or projected during this time all round the coasts of Great Britain, and even in Ireland, where he crossed over and resurveyed the Royal Canal in 1802. The most important of all these were the London Docks, completed in 1805, and the East India Company's Docks, opened in the following year. He did much for Glasgow, for Greenock, and for Leith, and he divined the great future of Southampton. His connection with schemes of national defence was an intimate one. At the request of Government he made a plan in 1803 for flooding the eastern side of London in the event of an invasion, he laid out the Hythe Military Canal across Romney Marsh, and he prepared in 1807 a report on the royal harbours and dockyards on which action was taken, though only after considerable delay.

An atmosphere of romance gathers round the lives of these early engineers, unable as they were as yet to harness and tame the grand forces of Nature, who yielded to them little of her wildness and beauty, and fell back undismayed by such petty inroads as they were able to make on her realm, whether among the mountains of Wales, Yorkshire, and Scotland, or among the rocks of the Firth of Forth or the storm-beaten North Sea coast. They had to struggle, too, to get their plans accepted. Their careers were no monotonous successions of accurate calculations nicely worked out, and unfailingly carried into effect by a machinery standing ready to be used. When Rennie advised upon the building of the Bell Rock lighthouse in 1805, the best example he could find was Smeaton's on the Eddystone, built under very different conditions nearly half a century before. When constructing the Humber Dock about the same time he could not clear the basins until he had invented the steam dredger. When repairing the pier-head of Ramsgate Harbour in 1813 he found himself in trouble until he had devised an improved type of cast-iron diving-bell. Nor had the engineer a strong staff to share his difficulties. There was not much margin for this. Rennie received only £350 from the Kennet and Avon Canal Company for constructing their works, and Telford's remuneration as principal engineer of the Caledonian Canal for twenty-one of the best years of his life averaged at £237 a year. Both were plain men. Telford loved darning his own stockings, and his heart was in the dale where he was born; but he had no pedestrian thoughts. Like more than one other inventor of his time he dabbled in poetry, and was the friend of poets. It helped him in a life of stress.

Telford, unlike Rennie, boasted no academic qualifications, but he had the spirit to feel that his professional gifts were wasted in his own country, though they were well appreciated in his own immediate neighbourhood. He was able to borrow the horse of his local laird to ride to London on, and after he had worked as stonemason and foreman for a few years, a son of the laird's who had changed his name from Johnstone to Pulteney, got him made Surveyor of Public Works for the County of Salop, where his career as a road-maker and bridge-builder began. He became, in particular, a great designer of iron bridges. One for a new London Bridge with a single span over the river was actually accepted after passing the ordeal of the scrutiny of the elder Watt, as well as Rennie and several other experts, and was only abandoned because the advantage of a height of sixty feet above high water was thought not to outweigh the disadvantages of such steep approaches to the bridgeheads. It was to have cost a little more than a quarter of a million. After this he was engaged under Government in various surveys of Scotland which led ultimately to a system of road and bridge construction, mainly in the Highlands, which took up the first twenty years of the century. At the same time his harbour works, particularly in Aberdeen and Dundee, transformed the conditions of navigation on the north-east coast of Scotland. One great work which he undertook for Government was the Caledonian Canal. Begun in 1804, at a time when something of the kind was believed to be essential in order to provide merchantmen with a highway across Scotland safe from privateers, it proved of very little use.

The name of Telford is connected most of all in men's memories with his very large share in the extremely practical work of removing the reproach which clung to the badness of British roads. But it is only fair to a plain man, typical of a country famous for its appreciation of the value of money, to repeat the words in which his admirer, Samuel Smiles, sums up his attitude towards the objects of human endeavour. " 'I admire enterprise', he would say: 'it is the vigorous outgrowth of our industrial life: I admire everything that gives it free scope, as wherever it goes, activity, energy, intelligence—all that we call civilization—accompany it; but I hold that the aim and end of all ought not to be a mere bag of money, but something far higher and far better.' "

CHAPTER II

INDIA AND THE EAST (1801–1806)

In an attack in parliament on the East India Company in 1801, Sir William Pulteney said that the character of traders and sovereigns was inconsistent, and that their union had never failed to prove ruinous to those counting-house kings, and to make their unhappy subjects suffer under all the evils of oppression and misrule. This unnatural combination of functions was the effect of only the past fifty years' working, out of the two hundred which had passed since the charter had been granted by Elizabeth; and those years had been marked on the part of the British Government and of the Company itself by constant struggles against the high destiny to which both were called. It was useless to battle against Fate, particularly in the continent of fatalism. It was inevitable, moreover, that the French and English trading settlements in India should attack one another whenever the mother countries were at war, that they should, in doing so, draw the large yet weak native powers to their aid, that they should help to organize their strength, and that the English, who were the more successful, should bring them gradually under their control, and from control to annexation was but a step. But this rivalry between the two nations did no more than hasten the natural course of events which made it impossible for the servants of the East India Company to confine themselves to the part of traders in such a country as India.

The government of the empire, which was growing up in this involuntary fashion, was regulated under Pitt's Act of 1784. A body of Commissioners, known as the Board of Control, was set over the Company to represent the Government. Its President was a Minister of Cabinet rank only when he happened to hold some other office which carried that rank with it. During the last years of

Pitt's Ministry he was Henry Dundas, whose knowledge of Indian affairs was—now that Burke was dead—unique in one who had never seen the country. He was succeeded, under Addington, by a President of whom very little is known, Lord Lewisham, afterwards Earl of Dartmouth; and so little account was made of the office that not only might it be held by a Minister who had another office, but changes were very frequent. There were no less than nine during the first ten years of the century. It was the Dundases, father and son, and Castlereagh, who clung to it the longest. They had just the bent of mind which enabled them to master the difficult subject of India, and they enjoyed the patronage which they indirectly possessed through their influence with the Directors. Of these there were twenty-four appointed by the Court of Proprietors of East India Stock, six retiring yearly by rotation. The Directors chose their own Chairman and a Secret Committee of three, whose duty it was to carry on correspondence of a secret nature—usually dealing with diplomatic or military affairs. It was through this Committee that the Board of Control usually exercised its authority, having the right to alter the Directors' despatches, and to require them to send them out so altered as their own.

By the same law the government of each of the three Indian Presidencies was vested in a Governor and three Members, but the head of the Government in Bengal had the title of Governor-General, and controlled the Governors of the two subordinate Presidencies of Madras and Bombay, particularly in questions affecting the Native States—known in Indian language as political matters. All three were shortly afterwards empowered to act without the concurrence of their councils in extraordinary cases. The smooth working of government within India itself was assured. But the relations of the three Governors with the home authorities were left in some uncertainty. The Court of Directors had the appointment of them, although it was usual to accept any recommendation made by the Ministry of the day, and the Directors, as well as the Ministry, could both censure and recall them. A high-spirited Governor General, regarding himself in all political matters, at all events, as the servant of the King's Government alone, was apt to chafe under the restraint of the India House. He was bound both by Act of Parliament and by the Company's regulations, as well as by the orders sent to him. They were not always adapted to affairs on the spot, as he understood them, and he was apt to disregard all three. There was one section of Pitt's Act which was of the highest importance.—"And forasmuch as to pursue Schemes of Conquest and Extension of Dominion in *India* are Measures repugnant to the Wish, the Honour, and Policy of the Nation: be it further enacted, That it shall not be lawful for the Governor General in Council of *Fort William* aforesaid, without the express Command and Authority of the said Court of Directors, or of the said Secret Committee by the Authority of the said Board of Commissioners for the affairs of *India*, in any Case (except where Hostilities have actually been commenced, or Preparations actually made for the Commencement of Hostilities against the *British* Nation in *India*, or against some of the Princes or States dependent thereon, or whose Territories the said United Company shall be at such Time engaged by any subsisting Treaty to defend or guarantee; either to declare War, or commence Hostilities, or enter into any Treaty for making War, against any of the Country Princes or States in *India*, or any Treaty for guaranteeing the Possessions of any Country Princes or States." Lord Cornwallis, who was Governor-General from 1786 to 1793, adhered faithfully to this injunction. But, as he pointed out, it involved difficulties, entailing in practice, as it did, a system of helpless inactivity. "Some considerable advantages have, no doubt," he wrote, "been experienced by the system of neutrality which the legislature required of the governments of the country; but it has at the same time been attended with the unavoidable inconvenience of our being constantly exposed to the necessity of commencing a war, without having previously secured the assistance of efficient allies." He was succeeded in office by Sir John Shore, afterwards Lord Teignmouth, who pursued the same policy. But the more vigorous Governor-General who arrived in 1798 refused to be strictly bound by the letter of the law or of regulations or instructions in this or any other particular.

The glorious family, of which this man was now the head, was composed of the children of an Irish peer whose ancestors had left England for Ireland in the sixteenth century. He was not rich, but he was able to send his eldest son, born in 1760, to Eton—an apparently trivial decision, which not only determined the boy's future, but had an indirect effect upon the world. Here the boy read about the glories of Ancient Rome. No one in that age of statesmen who were scholars thought more naturally in the language of Caesar and Cicero—no man's mind was more permeated with the imperial spirit than that of the boy who at forty years of age was to be raised to the rank of Marquis Wellesley for the conquest of Mysore. After leaving Oxford he was prepared for his Indian career by fifteen years of parliamentary life in the Irish House of Lords or the English House of Commons, ending with four years as a Member of the Board of Control. The duties of the office were light, but its opportunities of obtaining an insight into Indian affairs were great, and of these the future Governor-General fully availed himself. Although a man of genuinely liberal ideas, which were markedly apparent in the earlier and later stages of his long public career, he had no doubt that French Jacobinism was the enemy, and distinguished himself even in that parliament of the giants in eloquence by the magnificent periods in which he denounced it. He had an opportunity of proving the strength of his conviction immediately upon his arrival in India. Of the princes of the South, the Nizam of Hyderabad had an army officered by Frenchmen, and carrying the colours of the French Republic, the Sultan of Mysore had made proposals to the Governor-General of the French islands in the Indian Ocean for an alliance, and—it was afterwards discovered—the Nawab of Arcot, one of Britain's allies, was carrying on a treacherous correspondence with that prince. Wellesley at once compelled the Nizam to disband his French army, and in spite of the highest authorities both military and civil in Madras, who were for temporizing with the formidable Tipu Sultan, declared a war, early in 1799, which ended in two months with the loss of the despot's life and the conquest of his kingdom. The fate of the Nawab of Arcot, whose criminating papers were discovered on the capture of Seringapatam, the capital of Mysore, was the annexation of his country, the Carnatic, to the Company. The first effects of Wellesley's policy was to add nearly 90,000 square miles to the 53,000 square miles then included in the Presidency of Madras. The whole area of that part of India directly administered by the servants of the Company, and known as British India, had not previously been more than 195,000 square miles, almost all the remaining 142,000 being in Bengal. Bombay consisted of a couple of islands and a fort on the mainland.

But it was not for the territory which he annexed, but for the vast network of political relations which he established, that the system of Wellesley was remarkable. His horizon was not bounded by the million and a half square miles included between the Himalayas and Cape Cormorin. The Cape of Good Hope was his bulwark on the west. In the east he cast his eyes as far as the Philippines, which he wished to wrest from Spain to save them from falling into the hands of France. He had more serious designs on the French islands in the Indian Ocean, Bourbon and the

Isle of France or Mauritius, whose continual occupation by the enemy on the route to Europe round the Cape caused such loss to trade, and on the Dutch island of Java. Ternate in the Moluccas was actually taken from the Dutch in 1801. But he was diverted from other aims by the expedition to Egypt. He anticipated the orders for this as early as October 1800, and it was the fault of the Home Government and not his that Baird's force did not arrive in time to take a part in making prisoners of the French. He did not neglect the chiefs of the Red Sea and the Persian Gulf. But his great diplomatic successes were in Persia. In 1796 India had been disturbed by the last of the long series of invasions which she had suffered from the side of the north-west. The Afghan ruler of Kabul, Zaman Shah, advanced as far as Lahore with next to no opposition, and was only obliged to return by trouble at home. Wellesley found him further employment. He sent an Indian Agent to the Shah of Persia, and followed this up with a splendid embassy under the great political officer of the day, Captain John Malcolm. The Afghan was attacked from the west, and India was safe from that quarter. In January 1801 a treaty was made with the Shah providing for the exclusion of the French from Persia. It was just the moment when Napoleon Bonaparte and Paul of Russia had brought plans against India by land into definite shape.

But Wellesley was not content with this indirect security against invasion. Now that Southern India was to some extent off his hands, he was able to look more closely to the safety of the Company's northern possessions. Hitherto his annexations had been almost confined to the coast—always fearful lest the French should form a lodgment there. Mysore he cut off from the sea and restored the remainder, after other deductions in favour of the Company and its ally the Nizam, to the sovereignty of the Hindu family dispossessed forty years earlier by Tipu's father; and he felt that an apology was due from himself to Dundas for his moderation. Before he quitted India, the whole of the eastern coast down almost to Cape Cormorin was under direct British rule; and the intimate control which his diplomacy obtained over the powers on the western side secured him on that coast as well. But in the north the problem of defence was different. In the immense alluvial plain of the Ganges and its affluents between the Himalayas and the central highlands there is very little rise. At a thousand miles from Calcutta a watershed is reached where the rivers begin to run south-westwards instead of south-eastwards. Yet even here, in the country lying between Delhi and Lahore, the ground is not more than a thousand feet above sea-level. Thus the almost uninterrupted trend downward from the foot of the mountains of Afghanistan to the mouths of the Ganges appeared positively to invite attack. British rule now extended to five hundred miles from the sea. North-west began the dominions of the Wazir of Oudh, one of those rulers whose realm descended to him from a provincial governor of the Moghul Emperor.

But that country formed no barrier. On the contrary, it had become necessary for the British to undertake its defence, and the pacific Shore had concluded a treaty to that effect in return for a subsidy. The Wazir was unpopular with his subjects. He had to maintain troops to collect his revenue, and he asked for a British detachment to protect him from them. He offered to abdicate. Wellesey took a short way with him. He insisted upon an increase in the British force for which the Wazir had to pay, and obliged him to surrender territory of which the land revenue would be sufficient to cover the charges. The ceded districts now completely encircled Oudh except on the Nepalese frontier on the north-east. They amounted to nearly 35,000 square miles, the Wazir being left with just under 24,000. The cessions on the north-west were especially appropriate. Not only was this the quarter most exposed to attack, but it was already held by the Rohillas, a tribe of Afghan descent which had come in during a previous invasion. They had now settled down among the Hindu population and recognized the rule of the Wazir. But they were always likely to unite themselves with any foreign invader of their own race; and were distinguished, even among the landholders of Oudh, as turbulent and refractory revenue payers. The country was occupied with very little difficulty. Wellesley sent his brother Henry, who had come out with him as a Private Secretary and had negotiated the treaty in November 1801, as President of a Board of Commissioners to settle the revenue and reduce the Ceded Districts to order. In a few months the British were so firmly established that officers arriving at Bareilly, the capital of the Rohilkhand division, where he had his headquarters—800 miles from Calcutta—found the characteristic Anglo-Indian amusements of tiger-shooting, hog-spearing, and deep flirtation already in full swing. Henry Wellesley had, moreover, turned his attention to a subject painfully neglected by early Anglo-Indian administrators—communications. The old system of arranging for the maintenance of roads by means of forced labour, provided by the holders of the land by which they pass, had broken down as regards main roads in India, as it had in England. In the absence of any other system he took steps to inaugurate that of exacting a cess of one per cent. of the total land revenue for this purpose—thus distributing the charge equally among the landholders—a system which was only brought into regular use twenty years later.

It was at this time that in England the cry first began to rise against Lord Wellesley which waxed louder and louder until it almost brought him, like Warren Hastings, to stand in his defence against the Commons of Great Britain at the bar of the House of Lords. Writing in

September 1802, Castlereagh, now President of the Board of Control, remarked that the Government of India was now being accused of a systematic plan of territorial acquisition. Wellesley's methods had certainly been highhanded. But in the case of Oudh, at all events, his fault was rather that of doing too little than of doing too much. Travelling in 1800 from British India westward into a part of what afterwards became the Ceded Districts, Sir John Anstruther, the Chief Justice of Calcutta, noted the great difference in prosperity between British India and the dominions of the Wazir. Later on, a nobleman travelling in the old eighteenth-century way with a secretary who was also a draftsman, and made the drawings to illustrate his book of travels, wrote that, when he woke up in his palanquin after passing into Oudh, he could tell that he was across the border from the scene of desolation which he saw round him. Fifty years of misgovernment for Oudh followed, and so lasting were their effects that, even after the country had eventually been annexed, there would have been no great difficulty in judging where the border was reached fifty years later still. The policy of protecting an incompetent ruler from attack from outside, and also from danger at home, was bound to produce these unhappy results, unless assistance in the administration was forced upon him. In Mysore this was done. The Hindu sovereign who succeeded Tipu was a minor, and although the charge of the revenue remained in the hands of the excellent Hindu Minister who had been employed by the Muhammadan sovereigns, the control of government passed to a succession of British Commissioners.

The Directors at the India House were chiefly concerned with the Governor-General's encroachments on their own patronage and privileges, and with the state of their profits. They objected to the appointment which Wellesley had given to his brother Henry as one which should have been reserved for a member of their own civil service.

His reply was that in that case it would not have been made. The real cause for the virulence shown by the Court of Directors against him in 1802 on that and other topics was believed to be the delicate question of the private trade, a complicated subject which Wellesley did not neglect, but in which he took no special interest. It was mainly left to George Udny, one of the members of his council. The Company enjoyed by Charter a monopoly of trade in British ships with India. But they had no monopoly in purchases of Indian goods on British account, and of such private trade there was a considerable amount. The Company was obliged by law to furnish 3,000 tons of shipping to carry it to England. But the amount was insufficient, and the rates of freight in the splendidly built East Indiamen were too high. Even out of India's principal exports, furnished by the Company's factories or warehouses, there were some, such as sugar, which could not bear the rates. Its own ships were more suitable for silks, piece-goods, and indigo, the subject of a new, and then a very growing, industry, as that of fine piece-goods was a declining one. It was being gradually killed—so far as the trade to Great Britain was concerned—by the enormous duties. In the case of Indian calicoes these were raised in 1805 from about twenty-five to sixty per cent. in the interest of Manchester.

As foreign ships were allowed to trade freely to India, although British were not, the carrying trade passed to American and Portuguese. Udny was in favour of the encouragement of teak-wood Indian ships of which the iron and canvas requisites would be supplied by England, and this had the further advantage that—as the balance of trade was greatly in India's favour, that country being an importer mainly of specie—it would have obviated the necessity of one voyage for each ship. The Directors refused to yield on the general question. In 1801, pressed by the requirements of the force for Egypt, Wellesley hired, as a special case, three private ships on the part of the Company in infringement of the Company's monopoly. He did not repeat his offence, but, such as it was, it greatly exasperated both the Directors and the home ship-building interest.

There was one other matter, more nearly concerned with the regular functions of a Governor-General, which brought him into collision with the India House. The course of the growth of the British Empire in India had hitherto been of a most casual nature, and its administration was of a correspondent character. The Company's settlements had required troops for their protection, and had proceeded to lend them for that of neighbouring rulers, who, when the subsidies stipulated fell into arrears, were often only too glad to hand over the duty of collecting the revenue itself. This led to many of the early annexations. Almost every one of the rulers with whom the British had to deal on the east of India was a Muhammadan. He could not look back upon a line of princely ancestors. He had little attachment to his country. He was nothing if he was not a military governor, and that he was not this he had admitted by requiring protection. As the income of an Indian state consisted not of customs or excise, but of land revenue, to assign this to the Company to collect became equivalent to handing over the land administration itself. Even after this it often continued to make use of an Indian agency; when it had ceased to do so it made its own servants supervisors, the work of collection being performed by natives of the country; when these servants were at length made the actual Collectors, they evaded the task, and handed it over to agents. The administration of the land revenue carried with it the duty of maintaining order. This too was done after indigenous methods. When Bengalee offenders were brought to justice, judgement was pronounced in Persian by English Judges acting on the advice of Muhammadan lawyers.

The old Collector, of whom Thackeray's Josh Sedley was the type, was quite incompetent for the work of administration. Of the people and their customs he knew scarcely anything. If he knew any Oriental language, it was probably not an Indian vernacular but Persian, the official language of the Moghul Governments. When Cornwallis conquered Malabar from Tipu in 1792, he could find no civilian with enough knowledge of the language and sense of public duty to take a part in the administration. He selected four military officers. One of them was Thomas Munro. His letters describing a life spent almost entirely on horseback and in camp, whole hours passed in chatting to the country folk till the tents should come up, long strenuous years spent with no holidays and scarcely a single idle day, give a picture very similar to the existence which was soon to be led in the north-west of India by civilian administrators devoted to their duty and the people. An observant parish priest or lady novelist —a Crabbe or a Mary Mitford—hardly knew his or her fellow countrymen better than men like Munro the folk of their adopted country. But in Bengal the case was different. Englishmen did not, as a race, believe in the official anywhere concerning himself intimately with the lives of the people; and Cornwallis, a landed proprietor in his own country, looked for a system in Bengal under which the responsibility for internal order could be entrusted to a similar class, as it was in England, leaving the Josh Sedleys at the headquarters of their districts undisturbed. Properly to carry out the Indian system under which the State as supreme landlord collected from the superior proprietor or landholder an equitable rent under the name of land revenue, required an acquaintance with crops, agriculture, standards of living, and village economics generally, which these gentlemen neither had nor wished to have. Cornwallis substituted for the native system of a variable land revenue, irregularly collected from revenue payers whose possession was generally undisturbed, that of a fixed revenue punctually collected from payers whose land was ruthlessly sold up in default. Within a very few years of its institution in 1793 the faults of his permanent settlement had begun to appear. Although the State had sacrificed all the increment to be derived from the reclamation of waste, better cultivation, and higher prices, the assessments were such that many great landholders could not pay or could not pay in time, their property was sold by auction in default, and the list of those completely ruined includes several of those large Hindu proprietors who bore the title of Raja. The results were disastrous. The auction purchasers consisted largely of that execrable class, half attorney, half bailiff, which Cornwallis might have met with afterwards while Viceroy of Ireland, or at least read of in Maria Edgeworth's Castle Rackrent. But it was long before all this was realized at the headquarters of government, and Wellesley intended the districts ceded from Oudh to be permanently settled as soon as they had quieted down.

But he saw too—and in this lay his highest service to India—that a genuine efficient civil service was now required. In lofty language he pointed out to his masters the anomaly of styling their servants in an ascending scale, writers, factors, and junior and senior merchants, when they were required to discharge the functions of magistrates, judges, ambassadors, and governors of provinces. Boys of sixteen or seventeen on their first arrival in India were being prepared for these duties by copying letters and doing the other work of merchants' clerks, and lived among profligate surroundings in a society which provided no moral restraints. He established a College in Calcutta for all the young civil servants of India. To place them under discipline was the first object. But the course of studies was no narrow one. It included, besides vernacular languages, Persian, Arabic, Sanskrit, Hindu and Muhammadan

Law, Ethics, the History and Antiquities of India, Natural History and Astronomy. On the first occasion when His Excellency was able to be present in state at the examinations—in 1803—he listened to disputations in Persian, Hindustani, and Bengali on such subjects as the advantages enjoyed by the natives of India under British rule, the suicide of Hindu widows, or sati, and the effects of the caste system.

It was here that he again came into collision with the Directors. It was pre-eminently—even if it did not throw an increased burden on the Company's finances—the sort of scheme on which they should have been consulted. There was plenty of time. It was mentioned by him in a letter to Dundas as early as October 1799. Urgent despatches sent by land took no more than four or five months, those by sea usually only a month or so longer to pass between London and Calcutta. Wellesley did not actually issue orders for the establishment of the College until July 1800. When the Directors heard of it they ordered it to be closed at once on grounds of expense. Wellesley suspended the abolition. Castlereagh intervened, and consulted the three men who had held the office of Governor-General since its creation, all still living in England—Warren Hastings, Cornwallis, and Teignmouth. They approved generally of the idea. The College was allowed to continue for Bengal civilians only, and another was founded at Haileybury in Hertfordshire which prepared boys for it, and afterwards took its place. Writing to his father in 1809, Lord Wellesley's son Richard appeared to chafe somewhat at the lengthy period of discipline which he had inaugurated. "They ought to make something of me at last", he thought, after 3 years at Hertford, 2 at Calcutta College, and 2 of training with the Sudder Dewani, the supreme civil court of the province.

The grand scale on which the College was inaugurated, the magnificent new Government House in Calcutta, the splendid state barges, the mounted bodyguard, the pomp with which the Governor-General travelled when he went by river to Upper India accompanied by a thousand boats, all betrayed that he was suffering from a malady most incident to men of his station—megalomania. The insidious stages of its approach are clear from a familiar letter written home soon after his arrival, in which Wellesley describes the society of his subjects—as he calls them—as so vulgar, ignorant, rude, familiar, and stupid that he is obliged to entrench himself in forms for self-protection. But this unfavourable view of Anglo-Indian society was not confined to him or applicable only to Calcutta. This is clear from the observations made some years later by an intelligent lady traveller, Maria Graham, on the other side of India. She found the ladies in Bombay underbred and overdressed. The growing settlement had then the inestimable advantage of numbering among its denizens one of the first literary men of his age, Sir James Mackintosh, who was Recorder —an office corresponding in that small Presidency to the Supreme Courts in the other two. But even his presence in it, and the respect in which he was held, did not save society from being so uncouth that a thick veneer of forms was necessary to cover its barbarity. But Wellesley had also to impress the natives. He neglected no means for the purpose. Although a libertine, he lived, while in India, a decent life, went regularly to church, and, to show to the people that the Company's servants, too, had a religion, ordered the observance of Sunday.

In the most serious matter on which he withstood the Directors he was not alone. Both Wellesley himself and the Governor of Madras, Lord Clive, son of the victor of Plassey, had been subjected to a peremptory and presumptuous interference in the matter of appointments. In the southern Presidency the Directors had gone so far as to appoint to good posts men who had been sent home in disgrace. The Governor sent in his resignation in 1801, but the Governor-General got him to withdraw it by supporting it with his own. In January 1802 Wellesley asked for permission to embark for England in a year's time. At the same time he sent Addington a formidable series of indictments against the Court of Directors, concluding with what he described as the most immediate cause of his resignation, their treatment of Clive. In this he undoubtedly placed his finger on their gravest delinquency. Lord William Bentinck, who succeeded as Governor of Madras in 1803, complained bitterly of the way in which he found his position had been undermined before his arrival; and the evil seed sown by the Directors in a province always fertile in European intrigue bore fruit some years later in disturbances which threatened to shake British authority to its foundation. So far as Wellesley was concerned, the appeal to Addington had the calculated result in a formal request from the Court of Directors that he would remain. In the event he protracted his period of office beyond the end of the term of five years, after which experience has shown that the stay of a Governor General is apt to be unfortunate.

At the moment when he had sent his resignation, the schemes of Bonaparte had been successfully countered, and tranquillity reigned through India, so far as the British were concerned. But already a step had been taken which —although it was scarcely realized at the time—led almost inevitably to the greatest war in which England ever became involved in India, and committed her irrevocably to the great adventure of imperial responsibility. This was the Treaty of Hyderabad, which compelled the Company to enter into close relations with the only power then capable of disputing the supremacy of India. In the seventeenth century a Western Indian robber chief, Sivaji, had wrested an empire from the Great Moghul who reigned in Delhi. That empire became the Maratha confederacy. It was mainly divided between five great chiefs. One came of a junior branch of Sivaji's own family, the Bhonsla Raja of Berar. One was the hereditary Peshwa or Prime Minister. The others were descendants of the generals of the empire. They were men of low caste, the natural heads of predatory states. The head of Sivaji's family in the nineteenth century was a mere state prisoner. The Peshwa, Baji Rao, exercised a precarious supremacy over the whole confederacy from his capital at Poona—120 miles south-east of Bombay—where his own extensive dominions were. In the centre of India, as far as Orissa lying along the eastern coast, reigned Raghuji Bhonsla, weak both in personal character and in a military sense. On the west coast Anand Rao, after a disputed succession, was installed by the Bombay Government as Gaikwar of Baroda in 1802, and continued friendly, allowing his capital to be used by the British as a military base. The fourth chief was Jaswant Rao Holkar, by far the most formidable of the five, although—perhaps because—his territory was not large. It lay immediately to the east of the Gaikwar's. East and north-east of his was the wide dominion of Daulat Rao Sindhia, stretching from Hyderabad to the Himalayas. Each of these two chiefs had a number of European adventurers in his service, each was frequently at war with the other, and constantly at watch to raid a neighbour. They recruited by the lure of plunder men of the most diverse religions and castes from distant quarters of India; and the treatment which Maharashtra itself, the sacred land of the Marathas, received from this nondescript herd of rascals pointedly recalls de Rocca's account of how the Grand Army, consisting of French, Germans, Italians, Poles, Swiss, Dutch, Irish, and Mamelukes, marched from Germany into Spain in 1808, and treated France on its way as an enemy's country.

For years the Nizam had begged for a guarantee of protection against the Marathas. It had hitherto been steadfastly declined. In 1795 he had been left at the mercy of his enemies, and had been compelled, among other humiliations as the result of an unsuccessful war, to accept a Maratha Minister to govern his territories. He had applied for British assistance, which Shore refused; he had then obtained French help in disciplining an army, which Wellesley in his turn compelled him to disband. He had now no hope of defending himself without a British guarantee. Moreover his concerns, and even his actual territorial possessions, were so closely interwoven with those of the Marathas that it was quite impossible to hope to avoid the constant recurrence of fresh subjects of dispute. Besides he had now given the British substantial assistance in the war with Mysore, and that power, the only one which the Marathas feared, had been destroyed. It would have been unworthy longer to have refused him protection. The Treaty of Hyderabad, concluded in October 1800, placed the Nizam's foreign policy under British control, and guaranteed his dominion against attack. It was no longer possible therefore to be neutral as regards Maratha affairs. An alliance had, indeed, been concluded by Cornwallis with the Peshwa as early as 1789, and had never been denounced, but it was abrogated in actual fact by Sindhia, who had usurped authority over him, and would not allow him to help the British in the war with Tipu. In October 1802 that ruler's control of Poona was overthrown in its turn. In a battle near the city Holkar defeated the allied forces of Sindhia and the Peshwa, who fled to the coast and escaped in a British ship to his port of Bassein. about 30 miles north of Bombay. He was followed by Lieutenant-Colonel Barry Close, who had been the Governor-General's representative as Resident at Poona. On the last day of the year was concluded the Treaty of Bassein, another of those treaties of subordinate alliance which, defensive as they were in their terms, tended, apart from the small area directly ceded in return for the protection of a subsidiary force, to involve the British in larger and larger imperial commitments.

The task of restoring the Peshwa to his authority in Poona fell to a young major-general now well launched on his splendid career. It was Arthur Wellesley, the Governor-General's younger brother, and the sixth child of their father. He was born about the 1st of May 1769. Three more children were born after him in the family, Henry being the last of all. His childhood was spent in Ireland, his schooldays partly at Chelsea and Eton, and partly in France at the military academy at Angers. He received a commission at seventeen, and his name was borne on the books of several regiments, both horse and foot, in the course of the next few years, he was aide-de-camp to the Lord Lieutenant in Dublin, and he also entered the Irish Parliament. Although neither rich nor precociously clever nor particularly influential, promotion was so rapid before the Duke of York had reformed the system that he was a Lieutenant Colonel at twenty-four in the first year of the war with France. He saw service first in Holland in 1794 and 1795, and it was here that he had his first experience of commissariat defects and of a British army in retreat. Early in 1797 he reached India with his regiment, the 33rd, and his strong sense, exuberant vitality, and obvious capacity for high command at once attracted the attention and admiration even of so pacific a Governor-General as Sir John Shore. He was, indeed, far from being the plain soldier which a widespread tradition has since credited him with being. Besides showing great energy and ability in reorganizing the commissariat of the Madras army, he displayed considerable talent for political affairs —to use the word again in its Indian sense. He was, in consequence, at the Nizam's desire placed in command of the Hyderabad contingent in the Mysore war, and after it was over he was entrusted with delicate and responsible duties in connection with the settlement of the country. He had active military work besides in hunting down freebooters, but was prevented by ill health from going with Baird to Egypt. Little is heard of Wellesley's bad health during the remainder of his active life, and it was doubtless his Indian experience which confirmed in him two of those negative qualities which have often been imagined to be almost the principal causes of his success in life. They were abstemiousness and coolness of temper. "I know but one receipt for good health in this country", he wrote to Henry in 1799, "and that is to live moderately, to drink little or no wine, to use exercise, to keep the mind employed, and, if possible, to keep in good humour with the world. The last is the most difficult, for, as you have often observed, there is hardly a good-tempered man in India."

There could be little doubt that it was impossible for the British in India to keep either their health or their virtue without strenuous work. There were many who did not think of this. The old days of the Nabobs, who, after spending a few years in the Company's service, returned with large fortunes and bought modern mansions and rotten boroughs, had gone by; but there were still pickings. In 1797 the Commander-in-Chief in Madras was getting £14,000 to £16,000 a year in pay and allowances from the King, the Company, and the Nawab of the Carnatic. In the same year, Lord Bathurst was pressed to accept the Governorship of that Presidency, and told that the salary was £20,000, of which he could save half. Many of the servants of the Company, particularly those engaged in its mercantile interests, set the soldier a very bad example. They did not mind ruining their constitutions—coming home, as the saying was, with yellow faces—so long as they came with yellow guineas. In 1805 an officer who had just been through a succession of strenuous campaigns, came across one of the well-known Anglo-Indian family of Pattles at Murshidabad. He had seven pairs of carriage horses besides some of the best-bred saddle horses in India under a European coachman. But he was economizing.

He had already made his money once in India, returned to England and become a Director of the Company, spent it all, and had now returned to the service to make another princely fortune. But on the whole the soldiers resisted the temptation to follow such luxurious examples; their regimental pay was not high; if they acquired money (or credit) in the ingenious ways of which soldiers only were capable, they spent it on sport and horses. Besides for them fortunes meant active service. The prize money earned was enormous. After eight years of a strictly honourable life in India Arthur Wellesley accumulated between thirty and forty thousand pounds, mostly from the capture of Tipu's capital, Seringapatam. General Lake's prize money after the capture of Agra amounted to forty-four thousand.

In spite of the staff posts being mainly appropriated by King's officers, and the services of greatest responsibility and danger being allotted to the King's regiments, it was necessarily the Company's troops on whom the great brunt of the work fell. The return for the first day of the century gave of the troops of the Crown on the East India Station only four regiments of Light Dragoons and fifteen battalions of infantry, including a Swiss regiment—in all less than 16,000 strong. Several of these regiments were doing garrison duty in Presidency towns and elsewhere, or in Ceylon. Three years later the establishment was half as much again. But there were not more than six British cavalry regiments and twelve infantry battalions of the King's army in India in 1803, numbering with the artillery and the Company's three European regiments rather under 24,000. There were rather more than a hundred thousand native troops in the three armies among which India was divided. The men of the Madras and Bombay armies were small, averaging less than five and a half feet in height. But the former was generally confined to the highest castes, while the latter was recruited somewhat indiscriminately.

The Bengal army on the other hand had a taller, though not a more sturdy, stamp of man. They were not recruited in the unwarlike country from which the army took its name. Many of the infantry were Rajputs, thus belonging to the warrior division, the second of the four great divisions into which all the Hindu castes fell; the cavalry mainly Muhammadan. Upon such forces, differing little in material from those opposed to them, England depended for success in the great struggle which was now impending. There was nothing remarkable about the strategical or tactical talent on the British side. There was no marked superiority in armament. Everything, beyond the example which a few British regiments could bestow, seemed to depend on the British regimental officers in the native regiments. Yet these were most unaccountably neglected.

On first arriving in India, even in war-time, it might be months before a cadet found any notice taken of him. When posted to a regiment at last, he found that his brother officers had a very easy time. Parades were carried on by the adjutant and the European sergeant-major. The dress, in Bengal at least, was fifty years behind the times, the officers' heads were powdered all over, their queues were twelve or fourteen inches long, and above all this they wore the most enormous head-dresses. There was little regimental life. There was often no regimental mess. Lieutenant John Shipp in his Memoirs wrote of regiments in which every officer lived separately, each with his coloured female companion. When the time came for active service it was astonishing with what elaborate paraphernalia an Indian army moved—a luxury which naturally extended itself to the European troops. Shipp, when still sergeant of the King's 22nd, had his pony as well as his dog on active service. There were ten camp followers, male or female, to every fighting man. "The march of our army", wrote Major Thorn, "had the appearance of a moving town or citadel, in the form of an oblong square, whose sides were defended by ramparts of glittering swords and bayonets." Within were hundreds of elephants, thousands of camels, and all the mass of tradesmen and pedlars who make up an Indian bazaar. But an army in India had one merit of its own. As there were no roads, in the European sense of the word, the cumbrous machine was able to go anywhere, or it would not have been able to move at all. Luxurious as the officer of the Indian army was, he did his duty in the day of action. He only had to lead. The regiments were usually already welded together by common ties almost as strong as the strict discipline which bound an English regiment, or the love of glory which united the soldiers of the French Empire. They were like a union of families, for every private, or sepoy, almost, could claim some tie of kinship with a native officer or non-commissioned officer, whom he would follow to the end. No men had a finer sense of honour than the Rajputs, the chivalry of the East, and the high warlike castes of Southern India were not much behind them.

Arthur Wellesley was one of those who had led his brother to see in the Treaty of Bassein a guarantee of peace. In March 1803 he advanced to Poona with a force of nearly ten thousand men, Holkar retiring before him, and the Peshwa was restored without a blow. The treaty had been communicated to the other members of the Confederacy in the hope that they would recognize his authority, and at first there seemed to be some prospect of their acquiescence. Holkar retired into his own territory. The treaty had not infringed the rights of either Sindhia or Holkar, and both chiefs at first sent friendly letters. But their professions were deceitful. Even the Peshwa, whose chief minister was Sindhia's own man, appointed by him, was treacherous. It was so clearly in the interests of both Holkar and Sindhia not to press matters to a conflict with the British, that it was long before Arthur Wellesley could bring himself to believe that they could do so. But another figure now appeared on the scene in the person of Raghuji Bhonsla, Raja of Berar. At the end of May Sindhia had bluntly told Lieutenant-Colonel Collins, the British Resident at his court, that the issue of peace or war depended upon the result of an interview between the two chiefs. The Raja of Berar had peculiar claims on the score of his descent to a primacy among the Marathas, or at least to independence of what the Peshwa might do. He was, moreover, with good reason, afraid that the enforced pacification of Western India would bring the inveterate freebooter Holkar on to him in search of subsistence for his army. Weak man as the Bhonsla Raja was, the result of his intervention was decisive. The expected interview took place on the 8th of June. On the 26th the Governor-General invested his brother, who had marched north-eastward of Poona for the protection alike of the Peshwa's territory and that of the Nizam, with full powers of peace or war. The armies of Sindhia and the Raja of Berar were now menacing the Hyderabad frontier. Armed with his new powers, Arthur Wellesley sent a proposal, which perplexed from its very plainness, to the effect that the two chiefs should withdraw their troops to their usual stations, on which he on his part would withdraw his. Collins presented the notes on the 23rd of July. No subterfuge could enable the chiefs to evade the general's simple test of their good faith. They had played for time, and no more would be given. On the 6th of August war was declared on Sindhia and the Bhonsla Raja.

The Treaty of Bassein had been unsuccessful in its immediate object. Lord Wellesley was genuinely of opinion that the disturbances which had been rife in the Maratha empire in recent years would have disposed all branches of it to accept his general system of defensive alliance and guarantee. "This crisis of affairs", he wrote to the Secret Committee on hearing that the Peshwa had thrown himself on British protection, "appeared to me to afford the most favourable opportunity for the complete establishment of the interests of the British power in the Maratha empire, without the hazard of involving us in a contest with any party". That these were his real views is proved by their having been the views of his brother Arthur, whose confidential correspondence with him as well as with others shows how reluctantly he relinquished the belief in peace. In June, when he began to see that peace was not to be had, he wrote to Malcolm, then the Governor-General's right-hand man in political matters, that it had been a mistake to trust, as they all had done, in the authority of the Peshwa, adding in the rather sweeping way which he had: "We shall gain nothing by the treaty."

But, although the Treaty of Bassein was no ingenious plan of Lord Wellesley's to obtain a pretext for fresh conquests in India, it was justified not merely as a logical sequence of the Treaty of Hyderabad, but as part of a policy which preferred war, regrettable as it was, to constant unrest in the neighbourhood of the Company's territories. It was the vastness of the objects which he immediately showed that he expected to obtain from Sindhia's downfall that made him appear in the light of an imperial adventurer. Yet the entertainment of large designs in the event of a war was perfectly consistent with having no intention of forcing one on.

There was another circumstance likely to precipitate war with Sindhia independently of what went on in the south. Wellesley had freed India from the French menace, but those powerful convictions which had produced such energy four years before prevented him from feeling that he had really done so. During the European war the French possessions in India had been seized, and when, after the Peace of Amiens, he had orders to restore them, he—wisely as it turned out—withheld fulfilment. But in the north-west of India there existed, separated from the Company's territories by no natural barrier, what he called a French state. Here Sindhia had committed his forces to the command of a French officer, and assigned for their maintenance a considerable stretch of the historic country watered by the Jumna from the Himalayan mountains southwards to where the highlands of Central India begin, in which the Moghul capitals of Delhi and Agra were situated. The present head of the French state was Perron. The chiefs whose domains fringed the plain south-west of Agra were his vassals, and his enormous influence extended north-west of Delhi into the Punjab, the country occupied by the Sikhs, the votaries of the newest and most military form of Hinduism. In his determination to make the best of both the Hindu and Muhammadan worlds, Sindhia had added to his authority as Lieutenant of the pageant empire of the descendants of Sivaji that of Deputy of the pageant empire of the descendants of Akbar. His officer, Perron, styled himself a servant of the Great Moghul, whom he held a captive in the palace in Delhi, and called his army the imperial army. It was within Wellesley's knowledge that the Frenchman was on bad terms with Sindhia, and was only looking for an opportunity to retire to Europe on the fortune which he had amassed in his service. But, as he pointed out, this did not remove the danger. Perron might be succeeded by a more vigorous and more ambitious adventurer of the same nation, which he never ceased to regard as the enemy, although he did not yet know of the renewal of hostilities in Europe. The objects which he set before himself in the north in July 1803, every one of which was obtained by the end of the year, included, in northern India, the destruction of the "French state" and its annexation, the possession of the nominal authority of the Moghul, and the establishment of a protectorate over the petty states to the south and west of Agra. Seldom has so ambitious a programme been carried out with such rapid and complete success.

The war which followed was bewildering in its extent, being carried on simultaneously almost from Poona a thousand miles northward to Delhi, and over an equal distance from west to east—across the Peninsula from the Gulf of Cambay to the mouths of the Great River or Mahanadi. Vast mountain ranges and rivers separated the warring armies, but over all was held the strong control of Wellesley, who as Captain-General of India—an honour conferred upon him after the Mysore war—exercised authority over the troops of all three Presidencies. The campaigns conducted so far apart had many features in common. In the war as a whole courage, discipline, and pertinacity were almost the sole qualities in which the forces of the civilized West outdid those of the barbarous powers which had arisen on the decay of the Moghul empire. And even these troops had been partly disciplined by Frenchmen and Englishmen. The forces of Sindhia and the Raja of Berar were not very numerous. James Grant Duff, the historian of the Marathas, estimated them at a hundred thousand men, half of whom were horse, and almost a third regular infantry and artillery commanded by Europeans. But there was Holkar behind, and a crowd of smaller men ready to take advantage of a reverse. The strength of the enemy's cavalry prescribed the methods of carrying on the war. It had to be in the rainy season between June and October, when predatory raids by irregular horse were made impossible by the swollen rivers. Forts had to be rushed to save time. It was impossible to discover with any accuracy where the enemy was or in what strength, except by a cavalry reconnaissance in force, and this meant bringing up the main body to immediate action, however tired it might be with marching, for any retirement, even of cavalry only, and only for a few miles, would be a fatal encouragement to the enemy's horse. Such exigencies left little time for manœuvring. But it was desirable, if possible, before committing the infantry to a regular battle, to draw the powerful Maratha artillery out of the strong position in which it had been placed. The results were in every case decisive in favour of the British, comprising the complete dispersal of the enemy, and the capture of a large number of guns; the losses on the British side were small, though proportionately high in the European regiments. Such were the general characteristics of Delhi, of Assaye, of Laswari, and of Argaon. The two most important battles, Assaye and Laswari, had other points in common. The enemy showed an unsuspected talent for manœuvre. There were moments when the issue of the fight seemed to hang on a thread. In each of the two battles the General lost almost the whole of his staff, had two horses killed under him, and exhausted himself galloping up and down the field giving his own orders.

The officer upon whom success mainly depended was Lieutenant-General Gerard Lake, Commander-in-Chief in Bengal, one of several British soldiers who have so oddly distinguished themselves in a high command in a country, in which youth is deemed essential, at an age which would be thought too advanced for an active life even in Europe. He was just entering his sixtieth year. He had seen service so far back as the wars of the great Frederick under the English national hero the Marquis of Granby, whom he took for his model. Lake's greatest achievement hitherto had been in 1793, when with 1,100 men of the Guards he routed more than four times their number of Frenchmen in a frontal attack upon an entrenched position—a fitting prelude to his doings in India. His force now numbered about fifteen thousand men, including three regiments of British cavalry and one of British infantry, with 65 guns. He marched direct on Perron's force, which awaited him in the Doab, or land of two waters—that lying between the two rivers Ganges and Jumna. On the 29th of August he found him at Aligarh, seventy miles south-east of Delhi, and attacked him at once. Perron lost at the outset most of the British officers in Sindhia's service, who came over to Lake when he reached the border. His force in the field consisted mainly of cavalry. He refused to accept battle, withdrawing southwards to Agra. Soon afterwards he carried out his design of leaving Sindhia's service, and obtained for himself a safe conduct to France.

Lake now lost no time in storming the powerful frontier fortress of Aligarh, which fell on the 4th of September. He then made a rapid march on Delhi. Sindhia's general here was Louis Bourquien, another French officer of little skill, whose effectiveness was thwarted by intrigues and disputes between himself and his predecessor Perron. Confident in the enormous strength of his artillery—110 guns—he ventured to cross the Jumna in front of Delhi, and to fight with that river at his back. It was now the 10th of September. Lake had under five thousand for action against three or four times his numbers. He enticed the guns forward away from their positions, and made a rapid attack under very heavy artillery fire with his infantry, who fired a volley at a hundred yards, and then charged with the bayonet. The guns were taken, the cavalry took up the pursuit, the galloper guns which accompanied them were brought into action, and the enemy were cut down, drowned in the Jumna, or dispersed. His losses in this action were 478, and of these 137 were in the King's 76th. That devoted regiment had already had 90 casualties, including 5 officers killed, at Aligarh. The casualties in the battle of Delhi included two officers killed from the effects of the sun. The mere losses from the enemy's action are a very small measure of what the European troops especially had to go through in a campaign at the end of the monsoon, the most unwholesome and exhausting season of the year at all times, even though somewhat mitigated in 1803 by the partial failure of the rains.

The victory of Delhi laid that city open. The family of the poor aged blinded Emperor had watched eagerly for the result, and now joyfully welcomed the conquerors. Shah Alam was restored to his throne as sovereign of Delhi and the small surrounding district. Lake marched down the Jumna to Agra without opposition, and routed a force covering the fort, which surrendered to him on the 18th of October. The first phase of the war in the plains of northern India had ended gloriously indeed. But this was not the only work of the Bengal army. Some hundred miles down the Jumna from Agra, where that river changes its course from a southerly to a south-easterly direction, its right bank as far as Allahabad was fringed by the hilly districts of northern Bundelkhand—spurs and islands of rock thrown out from the central highlands—which, although poor, were of strategic value to the Company. Ill-adapted as a river is generally for a defensive frontier, this is never less the case than in India, where it is impossible to guard the numerous fords in the dry seasons of the year, or to watch the elaborate network of ravines which fringes the banks of such a stream as the Jumna. Wellesley had accordingly obtained the cession of this territory by a supplementary agreement to the Treaty of Bassein from the Peshwa, whose nominal authority was recognized there. But it was also necessary to go and take it, and a British force marching westwards from Allahabad, mastered eastern Bundelkhand after a trifling resistance in the month of September. The rest followed some weeks later. In the east of India a mixed force from the Bengal and Madras armies wrested the sacred country at the mouths of the Mahanadi, where the great temple of Jagannath stands, from the Raja of Berar; and the grateful inhabitants were relieved from the curse of Maratha extortion and the slave trade. The coastal districts were formed into the Orissa division of Bengal, whose seaboard now joined with that of Madras stretching as far as the extreme south of India.

The western coast was also in British or in friendly hands as far north as the Gulf of Cambay. Here Sindhia had a seaport in Broach, which was captured in August, and the district occupied, by a force acting under Arthur Wellesley's orders. That general had himself moved forward on the 8th of August with 11,000 men, including three British regiments, one imperishably connected with the name "Assaye", the 19th Light Dragoons numbering little over 405 men, and the 74th and 78th together making up 1,000. The same day he carried by assault the walled town of Ahmadnagar, a valuable base 70 miles north-eastward of Poona. Four days later the fortress itself surrendered. A tedious six weeks followed, during which Wellesley and Lieutenant-Colonel James Stevenson, who had a separate force of 9,000 men, were occupied in manœuvring to prevent Sindhia and the Raja of Berar from raiding Hyderabad. At length, on the 21st of September, he saw an opportunity of bringing them to action, and for the next few days, with a daring justified by his contempt for his opponents, successfully transgressed several principles of the art of war. He arranged with Stevenson to make a joint march on the enemy; but each army was to move by a perfectly separate road, and it actually happened that one found itself in action without being able to get any assistance from the other. With imperfect information as to the enemy's strength, he threw himself upon him in the afternoon of the 23rd with a tired force, crossed a river by a ford, of which he had only surmised the existence, exposed to the enemy's fire, based his plan on an assumption, which proved incorrect, that his opponent was unable to alter his front, and fought with the fork of two rivers at his back. With all this the battle which he fought on the 23rd near the village of Assaye on the northern border of the Hyderabad State, and 180 miles north-east of Poona, was a brilliant victory. He had with him 7,000 men and 22 guns, besides a few thousand irregular horse of the Peshwa's and from Mysore, which he kept for purposes of observation on the opposite side of the river. The enemy, fighting under the eyes of the two chiefs, consisted of 10,500 regular infantry and 30,000 horse, besides irregular infantry making up, with the men serving 100 guns, 50,000 in all. The infantry, under European leadership, were good, and the guns well served. The cavalry were formidable only from their numbers, and Wellesley had chosen his ground where his flanks were protected by the two rivers. The infantry carried the guns as at the battle of Delhi, but the right got into difficulties, and had to be extricated by a gallant charge of cavalry. The total loss was 1,584, of whom 428 were killed. How severely it fell on the Europeans is shown by the figures for the 74th, one of the regiments on the right. It lost 11 officers and 113 men killed, and 6 officers and 271 men wounded. The enemy, who had left 1,200 dead on the field, retired a few miles that day, but on Stevenson's approach they continued their withdrawal, and in the course of the next three weeks Sindhia lost all his possessions in the Deccan—the country south of the Narbada.

Before the battle that chief had sent seven good battalions to reinforce his northern army. These became in October the nucleus of a new force of 9,000 infantry, a few thousand horse, and 72 guns, which threatened to advance on Delhi under a Maratha named Abaji, who proved himself a much more formidable opponent than any hitherto. Lake came upon them on the 1st of November at Laswari, 80 miles south-south-west of that city, and almost the same distance from Agra. There was no great disparity of force, for Lake had about 8,000 men, including a strong body of cavalry. Confident in these, he first attempted to obtain the victory with his mounted troops alone, but failing in this, he brought up his infantry, which had already marched 25 miles since three in the morning of that day. Once more they carried the guns, once more, as at Assaye, a charge of cavalry—it was the 29th Light Dragoons—restored the fortunes of the fight at the critical moment of the action, and once more, as at Delhi, that handful of heroes, as Lake called the 76th in his despatch, bore the brunt of the action. They well deserved the emblazoning of "Lake and Victory" on their colours. That victory, though long doubtful, was complete. In this battle, unlike previous battles, the enemy left thousands of dead and wounded on the field. Lieutenant-Colonel James Skinner, the most celebrated of leaders of Indian irregular cavalry, described an incident after the fight. "As Lord Lake was returning from the battle, some of the Europeans cheered him. He took off his hat and thanked them, but told them to despise death, as these brave fellows had done, pointing to the Mahrathas, who were lying thick around their guns." Sindhia's power was now completely broken.

Meanwhile Arthur Wellesley had been watching for an opportunity to strike without allowing the confederates' cavalry to slip past him southwards. At last his patience was rewarded. Marching eastwards into Berar territory, he and Stevenson met with and defeated Raghuji Bhonsla's army supported by some of Sindhia's cavalry on November the 29th at Argaon. The victory was decisive. It now fell to Arthur Wellesley to carry through complicated negotiations affecting territories in very different parts of India, while occupied in laying siege to the very powerful hill fort of Gawilgarh. He was equal to both. Gawilgarh was stormed on the 15th of December. Two days later he had concluded peace with Raghuji, and on the 30th with Sindhia. The treaties gave his brother all he required. But that with Sindhia did not prove a final settlement.

All through the war the menacing figure of Holkar had loomed in the background, and the result had given him all—perhaps more than all—that he wanted. His rival was discomforted. Sindhia's disbanded troops could now join Holkar's standard, and make him more formidable than ever. The very success of the English was a point in his favour. He could now hope to work on the fears of a crowd of smaller men in the north—Rajputs, Jats, Muhammadans, and Sikhs—by showing them the danger in which all stood from this foreign Power which threatened to overrun all India. The new method of war had been discredited. Holkar believed, as Arthur Wellesley did too at one time, that the old way of warfare was what suited his people best. He had artillery and European officers as well as Sindhia, but he determined to trust mainly to his cavalry. He sent Lake, who had, as well as Arthur Wellesley, been invested with full political powers, the most extravagant demands, and backed them with a characteristic threat—"my country and property are upon the saddle of my horse".

Both Lord Wellesley and Lake had been most unwilling to try conclusions with so savage and so desperate an adversary. Even after he had put to death three British officers in his service for refusing to serve against their own countrymen in the event of hostilities, the Governor-General held his hand. But Holkar was determined on war. One of the small states whose protection had recently been guaranteed by the British was that of Jaipur, 140 miles west of Agra. Holkar made an incursion into that Raja's territory. Hostilities were now inevitable, and Lake arrived in the State only just in time to prevent the plunder of the capital itself, Holkar retiring precipitately before him. It was now the end of April 1804, the hottest season of the year was approaching, and the Governor-General would have postponed further movement. But he was at ten or twelve days' distance by post from the theatre of operations. Before his views could reach Lake, he had already moved. British officers had then little knowledge of what hot weather can be in Upper India, where the hot winds blow like a furnace-blast, and where even natives of the country die from exposure to the heat. But even

Lake withdrew his main army when he saw his men dying round him, leaving the duty of watching Holkar in the hands of Lieutenant-Colonel the Honourable William Monson. It was unfortunate that an officer from the British army should have been placed in command of a force consisting—except for a few European artillerymen —entirely of Indian troops. It was composed of five infantry battalions, and about three thousand irregular horse partly commanded by a treacherous officer of Sindhia. Though an excessively brave man, Monson was deficient in coolness of judgement, and it was that season of the year when such a gift was most essential. He followed Holkar, who drew him after him into the heart of a mountainous country, only to fall back upon his infantry and guns, and turn reinforced upon his pursuer. Monson came to a disastrous decision. On the 8th of July he began a retreat which could have but one result. He could make no permanent stand anywhere until, broken by incessant attacks, he at last reached Agra on the 31st of August with the loss of his artillery and baggage and half his force.

But Holkar, who had pursued Monson triumphantly almost to the walls of the city, was himself little better than a fugitive. A force moving up from Baroda in the west under Colonel John Murray took his capital Indore. Two months later, by the end of October, another, under Lieutenant-Colonel William Wallace from Poona, captured his possessions in the Deccan. But Holkar did not seem to care. He had no home and no responsibilities. But he was at the head of a force which Skinner estimated at sixty thousand horse, and fifteen thousand infantry and artillery, with 192 guns. He moved northward closely followed now by Lake himself, who was unable to bring him to action. Frustrated in an attempt to seize Delhi by the gallantry of the Resident, Lieutenant-Colonel David Ochterlony, and the Commandant of the garrison, Lieutenant-Colonel

William Burn, he slipped away with his cavalry across the Jumna, and made a path with fire and sword through the Doab. Lake followed him—350 miles in a fortnight—with a force consisting mainly of cavalry. Never did his vigour show better. At dawn of the 17th of November, after a march of 36 miles in 24 hours, he surprised Holkar at Farrukhabad on the Ganges within 90 miles of Cawnpore, and cut his force to pieces with terrific slaughter, himself scarcely losing a man. Four days earlier, Major-General John Fraser with the rest of Lake's army had won a complete victory over Holkar's infantry and artillery at Dig. Near a hundred guns were captured.

One of the petty states with which Wellesley had made treaties of alliance was Bharatpur, the home of the great agricultural fighting tribe of Jats. Its capital was 34 miles south-west of Agra, and 20 miles southward of Dig, which also lay in that state. When Fraser's men drove the enemy back they were themselves fired upon from the fortress. But Oriental treachery was usually impolitic, and often—as in this instance—belated. The Raja of Bharatpur had for months entertained the advances of Holkar, a fact which the British knew but preferred to overlook. Now that he had at length thrown off the mask and resolved to entertain the marauder, he found that he had himself to bear the brunt of Lake's wrath. Some of Holkar's guns which had escaped capture were taken into Dig, and Holkar himself reappeared with the remains of his cavalry. But he was unable to avert the capture of the fortress, which fell on the 25th of December. These British successes were followed by the disastrous siege of Bharatpur city.

It is one of Fate's ironies that it was only through Lake's unbounded confidence in his men, and theirs in him, that that terrible tale of useless heroism was rendered possible. Bharatpur was surrounded by an enormous mud wall almost impossible to breach, and a wide ditch very difficult to bridge in the face of an enemy. Lake had a very weak siege train, and engineers without experience, who were unable to judge when a breach had been made practicable. The siege began on the 2nd of January, 1805. Four desperate assaults were made. In most it was the European troops which led, but in the third, which at one moment looked nearest succeeding, the men who planted the colours for a moment at the top of the bastion were of a regiment famous for honours won at Plassey—the 12th Bengal Infantry. Sergeant John Shipp—most gallant of men—who was on all the other three occasions the leader of the band of twelve volunteers who led the storm, wrote an account of Lake on the morning of the next day, the 21st of February, when the last blood was fruitlessly shed. "His Lordship addressed every corps that passed him; but when the remnant of the two companies of the 22nd regiment marched by, he was seen to turn from them, and the tears fell down his cheek; but, fearful it might be observed, he took off his hat and cheered them. This was not the tear of Judas, for his lordship often shed tears of sorrow for our great loss at this place. He was a true soldier's friend, and valued their lives as much as his own." Nor did he spare himself, for they had had scores of occasions of witnessing his personal courage in the field. But, although that attack was another failure, and Lake was obliged to draw off with a loss during the siege of 3,000 men—half the total strength of his infantry at its commencement—yet his demeanour, and his obvious determination to renew the attempt as soon as a really efficient battering train should arrive, so imposed upon the Raja that he was glad to conclude a treaty of alliance which included the payment of £200,000 in consideration of the peace granted to him, and the leaving one of his own sons and the fort of Dig as hostages for his fidelity. The signatures were not affixed until the 17th of April; and in the meantime Lake had made several successful attacks on Holkar's weakened and dispirited force, which had hung about the neighbourhood of Bharatpur without power seriously to interfere with the siege. At the end of the month an example of still more belated treachery than the Raja of Bharatpur's gave the principal enemy another ally. Sindhia, without actually declaring war, joined Holkar with his army. Both moved themselves beyond striking distance of Lake, who was glad on his part to be spared another active campaign in the hottest season of the year. On the 25th of July the Governor-General addressed a final ultimatum to Sindhia.

It was the last important act of his administration. Wellesley had never ventured to stand boldly forth as a founder of empire. Castlereagh, who did not understand that the new arrangement gave British India a real strategic frontier, was puzzled by his long explanations of how a defensive policy inevitably entailed such enormous extensions of territory. But, writing in May 1804, when he was taking up the additional duties of Secretary for War, he was fully alive to what this meant for the British army. The establishment of King's troops in India, of 24,000 men, was already 6,000 deficient, and it was now desired to raise it to 31,000. Another difficulty was connected with finance. In 1801 the revenue of India had been roughly $7\frac{1}{4}$ millions for Bengal, $4\frac{1}{4}$ for Madras, and a quarter for Bombay, and the net revenue came to over a million pounds. From this, as well as the profits from trading to India and China, the Company had to find its own dividend of 10 per cent. for the Proprietors of East India Stock, and the expenses of its other possessions. It did not remit money to India when the expenses rose in consequence of war, and such charges were met by the Governor-General in Council raising a local loan at a high rate of interest. Wellesley had raised the debt of the Company from eleven to twenty-seven millions before he left India. It is true that by placing its finances in the best hands, those of St. George Tucker, he had immensely improved its credit. The eight per cent. paper, which was at 12 per cent. discount in

1798, was at par in 1806. The revenue would be fourteen and a half millions when the new districts had been settled, the charges not more than twelve. But it was difficult for anyone, and particularly for Wellesley, whose correspondence was too long for anyone but an Anglo-Indian or an historical student to read, to bring this home to Castlereagh or even to Pitt. The Ministers had no desire to disregard the growing clamour of the Directors. While Lake was made a peer and Arthur Wellesley a Knight of the Bath, the Governor-General, whose policy did more to consolidate British power in India than any other Governor-General's before or since his day, got nothing except the "pinchbeck Irish marquisate" which he had already obtained for Mysore.

An attempt was even made after his return to impeach him as Warren Hastings had been impeached. But that precedent was in his favour. The genius of Burke and Sheridan had breathed life into the dry bones of Indian state papers, but, though one of the two was still alive, there was no one able and willing to do it now. The result even of Hastings's trial had convinced Fox that it was impossible to get justice by so protracted a proceeding, unfair alike to prosecution and defence. "Strike but hear" had been the irritating requirement of Themistocles. "Strike but read" was the even more exasperating claim made by the Anglo-Indian official. Some members of the House of Commons tried to fulfil the condition. They read. Scores of motions were made for papers, hundreds of pounds were spent on printing reams intended to bring to light Wellesley's extravagance over his buildings, his journeys, and his establishments. But it would have been ludicrous to make such matters subject of impeachment. In the end it was decided to proceed by resolution. His treatment of Oudh and the Carnatic was arraigned. It was some satisfaction that resolutions of approval finally took the place of resolutions of censure. But it was only in June 1808 that

Lord Wellesley passed through the last of these ordeals. In the course of all these discussions the question whether the second founder of the British empire in India deserved any reward for his services passed out of sight. As regards the events which led up to the great wars by which he established it, the memorandum drawn up by his brother Arthur—a document which would have made a literary reputation for a lesser man—provided a complete justification. Very few men's actions have had as extensive an influence over the human race as Lord Wellesley's. Yet in the memorandum his brother was successful in justifying him with as little reference as possible to the views and intentions of the man himself, by showing how each measure followed almost unavoidably from things which had happened before. Wellesley was great, not by performing the almost impossible feat of governing the course of events, but because he did not drift helplessly on the current, but directed it through orderly channels towards an understood goal.

In India at least he got his due. Addresses poured in, and statues were voted to him by public subscription in Calcutta and Bombay. He was little known to the natives of the country which he ruled, but his regard for them is shown by the efforts to make the town of Calcutta habitable for Europeans and Indians alike, and to improve Indian agriculture. The range of his activities was indeed colossal. How he struck those with whom he worked can be abundantly illustrated. Lake loved him, and wrote that his kindness moved him to tears. Thirty years later Sir Charles Metcalfe, now acting as Governor-General, wrote affectionately of the time when, as a writer of fifteen, he was entering on his career, and was admitted to be a member of Wellesley's family—the attractive word then in vogue to denote the immediate staff of an administrator or general. "My public principles", he wrote, "were learned in your school, pre-eminently the school of honour, zeal, public spirit, and patriotism; and to my adherence to the principles there acquired I venture to ascribe all the success that has attended me."

Wellesley's successor was Cornwallis, who now became Governor-General for the second time. Sworn in on the 30th of July, 1805, he announced on the same day to Lake his earnest desire to put an end to what he termed this most unprofitable and ruinous warfare. The side of the shield which he looked upon was dark indeed. The mere circumstance that—as he expressed it—he found himself waging war against two chieftains who had neither territory nor army to lose, made success itself seem useless. The great ascendancy which British influence had obtained in the Courts of Poona and Hyderabad was another evil from his point of view, as tending to increase responsibilities already wide enough. He had not time to balance the assets and liabilities of the Company, but he could see at once that the immediate cash position was very bad. The troops and a part of the civil service were five months in arrears, and he had to send orders to detain £2,000,000 worth of bullion which was intended for China. On the 8th of August he set out on the tedious journey by boat up the Ganges swollen by the rainy season. It was necessary to be nearer to Lake, who still had charge of all negotiations, and who—as the Governor-General was not slow in realizing—was most unwilling to be an instrument of a complete reversal of policy. Cornwallis was intent on being lenient with Sindhia, who had gone so far as to detain the British Resident, Richard Jenkins, by force, and he actually wished to give up Delhi. But all his efforts were in vain. He was now 66. It had been, indeed, a desperate act, as he wrote himself, to embark for India at so advanced an age. He had been already failing, though only in body, when he reached Calcutta. He never got further up the Ganges than Ghazipur, 500 miles by river from the capital. Here he died on the 5th of October, 1805. The universal regret and the glowing tributes paid to his memory by those who—like Malcolm—were the most deeply opposed to his policy, indicate much more than mere recognition of the noble self-denial with which he undertook a charge which meant almost certain death. Whether right or wrong, he was one who compelled respect for his views—a proof how much greater character is than mere ability.

He was succeeded by the Senior Member of Council, Sir George Barlow, an experienced civil servant who had been a loyal colleague of Wellesley in all his imperial schemes, and was now an equally loyal supporter of the policy of his masters at home. The treatment of Sindhia offered no great difficulty. So firm had Lake's attitude been that he had already given Jenkins up. Sindhia received back a possession which Wellesley himself would now have been willing to restore, the powerful fort of Gwalior fifty miles south of Agra. He was allowed to push his boundary up to the Chambal, a tributary on the south bank of the Jumna. The Company acquired from him in round figures 10,000 square miles of the rich plains lying between the Upper Ganges and the Jumna, being the greater part of what afterwards became the Meerut division, 3,000 square miles on the right bank of the latter river round Agra, 1,300 square miles round Delhi, administered in the Emperor's name, and, in western India, the district of Broach of 600 square miles in the valuable cotton country, besides the 5,000 to 6,000 square miles in Bundelkhand obtained under treaty with the Peshwa and confirmed by conquest.

Meanwhile Holkar had pushed off north-west, with Lake once more in hot pursuit. He had some hope of rallying the Sikh chiefs to his side, notably the young chief who was afterwards called the Lion of the Punjab, Raja Ranjit Singh. But they had no quarrel with the British, and Holkar got no help. On December the 4th the intrepid Skinner showed the way across the Sutlej, and the first

British gun entered the Punjab. Holkar was brought to bay at Amritsar, 280 miles from Delhi, and here on the 7th of January, 1806, he signed a treaty with Lake, whose political assistant was the brilliant civilian Charles Metcalfe, then only twenty years of age. He too was to give up his possessions north of the Chambal as well as those wrested from him further to the south. All was well, but Barlow insisted on adding to the treaty certain declaratory articles by which the small barrier states west or south of the Jumna were generally sacrificed. Lake had to listen to complaints to which he could make no reply, and which were all the more galling as being of a character to which British officers were rarely obliged to listen. The Agent of the Raja of Jaipur said at one conference on the subject of the repudiation of the defensive alliance between the Company and his master, that it was the first time since the English Government had been established in India that it had been known to make its faith subservient to its convenience. Lake resigned, and was consoled on his return to England with a step in the peerage. He died in 1808.

The only important event of Barlow's Governor-Generalship was the mutiny at Vellore, a fortress nearly ninety miles west of Madras. Here the family of Tipu Sultan resided in honoured and opulent confinement. Innovations had been introduced into the native regiments as regards their dress and turbans, as well as the quantity and shape of the hair on the face, and the coloured marks of the foreheads indicating caste. The last order in particular appeared to point to the abolition of Hindu caste distinctions, and was absurdly interpreted as a design to make the Indian soldiers or sepoys into Christians against their will. A glance at the conduct of the Europeans in Madras would have convinced them that they had nothing to fear from the religious zeal of those set over them. All these changes had already led to trouble in a regiment quartered in

Vellore in May 1806. There was no violence—nothing more than disorderly conduct and disobedience. Order was restored by severe means, two ringleaders receiving 900 lashes. Encouraged by the presence in the fortress of the swarm of adventurers, idlers, and intriguers who follow the fortunes of Oriental princes, the offended sepoys led by the Indian officers meditated a terrible blow. Such was the European officers' neglect of them and their ignorance even of the language of the country that they remained perfectly innocent of the doom impending over them—a doom openly proclaimed in the bazaar—and a sepoy who tried to give warning of the plot was put under arrest. On the 10th of July the Indians who formed four-fifths of the garrison broke out, killed the British sentinels on duty, seized the magazine, and fired into the barracks. Over two hundred of the European garrison of 370 were killed or wounded. The rest defended themselves until the arrival from Arcot, nine miles distant, of a squadron of the 19th Dragoons and other troops under the command of Lieutenant-Colonel Rollo Gillespie. He had to retake that powerful fort before he could save the Europeans who were maintaining an almost desperate struggle within, but he and his troops were irresistible. The mutiny was now put down without difficulty.

The Special Commission which was appointed to inquire into the origin of the mutiny, although it consisted almost entirely of men who might have been expected to understand the country, furnished another example of the type of mind among rulers which provokes such outbreaks. After thinking it worth while to observe that "in this country the prejudices of the conquered have always triumphed over the arms of the conqueror"—as if it were possible for a handful of men to govern a teeming population without respecting their opinions—they sententiously remark: "Nothing would appear to be more trivial to the public interests than the length of the hair on the upper lip of a sepoy." They did not ask themselves why a matter trivial to the public interests should have been made the subject of general regulation at all, the facts, of course, being that experience has shown that men are better soldiers for having learnt to take a pride in their personal appearance, and that, once they do so, they begin to have their own views on the matter. Only three years before it happened that a serious mutiny was caused at Gibraltar partly by a series of meticulous orders issued by the King's fourth son, the Duke of Kent, extending to this very question of the hair upon the soldier's face. Had it been dealing with this mutiny, the Commission would not have been able, as in the case of Vellore, to discuss religious prejudices, and the obstinate adherence of unreasonable people to unintelligible customs.

The Court of Directors refused to be hoodwinked. They took the view that the obstinacy and ignorance were on the side of the authorities, and removed the Commander-in-Chief, General John Cradock, from his command. They also recalled the Governor, Lord William Bentinck, with whom they had already some reason to be dissatisfied. Nor did they fail to censure the aloofness of officers from their subordinates, although no proper steps were as yet taken to remedy this evil.

There was one possession which consoled the Honourable East India Company for all the troubles of an empire which, although it exercised a diligence and a regard for the well-being of its subjects which were new in the history of the world, it was not really competent to manage. This was the monopoly of the China trade. It brought a net profit of about two millions a year, enabling the shareholders of the Company to get their ten per cent. A Chinese writership was a fortune after a few years. The penetration of the Celestial Empire by Earl Macartney's magnificent mission in 1793 had been unsuccessful in its object of inducing the Emperor to receive a resident British Minister.

The Company had to be content for its servants to be permitted to reside at Canton, where their interests were represented by a body of three, known as the Select Committee of Super Cargoes. The homeward trade was mainly in tea and raw cotton. Canton imported cotton goods from India, and bullion and other metals and woollen from England, the Company claiming great credit for usually exporting these last at a considerable loss, a loss which, however, was obviously only nominal, as it was necessary to export something besides bullion to balance trade. It was not easy to find what the Chinese required, nor did the Super Cargoes make any effort to understand the people with whom they dealt. It is curious that at this time there was only one Englishman, Sir George Staunton, the son of a distinguished member of Macartney's mission, who could speak the language.

Though debarred from sovereignty in China, the Company had other territorial possessions outside India. Bencoolen, on the south-west coast of Sumatra, was the remainder of a larger dominion which had passed into the hands of the Dutch. On the opposite side of that island lay the Prince of Wales Island or Penang in the Straits of Malacca. It was a valuable gathering place for merchant ships awaiting convoy in time of war, as was another possession of the Company in the Atlantic Ocean, the island of St. Helena.

The Company had no authority over Ceylon, though it had to lend it troops. After its conquest from the Dutch in 1796, an attempt had been made to reorganize the land revenue system by the aid of Madras civilians with disastrous results, and the Colonial Office discarded Indian help henceforth, except in military matters. The first Governor, the Honourable Frederick North, found his capital, Colombo, a pleasant and sociable place. The chaplain has left it on record that the English circle (including officers) totalled 100 gentlemen and 20 ladies. Half of them lived in the fort, half outside. Beyond were 900 Dutch, and beyond these again 5,000 Portuguese, a people who had been there before the Dutch, and who were blacker than the natives themselves. Wine was cheap. Claret was £4 a dozen if from England, and 36s. if from Bordeaux; Madeira wine cost the same. Trade was flourishing, the principal export being £60,000 worth of cinnamon. More was done for the education of the people than in India. The Dutch, who usually left behind them a legacy of enslavement and inhuman punishments of the subject population, had set an example in Ceylon which England would have done well to follow. There were on the island in 1801, 170 schools. The people, moreover, although they would not accept a British revenue system from Madras, had accepted Christianity. There were several hundred Protestants, and an even larger number of Catholics who had been converted by the Portuguese. But the reduction of the amount allowed to be spent on education to £1,500 yearly, by orders from home, was a serious setback, and a far graver difficulty hampered the growth of the infant colony.

The Dutch and the British after them possessed only the coast. The centre was occupied by the Kandians, who were troublesome neighbours and interfered with trade. They would not allow a direct road to be made through their country between the two principal ports of the island, Colombo and Trincomalee. An unwise effort was unsuccessfully made in 1800 to negotiate a subsidiary treaty after the Indian model with the Kandian King. Two years later his people seized some goods belonging to British subjects. North showed exemplary patience, and spent months in a vain attempt to obtain compensation. Early in 1803 war was found inevitable, and columns marching from Colombo and Trincomalee entered the enemy's capital at the same moment. The King had abandoned it, leaving the task of expelling the invader to a far more formidable foe than any army of his own. Large numbers of the troops, of which there were never more than a very few thousand in the whole island, were struck down by jungle fever, and natives of India and Ceylon were almost equally affected with Europeans. Kandy was evacuated in June, four months after its capture: a claimant to the throne who had been supported by the British was basely sacrificed to die a horrible death at his enemy's hands; and the little garrison of thirty British who had marched out was shamefully surrendered to be massacred, as were their far more numerous comrades who had been left behind in hospital. The coloured troops deserted to the enemy. The elated King not only recovered his own possessions, but invaded British territory, threatening Colombo itself. Almost two years of useless and wasteful warfare, in which cross-raiding formed an eminent feature, followed, at the end of which North was succeeded by Major-General Thomas Maitland. The new Governor concentrated the troops and restored their discipline. Both sides were exhausted, and this disgraceful war came to a natural end; but the British soldier and those who had trusted them remained unavenged, and the blot of dishonour was not wiped from the shield of England.

CHAPTER III

THE MINISTRY OF ALL THE TALENTS

(JANUARY 1806—MARCH 1807)

PARLIAMENT was opened on the 21st of January, 1806. The Opposition was in high spirits. Pitt was called the soul of the Third Coalition, and its ruin was to bring about his fall. The two parts of the Opposition were now firmly united for a final blow—had not that blow been already dealt by another hand. The complete accord between elements, only three years before in such violent contradiction, is remarkable. Such had been Windham's known animosity towards Bonaparte that, during the peace, he was accused by the latter to Fox of having plotted to murder him. Such had been Fox's intimacy with Bonaparte that Cobbett charged him openly with the intention of betraying his country—a charge which Windham believed. That such men could have honestly met—and that while Bonaparte remained the hinge upon which all policy turned—seemed impossible. Yet it was the case. Fox and Windham were on opposite sides of Pitt, but—as it were—on the sides of a round table. They could draw together and, in doing so, become in greater opposition to him than before. While still a colleague, Windham's relations with his chief had been formal, and far from satisfactory to himself. He hated Pitt's efforts for peace. The moment the Preliminaries were known, he went into pronounced opposition. He thought the peace disastrous; and Pitt defended it, and was in part responsible. The chivalrous idea which was Windham's legacy from Burke—that England was champion of ancient thrones and churches to the death—had been sacrificed. It was never Pitt's view, but as long as the war continued it was not wholly out of court. At Amiens Fox had triumphed. He had promised that the war would lead to a disastrous peace; and it had done so, at least in the opinion of Windham and Cobbett, who thought almost the same. A war carried on by the help of burdensome taxes, which were transforming the nation from one of sturdy squires and peasants into one of fund-holders, industrialists, and paupers, taxes spent in subsidizing undeserving foreign Powers instead of in maintaining an army which would strike some blow for the glory of England, or in aiding patriots rising in defence of their King and their religion, such a war, followed by such a peace, was what they felt that Pitt had given them. Fox had at least not deceived them. He did not take the middle path of Pitt, the path which Windham and Cobbett hated. His love of liberty was a grand passion, and once he could be assured that Bonaparte was the enemy of liberty, he might still lead them against him in the spirit of a Crusader. As for parliamentary reform—that never stopped the way. Windham hated it; Cobbett had not begun to care for it; Fox did not love it. It was quietly dropped. It is not easy to find a single reference to it in speech, pamphlet, or newspaper in the whole of the decade until almost its close. Even Francis Place the tailor, leader in the reform schemes of twelve years before, had given up politics for the time, and had settled down to that business of deceiving his rich customers which he afterwards described with such exquisite relish. The army had been a greater difficulty in the way of union between Fox and Windham. The leader had been engaged on a history of what was then usually spoken of as the Glorious Revolution, and, as is the way with histories, he had a difficulty over bringing it beyond the introductory chapters. He never reached the triumphal year 1688. He lived back in the reigns of the later Stuarts —the age in which a devoted band of patriotic noblemen and gentlemen struggled against the servile tools of an effete despotism. Perhaps no British statesman of the first rank has ever lived so completely in the past as Fox. One of these servile tools was a standing army. It took him long to realize that the safeguards created by the Mutiny Act, and the control exercised over the army by a Cabinet responsible to Parliament, should remove all fear of the regular forces of the Crown becoming a danger to the liberties of the people. But in the end his good sense brought him to see that a defensive war diversified with pillage was nonsense, and that the possession of a striking force was essential.

Thus was Fox brought nearer to Windham and his supporter Cobbett. Grenville was never more than an ally. George III had well summed him up. Obstinacy, indeed, was with Grenville almost a principle of conduct. When he could not get Pitt to pursue not merely the same object as himself, but by the same means, he preferred to throw himself into opposition. But his principles, in reality, remained the same. He was never more than an ally of Fox. When the followers of Pitt after his death attacked Windham's military measures, he defended them upon the principles of the deceased statesman, whom he lost no opportunity of calling his dearest friend.

The leaders of the Opposition had all their plans ready for a vigorous attack on the Minister when they learnt that he was dying. Fox was moved, and Grenville burst into passionate grief. For two days controversy was hushed, while London watched in spirit by the bed-side at Putney. On the 29th the Honourable Henry Lascelles, Wilberforce's colleague in the representation of Yorkshire, proposed the interment of the deceased at the public expense in Westminster Abbey. Fox opposed the motion. He said he could not conscientiously vote for giving Pitt an honour granted only among statesmen to his father Lord Chatham, upon whose monument it was written that he had reduced the power of France to a very low ebb, and raised the prosperity of his country to a very high pitch. Windham opposed it too. He complained that his mentor Burke, who was on a level with Pitt, had not had that honour, but, not content with taking this ground, he added, in the extravagance of his devotion to his new allegiance, that he did not think that his life had been beneficial to his country. The debate was virtually closed by Wilberforce in a fine speech. It is noteworthy that he regarded as uncontested the success of a part of his friend's political life upon which posterity has entertained somewhat unnecessary doubts. Passing by all questions relating to foreign policy, finance, the army, and the navy, he alluded to the vigour and sagacity of the measures by which Pitt had stamped out sedition, and prevented the dreadful plague of the Revolution from reaching England. "This was the main source of his distinction; this was the great pedestal of his fame." In a House of 347 the opposition to the motion mustered only 89 votes. Subsequently the opponents of that proposal vied with each other in the zeal with which they supported a vote of £40,000 for the payment of Pitt's debts. Indeed, they regarded his complete neglect of his private affairs as a conspicuous merit.

The succession to Pitt had already been decided. The King first offered it to Hawkesbury, who refused. He then sent for Grenville, who replied that he could only form an administration upon a broad basis. There was to be no "principle of exclusion". He would have to consult Fox. "I thought so, and I meant it so", is the reply which George was believed at the time to have made. Such was the origin of the celebrated ministry which obtained the name of "All the Talents", from an expression used by Canning some years before to describe the ministry which he desired to take the place of Addington's. But it was not framed, as the name would seem to suggest, by a deliberate selection of all the ablest men in the country, irrespective of party. It was made up in the ordinary way. The Grenville and Fox Coalition was not strong enough by itself in parliamentary voting power. It therefore turned for support to one of the two remaining parties.

Grenville brought with him the personal followers of himself and his brother Buckingham, and the Portland Whigs who had come over to Pitt in 1792, with the exception of the Duke himself and his family. Fox had the Old Opposition, which was the strongest in debating power of any party in the House of Commons. To this was united the Prince of Wales's party, which included one indefatigable speaker in the House of Lords—the Duke of Clarence. Fox was also strengthened from another quarter. Lord Shelburne, the follower of the great Chatham, the depositary of some part of his tradition, and at one time the leader and mentor of Pitt, had, after he was thrown out of office by the North and Fox Coalition of 1783, pursued a tortuous course of his own. He opposed the war. He would not join Fox. Though without a political following, he had a very large circle of friends. He died as Marquis of Lansdowne in 1805, the year in which his son, Lord Henry Petty, came into notice as a speaker among the first in the House of Commons. This brilliant young man brought to the party the aid of financial talents trained in the same school as Pitt's. Finally Fox was strong outside parliament in the support of the advocates of peace and reform. Within it he and Grenville together could not depend on more than 150 votes. It was just possible to carry on the Government with that number, with the aid of those members who could be depended upon by the Crown. This body no longer existed in its former strength, but the remains of it were still substantial. Fox had suffered in the past from the precarious tenure occasioned by a Minister's exclusive dependence for a majority on this treacherous support. It was necessary to attach one of the remaining parties. The adherents of Pitt had been in office so long, several of them in places too high for their deserts, that they would be sure to demand a greater number of places in the Ministry than was reasonable as the price of their support. They were therefore left alone, and resource had to Sidmouth. There was some difficulty. It was agreed that he should have two places in the Cabinet, one for himself and one for a friend. The question was who that friend should be. Sidmouth first pressed for Buckinghamshire, but Grenville would have no nonentities. He had, however, one political friend of first-rate ability, Ellenborough, the Lord Chief Justice, who might—like Eldon before him—have taken the Great Seal. But he did not wish to become Lord Chancellor. His present office was for life, and the Chancellorship was not. Besides, he doubted his abilities as a judge in the equity cases which would come before him. He finally agreed to come into the Cabinet while remaining Lord Chief Justice. This extraordinary makeshift indicated in the clearest possible way that the Ministry of All the Talents was merely the result of ordinary party bargaining between three parties; and separate offers, afterwards made on different occasions to Canning and Perceval, were not unnaturally rejected without any hesitation, as the followers of Pitt conceived that they had an equal right to collective bargaining with the other three parties. But a Ministry of Talent the new Ministry undoubtedly was.

The Cabinet was small and very powerful. The posts of First Lord of the Treasury and Foreign Secretary fell naturally to Grenville and Fox. Lord Henry Petty took the Exchequer. Erskine was raised to the peerage and became Lord Chancellor. Windham naturally became Secretary for War and the Colonies. The Admiralty was taken by Grey, soon afterwards known as Howick, his father having been made an earl. Spencer, who had held this last post with such honour under Pitt's first administration, became Home Secretary. The Master-Generalship of the Ordnance fell to the Earl of Moira, the leader of the Carlton House party, as the Prince of Wales's followers were called. His abilities were then rather presumed than known. It was not until ten years later that the immense military combinations, which he formed with such signal success upon the uplands of Central India, revealed his consummate soldiership. Grenville introduced one more adherent in the new President of the Council, Earl Fitzwilliam, one of the Whigs who had followed Portland in 1792, and for some time Viceroy of Ireland. He made a third along with Spencer and Windham, thus balancing very fairly the three followers of Fox, including Petty along with Erskine and Grey, and excluding Moira as partly independent. Sidmouth as Lord Privy Seal, and Ellenborough as Lord Chief Justice, made up eleven.

The amount of talent dispersed in posts outside the Cabinet was quite as remarkable. Sheridan, excluded from higher rank as intemperate and a free-lance, was made Treasurer of the Navy. The companion post of the Secretaryship for War was held by Fox's most intimate friend, General Fitzpatrick. Lord Minto, a Portland Whig raised to the peerage by Pitt for distinguished diplomatic and administrative service, a high-minded public servant of the best type, became President of the Board of Control. The Chancellorship of the Duchy of Lancaster was given to the Earl of Derby. Grenville's nephew, Earl Temple, became one of the Paymasters-General. Sidmouth's party was represented by Auckland as President of the Board of Trade, Buckinghamshire as one of the Postmasters-General, and Vansittart as a Lord of the Treasury. Sir Arthur Pigott was Attorney-General, and the more famous Sir Samuel Romilly Solicitor-General. In Ireland, the Duke of Bedford, a brother of the Duke who was so firm a friend of Fox and patron of agriculture, became Lord Lieutenant, and George Ponsonby, who had recently made his mark in the House of Commons, Lord High Chancellor. The Chief Secretary, William Elliot, was a distant relation of Minto's. Irish affairs in parliament were in the hands of Sir John Newport, a baronet, member for Waterford.

Objection was soon entered in both Houses to the anomalous position of Ellenborough, as at once a Judge and a member of an executive Cabinet, a position which he himself recognized as exceptionable, because it might —in his own words—give a political bias to a judicial mind. But once it came to the task of making a formal attack on the appointment, the Opposition began to find itself in difficulties. It was first of all necessary to define the Cabinet, and it is interesting to observe the manner in which the attempt was made. No better description could be framed than "those members of His Majesty's most honourable Privy Council, whom His Majesty is advised to direct to be habitually summoned, and who are so summoned to that committee or selection of the said Council, which deliberates upon matters of state, and which is commonly known by the name of the Cabinet Council". It was moved that to summon to the said Cabinet Council a Lord Chief Justice of England was inadvisable. The high legal authority of Blackstone was quoted to support the contention that where the administration of criminal justice is united with the executive power, the public safety is in danger. It was replied that the passage was of no authority; Blackstone had merely taken it from Montesquieu, a foreign theorist. But a much more serious point was urged. The objectionable feature of the appointment was that Ellenborough might, as a member of the Cabinet, join in deciding upon the prosecution of a person whom he would afterwards have to try as a Judge. In reply to this, Government speakers were able to show that it was still the custom for political prisoners to be examined, previous to the decision to prosecute them, by judges along with the Cabinet Ministers. It by no means appeared that that separation of executive and judicial functions, which had been so much admired abroad, was as complete as was supposed. The Government allowed this boasted safeguard of British liberty to shift for itself, and appealed to the strict law of the constitution. Fox cited the King's prerogative, and affirmed that he had the right to take the advice of any of his Privy Councillors, that the Cabinet Council was neither known to the law nor recognized by Parliament, and that there was no such thing as collective Cabinet responsibility. No wonder that his nephew, Lord Holland, went to the point of saying that the constitution abhorred the idea of a Prime Minister. The result of the debates revealed the weakness of the Opposition. In the Upper House there was no division; in the Lower it mustered only 64 members, the majority being 158.

Having passed this obstacle, the Government proceeded with a confidence worthy of its strength. The Chancellor of the Exchequer had to borrow another £20,000,000, £2,000,000 being for Ireland, on which the interest worked out to five pence under five pounds per cent—an indication of the soundness of the country's finances. The total British estimate was for £43,600,000, exclusive of the Consolidated Fund. Petty boldly raised the war taxes to £19,500,000, and put up the income tax to ten per cent. Fox, in his support, laid down the principle that, at the beginning of a war, it was best to bring taxation at once up to the full amount to which it would be necessary to carry it. "The country", he added, in a style precisely the reverse of everything heard from him for the last dozen years, "wanted large taxes". The proposals were well received, but the usual demands were made for concessions to meet hard cases, and to this Petty was indisposed. Exemptions in favour of those who had children he rejected as in reality a tax upon those who had none. The net can seldom have been drawn wider. The tax was denominated a property tax, in order to justify its imposition on all who owned or occupied land, or had an income from investments, however small. An English farmer paid 1s. 6d. in the pound on his rent, whether he made any profit or not. Even those who had neither land nor stock were taxed, if they had incomes of more than fifty pounds a year, the only exception being labourers drawing no more than thirty shillings a week. Some abatements were also made in favour of small annuitants and tradesmen up to an income of £150. Another proposal for a tax of two pounds a ton upon pig-iron was more severely criticized. Birmingham was said to be in danger. German and even American competition was already keen. Finding its majority reduced to ten, the Government dropped this tax, and substituted one on private brewing—only to be given up in its turn for an increase in the assessed taxes.

The measures next submitted to Parliament were the repeal of the Additional Force Act, and the introduction of what Windham described as a permanent foundation for the Military Establishments of the country. In the debate on the subject, on the 3rd of April, Castlereagh took occasion to say that, so far as finance, the navy, and the army were concerned, the new Ministers were, by comparison with the difficulties which they said that they had found when taking office, upon a Bed of Roses. Fox instantly rose, and exclaimed with his characteristic "Gracious God!" that this was really insulting—he was torn and stung by brambles and nettles, whichever way he turned. It was long before Castlereagh was allowed to hear the last of the "Bed of Roses". But he was in reality right, as was shown in the case of the army by the nature of Windham's measure. It was not an expedient devised to meet a pressing emergency, nor could it be expected to produce immediate results. The manner in which Windham approached the subject was large and statesmanlike. A genuine attempt was to be made to put the "trade" of a soldier in a position to compete with other trades, and that without the need of bounties. The service itself was to be the bounty, as it had been thirty years before. Windham was convinced that as the inducements became understood, the bounties which it was necessary to offer would gradually be reduced to nothing. It would, he added, be a simple thing to obtain all the men who could possibly be required by raising the pay to five shillings a day. But this would render the army licentious; discipline would then have to be made more severe; and the service would grow unpopular again. He had decided upon enlisting men for seven years only on the existing pay; they could then re-engage for seven years more at an extra sixpence a day; after which they could re-engage for a third period of seven years at an extra shilling a day. In the case of cavalry and artillery the periods were different, the first period being ten years in the case of cavalry and twelve in that of artillery. Various benefits were offered as regards pensions, and three years service in the West Indies was to count as two. The system was supplemented by a Training Act which introduced the principle that all males capable of bearing arms could be ordered to be trained for 24 days in each year.

These measures eventually became law in the face of an Opposition, led by Castlereagh, Canning, and Perceval, and rioting in carping criticism. They had the excuse that the Government, which possessed more talent than experience, was constantly bringing itself into the most tempting confusion. The Opposition, on the other hand, had no recognized chief, and each of the leaders was eager to prove his mettle. But there was one matter upon which all parties agreed. The treaty of alliance between Prussia and France, which Haugwitz had signed in the preceding December, was not ratified in its original form. But delay did not help Frederick William. The final treaty of the 15th of February, which he was obliged to accept, was much more ignominious. In return for territorial cessions to France, he received Hanover as compensation, the term being used in the diplomatic sense of land taken from an unoffending third party. He was also compelled to close the rivers of the North Sea to British ships. The pretence that he was holding Hanover temporarily in order to keep the French out was given up. That he already held it in a sense hostile to England was manifest. By a declaration of the 1st of April he announced that the rightful possession of the territory of the House of Brunswick had passed to him. Great Britain replied on the 5th of April by an Order in Council blockading Prussian ports, followed, on the 23rd, by a Royal Message to Parliament announcing that Prussia's measures of direct hostility had left no alternative but the provisional adoption of measures of retaliation. Seldom did Fox appear to greater advantage than when he moved the address of thanks to the King. He commenced by a reference to the patience exercised by him when his electoral dominions had been seized. "It is impossible", he continued—and the speaker was the statesman whom George had, with some reason, regarded for nearly a generation in the light of a personal enemy—"not to feel grateful for that kindness and mildness which His Majesty has always shown to the subjects of this realm. It was with the most extreme reluctance that he could consent to involve them in war upon any ground that was not immediately and directly connected with British interests." He even went on to speak of the respect due to crowned heads, and to exempt from the censure which he was about to pass upon Prussia Frederick William himself, as "known to be of a mild and pacific disposition". That censure was indeed severe. He described the conduct of Prussia as "the union of everything that was contemptible in civility with everything that was odious in rapacity"—no other nation had been so degraded as to be the minister of the injustice and rapacity of France. But the general tone of the speech, as well as of that of Grenville in the House of Lords, and those of Castlereagh, Hawkesbury, and Mulgrave, who spoke for the Opposition in the two Houses, was far from being one of confirmed hostility. It was desired only to teach Prussia a sharp lesson; to show her that her notions of neutrality were not acceptable, and to indicate to her where her honour and interest really lay. Fox's own speech closed with some admirable observations on the subject of the principle "which", he said, "has been lately adopted of transferring the subjects of one prince to another, in the way of equivalents, and under the pretext of convenience and mutual accommodation". His objection was based equally on his love of freedom and on his regard for order. Human beings, he said, were not to be bartered like sheep and oxen. To do so was to strike at the foundation of every Government and the existence of every nation, for the attachment of the people to its form of government is a necessary condition of a nation's existence. These enlightened principles were then shared by few, and were even shortly afterwards to be temporarily thrown over by Fox himself.

Meanwhile, the Navy had not been idle. It had never been Barham's belief that a strict blockade of Brest was possible for a third winter. Now was the time for Napoleon to inaugurate his new scheme of diversions against commerce. On the 13th of December, 1805, a division of the French fleet in that harbour, consisting of eleven sail of the line with five smaller ships, escaped and divided into two squadrons, with orders to occupy various defined cruising stations and harass British trade. It was only on the 24th of December that news reached London; and it came from Gibraltar and not from Cornwallis. Two squadrons, under Warren and Strachan, left in pursuit in the following month; they had been detained by foul winds, and there had been no delay in issuing orders. Their despatch was the last important act of Lord Barham's life. But the first French squadron, after successfully reinforcing San Domingo, fell a victim, on the 6th of February, 1806, while still off that island, to neither Warren nor Strachan, but to Vice-Admiral Sir John Duckworth. He had hastened in pursuit from off Cadiz, where he had been blockading. He flew his flag in the Superb, still Keats's ship, as she had been in the Straits of Gibraltar in 1801. When he met the French he had two Rear-Admirals with him, Louis, and Alexander Cochrane, and seven ships in all. The enemy had only five ships. But as one of Duckworth's, the Agamemnon, commanded by the fortunate Berry, was only a 64, and the French Vice-Admiral, Leissègues, flew his flag in the 120-gun ship Impérial, claimed to be the most powerful ship ever built, not merely in the French Navy, but in the whole world, the odds were far from overwhelming. But victory was complete. Three French ships were captured, and the flagship and another driven ashore and wrecked. Rear-Admiral Willaumez, who commanded the second squadron, was more fortunate. His were the ships intended to have preyed on the eastern trade route, with his base on the Cape of Good Hope. Foiled in this, he sailed to the West Indies. After doing considerable damage to trade, his ships were scattered and much injured by a gale. In this condition, one fell a victim to Strachan's ships, one took refuge in America and was unable to get to sea again, the rest eventually returned singly to France.

On the 13th of March Warren in the London captured Linois, who was on his return from India in his flagship the Marengo. All these three French admirals had injured trade very considerably, and the capture of two of them, and the dispersal of the third's squadron, gave immense satisfaction to West and East Indian merchants. Even British Government transports had not been secure. The history of one capture and recapture is curious. Two transports had fallen victims to Willaumez at the mouth of the Channel, and the troops were being brought by a French frigate to Mauritius. She turned in at the Cape of Good Hope, where the Dutch flag was still kept flying after it had passed into British hands, and became a captive in her turn, and the troops were restored to their own country.

The most daring naval exploit of these years, and perhaps of the whole war, was Captain Charles Brisbane's capture of the West Indian island of Curaçoa. On the 1st of January, 1807, the Dutch were still heavy with drinking the New Year in, when he brought his four frigates through the narrow entrance of the harbour. In spite of the powerful forts by which it was defended, complete success was scarcely a question of hours. By noon the whole island had capitulated.

The change of Government, as was to be expected, gave Napoleon another opportunity of indulging his people in the prospect of peace. Almost immediately after he had come into office, Fox received an offer to assassinate the French Emperor. He wrote to Talleyrand in the informal French of which he was a master, to warn him that the man who had made this proposal was being expelled from England. On a hint from the side of France, he followed this up on the 26th of March with a proposal to negotiate for peace in concert with Russia. Talleyrand, however, adhered strictly to the constant French policy of playing off one country against the other, and the correspondence dragged on in this way until nearly the middle of June. Fox was determined not to concede the preposterous idea of separate negotiation.

But Talleyrand's resources were not exhausted. As a personal favour, Fox had been able to secure the restoration to their families of some of his friends who had paid for that admiration of French principles and customs which had led them to France during the peace, with an enforced indefinite stay in that country. Among these was Lord Yarmouth, afterwards distinguished, when he had succeeded to his father's title as Marquis of Hertford, not merely as the founder of the splendid collection of works of art known afterwards as the Wallace Collection, but as the prototype in Disraeli's and Thackeray's novels of the great English dissolute nobleman. It was in the latter capacity that he

THE MINISTRY OF ALL THE TALENTS

attracted Talleyrand. He was intimate with the mistress of a French marshal—Berthier. His own wife was intimate with a French general—Junot. With such connections he seemed framed to look kindly upon the interests of France. Before he left for England, Talleyrand interviewed him, and asked him to be the bearer of a secret and confidential communication to Fox. Peace was to be had upon the most favourable terms. France made no claim to Malta and Sicily, and would restore Hanover. A prospect was held out of finding some middle term between joint negotiation with Russia and separate negotiation. On arriving in London, Yarmouth was sent back to treat for peace. Once things were on this basis, even though he had not produced his powers, it was thought on the French side that a step back could be safely taken. Upon the plea of representations received by Napoleon from his brother Joseph, whom he had made King of Naples, Sicily was now demanded for France as an integral part of that kingdom. Talleyrand was now to find himself disappointed in Yarmouth, and perhaps in Fox as well. It is very probable that he never expected to see so firm an insistence upon British interests in the man who had delighted in 1801 in a peace which was glorious to France. Nor would Yarmouth recede, either over Sicily or over Russia being made a party to the eventual treaty. The attempt to rush some sort of agreement through before Pierre Jacovlevitch d'Oubril, who had been sent on the part of the Czar, could reach Paris, failed. The Russian Minister arrived on the 6th of July.

Matters now changed rapidly for the worse. D'Oubril offered such a feeble front to the French negotiators that in order to keep as far as possible in step with him Fox admitted the possibility of asking Ferdinand to accept some compensation for Sicily. But it was useless. Napoleon acted in diplomacy as in war. He attempted, and generally with success, to deal separately with his enemies before they could effect a junction. Foiled in this, as he had been by d'Oubril and Yarmouth meeting in Paris, he directed an overwhelming force against the weaker of the two. A favourite weapon, employed as it was later on in the case of Great Britain but without success, was to threaten some terrible consequence unless a treaty was signed within forty-eight hours. All the artillery of the Imperial diplomatic armoury was concentrated on the devoted d'Oubril. He was allowed no rest. Daily conferences were held of many hours. On the 19th of July Yarmouth reported one of fourteen. On the 20th the Russian was beaten into submission. Sicily was given up, and the treaty which had been extorted was altogether humiliating. The Czar refused to ratify it. But there was an interval of many weeks before his decision could be known, and it was a period of great depression for Great Britain. Yarmouth thought that as it was necessary to negotiate separately now, there could be no object in withholding his powers. He produced them; although he should not have done so until a basis as regards Sicily had been agreed upon. He proceeded to draft a treaty which went very far in the matter of concessions. So discreditable was their very existence that the British Government did not afterwards publish them. So discreditable was Napoleon's omission to seize the opportunity to close so favourable a bargain, that he equally omitted them when he published his version of the negotiations. The caustic style of the Imperial notes on the treaty suggests that the Emperor felt that he had people in hand whom he might treat like the petty principalities of Germany or Their High Mightinesses of the Dutch Republic. The negotiations had now reached so desperate a stage that, as a last effort to restore the British position, another negotiator was sent to act, first jointly with Yarmouth, and later on alone. Fox chose an intimate friend, Lord Lauderdale, for whose talents he had a special admiration, although his antecedents in 1803, when Whitworth had to complain of his unauthorized interference, did not seem to afford much prospect that he would adequately sustain the honour of Great Britain. But here again any hopes which Talleyrand may have entertained were disappointed. Britain's honour was safe in Lauderdale's hands. If he had a fault, it was a want of suppleness—a Scottish tenacity, in style at any rate, which made him appear more unconciliatory than he actually was.

But before Lauderdale had arrived, Yarmouth had taken a step which was a masterpiece in his own peculiar style of diplomacy. One of the companions of his drinking bouts was Herr Lucchesini, the Prussian Minister. Over his cups he confided to him that Napoleon had offered to restore to Great Britain Hanover, which he had promised to Prussia. The news was sent to Berlin on the 29th of July, and produced an almost instantaneous effect. Prussia had undergone many slights and injuries from France in the last few months, and now the prize for which she had made so many sacrifices—sacrifices of honour and of principle—was to be taken away from her. Yarmouth's object was attained, and France lost her last powerful friend. Two months later war was declared, and Prussia and Great Britain were again on friendly terms, although peace was not formally concluded until the following January. On the 25th of September the British blockade of the Prussian rivers had been raised. On the 9th of October Frederick William's Government issued a lengthy manifesto—an example of a singular mentality. It set forth in detail the humiliations and losses which Prussia had derived from her connection with France. It contrasted in column after column her own virtue and patience with the unprincipled usurpations of that country. Finally the climax was reached. "One single advantage remained." This was the possession of Hanover. An archangel could not have rebuked sin with a more edifying gravity. "Napoleon had solemnly guaranteed this state of things, yet he negotiated with England on the basis of the restoration of the Electorate. The King is in possession of the proofs. War", it continued, "was now in fact declared—declared by every measure taken by France."

Such was the unexpected result of Fox's efforts for peace. It was one of the two things which he left unaccomplished, the two "glorious things", as he called them, which he said that he could not abandon even to his nephew, Holland, when he found his health failing him. The other was the abolition of the detestable traffic in kidnapped negroes between the West Coast of Africa and the West Indies. This was, however, as good as done before his death. It is strange that it took so long to accomplish as it did. In the case of most reforms, the arguments against change have a certain weight. But here they were all on one side; the specious pleas upon the other, when examined, were found to have nothing in them but a narrow appreciation of the interests of a restricted class. Yet, though much had been done to prepare public opinion even previously to 1787, when the Committee for the Abolition of the Slave Trade was inaugurated, nineteen years' work remained. The prospects of success were bright in the first few years. In 1788 there was passed a bill, introduced by Sir William Dolben, to limit the number of slaves carried according to the tonnage of the vessel, and in other ways to mitigate the unspeakable horrors of the middle passage, which was the name given to the second stage of the round voyage to Africa and the West Indies, and back again to England. Indeed, abolition might almost have been carried through then. But it was the opinion of Thomas Clarkson himself, to whose indefatigable labours out of parliament greater honour is due even than to those of William Wilberforce within it, that such success would have been precarious. It was better that evidence should first be taken. But this allowed time for the first fire to die down, Liverpool shipping interests had the chance to assert themselves, and although in 1792 a Resolution was carried that the trade

THE MINISTRY OF ALL THE TALENTS 163

was to be abolished, Dundas obtained the insertion of the word "gradually".

The war now came, and it began to be felt that abolition was unsafe. It might mean the abandonment of a lucrative branch of trade to Great Britain's rivals—even to her enemies. A rebellion of the blacks had broken out in the French possessions in San Domingo in the West Indies, leading to shocking outrages. There was a vague fear of the untoward results which might follow any hasty application of humanitarian principles in any way similar to those which had led to the French Revolution. The objection upon principle to any act in restraint of trade remained strong, even where the trade was carried on in human flesh. During all this time Pitt enthusiastically supported the movement, and in particular did splendid service in demolishing by close statistical argument the theory that were it not for the constant importation of slaves it would be impossible for the West Indian planters to keep up their numbers. It was thought that he became lukewarm in the cause after the first five years of the movement. But Clarkson expressly defended him from this charge. He wrote that Pitt gave him all the help which he required. He had even free access to the Minister whenever he wanted it, without any previous appointment—a privilege which must have been rare even in days when Ministers had comparatively greater leisure. Pitt was hampered, moreover, by colleagues, some of whom, such as Dundas, offered opposition in its most intractable form, namely, that of supporters who are willing to proceed, but only to proceed slowly, and with what they style proper safeguards. Yet steady progress was made. In 1805 an Order in Council had forbidden the importation of slaves into new conquests in the West Indies. Even before Pitt's death a point had been reached which made success during the session of 1806 almost certain. The accession to power of a Ministry, at the head of which were two such uncompromising supporters of the cause as Grenville and Fox, put the event beyond all doubt. Preliminary measures were almost immediately taken. On the 10th of June Fox moved his last resolution in the House of Commons. It was that the House would proceed with all practicable expedition to take effectual measures for the abolition of the African Slave Trade. It was carried by 114 votes to 15. This was followed by an address to the Crown, and by the concurrence of the House of Lords. The way was now open for final abolition.

During this time the attention of Parliament was also occupied by charges brought against several distinguished persons. The impeachment of Melville had already been decided upon in 1805, and almost the first preoccupation of the new Ministry on assuming office was to carry it out without the delay and discredit which attached to the last trial of this kind—the impeachment of Warren Hastings. Twenty-three managers were appointed, including Fox, Grey, Petty, Sheridan, the Attorney-General, and the Solicitor-General. But the leadership was left in the hands of Samuel Whitbread, a supporter of the Ministry, though not a member. He was a free-lance, and did not work well with others. He gloried in his independence. In one of the debates in the preceding year he had boasted of being the son of the celebrated brewer, and of not being a man of family. "While others pride themselves on their remoteness from their founder, I feel a pride and satisfaction in being the nearest to mine." The aristocratic Whigs did not relish such very genuine independence. To be brought into close quarters with something so like real republicanism resembled the feelings of a professed lover of animals who all of a sudden finds himself embraced by a bear. They had no zeal to follow Whitbread's banner. Besides, by leaving the conduct of the impeachment largely in his hands, they could divest it in part of the appearance of a party measure. The result of this neglect was that the ten articles of impeachment were so badly drawn up that, had the object been to give as many peers as possible the excuse to acquit Melville of the particular offences with which he was charged, even when they thought him generally guilty, they could scarcely have been better framed for the purpose. If, instead of the words "convert to his own use", the words "apply to his own use" had been employed, he could hardly have escaped conviction, for though Whitbread was unable to prove that he had permanently misappropriated anything, there was no doubt whatever that he had constantly received advances of many thousands of pounds of Government money to the credit of his private account, directly contrary to the law. Besides the many loopholes which the imperfect wording of the articles allowed, another opportunity was afforded by the nature itself of an impeachment. The Lords were both judges and jurymen. They had before their bar a man impeached of "high crimes and misdemeanours". If it appeared to a particular peer that he had done what he was charged with doing in any article, but that this was not a "high crime and misdemeanour", he might see fair cause to acquit him.

The trial was conducted with an admirable despatch, for which Erskine, the Lord Chancellor, deserves great credit. It began on the 29th of April, and the evidence and arguments of counsel were completed on the 17th of May. Certain legal points were then referred to judges, and their replies delivered. The articles were then discussed at length. On the 12th of June Erskine put the question on the first article to each peer, beginning with the junior baron, Lord Crewe. "Not guilty, upon my honour", he answered, laying his right hand upon his left breast. This continued until every peer present had voted upon every article. There had been an open canvass. Grenville and Spencer did not vote, pleading that attendance interfered with their official duties, but they were probably torn between the wish to spare an old colleague and that to satisfy their new friends. Indeed, the voting mainly followed party lines. For example, it was not to be expected that Erskine would fail to find Melville guilty of the four best substantiated charges, or that Eldon would do otherwise than acquit him on every one. There was, however, considerable variation, and the Lords on the whole may be said to have come to an honest decision, and not one for which it is necessary to express regret. The nearest approach to conviction was on the second article, on which 54 found him guilty out of 135 voting. Erskine pronounced the decision of the majority as one of acquittal, and the last trial by impeachment in English history was at an end.

Parliament was also occupied with charges against St. Vincent for his administration of the Admiralty, against Wellesley for his conduct as Governor-General of India, and against an Irish Judge. None of these was to come to any result. But one undoubtedly flagrant case of misconduct on the part of Government servants claimed attention. The naval force which had escorted Baird's troops to the Cape of Good Hope was commanded by Commodore Sir Home Popham, a distinguished officer—better suited by nature to the command of a squadron of privateers than one of British ships of war. Three months after the Cape had been occupied, information arrived through the usual untrustworthy channel of neutral traders that the Spanish possessions of Monte Video and Buenos Ayres were ripe plums waiting to be plucked. The inhabitants were, it was said, ready for that insurrection which the Venezuelan adventurer, General Miranda, had for many years past dangled before the eyes of British Governments. Popham actually persuaded Baird to detach troops for an expedition to that quarter of South America; and on the 14th of April he sailed with his whole squadron, leaving the Cape defenceless so far as the Navy was concerned. He touched at Saint Helena and took on board fresh troops. A brilliant navigator, he skilfully threaded the intricate shoals of Rio de la Plata, where he landed Major-General William Beresford on the 25th of June, at a point eight miles below Buenos Ayres. The little force, raised by a detachment of seamen and marines to 1,600 in all, soon possessed itself of the city with its 70,000 inhabitants, defended by a body rather more numerous than its assailants. On the 27th a capitulation was signed, and within a few days Beresford was able to send home an account of the dollars he had taken—the principal object of a war with Spain.

Popham was not the only Englishman who projected himself into the spacious days of Elizabeth where hostilities with the Spaniards were concerned. Many Londoners must have thought that that time had come again when they beheld the eight wagons, containing a million dollars besides jewellery and precious stones, being ceremoniously escorted to the Bank. And to increase this enthusiasm, Popham actually sent a circular to British merchants describing the splendid market which he had opened for them. All that he had really obtained was the substitution of a direct traffic in British goods for an indirect. But this was not the way in which it struck people in England. Visions floated before them of fertile plains—where there were only ranches; and of mines of fabulous wealth—the silver mines of Potosi 1,800 miles distant from Buenos Ayres. In such circumstances it was completely forgotten that Spain was one of those enemies whom it was desirable to treat as possibly soon to become a friend again. The Government disapproved, and decided to recall Baird and Popham. The latter was tried by court martial and reprimanded. Nevertheless fresh troops were sent to secure the new acquisition. But before the reinforcements, which were on their way from both England and the Cape, could reach Beresford, the people had found their strength, and had risen against him and his puny force. On the 12th of August he and his men were made prisoners, and Buenos Ayres was once again in Spanish hands.

This was hardly a misfortune in all the circumstances. For in the autumn of 1806 Ministers embraced such large views of the area over which the war should be spread that some check was to be welcomed. Had this not been so, Windham's favourite officer, Robert Craufurd, would have been sent round Cape Horn to occupy a military post in Chili, and ultimately to conquer that province and establish a chain of posts 900 miles long across the Andes between it and Buenos Ayres. Grenville, not to be left behind, formed a plan for an invasion of Mexico from England in the East and India in the West, in which the precedent of the successful expedition to Egypt was to be followed in one point at any rate. As the author himself confessed, unity of plan would be wanting. Neither time nor place would cohere. His favourite general, Arthur Wellesley, was to have commanded. Fox had obtained for his own brother the command of the forces already in the Mediterranean, which were to assist his favourite ally, Russia. If Cabinet Government was to mean two or three ministers each carrying on his own little war with his own general, the Ministry of All the Talents provided a fresh and unexpected argument in favour of despotism. But the fall of Buenos Ayres destroyed these visions. The four forces which embarked for America between the autumn of 1806 and the spring of 1807 all went to the Rio de la Plata. The first to arrive was a body of 2,200 troops sent by Baird from the Cape, which made a lodgement on the mouth of the river. 3,000 more troops followed from England under Brigadier-General Sir Samuel Auchmuty, who decided to seize the strongly fortified town of Monte Video, though he had no requisites for siege operations. However, both he, and Rear-Admiral Charles Stirling, who had succeeded Popham, were men of resource; bluejackets did not fail to drag guns through the sand; the absence of a

THE MINISTRY OF ALL THE TALENTS 169

qualified engineer officer to direct the batteries to the best advantage was made up by the gallantry of the troops, who dashed through a scarcely practicable breach—some even over the top of the wall; and the town was carried by assault on the 3rd of February, 1807, with a loss of 118 killed and 279 wounded. The next force to come of any strength was a small body of 1,800 under Lieutenant-General John Whitelocke, who had been Inspector-General of Recruiting, and was sent to command the whole. Finally, Craufurd arrived with 4,800. He had come by the Cape of Good Hope where he was diverted from his Cape Horn voyage. It was the middle of June before the whole of his force had reached Monte Video.

A more memorable fortune attended British arms in southern Italy, followed not, as in South America, by disaster, but by failure to reap its full advantages. The kingdom of Italy had been rapidly overrun by Masséna's troops in punishment for the treachery of the Court of Naples. By the end of March Joseph Bonaparte was firmly seated on the Neapolitan throne, and the fort of Gaeta was the only place of importance on the mainland which still held out for Ferdinand. The Royal Family had taken refuge at Palermo in Sicily. That island was protected by Craig's force, covered by a British squadron which Rear-Admiral Sir Sidney Smith came out in April to command. That officer did nothing to enhance the fame won by his glorious defence of Acre in 1799. He had no idea of regular warfare. The same may almost be said of the officer on whom the command on land devolved owing to Craig's retirement through ill health. This was Major-General Sir John Stuart, who had fought well in Egypt under Abercromby. Smith's first act was, very properly, to throw supplies into Gaeta, and to make other arrangements for its defence. He also captured, with very little loss, the fortified island of Capri off the southern entrance of the Bay of Naples. After this, like other vain men, he fell a victim to the glamour of a court. He got himself made Ferdinand's Viceroy for his lost possessions on the mainland, and set himself to stir up insurrection in the extreme south of the Peninsula. It was a cruel policy, unless there was almost a certainty of success; and there was very little, without the aid of regular troops, in the presence of a French army of 50,000 men. Realizing this, he asked for assistance from Stuart, who had hitherto held strictly to Craig's policy of using his army for the defence of Sicily, which the Navy was unable to guarantee against a possible surprise by a force conveyed across from Italy in a number of small vessels. Smith's view was that, for this very reason, it was desirable to keep the theatre of war at a distance from the Straits of Messina. The alternative view was that a flotilla of small boats should be collected, able to frustrate any attempt of the enemy to row over in a calm, and meanwhile everything possible done to interrupt movements along the coast towards the part of Italy facing Sicily, and that no other land operations should be attempted. In the end Stuart decided that the defensive could be maintained in theory, while doing what Smith wanted. It was possible to combine the idea of a blow in favour of the insurgents in the province of Calabria in the extreme south of the peninsula, with that of breaking up the collections of stores and ammunition being prepared for the invasion of the island.

On the 1st of July Stuart landed with nearly 5,500 men at St. Euphemia, the narrowest part of the toe of Italy. General Reynier hurried up from Reggio to meet him, and on the 4th was known to be at Maida, a few miles inland. Stuart determined to strike before he could collect all the troops within call. He was himself rash. He chose to fancy that Reynier had only collected 4,300 men, whereas he had already 6,400. With the object of turning the French left, he made a long and tiring march in that sultry weather, over an open plain on which all his movements were distinctly visible. But such manœuvres, where they do not completely exhaust troops, add to their zest for action; a battle purchased at the price of such hardships is felt to be worth fighting. He knew on his part that Reynier—the officer who had, after seeing the earlier part of the campaign of 1801 in Egypt, learnt so little that he had written a foolish book well known to British officers, to show how contemptible their army was—would act with his "characteristic confidence", to quote the words of Stuart's own despatch. In fact he left a strong position and came down to meet the British General on the open plain. The flanking movement merely had the effect of the British right and the French left becoming engaged first. Nor had Stuart succeeded in throwing a superior mass of troops upon the point chosen for the attack. The right hand brigade of 1,200 men, Colonel Kempt's, found itself faced by General Compère's, of 2,800 men. As the French came down with a rush, certain of the success which had followed their arms in almost every battlefield in Europe for fourteen years, they found themselves drawing nearer and nearer to a thin sturdy line which waited motionless to receive them with ported arms. Nothing could have unnerved them more. It was vain to encourage themselves and to discourage the enemy in the customary way—throwing their caps into the air, uttering yells of triumph, and calling out the Emperor's name. All this noisy prelude of onset broke harmlessly upon the silence of those imperturbable ranks. The French were utterly disconcerted. They were as good as defeated when their enemies' fire, so long and so wisely reserved, rang out. The British broad front and good markmanship told so well that the lines had hardly met when the enemy turned and fled. Compère, who could not recognize defeat, galloped wildly into the British ranks and was taken. A similar result took place all along the line, as the different brigades got successively into action, as far as Stuart's extreme left, where timely help was given by Lieutenant-Colonel Robert Ross. He had landed with the 20th regiment that morning, and brought it at once into action. The conflict had only lasted two hours when Reynier, beaten on every side, withdrew across the Peninsula. Stuart had no cavalry to pursue. His losses were 327 officers and men, of whom one officer and 44 men were killed. The French losses in prisoners alone were above a thousand, and five to seven hundred dead were buried on the ground. The French owed their defeat to the overweening confidence of all ranks, from the General downwards. It was the first which they had sustained in Europe since the successes of Souvaroff against them in 1799, and the first which they had received in that continent at the hands of the British since Minden in 1759.

The French had now lost all that part of the toe of Italy which stretched from some distance north of the battlefield down to the Straits of Messina. But Stuart and Smith made no other use of their victory. The General had no idea but to return to Sicily. While the Admiral was carrying out his duty as Viceroy to the King of the Two Sicilies of making one part of his dominions a scene of anarchy and carnage, Reynier was left alone, Gaeta was allowed to surrender, and Masséna was now free to turn his attention to the south. Meanwhile Lieutenant-General Fox, who was, though now past active work, an officer of sound judgement, arrived in Sicily as Commander-in-Chief, with Moore as his Second-in-Command. There was now little left for Stuart to do, and he returned home. Moore found that the predatory bands, which the policy of the Court at Palermo and the efforts of Smith had called into existence, could not be organized for the purpose of any effective resistance, and by the end of the year almost the whole of southern Italy was once more in French hands.

A more important ally than Ferdinand was now threatened, one, moreover, whose dominions still remained

almost intact. This was the Prince Regent of Portugal.
Lauderdale had been sent to collect and straighten out the
threads of the Paris negotiations with instructions which,
as regards Sicily, were vague in the extreme. He was told
that compensation was to be claimed for Ferdinand on
surrendering that country, and, most of Europe being
already ruled out, the suggestion was actually made that
some place might be found for the expatriated sovereign
in South America or the West Indies. But there was no
weakening upon the general basis of the negotiations being
that of actual possession. Napoleon resisted strenuously,
although this had been the basis on which Talleyrand
originally led Yarmouth to believe that he was ready to
treat. Such a position, which could hardly be upheld
diplomatically, needed some other support. Napoleon
provided it by collecting an army close to the Spanish
border to threaten England through Portugal, her oldest
ally. As the British Foreign Office stiffened, the French
menace became more pronounced. It was found desirable
to take some steps to meet it; and St. Vincent, now once
more in command of the Channel Fleet, was sent to the
Tagus with a squadron of ships of the line and some high
military officers to concert with the Prince Regent for the
defence of Portugal, or in the alternative the withdrawal
of the Royal Family to their possession of Brazil. But early
in September all the French troops available were required
for the war with Prussia, and the menace was, for the time,
removed. The news now came of the British successes in
South America and in Italy, and early in September it
was known that the Czar had refused to ratify d'Oubril's
treaty. Fox fell ill, and the despatches to Lauderdale during
September are over the signatures of Spencer or Windham.
But the change made no difference. Talleyrand was still
making the same efforts which he had made six months
before, when he was in direct communication with Fox
himself, to separate Great Britain from Russia. He still

insisted that Joseph should be King of Sicily. On the 6th of October Lauderdale put an end to the negotiations, at the same time assuring Talleyrand that his own intimacy with Fox enabled him to affirm that the latest instructions which he had received would have had the complete concurrence of the great man whom England had lately lost.

For Pitt's great rival had followed him to the grave after less than eight months. Fox was now 58 years of age. He had always lived with that intensity of which only a certain type of idler is capable. He had drunk the cup of life to the full. Travel, drinking, gambling, women, art, literature, popularity, the senate, domestic happiness,— he had drained them all. Called back to office and to steady work, his strength was overtaxed. As Foreign Secretary he was extremely thorough, and displayed an industry which was—in him—astonishing. Parliamentary labours were, no doubt, a comparative relief. But he was intensely harassed by a very persistent minority; and for various reasons he received very little help from the best debaters on the Government side, such as Windham and Sheridan. Dropsical symptoms appeared as early as March. During April he was medically advised to give up all business, but refused. By the middle of June he ceased to attend parliament. Six weeks later he had to give up work altogether, though he continued to keep himself informed of what was going on. For a time he entertained the idea, characteristic of an old Whig, that he might hand over the Secretaryship of State to his nephew Holland, while himself remaining in the Cabinet and retaining the virtual direction of foreign affairs. He was tapped for dropsy on the 7th of August, 16 quarts of water being removed. The operation was repeated on the 31st, but recovery was found to be impossible; and after the 7th of September he gradually sank in strength. It was on that day, as Howick told the House of Commons in the following January, that he had his last conversation with him. Fox named three cardinal points in connection with the peace negotiations: the security of British honour, in which Hanover was materially concerned; Russian connection; and Sicily. Upon this last question he explained to Lord Holland that the Government was bound in honour to the Queen and Court of Naples, bad as they were; that Sicily was of great importance besides; but that, above all, it was the shuffling insincere way in which the French were acting that convinced him that it would be the greatest imprudence to yield to them. He was always fond of maintaining that there was nothing worth fighting for but honour. A few days before his death he was removed to a beautiful villa of the Duke of Bedford's at Chiswick. Here he was joined by Holland and other relations and friends, such as Fitzwilliam and Fitzpatrick. But it was not to politics that his last thoughts turned, as Pitt's had done. One of the last things read to him was the favourite eighth Aeneid, in which Virgil throws into his poem of war and empire a picture of simple living and domestic peace. Another was Crabbe's Parish Register, still in manuscript. He took pleasure in finding it to be a brighter account of rural life life than the same poet's "Village". He lived only till the 13th of September. Before he died, Mrs. Fox had prayers read at his bedside, and joined his hands. His last thoughts were for her, and the last sentence which he uttered "I die happy". Certainly he had lived so. But his work for peace had been a failure, as had Pitt's for the Third Coalition, and he hardly left his country in a more hopeful state as regards the inevitable continuation of the war. The same want of co-ordination of effort was to mar the effect of the alliance of 1806 as had that of 1805.

In the historical work which occupied some of the last years of his life, Fox suggests that there are periods in the histories of nations where it is possible to take a stand and to pause, in order to consider the immediate and remote effects of the conditions then existing. His own death furnishes a turning point of a similar character. Within eleven months, the three greatest Englishmen of the day had died. A century is an arbitrary division of time; nevertheless custom has made it to stand for something more; and it is impossible to regard Nelson, Pitt, and Fox as belonging to the nineteenth century. A number of men who had held very high place in the history of the age just passed away, such as Lansdowne and Rosslyn, better known by their eighteenth-century names of Shelburne and Loughborough, had only recently died. Of eighteenth-century names there still remained a few, such as St. Vincent, the Grenvilles, Dundas (now Melville), Windham, and Sheridan, but they were to take but small parts, if any, in the events to come. The year 1806 itself was not a definite turning point in letters, but it is not far off from being one. British literature was to be led to a great extent in the early nineteenth century from Scotland, and it was in 1802 that the Edinburgh Review was started, in 1805 that Scott published his first great poem, the Lay of the Last Minstrel, and in 1809 that the Quarterly Review first appeared, largely a Scottish venture. It was about this time that Coleridge and Wordsworth began to be known, and in 1807 a new star rose above the horizon. Lord Byron, then a youth of nineteen, published his first book of poems, Hours of Idleness, and soon found himself at issue with the Scottish Reviewers. He felt driven to attack, along with the reviewers, the whole of the romantic school of poets, and himself made a serious effort to live back nearly a century, and to write in the style of Pope. Had he been born only ten years earlier he would have found the effort an easy one. As it was, he soon had to drop the style, and to confess that he was a romantic in spite of himself. Several other writers who belonged to a class which is in far closer touch with the spirit of the age than graver authors, or even poets, were now just beginning to be known—William Hazlitt, Charles Lamb, John Jeffrey, Henry Brougham, Francis Horner, and the two Hunts. It is impossible to think of them as belonging to the eighteenth century. All of these were strongly liberal in their views. It was a new liberalism, sharply divided from the revolutionary liberalism of fifteen years before. The very name for that temper of mind, Jacobinism, was almost extinct. The establishment of the most aggressive despotism of modern times upon the ruins alike of the prerogatives of princes and the rights of man, was turning early enthusiasts like Wordsworth, Coleridge, and Southey, into conservatives. Among the people, the last dying fires of Jacobinism flashed up in the excesses of the Nottingham and Middlesex elections four years before, as well as in the delight of the mob at the sight of Governor Wall's dead body—partly because he was nobly connected—and the applause which some gave to the last defiant words of the traitor Despard.

Within parliament the position had grown clearer. There was always something unreal, or at least merely personal, about Pitt's disagreement with Fox, acute as it was. After they had combined to attack Addington, and had been willing to serve together, it had grown more unreal than ever. It was partial, and confined to administrative matters, and no longer extended to any question of principle. Pitt was not a Tory, but his followers were; and now that he was dead the followers of the two deceased statesmen fell naturally into the old divisions of Whig and Tory, instead of the clumsy "Foxites" and "Pittites". There was, it is true, no great division between them upon principle. Even Catholic emancipation was an imperfect test to apply. Sidmouth and his supporters, who opposed that measure, were to be found on the wrong side of the lobby for a few months longer. Reform was quite left on one side. But that a new order of things was in being, was clear. In one party the two branches represented by Grenville and Grey had come to understand each other after two years of joint opposition and nine months of office. The other had recovered from the chaotic state in which it had been thrown by the death of Pitt.

The change in the aspect of the war was very marked. Napoleon had long given up the idea of invasion, and was well on his way to the goal of starving the United Kingdom out by excluding her from the trade of Europe. No fleets were required for this. Until Trafalgar, and beyond it, as far as Strachan's and Duckworth's actions, the Navy had had all the honours. Now the Navy had done its work, and the turn of the Army was to come, ushered in by the victory of Maida, the importance of which as re-establishing the prestige of the British soldier was fully recognized at the time, however much it may afterwards have been forgotten. Even in training there was an inversion of parts. The men who had done so much to shape the Navy had gone. The senior service reposed under its laurels, and seemed to be losing rather than gaining in efficiency. It was suffering from what St. Vincent called frippery and gim-crack. The Army, on the other hand, was only just beginning to be penetrated with a new vigour. In the two or three years since the peace Moore had been showing with his Light Brigade at Shorncliffe what could be done. Those who composed it were recognized as the veterans of the army as soon as they had joined the troops in the field, and before they had fired a shot. General Sir William Napier, himself one of the most zealous of the school, has observed that the ninety field officers who passed through the regiments which he had trained included many men of great distinction afterwards, in the Peninsula and elsewhere. The example of the men who passed through Moore's hands, trained to act with independence under captains who understood responsibility, converted into a professional army what had formerly been bumpkins tricked out with pigtails and pipeclay.

Fox's own contribution to the new order had been the

very last which he could have wished to make—to prove the unmistakable necessity of a war to the end with Napoleonic France. If he could not make peace, it was abundantly clear that no one else could; and his country owes him a debt for placing this beyond a doubt. This was done when his plain honesty was placed side by side with the sophisms of Talleyrand. It was an honourable effort to have made, and failure in it was a principal step on the road to ultimate success in the only way in which it was possible. The country was now united in a struggle which could end only with the end of Napoleon's dominion. The mail coaches which brought the news of Lauderdale's return were greeted in the Kentish villages with triumphant acclamations. "Eternal war", was the cry, "rather than a dishonourable peace". Such feelings were in the main honourable, but the shouting of the merchants and stockbrokers in London was shamefully occasioned by visions, doomed to bitter disappointment, of the wealth of South America.

Fox was replaced as Secretary of State by Howick, who also took the lead in the House of Commons. He exhibited, in both capacities, abilities and a force and rectitude of character which make it all the more regrettable that after a few months he was to cease for almost a quarter of a century to have any share in the Government. Thomas Grenville, with more popularity than his brother, though not so much ability, took the Admiralty in his place. Holland, who had eagerly hoped for his uncle's legacy of the Foreign Department, had to be content to come into the Cabinet as Lord Privy Seal. Sidmouth became President of the Council, and Fitzwilliam remained in the Cabinet without an office. An unsuccessful attempt earlier in the year to force Fox's friend Lauderdale upon the Directors of the East India Company, had prolonged the interval between Cornwallis's death and the appointment of a new Governor-General for some months, until the difficulty was solved by the excellent choice of Minto, who left for India in the following February. This brought Tierney into the Ministry as President of the Board of Control.

The reorganization of the Ministry was completed by October the 24th, 1806. Its first act was to dissolve Parliament, when it had still nearly three years to run under the Septennial Act. It was given out that the Government wished to obtain the country's confirmation of its determination to pursue the war to the end. This was unnecessary. The Government's main object was to strengthen itself. It had every hope of doing so in an age when the distribution of patronage in the hands of ministers always brought them numerous friends on such occasions. On the other hand, there was no reason to fear the sort of charges commonly brought at the time of a general election during a later generation, of the failure of Ministers to fulfil pledges made when in opposition or on accepting office. As it was, they did not do quite so well as they expected, and obtained some discredit. It was unusual in the reign of George III for changes of ministry to be accompanied or followed by dissolution. Parliaments invariably lasted six sessions or about six years, the only exception being the necessary dissolution by Pitt, soon after he had taken office with the Parliament hostile but the country friendly, upon the dismissal of the North and Fox coalition.

Neither did Ministers escape severe criticism when Parliament met in December. The position was indeed singularly analogous to that of the former Government when the last session opened a year before. Not merely had they in their turn to face the House of Commons without the leader to whom they looked for guidance. Not merely had they to admit that Windham's Act had not done for the Army what it was expected to do by comparison with Pitt's, just as Pitt's had failed to outdo Addington's. But they also resembled their predecessors in meeting Parliament under the shadow of another great calamity

THE MINISTRY OF ALL THE TALENTS 181

upon the Continent. Another mighty Power was overthrown, and its capital was in the hands of the enemy. On the 14th of October Napoleon broke the main Prussian army at Jena. On the very same day Marshal Davout disposed of the other at Auerstadt. What followed was an unprecedented history of flight and capitulation. In a few weeks Berlin and almost all Prussia West of the Vistula were in French hands. Grenville's Government was criticized for this, but was no more to be blamed than the previous one for events which had resulted in both cases from the unaccountable vacillations of an invertebrate character. Weak timidity in the Prussian councils, which had been one of the causes of the failure of the allies in 1805, had been succeeded by weak temerity, which had proved fatal in 1806. The British should, it was said, have helped Prussia. It was true, but they were given no time. That Government, which had delayed the recall of its ambassador from London in consequence of the declaration of hostilities in April, allowed him to leave on the 15th of August, precisely at the wrong moment. It then left Great Britain so long in total darkness as to the probability of a war between Prussia and France, that there was no time even to settle the form which assistance should take, before the blow fell.

The capture of Berlin enabled Napoleon to give a somewhat dramatic turn to the struggle for the destruction of British trade. By a strange irony France, who stood forward as the champion of the rights of nations against the yoke of the tyrant of the seas, had since 1793 molested and discouraged neutral trade; while the supposed tyrant, Great Britain, had encouraged neutral at the apparent expense of her own trade, though not against her own interests. It was necessary for her to have British seamen to man her fleet; with ships to carry her trade, however manned and under whatever flag, she was equally unable to dispense. Consequently, while the total tonnage of shipping entering and leaving her ports between 1792 and 1800 had increased from 3,600,000 odd to over 4,200,000, the British share showed a positive decrease, and the foreign share rose from just over one-eighth to one-third. On the other side of the Channel a resolution of the Council of the Five Hundred, passed on the 2nd of November, 1796, had gone so far in severity to neutrals as to declare any ship, under whatever flag, on which British goods were found, liable to forfeiture. No better compliment could have been paid to the enterprise of her manufacturers and merchants than the list, which it contained, of goods which were to be regarded as British. It comprised cotton, woollen and muslin stuffs, buttons, cutlery, hardware, saddlery, tanned leather, refined sugar, and pottery. It was almost impossible for France to undertake a commercial war against a country possessing such a monopoly as this. If she persuaded or compelled her allies to exclude all this merchandise, she turned friends into enemies, and impoverished those friends who still remained. Fox took an ingenious advantage of the opportunity. After Frederick William's ordinance of the 1st of April, 1806, excluding British ships from Prussia and Hanover, had been answered by the blockade of the coasts, this last measure was followed on the 16th of May by an Order in Council extending the blockade to the whole of the north coast of France, and to Holland and North-West Germany, but permitting neutral ships to enter on most of this coast if not laden at, and to leave it if not bound for, an enemy port. The Government believed that free trade in neutral vessels even with the ports of France was a British interest, and the concession was particularly agreeable to the United States. Trade, however, with that part of the coast which lies from the mouth of the Seine to Ostend remained forbidden. But Napoleon had no intention of leaving even this partial blockade without a reply. He waited until he was in possession of Berlin, and then, from the capital of the country which had made the greatest (though

THE MINISTRY OF ALL THE TALENTS 183

ineffectual) sacrifices to preserve her neutrality, he issued on the 21st of November the celebrated Decree pronouncing Great Britain in a state of blockade, forbidding all commerce with her, and declaring all goods of British origin forfeited, wherever found. The Coalition Government had, under a fire of very severe criticism, consistently upheld a moderate and liberal policy in commercial matters. It had notably improved relations with the United States, and had concluded a commercial treaty, which was, however, not ratified by the American Government. It now contented itself with issuing, on the 7th of January, 1807, an Order in Council forbidding all trade between one port and another belonging to France and her allies. The exchange of these heavy missiles at long range between France and England, neither of them able to do the injury intended, closed the first stage in Napoleon's attempt to bring about what he called the conquest of the sea by the land.

A considerable amount of parliamentary time during the first three months of 1807 was taken up by two proposals which led to no result. The vigorous steps which Petty had taken in the preceding year made his present task an easy one. The budget for 1807 contained no important features. But now that the country was settling down for a long war, he conceived an elaborate scheme—to which other members offered alternatives—of placing the system of loans and sinking funds upon a permanent basis. It was assumed that the war might continue for any period up to another twenty years, and that eleven millions would be borrowed annually. A plan on a subject of greater interest was introduced by Whitbread. Prefacing that by the latest returns, which referred to the year 1803, out of a civil population in England and Wales of 8,870,000 souls, 1,234,000, or nearly one-seventh, were recipients of poor relief, he made a number of proposals. In the first place he contrasted the condition of Scotland in 1698 when Fletcher of Saltoun wrote—filled with beggars, vagabonds, and poor families living out of the church poor boxes—with the general order and freedom from crime which now characterized that country. He believed that it was due to her system of national education, and drew the conclusion that such a system was a crying need for England as well. But he failed to realize that the poverty and crime of a hundred years before in Scotland had been a mere survival of barbarous manners, and not due to the same causes as in England, and that the same qualities of resolution and self-reliance which had enabled them to rid themselves of ignorance, had assisted to rid them of poverty and crime. To help the poor to save, he outlined a scheme of a national savings bank. The deposits were to be laid out in Government stock, and the post offices were to assist in the operations. His other plans were of a technical character. Owing to the strange fatality by which over a period of fifty years critics invariably had the better of anyone from Pitt downwards, who suggested any remedy for national pauperism, his proposals came to nothing. But at least Whitbread's measure, together with the sympathetic manner in which it was received, is a ray of light amid the prevailing darkness of indifference on the subject.

A third measure unsuccessfully introduced into Parliament was that which led to the fall of the Ministry, thanks to an almost incredible combination of weakness and obstinacy. Ireland had long been the quarter on which the party led by Fox and afterwards by Howick leaned for support. But in their anxiety to take advantage of any unrest in that island, it almost appeared as if its present leaders forgot that they were in power and no longer in opposition, and might find themselves to be merely preparing a rope for their own necks. The occasion soon arose. Disturbances broke out in Sligo. Ponsonby, the Irish Chancellor, gave it as his opinion that the disturbed areas must be proclaimed, unless something was done immediately to conciliate the Roman Catholics. To do the first would have been to trust the magistrates with increased power—a proceeding thoroughly alien to the temper of men like Howick and Holland. Although, even in their own opinion, the disturbances were not political, this section of the Ministry decided upon a political remedy. It was gratuitously suggested to the Viceroy, the Duke of Bedford, that he should write an official letter explaining that the Catholics of Dublin were on the point of petitioning Parliament, and informing Government what measures of relief short of complete emancipation would pacify them. This the Duke did on the 4th of February. The grievance finally selected for removal was one which, however genuine, cannot have been widely felt. In 1793 all military ranks in the Irish Army below that of general on the staff had been thrown open to Roman Catholics. Although the armies of the two countries had been united in 1800 by the Act of Union, the anomaly still remained whereby the Catholic officers of an Irish regiment, landing in Plymouth or Gibraltar, would be subject to heavy penalties, if it occurred to anyone to enforce the letter of the law. No such thing took place, but it was no doubt desirable to guard even against its possibility. It was also desirable to open the army to the loyal body of English and Scottish Roman Catholics, although little stress was laid upon this. Ministers were more impressed with the typically Whig idea of meeting the agrarian and economic grievances of the almost barbarous peasants of the West of Ireland with the boon of extending to Irish gentlemen the privilege of safely exercising military commissions in England. It appealed specially to Grenville, who had plans—in what should have been the province of the War Secretary—to encourage Irish recruiting by satisfying the military ambitions of the gentry.

It was with some difficulty that the King's consent was obtained, and not before the Cabinet had stooped to represent their measure as desirable, not merely in order to unite the whole kingdom in resistance to France, but to avert what was termed a still greater danger. Rebellion was clearly indicated, and Ministers were merely encouraging themselves in fears which sensible men would not have cared to formulate, even to themselves. But the real justification of the measure was that it was a simple corollary from the Act of 1793. This was the view of Erskine, of Sidmouth, and of Ellenborough. It was upon this representation that the King's consent was at last obtained. The letter communicating the Cabinet's decision laid the utmost stress upon the point, and on the fact that the faith of Government had been pledged in that year. "It is judged highly important", he continued, "that you should declare that it is not adopted in any view of compromise, or with any purpose of thereby obtaining the abandonment of any intended or projected petition to Parliament." The letter laid such stress on this point of view—in striking contrast with the real facts as to how the proposal started, on what grounds it was pressed on the King, and the terror betrayed at the idea of a Catholic petition being discussed in Parliament—that Sheridan must have been reminded when he heard of it of his Bob Acres stammering out "We won't run" in the duel scene of the Rivals.

When the Roman Catholics in Dublin were informed that the measure was not adopted in any view of compromise, they at once brushed the subterfuge aside. They saw that they were dealing with men who had embraced what is called a policy of conciliation, that is to say a policy guided not by justice or even consistency, but by consideration of the expediency of yielding to force or the fear of it, while pretending not to do so. One of them asked Elliot whether Catholics would be capable of being appointed generals on the staff. The wording of the letter left the point in some doubt; but as this would have been in no sense a corollary of the Act of 1793, he might well have taken the safe line, and replied in the negative.

THE MINISTRY OF ALL THE TALENTS 187

Instead of this, he encouraged the idea. When his report reached London it caused a split in the Cabinet. Sidmouth and Ellenborough as good as resigned. Erskine would not continue to attend. Spencer and Fitzwilliam, who were strongly in favour of the Catholics, but were prudent in council, unfortunately fell ill. The rest of the Ministry agreed to the extension of the concession to generals on the staff. A misunderstanding now took place with the King. On the 4th of March he gave Howick an audience. Both were clear-headed men, and Howick was a frank and loyal servant. But the King was ageing, his brain was weakening, and the subject upset him. There can be no doubt that at this interview he spoke strongly of his objections to any scheme at all. But he did not make it clear to Howick that he positively refused to consent to the enlarged proposal. He ought to have known what it was from the papers which had been sent to him, though even these were not absolutely clear. On the following day Howick brought in a Bill for securing to all His Majesty's subjects, including dissenters as well as Catholics, the privilege of service both in the Army and the Navy. Perceval spoke strongly in opposition. The King took the next opportunity of seeing Lord Grenville—on the 11th—to declare his objection to the extended measure in unmistakable terms. On the 15th a Cabinet Council met of those favourable to the Bill. Lord Grenville and his brother, Holland, Moira, Howick, Petty, and Windham were present. Even this reduced body was not unanimous. By four votes to three—the minority consisting of Holland, Howick, and Windham who were for immediate resignation—it was decided to draw up a minute which contained at once a surrender and a challenge. The Bill was given up altogether. His Majesty was moreover informed that in the discussion on the Catholic petition which could not now be prevented, it would be indispensable that Ministers should openly express their individual opinions that the policy which it had been their painful duty to adopt as members of a Cabinet was wrong. The seven Ministers thereby announced their intention to drag cabinet disagreements before the public gaze, and—worse still—to inform the world that the King had refused to accept the advice of Ministers who still kept office. No wonder Holland wrote: "I passed the most unpleasant night that I ever experienced from political anxiety." No wonder if Moira behaved as the Prince of Wales twenty years afterwards told Croker that he did—going over to the chimney piece and fiddling with the china on it in the great bedchamber in Carlton House where the Prince lay in bed at seven in the morning, until at last he summoned courage to tell him what was done; that he knew it to be both foolish and wrong; but that he himself had signed from considerations of honour.

The King replied to the minute that his mind could not be at ease unless he received a positive assurance that no future Catholic concessions would be pressed upon him. Such a demand was a very natural answer to the outrageous paper which he had received. But it was unconstitutional, and although Pitt and Melville had voluntarily given a similar pledge, it was preposterous that a whole Cabinet should thus be compelled to fetter themselves. A dignified minute of refusal was drawn up at Lord Spencer's, who was well enough to be present, and the Ministry resigned. The last phase of its existence was honourable. It was in the position of a force which has occupied one untenable ground after another, and been beaten in front and in flank, but has at least brought off its guns in triumph.

In another and a more important respect the Ministry was covered with glory in this, literally its last hour. When its impending fate was known, the Slave Trade Abolition Bill was rushed hastily through its remaining stages. At mid-day on the 25th of March the royal assent was given by commission in the House of Lords. Immediately after-

THE MINISTRY OF ALL THE TALENTS 189

wards Lord Grenville and his friends were seen sitting on the Opposition side. The Ministry of All the Talents was at an end. It is fair to add that Perceval had arranged for the passing of the Bill in any event. Wilberforce had obtained this. The day's work was the crowning triumph of a devoted life. His palm and Clarkson's were won.

Sheridan's bitter account of the Ministerial plight was so apposite that it became the subject of one of the most telling of contemporary cartoons. He had often known men knock their heads against a wall, he said, but he had never before heard of any man who collected the bricks and built the very wall with the intention of knocking out his brains against it. Petty afterwards was so incautious as to admit in the House of Commons that the measure for which Ministers had sacrificed themselves could not have been carried through Parliament. So gratuitous had been their self-destruction. There had certainly been no plot against them. The King had not led them into a snare. It is true that on the 12th of March the Duke of Portland had written to him, in much the same manner as Pitt had three years before, offering to form a Ministry. He ultimately accepted, but not eagerly. He knew that it must include —in all probability as its virtual leader—Perceval, who had just involved himself in a very unpleasant business, and become obnoxious to the Court. Charges of immorality had been brought against the Princess of Wales. Four Ministers were appointed Commissioners to enter upon what was known as the "Delicate Investigation." She was ultimately convicted of indecorum and levity, and form lly reprimanded by Erskine as Chancellor. The delicacy was on the side of the judges only. Perceval drew up a defence of this worthless woman, much of which was published in the newspapers. All this was embarrassing to the King, who did not wish to receive her at court, and it was only the change of office that compelled him to do so.

While the Government was being overturned at home

by an imaginary Irish rebellion, it was faced by genuine difficulties abroad. During the winter of 1806-7, Napoleon had succeeded in transferring the theatre of the continental struggle to two parts of Europe at the greatest possible distance from England. In Poland, where the armies of France and Russia were in contact, Great Britain was unable to assist. It was undesirable to attempt to land troops in Northern Europe in the heart of winter. But there was another quarter, where a British fleet might act. In Turkey the contest assumed a diplomatic form, both sides being supported by military forces which did not themselves come into contact. The French and Russian armies in the Balkans were watched by a third Turkish army. To reap the full advantage of this state of affairs, General Sebastiani, that most effective instrument of Napoleonic diplomacy, had been sent as Ambassador to Constantinople. By September 1806 he had created a panic, thrown the Porte into the arms of France, and exasperated a dispute between it and Russia. A Russian army now invaded Turkish territory. Force seemed the only remedy. At the end of September Charles Arbuthnot, the British Ambassador, had already been mentioning the need of that time-honoured support of British diplomacy—a naval armament. His wishes were anticipated. The Russian Government had long expressed a desire that a British fleet might be sent to Constantinople. It was the only way left of helping the Czar in the severe struggle which he was carrying on almost singlehanded with Napoleon, and it would have been preposterous to have refused. But there was a lack of judgement and vigour in the steps taken.

It was not till the 22nd of October that the Admiralty sent orders to Collingwood for reconnoitring the forts of the Dardanelles, which commanded the passage to Constantinople. By the time Rear-Admiral Sir Thomas Louis had carried out this errand it was almost the end of December. Turkey declared war on Russia on the 24th of that month. Although Louis's visit had been a friendly one, it was regarded as the forerunner of another of a different character, and the Porte availed itself of the offer of French engineer and artillery officers. By the 25th of January, 1807, relations had grown so strained that Arbuthnot thought fit to take refuge on the British frigate which had carried him to Constantinople. Definite orders for a decisive stroke had only left England on the previous 22nd of November, and, not being sent by the most rapid way, did not reach Collingwood off Cadiz till the 12th of January. And although this was altogether too late to enable him to take Turkey by surprise, it was too early to enable him to enjoy the advantage of Louis's report as to the strength of the force necessary, before he detached a squadron to the Dardanelles. Vice-Admiral Sir John Duckworth was placed in command by orders from home. In spite of his victory at San Domingo, there were episodes in his career which betrayed that he was not the right man for a task demanding exceptional judgement and resolution. Either Collingwood himself or Sidney Smith would have been a better man. There was some vagueness about the instructions. But they laid down clearly that, once Arbuthnot had decided that hostilities should commence, the Admiral was to place his ships where he could enforce compliance with the British demands. So stringent were they that the sole alternative to compelling their acceptance in full was to throw the Porte into the arms of France. He was to claim the surrender of the Turkish fleet and stores, on pain of an immediate bombardment of the town, and to refuse to allow the Porte to gain time by negotiating. The appearance of Arbuthnot in Louis's squadron was unexpected. But in reality it simplified matters. The point had clearly been reached when it became the Admiral's duty to sail up as close to the Turkish capital as possible, and there demand the Turkish fleet, threatening a bombardment if refused.

Duckworth lost no time in reaching the island of Tenedos,

where he arrived on the 10th of February, after being joined by Louis and Smith. Here he was kept by foul winds till the 19th, when he entered the channel, nearly fifty miles long, by which the Sea of Marmora is approached, and the narrowest part of which—not three-quarters of a mile wide—was strongly fortified. He now had with him seven sail of the line, ten frigates, and two bomb vessels. On Arbuthnot's suggestion, no reply was at first made to the fire from the forts upon the ships as they passed, the fiction that Great Britian and Turkey were not at war being kept up as long as possible. But since the Turkish protest took the form of stone shot, 800 pounds in weight and six feet in circumference, each capable of sinking a ship if striking her between wind and water, or of cutting a mast in half, it was impossible to maintain this dignified attitude for long. Before the squadron had passed the Narrows, the firing was allowed to become general. The ships sustained but little damage; six men were killed and 51 wounded.

When entering the Sea of Marmora, Duckworth detached Smith with the rear division to destroy a small Turkish squadron which lay off Point Pesquies close to the entrance, and had fired on the British as they passed. This was done with characteristic thoroughness. The Turks were superior in the number of their guns, but their practice was inferior, and in four hours they lost all their ships—one line of battle ship and ten small vessels burnt, and two small vessels taken. A landing party attacked a formidable redoubt on the point, and spiked the guns, 31 in number. The British lost only four killed and 26 wounded. Smith rejoined Duckworth before nightfall, and there was now no obstacle on the hundred miles of open water which separated him from Constantinople. But the wind would not allow him to sail right up to the town, and he dropped anchor off the Prince's Islands eight miles from it at 10 p.m. on the 20th. Constantinople was in terror. The Sultan

THE MINISTRY OF ALL THE TALENTS

warned the French Ambassador that he could not be responsible for his safety. But Sebastiani remained firm, and the fortunate arrival of a letter from Napoleon himself dated only a month before, addressed to the Sultan, changed the whole aspect of affairs. Duckworth might have sailed up on the following day. But he listened to Arbuthnot, who entertained the notion that negotiations with the Turks could be carried out with a better prospect of success if that which Nelson had called the best negotiator in Europe were still kept at a little distance. The Porte refused even to allow the flag of truce carrying Duckworth's ultimatum of the 21st to land. This pointed clearly to the only course compatible with honour. The wind was once more fair on the 22nd. But the opportunity was not taken, and all hope of a bombardment was lost. But Fortune did not even now desert the British. The Ambassador fell ill. The negotiations were now in the hands of a sailor, and it might have been expected that they would have been brought to an immediate issue. But there was no change in their spirit. The Turks took courage, and although every moment was of value to themselves—as they were strengthening their defences with desperate energy—they went so far as to accuse Duckworth of trying to gain time. Even this taunt did not make him act. He replied by merely pointing out that he had the power to cut off the supplies of Constantinople which came from the Asiatic side. But he was not equal even to this moderate measure of hostility. Everything possible had now been done to rouse the energies of the Admiral, and everything had failed. It was one of those occasions on which British interests have been sacrificed to an unnecessary fear of being thought warlike and aggressive. Some days more were spent in negotiations as to the place where, and the persons between whom negotiations were to begin. All this time the Turkish defences were growing stronger and stronger, and there was even some desultory fighting on one of the Prince's

Islands, where the Turks were erecting a battery. Every hour Duckworth's mind was bent upon the forts which were being strengthened in his rear. At last, on the 1st of March, he sailed for the Mediterranean. The Turks had made such good use of their time that they were able to show better results with their immense projectiles on the squadron as it passed down the Dardanelles than they had on the 19th. But the ships escaped serious injury, and only 29 men were killed and 138 wounded.

In his letter to Collingwood of February the 5th, written when it was not known that Duckworth was already on his way, Louis wrote that a force of ten sail of the line would be required, including two three-deckers, besides smaller vessels, and also troops to capture the forts. The actual strength detached in ships of the line was one three-decker and seven other ships, one of which was accidentally burnt before the squadron entered the Dardanelles. It would have been safer, if a stronger force could not have been spared, to have obtained the co-operation of the Russian fleet then cruising in the Archipelago. But the squadron which actually went up was sufficient. There were other courses open if it was thought imprudent to bring the ships close up to the town where they would be at the mercy of the currents, supposing the wind to fail them. Smith recommended a bombardment without at first going near the new batteries. There was also the alternative of a blockade. The Turks could be starved into surrender, while there was no fear of the British squadron's provisions being exhausted. The change of Government which took place almost immediately afterwards was fortunate for Duckworth; in fact it was those who planned the expedition whose conduct ultimately came before the House of Commons.

General Fox had had no doubt that the flight of Arbuthnot from Constantinople meant war. When the news reached him, on the 18th of February, he at once acted upon instructions which he had received as to what to do in the event of hostilities, and ordered the despatch of a force of nearly 6,000 men to seize Alexandria. The expedition was the last venture for which the Ministry of All the Talents was responsible. It was no doubt a dissemination of strength which could have been better employed in Italy, or in getting in the rear of the forts in the Dardanelles. But there was much to be said in favour of anticipating Napoleon in Egypt. The Emperor had not forgotten his dreams of nearly ten years earlier. Even before disposing of Russia he had sketched a plan for mobilizing the Sultan of Turkey and the Shah of Persia, and throwing a mixed force on the Indus. But had he attempted another military occupation of Egypt it would have been what his enemies would have most desired. The alternative was to bring Egypt over to the French interest by means of an agent, and this he was actively attempting. All that was required to meet his plans was an equally intelligent British agent, who would have had the advantage—as against his French opponent—of the presence of a British fleet in the Mediterranean. One diplomatist might then have done what six thousand were sent to do. As things turned out, the officer who was looking after British interests in Egypt, was unwise, and brought the troops to disaster. But the result of this expedition was one more of those legacies left by Grenville's Ministry to its successor to disown or to maintain.

CHAPTER IV

THE DUKE OF PORTLAND'S ADMINISTRATION

(March 1807—September 1809)

It might have been supposed that in 1807 the time had arrived when party differences could be waived in face of the common danger. The two great political rivals were dead. The war had been the main subject of dispute, and that party which had believed that it might be possible to withdraw without dishonour had now proved itself to be mistaken. It was, moreover, in alliance with some of the most warlike members of Pitt's first administration. While Grenville's ministry existed, there had been some prospect of its being joined by both Canning and Lord Wellesley, thus further extending the principle of coalition. When it fell, its fall was due to an issue of no immediate importance. So far as regarded the removal of some of the disabilities of the Catholics, Grenville had had three members of his Cabinet opposed to him—Erskine, Sidmouth, and Ellenborough, while of that now being formed three at least—Portland himself, Castlereagh, and Canning—had been in favour of admitting them to Parliament itself. But it was soon to appear that when there was nothing to separate the new ministry from the old except the spirit of party itself, that spirit could become a far more fruitful ground of quarrel than any mere difference of principle.

At first the outgoing ministers could not take their own fall seriously. They pointed to their successors with derision. These were the same men who, on the death of Pitt not many months before, had admitted their own incompetence to govern. The only difference was that the accommodating Duke, who had been a figurehead in two preceding coalitions, and was now almost in the seventieth year of his age, had hobbled out of his gouty chair to lead them.

The task of forming a cabinet at least did not present any formidable difficulties. Portland himself took, of course, the part of First Lord of the Treasury. Several fell naturally into their old places. Eldon went back as Lord Chancellors, Camden as President of the Council, and Westmorland as Lord Privy Seal. Chatham again took the Ordnance. Two went back as Secretaries of State to their old departments, Hawkesbury to the Home, Castlereagh to War and the Colonies. Lord Wellesley was offered, and refused, the Secretaryship for Foreign Affairs. It was given to Canning, who could not now be passed over, and who was qualified for the office by service some years before under Grenville. Perceval was thought to have earned the leadership of the House of Commons. While Castlereagh and Canning had been fettered by their known convictions on the subject, he had been free to raise the banner of opposition to Howick's bill in favour of the Catholics when it was brought in, and was in this way closely connected with the fall of the late ministry. He had, besides, the gift of not making personal enemies. In order to assume the leadership it was necessary for him to take the Chancellorship of the Exchequer, in spite of the jeers of Sheridan, who contrasted the exuberance of other members of the party on the subject of finance with Perceval's unbroken silence. The former Foreign Secretary, Lord Mulgrave, was selected for the Admiralty. He was no great administrator, but he had one qualification for the office—a conciliatory and ingratiating disposition. The number of the Cabinet was brought up to eleven by the introduction into it—following Pitt's precedent—of the President of the Board of Trade. This was Earl Bathurst, a nobleman of great good sense, but of no particular aptitude for affairs of commerce or finance.

Outside the Cabinet, Melville's son, Robert Dundas, was made President of the Board of Control, George Rose Vice-President of the Board of Trade and Treasurer of the Navy, Huskisson one of the Secretaries of the Treasury, and Sir

Vicary Gibbs Attorney-General. The fourth Duke of Richmond went to Ireland as Lord-Lieutenant, with the distinguished Indian general Sir Arthur Wellesley as his Chief Secretary. Foster was once more Irish Chancellor of the Exchequer. One of the family of which the Duke of Rutland was the head, raised to the peerage as Lord Manners, became Lord Chancellor of Ireland, an office which he filled for twenty years.

Could they have looked over the cards which destiny had still to play, the critics of the administration would have been greatly astonished. Four out of the eleven members of that despised Cabinet were to hold the office of Premier, Portland himself for eighteen months, followed by Perceval for two years and a half, Hawkesbury after he had become Earl of Liverpool for nearly fifteen years, and Canning for a few months till his death. After a short interval of four months the rule of the Tories was to be closed by the three years administration of another member of Portland's ministry, become Duke of Wellington. Yet a sixth member, Viscount Palmerston, was to continue Premier, with a short interval, for ten years beginning in 1855. Born the 20th of October, 1784, and destined to be a splendid link between the old world and the new, he was already a Lord of the Admiralty.

Unaware of any such possibilities, Ministers thought hardly less meanly of themselves than their opponents did. They supposed that they would have to face a hostile majority in parliament, like Pitt in 1783, and decided to take the sense of the country. Perceval prepared the ground for a dissolution at once, and in an extremely questionable way. His acceptance of office necessitated a by-election in his constituency, Northampton. In his address to the electors he explicitly raised the cry that the established religion of the country was in danger; and the language of his advertisements and handbills amounted to an appeal to the passions which had set London on fire in 1780. It was peculiarly disgraceful to suggest a charge of hostility to the established church against Grenville, who was no latitudinarian, but a most zealous member of it. It was the first occasion when a cabinet minister had descended to raise a whirlwind of mean passions on the eve of a general election. Perceval had the excuse that he was a sincerely religious man of the narrow evangelical school; he reasoned out the possible consequences of Grenville's proposals, and then set them down as probable; and, like other counsel learned in the law, he began by convincing himself. When the new ministers succeeded by a majority of 32 in meeting the first attack made upon them in the House of Commons, they were as surprised as their opponents had been. In point of fact, apart from the number of placemen who crossed over when the ship of state went about on the opposite tack, some who were not party members did not think it the province of Parliament to question the King's choice of his advisers. It might, they held, express its want of confidence in them, but it was premature to do this before a trial. Moreover, the principle of toleration was far from popular. Ministers were emboldened to go on with their plan of a dissolution before the No Popery cry had time to cool, and the writs were issued for a new Parliament without delay.

The general election of 1807 was fought on Perceval's cry with fair success. In Yorkshire, for instance, a broadside, ending "Wilberforce and Lascelles for ever", set out that Popery and Slavery always had and always would go hand in hand, and pilloried Windham among the late ministers as a strenuous Advocate for the Slave Trade. It so happened that Wilberforce's colleague failed to be re-elected owing to the discontent of the clothiers with his opposition to the agitation against the use of gig-mills. To the delight of the Whigs the Fitzwilliam interest regained some of its control, Lord Milton, the heir of the house, coming in in Lascelles' place. Forty-three out of the hundred Irish members were supporters of the Opposition—a fact suggesting that, after all, Catholic interests could safely be trusted in Protestant hands. But in England the election enabled Perceval to command a majority of nearly 200 in any important division, and thus fulfilled his expectations. The general result was thought by the writer of the Annual Register of the year to mark the rise of a disgust with parties, and unwillingness to credit them with honest differences of opinion, which has since characterized generations of intelligent British observers. It was now that they first began to be familiarly called the Ins and the Outs. The former accused the latter of being an overweening aristocracy, endeavouring to encroach upon the royal prerogative, while they were charged in their turn with being subtle courtiers and chicaning lawyers. The public believed both. The effect was unfortunate. Neither side had any single man with that warm attractive personality which might have turned back this tide of mistrust. Both Fox and Pitt had been popular figures. But no Westminster mob would have cheered Grenville or Grey, no City of London crowd pulled the horses from the shafts of Perceval's or Canning's carriages. The man in the street did not know their Christian names as he knew "Charley" and "Billy". The result in Westminster—heralded by the somewhat inconsistent cry of "Measures not men"—was the return of two popular personalities, the old favourite Burdett and the intrepid sailor Lord Cochrane. Unable and unwilling to contend with such adversaries on common ground, both the great parties entrenched themselves in close boroughs and obsequious counties, and lost touch, in great measure, with the living spirit of the nation.

Parliament opened on the 26th of June in the shadow of two calamities. The announcement of the failure in the Dardanelles had been followed by bad news from Egypt. The force, of less than four thousand British and over two thousand foreign troops, which had been despatched

DUKE OF PORTLAND'S ADMINISTRATION 201

from Sicily on the 6th of March to seize Alexandria, had, indeed, begun well. It arrived on the 16th, and took possession of the place on the 20th after a short resistance. Major Missett, the British Agent, was in the town all the four days, and was permitted to communicate with Major General Alexander Fraser, who commanded the expedition. He had fallen into the post which he occupied because he had been Stuart's Military Secretary during the former occupation, and was left by him in March 1803 when Egypt was evacuated. He was a cripple, and relied on inaccurate reports of whatever he wished to be considered as true, and he passed them on to Fraser as authentic with fatal results. He had already told him that the population of Alexandria would rise in his favour when he appeared, whereas they actually manned the walls in its defence. He now informed him that there was only a few days' food supply in Alexandria, and that it was essential to seize two towns at forty miles distance, Rosetta on the most westerly mouth of the Nile, and Rahmanieh higher up the river. The Albanians who protected those places were, he said, a mere rabble; and the Mamelukes would come to the help of the British. All this was false. A general had to be almost completely in the hands of the political officer upon such matters in an oriental country. But Fraser had once already been deceived by Missett. He would have done well not to trust him implicitly, but to have probed the ground and walls in selected parts of the city with spears. He would probably have found plenty of grain. In the event the army was able to remain in Alexandria for six months with very few supplies by sea. But at the time Fraser saw no alternative but to attack Rosetta at once. It was contrary to his instructions, but he believed it to be essential to the very existence of his force. He was led to suppose that 1,600 men would be sufficient to reduce the place, and Major-General Wauchope, who was in command, entered it on the 31st of March without expecting any resistance. He was all at once fired on when inside the town from the roofs and the walls of the houses. Wauchope was killed along with nearly 200 of his men, and the remainder compelled to retreat. Fraser now sent 2,500 men under Brigadier-General the Honourable William Stewart with all that was necessary for a regular investment. But the wiser—as well as bolder—course was committed by Moore to his diary in Sicily before the news of the first mishap arrived. Fraser should have left a few hundred men in Alexandria and on his communications, and marched with his main body upon Rosetta. Stewart could only invest it from the western side. Here he remained from the 7th till the 21st. The enemy were indifferent to bombardment, and even took the offensive, though not really good fighters. Stewart felt that his success depended on the expected arrival of the Mamelukes. By the 21st it was apparent not only that he was deceived as to this, but that numerous reinforcements were reaching the enemy down the river in boats. It was useless to persevere. He effected his own retreat in good order, but a detachment of 800 men on his right took a wrong direction. It was surrounded by horsemen. Nearly 300 were killed and the rest captured. It was noted as a new departure that the Turkish General, the Albanian Muhammad Ali who was afterwards famous, did not sell the prisoners as slaves, but treated them well.

It was now a question of maintaining the troops in Alexandria from the town's own resources, or of evacuating Egypt altogether; so that it became as desirable from Missett's point of view that the reports should show that there was plenty of food as it had previously been that they should show the reverse. As happens in oriental countries the required reports were very soon procured. A reinforcement of 2,000 troops was sent from Sicily, and Fraser held on till September, when Alexandria was evacuated. The British prisoners were also liberated. Active hostilities against

DUKE OF PORTLAND'S ADMINISTRATION

Turkey were suspended, but attempts to convert this condition of things into a regular peace were long unsuccessful.

Whitelocke's expedition to the Rio de la Plata was the principal remaining legacy of the late Government. He was to reconquer the province of Buenos Ayres. On the 28th of June he landed, at the head of a round ten thousand men, at a point thirty miles below the town. The march on Buenos Ayres was ill-planned and ill-carried out. But by the 4th of July the troops were in occupation of the suburbs on the west and landward side of the town, which occupied two miles of river frontage, having the fort in the centre. Wearied as the men were with heavy marching, they could still have taken the place had they pushed on at once while the enemy was flying in confusion into the town. But time was given to organize resistance. An elaborate plan was drawn up for the next day by Major-General Leveson Gower, Whitelocke's Second-in-Command. Six thousand troops were to be employed in the attack. A demonstration was to be made in the centre, the real attacks being upon the two flanks, so as to seize the extreme points of the town upon the river, each a mile on opposite sides of the fort. No proper provision had, however, been made for communication with headquarters, much less for lateral communication and mutual support. The Spaniards showed some of that aptitude for defending a town which they showed afterwards in the Peninsular War. Not merely did the British only reach their positions on the river face at the cost of a loss in killed alone of 400 officers and men, but it was found at the close of the day that almost 2,000 had been compelled to surrender in different isolated bodies. Of these the largest was a part of Craufurd's brigade. His Staff Officer had omitted to copy out an important paragraph of his instructions; and the Brigadier, whose fault was always on the side of excessive boldness, ventured into an exposed place where he had not been intended to go, and was captured. Whitelocke's attacking force was now reduced by half, but he had 3,000 more in reserve; whom he ordered up early on the 6th; and he had taken over a thousand prisoners and thirty-two guns. This was the state of affairs when a specious proposal arrived from General Liniers, who commanded the town. It was to the effect that all prisoners—including those previously captured under Beresford—should be exchanged, and that Whitelocke should evacuate the province. Liniers also intimated that the populace was so infuriated that he could not answer for the safety of the prisoners. A man of honour, the General was a French emigrant, and it is not to his discredit that he was unable to control the turbulent Spaniards. But so far as this point was concerned a bold course would almost certainly have been safe. The Spaniards would hardly have dared to proceed to extremities with so many prisoners, and so much of the town in British hands. Whitelocke was mainly influenced by other considerations. He had from the first expressed a strong dislike of street fighting. He disliked Leveson Gower, and did not wish for the success of his plan. He realized—what had before been doubted—the confirmed hostility of the inhabitants, and he feared that, even if he succeeded in occupying Buenos Ayres with a total force perhaps reduced by casualties to half its original strength, he would end by meeting the same fate as Beresford. Further, one object of the expedition, the release of the troops who had surrendered eleven months before, was attained. After a consultation with Gower and Auchmuty he, to use his own words, "resolved to forgo the advantages which the bravery of the troops had obtained", and accepted what Liniers had offered. The indignation was extreme. His soldiers scrawled such things as "General Whitelocke is a coward or a traitor or both" on the walls of Buenos Ayres. When he reached home he was brought before a general court martial and cashiered.

There had, moreover, been disturbances in the Madras

Presidency, and it had, in consequence, become necessary to despatch 4,000 of the 40,000 available troops to India. There were now 109,000 of all ranks of the regular army—cavalry and infantry—serving abroad. Those at home, including those not fit to take the field, amounted to 96,000. The militia counted 86,000, and so large a body of men, some thousands of whom were now completing their time, attracted the greedy eyes of the Secretary for War. The scheme of his predecessor, Windham, had met with the fate of most of those which had preceded it. It gave good results in appearance—eleven thousand in six months. But it had in reality broken down. The special attractions of Windham's scheme—short service and better pay and pensions—had fallen into the background. He had been driven to employ machinery of a very questionable character. Recruiting parties had been almost trebled in number, and Windham, in his anxiety to avoid the system of offering rank as a reward for recruits, had fallen back on the complementary device of punishing officers by deprivation of pay if they could not produce them. Upwards of fifty second battalions had been told to raise 400 each in six months. If they could not do so, the officers would be placed on half pay. Two-thirds of the eleven thousand had been raised in this way. Castlereagh determined to bring this state of things to an end. He introduced a Militia Transfer Bill, by which nearly 29,000 of that force were to be induced by bounties of ten pounds to volunteer for the line. The plan proved a success. But it was fiercely criticized at the time. It entailed the temporary disorganization of the militia, until its men could be replaced by the ballot. There was certainly nothing brilliant about Castlereagh's scheme. It was a makeshift. Moreover, some danger had to be faced. During the period of transition England would be left with a weak army and a depleted militia. Nor were the volunteers of much value. That force now amounted to no more than 289,900 men. It had, moreover, suffered from old age. It was observed that time, while it improves the discipline and efficiency of a regular unit, has exactly the opposite effect upon volunteers. Home defence was now practically disregarded. It was necessary in the words of the Earl of Selkirk in the House of Lords, that England should entrench herself behind a miserable ditch. In other words she had to trust to her naval supremacy, and that to a greater extent than even in 1805. Viewed in this light, the extreme anxiety of the Government of 1807 that no neutral men of war should be added to the enemy's fleet becomes intelligible.

Yet bounded as was Castlereagh's horizon, the speech in which he introduced his measure on the 22nd of July was remarkable for one notable prediction in the manner of Pitt. "That individual," he said speaking of Napoleon, "who, unfortunately for the world, had acquired such an ascendancy on the continent, was little aware, that by that very ascendancy he was creating in this country a power to which the world might ultimately look for deliverance; and that out of the ascendancy which his inordinate ambition produced, the military character of Great Britain would probably be raised to a greater height than any to which it had hitherto attained." Three months earlier Windham, speaking of the gallantry of British troops in the assault of Monte Video and of Spanish in its defence, had observed that after all France was the common enemy of both. "If a little of this spirit was displayed in Old Spain, it would be attended with consequences at which Europe would have reason to rejoice." The two predictions taken together showed the country the road along which circumstances compelled and glory led her.

Partly through absorption in the war and in foreign affairs, and partly owing to the character and bent of mind of its leaders, Portland's ministry adopted in internal affairs the attitude which was to mark the Tory party for many years. The distinction between the party which upheld the prerogatives of the Crown and that which upheld the rights of Parliament now began to give place to that between the party of order and the party of progress. Though nominally led by a Whig, the Ministry was Tory; and it was now that that word, which had meant so many things in its history, first began to connote a disposition perplexed with unreasoning fear of change. The Government had the energy to press through an Arms Bill and an Insurrection Bill for Ireland. In this it had the support of Grattan, as there was sufficient disorder in certain parts of that country to justify coercion, and the principle of both measures had been accepted by the late administration. But Ministers refused to treat the Irish question in a large way. Their predecessors had been considering plans for dealing with the tithe question—the mainspring of Irish unrest—and Howick suggested that it was a question for the Government of the day and ought to be taken up. But the Ministry would not act. Nor did it listen to Sheridan when he raised the general question of the state of Ireland at the end of the session. Even Howick had only partially realized the importance of the point to which he had himself called attention. But Sheridan had no doubt on the subject. The late ministry's notion of removing the grievances of the higher orders of the Catholics he dismissed with more frankness than party loyalty as an attempt to commence the measure of redress at the park and the mansion. "The place to set out with in Ireland for the relief of the people", he said in a memorable sentence, "is the cottage."

So far as Great Britain was concerned there was very little movement. Whitbread failed to pass his Poor Laws Bill and Parochial Schools Bill. The latter was unpopular in the country. It was based upon the unacceptable principle of compulsion by local option, and the House of Lords was probably justified in throwing it out. But the speeches during the discussions were of more significance than the result. In moving the rejection of the Bill, Hawkesbury said that he would not deny that education for the lower orders of the community, in the extent proposed, under proper directions and limitations, might be desirable. It was well to avoid all possibility of misunderstanding, for there were many who objected even to this. They foresaw a double rise in the poor-rate, both for maintaining schools —if Whitbread's bill passed, and in any case—if education was more widely diffused—from children of between seven and fourteen being at school instead of earning something in the fields for the support of their families. The ludicrously cautious ideas which prevailed were further illustrated by the debate on the subject of a second reward to Doctor Jenner for his discovery of vaccination and the labours of his life. Perceval was afraid of a possible objection to a discovery which tended to increase population. Malthus's Essay on the Principle of Population was now nearly ten years old, and his conclusions commanded general acceptance. In the end Perceval's proposed £10,000 was doubled. In one other matter some progress was made. The impetus given by Petty to the cause of financial reform had not yet spent itself. A Committee of the Public Expenditure was sitting, and its labours promised to have useful results.

While Parliament was sitting the Government was engaged in setting powerful forces in motion abroad. On the very day on which Castlereagh introduced his measure for the increase of the army it had come to a momentous decision. On the 14th of June Napoleon defeated the Russian army at the battle of Friedland. On the 25th he had a friendly meeting with the Emperor Alexander on a raft moored on the river Niemen. The negotiations which followed culminated in the Treaty of Tilsit, signed on the 7th of July. Prussian interests were sacrificed, and Great Britain was deserted. But there was some excuse. It is true that Great Britain had loyally refused to sacrifice Mediterranean interests which were thought essential by her Russian ally. It is true that she had gone to war with Turkey for the sake of the same ally. But she had not made a useful employment of her troops in Southern Italy. She had behaved in a half-hearted manner in the Dardanelles, and made the war with Turkey an excuse for what was not much more than a filibustering expedition to Egypt. She had made no diversion of any value in Northern Germany. She might have provided money if she had no men, but she had refused, in somewhat harsh terms, to facilitate a Russian loan on London. Such an act would of course have been tantamount to lending Russia money herself, as British bankers refused to lend money without Government security. The policy of Grenville's ministry had in this last respect been prudent, but it only threw her failure in a military sense into stronger relief. When Portland's ministry succeded it found its hands tied. It had been Pitt's policy to keep transposts constantly ready, but there were now only 25 ships fit for use, with a tonnage of less than 8,000, and further reductions had been ordered. Such had been the situation when the new Cabinet decided to make some effort to help the King of Sweden, whose territory south of the Baltic Sea was being attacked. But while transport was being collected and plans discussed with Lieutenant-General Lord Cathcart, who had been appointed to the command, Napoleon's blow had been struck. It was not till a few days after the battle of Friedland that eight thousand troops of the King's German Legion left for the island Rügen, a Swedish possession off the coast of Swedish Pomerania. Alexander had had some reason to be exasperated at such delay.

The Treaty of Tilsit was supplemented by a secret treaty of alliance, the terms of which were not fully known to the world till nearly a century later. Russia was to offer England her mediation. Should it be refused, Denmark, Sweden, Portugal, and Austria were to be summoned to make war upon her. But the British Cabinet did not wait for information of this. Some members or member of it, probably

Canning, was able to divine the intentions of Napoleon with regard to Denmark in the same manner as an experienced general can those of his adversary. Nor was this difficult. It was obvious that Britain was the enemy, that without a fleet Napoleon could not compass her destruction, that he had no fleet worth the name, and that he could only obtain one within a reasonable time by incorporating the ships of subject allies with his own as he had done those of Holland, and threatened to do those of Portugal. The object of St. Vincent's mission in the previous year had been to secure the Portuguese fleet—by force if necessary—in the event of France attempting to obtain possession of it. There was a difference, however, between that country and Denmark. The former was England's traditional ally; the latter, while professing neutrality, had shown that she was almost as unwilling as she was unable to resist the encroachments of France. Early in the year postal communication between Altona in Holstein and England had been interrupted, just as if Denmark were at war, the officials alleging that Napoleon had compelled them to refuse to take letters. Henry Crabbe Robinson, the correspondent of The Times there, and no friend of the Tories, afterwards regarded this as, by itself, a justification of the action taken by the British Government. After the battle of Jena, Danish territory had been violated; and how this might be done on a large scale by a French force coming in the guise of an ally was very shortly to be seen in the case of Spain. Such an invasion would have provided the Crown Prince with an inducement to hand over his ships and dockyards to Napoleon. So unfriendly had been the Danish attitude that Howick had actually instructed Benjamin Garlike, the Minister at Copenhagen, to inform that Government that in the event of its submitting to the control of France, His Majesty could never suffer any part of its navy to be placed at French disposal. Rist, the Danish Minister in London, felt, on his part, that his

DUKE OF PORTLAND'S ADMINISTRATION 211

position was so bad that with no other British Foreign Minister could it be worse. The succession of Canning was welcomed. Tempted possibly by the change of ministry, Denmark now adopted an even higher tone. Canning and Garlike each complained to the other of the overbearing and ill-tempered manner in which Danish objections to the Orders in Council had been urged.

On the 5th of July Garlike wrote to Canning on the subject of Danish apprehensions from a French military occupation. The letter reached London on the 16th. On the same day other information, which proved to be greatly exaggerated, arrived regarding the forward state of preparation in which the Danish fleet was supposed to be. The Cabinet was now convinced of the necessity, if Denmark's balance was to be maintained, of administering as great a pressure from the side of the sea as France was doing on land, so as to ensure her standing upright. It was imperative to counteract the menace of Napoleon's armed diplomacy. No time was to be lost before the winter months put a stop to operations in the Baltic. Orders were issued for a fleet to be ready to proceed on a particular service.

On the 21st of July news reached Canning direct from Tilsit that in the interview with Alexander on the 25th of the previous month, at which several persons were present, Napoleon had proposed the conclusion of a maritime league to which he represented the accession of Denmark to be as certain as it was essential. The mind of the Cabinet was now made up. Once the 16 Danish ships of the line were added to the French navy, there could be little doubt of the adherence of the 11 Swedish, besides 19 or 20 Russian. There were 14 in Dutch ports. Sixty sail of the line in the North and Baltic Seas, in addition to an equal number in the rest of Europe, was more than the British blockading squadrons could manage. On the 28th a special mission was entrusted to Francis Jackson, the former Minister in

Berlin. He was to demand the deposit of the Danish fleet in British hands during the war; and to offer Great Britain's alliance, and the yearly payment of £100,000 while the fleet was held in pledge. The Government was afterwards blamed for showing insufficient confidence in the British navy. But it was the duty of Ministers to place the safety of their country beyond a peradventure, and not to provide opportunities for future Nelsons. The threat was supposed to be directed against Ireland, which had been successfully reached by the enemy in 1795 once, and on two occasions in 1798. The Chief Secretary, Arthur Wellesley, took the danger here seriously, even after the Copenhagen expedition. It was vain to hope to seal up this enormous fleet of nearly fifty vessels in the Sound with complete security. There was no mistrust of the British seaman, but to expect that the enemy could always be successfully brought to action was to detract from the glory of Nelson. It was a thing which only he and a very few who approached him in genius were able to do. This was particularly the case just now. The weakness of the naval command about this time was remarkable; and it was forcibly exhibited in the following year, when the escape of the Brest fleet and its junction with another squadron in Aix Roads produced such apprehension at the Admiralty, that the work of cutting their wings was specially handed over to a junior captain who possessed in an eminent measure the Nelson spirit.

Pressure was being brought to bear upon the unfortunate Danish monarchy from both sides at the same time. On the 31st of July Napoleon was instructing Talleyrand to inform the Danish Minister in Paris that should England refuse the mediation of Russia, Denmark had to choose between war with her and war with France. He followed this up two days later with a letter to Marshal Bernadotte at Hamburg telling him that the force under his command was to be raised in the course of the month to over 30,000 men. On the same day he instructed it to be intimated to

DUKE OF PORTLAND'S ADMINISTRATION 213

Portugal's representative that that country was now to declare war on England, as she had in fact been ordered to do a fortnight earlier. It was not Napoleon's way to keep his plans to himself. The objects which others endeavoured to reach by secrecy he attained by headlong vigour in execution. In two days more the world was as wise as Bernadotte. An announcement was published at Frankfort on the 4th of August to the effect that if Great Britain could not make peace, this army of 30,000 Frenchmen would, in conjunction with the Danes, close the Sound and erect batteries to defend Copenhagen. All this was reprinted in the North German and Danish press. It had been preceded by rumours to the same effect officially reported from Hamburg during the whole of the previous month to the Danish Government. The notorious existence of these designs had been during July and August the constant theme of English newspapers. The Times had all along urged the necessity of the Danish expedition. Even the Morning Chronicle, which—although somewhat doubtingly at first—embraced the view that it was unnecessary and wrong, published on the 3rd of August a letter from Hamburg giving currency to Napoleon's intentions.

But the Emperor had for once been anticipated. On the 1st of August Jackson left for Kiel, which he reached on the 6th. Here he saw both the Minister, Count Bernstorff, and the Crown Prince Frederick himself. The latter, after refusing his proposal, set out for Copenhagen to put matters in order for resistance. Jackson followed him to make one last effort to avert the threatened calamity, only to find that, distracted between his fears of a British attack from the sea and a French attack from the land, Frederick had returned to the mainland. It was now the 12th of August. Admiral James Gambier had already been long waiting. He had left England on the 26th of the preceding month with 17 ships of the line besides smaller vessels of war and transports containing 20,000 troops. General Lord Cathcart who had the military command, had now joined him before Copenhagen, followed by his troops from Rügen. The island of Zealand or Sjaelland, on the east of which the capital lay, was carefully invested by a squadron under Keats as Commodore. It only remained for the British envoy to join Gambier with the announcement of the failure of his mission, which he did on the 14th, for hostilities to begin.

The Danish ships were drawn up in the arsenal, and protected by batteries from any attack by sea. The main operations were left to the military, but at the outset an incident occurred to show that British seamen had that superiority to Danish which they had so often displayed against French and Spanish and Dutch. On the 12th a frigate, the Frederickscoarn, escaped from Elsinore Road. The Comus went in pursuit to detain her. An action followed. The British vessel had fewer guns and a much smaller complement of men. After only three quarters of an hour the Frederickscoarn was easily carried by boarding. So easy a victory deserves chronicling for the striking illustration which it offers of the superiority of British gunnery. The Danish ship had been riddled and disabled, and lost 12 killed and 20 wounded. Close as the action was, the Comus escaped almost untouched, and had only one man wounded.

On the 16th the disembarkation of the troops, which now amounted to nearly 30,000, began, a few miles north of Copenhagen. Every possible measure had been taken to ensure success. Denmark was no despicable foe. The Danish dominions included Norway, and the number enrolled in the army and militia was put by Arthur Wellesley, who commanded a brigade, at no less than 170,000 men. In point of fact the Danish regular army numbered 35,655, and the second line troops less than 40,000, besides which there was a third line of coast militia, the strength of which was uncertain and the quality negligible. Wellesley, however, wrote somwehat doubtingly to Castlereagh upon the British chance of success, and explained the urgency of acting before the older men could be embodied. As it turned out, it fell to him to strike the only important blow in the field during this short campaign. He was sent to repel an enemy force of 7,700 men which had appeared to the south of Copenhagen; and he did so successfully on the 29th, taking 1,500 prisoners and fourteen pieces of cannon. The island of Zealand itself never contained more than four or five thousand regulars outside the city, and the navy saw to it that no reinforcements were thrown in. Copenhagen had only 5,500 regulars besides 7,500 in the second line. The batteries were now ready. A final summons was sent on the 1st of September and refused.

Those within the beleaguered city were fatally blind to their danger. The General did not even order the women and children away from the exposed parts. Strange beliefs were held as to the harmlessness of bombardments, and, eight days after the invading troops had begun their landing, a Copenhagen Newspaper, the Nyeste Skilderie, had given utterance to the untimely reassurance that Old England's last hour had struck. Such phrases rang as if minted in Paris. Napoleon's mobilization of public opinion had, in fact, been astonishingly effective, and as rapid as that of his own armies. Not that this was any mere sudden effort on his part. In the previous year Niebuhr, a Dane by birth, found it necessary to combat what he even then found to be the received opinion on the Continent—that Great Britain, so prodigal of subsidies, was to be shunned as a vampire which sucked the life-blood of Europe.

It was found impossible to reduce the place by a blockade, the course which Wellesley, who was deep in the confidence of his Commander-in-Chief, would have preferred. Cathcart now most unwillingly subjected the city, which was ill defended, to three nights' bombardment. It was only when there appeared to be danger of the whole city being burnt to ashes that the Danes surrendered. A capitulation was signed on the 7th September providing for the delivery of the ships and naval stores to the British Commanders-in-Chief, who undertook on their part to evacuate Zealand within six weeks.

Governments have sometimes been charged with having insufficiently recognized successes which were bought with very little bloodshed. This could not be said here. The whole venture cost only 56 men killed in navy and army together, and the honours lavished on the leaders included the bestowal of a peerage on Gambier and the promotion of Cathcart, who was a Scottish peer, to a peerage of the United Kingdom. There was much criticism of this, and a long and bitter attack was made inside parliament and out on the justice and expediency of the expedition itself. Canning had made some mistakes. He had miscalculated the strength of Denmark's reluctance to give up her fleet without a struggle. He was certainly unfortunate in his choice of the man on whose tact the success of the plan depended. Jackson was no doubt from one point of view the obvious instrument to select. The chosen confident of Gentz, the first political writer of his day, he had a unique knowledge of the affairs of northern Europe. But he was stiff and abrupt, and—as the event proved—required more exact instructions than he was given. Had he begun his conversation with the Crown Prince with some account of the circumstances which made a maritime league between Denmark and Great Britain desirable from the point of view of both countries, and then passed on to the proposal to unite the two fleets, he would certainly have had a better chance of success than by acting as he did. He bluntly demanded the Danish fleet directly he was introduced into the royal presence. It was a far from impossible suggestion had it been put in the right way. Five years later the Great Czar himself obtained leave to send his fleet to a British harbour to be safe from capture by the French. The Crown

Prince of Denmark refused, not because the proposal was a dishonourable one for him to accept, but because all who had embraced England's alliance hitherto had bitterly rued it, because the guarantees which she offered were insufficient, and because the overwhelming probability was that she would not be the eventual winner in the struggle with Napoleon.

Afterwards Canning had trusted that hostilities would end with the capitulation. A declaration of war had been issued in the name of the poor demented Monarch of the Wends and Goths as early as the 16th of August. That of the United Kingdom did not appear until the 4th of November. The interval was taken up with ineffectual efforts to reopen negotiations, and—on the other hand— with discussions as to the reoccupation of Zealand—a dangerous suggestion which was fortunately negatived. For a time it was intended to employ some part of the force in defending Sweden, but this too was dropped. The effective gains from the expedition amounted to the bringing home of fifteen Danish sail of the line, four of which were found fit to be repaired for the British navy, and upwards of ninety transports full of naval stores. The loss to Denmark was much greater from a merely monetary point of view. Debarred from service in their own navy by British action, and cut off from the large carrying trade which they had enjoyed by their own Government's refusal to make peace, the Danish seamen became privateers; in the course of the next few years millions of pounds worth of goods were carried as prizes into the harbours of Denmark and Norway. Nowhere did the British Navy find its task of protecting trade more difficult than it did in the Sound from the persistent boat attacks of that intrepid people. The Government cannot, however, be blamed for this. It was its duty to provide against the immediate danger, and this it effectually did. It had disposed of the Baltic peril.

In dealing with the difficulties with which the Government was now beset, Canning committed the mistake which might have been expected from him. He was too clever. It was not until some days after Jackson had sailed that it was known that the conversations at Tilsit had resulted in a treaty. It was not even then known in London that there were any secret articles. There was therefore no mention of Tilsit in the British declaration which was issued on the 25th of September regarding the expedition, and on the 2nd Leveson Gower, the Ambassador in St. Petersburg, justified the action of his Government on the ground that it had long been in possession of positive information which left no doubt of France's intentions, and that the peace with Russia and Prussia had now given her the opportunity of carrying them into effect. He added that these projects could not have escaped the Emperor's penetration. They were in fact notorious throughout Europe. Yet Canning afterwards chose to indulge his love of mystification by bringing into prominence the secret information which he had received, the source of which as well as its nature he refused to disclose. As if to create greater confusion in men's minds, a reference to the result of the negotiations of Tilsit was made in connection with the expedition in the King's Speech at the opening of Parliament in the following January. If the sensational legend of the man behind the curtain of the tent of the raft upon the Niemen, who was listening to the conversation of the two Emperors, emanated from Canning himself, it goes some way to prove the truth of Malmesbury's complaint that even when Foreign Secretary he had not given up the schoolboy habit of quizzing people. No British subject could have been in a position to overhear any conversation which was intended to be secret. But several persons, including one Englishman—the adventurous Colin Mackenzie, at that time attached to the Czar, were present among whom Napoleon had no objection to being as open regarding his intentions as he was six weeks later in the press. There was no one present who was likely to be shocked. Russians needed no conversion on the subject of the coercion of neutrals. A strong party in that country had been seeking to drive Denmark into the alliance against France. There was already a French party, which aimed at forcing her into the alliance against Great Britain. If, as is almost certainly the case, the party which favoured the latter country took its revenge for its failure by disclosing to the British Government the plans embodied in the secret articles, the information had nothing to do with the situation as it stood in London on the 22nd of July, and is almost irrelevant to the rights and wrongs of the whole question.

It was no wonder that in the following year Ministers were subjected to violent attack on both the justice and expediency of their action. The position in regard to international law was stated, with his accustomed weight and clarity of expression by Grenville. Criticizing the Government's policy in the House of Lords on the 21st of January, 1808, he said: "Where you have certain evidence of the intention of an enemy to seize upon a neutral territory, neutral vessels, or property, such neutral being incapable of resisting, and thereby to place you in imminent danger, you have a right to seize such neutral territory, vessels, or property, in order to secure your own safety." Canning possessed such evidence, not in the form which would satisfy a jury in a trial for murder, but such as would justify a careful general, for example, in throwing all his troops on to one side of the field of operations, and leaving his other flank unguarded. To risk anything on Denmark's will and capacity to resist would have been folly. In the best speech made on this subject in either House of Parliament, Lord Wellesley said: "Here was an instrument of war within the grasp of our inveterate enemy: we interposed and seized it; and this act of energy and wisdom was to have the hard epithets of rapine and impiety ascribed to it! To shew that injury had been done to an innocent party in a transaction, was not to prove its iniquity." For, as he pointed out, all war had this effect.

Such was the defence of the Government in the House of Lords, where the highest level was reached by both sets of disputants. Outside parliament the great Whig divine, Samuel Parr, complained that nine persons out of ten were disposed to approve of all that had been done. Yet the controversy was frequently renewed in both Houses, the voices of the Opposition growing weaker as time went on. The Ministry was accused of wishing to set off a contemptible success at the expense of a puny and unresisting nation against the long series of failures which had recently attended British arms and British diplomacy. It was, indeed, all these misfortunes and their own acute consciousness of their weakness which determined the members of Portland's Cabinet to take no further risk. They were told that Denmark could not have been intimidated into a hostile alliance. But she had been in 1801; and in 1807 a much greater power, Russia, had been, if not intimidated, at least induced almost literally upon the stricken field, to reverse her system. It was said that the Crown Prince would have resisted; he would have sacrificed his continental possessions, and held on to his arsenal and his ships in an island made impregnable by the British fleet. Such had been England's wish; but she had hoped that his decision to do so would have been formed without waiting for an actual French invasion to be made at a time when the approach of winter would have rendered naval assistance difficult, if not impossible. At such a season no confidence could be reposed in the insular position of Zealand. Charles Gustavus had availed himself of a winter of extraordinary severity in 1658 to cross the two great belts of ice which separated it from Jutland at that season. That was a mad exploit, never to be repeated, perhaps; and yet what had armies done in the past which French soldiers could not

DUKE OF PORTLAND'S ADMINISTRATION 221

repeat? What naval expert could ever have believed it possible for a body of horse to capture a fleet? and yet that had been done by General Pichegru's cavalry in 1795 before the day of Napoleon Bonaparte's invincibles. Even were unparalleled weather conditions not again to come to the aid of unparalleled enterprise, there was no confidence in sea-power presenting an impassable barrier to troops which had only to collect a flotilla and wait for a calm. In an ordinary winter blocks of floating ice intercepted the passage on the Danish coasts for ships, and when wind and current alike drove down the Belt, it was impossible for them to maintain their stations, and prevent troops from crossing. It proved impracticable during the Walcheren expedition two years later to stop the French from throwing troops time after time across the broad mouth of the Scheldt into Flushing in the height of summer. No one, not Nelson himself, ever believed even in Sicily being safe from invasion. It was not for Ministers to occupy themselves in balancing possibilities, but to assume that their inveterate foe would do all that man could do or had ever done, and to play for the highest degree of safety.

As the event proved they were to lose four former allies before the end of November. On the arrival in London of news of the signing of the Treaty of Tilsit, the Russian Minister had offered his Emperor's mediation. But the failure of the negotiations started by Fox in the preceding year had made the British Ministry wary. Canning replied by asking for a communication of the Articles of the Treaty, and of the principles on which France was ready to negotiate. Three days later, on August the 4th, he wrote to Leveson Gower for any secret articles which the Treaty might contain. The Russian Court refused to give them. It was now certain that they were to Great Britain's disadvantage. Of their general tenour there could be very little doubt. Relations were further complicated by the attack on Copenhagen. But this was far from being a deciding factor in the

Emperor's policy. The news of the ultimatum to Denmark and of the arrival of the fleet had made no difference; in fact Leveson Gower was able to report that on the 1st of September the Foreign Minister's tone had grown more conciliatory. Alexander had, in fact, no intention of allowing himself to fall in with Napoleon's plans too rapidly. On the 23rd, however, he made the intelligence that the ultimatum had followed up by action—that Copenhagen had been bombarded—the occasion for a vigorous protest. Even now he waited another six weeks before proceeding to extremities. On the 2nd of November he declared war with a country which, he averred, had wronged Denmark, and scattered afresh the seeds of war.

Such a declaration, postponed as it was till ten weeks after the act of which complaint was made, was put down to its true cause—the Czar's desire not to offend his new ally. Condemned to follow on the same frivolous ground—that England persisted in continuing to be the firebrand of Europe, Austria confined herself to breaking off friendly relations. Prussia similarly fell into line.

The fourth country was Portugal, England's oldest ally, for even she for a time threw herself into the arms of France. On the 19th of August the Prince Regent had written to King George to the effect that he would abandon Europe rather than agree to the French demands. These had taken definite expression long before any threats had been made to Denmark; indeed it had appeared to the Portuguese Ambassador in Paris that his country was to be made the example. No time was to be lost if that fleet was to be secured from falling into British hands. On the 19th of October a French force under General Junot crossed the Bidassoa into Spain. On the 8th of November Prince John found himself compelled in Napoleonic phrase to adhere to the cause of the Continent, and to comply with the French demands. On the 10th the British Minister, Lord Strangford, demanded his passports, and on the 17th he joined Sidney Smith, who was cruising with six ships off Lisbon. Heedless of the Portuguese fleet of eight ships of the line, or of the Russian fleet of nine which had recently entered the Tagus, the Admiral and the Minister decided to announce a blockade of that estuary. British naval pressure could be felt before Napoleon's armies could be seen. Moreover, the Prince saw that his efforts to temporize had been of no avail. The Moniteur of the 13th of November had in fact, as was afterwards learnt, announced the impending deposition of the House of Braganza. The die was cast. In a last effort to persuade the Prince to accept the escort of the British fleet Strangford found himself met half-way. Landing at Lisbon on the 28th, he found the Prince already in course of embarcation for his dominion of Brazil. He had only to hasten his departure. Junot was quickening his approach at a speed which converted his army—that part which kept with him—into a ragged handful of scarecrows. He had instant orders from his imperial master to be in Lisbon by the 1st of December. He was there a day earlier. But it was still a few hours too late, for on the morning of the 29th the coveted Portuguese fleet had put to sea, to be escorted by Sidney Smith himself to the new royal capital at Rio de Janeiro. Napoleon had been once more anticipated.

At the same time the safety of the island of Madeira was insured by its being handed over to Great Britain to retain until the re-establishment of the Portuguese monarchy. The capture from the Danes of Heligoland, a useful point of vantage from which British goods could be smuggled on to the continent through the French blockade, and of the Danish West Indian Islands, completes the naval history of the year. Plans of South American conquest and emancipation, what the Foreign Secretary afterwards styled calling a New World into existence to redress the balance of the Old, floated before the eyes of Ministers as they had before those of their predecessors a year earlier. Fortunately the country was not committed before the events of the following spring in Spain demonstrated clearly the right quarter for the employment of British troops.

Of much more importance for the New World was the issue of the complicated and confused body of enactments conveniently known as the Orders in Council of the 11th of November, 1807, but which includes certain later supplementary orders. They had been preceded by a long series of encroachments upon the rights of neutrals, for the first of which, by a curious irony, the blame lay with Fox, who was responsible for the institution of the unreal blockade of the whole northern coast of Europe from Brest to the mouth of the Elbe in the spring of 1806. After Fox's death the Ministry, in the preamble to their Order in Council of the 7th of January, 1807, actually claimed for the naval forces of the Crown the ability to make the approach towards the whole coast line of the enemy manifestly dangerous. But this was impossible, in the sense in which those words were understood in international law outside the United Kingdom, even as regards the 800 miles from Brest to the Elbe. The coasts should have been invested in such a manner that a vessel attempting to reach them would, unless favoured by a fog or an exceptionally dark night, be certain to be seen, and to have to run for it. Not only was this in no wise the case, but in the course of the year 1807 a system of exceptions was introduced which had the effect of throwing into yet higher relief the illegitimate use which was made of the term "blockade".

The heterogeneous mixture of the perfectly justifiable with the manifestly illegal which comprised the Berlin Decree of the 21st of November, 1806, has the mark of deep policy. By it Napoleon excluded British merchandise from France, as he had a perfect right to do. He had an equal right to induce as many governments as he could to do the same. There was no good ground, for example, on which Denmark could object to a prohibition of Manchester piece goods from entering a Prussian port, whether the Government issued that order of its own free will or upon French compulsion. It was a reasonable, and indeed the only possible way of attaining his professed object of conquering the sea by the land. But he went very much further. In the very forefront of his Imperial Decree he declared the British Isles to be in a state of blockade. He justified this declaration by the illegitimate orders of blockade issued by Great Britain. His own measure was not merely illegitimate, but absurd. It amounted, however, to this, that any neutral vessel carrying neutral goods to England might be seized by one of his privateers and condemned. But when inquiry was made in Paris on behalf of the United States, it appeared that Napoleon did not mean to enforce his so-called blockade even to this extent. Other articles of the Decree recited that it was English or English colonial merchandise which was forbidden, and that neutral vessels sailing from England or English colonies could not be received in a French port. Their right to enter and to leave ports within the dominions of George III remained undisturbed. The declaration that the British Isles were in a state of blockade was thus reduced to a piece of braggadocio, intended partly as a challenge, and partly to veil the fact that the country whose blockade had been declared was in reality France.

But it had had its effect in irritating Grenville's Ministry. Before waiting to see how far the Berlin Decree would be carried out, it had issued its Order in Council of the 7th of January, 1807. Howick was of the opinion that it would have been justified in going to the full length to which France had gone, and declaring all the countries occupied by the enemy in a state of blockade. But he contented himself with obtaining the prohibition of trade between one port of France or her allies and another. This was another measure which was all the more patently illegitimate because it was partial. A vessel might trade direct between New York or Copenhagen, and Marseilles or Barcelona. But if she attempted to pass from one of the two last-named ports to the other she was liable to capture and condemnation. This was bitterly resented both by the United States and by Denmark. They suffered directly from the enforcement of this order, and they were not satisfied with the reply that the French decree had been a much greater contravention of the Law of Nations.

Howick had plainly intimated to the representatives of both these countries that he expected their resentment to be converted towards France, and that they would refuse to submit to the pretensions advanced in the Berlin Decree. The successors of Grenville's Ministry were equally unable to grasp a point of view which limited resentment to injury actually experienced by the neutrals themselves. Recourse to the larger measure which Grenville's Ministry had threatened was justified on Howick's own ground. The principal Order in Council of the 11th of November recited that: "His Majesty's Order of the 7th of January last, had not answered the desired purpose, either of compelling the enemy to recall those Orders, or of inducing neutral nations to interpose, with effect, to obtain their revocation." Under the influence of this idea, a Cabinet almost ignorant of commerce was persuaded to order that all countries from which the British flag was excluded should be subject to the same restrictions as if actually blockaded. But neutrals were permitted to trade direct with enemy colonies, to trade between them and certain ports in the British colonies which had been declared free ports, and to trade with enemy ports generally in British goods, or, with some exceptions, in foreign goods, provided that they touched at British ports on the way, and, in some cases, landed and then reshipped their cargoes, paying a duty on the transit. They were equally compelled to call in the United Kingdom after leaving a hostile European port. The enemy had declared that Britain should have no trade. The reply was that the enemy—and the word was used in its widest sense —should have no trade except through Britain.

What was regarded by the English Cabinet as concession was treated, very naturally, by Thomas Jefferson, President of the United States, which now represented all that was comprised in the term neutral, as extortion. It is clear from a paper which was circulated, a month before the issue of the Orders, by Perceval to the Cabinet, and from his colleagues' notes upon it, that the original object was to retaliate on the enemy while sparing neutral trade as much as possible. But other ideas were in the air. Pamphleteers like Lord Sheffield and James Stephen thought that neutrals had unfairly jockeyed England from the ocean trade while she was engaged in the war, and that it was necessary to restore the balance. According to Lord Erskine Ministers spent some of the period between the 11th and the 25th of November undergoing a siege from the merchants of London, and it was only on the latter date that a definite permanent character was given to trade with hostile countries through the United Kingdom. Neutrals were still to be allowed to carry on a trade with the enemy. But severe conditions were imposed. Where they included the obligation to unload cargoes, and to load them again at British ports, and, still more, the payment of heavy duties, the expense was expected to make up in part for the difficulty which the English trader had in smuggling his goods past the barrier. In the case of that most important American staple, cotton wool, the motive was clearly avowed. France had encouraged her own cotton manufacture, and it was deemed necessary for this reason to compel the raw material to be landed at a British port, and to pay a heavy duty in transit. Such orders certainly bore the appearance of attacks upon neutral trade under cover of military measures against France.

Another objectionable provision of the Orders in Council had reference to the certificates of origin. Vessels sailing to French ports from neutral countries had been compelled by French orders to obtain these documents from the consulates of that nation at the point of embarkation as proof that no part of the cargo was British. It was actually ordered that any vessel on board which such a certificate was found might be captured. Napoleon countered on the 17th of December with the Milan Decree. This emulated the harshest provisions of the Orders in Council in barbarity. Every neutral vessel submitting to British search or to a compulsory voyage to a British port was denationalized and decreed subject to capture. Every vessel sailing to or from a British port was good prize. The first article of the Decree of Berlin, that imposing the blockade generally, was now interpreted in its strictest sense. This completed the Continental System, to which the allies of France embracing almost the whole of the Continent, generally adhered.

It was to be supposed that if one Power ordered that no neutral trade should reach the Continent except by way of the United Kingdom, and the other that none should reach it by that way, the result would have been that there was none at all. This was, generally speaking, the case, and there was additional and much more cogent reason for it. For years the high-handed action of Great Britain in enforcing rights claimed by her such as those of impressing British seamen in American ships, and searching those ships for deserters, had caused very bitter feeling. Hitherto it had been usual not to molest men-of-war. But in June 1807 the British frigate Leopold enforced a demand to search the American frigate Chesapeake by firing a broadside into her which killed three men. The Admiral who had given the order was deprived of his command, and the Government expressed its regret. But the injured nation was not pacified. Exasperation throughout the country was general. It became necessary on the British side to reinforce Canada. But the United States was not prepared for hostilities.

Jefferson held his hand, and finally obtained from the American Senate a measure which he regarded as the only alternative to war. The Orders in Council of the 11th of November had not reached him. But their general sense was already known on the 22nd of December, when the Embargo Act was passed by which American ships were not permitted to leave the States at all. The injury suffered by American trade was considerable, particularly in the Eastern States. But Jefferson considered this preferable to the losses which it would undergo from capture, combined with the danger of the outrages of the belligerents leading to actual warfare with Great Britain or France or both. Impartial as this measure was in form, the President took no trouble to disguise the fact that he regarded England as the eventual enemy. He was energetically strengthening the land forces, and no part of the States marched with any French possession. The opinion in America, as in Denmark, had been that Napoleon was the winner. It was reported at the time that on the 18th of December Jefferson had said at his own table that Britain would cease to be a nation in less than two years.

Surrounded by enemies, cheered only by the belated adherence of one ruler who had just lost a kingdom and the failing support of one ruler who was shortly to lose his, England's Parliament was opened in January 1808 with a speech from the throne breathing all the inflexible resolution of Pitt. "This war", it ran, "is in its principle purely defensive. His Majesty looks but to the attainment of a secure and honourable Peace; but such a peace can only be negotiated upon a footing of perfect equality. The eyes of Europe and of the world are fixed upon the British Parliament." It continued in the same strain, expressing unabated confidence in the ultimate success of Great Britain. During the exceptionally arduous session which followed, the foreign policy of the Government was keenly criticized. For once in its history the leadership of a British party in the House of Commons fell to an Irish member. The death of his father, the first Earl Grey, in November 1807, had given Howick his title and place in the House of Lords. The ablest speaker on his side left in the Lower House, Sheridan, had not the qualities of a leader; and others who had some claim, such as Windham, Whitbread and Tierney, were almost as unfit. Petty was young, and did not aspire to the position. Hence the choice fell on George Ponsonby, the former Lord Chancellor of Ireland. Though a fluent and graceful speaker, his negative gifts for the leadership were quite inadequate to the task of welding his party together. In the Lower House Ministers held their own; but in the Upper they could make but a feeble reply to a most damaging attack made by Lord Erskine on the Orders in Council on the 8th of March. He pointed out that up to the date of the Orders the United States had been taking millions of British manufactures. "America, as I have said, continued to smuggle your goods into France for her own interest, and France continued to buy them for hers. The people huzzaed their emperor in the Thuilleries every day, but they broke his laws every night." Not a complaint of bad trade was to be heard throughout England. But now Parliament was beginning to be surrounded by cries of distress and discontent from every quarter. There was some exaggeration in the contrast drawn by Erskine, for the Berlin Decree had had the effect of raising the rate of insurance even on American ships sailing between their own country and England from $2\frac{1}{2}$ per cent in 1806 to $3\frac{3}{4}$ in 1807, and during the month which preceded the issue of the Orders underwriters had ceased to quote any rate at all for voyages between England and the Continent. Moreover, the City of London was in favour of the Orders in the main. But even from this quarter an influential petition was presented to Parliament under the sponsorship of the banker Alexander Baring, and Liverpool and Manchester followed. Three weeks later the brilliant young advocate Henry Brougham—not yet a member of Parliament—summed up the evidence in their support in a great speech at the bar of the House. But the last word had not been said. More petitions were presented; more evidence was taken; and the Opposition, united as they were against the Government policy, shrank for the present from putting the question to a decisive issue.

The sufferings of those engaged in the cotton industry had, as the Lancashire petitions suggested, been intense. Most of the raw cotton came from the United States. The embargo had greatly restricted the supply, and the price had doubled. The consequent distress was spread over the whole industry. On the 19th of May George Rose, who was a great admirer of the Spitalfields system of regulation of wages, went so far as to take the sense of the House of Commons on a minimum wage bill, which he introduced, as he said, not from a conviction of its propriety, but from sympathy with the peculiar hardships of the persons affected. It met with universal disapproval. Perceval expressed the hope that those who had applied to Rose would realize that the House was far from being indifferent to their sufferings, and only refused the measure because it could do no good. The news of the failure was immediately followed by a violent agitation. The Manchester weavers sent delegates to the magistrates giving a ghastly account of the state to which they were reduced. In a six-day week of fourteen or fifteen hours a day they could not possibly earn more than seven or eight shillings, on the present piece work wages. A formidable crowd collected, which was dispersed with difficulty by charges of cavalry. The master manufacturers offered a 20 per cent. advance, which the men at first refused, and disorders continued for several weeks. Shuttles were seized from the homes of men at work on their looms, and Rochdale jail was burnt to the ground. The unrest spread into agricultural districts, where there was rick-burning and cattle-maiming. Vigorous steps were, however, taken to protect those willing to work, and gradually the men came back, having got nearly two-thirds of the rise of 33⅓ per cent which they had demanded.

The most important internal question of the year—that of the Budget—offered little difficulty. The revenue was steadily expanding. The charges on Great Britain for the year were £80,000,000, including a Swedish subsidy of £1,100,000. The new Chancellor of the Exchequer adhered, with some unimportant deviations, to the principle agreed upon in the previous year, of imposing no fresh taxation for three years. After obtaining a loan without interest of £3,000,000 from the Bank of England, in return for the advantage which it enjoyed of holding public balances of almost four times the amount, and taking £500,000 of fundholders' unclaimed dividends, Perceval had to raise £8,000,000 by public loan. He did so at four per cent instead of three, and at a price which made the interest payable on every hundred pounds in cash lent to the Government a little under 4¾ per cent. The requirements for Ireland were upwards of nine and three-quarter millions Irish money, or rather over nine millions English, which, as Foster said in introducing the budget, was a very large sum indeed for that country. Almost half of it had to be raised by loan of one sort or another. A third of a million was estimated from extending the malt duties to raw corn used in distillation.

The West Indian Colonies were at this time suffering from an evil for which no complete remedy was possible—a fall by almost one-half in the price of their chief staple. Sugar, which had been 65s. the hundredweight in 1800, was only 34s. in 1807. And now it was feared that it would be no longer feasible to export to the Continent the usual million out of the three and a half million hundredweight yearly imported into the home country. But it was found that some relief could be provided for this as well as for another evil nearer home at the same time. The average annual importation of grain into Great Britain from foreign countries was 770,000 quarters. By prohibiting the use of grain in distillation, and substituting sugar and molasses, it was possible to help the West Indies and at the same time to set free for the food of the people the 470,000 quarters usually consumed in distilleries. This strong measure of restriction of trade had been adopted on three occasions in the past—the last in 1800—but only in times of actual scarcity. At present wheat was only at 70s. a quarter, barley at 40s., and oats at 34s. There was some risk in trenching on this useful reserve before the actual crisis had arrived, and the measure was not passed without loud complaints from the agricultural interest, headed by its doughty Whig champions "Squire" Western and Coke of Norfolk.

Parliament also gave some part of its time to certain minor reforms. The House of Lords could no longer resist a measure to prevent the grant of offices for life, or the prospective grant to any individual of an office upon the death of the present incumbent. It was in this year, too, that Romilly successfully inaugurated his noble crusade against the severities of the criminal law. But other attempts at reform were unsuccessful. Perceval himself, when for once he came forward as a reformer, met with no better fortune. A fourth attempt of his to oblige non-resident clergy to make adequate provision for their curates' salaries failed before what amounted to an unnatural alliance between the Whigs, Manners Sutton, Archbishop of Canterbury, and the halting Eldon. A very different measure of Perceval's exhibited a narrowness and even pettiness of nature with which Sydney Smith made excellent play in the brilliant political tract, Peter Plymley's letters. The drug first isolated in 1809 under the name of quinine then existed in the compound known as Jesuit's bark. Perceval carried a law prohibiting its export to the ports of France and her allies. When attacked by Whitbread for his inhumanity he explained, in the spirit of a salesman pushing the wares of a new emporium, that the measure had been misunderstood, for the French and their friends might have the drug if they consented to purchase British manufactured goods along with it. He obtained support from an unexpected quarter. Cobbett cracked a few jokes in his Political Register at the expense of Whitbread's advocacy. He disliked brewers, not because he was an abstainer, but because he believed in people brewing their own ale at home.

So far as the foreign enemy was concerned, the Ministry felt at last safe. Castlereagh's Militia Transfer Act had added 40,000 men to the regular army, which now amounted with the militia to 200,000 men at home, exclusive of the artillery. These together he regarded as the first line of defence. The second was the volunteers, who numbered 240,000 for Great Britain at the last inspection, besides Ireland's 70,000. Behind these he proposed to have a third line of militia, 60,000 in the first instance, to be gradually increased in number so as to supersede the volunteers. They were to be embodied for 21 days in the year in their own counties, and would not have to march outside them except in case of invasion. 200,000 men were, moreover, to be trained under Windham's Training Act, and to be liable, in case of invasion, to serve in the Line. For this purpose the Local Militia Act was passed. The measures now adopted formed a comprehensive scheme of national defence, which continued without radical alteration until the end of the war.

It was not easy to find employment for such troops as could be sent abroad. But it was not possible for a British Cabinet to hold its hand and wait quietly for a good opportunity. In May, Moore was sent to Sweden with 12,000 men. It was certainly desirable, if possible, to assist the last sovereign on the Continent who maintained the struggle with Napoleon; and in February a subsidiary treaty was concluded with Gustavus who was to receive

£1,100,000 in all. But Napoleon had succeeded in setting Russia and Denmark on the doomed and now almost demented monarch, and his cause was hopeless. Moore's instructions from home were quite impracticable; he was unable to achieve anything, in fact he could not even land his troops. He returned in July to find that the day which Castlereagh had foretold, when Britain was to manifest her military power, had come at last.

Napoleon had been exasperated by the defiant tone of the speech with which Parliament had been opened. He regarded it as a manifesto calling for immediate action, and wrote on the 2nd of February to Alexander that it was only by grand and vast measures that the peace which both desired could be obtained. The adherence of Sweden to the continental system would complete all that he hoped in the north, and he left this to his imperial brother. His own eyes were turned southwards and eastwards. Early in 1807 he had concluded a treaty with the Shah of Persia, securing for an army of invasion a passage through that country to India, and had sent a mission under General Gardane to follow up his advantage, the British countered with another under Sir Harford Jones, and the country became during 1808 the battle-ground of rival diplomacies. Napoleon saw the necessity of supporting such a policy by force, as could be done once the Turkish question was laid to rest, and in the letter to Alexander he sketched a seductive plan. An army of 50,000 men, Russian, French, and perhaps in part Austrian, was to cross the Bosphorus and strike such a panic into the desert spaces of Asia as would bring England on her knees as soon as it had touched the upper waters of the Euphrates. It was moreover necessary to secure the Mediterranean, to drive the English from the Levant, to get possession of Egypt. He sought to concentrate as much of his naval power as possible in those waters, and actually Rear-Admiral Allemand with the Rochefort squadron succeeded once more in escaping, and passed through the Straits of Gibraltar. The last post held by British troops on the Italian mainland, Scilla, had fallen in February, and Napoleon now hoped to take advantage of the defenceless state of Sicily, which was very short of troops just at that time. But first of all it was necessary to look to the safety of French possessions. The Republic of the Seven Islands, as the Ionian Islands were then called, had been handed over to Napoleon by the Treaty of Tilsit. Of these the most important was Corfu. Napoleon's Indian schemes had been fluttered before Alexander's eyes before there was any prospect of bringing them into effect. But his designs upon Egypt were genuine enough; he would move by Italy, and must secure the mouth of the Adriatic. At that moment, he wrote, the loss of Corfu would be the greatest misfortune which could befall him, and that island first claimed attention. On being joined by Allemand early in February at Toulon, Ganteaume, the French Admiral in command there, sailed out and successfully evaded Collingwood's vigilance for two months. But all he was able to do was to revictual and strengthen Corfu. He returned to port, and the concentration had no further result.

In March a treaty had been concluded between George III and Ferdinand to secure the latter in the possession of what remained of the kingdom of the Two Sicilies. He was to receive a subsidy of £300,000 a year, afterwards raised to £400,000. A British force of 10,000 was to be maintained for the defence of Sicily, and that island was now safeguarded against enemy attack. Yet one last brilliant success was to crown French arms in Italy before the year 1808 closed—the capture in October by Marshal Murat, Joseph's successor as King of Naples, of the island of Capri in the face of Britain's sea power. Meanwhile Napoleon's plans as regarded the Western Mediterranean had been matured. Under the pretext of supporting Junot he had filled northern Spain with troops. On the 23rd of March 25,000 men entered Madrid. A few weeks later Napoleon took advantage of the dissensions between King Charles IV and his son Ferdinand to get them both into his clutches at Bayonne; and in the first days of May he compelled them to renounce their rights to the Spanish throne, which he bestowed on his brother Joseph.

But even before this there had been expressed one of the most unmistakable pronouncements of a national will known to history. On the 2nd of May, a day which was to live in the memories of Spaniards, the people of Madrid made an ineffectual rising against the French garrison. The news spread like fire. The ancient provinces of Spain, entrenched though they were in their provincial—almost national—exclusiveness, received it with one mind. The whole country rose in arms against the usurper. There was one friend, the general friend of the oppressed, to whom it could turn. It fell to the northern province of Asturias to make the first move. The Provincial Council was already in session. On the 30th of May it despatched two emissaries to England. They reached Falmouth on the 6th of June and London at 7 the next morning. Canning saw them at once, and assured them of the help of the British Government. He was able to do so officially on the 12th. Succours were sent in money and arms, and peace was proclaimed with Spain on the 5th of July. The people of London were deeply stirred. One of the two deputies, afterwards the Conde de Toreño, became the historian of the war. He related that on one occasion when they were seen in the theatre, there was such a demonstration in their honour that the performance had to be suspended for an hour. The party of reform in England was not behindhand; and the veteran Major Cartwright addressed a public meeting of the freeholders of Middlesex in favour of the Spanish cause. In Parliament Sheridan told Ministers that he was convinced that since the first burst of the French Revolution there never existed so happy an opportunity for Great Britain to strike a bold stroke for the rescue of the world.

He added that he hoped that nothing now would be done in driblets, and that the petty policy of filching sugar islands would be abandoned.

It happened that a small force was already being assembled at Cork in connection with designs on the Spanish colonies, and that Arthur Wellesley, back at his duties as Chief Secretary for Ireland, was in close consultation with Ministers as to its employment. Already in May he suggested its being sent to Spain. The proposal was approved; he was given the command; and his peculiar position gave him the inestimable advantage of inspiring his own instructions. There were those who thought that operations should have been begun in some part of Spain—in the south where there was already a force under Major-General Brent Spencer, and where Gibraltar was available as a base, or in the north which was nearer home, and whence the first requests had come for help, even though the requests had been for money and arms, and not for men. But it was mainly due to Wellesley that Portugal was chosen and maintained as a basis of operations; although the attitude of the people was in some doubt, it was at a greater distance from Madrid, and its rugged character promised difficulty in furnishing supplies. The choice was justified by the results. Outside Lisbon, which remained quiet and sullen, the Portuguese, although disarmed and short of officers, rose during June in sympathy with the Spanish rising. The many obstacles which intervened between the west coast of the Peninsula and Madrid made it eventually more difficult to overwhelm the British when a superior French force could be brought against them. Finally the fact that they were operating in a country which normally drew almost half its food supplies from abroad told more in favour of that belligerent who commanded maritime communications and paid for what he took from the country than the belligerent who did neither.

On the 13th of July the first force destined for the

DUKE OF PORTLAND'S ADMINISTRATION 239

reconquest of Portugal sailed from Cork to the number of nearly ten thousand men, exclusive of a veteran regiment destined for garrison duty at Gibraltar. It was very short in horses. The only cavalry regiment was the 20th Light Dragoons, and it had 215 horses for 381 officers and men. A dragoon, in the old official phrase, was able to fight indifferently whether mounted or on foot. But guns and supplies for troops on the march had no corresponding advantage. Without some method of transport they were useless, and Wellesley had so much trouble in personally arranging for them that he left the cavalry to shift to a great extent for itself. That arm fell into the background from the very outset of the Peninsular War.

Scarcely had Wellesley started when the Government learnt that Junot's force was much stronger than it had supposed. It determined on raising the expeditionary force to thirty thousand men. Sir John Moore's corps was included, and that officer, as the most distinguished in the army, might naturally have expected the command. But he was no favourite with Ministers, as Wellesley was, and on the Duke of York objecting to so important a force being entrusted to so junior a Lieutenant-General as the latter was, it was decided to give the command to Lieutenant-General Sir Hew Dalrymple, with Sir Harry Burrard as second, both officers of little war experience. Besides Moore three other officers senior to Wellesley were sent.

Wellesley's first care was to discuss the situation with the Spanish executive council or Junta at Coruña, and the Portuguese Junta at Oporto, as well as with Vice-Admiral Sir Charles Cotton off the mouth of the Tagus. A landing on the coast anywhere between that river and the Douro was a difficult operation, almost certain, in the most favourable conditions, to be attended with delay and some loss of life. Wellesley chose Mondego Bay, about half-way between the two rivers, as being far enough from the neighbourhood of Junot's force in Lisbon. The landing began on the 1st of August and was completed, along with that of Spencer which joined it from the south, by the 8th. Wellesley exhibited from the first the vigorous offensive spirit which had always distinguished him. He insisted on estimating the enemy's total force in Portugal at only from 16,000 to 18,000. He expected the co-operation of 5,000 Portuguese, but when that force failed him, with the exception of 1,400 infantry and 260 cavalry, he still pressed on southwards. On the 17th of August he found his way strongly barred at Roliça by General Delaborde with rather over 4,000 men. The Frenchman had to fall back before superior numbers, but not without a severe struggle in which he inflicted a loss of 487 in killed, wounded, and missing. Burrard, who had already reached Mondego, became alarmed. Wellesley had suggested that Moore's force, which was immediately behind, should make a movement on Santarem, fifty miles north-east of Lisbon on the Tagus, where it would be able to cut off Junot's retreat. But Burrard would not allow this. He thought Sir Arthur had already advanced too far, and ordered Moore to remain between Oporto and Mondego so that in case of a check he might have something to fall back upon.

Wellesley on his part felt the need of reinforcements seeing that the main body of the Portuguese had disappointed him. He had intended to march straight on Lisbon by the direct road through Torres Vedras. But the determined and gallant resistance which had met him at Roliça decided him to turn aside south-westward to Vimeiro, where he could cover the disembarcation of his first reinforcements from England. These 4,500 men being landed, he would have pressed on at once on the 21st. But fortune forced upon him the rôle, which he was so often afterwards to fill, of a defensive general. Burrard arrived in the bay as well as the troops. Wellesley anticipated his landing by going on board his ship to report, and to obtain his approval of the proposed advance. Burrard peremptorily forbade it.

DUKE OF PORTLAND'S ADMINISTRATION

It was left for Junot to make the attack. He did so with the confidence of a race which had been for the last fifteen years the conquerors of Europe. His force was superior in cavalry and artillery only. Out of the 26,000 men whom he had in Portugal he could only collect 13,000, and it was with these that he hoped to drive a force of close on 20,000 into the sea. Wellesley's men were excellently posted on two steep ridges, and on a hill which stood near the entrance to the gorge separating them. The position looked south-east with the sea behind, and was too strong on the right to invite attack. Two successive attempts which were made to force the British centre failed, though in this part of the field the last French reserves were thrown in. It was here that the new shell invented by Major Shrapnel obtained its first important results. Meanwhile, a wide flanking movement, which Junot had ordered against the British left, had developed with even less success for the assailants. The brunt here was borne by Major-General Ferguson's brigade. Waving his hat at the head of his men he led them to meet the enemy with bagpipes playing, and made them reserve their fire till the moment came to pour in a shattering volley. Wellesley said that Ferguson's personal gallantry struck him as the finest thing which he had ever seen in his military service. The two French brigades on this flank lost both their commanders, and fell into the greatest confusion. Ferguson was now edging them away towards the north, and proposed to cut them off altogether. Wellesley was for doing more than this. His own right was nearer to Torres Vedras than the enemy, and he had ample troops to cut off his retreat to the southwards while pursuing his own victory in his immediate front. But Burrard, who had landed during the day, thought it was time to interfere. He considered that Ferguson's brigade was getting too far, and ordered all the troops to be halted where they stood. Thus the fruits of Wellesley's victory were snatched from him. Even so it was a signal success. He had captured

14 guns with a loss of 720 men, that of the enemy being 1,800. He had done more; he had already captured the hearts of those whom he commanded. Two members of the Opposition spoke warmly on the subject, when a vote of thanks was moved to him and his troops in the House of Commons in the following January, and another member, Brigadier General Charles Stewart, Castlereagh's brother, spoke of the universal enthusiasm in the army from general to drummer, which he found when he joined it shortly after the battle. A piece of plate of the value of one thousand pounds was presented to him by the seven general officers who had served under him in this small campaign, and a similar presentation was made by the field officers.

Sir Harry Burrard had not been twenty-four hours in command when he was superseded in his turn. It so happened that the officer destined for chief command arrived from Gibraltar on the morning of the 22nd. Sir Hew Dalrymple was from some points of view the person naturally indicated for the general command of the forces operating in Portugal and Spain. He had been commanding the troops in Gibraltar, and as such had been long in correspondence with Spaniards disaffected to France, and after the rising had been actively helping them with arms, ammunition and money. For all that the Government knew when it made the appointment, Spencer was already carrying out operations under his direction. He was of no use in the field, and Castlereagh had recommended him to trust to Wellesley. But on his arrival he refused to repose any more confidence in him than Burrard had done. He would not accept Wellesley's plans, and postponed the advance till the next day. Meanwhile Junot had sent one of his generals of division, Kellermann, to propose an armistice with a view to the evacuation of Portugal by sea. Wellesley at once appreciated the situation. Dalrymple was not the man to carry out a campaign. Every plan which Wellesley had proposed for pressing the enemy close had

DUKE OF PORTLAND'S ADMINISTRATION 243

been scouted by him or by Burrard, and the only outcome of further operations would be a leisurely advance in which the enemy would be given time to dispute every position, to end in the reduction of the last fortress in Portugal somewhere about the beginning of December. Once Junot's army was cleared out of the way, the British forces would be free to act in Spain forthwith, whether under himself or Moore, or any other active general, while Dalrymple and Burrard might remain in Lisbon. Nor did so proud a man relish being constantly in the position of one whose advice is right but is never taken. Consequently when asked his opinion as to whether the French army should be allowed to leave Portugal by sea, he agreed that there was no objection. He went further. It would not have been regular for the Commander-in-Chief to sign the agreement with Kellermann, and Sir Hew asked Sir Arthur as an officer of similar rank to do so. Wellesley did not regard this as a definite order, which it would have been insubordinate to have disobeyed. But to have refused would, as he explained privately to his friends, had been to place himself at the head of a party in opposition to the Commander-in-Chief on the very day of his assuming the command. As he told the House of Commons afterwards, it was the duty of an inferior officer to carry out his commander's plans. The armistice, as negotiated between Kellermann and Dalrymple, contained unusual details for which Wellesley was in no way responsible. When shown it he told his chief that it was an extraordinary paper. But he said that he would sign any paper he was desired to sign, and signed accordingly.

The Armistice of the 22nd of August was followed by a Definitive Convention for the Evacuation of Portugal, concluded on the 30th. A separate Convention was made on the 3rd of September between Admirals Cotton and Siniavin, by which the latter surrendered the Russian fleet till six months after a peace, while the officers and men were to be conveyed to Russia at British expense. When the contents of these documents were known in England they raised a tremendous outcry. The three generals were caricatured hanging on gibbets. It rained petitions and demands for justice on the offenders. A singular unanimity prevailed throughout the country. Even one who took so little part in public life as the poet Wordsworth was ready to address a meeting in his native county, and denounced the Convention of Cintra, as it was called, in a vigorous although unwieldly pamphlet, the earlier part of which appeared in the ministerial newspaper, the Courier. Portland, Castlereagh, and Canning were equally indignant. In November the Government ordered an inquiry to be made into the conditions of the armistice and military convention by a Board of seven general officers.

On several points the agitation was unjustified. It was wrong to blame Wellesley, as the public did, for not having refused to sign the armistice. Great objection was made to the French army being carried home in British ships; but if the evacuation of Portugal were to be permitted at all, this was obviously better than merely marching the enemy across the frontier into Spain. Objection was also made to the Russian sailors being taken to their homes at British expense, and Dalrymple was blamed for this. But this arrangement was Cotton's, and had been believed by him—although mistakenly—to be in accordance with the policy of the Admiralty. What the British required was not men but ships, or rather to keep ships out of Napoleon's reach. To refuse to treat Admiral Siniavin, who had on his part refused to land men to help Junot, as an enemy, was to prepare for the day when the enforced hostility of Russia would cease, and she and Britain would once more be allies; and Cotton's mistake had the best results. It was also wrongly supposed that the permission given to the French to carry away their private property had enabled them to take great quantities of plunder back to France in British ships. But on the main question the instinct or the public was right. The natural unwillingness of high-placed officers to pass an adverse judgement upon the action of one of their own number in the exercise of his discretion in a position of great responsibility saved each of the three generals from censure. Moira was the only member of the Board who disapproved of both the armistice and the convention; but he was the ablest British soldier not actually in the expeditionary force. At the same time he agreed with his colleagues that no further military action should be taken, and that only an error in judgement could be imputed to the officers responsible.

In these circumstances it was quite impossible for the Government to make a satisfactory pronouncement. It had been itself to blame for the unfortunate circumstance that a double change of command within forty-eight hours had happened to coincide with a situation requiring wise and rapid decision. The letter, dated the 18th of January, 1809, in which Castlereagh, as Secretary of State for War, conveyed the King's decision to His Royal Highness the Commander-in-Chief, is incidentally of some constitutional interest as showing that it was still possible for a letter determining a great question of state to make no mention whatever of "His Majesty's Government" or even "His Majesty's Ministers". As regards its contents it confined itself, so far as the convention was concerned, to disapprobation of those articles in which Spanish and Portuguese interests and sentiments had suffered injury. The garrison of Almeida, for example, then actually being besieged by Portuguese troops, had been included in the evacuation, and the safety of French subjects residing in Portugal was guaranteed, and an indemnity granted to Portuguese who had embraced the cause of the invader.

In parliament Wellesley afterwards made a powerful defence of the Convention on the ground that it enabled the British Army to pass at once into Spain. But there was no attempt to take advantage of this opportunity. Very soon after the convention was signed Sir Arthur himself left the army to return to his duties as Chief Secretary for Ireland, a post which he still held. Dalrymple found occupation in assisting the Portuguese to form a new Council of Regency in Lisbon and in restoring order. He was also expected to have his force ready to move forward into Spain on receipt of orders, and might even, had he obtained the necessary permission from the Spanish authorities, have done so in advance of them. But he was no organizer. "The confusion which exists in the different departments exceeds anything I have ever witnessed", wrote Moore in his diary on the 8th of September. Early in October Dalrymple was recalled. But before he left he had sent a good officer in Major-General Lord William Bentinck, the former Governor of Madras, as military representative in Madrid, which had been evacuated by Joseph Bonaparte on the 1st of August. The diplomatic representative with the Central Junta now established there was another able man, Charles Stuart, to be succeeded in October by the former Minister in Spain, Canning's gifted friend, John Hookham Frere, who knew the Spaniards well, and was devoted to the cause of the country. Nor were Ministers at home wanting in covering northern Spain with a network of military and civil agents. Sir John Moore, who now succeeded to the command, had a special source of information of his own in that most fiery and quixotic of men, Thomas Graham. A temporary colonel of the 90th Regiment or Perthshire Volunteers, which he had himself raised at enormous cost, he did not yet despair of attaining permanent rank in the army, as Lord Paget had done in somewhat similar circumstances, and attached himself to the Commander-in-Chief in Spain as a volunteer aide-de-camp. It was now fifteen years since his military talents, as well as his extraordinary gallantry, had attracted the notice of Lord Mulgrave, then commanding a brigade before Toulon, and he had discovered his own taste for a soldier's life; and yet after many years of active service he had not been able to overcome the Duke of York's reluctance to admit of any exception to the rule of promotion through the regular line. Graham was past sixty years of age on the 23rd of December, 1808, when he noted laconically in his diary: "Frost in the morning. Tossed by a bullock in the convent yard." Nothing more is recorded of this shock to his system. Yet he not only survived the hardships of the retreat which followed without injury to his health, but the campaign turned out to be the introduction to a new career. The dying recommendation of Moore was to do more for him than Pitt or Melville, or any of his numerous friends in the army or in parliament had been able to do, and he was to find himself at last in the enjoyment of regular rank as a Major-General.

Yet trustworthy channels of information on Spanish military affairs were not established. Several of the officers sent, as must often happen when the authorities have to make their selection from the very few who happen to possess some knowledge of a particular language and people, turned out to be enthusiasts without judgement, and competed with the provincial Spanish juntas themselves in presumptuous self-confidence. The Spanish love of boasting infected even prudent and experienced soldiers. Writing as late as the 14th of November, after the first blows of Napoleon had sent the Spanish left and centre flying, Bentinck actually endorsed an opinion of Graham that the wretched army which remained on the right, in want of clothing, of money and of provisions—much of it made up of wholly untrained troops—could confidently await the event of a battle with a superior force of the armies of France. It is not to be wondered at that he should have been even more at fault in appreciating a distant situation, and that on his first arrival at Madrid at the end of September he should have written home about the operations to be undertaken on the expulsion of the French from Spain. But the disease was caught in its worst form by Frere. He proved to be completely wrong-headed, and because Moore refused to attempt what was impossible, insulted him, and wrote to him as if he was the enemy of Spain.

Besides being guilty of having bad advisers, Ministers in England, as well as everyone else, went wrong in what should have been a matter of ordinary common sense. While all these schemes were being hatched for descending the northern slopes of the Pyrenees, no one seems to have considered what Napoleon would be doing. The Emperor had no greater matter on his hands. His armies were unemployed. It was not to be supposed that he would allow them to remain passive while his brother was driven out of Spain. Throughout September and October he had been marching them out of Germany, where he himself repaired to meet Alexander and to ensure that all would be safe on the side of Austria while he dealt with Spain and Portugal. A famous meeting took place at Erfurt. Kings came there merely to do homage to him and to realize their own insignificance, while the two Emperors signed a treaty of alliance and a joint letter to the King of England, inviting him to listen to the voice of humanity and to enter upon peace negotiations. In replying, Canning asked that the existing Spanish Government should be included in the negotiations. This was refused, and the proposal dropped. But Napoleon had not waited. On the 6th of November he was at Vitoria, twenty miles from the Ebro, at the head of 180,000 men. And it was the line of this river that the Spaniards undertook to hold with just two-thirds of that number, and it was here intended that they should cover the concentration of the British troops at Burgos a few marches behind. Moore was then to co-operate with the generalissimo of the Spanish army. But he only left Lisbon on the 27th of October, though the

DUKE OF PORTLAND'S ADMINISTRATION

bulk of his troops had preceded him some ten days earlier. When he reached Spain he found no generalissimo and no army. Napoleon had proceeded according to plan. While his marshals dealt heavy blows to his right and to his left, scattering the Spaniards like chaff before the wind, he pressed triumphantly on and entered their capital on the 4th of December. There he was waiting to concentrate his strength for a last dash forward to fulfil the remainder of what he had publicly undertaken to do—to plant his eagles on the towers of Lisbon—when his plans were completely overturned by one of the most daring exploits in the annals of war.

Its author, Lieutenant-General Sir John Moore, had now reached the crown of his career. Though not himself to be numbered among great conquerors, he had reached the period of life at which great victories are won; that reached by Nelson at the Battle of Trafalgar, and by both Napoleon and Wellington when they met at Waterloo. He was forty-six years of age. They were years strenuously spent, yet by no means—or even chiefly—in the camp or garrison. Indeed, a more complete specimen of British manhood than Moore it would be impossible to name. It would be hard to find one who evoked more eloquent words of praise from all who knew him. As time passes, and as records come to light which do him more and more honour, it becomes increasingly difficult to appraise him in expressions which do him justice. It is so easy to expatiate on some virtue or merit which will suggest a corresponding defect. The most outstanding feature of Moore's character was that overwhelming ascendancy which enabled him to treat with lofty scorn the follies of a sovereign, the intrigues of a diplomat, or the injustice of a cabinet of ministers, merely because he felt it to be his duty to himself so to do, and his capacity after having done so to banish the whole thing from his mind as one wipes off a spot. Yet he was no hard stern man. No officer was more beloved by every individual who served under him than Moore. Not the least of his claims upon his country was his having trained as his professional sons such men as the illustrious brothers Charles William and George Napier, each of whom performed many acts of heroism, was several times wounded and distinguished in battle, and rose to be a general. He had a fascinating wit in conversation. He shone in society as in the field; he was the favourite friend, and might, had he wished, so far as such a thing may be predicated of any event dependent upon the fancy of a girl, have become the husband, of the niece of either of the two great rival statesmen of his time, of the gay and witty Hester Stanhope or the quietly brilliant Caroline Fox. He was perfectly honest and simple. Yet he was far from being unread in books and in the affairs of civil life, and he was as much at home in a court or in the room of a Minister of State as anywhere else. He had the faculty of being almost always right, and of looking on matters from a large and lofty standpoint—gifts apt to irritate others, but not in the case of one who, as Moore's letters and his wonderful diary show, reached his conclusions so easily and so simply, who was too much a man of the world to be importunate in pressing his views, and who had too good a sense of humour and of fitness to talk big without occasion. His perfect features were redeemed by a mouth expressive of playfulness and refinement, his great vigour of body by a singular grace of person.

Such was the man to whom was given the heavy task of saving a ship which was already sinking. In the course of the campaign which followed, Francis Jackson was reminded of Haugwitz having said to him in what he called his impudent cool tone, soon after his arrival as Minister at Berlin, "You Englishmen are always two months too late." For most of the delay the Government at home and Dalrymple in Lisbon were responsible. In particular the Ministers, who had lavished their dollars on the juntas, kept their own generals short of cash, hoping by these means to induce the two nations of the Peninsula to accept a paper currency. This embarrassed the Commissariat, already inefficient enough, consisting as it did of civilians appointed by the Treasury, who were little better than bankers' clerks. Moreover, Moore himself had been trained in an extremely deliberate and cautious school. He was unable to satisfy himself that artillery could pass by any of the roads running directly north-east towards Burgos. He consequently sent his guns and cavalry under Lieutenant-General John Hope by a wide detour south of the Tagus.

There was another cause of delay. Moore had been given his choice whether to carry his troops to northern Spain by sea or by land. He was fortunate to have chosen the latter, for Lieutenant-General Sir David Baird, who reached Coruña on October the 13th in command of 15,000 officers and men, was kept for nine days till the Spanish authorities gave him leave to land, and when he did so he was embarrassed by the same want of transport animals and money as Moore. The force was followed by the cavalry brigade, nearly 4,000 strong, under Lieutenant-General Lord Paget. This in turn was not completely disembarked until November the 13th, by which date Moore had already marched the 250 miles which separated Lisbon from Salamanca. Here he was met by the news that Burgos, the original point of concentration, still nearly 150 miles distant, was occupied by the French. It was useless for the present to proceed. He halted to allow Baird time. Here he learnt the successive defeats of the Spanish. On the 28th he heard that their right had been routed. No army remained between him and the French. The natural line of march from France by Bayonne south-westwards into Spain, if continued from Burgos, lay direct on Salamanca and Lisbon. The French covering cavalry were already several marches ahead of Burgos. He had no means of knowing that the mass of the French army had been directed southwards upon Madrid. To attempt to effect a junction with Baird at some point in advance, or even at Salamanca itself, was to risk being defeated in detail. He sent him orders to return to the coast and come round to Portugal by sea, while he himself determined to remain where he was as long as possible, so as to give Hope an opportunity of joining him. That general reached the neighbourhood of Salamanca on the 4th of December. Moore now had the whole of the force which had come from Portugal under his hand, amounting to 20,000 men with thirty guns, and might have commenced his retirement. But news came that Madrid was resisting, and he still stood fast. On the 5th he wrote to Baird countermanding the retreat, and the next day he called him up. "I mean to proceed bridle in hand," he wrote; "for if the bubble bursts, and Madrid falls, we shall have a run for it." He waited another week for Baird to get nearer, and then set out north-eastwards in the direction of the enemy's communications at Burgos. As he did so he learnt from an intercepted letter from the French headquarters to Marshal Soult that Madrid had fallen, but that there was still the chance of a diversion. The effect of Hope's curious circular march, which had brought him round by Escorial only two marches from Madrid, had been to suggest to Napoleon's mind that the British had reached that place, and then retired, and were now in full retreat. On the assumption that there were no English in front of him, Soult was to sweep the country in a westerly direction. On reading the letter Moore decided to incline to his left. He would thus be enabled to join Baird earlier, and they would together fall upon Soult's sixteen thousand troops, which were evidently isolated and further to the west than he had supposed. Moore turned almost due north. On the 18th Baird had reached Benavente, 213 miles south-east of Coruña. Two days later the two converging lines had met. The whole army of 27,000 men, exclusive of troops which had not come up, was concentrated at Mayorga, 25 miles further to the north-east of Benavente.

Moore continued his march with his usual deliberation. He had already 4,000 men sick, as the weather had been exceedingly severe and cold. There were the usual transport difficulties, and a brigade of Baird's was still on its way. At Sahagun, 20 miles further on, he halted for two days. He had already been in touch with Soult through his cavalry, which showed itself superior to the enemy's in quality as well as numbers. It was now the 23rd of December, and Moore had made every preparation for a couple of night marches so as to attack at dawn on the 25th, when news came which convinced him that the diversion had had its expected effect. Napoleon had countermanded his advance south of Madrid, and was now known to be in rapid movement to cut off his retreat. In one of the great objects of strategy Moore had succeeded. The great master of the art of war had been thoroughly mystified. Even now he failed to take the right direction. In terrible weather he succeeded by almost incredible personal exertions in bringing 42,000 men from Madrid over the bleak mountains which separate New from Old Castile in a week from the time when he had decided upon his march. On the 25th of December his headquarters were at Tordesillas, the southern point of a diamond-shaped figure whose sides are roughly fifty miles, and the western, northern, and eastern points are represented by Benavente, Sahagun, and Palencia respectively. He now felt confident. "Put in the newspapers, and make it universally known", he wrote two days later to his brother Joseph who was left in Madrid, "that 36,000 English are surrounded, that I am at Benavente in their rear, while Soult is in their front." But he was too sure of his prey. He did not march from Tordesillas to the north-west direct upon Benavente; although even had he done so it was still possible for the British to have escaped further to the northward. He marched due north upon

Sahagun. He was delayed, moreover, by very heavy rain. He was still at Medina de Rio Seco, less than half-way to Sahagun, and about the same distance from Benavente, on the 28th, when he realized that the British general had already crossed his front and arrived there.

Moore had been in no undue haste. After he had decided that there would be no time to attack Soult, he still remained at Sahagun for nearly 24 hours, and then having three roads to choose from for his retreat to Astorga on the way to Coruña, he allowed the Spanish general, the Marquis de la Romana, who had joined him with 7,000 men, to take the shortest route on the north, sent Baird by the central one, and himself took that nearest the enemy by Benavente. Here most of the troops arriving successively on the 26th and 27th, were able to halt for a day. Here also Napoleon's best troops, if not the Emperor himself, who was still a few miles back, were for the only time in direct contact with the British. The 10th Hussars and the 18th Light Dragoons had already learnt to attack with success twice or three times their number of Soult's cavalry, and now joined by some Hussars of the King's German Legion and headed by Paget and Charles Stewart, obtained a notable success under the walls of Benavente against a slightly inferior force of the cavalry of the guard, capturing their general. But Moore would not allow himself to be approached more closely. Napoleon was not yet to see a red-coat in action. By the 30th, Moore, Baird, and Romana were united at Astorga 38 miles from Benavente. Napoleon still pressed on in pursuit, hoping that Moore might have made a stand. But there were only two days supplies to carry the British the next fifty miles to Villafranca, and Sir John had already reached it when the Emperor entered Astorga on the first day of the new year.

It was useless for Napoleon to pursue further. He had little hope of doing so with any better prospect than that of fighting some more or less indecisive action, and then

DUKE OF PORTLAND'S ADMINISTRATION 255

watching the British embark. It was impossible to make use of his cavalry, his artillery, or the superior numbers of his infantry effectively on a single mountain road. Time had been lost, and affairs nearer home now called him back. There was no haste. He made his way at leisure back to Valladolid, which he only quitted for France on January the 17th, 1809, the day after the Battle of Coruña. But there was no time to carry out the second part of his programme—to plant his eagles on the towers of Lisbon. Moore's adroit diversion had, as he himself claimed, answered completely. On this, the first occasion on which a British general had crossed his path, all Napoleon's plans had been deranged. That the Spanish generals did not take better advantage of the opportunity which Moore had given them was unfortunate. They did make head again, only to be once more defeated; and this was to happen again and again. The one chance—as Napoleon saw—of subduing this people with even 180,000 men, was by the prestige of a victorious march in two giant strides through the whole length of the Peninsula, taking a capital in each stride; and he was baulked of the second one. The pursuit was left to Soult, who had already joined Napoleon by the northern road which Romana took, inflicting a heavy defeat on him on the road.

Many officers and men who passed through that terrible experience have related the horrors of the British retreat over the Galician mountains to Coruña, the soldiers' wives —whom a mistaken kindness had allowed to follow the army in even greater numbers than the rules permitted— giving birth to children in the snow, their babes perishing of frost, the soldiers turned drunken marauders, left insensible, and slashed by the French troopers as they rode by scorning to make such men prisoners, or hanged by the peasants in revenge for their ill treatment, those who still kept in the line famished, shoeless, and footsore pressing forward on the unending road, the stores necessarily or unnecessarily destroyed, the foundered horses shot in heaps, the guns abandoned, even the military treasure heaved over the cliff. Yet Charles Stewart wrote that the most harrowing accounts which he had seen published fell short of the reality. There was no respite but once, at Lugo, where Moore turned at bay. But Soult was too cautious to attack and too strong to be attacked, and after two days halt the race went on. The cavalry which was in touch with the enemy, and the rearguard under Lord Paget's brother, Major-General Edward Paget, kept their discipline, and the whole army whenever, as at Lugo, and again at Coruña, there was word of fighting, became itself again. But for the most part it was as Stewart afterwards wrote—after Astorga the army no longer resembled a British army.

It was necessary to press on without respite, for Moore could not know how many troops were in his rear; and indeed Ney had been ordered to support Soult. The marching had been terribly severe; the distance covered by the British from Sahagun by Benavente to Coruña was 258 miles, and it was accomplished in 19 days; the men were often called up from sleep by false alarms; shelter from the pitiless storms there was little or none; and there were occasions, such as the first fifty miles after Astorga—covered in two days—when the calls made upon the endurance of the troops had been particularly exacting. One brigadier, Robert Anstruther, succumbed before the end of the retreat, and a major-general, Coote Manningham, died soon after his return. Such a toll taken from the leaders gives an idea of what the men must have suffered. There were other things trying to discipline. Second to none in fighting a battle a few hours or days after landing, such as Maida or Vimeiro, British troops had little or no experience of long marches, and of many of the most ordinary hardships of a campaign. Many were young soldiers, and few had mastered the difficult lesson that fighting is one of the least of a soldier's duties. When the order to advance was countermanded at Sahagun, the grenadiers waiting at the foot of the convent stairs were transfixed with dismay. "Nothing", wrote a young officer, "was heard on every side but the clang of firelocks thrown down in despair, which before they guarded as their dearest treasure, and from the high order they were in had placed in them implicit confidence." It was after the second disappointment at Astorga, where it was confidently believed that a stand would be made, that discipline finally gave way. The men wreaked their wrath on the Spaniards through whose towns they passed. It was difficult to understand that character in which the coldest indifference alternated with the warmest enthusiasm. "Why is not every Spaniard under arms and fighting? The cause is not ours; are we to be the only sufferers?" Such are the words which a private soldier used to describe the common feeling in the ranks. Many of the regimental officers were much too incapable to be able to cope with this sort of spirit, or to restrain the men when exposed to the temptation of almost unlimited supplies of wine. Nor was the staff much better. Sir John had been so short of general officers that he was forced during the campaign to call back two military agents, Major-Generals Lord William Bentinck and Charles Leith, and give them brigades. Not even Moore himself had had any long experience of the requirements of march discipline. Baird had, but it was in the luxurious conditions of Indian warfare. Speaking, as he himself said, after the event, the Duke of Wellington could find but one error in Sir John Moore's campaign; "when he advanced to Sahagun he should have considered it as a movement of retreat and sent officers to the rear to mark and prepare the halting-places for every brigade." The same advantage makes it possible to add that he should have taken officers and men more fully into his confidence as to the reasons why so rapid a retreat was necessary.

"I would not have believed, had I not witnessed it,"

wrote Moore in his last despatch, on the 13th of January, 1809, "that a British army would in so short a time have been so completely demoralized. Its conduct during the late marches was infamous beyond belief." But when there was a prospect of fighting, he added, in a phrase which strikes like a refrain through his writings and his life, the men seemed determined to do their duty. That opportunity, so long desired, had at last come. On the 11th he had reached Coruña, only to find that a part of his transports had not yet come in, and that it would be necessary to fight. But Soult was deliberate as usual; it was not until the afternoon of the 16th, when the whole fleet had come in, and Moore had embarked his cavalry and fifty of his guns, and—it was thought—a part of his infantry, that he decided to attack him in the position which he occupied on a ridge south of the town. Of the British army, two brigades had gone round to embark at Vigo, and the four infantry divisions which took part in the battle afterwards disembarked in England 18,854 strong. About 3,000 of these were absent from the action, having been put on board sick. Including the two or three hundred who were killed or missing in the actual battle, as well as two hundred artillerymen, the British general can scarcely have had less than 16,000 men. He thus slightly outnumbered the French, whose 3,000 cavalry were moreover unable to be of much use in so enclosed a country. He had, however, a worse position, and was markedly inferior in artillery, having nine six-pounders not embarked, against the ten heavy guns which Soult had posted on a commanding point of his position, besides ten others elsewhere.

The Battle of Coruña attained a fictitious importance as a set-off to the disastrous retreat. Soult called it a mere reconnaisance in force in his first despatch, and, though it was more than this, it was something less than a regular battle. Only about half the troops on either side took part in the action, and the losses in killed were 192 on the

English and 154 on the French side. It should not have been postponed until there were only four hours left of daylight, had it really been his intention to drive the British headlong into the sea. But thanks to the vigour of his subordinates, the somewhat desultory attacks which he ordered were firmly pressed home. The stress of the fighting was about the village of Elviña, lightly held as an advanced post on the British right; it was captured and recaptured; but the French advanced once more, and had effected a lodgement in it at the close of the action. It was here that Baird, whose division bore the brunt of the fighting, and later on Moore himself, who had followed the unfortunate example of Abercromby in choosing his place in the hottest fire, were both severely wounded by cannon shots, and carried to the rear. The command now devolved on Hope. Moore had not intended to remain merely on the defensive. He had kept two divisions, or one-third of his force, in reserve and, as soon as he saw the French committed against his right, he had launched a counter attack against the enemy's extreme left. The first of these divisions, Edward Paget's, had successfully advanced, and was beginning to menace the battery which had done such deadly work, when night fell. Sooner than fight in the dark Hope decided to persist in the original plan of embarking that night, when the failure of the enemy's attack had left him in some disorder, and the embarkation might proceed unmolested. The French losses in killed and wounded had been 700, and those of the British, who had suffered severely from the artillery fire, perhaps a couple of hundred more, but they had made more prisoners. Each side at the end of the action was holding a more advanced line than at its commencement. Writing at four o'clock the next morning Soult had no notion that Hope had already withdrawn; he half feared an attack on himself, and for his own part, he said, had no intention of doing anything until he could receive reinforcements.

Meanwhile Moore had been carried into Coruña. He recognized at once that his wound was mortal. Meeting an old friend, Colonel Anderson, he said, "Anderson, you know that I have always wished to die this way." He was buried as he wished, near where he had fallen—on the rampart of Coruña, wrapped in his military cloak. Hope compared his death to Wolfe's, whose last moments were cheered by the assurance of victory. The army which he had saved was embarked without serious mishap. It sailed direct for England, as it was unfit to try the fortunes of war elsewhere in the Peninsula until it had been restored. It landed as many as 26,551 strong, and many of the devoted followers of the regiments survived as well, 450 women and children arriving in a destitute condition in Plymouth alone. The total number of fighting men, including the sick and those on lines of communication, had been over 35,000 before the retreat began. The losses of the campaign had thus been about 8,000: Soult claimed 5,000 prisoners, although no more than 2,000 reached France. Perhaps almost as many were men whom he had only been able to capture because they had been left behind in a dying state; and about 600, whether they had been prisoners or not, escaped into Portugal, and afterwards fought honourably at Talavera. But it was not the losses but the condition of the survivors, which struck the public at home with horror. After a rapid and stormy passage Moore's war-worn soldiers were thrown on to various parts of the English south coast almost in the same state as though they had just come from the march and the battle-field—many too in the last stage of typhus, a disease whose ravages continued to spread among the troops long after they had landed. All this shocked a people so unused to the practical horrors of war that it broke into parties violently censuring either the ministers or the deceased general for the state in which it beheld them. Many of those in opposition saw their opportunity and set themselves to canonize Moore, who had been a lifelong Tory, or follower of Pitt, at least, as a Whig martyr to politica intrigue. This was harmless enough, but several went further and began to embrace a view which proved disastrous to themselves as a party and, had it not done so, would have proved disastrous to the state. It was expressed by no one more strongly than by Grenville, who still saw nothing between the old policy of promiscuous descents and abortive expeditions, and one of remaining entirely on the defensive. He was thoroughly convinced, he said in June, that no possible advantage could be derived from continuing to keep up a British force in Spain.

But the House of Commons, at least, was soon spared the necessity of dwelling upon such unhappy affairs by a diversion peculiarly to its mind—a royal and military scandal. The Duke of York's mistress, Mary Anne Clarke, was proved to have systematically sold her interest with him as Commander-in-Chief in military commissions and promotions. Now that she was discarded and in want of money, she roundly accused him of corrupt connivance. The House had the pleasure of several times examining and cross-examining the lady, who treated it with very little respect. For many days and nights the examination of Mrs. Clarke and the other witnesses went on, and at the end a fortnight was spent, while almost every prominent member delivered his judicial opinion. However conscientiously held, it nearly always coincided with party. Speaker after speaker on the ministerial side thought the Duke innocent, while those on the opposition benches pronounced more or less for his guilt. It was obvious that, in such a case, the majority would follow the lead given by Perceval in what was probably the best speech which he had ever delivered, and refuse to find York guilty. But, as previously in the case of the charges against Melville, there was one quarter to which the House might look for an opinion unbiassed by faction or favour. Wilberforce, the leader of the small party known derisively as the Saints, acquitted the Duke of corruption, but gave his opinion that it was unlikely that he could have been free from any suspicion of Mrs. Clarke's practices. Such must have been the judgement of almost anyone who carefully and without bias studied the voluminous evidence; and accordingly, York, in spite of his having obtained a resolution of the House in favour of his innocence, resigned, and the matter was allowed to drop. Shameful as all the revelations had been, it did not come out that any incompetent person had been able to purchase a commission or a step by a corrupt channel. On the contrary there was considerable evidence of the upright and business-like way in which the Duke's office worked, and a letter written to his Darling Love, as he called her, gave unimpeachable proof of the energy with which he had been carrying out his inspections. It is significant that among the first fruits of his succession by General Sir David Dundas was the irregular promotion of Lord Burghersh, the son of a Cabinet Minister, a deviation from rule which it was observed in both Houses that the past Commander-in-Chief could never have committed.

The author of the account of Mrs. Clarke's examination in the Annual Register was led to reflect upon the change of manners which had taken place, and the very different treatment which the gaiety and levity of that pert hussy had received from a somewhat dissolute and frivolous House of Commons from what she would have experienced at the hands of the Long Parliament. Out of doors the attitude was very similar. Instead of tossing "heads and tails" in the streets, it was "Duke and Darling". But there was a deep undercurrent of exasperated feeling. Several scandals were brought to light either in the course of this proceeding or through the reports of the various bodies which had been appointed under successive governments to investigate abuses in public offices, the navy, the army, the West Indies, Ireland, the patronage of the East India Company, and the disposal of captured Dutch property. One of the Bishop of London's chaplains had left a note at the Prime Minister's house offering him £3,000 for a deanery. Another aspirant tendered Mrs. Clarke money if she could get him made a bishop, and she actually succeeded in getting for him the opportunity of preaching before royalty. A firm which carried on the business of the sale and brokerage of offices was prosecuted by Government for conspiracy, and Perceval got a bill passed making the trade a punishable offence if carried on by an individual. The Select Committee of the House of Commons appointed to inquire into East India appointments found that as much as £3,500 each had been paid for writerships. It made Castlereagh confess that he had been implicated in a curious transaction. When President of the Board of Control, he had been given a writership which he had placed at the disposal of a political supporter to facilitate his coming into parliament. Castlereagh was made to recant his error, and somewhat narrowly escaped the censure of the House. Scarcely was this over when he was again arraigned along with Perceval. A resolution of the House of Commons in the days of Lord North's administration had declared it to be a high crime and misdemeanour in any minister or servant of the Crown to interfere in the election of members of parliament. It had been notoriously neglected by both parties at the last two general elections, and when it was now brought forward in the case of Perceval and Castlereagh on account of a seat which had been purchased from the Treasury, an immense majority was found to be against any enquiry. Wilberforce, however, spoke and divided for the minority, and his name as well as Grattan's appeared in the division list along with those of implacable members of the Opposition such as Samuel Whitbread and Sir Samuel Romilly, and staunch radicals such as Lord Cochrane and Sir Francis Burdett. But the worst scandals of all were dragged to light in the case of Ireland. The frauds committed on the revenue by the licensed distillers in that country amounted in a year to £856,000; and of 32 excise officers examined by the Commissioners appointed for this particular enquiry, 30 had admitted receiving regular presents from the stills in their walks. John Croker somewhat cynically defended this on the ground that it was sufficient proof of their corruption that they were alive, as, until recently, their salaries had been, even in the case of surveyors, no more than £65 a year as settled in the reign of Charles II. The Government wished that they should be indemnified against any proceedings. But this was too much for the House of Commons, and it threw out the proposal.

All these revelations, combined with the growing pressure of high prices and high taxation, produced a burst of feeling outside the walls of Parliament. Cobbett, who had by this time come clearly forward as a radical reformer, published a lively calculation by which he showed that the persecuted Castlereagh had divided with five or six of his relations about three millions of public money in the past thirty or forty years. It was felt, in fact, that public money was not being properly spent; and when Lord Grenville, who could not be happy until all the world was as gloomy as himself, complained loudly of the indifference of the people to an increase in the expenditure of £9,000,000 in two years, he underrated the effect of the finances on the prevailing discontent. A genuine popular agitation for parliamentary reform had now begun, and, as Tierney told the House of Commons, what many understood by it was a relief in taxation. The cause was that of a small body of men much stronger outside parliament than inside, known as the patriots. It did not receive much countenance even from the leaders of the Opposition. Windham, who was indefatigable during this session in pointing the moral of his old master Samuel Johnson that people erred in ascribing to governments what was the effects of their own vices or folly, told the House that there was one remedy, which he knew that they would not adopt, but which would do away with all the prevailing troubles as by a charm. "Let every man resolve to live with no greater measure of enjoyments than his father did before him, than people of the same rank and class did forty years ago." The standard of living had certainly, as the elasticity of the revenue showed, kept pace with the demands of the tax-collector; and that personage stood exculpated.

But, as no one would have taken Windham's advice, discontent continued to prevail. Meetings were held. One at the Crown and Anchor in particular attracted great notoriety. Fresh from it one of the patriots, William Smith, convulsed the House of Commons by slipping inadvertently into the words "And now gentlemen". Canning asked it whether it was to listen only to those among its members who came reeking from those meetings. Yet the tables were turned on him a few days later when Whitbread pointed out that he was himself a taverner. Canning had —most indecently and unconstitutionally according to him —made a declaration of foreign policy at the London Tavern. He was abreast of his time, and Whitbread was here the reactionary. This growing sensitiveness of Parliament to what was thought of it outside actually resulted in the passing of a mild measure of reform. Introduced by John Curwen, a conscientious Whig country member, who thought that the legitimate landed interest had, ever since Pitt had transferred so many great proprietors to the House of Lords, been unfairly swamped by the interest of those speculators and fundholders who were the aversion of Cobbett, it fell into the hands of Perceval, who saw to it that the measure, a very modest one at the outset, should be rendered even more harmless. As passed it made illegal the sale of a seat in parliament, as well as any express agreement to barter places in return for parliamentary support. Perceval would not even have gone so far as this but for the powerful intervention of the Speaker, and he was severely criticized for emasculating the bill. But few of those who did so saw that the whole subject of reform was being attacked at the wrong end. Romilly was one of the reformers; yet he conscientiously thought it the most honourable thing which he could do, under prevailing parliamentary conditions, to buy a seat. So long as parliamentary interest was closely attached to property it was capable of being bought and sold, and a candidate for parliament had usually either to buy or to attach himself to someone who possessed the interest as patron. The right remedy in both cases was not to make the thing illegal, but to make it not worth doing. The way to prevent the sale of seats was to put an end to the intimate union between political interest and property. The way to prevent the use of official patronage to obtain parliamentary support was simply to deprive ministers of their patronage by devolving it on independent boards of advisers, or throwing posts open to public competition. This last idea as yet occurred to no one. But Burdett was emboldened at the end of the session to sketch a comprehensive scheme of parliamentary reform, including equal electoral districts with similar qualifications, voting to be in each parish and to be concluded the same day. He got 16 to vote with him.

During the session Perceval had developed a high talent for obstructiveness. He refused to allow the burning question of the Irish tithes to be touched, although it was to the interest of the Church to do something, and although such good Tories as Redesdale and Arthur Wellesley had recognized the fact and put schemes before him. The eloquence and sincerity of Erskine had carried through the House of Lords a Bill for the Prevention of Cruelty to Animals, which would have been the first enactment to vindicate the rights of the animal world in Europe. Perceval joined with Windham in obstructing its progress, and it was thrown out. On the subject of sinecures he surpassed himself. Henry

Bankes, a supporter of his own, had proposed their abolition. Perceval replied that as the means of rewarding public service, they were a fundamental principle of the constitution. This doctrine actually found general support even from leaders of the Opposition, partly because it was feared that if sinecures as a means of rewarding past services were replaced by pensions, the latter would cost the public more. In a House so disposed Perceval had very little trouble over his budget, particularly as he proposed no new taxes for Great Britain. The loan of £14,600,000 of which £3,000,000 were for Ireland and £600,000 for Portugal, was raised at an interest of £4 12s. 10d., the lowest ever known. He claimed, and his predecessor at the Exchequer agreed with him, that it was a proof of the prosperity of the country. But it was also the fact that there was not much commercial speculation, and idle money was forced into the stocks.

The presumption of a foreign government had caused some small embarrassment to the finances of the country. Much in the same way as a son who has thrown off his father exhibits the first intimation of returning good will in the shape of a cheque upon his account, Austria having again gone to war with France and become in consequence once more a friend of England, had drawn bills upon that country to the amount of a round £300,000. This confidence was not misplaced. Parliament accepted the Government's proposal to honour Austria's drafts, provided that the practice should not be drawn into precedent.

In the efforts which Canning was making to restore good relations with as many Powers as possible, he did not allow narrow party considerations to limit him in the matter of his agents. One of these was Robert Adair. Entering public life as the close friend of Fox, he enjoyed the full confidence successively of two Whig and two Tory Foreign Secretaries. It is significant that at a time when England was stigmatized by the rulers of France and Russia as delighting in setting other countries by the ears, Adair, with a long-sighted view of the true interests of his country, was bent on reconciling successively Prussia with Austria, Russia with Austria, and Russia with Turkey, even at a time when the first country at least in each pair was in a state of hostility with Great Britain. In spite of the minatory thunders of France he succeeded in negotiating a peace between George III and the Sultan in January 1809, by pressing upon the Turkish Government the danger to which it was exposed in consequence of arrangements concerted between Napoleon and Alexander at Erfurt.

Another Whig, who was Minister at Washington, the Honourable David Erskine, the son of the late Lord Chancellor, did not serve Canning so well. The American Embargo Act of 1807 had been replaced in March 1809 by a Non-Intercourse Act, prohibiting commerce between the United States and Great Britain or France and their dependencies. A few weeks earlier Canning had taken advantage of the election of a new President, James Madison, to open negotiations for the withdrawal of the Orders in Council so far as the United States was concerned, provided that the Non-intercourse Act was suspended as regards Great Britain, remaining in force as regards France. But Erskine exceeded his instructions. He promised the withdrawal of the Orders with effect from the 10th of June without obtaining any stipulation that the United States would shut her ports against France. His action was repudiated, but not in time to prevent a very large number of vessels sailing for England on that day. Both countries had, however, been the gainers, Great Britain because she had had successive bad harvests, and was faced with a severe scarcity. Wheat was never below £4 a quarter, and rose to over £5 by the end of the year. It was essential to import. Fortunately wheat or wheat-flour was forthcoming not only from the United States, but from France and Holland. The farmers in the last two countries were distressed, so that Napoleon, who regarded gold and not grain as the sinews of war, granted licences for export in order to drain England of her money; and the astonishing spectacle was seen of two belligerents, who had with the grossest injustice thrown the whole commercial world into a ferment in order to destroy each other's trade, trading directly with one another. The import of wheat and wheat-flour into Great Britain during the year amounted to nearly 450,000 quarters. Nor had trade suffered in the aggregate. So effective were the reciprocal systems of license, evasion and smuggling, that Great Britain could show a large increase in 1809, both in exports and imports, over previous years.

By the end of this year almost the whole of the New World, outside the United States, was in the hands of Great Britain or her allies. Early in 1809 a combined British and Portuguese force compelled the distinguished general Victor Hughes to surrender Cayenne and French Guiana. A British and Spanish force reduced San Domingo in the summer. Attention had been earlier directed to Martinique, which had the finest harbour in the West Indies, and furnished the French flying squadrons and privateers with their principal base. When so little remained in the enemy's hands, an effort to wrest from him his capital in that part of the world was worth while. Nothing was left to chance. A force of ten thousand men under Lieutenant-General George Beckwith was conducted in January by Rear-Admiral Sir Alexander Cochrane, and landed in various parts of the island. In order to win over the militia which had a large coloured element, the two commanders issued a proclamation in which they actually apologized for the restoration of the island to France in 1801, and added that they had now come to restore it to prosperity. British rule cannot have left disagreeable memories, for the militia did not resist, and, deprived of support, the regular troops were unable to make a long resistance. On the 24th of February

Martinique was in British hands, the islands called the Saints followed a few weeks later, and after the summer Guadeloupe only remained. Another French colony, on the west coast of Africa, was conquered for a similar reason in July. A small expedition was led from Goree by Commodore Henry Columbine and Major Charles Maxwell of the Royal African Corps against Senegal, which had become a nest of privateers, and obtained its surrender with little difficulty. One desired result of such acquisitions was to relieve the Navy of some of its blockading duties, which it was never possible to perform effectually for any length of time. There had been an example of this in European waters.

In the month of February 1809 when westerly gales had driven the blockading squadron from its station off Brest, the French fleet escaped, but was shortly afterwards discovered to have gone southwards, and joined another squadron lying in Aix Roads. Here they were again blockaded by Admiral Lord Gambier, who lay in Basque Roads, the outer part of the estuary. It was their known intention to make a dash for the West Indies, and save Martinique and Guadeloupe, and it was important to cripple the armament at once. The eleven French sail of the line drawn up in two lines, flanked by batteries, guarded by a boom, and defended on all sides by the network of shoals which protect the intricate channels at the mouth of the Charente, were in much too strong a position to be attacked in the ordinary way. Fortunately the right man for the work was at the very moment available.

Lord Cochrane, heir to the Scottish earldom of Dundonald, was only born in December 1775, but he had already for some years made himself known as an original figure in parliament, while in the Navy his reputation was unique. The most celebrated of his countless acts of daring had been the capture in 1801 of the Spanish frigate El Gamo of 32 guns with a complement of 319, by the Speedy sloop with a complement of 54, and 14 guns of a much weaker calibre. Cochrane once appeared with a whole broadside of her four-pounder guns in his coat pocket. "The great disparity of force", he wrote, "rendered it necessary to adopt some measure that might prove decisive; I resolved to board." The casualties sustained by the Spaniards were more in number than the whole crew of the Speedy. Cochrane was in 1809 a captain commanding a frigate, the Impérieuse. He seemed privileged to go where he pleased, and specialized in attacks on forts and on vessels lying under their protection. Only a few months before, he had signalized himself by his gallantry in assisting the Spaniards to defend the fortress of Rosas, and they admiringly related how when the Spanish flag fell off the wall into the ditch, he alone, regardless of the showers of balls, went down and returned with it. Happening to be in London, he was consulted by Mulgrave on the proposal to attack the French fleet in Aix Roads, already the scene of one of his own most daring exploits. He was told that it was to be by means of the small but formidable class of vessels known as bombs and fireships. The young captain coolly replied that it was a service very easy to be executed. When asked if he would undertake it, he said that he would. The attack was made on the night of the 11th of April. Preceded by explosion vessels which were under Cochrane's personal direction, the fireships drove forward under a strong gale, the boom was broken, and the fireships swept into and through the French ships, scattering them in wild panic. Eleven ran ashore. On the following day Cochrane in the Impérieuse led the attack on the line of battle ships in their disabled state. One French ship of the line struck to his frigate and was burnt. Two more struck to other ships and were burnt, and a fourth was burnt with the French flag still flying. Others were badly damaged by grounding. The fleet was severely crippled for months, apart from the loss of four ships. All this was done in harbour in the sight of thousands of Frenchmen ashore, whom it was in this instance impossible for Napoleon to mislead. No British vessel was disabled, and the losses in officers and men were only 46. But Cochrane was not satisfied. More could certainly have been done had Gambier followed up the attack of the fireships more promptly, and the Commander-in-Chief felt himself obliged to get his reputation cleared by demanding a court martial on himself, which had the expected result.

After an attempt to transfer the line of operations in the Peninsula to the south of Spain had been foiled by the unwillingness of the Central Junta to admit British troops into Cadiz, the Government decided, on Wellesley's advice, once more to try the issue of a campaign in Portugal. The Portuguese Government had bid high for British assistance. It had offered the command of its army to a British officer, and the choice fell on Major-General Beresford, among whose several qualifications was that of knowing the language of the country. It would now be possible to see that the subsidies sent from England to Portugal would not be wasted. It was Wellesley's opinion that an army of only 20,000 British, in aid of 40,000 Portuguese militia and 30,000 regulars, would be able to provide employment for 100,000 French troops, and that there was good hope that, if the Spanish maintained their part of the contest as they had hitherto done, the enemy would be eventually worn out. His view was accepted. He resigned the Chief Secretaryship for Ireland into the hands of Robert Dundas, and departed on that journey from which he was not to return until five years later, and that by way of Paris as a conqueror.

Arriving at Lisbon on the 22nd of April, he found Portugal invaded from the north and threatened from the east. According to Napoleon's last instructions before leaving Spain, Ney was to complete the subjugation of the north-west of the Peninsula. Thus supported, Soult was to overrun Portugal from the north. According to the Emperor's time-table he should enter Oporto and Lisbon itself in the month of February, and so drive the British into the sea. He was to be supported on his left flank by a force of nine thousand men under General Lapisse which, marching south-westward from Salamanca, would form a link with Marshal Victor's army between Madrid and Lisbon. But Portuguese resistance had delayed Soult, who had not gone further than Oporto. The most brilliant British partisan soldier of his day, Brigadier-General Sir Robert Wilson, who had won an Austrian order of knighthood when still a boy, a dashing cavalryman whose life history had been a long romance, had been deputed from England to raise a Portuguese levy long before there had been any thought of placing the whole army of the country under a British officer. With this force, known as the Loyal Lusitanian Legion, he garrisoned the important fortress of Almeida on the north-eastern frontier of Portugal after the troops of his own countrymen had been withdrawn, and, drawing Spanish troops to him by virtue of his military genius, crossed the border and, with a few hundred men, produced such an impression on Lapisse that he gave up all idea of invading Portugal or even opening up any sort of connection with Soult, and turned down southwards to join Victor.

After due consideration Wellesley concluded that Portugal was safe on that side for the moment, and that he was free to carry out his instructions to deliver the country from invasion by turning on Soult, who could now put 21,000 men in the field. He had 25,000 men himself, including the troops which he had brought with him from England, besides the Portuguese. Leaving a force to watch Victor, he took the field himself with 16,000 men, with whom as Marshal-General of that army he was able to brigade 2,000 picked Portuguese troops. On the other hand he detached one of his brigades, 1,500 men, to serve with the main Portuguese force of over 4,000 men under Beresford, which was intended to operate on his right, and to cut off Soult's retreat eastward into Spain. Rapidly and secretly concentrating his force at Coimbra about 100 miles south of Oporto, he was ready to move forward his main body on the 9th of May. He threw Soult's advanced troops back upon Oporto in two engagements, and on the 12th was on the south bank of the Douro opposite the town. Everything pointed to his crossing the river lower down, and the daring operation of that day was a brilliant example of a victory gained by taking a less obvious course. He caught Soult napping, and threw his troops over in two places, one just above, one four miles from the town, right across the line of the retreat which the Marshal had already begun. The danger spot was commanded by guns on the height south of the river on which Wellesley stood, the French resistance soon slackened, and the retreat now began to resemble a rout. Beresford, who had been joined by other Portuguese troops making his force now 10,000 strong, did his part on the right, and shut Soult off from the east, forcing him to take refuge by miserable mule-tracks in the Galician mountains, and almost cutting him off altogether. The French Marshal lost nearly 2,500 men in this retreat, and left behind 1,500 sick, all his guns, his ammunition, his military stores and his baggage. Wellesley had had one loss which was of consequence, and of which he wrote in the most feeling terms; Major-General Edward Paget had been severely wounded just after the first crossing. A few weeks later the whole of Galicia was evacuated by the French. But Wellesley had not pursued Soult beyond the Spanish frontier. On the 19th of May he turned southward to deal with Victor.

He had now obtained the desired permission to advance into Spain, and prepared for a campaign on the Tagus which, passing by Toledo, 45 miles nearly south of Madrid, runs past Talavera, Arzobispo, and Almaraz almost due westward until it reaches the Portuguese frontier soon after passing Alcantara, 130 miles from Toledo. Victor was endeavouring to maintain himself in the rugged inhospitable country lying between that river and the Guadiana, which takes an almost parallel course about sixty miles to the south. He was too weak to advance either into Portugal or southwards into Andalusia, and in the middle of June he was compelled by want of food to evacuate the whole country and fall back on the upper Tagus. Wellesley was confident of driving him back on Madrid, and recapturing the capital. He had 20,000 men with him, and the Spanish General Cuesta was marching up from the south with 40,000. Victor had 25,000. A diversion by means of another Spanish force operating from the south-east under General Venegas was intended to make it impossible to reinforce the Marshal from Madrid. But Wellesley was much delayed, principally from want of money, which also prevented his reinforcements from reaching him rapidly. It was not until the 3rd of July that his advanced guard entered Spain. On the 23rd an opportunity was lost of attacking Victor at Talavera before he could be reinforced, owing to the impracticability of Cuesta. The French Marshal escaped eastwards, to be joined two days later by the corps of General Sebastiani, and the troops of the intrusive King of Spain, Joseph Bonaparte himself, who was in chief command, with Marshal Jourdan as his Chief of the Staff. The French force consisted now of 46,000 men and 80 guns. Venegas had not conformed with his instructions, and the diversion had been a failure.

The French were now the attackers. The allied army was composed of nearly 21,000 British and 32,000 Spanish, each force having 30 guns. The main battle was preceded by two very unfortunate incidents. In the afternoon of the 27th Major-General Alexander Mackenzie's division, which had been in advance of the main body, was surprised while resting in a wood, and lost nearly 450 men. Wellesley himself narrowly escaped capture. There was almost a panic among some of the younger soldiers, and the situation was only restored by the firmness of the 45th regiment, and five companies of the fifth battalion of the 60th Rifles which were with Mackenzie's division, the other five having been distributed among five other brigades to provide them with skirmishers in order to meet the skirmishing tactics of the French. Nor did the unfortunate effects of the episode end here. So occupied was the Commander-in-Chief with seeing that the subsequent withdrawal to the main position was carried out in good order that he was unable to be present when the different divisions took up their ground to await the French attack, and some confusion resulted. In the evening Wellesley's attention was distracted by another untoward incident. A disgraceful panic occurred among four Spanish battalions, appalled by the presence of a few French horsemen who discharged their pistols at them and by the noise of their own musketry. That part of the line was short by some thousand men and some guns on the following day.

The Spanish army was not destined to undergo further trials in the battle of the 28th of July. It occupied a strong position only a mile long, covered with small enclosures, its right resting on the walled city of Talavera. The line was prolonged northward for another mile and a half by Campbell's division standing on somewhat similar ground, and by Sherbrooke's and Hill's along an open ridge. The remaining infantry division, Mackenzie's, took ground where it could, one of its two brigades, Colonel Donkin's, finding a place in front of Hill's division on the most northerly and highest part of the ridge. Beyond this, still to the north, was left a narrow plain where it was possible for cavalry to operate. It is characteristic of the methods of the high command of that day, particularly under Wellesley, that in scarcely one of the numerous accounts of the battle is there a single allusion to any act of any member of the headquarters staff. Wellesley was not there on the evening of the 27th, and consequently brigades which imagined themselves to be in second line were really in first line.

DUKE OF PORTLAND'S ADMINISTRATION 277

The key to the whole position, the highest point of the ridge, was moreover not occupied at all, and the ground in front of it was weakly held by Donkin's brigade. The 37,000 French infantry were mainly aligned on a slightly lower ridge also running north and south, separated from the British by a brook, the Portiña, celebrated ever since that day for one of the strangest of the amenities which have alleviated the ferocity of war.

The auspices were far from favourable. Mistakes had been made in both the allied armies and considerable losses had been sustained, while the French had scarcely suffered. The British had several second battalions whose ranks were filled with young soldiers; and it was observed that in these were more knapsacks with the names of the militia regiments from which the men had recently been drafted than of numbered regiments. Yet almost every one had entered the army provided with a tranquil belief, somewhat extraordinary in the light of the history of the preceding fifty years, that nothing could stand up against a British soldier; and this stood them instead of discipline and experience. This stoutness would hardly have saved them had it not been for the presumption and want of judgement of one of the French commanders. Marshal Victor, who knew the ground, and possessed the ascendancy always enjoyed by him who can devise a plan when others cannot, was able to enforce his will upon the rest of the army. He at once saw that the key of the British position lay exposed. Soon after nightfall on the 27th he sent one of his divisions against it, and easily made himself master of the height. Major-General Rowland Hill was on the alert. He galloped to the top to see what was the matter, and found himself among the French. One of the men caught hold of him, and he broke away with difficulty, and galloped down under a volley which killed his brigade major who was with him. A few minutes later he had re-formed one of his brigades, and swept the single regiment which had been able to find its way up, off the height. The danger was now past. Shown where his weakness lay, the British Commander in Chief strengthened the position, himself taking post there with his staff, and brought up four guns.

Victor had intended his capture of Wellesley's position to be a surprise for his own chief, Joseph Bonaparte, as well as the British; but he did not renew the effort without informing him of his intention, and he was actually allowed to repeat his partial attack. At dawn of the 28th the same troops again advanced, supported by a violent cannonade. Once more they reached the height, and once more they were disastrously thrown back by the same men as before. Wellington had made Hill's division lie down behind the brow of the hill, and when the artillery fire ceased they rose and poured in a volley of musketry. As the French column wavered, exposed to the fire of the long British line and to a flanking fire as well, the order to charge was given, and one wing of the 29th regiment and the first battalion of the 48th dashed down and pursued the flying Frenchmen across the ravine.

The battle was now stayed. The heat was excessive, and induced a temporary truce; and the troops so lately in violent conflict descended and drank together of the loathsome water of the Portiña and carried away their wounded. The battle was renewed about noon. Victor still professed himself confident of success. He undertook to capture the height for which he had twice so fiercely striven, if a simultaneous attack were made on the British centre and right. Wellesley on his part now made a final provision against the danger. He obtained a liberal supply of troops and guns from Cuesta. Having nothing of his own sufficiently powerful to cope with the French heavy artillery, he occupied the height with two Spanish twelve-pounders, whose plunging fire afterwards did good execution on the enemy's columns. He massed his own and the Spanish cavalry in the narrow plain to the northward, and placed a Spanish division on the slopes of the mountain on the further side.

The French attack, when it came, was beaten back everywhere. It was nearest success against the division of Wellesley's second in command, Lieutenant-General John Sherbrooke, in the centre. Here the Guards, advancing too freely after thrusting off their opponents, were caught in disorder and themselves thrown back. Mackenzie brought up the brigade under his own personal command and averted disaster, but was himself killed in doing so, as was Brigadier-General Ernst von Langwert, who commanded one of the heavily taxed brigades of the King's German Legion further to the left. Here the fight was restored by the First 48th, which had already done so much. It was at that moment free to be sent down from the height by Wellesley to cover the retreating Germans. Further still to the left, where Victor's troops were engaged, the division which had the duty of advancing straight across the Portiña ravine failed, its general, Lapisse, falling at its head mortally wounded. The attack round by the plain against the key of Wellesley's position was never pressed home. As Victor's remaining two divisions were advancing, they were met by a charge of the 23rd Light Dragoons. There were no ground scouts, and the regiment, thrown into disorder by an unexpected water-course, was unable even to attack the French squares, and broke against the cavalry held in reserve beyond them, passing through and circling back with the loss of nearly half its number. But the infantry had been checked; they could still see many thousands of cavalry, British and Spanish, in reserve, while the Spanish division was ready to open a fire on their right flank if they advanced. The battle came to a standstill. Joseph's reserves —6,000 men—were never used.

Both armies kept their positions while daylight lasted, but during the night the French retired, and the allies remained undisputed masters of the field. The British losses in the two days were 5,363, of whom nearly 4,000 were wounded. The French lost 7,268, besides 17 guns captured on the left of the line by an advance of Brigadier-General Alexander Campbell's division, and a bold and well-timed charge of the Spanish cavalry regiment known as the King's. The Spanish losses were about 1,200. In spite of the share which these troops as well as the British cavalry bore in the action, the general description of it as a battle in which between 15,000 and 16,000 British infantry successfully repelled the attack of about double their number of French troops supported by a much more powerful artillery, is justified. It was a glory to British arms, won by hard fighting under terrible conditions of thirst and almost starvation on the British side against an enemy consisting—but for one division of Germans—almost entirely of seasoned French troops. Stewart wrote to his brother Castlereagh that there was scarcely an officer in the army who could not show the marks of the enemy's fire about him. Wellesley himself was struck by a spent musket ball. He wrote to Richmond that he could not tell how he had escaped.

Talavera was one of the several fruitless battles of the Peninsula War. Its place in the campaign of which it forms a part much resembles the presumed place of Moore's battle in his campaign, had he fought Soult before beginning his retreat. Indeed, the situations of the British army in the last days of December 1808 and of July 1809 were much alike. Like Moore, Wellesley was to find that he had brought five enemy corps on his head. He had received welcome reinforcements, Craufurd's Light Brigade and the almost equally celebrated Chestnut Troop of Horse Artillery, on the day after the battle. But the rest of his men had been on short rations, and, exhausted by heat and fighting, were in no condition to pursue for a day or two. On the 30th he heard that the Puerto de Baños, the pass on his left rear over the mountains separating the Tagus valley from Leon and Old Castile, was threatened. The enemy in this quarter was Soult, who, a month earlier, had been placed by Napoleon in command of three army corps, his own and those of Marshals Mortier and Ney, a force amounting to 50,000 men. So possessed had the ardent British general been of the spirit of the attack, that he had left it to the Spanish general to secure his flank against a raid, which was all he feared. Cuesta had merely posted two very small battalions at the Puerto de Baños.

On the day when Wellesley's apprehensions were first aroused, the first of the three corps from the north, that of Mortier, was already forcing the pass, with the other two close behind. Soult would have been earlier had he not been obliged to wait for artillery to replace that which he had lost in May. On the 2nd of August it was known that the French were in Plasencia, only fifteen miles from the north bank of the Tagus, cutting off the British army's communications with Portugal by the road by which it had come. Wellesley turned right-about to face the force threatening his rear, leaving Cuesta behind to watch Victor. The direction of the three corps on the Tagus valley had been known in the British camp as early as the first week of July. It was hardly to have been supposed that their commanders would have helplessly marked time while the allies drove Joseph from Madrid; it was no unexpected stroke of genius to have concentrated them round about Salamanca on the road to Plasencia in the time; the former town was only fifty miles from Ciudad Rodrigo, where Beresford was and might easily have organized a system of intelligence. But till the last Wellesley, who at this period of his life almost systematically underrated the enemy's numbers, would not believe that there were more than a few thousand men. Even on the 3rd of August, after he had marched a day's march westward from Talavera to Oropesa to encounter the new enemy, he wrote to his ally making light of the danger. "Depend upon it", he said, "you are mistaken in Soult's strength." But the Spanish

general knew better. His view was confirmed on the same
day by an intercepted letter which he was able triumphantly
to despatch to Wellesley, and which put the matter beyond
all doubt. He followed it himself with the whole of his
force, with undue precipitancy abandoning the hospitals
at Talavera, where 2,000 British wounded, who were unable
to get carriage or to limp after the army, either perished
on the way or fell into the hands of Victor. The French
marshal once more advanced. He had been distracted by
Wilson's mixed force of 4,000 men magnified to 10,000—
that enterprising leader having, in Wellesley's own words,
pushed his parties almost to the gates of Madrid, and
showing no great haste to retire—and was without the
support of Joseph and Sebastiani, who were watching
Venegas. But, slow and cautious as was his advance, it was
sufficient to decide Wellesley. Situated as he was, with
18,000 men of his own and 30,000 of his allies, the British
Commander in Chief was in no position to face northwards,
and fight Soult with a river at his back and Victor advancing
on his right rear. He determined, in spite of Cuesta's
objections, to place the Tagus between himself and the
enemy, and that by the nearest way. On the 4th he crossed
it at Arzobispo, 9 miles from Oropesa. Cuesta followed on
the 6th without disaster. But two days later Soult forced
a ford just above Arzobispo, and routed the Spanish rearguard with the loss of thirty guns, including fourteen of
those captured at Talavera and made over to the Spaniards.

Wellesley had been in what he called himself a bad
scrape. But the French thrust was now spent. Soult wished
his advantage to be followed up, but Joseph refused to give
the order. The allies had now taken refuge in the network
of inhospitable defiles between the Tagus and the Guadiana,
a country terrible to any army—most of all to an army
in pursuit, and to which the inhabitants were hostile. The
British soldiers on their part experienced a return to that
golden age the passing of which had been so deplored by

Don Quixote, when men made meals off acorns. A goat's offal sold for four dollars. Bread was fetched from many miles round at three or four shillings for a piece the size of a threepenny loaf. The French had no mind to follow them, in the stupefying heat of a Spanish summer, into the country which Victor had exhausted and abandoned only two months before. Wellesley on his part moved off slowly, lingering as long as there was any hope of resuming the offensive in conjunction with the Spaniards. For a time he feared an invasion of Portugal, and ordered Beresford southwards into the Tagus valley, but by the 21st of August his mind was at ease. He moved southwards to the Guadiana, and finally reached the Spanish frontier fortress of Badajos on the 3rd of September, where he could best watch any attempt at an invasion of Portugal without deserting Andalusia.

His army was in sore need of repair. Supplies had entirely broken down, the army was ravaged by typhus, dysentery, and the Guadiana fever, and there were ten thousand men in hospital, half of whom perished. Discipline among starving men could not exist. Even in his advance Wellesley had found much the same difficulties as Moore. The army, he complained, was a rabble; "we are worse than an enemy in a country". A pause was necessary to give time to restore health and discipline, and to reorganize the commissariat. The whole campaign of the summer of 1809 was no more than an experiment in the possibility of making warfare in reliance on Spanish help over transport and supply and Spanish co-operation in the field. The real struggle was not to begin for another year. Wellesley had started with every fair prospect of success in the attempt at co-operation with the Spaniards. The pains which he had taken to master the language enabled him, a few days only after he had entered the country, to receive and understand a Spanish deputation. In July Samuel Whittingham, then serving as a Spanish brigadier-general, wrote in high praise of his conciliatory manners. "He is just the man", he added, "to please the Spaniards." But Wellesley now found Spanish co-operation to be impossible. One hope remained. On the first day of August his brother, Marquis Wellesley, had arrived at Cadiz on a special mission as Ambassador to conclude a treaty of alliance with the Junta, and had enjoyed a magnificent reception. He did the work for which he had come. He further placed the members of the Junta under a personal obligation by revealing a plot against them which had come to his knowledge. By his advice an early date was fixed for the summoning of the Cortes, in order to bring into one focus the warlike enthusiasm disseminated through Spain. But he was unable in so short a time to induce the Spanish authorities to organize a satisfactory system of supply. Co-operation from that quarter had to be recognized as hopeless. Arthur Wellesley, now created Viscount Wellington, prepared himself to take the field on a new system by which Portugal was to be England's chief ally.

In other parts of Europe attempts were made during the summer to give some help to Austria in the struggle which she was maintaining for the liberties of Europe. During June Sir John Stuart, with the aid of the vessels of Collingwood's fleet, recaptured for the expelled King of Naples two islands off that city, Ischia and Procida. It was an exploit calculated to make Murat tremble for his capital, and fear that the troops facing the Austrian army in the north of Italy might be taken in the rear. But once more Great Britain was two months too late. Napoleon had entered Vienna on the 13th of May. It was found useless and dangerous to retain such conquests, and before the end of July they were again abandoned. On the return of this expedition Stuart sent troops to carry out a service in which both Collingwood and Robert Adair took considerable interest. By his acquisition of the Seven Islands, that small archipelago stretching along the Grecian coast nearly as far as Crete from the mouth of the Adriatic, Napoleon had hoped to convert that sea into something resembling a French lake. He had succeeded in attaching Corfu strongly to his interests. The inhabitants of the remaining islands were anxious to throw off the French yoke and receive the British. As a counterpoise to Napoleon's possession of Corfu, the weaker islands of Zante, Cephallonia, Ithaca, and Cerigo, the last a nest of privateers, were occupied without difficulty during September and October 1809, and the Septinsular flag hoisted along with the Union Jack.

But the diversion made under the direct orders of the Government in London was later even than the only Mediterranean operation intended to affect the Austrian campaign—the capture of Ischia and Procida. Following Austria's declaration of war there had been movements of revolt against Napoleon's dominion in Northern Germany, and the Cabinet first turned its attention to a possible expedition in that part of Europe. It was eventually decided to operate a diversion while pursuing an essentially British object. The Admiralty, habitually uneasy at the accumulation of a naval force in any hostile port, was particularly so as regards the lower waters of the Scheldt. The celebrated saying of Napoleon that that river was a loaded pistol pointed at the head of England applied accurately alike to the river's shape and its direction. An easterly wind would take ships straight down its most important or western channel, across the North Sea, and up the Thames, safe from any interference except from the North Sea Fleet. Since Trafalgar Napoleon had lavished money on the improvement of Antwerp—at the handle of the pistol—while he had obtained from his brother Louis, King of Holland, the cession of Flushing—at the barrel's mouth. Here were ten sail of the line already afloat, and arrangements were being rapidly made to bring the number up to twenty. A joint naval and military expedition was now designed to capture or destroy these ships, and to destroy the dockyards and arsenals of Antwerp and Flushing. It was also intended to maintain possession at the river's mouth of the island of Walcheren on which Flushing is situated. A British squadron riding at anchor here would be able not only to seal up the passage of the Western Scheldt down from Antwerp, but also to command a position to windward of any attempt made upon the Kentish coasts from Ostend with an easterly or north-easterly wind.

As it was necessary to employ the depleted and demoralized regiments which returned from Coruña, the expedition could not have started immediately on the outbreak of war between France and Austria. But by the end of May the effects of the terrible retreat had been removed—Craufurd's Light Brigade, in fact, sailed for Lisbon in the last week of the month—and it was at this time that the Archduke Charles succeeded in administering a severe check to Napoleon on the Danube. The good news did not of course reach England till the second week of June. The occasion had now come. The men were ready; but the transports were not. Meanwhile Napoleon gained a decisive victory over the Archduke at Wagram on the 6th of July, and an armistice was concluded on the 12th. At last on the 28th the expedition sailed. It was the most powerful which had ever left England. The military force was upwards of 39,000 strong. The Cabinet selected one of themselves for the command. It was thought that the return of the Master-General of the Ordnance from a successful exploit on the Continent would give him a prestige which would enable him to be easily accepted as Premier, thus meeting the difficulty expected from the inevitable retirement of Portland on the ground of health. The Earl of Chatham had commanded a brigade creditably in Flanders in 1799, when he had been wounded. For most of the past seven years he had presided over a military department as Master-General of the Ordnance. He was generally recognized as

DUKE OF PORTLAND'S ADMINISTRATION

a man prudent in council, and he showed his prudence in nothing so much as in the cultivation of a dignity and taciturnity which caused him to be thought wiser than he was. But, wise or not, there was a quality more essential in a soldier which he conspicuously lacked. It is strange that an expedition, the success of which depended before all things on rapidity, should have been confided to a man whose sloth was so notorious that he was commonly known as the late Lord Chatham, and whose habits of luxury and reserve were illustrated by a story retailed by Earl Temple that an officer on the staff of this expedition had said that he should not have known of the existence of a Commander-in-Chief had he not seen in his garden at Batz two turtles sprawling upon their backs. The naval force, which reached the enormous total of 35 sail of the line and 208 other vessels of war, accompanied by 400 transports, was under Rear-Admiral Sir Richard Strachan, an officer who had fought gallantly and successfully in the past, but a man of indifferent judgement, and of a hasty and uncertain temper. But the work of dealing with the tortuous sandbanks—the principal foes which the fleet would have to meet—was entrusted to Sir Home Popham, probably the best pilot in Europe.

The trifling result of all this preparation may be dismissed very shortly. Southerly gales compelled the transports to take refuge in the East Scheldt off the north-east coast of Walcheren. Sir John Hope landed his division on the island adjoining it to the eastward, South Beveland; and by the 2nd of August he was in possession of the whole as far as Batz or Bat at its south-eastern extremity, where the West and East Scheldt unite, only twenty miles below Antwerp. Walcheren itself presented more difficulty. Flushing underwent a heavy bombardment of two days, in which the principal part was taken by the Navy. It did not surrender until the 16th. But it was no part of the original plan to wait for this before pushing on to Antwerp. Unfortunately, however, in face of the difficulty of disembarking the cavalry and field-guns, marching them across South Beveland, and then re-embarking them to cross the Scheldt at Bat, to say nothing of the impossibility of doing the same with the heavy ordnance, the transports found themselves committed to the narrow and intricate passage between the two islands. The southerly gales continued longer than was expected, and the inexpressibly tedious labour of warping the transports, or—as Strachan afterwards expressed it for the benefit of those who appeared, like Chatham, to be unappreciative of naval difficulties—hauling them by human labour, southwards against a head wind, lasted so long that it was not till the 23rd that they were in the West Scheldt. They arrived off Bat a day or two later.

Chatham himself did not succeed in reaching Bat till the 24th. It was now found, not only that Antwerp, where the enemy's ships had long removed themselves, was much stronger than had been supposed in London, but that a large force, estimated at 35,000 men, had been collected for the defence of that city and the neighbouring forts. On the 29th the evacuation of South Beveland was begun. All that remained of the acquisitions of this inglorious expedition was the island of Walcheren, a fine frigate, the timbers of a 74, and over 7,600 prisoners or deserters from the French army. The British losses in killed, wounded and missing were not much more than eight hundred in both services. At this cost considerable alarm had been created both in Paris and in Vienna where Napoleon had his headquarters during the armistice between France and Austria. Not only were detachments on their way to the Grand Army diverted, but the Emperor wrote as if it might be necessary to return himself and take command. Had this been merely said in order to stimulate the activities of his Minister of War in Paris, there would have been no reason to allow it to be believed in Austria. Yet such was the case. In a letter to Canning, Gentz wrote that Francis had twice refused a prolongation of the armistice for six weeks to permit Napoleon to take a journey to the low countries and back. How the situation was regarded in Paris appears from a report of the Minister of War to the effect that 150,000 national guards had been collected and formed into three redoubtable armies under three marshals.

The expedition would have justified itself, even though too late to be of substantial use to Austria, but for one circumstance. The unwholesomeness of Walcheren was notorious. It had been the subject of conversation between Popham and the responsible ministers before the expedition sailed. Castlereagh, in fact, had long been fully aware of it, and acted with the blindness to a salient fact characteristic of those who immerse themselves in detail. Napoleon had carefully avoided placing troops there in force for this very cause. British soldiers, partly through the national carelessness, partly through that liberal indulgence in meat and intoxicants called in the language of the day a "full habit", were much more liable to climatic and seasonal disorders than the troops of other nations. Walcheren was occupied just when the unhealthy season was about to begin. The dykes were cut, and the whole country—even the town of Flushing—was under water to the men's knees. Before the middle of August a disease afterwards diagnosed as a bilious remitting fever broke out among the troops. They dropped down with it on parade. Almost the whole of one regiment, the 23rd, was in hospital at one time. South Beveland was not much better than Walcheren. By the 8th of September, two or three days after the evacuation of the former island had been completed, the number of sick in the whole army was almost eleven thousand. But Walcheren was still retained. The members of the Cabinet were so much occupied with one another that they found no time to attend to the situation of the troops left there, still numbering nearly eighteen thousand men.

At the time when the Convention of Cintra was the topic

of the day, Canning had begun to find himself in sharp difference with some of his colleagues. His attitude towards the soldier in the field was far from generous. The Cabinet had, in his view, lost ground in public estimation by assuming responsibility for events for which it was not itself to blame. The last of these was the result of Moore's campaign. On the 24th of March he wrote a letter to Portland, offering to resign. His principal objection appears to have been to the inadequacy of Castlereagh's defence of the conduct of the war, but at the same time delicate questions, in which foreign relations and military dispositions reacted upon one another, had undoubtedly arisen in the Peninsula. It was no secret, even to outsiders, that there was a struggle in the Cabinet. It was obvious that the less able of the two ministers responsible should give way. The King preferred the solution of removing Castlereagh from the War Office. There can be no doubt that Canning was actuated in part by a natural—though unpatriotic—desire to withdraw to a position in which he might escape being involved in the confusion of the impending breaking up of the Ministry, and make a surer grasp at the vacant Premiership. For it was obvious that Portland, aged and broken down with the excruciating torment of the stone, was, as he recognized himself, no longer adequate to his duties, even according to his own mild conception of them. He was an unique example of a modern Prime Minister who does not appear once as a speaker in Hansard's Parliamentary Debates during his two years and a half of office. Nor was this silence in public set off by any fertility of resource in council or energy of action. On the contrary it was only thanks to the superior vigour of the King that any decision was come to at all upon Canning's repeated importunities. The ill health of Portland worked, however, in a way different from that which the Foreign Secretary had hoped. It made him first unwilling to decide upon Castlereagh's removal, and then desirous to put it off on one pretext or another.

He was seconded in this by another member of the Cabinet, Camden, who as a near relative of the Secretary for War had to see that his feelings were spared as far as possible in the manner in which the change was made, and who had agreed to facilitate the arrangement by retiring himself. It was intended that Castlereagh should remain in the Cabinet, being succeeded in the War Department by Lord Wellesley, then about to set out on his mission to Spain. Finally Canning was obliged to agree to the change being deferred till after the termination of the expedition to the Scheldt.

Meanwhile he had become engaged in a correspondence with Perceval relating to a yet higher interest. In August Portland had a fit in his carriage, and his life was for a time in danger. His retirement was now imminent. Perceval and Canning were at one in desiring to see him succeeded by a really responsible Prime Minister. One thought of Harrowby who had in July succeeded Dundas as President of the Board of Control, the other of Chatham. Harrowby refused. The failure of the Walcheren expedition made Chatham impossible. Canning now thought that the game was at his feet. "I have for some time been convinced—and every month's experience tends to confirm that conviction more and more", he wrote on the 31st of August, "that a *Minister*—and that Minister in the *House of Commons*—is indispensable to the well-carrying on of the King's Government in these times." For the moment Perceval patriotically intimated that he was willing to serve under Canning. He would have had to cease to be Chancellor. For the traditional preponderance of the Chancellorship of the Exchequer was so great that it was then supposed that if the Prime Minister was in the House of Commons—and he had been so with only one short interval for nearly a quarter of a century—he could not be merely the Foreign Secretary. But Perceval found that his own friends and a large section of public opinion would have objected to the sacrifice which he was inclined to make. He now wrote that he was unprepared to give up the Chancellorship. Worse followed. On the 6th of September Canning heard from Portland that Castlereagh's removal was again postponed, that other ministers, or at least one other minister, would resign in that event, and that the Premier himself had also determined to retire. He now tendered his resignation through Portland to the King, who accepted it, asking him to carry on the duties of his department until relieved. Portland's own resignation followed, as did Castlereagh's on hearing all that had been intended for him; and Canning now found himself forced to the most desperate shifts in order to get Perceval out of the way at any price. He might be made a Peer and President of the Council, with the Duchy of Lancashire for life. He even got Portland to suggest his being made Lord Chancellor, to Eldon's extreme annoyance. He obtained an audience of the King, and told him that he would readily undertake to form an administration. George saw clearly how ill-considered as well as presumptuous the proposal was, although it had Portland's support; he told Perceval that Canning's conversation was the most extraordinary that he had ever heard. All the efforts of the younger man were unavailing, and when the eight members of the truncated Cabinet—shorn for the moment even of the counsels of the Earl of Chatham—met at the house of the Chancellor of the Exchequer to deliberate on the future of the administration, it could no longer be doubted who would be its head.

But before a new Ministry was in office there occurred an act of blind folly, for which the blame must be very widely shared. On the 7th of September Castlereagh learnt for the first time of the decision to remove him. He made the exasperating discovery that those with whom he had been associating for months had been in possession of a fact to his disadvantage, the knowledge of which they had sedulously concealed from him. But Castlereagh was dull-witted enough to mistake this natural feeling of irritation for a sense of insulted honour. He could not, and did not, resent the demand for his removal from his office. So far as the practice of secrecy towards him was concerned, his own relative Camden, Portland, even the King himself, were even more responsible than Canning, who had pressed for disclosure, and had at one time believed it to have been made. But Castlereagh chose to visit only on the last his wrath at having been deceived, and having thus been induced to remain in a situation which he would have left at once had he known the facts. He discovered a distinction between the kindly motives of his friends and those of Canning which were the reverse—a perfectly logical deduction from the diabolical malice which he had chosen to impute to him without any grounds. On the 19th of September he sent him a challenge. The custom of the time left Canning but one reply. On the 22nd of September the two former colleagues met, fortunately without any fatal result. The duel was ended by Canning receiving a bullet from Castlereagh's pistol in his thigh at the second discharge. His overbearing demeanour, his far from scrupulous ambition, and those elaborate movements which made every step he took appear to be part of a grand intrigue, disgusted everyone with him outside the circle of his personal friends, and his conduct was generally condemned. But he was able to publish a complete vindication of his proceedings in this particular at least. He had in fact shown throughout a scrupulous regard for the susceptibilities of Castlereagh.

CHAPTER V

PERCEVAL'S ADMINISTRATION TO THE ESTABLISHMENT OF THE REGENCY

(OCTOBER 1809—DECEMBER 1810)

THE task of carrying on the King's government left after the break-up of the Portland administration in September 1809, seemed to be almost a desperate one. Only one of the remaining cabinet ministers, Perceval himself, was in the House of Commons. Of the rest it could be said of three that they were men of weight, and had even been considered brilliant speakers in their time. These were Eldon, Hawkesbury, and Mulgrave. The other four, Camden, Westmorland, Chatham and Bathurst, were able only to serve as buttresses to an administration. Ministers could expect no help from Portland, who, in fact, died within a few weeks. Meeting with rebuffs and uncertainty on every side, they were driven to the extreme step of asking permission to open negotiations with Grey and Grenville, a matter made difficult by the King's unwillingness to run any risk of the Catholic question being reopened. Perceval explained that under a combined administration this would be impossible; and on this assurance leave was obtained. The two statesmen were at their homes in opposite ends of England. Grey could not leave Northumberland. Grenville came up from Cornwall, only to send a flat refusal. Neither of them had a strong desire for office, and without such desire, or—in its place—an overmastering sense of patriotic duty, it was not to be expected that any man would have sprung forward to grasp the helm of the—so it was thought—sinking ship of state. Yet had a stronger sense of what he owed to his country induced either of them to make a few enquiries before coming to a decision, he might have discovered that there were few obstacles in his path. Either of them would have been accepted as Prime Minister, and the Chancellorship of the Exchequer and two of the Secretaryships of State, and almost any other particular office which he desired, would have been placed at his disposal.

The Cabinet now sent Eldon to the King to convey their request that His Majesty would appoint a First Lord of the Treasury, together with their unanimous opinion in favour of Perceval. The new Prime Minister kissed hands on the 4th of October. Never have England's destinies been presided over by a commoner who had so little genius to compensate for the absence of the influence accompanying title and property. Yet this man was given her at a moment when her cause on the Continent seemed almost hopeless; when relations with the great State across the Atlantic were approaching a climax; and when one who seldom failed in what he undertook was determined to destroy her through her trade. It was also a time when it was desirable, in order to meet the growing discontent at high taxation, to put an end to what was known as government by departments —when, in Canning's phrase, a Minister was indispensable— a man strong enough to resist that tendency of the heads of departments to dip their hands into the public purse without mercy, of which Rose complained. Nor was it by any long apprenticeship that Perceval had won his way to that high place. Born on the 1st of November, 1762, he was of the same age as that at which Nelson and Moore had reached the climax of their lives. But it was less than nine years since he had been first introduced into the Ministry as Solicitor General, and only two years and a half since he had become a Cabinet Minister. He owed his advancement partly to an even temper and sweet reasonableness which brought him friends on every side at a time when distinguished politicians were remarkable for the art of making enemies, and partly to that courage which, as Lord Beaconsfield told Lord Salisbury, was the rarest of all qualities to be found in public men. One of several to whom Perceval unsuccessfully offered the Exchequer, Robert Milnes, spoke of him to Palmerston as an honest little fellow and hoped that it would be possible to fix him firmly in his seat. Such was the sentiment which prevailed among many who refused, as well as those who accepted office.

For Perceval had added to his other difficulties the idea of giving up the Chancellorship of the Exchequer. He hawked it round; but all refused—even old Rose, who preferred to press his views on finance upon the Cabinet from a position of less responsibility. Palmerston, with his usual precocious wisdom, after consulting with another subordinate minister, Robert Plumer Ward, who told him that he thought him quite equal to the task in point of capacity, quietly decided that he was not quite good enough, and chose the post of Secretary at War. Perceval had to keep the Exchequer himself, though he refused the salary. In filling other offices he met with enormous difficulties. Many of his wellwishers were not free agents. Robert Dundas's father, Lord Melville, would not allow him to become Secretary of State for War. Charles Yorke's brother, Lord Hardwicke, would not let him join the ministry at all. It was indeed supposed to be a duty to put ties of family and friendship before the requirements of the public service. A subordinate member of the Government, William Sturges-Bourne, a man of high principle, wrote of Canning: "I cannot hesitate to abandon office, and perhaps Parliament, rather than be suspected by him, or even my bitterest enemy, of having sacrificed obligations and friendship to the love of place." Huskisson was another of the handful who followed Canning in his defection. Sidmouth, moreover, prevented any of his own small party from joining the new Ministry. At last it was determined to give the War Department to Hawkesbury, soon afterwards by the death of his father become Earl of Liverpool. He was succeeded at the Home Office by the Honourable Richard

Ryder, brother of Harrowby, whose own bad health would not allow of his being in the Cabinet. In fact he retired from the Board of Control, where Robert Dundas was permitted by his father to resume his place as President. Leaving Rose to carry on the business of the Board of Trade, Bathurst temporarily took the Foreign Office. He had the opportunity, during his short time, of assuring the deputies from the Austrian Tyrol of his country's warm sympathy with the Tyrolese in the desperate struggle which they were then maintaining against the power of Napoleon, but without encouraging false hopes of assistance. It was not until the 23rd of November that Perceval received news impatiently attended by all the Cabinet. The seals of the Foreign Office had been offered to Lord Wellesley, then Minister with the Spanish Junta in Seville. His decision had been in considerable doubt; he had refused office before; and it had been put about that he was irremovably wedded to the Canning interest. But he took the same view as his illustrious brother was to do on a famous occasion thirty years later—that his sovereign's government must be carried on. He accepted and returned at once, and kissed hands for the Seals on December the 12th. Bathurst went back to his duties at the Board of Trade. With the accession of the great Proconsul the administration felt strong enough to meet Parliament in the following year. But before this took place the capital became the scene of a series of disturbances on a small scale which were the precursors of much graver disorder.

Covent Garden and Drury Lane theatres, the only two regular theatres in London, had both been burnt down within a few months of one another in 1808 and 1809. On the 17th of September, 1809, the proprietors of the former theatre opened their new building. The prices were raised for the boxes from 6s. to 7s. and for the pit from 3s. 6d. to 4s. The theatre-going public became outrageous. It determined to make the performances inaudible till they had the old prices restored. The Morning Chronicle characteristically supported the O.P. men, as they were called. The argument was that the public had a right to express in its usual manner its disapproval of a performance submitted to it, hence rowdiness in the theatre was justifiable. It was useless to attempt either to conciliate the rioters by producing a report signed by eminent city men showing that higher expenses justified the prices, or to put them down by the help of constables, Bow Street runners, boxers, Jews, chairmen and butchers. Nor could much help be got from the courts. Indeed, the law sometimes appeared to be on the other side, and it looked as if the injured Actor Manager, John Kemble, might be indicted for keeping a disorderly house. At last, on the 15th of December, the affair was settled by the pit price being restored to 3s. 6d. But it was long before the O.P. designs on hats and clothes, the O.P. fandango, and the O.P. call, were forgotten.

King George III's jubilee was celebrated on the 25th of October throughout the country by church services, by tawdry displays of temporary architecture and transparencies and other illuminations characteristic of the time, and by generous entertainments of the poor, recognized as the most suitable mode of public rejoicing. A proclamation was also issued pardoning all deserters from the fleet unconditionally, and those from the land forces if they surrendered within two months. But if the ministers of the day derived some strength from royal support, the King on the other hand had to share in the disrepute incurred by servants who had brought so many misfortunes upon the country. The Government met Parliament on the 23rd of January, 1810, in a very chastened mood. Austria had made peace with France on the 13th of October. But the Government was so unwilling to abandon Walcheren that it was not until the 13th of November, or a fortnight after this news had been received in London, that it had been finally decided to evacuate, and not until the 23rd of the following month that, the defences and naval basin having been demolished and a fair wind assured, the last man was withdrawn. The deaths through sickness amounted to nearly 4,000, and the number of soldiers still in hospital when Parliament met, five months after the expedition had been given up, was about 11,500. The evil did not end there, nor indeed until long after the close of the general war. Men were at all times liable to a recurrence of the fever. The Rifle officer, John Kincaid, for example, related that he and a brother officer simultaneously experienced two returns of it, the first five years, and the second eight years after they had first had it.

An enquiry by a Committee of the whole House of Commons was insisted upon, Perceval being defeated by nine votes on the question, and a number of persons were examined, including the general and flag officers engaged in the expedition, those who were in any way concerned in its inception, and the high medical authorities of the army. Having constituted themselves judges of a number of professional subjects, often extremely technical, and especially so where the Navy was concerned, Members made a very poor use of the material accumulated. The most thoughtful and valuable speech of the debate which followed was that of Robert Craufurd's elder brother Charles, also a general, who had succeeded to his seat. But Whitbread expressed the sense of the House when he said that he had indulged in a gentle slumber during a part of the fatigues of the gallant officer's campaign, and did not wake up till he had reached Bergen-op-Zoom. When Sir Home Popham, who knew more of the naval side of the expedition than anyone else, got up at the end of the debate to clear up two or three points, the House took advantage of the Captain's use of a Dutch name in an unfortunate connection to burst into ribald laughter and shout him down. The divisions which took place in such a mood at seven o'clock in the morning of the 31st of March were on party lines, but not entirely so. The Opposition had failed to make out their case that there had originally been no reasonable hope of success. Ministers obtained a majority of forty on the question generally, though they only got one of twenty-three in favour of their prolonged retention of Walcheren. If those inside were puzzled, those outside the House were unable to draw any better conclusion from the evidence, in which the mutual recriminations of the naval and military commanders formed the most outstanding feature, than that which appears from the lines published in the Morning Chronicle of the 26th of February as an Abstract and brief Chronicle of the Documents and Evidence concerning the Expedition to the Scheldt :—

> "Lord CHATHAM, with his sword undrawn,
> Kept waiting for Sir RICHARD STRACHAN :
> Sir RICHARD, eager to be at 'em,
> Kept waiting too—for whom?—Lord CHATHAM."

The honour to Wellington was very badly received. The faults of his campaign were not spared, and his victory put down to the invincible valour of British troops. One veteran officer whose own gallantry in the American War was commemorated on the canvas of Reynolds, General Tarleton, censured his despatches in the House as vainglorious, partial and incorrect. The pension of two thousand a year for three lives, a usual accompaniment of a military title—though it was scarcely necessary in this case—was severely criticized. The Common Council of the City of London presented a petition against it to Parliament. It drew the comparison which had now become fashionable between the treatment of Moore and that of Wellington, and pointed out that, since their return to Europe, the Wellesley family had been in constant possession of the most lucrative offices and emoluments of the State. An amusing imitation of Sterne's Tristram Shandy, applied to the Walcheren expedition, in the Morning Chronicle of the 5th of March, suggested that it was only politicians who could now get the command of armies. The analogy was hard upon Wellington, who thus had to suffer in his own reputation for Chatham's failure, besides seeing crippled the forces on which he had relied for reinforcements.

The parliamentary enquiry into the Walcheren expedition led incidentally to two unexpected trains of events. Each was connected with a constitutional question, the discussion of which furnished a strong illustration of the peculiar English way of political thinking. The first rose out of a narrative which Chatham presented direct to the King justifying his conduct of the expedition, and moreover accompanied by a request for secrecy. When the enquiry was about to begin His Majesty directed him to hand it to the Secretary of State for War, and it was placed on the Table of the House of Commons accordingly. Chatham's proceedings had been entirely out of order, and they were the more objectionable because, in defending himself, he had imputed responsibility for failure to the naval service. But this was not pressed. Chatham had a high character as a man of honour, and no one supposed that he really wished Strachan to be condemned unheard. It might have been supposed enough for some Opposition leader to have observed that the narrative ought to have gone through the regular departmental channel. But Chatham's offence was regarded from a much wider point of view. Whitbread brought up some damnatory resolutions on the subject. Here was a document secretly presented to the King, and intended to influence his opinion on an important question of state, of which none of His Majesty's advisers had, as such, any cognizance. All this called up visions of that secret influence behind the throne, greater than the throne itself, of which the Earl's own illustrious father had so bitterly complained. That there was much exaggeration in this view of affairs was freely admitted by the veteran constitutional lawyer, William Adam. That powerful speaker had, however, little difficulty in showing that the secret presentation of this document was, as it stood, a blow struck at what he called "the three grand and leading features of the constitution", namely, "the responsibility of the King's advisers, the irresponsibility of the sovereign, and the inquisitorial power of parliament". He actually went further and, with an immense display of historical precedent, attempted to show that there never was a period when the King, according to the constitution, acted in public affairs on his own personal authority. The House was extremely sensitive on the old grievance of the King's friends, and it was unanimous in the opinion that Chatham deserved censure of some kind. Perceval was unable to save his colleague; Whitbread carried his constitutional question, as he called it, on the 23rd of February; and the Master-General of the Ordnance was obliged to resign.

It was easy to find a successor. Mulgrave had been finding the duties of the First Lord of the Admiralty beyond his strength. He had been far from a success. The mismanagement, so far as the susceptibilities of naval officers were concerned, of the Basque Roads affair, the one great naval exploit of his three years' period of office, was a crowning instance. Economy was the cry of the day, and, though he had not disregarded, he had done little to advance the claims of the increasing number of men battered and broken, who had lost their health or limbs in their country's service. Cochrane pressed the point with telling effect in the debate on the navy estimates a few days after Mulgrave had left office. "Should thirty-one commissioners, commissioners' wives, and clerks, have £3,899 more among them, than all the wounded officers of the navy of England? I find, upon examination, that the Wellesleys receive from the public £34,129, a sum equal to 426 pairs of lieutenants' legs, calculated at the rate of allowance for lieutenant Chambers' leg.—Calculating by the pension for captain Johnson's arm, viz. £45, lord Arden's sinecure is equal to the value of 1022 captain's arms." But the darkest stain on Mulgrave's record was his treatment of the most distinguished naval officer of the day.

Collingwood had been commanding the Mediterranean Fleet ever since Nelson's death. Only a year after that event he complained that he was almost worn out. But a sense of duty, in which he was not surpassed by any man of his time, kept him at his post. Nor had the bestowal of a title, which was not made to pass through the female line —and he had no sons—quenched his thirst for professional distinction. But in August 1808 he could bear it no longer, and applied, very reluctantly, for leave. He had, as he wrote a few months later, seen all the ships and men out two or three times. But Mulgrave thought this grand lone figure indispensable. It was true that no one could have adequately filled his place. He was in almost independent control of political relations with most of the countries bordering on the Mediterranean. By the constant interchange of such courtesies as were compatible with a state of war between himself and Spanish and Turkish authorities he had been steadily laying the groundwork for peace with those countries. He did much to prevent the war extending by smoothing relations with the half-civilized chiefs, Beys and Deys, who ruled the southern Mediterranean littoral. This was a most valuable service, committed as those relations were to an unsatisfactory class of restless and often mischievous men. Typical of them was the Consul at Tripoli—panting, as Collingwood observed, for "a political intrigue, a little snug war of his own making". All these duties tied the Admiral so closely to his desk that he could hardly show himself on deck. They were in any case too much for one man, and the command should have been divided. In the existing dearth of good flag officers, Mulgrave took a cruel advantage of his zeal and made him stay, although there was no excuse, for Vice Admiral Sir Charles Cotton, who eventually succeeded him, was already available in 1808. Collingwood remained at his post till the 3rd of March, 1810, when he was obliged to hand over the command to Rear-Admiral George Martin and start for England as the only chance of saving his life; but it was too late. Four days later he died. He was worn out at fifty-nine. His death was due to confinement on board ship and to continually bending over a desk. In October 1809, a few months before his death, one last bright ray lighted up the darkness gradually closing on him; the darling wish of his heart was partly gratified. Barcelona, which was in French hands, was, he knew, in need of supplies. He pretended to raise the blockade of Toulon, and a part of the French fleet came out with a convoy. Martin's division was the one which was lucky enough to get near the enemy, and two of the three sail of the line were driven ashore and burnt by their crews; the convoy was afterwards destroyed. One of Collingwood last wishes had been that he might live to fight the French once more; and yet there is no better tribute to the memory of that grand forlorn sentry left by his own countrymen to die at his post, than in a Frenchman, Comte Alfred de Vigny's, description of how one of Napoleon's young admirers first learnt from him what veritable grandeur was.

One of the last important services rendered to his country by the King before the ever-impending malady finally removed him from active life, was to save Perceval from the fatal mistake of putting in Gambier as First Lord. "His appointment to the Admiralty", he wrote, "would not be a popular one with the Navy, in which his professional abilities are not held in the highest estimation." After an attempt to get Robert Dundas, foiled once more by his father's veto, Perceval obtained Charles Yorke, who possessed just the steady-going administrative qualities dear to the King's heart. The Premier had—at least so it was thought by some of his supporters—made some sacrifices. The Tellership of the Exchequer, a sinecure worth £2,700 a year, had fallen vacant. Perceval refused it for himself, though he was certainly much worse off as First Lord of the Treasury than he had been while earning money at the bar. He gave it to Yorke as a sort of pension for his services as Secretary for War under Addington, and thus made him a friend. The cry was all against sinecures in the country. When Yorke presented himself to his constituents in Cambridgeshire for re-election after accepting a place of profit under the Crown, he was rejected. But although his subsequent acceptance of the office of First Lord of the Admiralty did not strengthen the Government in parliament, it rendered it more efficient. Mulgrave passed to the Ordnance, where a soldier was in his proper element.

In the other series of events which rose indirectly out of the Walcheren enquiry Yorke played an important part. The House of Commons bitterly remembered being made a laughing-stock by a worthless woman in the enquiry which took place the year before. To safeguard its dignity on this occasion Yorke moved the enforcement of the standing order for the exclusion of strangers. This was agreed to as a matter of course without any object of concealing anything which might come to light at the enquiry. The minutes were taken and published in full. Sheridan, however, objected to the rule which enabled any member at any time to enforce an order of this kind, and attempted to open up the whole subject, arguing in a powerful speech that this was not the occasion for it. His motion failed, and Windham took the opportunity to make an attack on the press. In a few days placards were seen all over London advertising a meeting of one of the debating societies which were held in imitation of Parliament. It ran:

"WINDHAM and YORKE. *British Forum*, 33, *Bedford-Street, Covent-Garden.* Monday, February 19, 1810. QUESTION: Which was a greater outrage on the public feeling, Mr. Yorke's enforcement of the standing order to exclude strangers from the House of Commons, or Mr. Windham's recent attack on the liberties of the press?"

U

It is usually a miserable subterfuge to attempt to escape from an inconvenient contest by treating an opponent with what is called the contempt which he deserves. But on this occasion it would have been prudent in Ministers to have induced Yorke and Windham to drop the matter, or, if they pursued it, to do so as individuals. Nevertheless the more obvious and usual course was taken. Acting for both Yorke was allowed to bring the matter up as a high breach of the privilege of the House. The printer was reprimanded and discharged. Proceedings then began against the author, who turned out to be John Gale Jones, a noted member of the old Corresponding Society. The culprit acknowledged his offence in language which ought to have been satisfactory. He begged to express his sincere contrition, and threw himself on the mercy of the House. But Yorke was not satisfied. He carried, without a dissentient, a motion to commit Jones to Newgate. A few days later, on the 12th of March, Burdett, who had not been present on the former occasion, proposed his discharge. He contested the right of the House to imprison anyone who was not a Member for an offence punishable in the ordinary course of law. Viewed in this light he found no one to agree with him on the subject, though several were for releasing Jones as having expressed contrition and been sufficiently punished. The ominous name of Wilkes had been mentioned, and warning might have been taken by the discreditable plight in which the House had involved itself on a previous occasion. But Perceval refused all compromise. It had been the custom not to discharge such a prisoner without a humble petition repeating what had already in this case been said verbally. Jones had, it appeared, reconsidered his position while in prison. He now refused to petition, and Perceval had the House with him in saying that it could not set him free without a compromise of its dignity.

The baffled patriot in the House of Commons determined to bring the point to an issue. The Ministry had objected to a few words derogatory to the dignity of Parliament being placarded about London. Burdett decided on disseminating a much longer and a much stronger indictment throughout England. The instrument was ready to his hand. Cobbett's lively Political Register now catered widely for the needs of newspaper readers dissatisfied with the jejune fare provided by the provincial newspapers, and even supplemented or supplanted those of the metropolis itself. He was incomparably the most influential man then living outside Parliament. Ministers had long had their eyes on this dangerous fellow, who combined the parts of scribbler and Hampshire farmer. At last, in June 1809, he had brought himself within their clutches. A trifling mutiny in the Cambridgeshire militia had been suppressed by the arrival of a detachment of the King's German Legion, and five ringleaders were sentenced each to five hundred lashes. The old jealousy of Hanoverian troops in England was hot within him, and found vent in a characteristic outburst of savage irony. " 'Lash them daily, lash them duly.' What! shall the rascals dare to *mutiny*, and that too when the German legion is so near at hand." Yet even now the Government was in no haste to take the matter up. Eldon was inclined to taunt his colleagues with their remissness in prosecutions compared with the vigorous days of fifteen years ago when he was Attorney-General. But in February 1810 they unwisely prosecuted Perry of the Morning Chronicle for an article reflecting obliquely on the King. Ellenborough, the Chief Justice, summed up for an acquittal, and the jury followed him.

Whether he needed this encouragement or not, Cobbett was not the man lightly to be intimidated by a pending prosecution. The Register of the 24th of March came out with the Member for Westminster's manifesto under the title, in large capitals: "Sir Francis Burdett to his constituents, denying the power of the House of Commons to imprison the people of England." It was read out by the

Clerk to the House on the 27th. Even in the first sentence there was a stinging gibe which strung the passions of the listeners to the highest pitch. The House of Commons was called "a part of our fellow-subjects, called together by means which it is not necessary for me to describe". But as the reading proceeded, members were not a little staggered by the learned arguments adduced to show, from precedents back in Plantagenet times, that Parliament had no such power of imprisoning as it had exercised in the case of Jones. They were only reassured by the even more learned argument of Adam, who was, besides, able to quote in his favour the opinion of one whom he called the greatest of all parliamentary lawyers—that staunchest of champions of popular right, Charles James Fox—to the effect that either House of Parliament had the right to commit for libel. So much for the legal argument as to the powers of the House. There was hardly a doubt as to Burdett's paper having been scandalous and libellous, though there was some question as to whether it would not have been enough for him to be reprimanded by the Speaker in his place. But he had frequently insulted the House in his place in the past, and it was apprehended that he would not miss the opportunity of creating a scene which would not tend to enhance its dignity. Still as many as 152 members voted for that course, and there was a majority of only 38 in favour of his committal to the Tower.

It was not until broad daylight of the next morning, which was the 6th of April, that the debate came to an end. The Speaker lost no time in signing the warrants and delivering them to the Sergeant-at-Arms. From the emphasis which Burdett had constantly placed on the illegality of imprisoning one who was not a member, it had been inferred that he would not contest the right in his own case. Such was the impression of the Sergeant-at-Arms. That unfortunate officer was now bandied about between Burdett and the Speaker. Told by the former to come again next day, he returned to the latter, who told him to execute the warrant immediately, and to get help from the Secretary of State. Ryder refused to help, and when the Sergeant next called upon Sir Francis accompanied only by his Deputy, the Member for Westminster refused to come unless compelled. By this time a large mob had collected. Still left with little help from the Home Office and the Magistrates, the Sergeant had to attempt his task again the next morning with only a few police officers and with the same want of success. The mob now had things their own way. Everyone who passed by Sir Francis's house in Piccadilly was made to take off his hat and cry "Burdett for ever!" and the windows of several Ministers and others were broken. The guards were called out, and the Riot Act read. But authority was far from being only on one side. The British inveterate jealousy of a standing army found support among the City dignitaries, and while the people employed the materials of two half-built houses in an attempt to barricade Piccadilly, the sheriffs threatened the military officers. A plan was actually set on foot, in which the tailor, Place, now once more active, took the lead, to get as many householders as possible sworn in as constables to support Sheriff Matthew Wood in arresting the officer in command of the troops if he refused to withdraw them. Should he decline to submit to arrest, he was to be threatened with an action. But the Government was too quick for the conspirators.

On Monday the 7th an overwhelming force of artillery, cavalry, infantry, and volunteers were collected, the house door was forced and the arrest was made. The great event was well staged. Sir Francis was found surrounded by his family and friends, persons of title and others. He had finished breakfast and was hearing his son, an Etonian of fourteen, translate Magna Charta. If the boy did so correctly, he must have seen that there was nothing in it to bear out his father's contention. It was there laid down that no freeman could be arrested except by the law of the land. But it was only lawyers who could say what that law was, and the best lawyers had unequivocally decided that it included the law of Parliament, which enabled it to punish a libel upon itself with imprisonment for contempt. Burdett had indeed fallen into a confusion of thought which he shared with many other Englishmen. " 'The law of England,' says the great Lawyer Plowden, 'is no other than pure and tried reason.' " So ran the argument in the paper for which he was now under arrest. Authorities were quoted to the effect that no orders could stop the Common Law. It was shown that there were a number of rights under the Common Law all of which were violated by the Parliament's arbitrary act. So Burdett went cheerfully to the Tower relying on being able to prove the illegality of the warrant. When he brought his action against the Speaker and others in due course, the Judges of the King's Bench also held that the privileges of Parliament were part of the law of the land, and were not cognizable in a court of law. The English trick of bringing about a revolution under the guise of merely asserting ancient rights had failed. Burdett was perfectly right in his object. He should, however, have urged Jones's release on the ground that the privilege of Parliament under which he was imprisoned was so clearly incompatible with the principles which underlay the Common Law that it ought to be abandoned. Nor was there any occasion to complicate by an attack upon the constitution of the House one upon what were very judicially described in the petition from the City of Rochester as its overstrained privileges.

Those four days were the culminating period of Burdett's life. He lost credit from the hour when the people of London who had followed him to the Tower left him there. In their return a disgraceful attack was made on the military who were obliged to fire, and two lives were lost and a few persons wounded. It was not the first time ball had

PERCEVAL'S ADMINISTRATION

been fired in those few days, nor had the firing been only on one side. Burdett was bound to be released when Parliament rose, and the date was eagerly awaited. A committee of his friends was formed, in which Place was conspicuous, and a programme published of the triumphant procession in which he was to return from the Tower to Piccadilly. There were to be trumpeters leading, gentlemen on horseback ond on foot, and a large dark blue streamer was to be carried bearing the motto "Hold to the laws". But while all these preparations were going on, Burdett was reflecting. The agitation which he had set on foot was on both too large and too small a scale. The nation did not really much care whether the House of Commons had or had not the power to imprison the people of England, as it knew that there was very little fear of its doing so. Many thousands of people up and down the country were now beginning to care for reform, but it was unlikely that they would regard Burdett as a martyr to that cause merely because he was imprisoned for insulting an unreformed Parliament. A riot took place at Bristol on the 16th of April in sympathy with those which had occurred in the metropolis. But as a whole the nation was unmoved. There were several petitions, but only two were from counties—Middlesex and Berkshire; and outside London the only important towns petitioning were Liverpool, Kingston-upon-Hull, Nottingham, Worcester and Coventry. Some petitions were for parliamentary reform and some for Burdett's release; but in most of them the two questions were mixed up together, as were the high taxation, the failure of the Walcheren expedition, the mismanagement of the war generally, the existence of sinecurists, placemen and pensioners, and the particular misdeeds of Perceval and Castlereagh, as brought to light in the previous session.

Burdett was not the man, even seconded by Cobbett, to send the fiery cross through the country and focus all these grievances upon one point. Moreover, he had at last succeeded in producing unanimity within the House of Commons itself. He had written a letter to the Speaker on the reception of his warrant, which the House agreed on the 10th of April to be a high and flagrant breach of its privileges. Whatever might have been his object at first in barring his house and refusing to go to the Tower until compelled by an armed force—and revolutionaries have small time to realize to what end their actions inevitably tend—there could now be little further doubt of what the agitation meant—the intimidation from without of an united Parliament. Burdett was a brave man, but his spirit began to quail before the enlarged prospect which was opening before him.

The means at his disposal were not adequate to the end. It looked as if he would, after all, have little more to rely on than that rabble from Saffron Hill which had been accused of swarming into the Guildhall and compelling a petition to be presented in the name of the Liverymen of London. The "fifty two gentlemen on horseback" contemplated by the Committee did not seem to be forthcoming. There were no leaders; even his colleague Lord Cochrane held aloof. There was a little too much "Burdett for ever!" for Sir Francis. As for "Hold to the laws", the Government was doing that as well; he had himself not dared to sue out a writ of Habeas Corpus; and it did not look as if he would prosper in his action against the Speaker. Rather than establish any principle of law, he was likely to find himself the centre of a disreputable tumult. And as the Times unkindly published afterwards, it was the rumoured intention of the mob to place his fellow prisoner Jones, due for release from Newgate at the same time, into the baronet's carriage, when the procession should pass the Old Bailey; and this was by no means to his mind.

On the 21st of June the procession arrived at the Tower. An Irishman of family was found at its head, the eccentric and rather disreputable Colonel the Honourable George

Hanger, who, having been himself confined for debt, had some sympathy with a fellow prisoner. When the people arrived, the news was broken to them that their idol was gone. Sir Francis had decided to depart by that way by which so many genuine martyrs to the cause of civil or religious freedom had arrived at the Tower, never to leave it—by water. He explained afterwards that he would never have forgiven himself had there been any blood shed during the course of the procession. In vain was he asked why a satisfied crowd should be more dangerous than one exasperated by disappointment. When asked why he had not countermanded the procession he replied that he had wished to have the demonstration—even in the absence of the principal performer. There was an illumination that night, compelled by the mob with the usual cry of "Lights up!" those buildings whose owners refused, such as the offices of the Morning Post, having their windows broken. But quiet was soon restored and Burdett forgotten. The dinner to him a few days later was a tame affair. Romilly, who had supported Burdett as much as any member of Parliament, refused to be present.

Meanwhile the Government had at last taken orders with Cobbett. On the 15th of June he was tried before Ellenborough for criminal libel on account of his flogging article. He was injudicious in his defence, and Sir Vicary Gibbs, the Attorney-General, had no difficulty in obtaining a verdict of "guilty". Cobbett, who had a large family and other interests besides politics, was willing publicly to undertake never to write for the press again if he was not sentenced, and Perceval would have been wise to have accepted. But the negotiations fell through. On the 9th of July Gibbs prayed judgment against Cobbett, and he received his vindictive sentence. He was to pay a fine of a thousand pounds, to undergo two years' rigorous imprisonment in Newgate, and to give security to keep the peace for seven years after his release. Yet he was allowed to continue to carry on the Register from prison.

Ministers—Ryder in particular—had little reason to pride themselves on their own share in these events. Yet on the whole they had gained some strength. Earlier in the session they had suffered several defeats in parliament. On the occasion of the division on Chatham's misconduct, the Morning Chronicle triumphantly published a division list with asterisks attached to the names of county members. There were more of them for the Opposition than for Government. But after the Burdett riots there was a change. "A few well-meaning Country Gentlemen have taken fright", wrote the same newspaper on the 14th of April. It would have been more fair to say that as honest Englishmen they rallied to the side of those whom they saw persecuted, the party so treated being not Burdett but his opponents. Sir Robert Salusbury, a private member, who had moved for his commitment to the Tower when no one else dared, was obliged to go into the country to avoid the mob, and afterwards found no hotelkeeper hardy enough to harbour him for the rest of the session.

Perceval seemed to thrive under adversity; and this was one of the things which exasperated people so much against him. Early in the session, after he had been defeated in the House time after time, Whitbread compares his inexhaustible vitality with that of Punch. "At the very moment when you expect to hear nothing more of him, up jumps the little fellow and says 'I am alive'. " Towards the end of the session after a long debate in the Upper House on the State of the Nation, a grim comparison was suggested to Grey's mind by the fact that if anyone, three years before, had contended that the country would be governed by those who were now ministers he would have been esteemed little better than a madman. "Who would have thought at the time Augustus was emperor of Rome, that in the reign of Caligula, the people could have submitted to have a horse

PERCEVAL'S ADMINISTRATION

for their consul?" But Perceval had one great advantage. Grenville did not desire office. The Opposition was in disorder. The death of a brother had removed Petty to the House of Lords as Marquis of Lansdowne—strengthening a party already strong enough in that House. In the Lower House Thomas Grenville was ceasing to take an interest in parliamentary affairs, and more and more devoting himself to the collection of that splendid library which forms his principal title to fame. Another Cabinet Minister of the Talents, the brilliant high-souled Windham, died in June. A few days later Whitbread took occasion to deplore the absence of one whom he called "the last star in that brilliant constellation of orators who were at the same time the pride and ornament of their age and nation"—Sheridan, now a waning star. Tierney was another whose powers were weakening, and Ponsonby, the titular leader of the Opposition, never found his feet or won the confidence of his colleagues. Constituted as the House of Commons then was, with a number of independent members ready to be turned by argument, some definite superiority of debating power was necessary before the Ministry could be compelled to resign. This the Opposition members had not got, and they constantly saw themselves baffled by one who was not merely no statesman but who frequently, as they legitimately complained, was wanting in common sense and judgement.

Perceval's lack of these qualities was conspicuous in the efforts which he constantly made until the autumn to strengthen his administration. The questions with which he had to deal were certainly intricate. Could Canning and Castlereagh be got to serve together? Would either of them serve except in his old office? Would Sidmouth serve with Canning? Would Perceval's colleagues allow him to select one or two out of the three? And if so, would not any one of the three who was left out go into open opposition and make the situation worse than before? Wellesley was now ready to sacrifice not merely all claims on his own part but even his present office to help Perceval to get something done; but every attempt failed. Yet the genuineness of the Premier's offers and the pertinacity with which they were made had the effect of strengthening him. It was impossible now for any of the three to refuse his support. Canning gave valuable assistance in parliament by one of his magnificent orations on Peninsular affairs which reduced the Opposition to silence. Sidmouth, finding that Grenville refused to unnail his colours from the Catholic mast, concluded that further support of him would be mere faction, and inclined more and more to the right. Had he still been in the House of Commons, however, he would have been a severe critic of Perceval's financial arrangements. In providing for a total expenditure for the year of just under £85,000,000, the Chancellor had refused to impose fresh taxation. With some financial audacity he pointed to an unexpected rise in the receipts from existing taxation as providing for the interest and sinking fund on the new loan of £8,000,000. He was able to raise on terms only a little worse than those of 1809 both this and a loan of £4,000,000 for Ireland. That unfortunate country did not escape extra taxation.

In one matter Perceval also failed to secure the support of Canning's small party. In 1809 David Ricardo had published his first work: "The high price of bullion a proof of the depreciation of bank notes." In the following year the general rise in prices and the fall in the foreign exchanges forced themselves on the attention of Parliament. The price of gold had risen to £4 10s. per ounce, or $15\frac{1}{2}$ per cent above the mint price. The foreign exchanges had fallen as much as 20 per cent at the end of 1809, although in the course of 1810 there had been a considerable recovery. Horner, who, keen opposer of the Tories as he was, approached the subject without bias, brought the question before the House. A Committee was appointed in which the leading spirits were himself as Chairman, Huskisson,

Thornton the well-known authority on currency, and Alexander Baring. Perceval was a member, but filled a very secondary part. Had it been then the custom to publish minority reports, the Chancellor of the Exchequer, dissenting from the Chairman, might have produced three signatures besides his own in a Committee of twenty-one. Huskisson had no hesitation in supporting the views of the majority both by assisting Horner to draw up the report and independently in the press. The Committee found that the evils complained of were not due to the demand for gold on the continent or to anything connected with the course of trade, but to the excess of Bank of England notes. This in its turn was the cause of the excessive printing of notes by the seven hundred odd private banks, for their circulation was based ultimately on the notes of that bank. If presenters of their notes at country banks could not obtain Bank of England notes in exchange, the country banks would break. But the currency sent into the market by the Bank of England was based upon nothing. The Committee estimated, on grounds which did not indeed bear a close examination, that in the year 1809 there had been an addition of between four and five million pounds to the circulation of Great Britain. In any case the addition was certainly large, and was not warranted by the requirements of legitimate trade.

The witnesses before the Committee who represented the Bank contested this. They explained that notes were issued when required by safe persons for genuine transactions. But this, as the Committee showed, would not have prevented the inflation of currency. A perfectly safe person often required a loan for what turned out an unprofitable speculation. The Bank rate, fixed by the usury laws at five per cent., wholly irrespective of the demand for money, presented an irresistible temptation. There had been many wild ventures recently in the South American market. Nearer home there had been speculation in continental grain and other goods. There can be no more legitimate trade in the world than the methodical purchase of necessary provisions in order to keep the markets adequately stocked. But the present case was that of a trade precariously existing by the arbitrary fiat of a hostile despot, with the object of draining his enemy of gold, which partly enabled his own people to pay their taxes and rents, and partly swelled his own treasury direct in the form of heavy license fees. A trade which depended merely upon the continuance of a certain policy of the enemy bore a speculative character. To replace the currency of the country on its only secure basis, the Bullion Committee recommended the repeal of the law of 1797 which suspended cash payments by the Bank of England. It would then have to pay gold for its notes whenever required to do so, and would restrict its issue accordingly, and the country banks would correspondingly contract their own issues. But the Committee aimed at setting a period ample enough to prevent any such sudden deflation as would cause a commercial crisis. It suggested two years from June, the time of report.

But the proposal itself caused a panic. The Bank of England had no intention of lightly submitting to the reversal of an arrangement under which it had enjoyed unexampled prosperity for the last thirteen years and brought its stock to a premium of 170 per cent. The publication of the report was followed by a cry that enterprise would be stifled and the empire ruined. The alarm was spread among those who feared that the Bank would no longer be able to furnish the accustomed credits. There were many bankruptcies in London, and some country banks failed. For once the jobbers whom Cobbett held up to the country as sucking its life-blood were badly hit. The joint contractors for the new loan were Abraham Goldsmid and Sir Francis Baring. It fell in October to 8 per cent. discount. Before it was at its worst, Goldsmid committed suicide.

Another Francis Baring, a relative of the loan contractor, did the same, and his act was also ascribed to the prevailing financial depression.

The Committee in fact had, in their somewhat pedantic way of treating the subject of Pitt's drastic remedy for the crisis of 1797, proved very little more than that the case before them was an instance of remedies for evils being in themselves unwholesome things. They had neglected the further consideration whether the disease in question was sufficiently cured to make it possible to discontinue the medicine. Of course if a gold currency were restored the exchanges would rise. But this would be because the Bank would have to contract its credits. So far as these enabled speculative purchases of corn to be made, the country would have starved if they were stopped. So far as they enabled a precarious trade to be continued in the face of imperial edicts and other perils, and in untried parts of the globe, the country would, if they were stopped, have lost opportunities of opening markets by methods necessary in war time however little they might recommend themselves to steady mercantile enterprise during peace.

If a train of bankruptcies and suicides were to follow the mere publication of the report, there was something to be said for bearing generally the existing ills of the present inflation, and providing such remedies as the special cases would admit. Among those injured by the prevailing high prices were annuitants and creditors, particularly those of Government. On the other hand, Government itself suffered from the necessity of raising the pay of its servants to meet the increased cost of living, and in anticipation from the difficulty of reducing it again when prices should reach their former level. But none of these evils, once it was remembered that the difference in prices caused by inflation could not be more than twenty per cent, was worth a measure which—absurd as such a result might be—threatened a commercial panic. By far the most important effect of the increase of prices, in the Committee's opinion, and one on which Horner admitted to Dugald Stuart that more might have been said, was the loss to the common labourer, the rate of whose wages, in the words of the report, adapted itself more slowly to changes in the value of money than the price of any other species of labour or commodity. It was certainly wrong to have left him out of account. But there would have been very little to say. There were as yet no complaints from Lancashire, though wages were no longer what they had been a few years back. Indeed a militia officer wrote to the Home Office in February to say that he was afraid of losing some of his men, it being a common practice in the manufacturing districts for men to allow themselves to be bound to relations by nominal indentures, so that they might enlist when trade was bad and be claimed back as runaway apprentices when it recovered. The agricultural labourer was in no distress. The state of Ireland was, upon the whole, reassuring. Constitutional movements had taken the place of thresher outrages. It was during the summer of 1810 in Dublin that the cause of the Repeal of the Union first reared its head, and that the voice of Daniel O'Connell first became formidable. He asserted with characteristic wildness that 70,000 out of 120,000 men fighting England's battles were Irish. But the true figure was no doubt large, and pointed to economic conditions favourable to recruiting. Still there was nothing even here which called for any drastic financial remedy.

Napoleon's continental system had hitherto met with little success. The average trade of Great Britain with Europe for the year which preceded that of the Berlin Decree was only two-fifths of her whole trade outside the United Kingdom. He could operate only upon a fraction of this fraction, namely upon that part of Europe which from time to time entered into his system. His want of success was now apparent. The system had failed as regards Spain, seeing that since she had risen against him it could only be enforced in those parts actually occupied by his troops. It had failed in Portugal for the same reason. It had produced the greatest distress in the north of Europe; yet it failed there too. In Holland it had been enforced only by the introduction of French customs-house officers, and even this was found not to be enough: French troops were sent in to compel compliance with the imperial system in all its rigour; the King, Napoleon's brother Louis, abdicated in disgust; and the country was annexed to the Empire in July 1810. Further to the east there was incessant evasion. Heligoland, that useful acquisition from the Danes, was the great depot for smugglers who plied, on the whole with success, their precarious trade. "A gentleman, very lately returned from that fortunate island," wrote Sir Philip Francis, "assured me that, from the beach to the stairs, he had walked up to his ancles in salted sugar and rotten coffee." These words were written early in 1810, when Napoleon, relieved from the Austrian war, had time to devote specially to the task of drawing his cordon tight in North Germany. In the previous summer, when both he and his armies were fully occupied, Cuxhaven was almost as open to British ships as Heligoland itself. It was then the British who resented the predatory excursions of French troops in the neighbourhood, and they were able to use the town itself as a base for a retaliatory expedition.

But it was in the Baltic that Napoleon's failure had been most apparent. The commercial summary in the Literary Panorama for the 1st of January, 1810, ran: "The merchants declare that there never was so vast a trade carried on with so little loss as that to the Baltic has been during the present year. The number of vessels that have passed through the Belt, under the protection of Admiral Dixon's squadron alone, between the 25th of June and the 8th of November, amounts to 2,210, not one of which has been captured by the enemy." Yet at the end of 1809 Napoleon had won another triumph. Sweden was forced to make peace with Russia and to close her ports to Great Britain. A year later, after she had chosen one of his marshals, Bernadotte, for her ruler and future King, she was obliged to declare war. But she made no attempt to carry out the almost impossible task of watching her intricate network of harbours. Count Rosen, Governor of Gothenberg, expressing the views of the Government, announced to Saumarez, who now commanded the British fleet in those waters: "The Swedish Government declares war, it is true, against Great Britain; but it is not said that any measures of active hostility are to be had recourse to." If a French marshal was chosen, it was pointed out that this was because he was the only candidate capable of opposing Napoleon and promoting a national policy. In October 1810, when Bernadotte crossed over to his new kingdom, obtaining leave to pass in the Swedish Royal Yacht through Saumarez's fleet, he saw a sight calculated to give a direction to his future ideas. The Belt was white with the sails of a thousand vessels then on their way to England escorted by six British ships of the line and other men of war. All this activity was reflected in the statistics of trade. So far as exports were concerned, the total value of British produce and manufactures, which had fallen for the North of Europe from over ten million pounds in 1805 almost as low as two millions in 1808, rose in 1810 to nearly seven and three-quarter millions. The exports from Great Britain to the same quarter of foreign and colonial merchandise had not fallen so much. They too recovered, and reached in 1810 to within a couple of hundred thousand pounds of the six and a third millions of the year preceding that of the Berlin Decree.

Napoleon had made little progress towards his goal as regards British trade with the countries nearest to his capital. He made less as regards those bordering the Mediterranean, and could of course do nothing with America, except so far as his efforts to excite the unfriendliness of the United States were seconded by the injudicious policy of Great Britain herself. Both in the Mediterranean and in the West Indies he had driven his enemy to secure her trade by further conquests from him. In April 1810 a mixed force mainly of British and Italians, under Brigadier-General John Oswald, liberated one more Ionian island, Santa Maura, and the British Government was now enabled to declare a blockade of the channel separating Corfu from the mainland, and with the assistance of Ali Pasha, the ruler of Albania and Morea, to counterweigh that island's commanding position at the head of the Adriatic. But it was not possible to go further. Corfu remained French till the end of the war, and Sir John Stuart was thrown on the defensive in Sicily, face to face with Murat who had marched at the head of a formidable army to the extreme point of Italy, and there sat in state overlooking the Straits as his master had done at Boulogne. In September the event occurred which had been so long expected, and which Nelson himself had not been confident of preventing. Three thousand men effected a landing some miles southwards of Messina. But dissensions among his officers intervened to prevent Murat from throwing across the mass of his army. Yet the ease with which the invasion, such as it was, was repelled proved to Murat that the British could count—and not in vain—on the help of the peasants in their defence of Sicily. Henceforth Murat left that island undisturbed, and the Central Mediterranean ceased for the time to be of importance in the war.

Meanwhile, the reduction in February by Sir George Beckwith of Guadeloupe, followed by some minor captures, had completed the work of hauling down the flag of France or any of her allies wherever it flew in the West Indies. British export trade to other parts of America and the West Indies was now no longer in the same fear of privateers. It had already been relieved of a formidable competitor in the United States, first by the Embargo, and then by the Non-Intercourse Act which prevented the carrying trade in British manufactures. It rose from eight and a half million pounds, which it was in 1805, to nearly twenty millions in 1809. In May of 1810 the Non-Intercourse Act expired. Disturbances also broke out in a part of Spanish South America portions of which, headed by Venezuela, declared their independence. The trade now dropped below eighteen millions. But it was compensated by the trade with the States itself. British exports to that country, which had been only seven and a half millions in 1809, now rose to over eleven millions, or not much less than they had been in 1805. Swollen by the prosperous Mediterranean trade, exports to the continent of Europe, twenty-four millions, were actually almost four millions higher than they had been five years before. The total exports of Great Britain to the whole world, which had been valued at fifty-one millions in 1805, had remained round about fifty millions for the next three years, reached the unprecedented amount of sixty-six millions in 1809, and fell to not much below sixty-three millions in 1810. British goods continued to be bought in spite of every difficulty placed in their way, because they were better at the price—the only reason why, in the long run, one class of goods is preferred to another. The French view was that the English compelled Europe to buy their goods, and they made use of expressions which concealed from themselves as well as others the irresistible penetrative virtue of trade. They failed to see that such a phrase as "forcing a market" is a contradiction in terms, for a market is a place of voluntary sale and purchase. England's sea power alone could merely drop her goods down on the beach, and it was the willing hands of the people whom Napoleon claimed to be rescuing from her commercial tyranny which did the rest.

The year 1810 was one of special effort on Napoleon's part. He inaugurated a policy of direct annexation to carry through his system. By the end of the year he had incorporated the whole of the north coast territories, and the Holstein frontier as far as the Baltic with France. Pressed relentlessly forward by a logic which he could not escape, he was driven on the 19th of October to issue an edict which obliged the impoverished people of every land occupied by his troops to see articles of British manufacture taken from their possession and publicly burnt. Without command of the sea he could not strike his enemy through her imports, nor did he wish to, if he could drain her of gold. Nor did he rigorously enforce the exclusion of colonial produce. It was through the destroying of the markets for British manufactures—or the destroying of the manufactures in the markets—that he now hoped to bring that country to her knees. It seemed as though for the past four years the war on its commercial side, intense as the suffering was which it had brought, had only been half waged, and that France and Great Britain were only now at last at grips.

The most effective of the ways in which the Continental system had been met had been the forcing of the trade barriers so far as that could be done, and—so far as it could not—the opening of new markets where such barriers did not exist. The Orders in Council of November 1807 had been rightly replaced by the less extensive measure of April 1809. The irritation was now reduced. But the vicious principle remained. The fixed idea of men like James Stephen was that the United States was gathering up more than its legitimate share of the trade of the world, and needed to be curbed. They had an exaggerated idea of the possibilities of the British mercantile marine. In reality the people of the United States were no dangerous competitors. In manufactures, at which Napoleon directed his principal aim, they did not compete at all; to quarrel with them was merely to lose a market. There was no great harm if they sent their raw produce, cotton and tobacco, to Europe, so long as the British West Indies could supply it with sugar and coffee. It was these last staples which furnished the principal complaint against the States, whose ships brought them from the colonies of France and her allies to Europe. The proper remedy was to blockade or reduce them all, and this it was eventually found necessary to do.

Claiming to be the carriers of Europe, the Americans competed with Great Britain in that trade also. Had Stephen looked further into the matter, he might have been content to allow that trade to go on increasing at the expense of his country in time of war. The seafaring population even of an island nation had its limits. Already in 1810 the strength of the navy had been raised from 130,000 to 145,000 seamen and marines, and the increase was necessary in view of the probability of war with the United States. Yet it was difficult, even with the enormous powers which naval officers had, to make up the crews. It was impossible to do without a large foreign element. In 1807 Collingwood found that there were over two hundred Americans serving in a part only of the Mediterranean Fleet—some compensation for the British seamen decoyed into the mercantile marine and even the Navy of the United States. In 1808 Captain Byam Martin found that his own ship contained 27 foreigners from Northern Europe and 11 from Southern Europe, 28 Americans, and several other foreigners. Out of the total ship's company of 558, 130 were Irish, and this proportion of a race which did not take naturally to the sea, and which was undesirable in other respects, was greatly exceeded elsewhere. It followed that in the merchant service an even greater proportion of the ships' companies would be foreign. Cochrane once said in the House of Commons—no doubt with some exaggeration—that men of war were allowed to remain on the East India Station until the greater part of their crews had died off. Rose had known merchant ships sail for those seas without a single regular bred seaman on board. This terrible state of things is reflected possibly in the disappearance in 1807 of the Blenheim, the flagship of Rear-Admiral Sir Thomas Troubridge, the exact cause of which cannot be known, as every man on board of her was lost; and certainly in that of some, at any rate, of the seven East Indiamen belonging to two successive fleets, which similarly disappeared three years later.

Viewed in this light, the gloomy vaticinations of pamphleteers and Members of Parliament about the future of British shipping were beside the mark. In 1806 3,792 foreign vessels had entered British ports, and that number had mounted in 1810 to 6,876. The figure for British ships, 12,110, had on the other hand only risen to 13,557. But even the total of a little over 100,000 merchant seamen was only being maintained by increasing drafts upon foreign sources of supply. There was shortage of men, now that adventurous spirits were finding the army more and more popular. There was shortage of hemp and timber. There would have been no seamen begging their bread and no ships laid up for want of freights even had the Orders in Council never issued. And so far as there had been an inevitable increase in foreign shipping, the Orders had given it a wrong direction. Out of the 18,000 licences to trade issued by Great Britain in 1810, a very considerable number were granted either openly or under a subterfuge to enemies. With some reason Grey accused the Government of rearing an enemy navy.

It was this which caused so much bitterness across the Atlantic. Americans saw in the Orders a design to destroy their trade rather than to injure France; and certainly, when the belligerents closed one another's ports to neutrals and traded with one another, there was some excuse for regarding the Napoleonic war in the light of a conspiracy to prevent a New world from coming into existence, and, as Jefferson and Madison did, for declaring commercial war on both parties alike, so as to bring the Old World to its senses. "Do not believe", said a French Minister to General Armstrong, the American Minister to France, "that peace between us and England is impossible. If we offer to her the commerce of the world, can she resist it?" It was in this mood that in January 1810 some confused and unacceptable advances towards peace were made in which the principal part was taken by Pierre Labouchère, the son-in-law of Sir Francis Baring, and the head of the greatest international banking firm in the world, that of Hope and Company of Amsterdam. Nothing came of them. Nor even did the negotiations which went on somewhat later for an exchange in mass of the 41,000 French prisoners of war against the 11,000 British have any result, though they were protracted almost through the year. But there was much in the relations between Great Britain and France during the earlier part of 1810, to flatter the young republic across the Atlantic with the idea that it was she herself who was the enemy.

That nation entered upon the year 1810 in a disappointed and irritable mood. Every measure had been a failure by which it had been hoped to bring the two belligerents, or one of them, to reason. The last of these, the Non-Intercourse Act, was shortly to expire, and some action had to be taken. After some shifts and changes Congress passed a law, on the 1st of May, providing that, in case either Great Britain or France should before the 3rd of March next, so revoke or modify her edicts as that they should cease to violate the neutral commerce of the United States, the President should by proclamation revive the prohibition of commercial intercourse as against the other nation. While this was going on in Washington, Napoleon was showing how much regard he had for American interests. He wanted money. He was confiscating American ships if they entered Spanish ports under his control, as a reprisal for their being forbidden to enter France under the Non-Intercourse Act. He was confiscating them if they entered France because, as they had been forbidden by their own Government to do so, they could not be law-abiding Americans, and might be treated as British. But on hearing of the last measure which the Congress had passed he changed his tone. He determined not to miss so golden an opportunity. He explained that, now that the dignity of France was no longer outraged by the preferential treatment accorded to Spain, Naples and Holland (governed by his own brothers), he had no fault to find with the treatment of her by the United States. "In this new state of things", continued the letter of the 5th of August from his Foreign Minister, the Duc de Cadore to Armstrong, "I am authorized to declare to you, sir, that the Decrees of Berlin and Milan are revoked, and that after the 1st of November they will cease to have effect—it being well understood that in consequence of this declaration the English are to revoke their Orders in Council, and renounce the new principles of blockade which they wished to establish; or that the United States, conformably to the Act you have just communicated, cause their rights to be respected by the English." The letter concluded with many expressions of affection for the Americans on the Emperor's behalf.

It was afterwards considered as a crowning example of Corsican perfidy that on the very date of this letter Napoleon should have signed a secret decree condemning about fifty more American ships which had been sequestrated and as yet not ordered to be sold, and an arch-promoter of war with Great Britain, Albert Gallatin, was aghast with indignation years afterwards, when he learnt it. Had the decree been communicated to the United States at the time, he wrote, his country would never have taken the ground which ultimately led to that war. It might have been that Madison's cup would have brimmed over. But it was already full enough. On the 25th of May, when he heard of the seizures in the Spanish ports, he broke into honest indignation. "The late confiscations by Bonaparte", he wrote to

Jefferson, "comprise robbery, theft and breach of trust." But this was not to be allowed to deflect the policy of a lifetime. He was not the man to surrender to what he had called thirteen years earlier the British faction. Naploeon's offer or promise to revoke the Decrees gave him ground sufficient, as he thought, to proclaim under the Act of the 1st of May that the necessary conditions had been fulfilled by France, and to condemn Great Britain to a renewal of commercial non-intercourse. He had received neither from Armstrong nor from anyone else any sort of guarantee that the neutral commerce of the United States, a commerce which was, indeed, principally carried on by those Eastern States which were the stronghold of the British faction, would be no longer violated. It was affected by other imperial edicts and proceedings besides the Decrees of Berlin and Milan, and, as a matter of fact, not only did American vessels without French licences continue to be sequestered after the 1st of November, but the Foreign Minister publicly announced in December that the Emperor would persevere in his decrees. James Madison was heading straight for war with England and he knew it, and that at a time when his friend Napoleon was filling his pockets with American treasure, and his enemy George III was protecting American ships from Danish privateers. But he was carrying out Jefferson's policy and his own. On the 2nd of November the fatal Proclamation was issued.

One hope of peace remained. In England a Foreign Secretary whose tone of patronizing insolence had cut Americans to the quick had been succeeded by one whose tone was conciliation itself. William Pinkney, the American Minister in London, had some reason for hope when he pressed Lord Wellesley to obtain from the Government of which he was a member a revocation of the Orders to which both France and the States objected. The Foreign Secretary was personally in favour of giving up all the Orders in Council as far back as Fox's blockade of May

1806. But there were strange delays, and Pinkney's letters were left unanswered for months. In truth Wellesley could not carry his point in the Cabinet. His was no unique case. For years he had been accustomed to feel his will to be law during a splendid administration of the great Eastern dependency. Now that he was called to press his views as an equal in the council chamber, he did not know how to do so, and was baffled by the very inferiority of his colleagues. He had soon found that, although incomparably the ablest man in the Cabinet, he had no weight whatever. He could give Pinkney no answer, or at least not the answer he wished to give. Intense suffering was caused to the country, ending in another war, and further suffering across the Atlantic, merely because, owing to some defect in tact or persuasiveness, the wisest man in the Ministry could not make his views prevail. At last Pinkney brought him the letter of the 5th of August. Wellesley could do nothing, except point out that the letter was a blind; and things were left to take the course determined at Washington.

Meanwhile his brother was passing through a period of his life which called for almost as much of the qualities of tact and management as if he too was a cabinet minister, a period in which the patience which he had acquired as a negotiator in India stood him in good stead. Wellington had to convince Spain that he could not help her, at least not in the way in which she expected, and to persuade Portugal to allow herself to be helped in a way which he was able to approve. On the 10th of October, 1809, he visited Lisbon, and while there, obtained from Lieutenant-Colonel Robert Fletcher a report on the best situation for an entrenched position to cover the embarkation of his army. Indeed, it appeared as if, as soon as Napoleon should have Austria off his hands, the expulsion of the British from Portugal could not be much longer delayed. From Badajoz, where he still kept his headquarters, Wellington was compelled to watch the successive defeats of Spanish armies which had refused to attend to his advice to adopt the form of warfare to which they were suited, and to fight in large masses and in strong positions. By the end of the year he had abandoned Spain and concentrated upon the defence of Portugal, marching the mass of his troops to places north of Lisbon, and leaving Hill with one division on the Tagus. But the expected blow was deferred. It was the best season of the year for a campaign in Andalusia, and Joseph could not resist the temptation to turn aside and recruit his depleted finances from the richest province in Spain. There was scarcely anything to stop him. On the 1st of February, 1810, he was in Seville, the Junta flying before him into Cadiz, and the authorities which a year before had refused to admit British troops within the town were obliged to beg for aid. Out of nearly a hundred thousand men whom they had had in the field three months before, they could not find the few thousand necessary to man those almost impregnable defences. They were reinforced by two British battalions, some artillery, and a Portuguese regiment. In March Major-General Graham came to take command of the British force, which was raised by June to eight thousand men.

The French high command in Spain had committed a strategic error, of which Napoleon's disapproval came too late, in allowing itself to be diverted from the enemy's strongest point—Wellington's army; and that general turned the respite which he had obtained to good effect. On the 20th of October, 1809, he drew up for Fletcher the memorandum which formed the foundation of the scheme of defence behind the Lines of Torres Vedras of a year later. To have allowed the details of it to get abroad, even to have permitted his own officers to think that he expected much from it, would have been fatal. For no secret was kept. On one occasion about this time he complained that an English newspaper had published the precise line of operations which he meant to follow in a certain event.

He was precluded from doing anything to raise the hopes of the troops. He had no high expectations himself. His letters and despatches were full of arrangements for re-embarkation, not as a mere possible eventuality, but as a thing most likely to occur. "If the Spaniards had not lost two armies lately, we should keep up the ball for another year. But as it is!—But I won't despair!" So he wrote in December, and it is not strange that all the following spring letters from the front expressed the conviction that evacuation was inevitable, and that the most despondent views were entertained by all officers whom Ministers were able to consult at home. Natural as all this was, Wellington felt it deeply. He shrank into himself. The Wellington of the year following Talavera was a very different man from the popular Arthur Wellesley of the brilliant three weeks campaign which ended in Burrard's refusal to allow him to follow up the success of Vimeiro. His army was full of the faults of the Talavera campaign, and long refused to forgive him the prolonged stay which followed in the feverish swamps of the Guadiana. He could say that he had done his duty in standing by his allies as long as there seemed any possibility of helping them; and yet he had had small thanks for that from them, while with his own people Charles Napier found in July 1810 that he was even less popular than was supposed at home. He had other reasons for reserve. He had now the responsibility of a large army and of making decisions on the most important matters, civil as well as military, for everything seemed to come to him; he was still only forty, and he was obliged to assert his authority over generals in his own army some of whom were older than himself, while among the Spanish and Portuguese sixty or seventy was no uncommon age. He had lost almost all his divisional generals after Talavera for one reason or another, including Sherbrooke, his Second in Command; nor was he much more fortunate as regards his brigadiers. He obtained two excellent major-generals from home in Thomas Picton and the Honourable Lowry Cole. But he was not altogether happy either about those who remained or those who came out. He was not chary of reposing confidence in subordinates where such confidence was deserved. He erred rather in the opposite direction, particularly before experience taught him the danger of such errors. When Spencer first joined him as Second in Command in 1808, he gave him the greatest latitude as regards issuing orders; yet in 1810, when he obtained him again in the same capacity, he found him very far from satisfactory. Several incidents of the same year showed that he gave Craufurd his head at least as much as was safe. Men like Graham and Hill enjoyed his full confidence.

He was by nature warm-hearted—one of those men who find it almost impossible to refuse anything which duty does not compel him to refuse. The man who complained in later years that such advantage was taken of his disposition that, though the costermonger's donkey had some rest, the Duke of Wellington had none, was the same man who in 1809 wrote in reply to a preposterous request for leave enlarging upon the concern which it gave him to refuse a request made to him by any of his officers. Yet it was absolutely necessary to harden himself in the face of such a serious lack of discipline as prevailed. There are many passages in his despatches and orders which throw light from the point of view of a Commander-in-Chief on the vagaries of the army during its enforced period of inactivity in Lisbon and elsewhere; of which so gay a picture is given in Lever's Charles O'Malley—the plundering commissary, the field officer sacrificing the necessities of his men to his own comfort, the subaltern lurking about the town—instead of being at the front—in quest of disreputable pleasures. Good regimental officers were not forthcoming to cope with the increase in the army; nor indeed, outside the Light Division, was even the older class of regimental officer aware that his duties did not end when the men had left the parade ground. It was not to be supposed that such men would be of much use in controlling the partially disciplined men of the second battalions, spread far and wide over a friendly country where there was abundance of wine, though little to eat. As early as September 1809 he wrote: "I really believe that more plunder and outrage have been committed by this army than by any other that ever was in the field", and, in the following year, "they have never brought up a convoy of money that they have not robbed the chest." Meticulously accurate as he was over details, Wellington seldom made a general statement without some exaggeration, and in the case of the former of these two statements, at least, the exaggeration was obvious. But the instances which actually occurred of murders and other outrages were enough to justify the sternest attitude. His own aversion from severity is apparent from the mild character of some of his orders themselves, as well as the frequency with which it was necessary to repeat them. The first execution of a soldier for plundering was not until October 1810. But he supported the severity of such almost ferocious disciplinarians as Sherbrooke and Craufurd, and he specially asked for Picton, whose reputation in this respect threw that of every other in the shade. For himself he fell back upon a sternness of demeanour which made him personally feared, and effectually masqued the real kindness and even softness of his nature.

Another circumstance helped to produce a change in him. He had hitherto been almost invariably venturesome to a fault. Such seemed the opinion of two observant young officers, both afterwards famous, Charles Napier and William Gomm. The Times condescended to voice the general censure with its solemn ribaldry:—

> "What chief with Wellington can vie
> Who flies to fight, and fights to fly?"

True to the general belief in his foolhardiness he refused to relinquish the offensive. For three months he still kept his headquarters at Badajoz. He clung to the hope, in spite of past disillusionments, that he might yet strike some blow along with his Spanish allies. Viewed in broad outline the history of the next year seems to be that of a period in which all went according to a carefully conceived defensive plan, in which the fortresses of Ciudad Rodrigo and Almeida were to hold out just long enough to allow him to develop his powers of resistance. But his correspondence tells a different story. He had serious plans for raising the siege of both those places, which he regretfully relinquished. It was not without severe pain that he grew into the Wellington of the famous Lines.

The Fabian part was forced upon him by political exigencies, as he himself explained. Compelled to a reserve which was not natural to him, he was apt to disburden himself, when he could, to anyone who was not an officer actually under his command. One of these was Major Charles Napier, who had been made prisoner of war at Coruña, and chivalrously granted leave by Ney, and was now in Wellington's camp as a spectator only. Another was his cousin, the other Charles Napier of the Royal Navy, who had all the fire-eating characteristics of the family, and who was equally successful in getting wounded in a battle in which he had no concern. "I could easily beat the French", Wellington once told him in a moment of expansion, "but England has no other army, and it would cost me ten thousand men." England could not spare them. In March the Earl of Darnley twice called the attention of Ministers to a rumour that it was intended to send every disposable soldier fit for foreign service out of the country, without eliciting any attempt at a satisfactory reply. Fully aware of these difficulties, Wellington confined his demands to 30,000 men; but these were rank and file, exclusive of officers and sergeants, and inclusive only of cavalry and infantry. It soon appeared, however, that even this was not intended to include the sick, whom he reckoned at ten per cent of his force, or garrisons and casualties, amounting to another couple of thousand. The Cadiz force was also separate. The total required for the Peninsula, outside Gibraltar, was found to exceed fifty thousand men. The Secretary for War on his side was as ingenious in lowering his performances as the General had been in raising his demands. Liverpool told him he should have everything he wanted, but in the list he gave he took care to include some units from other parts of the world, none of which—as it turned out—could then be spared. Wellington occasionally gave way to somewhat bitter complaints. He wrote contemptuously of the Government to the admiral on the Tagus, Vice-Admiral the Honourable George Berkeley, a very near connection of Lord Buckingham, the head of the Grenville family—"What can be expected from men who are beaten in the House of Commons three times a week?" Already in November he had told Buckingham himself that he wished old friends would unite and form a strong Government. But peace at home was a forlorn hope; and he set himself to maintain the firmness of those among his own political associates who were in the fighting line on the parliamentary benches. He indited to Liverpool one of those letters characteristic of him, in which great political wisdom is so clearly and cogently expressed as to give the impression of nothing more than ordinary common sense; he pointed out that the war had to be carried on somewhere, and if not on the Continent it would be in the United Kingdom, where it would be much more expensive and disastrous to the country's future prosperity.

The Secretary of State was far from being blind to this point of view. It is possible, indeed, to trace a steady progress in the war policy of the various cabinets which had held office in past years. After the unfortunate results of the attempts to co-operate with allied armies in Flanders and elsewhere in Pitt's first administration, there had been a long period under both Windham and Castlereagh, when the notion of independent amphibious warfare was in the ascendant. Hence came, among many failures, such almost fruitless successes as the battle of Maida and the capture of Flushing. Wasteful as all such efforts were, the Cabinet had been so apprehensive of running any serious risk that Moore was actually ordered, during the expedition to Sweden in 1808, to arrange plans with her King in such a manner as to avoid taking his troops to any distance from the coast. In his last campaign that officer was no longer hampered in this way, but, forgetful of Blenheim, everyone was most anxious for the fate of a British army in the heart of a foreign country away from the friendly ships, and there was a tendency to fetter both him and Wellesley with instructions. At last in 1810 Liverpool realized that a new policy was imperative. The Commander-in-Chief must have a free hand, both as regards instructions from home and co-operation with the allies. The responsibility would be his. But he would at the same time understand that the effort to support him was limited by the Empire's resources in money and man power. The weakest Cabinet of the age was showing itself the best able to conduct a war.

Wellington had good reason for not wishing for more troops. He would have had greater difficulty even than he had already in organizing his commissariat, and their pay would have been in even greater arrears than it already was. Until Canning's resignation drew Huskisson's along with it, the financing of the troops had been in the hands of the latter as Secretary of the Treasury. Both in Walcheren and in Portugal he had created difficulties by attempting to compel military expenses to be defrayed by bill on London. To the shame of England many debts on account of Moore's army were still unpaid in 1810, and he and Wellesley and Chatham had all been held up in the course of their campaigns by want of specie. This difficulty was increased by Portugal's own requirements. Great Britain had undertaken to keep 20,000 Portuguese troops in her pay at a cost originally estimated at £50,000 a month, and that country received a subsidy besides. It was Wellington who pointed out that now that Great Britain carried on a trade direct with Brazil, which under the old mercantile system would have been confined to the mother country, the customs revenue was reduced almost to nothing, and in spite of every economy Portuguese finance showed a deficit for 1809 of over £1,200,000 at four shillings the dollar. Finally the whole subsidy, a considerable part of which was sent in kind, was raised to £980,000. The finance of the war benefited by the loss of Huskisson. Perceval's Secretaries of the Treasury were neither of them men who could take on this work, and he was obliged to go into the matter himself, which he did with a thoroughness and an appreciation of the difficulties of others which left nothing to be desired. It was another of the compensations which the country obtained for the weakness of ability in its Government.

The most important business of the war during the year of waiting for the invasion of Portugal was the training of her army. Already in May 1809 during the advance on Oporto, Wellington had had occasion to observe the gallantry of a Portuguese regiment which can have owed little or nothing to any foreign training. But no general confidence could as yet be placed in that army as a whole. It was true that no troops could be relied upon to be always firm. The Light Division itself, only two months after behaving so splendidly on the Coa, and a day or two before behaving equally splendidly at Bussaco, was attacked by an extraordinary, and to all intents causeless panic. But it was felt that the Portuguese army could not as yet be even generally relied upon. Now that it was no longer necessary for it to remain in the field, it was possible to take up its reorganization seriously; and Beresford was fortunate in being able to set himself to this task almost as if it had been in time of peace. In December he obtained the institution of a central depot with a British general officer in command for training recruits for the infantry and artillery. The mounted arm was necessarily so small in a mountainous country where there was no good natural breed of horses, that Beresford did not concern himself with its training; though as a matter of fact the cavalry distinguished itself considerably on one or two occasions, notably in September 1810, when a brilliant charge under Brigadier-General George Madden, a former officer of the British army, rescued Romana's army from disaster. Within the regiments Beresford's system was a different one from that commonly followed when the army of one nation is trained partly or wholly by officers belonging to another. Instead of being attached to divisions or brigades as inspecting officers, or to commanding officers of battalions as adjutants, they were introduced everywhere at what seemed haphazard. The men were very apt to learn, and there was considerable zeal among the officers, but there was a tendency in both to fall back into what Benjamin d'Urban, Beresford's Chief of the Staff, called slouching and slovenly habits. To remedy this it was advisable to encourage the spirit of emulation, and at the same time to keep in touch with the regimental officers and their ways by having British officers in the lower grades as well as the higher. Among the 164 British officers in the Portuguese service, of whom all but twenty surgeons were combatant officers, 20 were majors, 34 captains, and 21 subalterns. The last included men who were sergeants in the British army before exchange, such men being needed to teach the English exercises. The method of interspersing—the word is Beresford's own—the British regimental officers with the Portuguese, put the newcomer upon his mettle. He had already, on entering the new army, obtained a step in rank, and he set himself to deserve his position, and to make himself an example to officers to whom in other circumstances he would perhaps have been little, if at all, superior. To complete the system under which the Portuguese army was penetrated with British officers, Beresford arranged for the command and the post of second in command of a regiment to be divided between the two nations; while as there were 13 British brigadiers and 17 British full colonels in that army, it was easy to secure the commands of brigades. Only one of the ten at Bussaco was commanded by a Portuguese. Artillery offered little difficulty. There was here no question of revolutionizing drill; and the bestowal of a few divisions, as the command of two batteries was called, upon British captains, with a step of rank as Portuguese majors, merely intensified the spirit of emulation already characteristic of the scientific branches of the service. The total of the regular army in the first half of 1810 was about 55,000 men, including nearly 5,000 artillery, 4,500 cavalrymen actually mounted, and, besides the regular infantry, nearly 4,000 light infantry or caçadores who were trained in the manner of British riflemen, and armed with a rifle of British manufacture.

For the militia, which was put at the same strength, an arrangement was made in December 1809 on the initiative of Miguel Pereira Forjaz, a good soldier in the earlier days of the war and now Secretary to the Regency, to pass the officers through a course of training in a central school. But it was never possible to trust much to this line of defence. The regiments, placed under native generals with occasionally a British second in command, such as Nicholas Trant or John Wilson, were, if mobilized at all, left outside the regular theatre of war. Descending from north of the Mondego or south of the Tagus, they might harrass the enemy on the march or intercept convoys. They also occupied redoubts and entrenchments, and formed the greater part of the garrisons of the fortresses. The levy in mass or ordenanza did somewhat similar work to the militia, and it was these, chiefly, who made and destroyed military roads, and constructed those entrenchments which afterwards became the wonder of Europe. It was owing, to a great extent, to the authority which as Marshal-General he thus possessed over the whole manhood of Portugal called out for military service, that Wellington was able to enforce his will upon the country.

It was no new thing for Portugal to place her army under foreign control. The traces still remained of the reorganization by a German, Count Lippe, fifty years before. When the Peninsular war began, one of the British adventurers who took service under him, John Forbes, was Governor of Rio Janeiro, and the Prince Regent, after being escorted to his transatlantic possessions by an English admiral, was being guarded there by a Scottish marshal. It is because it was in the tradition of the Portuguese army to be partly officered by foreigners that Beresford's system worked so smoothly. Much was also due to the character of the chief. Beresford could scarcely have been called popular. He was regarded as harsh and even cruel, but this was only because, habituated to the strict disciplinary methods of the British army, he could not but adopt a severe attitude towards the characteristic faults of the Portuguese. But he was really averse from all undue severity. The choice which he made of British officers was excellent. Service in the Portuguese army was popular, and some of the best officers applied, encouraged by the single or double step in rank, and the scope for distinction. It was not possible to find more like Robert Wilson—a man equally at home in any part of Europe, whether cracking his camp jests with the Emperor of Russia or concerting the defence of Portugal with the Bishop of Oporto. His Loyal Lusitanian Legion, a forerunner of the reorganized Portuguese army, was absorbed into it, and he himself, unable to submit to a similar fate, retired to England. But there were not wanting men capable of exercising that sportsmanlike easy-going control of men of a different nation in which his countrymen excelled. Some of these belonged, like the future Lieutenant-General Sir William Warre, to families long associated with the country. By their means Beresford was able to remodel the Portuguese army, and, thanks to the unexpectedly slow movements of the enemy, he got almost a year in which to do so undisturbed.

Napoleon's final admission into the ranks of European sovereigns by a matrimonial alliance with the Emperor of Austria in February 1810, was followed by some relaxation of his military vigour. He did not attempt to redeem his promise of personally planting his eagles on the towers of Lisbon and driving the leopard into the sea. He sent, indeed, that one of his officers who alone could point to battles won and honours gained while he himself was still but a general—the spoilt child of victory as he called him—Marshal Masséna. But in choosing him he chose one who had no heart for the work. Masséna was now fifty-two. He had spent the last seventeen years of his life almost continually in the camp, and now thought himself too old. Napoleon only passed his order placing Masséna in command of the three corps of Ney, Reynier, and Junot, united as the Army of Portugal, in April. It was not until the summer was well advanced that he had finished filling the Peninsula with troops.

The numbers shown in the imperial master rolls of the 15th of July appear enormous. Including 29,000 detached, and nearly 48,000 sick, the total amounted to 356,729 men. But out of these almost 90,000 found employment in the two north-eastern provinces of Aragon and Catalonia alone, particularly in the latter province, where much weaker Spanish forces, aided by British command of the seas, kept them fruitlessly moving from one quarter to another. Something of the same kind was done on a smaller scale in the north-west. Three corps, nearly 73,000 men, were kept at work in the south owing to the unfortunate committal to Andalusia. The active portion of the Army of Portugal was nearly 87,000 men, including General Montbrun's cavalry with the corps of Ney, Reynier, and Junot. There were more than a hundred thousand men on the lines of communication, in the north-west and in other parts of Spain. All of this was necessary, and, to bring the war to a fortunate conclusion, called for a rapid and vigorous hand, every month increasing the difficulty of maintaining so large a force in such a country as Spain. Yet Masséna only arrived at Salamanca on the 15th of May, and did not break ground before Ciudad Rodrigo, the Spanish fortress which barred the nearest way to Portugal, till a month later, nor did he take it until the 10th of July. He was more fortunate with Almeida, the fortress on the Portuguese side, which was not invested until after another five weeks' delay. Scarcely had his batteries opened when a magazine exploded, on the 28th of August the place surrendered, and the road into Portugal was open. But still there was delay, and it was nearly another fortnight before he had begun to concentrate the whole of the Army of Portugal on the roads which led south-west from the frontier at Almeida to Coimbra, and thence more nearly southwards to Lisbon.

During the operations about Ciudad Rodrigo and Almeida, the main body had been watched by Robert Craufurd. In the years when an invasion had been believed to be imminent, Moore had welded the 43rd, 52nd, and 95th regiments into what was afterwards to be celebrated as the Light Brigade. The last regiment, that of Rifle Men as they were then called, had a weapon which was an arm of precision at 300 yards, whereas the smooth-bore Brown Bess, with which almost all the rest of the army was armed, could not be depended upon at 100 yards. Trained as marksmen and skirmishers, they were naturally adapted to cover a much wider front than other regiments. Hence Colonel

Coote Manningham, who originally raised the regiment in 1800, introduced the system under which each company was treated as independent, and the captain made responsible for the whole training of his men. A tie of comradeship was encouraged between officers, non-commissioned officers, and men, which had not been known in other regiments. Moore had long realized the importance of treating the private soldier with a more considerate interest. He extended the company system three years later to his other two light infantry regiments, and the three together became a model for the rest of the army as the 95th had been a model for the 43rd and 52nd. But march discipline was so little understood in the early days of the Peninsular War that, on the retreat from Sahagun, even this fine brigade was very far from perfect. Craufurd cured that fault partly by severity in punishment, partly also by careful arrangement and attention to the wants of his men. Rifleman Harris of the 95th has left a vivid picture of him mingling among the men during that terrible time, encouraging them individually and by name, and sharing in their hardships —even bringing rum to them when visiting the outposts at night.

Craufurd had another gift almost essential to the commander of an advanced body in such a country as the Portuguese frontier. "As a commissary", wrote George Napier, "he was perfect." This, and the special suitability of the troops which he commanded, led Wellington to reject the obvious course of keeping the enemy watched by means of a division of cavalry. Craufurd did the work much better. He was not, however, kept without cavalry. As much was sent him as could be put under him when no cavalry brigadier junior to him was available. He was given one regiment which was far superior to any British regiment, the First Hussars of the King's German Legion. There was a special justification for placing it under Craufurd. He had the unusual accomplishment of being not only fully conversant with German military methods, but also capable of addressing the men in their own language. Strengthened with two brigades of Portuguese Light Infantry his force became the Light Division, and was divided into brigades commanded by two of his lieutenant-colonels, Sydney Beckwith, a man cast in a heroic mould, and Robert Barclay of the 52nd.

For three months Craufurd successfully maintained his division, which amounted after all to no more than 4,300 men, unsupported, within two hours march of the advanced posts of an enemy of close on 60,000. It was an extraordinary feat, calling for the most perfect organization and ceaseless vigilance, and would even then have been impossible without the skill of the 95th Rifles and the First Hussars of the King's German Legion. But this success was temporarily eclipsed by a misfortune which was due to the General's own characteristic faults of presumption, and a desire to distinguish himself and his division. Previous to the investment of Almeida he lay with his troops close to the fortress with the river Coa in his rear, virtually inviting attack. Here Ney fell on him on the 3rd of July with his whole corps of 24,000 men. His troops extricated themselves across the river bridge with considerable courage and skill, but with the loss of 333 of some of the best soldiers in the army. Charles Napier was a spectator of the action; and the future conqueror of Sindh noted for his own instruction a list of nine distinct errors on Craufurd's part, besides the capital one of accepting battle contrary to the express direction of the Commander-in-Chief. The French success was marred by Ney, who with equal presumption obstinately endeavoured to force the passage of the bridge, which cost him the greater portion of his 527 casualties. The Light Division escaped terribly mauled, and had to be replaced at the outposts by the Cavalry Division under Lieutenant-General Sir Stapleton Cotton. Had it not been for this reverse, and for the premature surrender of Almeida, it is possible that there would have been no British retreat to the neighbourhood of Lisbon, that the Lines of Torres Vedras would have been no more famous than those of San Juliao, and that the detractors of Wellington would have lost the opportunity of hastily substituting for the legend of the foolhardy Sepoy General that of the unimaginative Fabius who fought from behind stone walls and conquered by starvation.

Masséna's invasion of Portugal was a campaign of discoveries in which nothing on his side, and not very much on his adversary's, went according to plan. The beginning was regular enough. It was the French marshal's object so to conceal his movements as to draw Reynier's corps to him from the south and make a combined dash on Coimbra, before the British army was concentrated. But he was foiled in this part of his plan by the excellent scouting services of a reconnoitering party under the enterprising Colonel Waters of the 11th Foot, and by the prescience of Hill himself. That general, left to keep Reynier from making a dash with his 16,000 men upon Lisbon by Abrantes and Santarem, got information in time that he had destroyed his boats on the Tagus. He immediately divined that he was on his march northward, and made a parallel movement to join Wellington. The concentration of the British army in advance of Coimbra was completed by the 22nd of September.

In his advance Masséna had the choice of roads running on either side of the Mondego, which takes a somewhat similar south-westerly course through Portugal as the Tagus, at a distance of about sixty miles to the northward of that river. Many of those whom he led had been in Portugal before—notably Generals Junot, Loison, and Foy. He was accompanied by several Portuguese who sympathized with France, and, had these gentry intended a double treachery, they could have hardly have informed him worse. Wellington had thrown up entrenchments on the direct road south of the Mondego. Masséna knew at least of this, and, misled by his Portuguese friends, elected, after being joined by Reynier on the 19th, to cross the Mondego, and advance by the roads northward of it, choosing for his artillery and baggage what William Napier described as the worst road in Portugal. He found all the country through which he passed empty of people and devastated, supplies removed or destroyed, even the mills broken up, Wellington having obtained from the Regency orders to that effect which were faithfully carried out. He had execrable maps. He had no idea of what alternative roads were in his front by which Wellington's position might be turned, and could get no information. On the 22nd he found himself in touch with the enemy, and for the next three days he was pushing the British advanced troops back until, on the 26th, he was brought up before the ridge of Bussaco, where Wellington had determined to make his stand.

Other considerations had determined the British general besides the temptation to offer battle in a position in which he had good hope of victory. There had been difficulties with the Portuguese Regency. Some members had been profoundly discontented with the failure to relieve Almeida, and were calling violently for a blow to be struck. They had, moreover, neglected to carry out the agreement to waste the country between Coimbra and Torres Vedras as the country had been wasted between Almeida and Coimbra, and had thus deranged the whole of Wellington's plan. A battle here would give him more time, even if a further retreat became eventually necessary. He drew up his troops accordingly—on the extreme right Hill's division, then Leith's, Picton's, Spencer's, Craufurd's, and Cole's. The Portuguese infantry, almost exactly equal to the British in number, were for the most part brigaded with them, and the total force on the ridge, including the 2,000 artillery and a couple of hundred cavalry, was nearly 57,500.

Masséna had learnt little of the natural features of Wellington's position, and was completely ignorant how it was occupied. General Éblé who commanded the artillery, and whom Foy styled the best officer of that arm in Europe, represented to him the danger of hurling his columns of attack against a position upon which his guns could not bring an effective fire. It was no longer possible to despise the British. In fact a month earlier Foy had recorded in his diary—a thing which he added that he intended to keep strictly to himself—that they were better soldiers than the French. But the Portuguese, at least, were an unknown factor. Masséna needed a victory to establish his authority over his almost mutinous corps commanders; and he trusted in his star. He made his attack on the morning of 27th of September. He had entered Portugal with 65,000 men. But in effective infantry alone he was now outnumbered by almost 2,000 men by Wellington. The result of his ill-planned adventure was not long in doubt. The attack was to be made by Reynier's corps on the left, followed by Ney's on the right, Junot's being held in reserve on that wing. Preceded by the usual cloud of skirmishers, the seasoned troops belonging to those two corps mounted the steep rocky slope of between four and five hundred feet with a determination which would not be refused. But reaching the top disordered and out of breath, Reynier's columns were unable to deploy, and stood for the most part helplessly exposed to the devastating fire of the well-placed artillery, until they were hurled down the slope by a vigorous counter attack. One brigade in particular, which had effected a lodgement on that part of the ridge occupied by Picton's division, was repelled by Lieutenant-Colonel Wallace, a regimental officer of marked tactical initiative, personal courage, and control over his men. He charged with his own men, the 88th Foot or Connaught Rangers, and half a battalion of the 45th, supported by the 8th Portuguese regiment. Wellington wrote that he had never witnessed a more gallant attack. On the British left, where the ground was steeper, the advance was prematurely made before Reynier was master of the heights. One brigade only succeeded in reaching almost to the top, watched intently by Craufurd, who stood on a rock alone until the moment came when he gave the word to charge. The 43rd and 52nd now sprang forward from a hollow where they had been concealed from view, opened a devastating fire, and within a few minutes thrust the enemy from the top to the bottom. Masséna lost over 4,500 men in the battle, about a sixth of the four divisions which alone were really engaged. On the Anglo-Portuguese side the losses amounted to about 1,250, being equally divided between the two nations. When Wellington's despatch was read to the King at home, now almost blind, and with the clouds which darkened the last years of his life gathering round him, he saw at once who deserved the honours of the day. It was only to be expected that the flower of the British army would do its part. The issue of the fight depended on the Portuguese, and these had quitted themselves almost like veterans. George III's last notable act before he sank into oblivion was to insist on a knighthood of the Bath being given to Marshal Beresford.

Masséna now made a fresh discovery. It was after all possible to turn Wellington's position. His cavalry found a peasant who expressed surprise at so unnecessary a battle having been fought, when the French, by retracing their steps a few miles eastwards and then turning to the north-west, could strike the main road which runs southwards from Oporto upon Coimbra, and so on to Lisbon. Wellington had foreseen this, and might have detached one or more divisions to occupy the pass. But had he done so, in case of defeat the line of retreat of such a force would have been north-westwards, and then northward by the main road to Oporto, and he would have had to enter the Lines without it. He preferred to keep his own army intact, and directed Brigadier-General Trant to occupy the pass with his division of Portuguese militia. As it turned out, the route prescribed to him by the Portuguese general officer commanding in the north did not permit him to be in time. But Trant could in no case have done much with a few thousand untrustworthy militia against the whole French army even in a defile or series of defiles. All that the French found in the pass was a few German Hussars, who were easily brushed aside. It is easy to understand why, playing as he did for the highest degree of safety, Wellington made no detachment strong enough to offer any substantial resistance. It is less intelligible why his cavalry, which had only a few days before been conducting some admirable reconnaissances, failed to watch a beaten enemy closely, and harass him while carrying out a flank march across the front of a victorious army in position. There must have been some thought of preserving that arm for its duties as rearguard on the now inevitable retreat. Cotton, too, was not enterprising. But the principal explanation is to be sought in the fact that every part of an army is affected by any want of vigour at the head, and that at this time even the colossal energies of Wellington were unequal to any enterprising line of conduct. He had recently found he could not depend upon his second in command, Spencer, for anything. He complained that he was not supported either by his own officers or by the Portuguese Government. Even his thoughts were not expressed with his usual clearness. In his despatch to Liverpool of the 30th of September, immediately after explaining that he was in full retreat, he inconsistently added that Trant's delay might prevent his effecting his object in occupying the Bussaco ridge. That object—the rolling back the tide of invasion—had admittedly been already abandoned. A similar unwillingness to look facts in the face, very rare in Wellington, recurred on the 4th of October, when he wrote in a letter home that he would have stopped the enemy entirely if it had not been for the blunder of the Portuguese general who sent Trant by a circuitous road. But he was clear on one thing. He had fought and won what, regarded merely as a political battle, was of value at all events in animating the Portuguese, and justifying the confidence placed in them. He was now free to proceed with his general plan, and to draw Masséna after him to the south. At nightfall of the 28th he began his own retreat westward by the shortest way to Coimbra, at the same time as Masséna was moving away from him in precisely the opposite direction, in order to reach the same place by a more circuitous route.

The retreat was steadily continued for the next twelve bays, and by the night of the 10th of October the allied army had safely reached the Lines. They had been pressed by General Montbrun's cavalry, but without effect. The rearguard was successfully protected by the British cavalry, which had the best of it in several small encounters. It was Masséna who met with misfortune. He had left his wounded with a small guard at Coimbra, and after he had gone, Trant, advancing at his heels from the northward, swooped down with four thousand militia and a few cavalry upon the place, captured the whole number, and carried them into Oporto. The Englishman was able, after the first few moments, to restrain the outrages of his followers, exasperated as they were at the condition in which they found Coimbra after Masséna had left. He afterwards received a warm acknowledgement of their gratitude from the captured officers. Nevertheless, the news that their wounded had fallen into the hands of an ill-disciplined body of the enemy from whom they could expect little mercy, came as a rude shock to the French army, and reduced confidence in its Chief. The defence afterwards made for Masséna was that he could not spare a larger force, and that he expected to finish the campaign in a week.

It was now that he made two further important discoveries. He had already heard after crossing the Mondego something of the existence of entrenchments in front of Lisbon. But now that he was before them, he was able to take note not merely of the Lines which Wellington had thrown up, but of the configuration of the country as well. He had actually been led to suppose that there would be nothing but undulating plateaux, and he was surprised to discover mountains between himself and Lisbon. Had Junot, when he was hastening northwards in 1808 in such anxiety to meet Wellington, turned his head behind him when he reached the high land south of Torres Vedras, he would have observed a powerful natural line of defence from the sea to the Tagus, which it needed comparatively little labour to make almost impregnable.

The incredible tradition that Masséna arrived quite unexpectedly in front of an impenetrable barrier, before which his army was starved in a wasted and driven country until he was obliged to retire, is thus only a slight heightening of the truth. He knew very little indeed of the Lines before their existence was reported to him by his cavalry. The first line could certainly have been forced without a train of siege artillery, although only at very great loss. Although the country was not completely wasted, difficulties over supplies had much to do both with the withdrawal after a month to Santarem and his eventual retirement. But there can hardly be a stranger travesty of the facts than to represent the moment when Masséna found himself before the Lines as the crowning success of Wellington's career in the Peninsula. His whole plan had been thrown out of gear, and it would be difficult to find a period in his life in which his correspondence displays less satisfaction and more exasperation.

The construction of the Lines had indeed been a success beyond his hopes. The general idea was his, and owed much to that eye to country in which he excelled, and which, judging from the failures of his highly esteemed opponents, was no common gift. But all details were left to Lieutenant-Colonel Fletcher and his subordinates of the Royal Engineers, and the scheme gradually grew under their hands. The Lines took their name from the powerful isolated work begun at Torres Vedras at the most advanced point of the whole system as early as November 1809. Another was begun at the same time south-eastwards of it on Monte Agraca, eight miles west of the Tagus. These two works commanded the western and eastern sections of what became the first line. Here Wellington made his stand, but it is doubtful whether he would have done so had it not been for the very heavy rains which had fallen during the first days of October. These made it possible to flood the Zizandre for six miles between the sea and Torres Vedras, which, together with some minor redoubts, commanded the remainder of the twelve miles of the western section. The eastern section of seventeen miles ran almost due south for seven miles, still in October 1810 almost without defence. The remaining ten miles, running eastwards and southwards to the Tagus, were strongly fortified. The real line of resistance was the second line. This was carried over a bolder series of heights than the first, separated from it by valleys and undulations over a breadth of about five miles. It stretched across the Peninsula on which Lisbon is situated for 22 miles from the Atlantic to the Tagus. What is generally known as the third line was a small line of two miles covering the place of embarkation on the mouth of the Tagus at San Juliao westwards of Lisbon.

As the first line was far from being an impassable barrier even to a field army, Wellington had been in expectation of a battle upon ground of his own choosing. A starving army was bound to fight or to surrender. But he was woefully disappointed. Even the stand at Bussaco, though it had enabled much, had not given time to enable all supplies to be carried off. The maize harvest was still on the ground. The Regency had delayed enforcing the orders to abandon and waste the country, the civil magistrates were not warned in time, and it was not until the army was at their heels that the inhabitants from Coimbra southwards hastily gathered up what they could, only partly destroying the remainder, and took refuge either in Lisbon or in the mountains out of the path of the invading army. But the failure to overcome the stupendous difficulty of removing everything capable of feeding an army was not confined to the civil authorities. Wellington was unable to complete the removal or destruction of his own stores. At Villafranca, just outside the lines, good magazines of barley and corn, and at other places along or near the Tagus imported foodstuffs such as rice, sugar, coffee, and cod, fell into the hands of the French. Where the British army had not passed, as in the area about Santarem, only twenty miles north-eastward of where Masséna's troops were, very little had been done. But food was found nearer still. "At this moment", Wellington complained bitterly to Berkeley on the 16th of October, "the enemy are living upon grain found close to the lines; and they grind it into flour with the mills in our sight, which the Government were repeatedly pressed to order the people to render useless, and which could have been rendered useless only by taking away the sails". But it was the fact that many mills had been dismantled, and at this very time the sufferings of the enemy were severe. They were on quarter rations. They made this up by foraging for themselves; they got maize, chestnuts, vegetables, and occasional goat's flesh. As Hill wrote, it was a difficult matter to starve a Frenchman.

    Wellington did not allow himself to be long depressed by the miscarriage of his plans. The traveller and archaeologist, Sir William Gell, who met him a few days later at Beresford's headquarters, gave a remarkable account of that vitality which is the most prominent characteristic of truly great men. "More animation and merriment I never saw. He has none of the airs of a great man at the head of 100,000 men—all life and good humour." The Chief had his own headquarters near the centre of the line—at the southern extremity of the seven miles which had not yet been fortified. He garrisoned the works with militia and men of the levy in mass, having his whole field army free. He thus had under his hand a mass of manœuvre consisting of three divisions, available to defend the weakest part of the line with complete security for its flanks and rear, or to be thrown upon any other part of the line which should be attacked. The eastern and western section were actually separated from one another on the attackers' side by a steep range, but on that of the defenders communication was easy. His semaphores, worked by seamen, enabled him to communicate with either end of the line in four minutes.

None of the arrangements were called into play. The resistance which Masséna had experienced at Bussaco made him pause, and he finally decided not to attack. He was still able to claim that with under 49,000 men he had blockaded an army numerically half as strong again in regular troops, while, including troops of the second and third line, it was almost double. For the British were now 42,000, of whom 7,000 were sick or detached, the Portuguese regular troops 27,500 of whom 3,000 were sick, and Romana, who was at this time in little apprehension from Soult, was able to bring 6,000 into the Lines; and these totals did not include two battalions of marines left on the embarkation lines. The militia and levy in mass amounted to about 30,000. Berkeley had, moreover, supplied gunboats to protect the right of the Lines resting on the Tagus.

All these elaborate efforts of the army and navy, the flooding of rivers, the scarping of precipices, the clearing of forests, the great trees dragged into the valley with all their roots and branches, the thick stone walls piled on the tops of the mountains, the 59 redoubts mounting 232 guns on the second or main line of defence alone, to resist less than fifty thousand half-famished men who had marched hundreds of miles from their own country, seem at the first view a source of shame rather than of pride. But it would be unworthy to grudge Wellington the credit of having, almost in a literal sense, left no stone unturned to be able to say to Napoleon's legions, "Thus far and no further," for the first time since Sidney Smith turned them back at Acre, and to be able to disprove the predictions of a few months before of every Frenchman and every Englishman as to his prospects of maintaining himself in Portugal at all. Moreover, he had brought about a revolution in accepted theory as to the reliability of field fortifications, and the possibility of counterbalancing the advantages inseparable from the free and concentrated attack. Nor was the expense of teaching this lesson to the world considerable. The guns, 521 in all—ancient rusty pieces, many of them—were provided out of the Portuguese arsenal. The cost of the Lines at the time when the army entered them was less than £100,000—doubled before the end of the war by subsequent charges, including compensation for damage to property, and the construction of another line south of the Tagus to prevent the enemy from establishing a battery there in order to annoy the shipping during embarkation. The price paid by the inhabitants whose homes were devastated was a high one; but they would have escaped very little had they remained in their homes, and placed their stocks at Masséna's disposal. Wellington felt for their sufferings, and made a suggestion to Liverpool for a British subscription for their relief, which bore fruit in due course.

A month passed, during which Masséna's foragers were obliged to go farther and farther afield in search of supplies, and—harried as they were by parties of Portuguese militia from the north and from Peniche and Obidos on the north-west—in larger and larger parties. On the morning of the

15th of November a thick mist covered Masséna's position. When it had cleared, the British on Monte Agraca saw nothing in front of them. The Army of Portugal had slipped away in the night, and had marched to Santarem. Here Masséna looked not only for fresh supplies, but to reopen his communications with Spain, which had been interrupted since his march to Bussaco. Couriers with their escorts were intercepted. Napoleon's earliest information of his movements was through the English papers. At the end of October Masséna had sent to Paris a general of brigade with several hundred men. It was Foy, who, on his way, transmitted Masséna's orders calling up reinforcements and supplies from that part of the Army of Portugal left in Spain. He reached Paris on the 21st of November, and was thought to have performed a feat in reaching it at all. Complete as was Foy's report, the Emperor scarcely realized the situation. He played Wellington's own game. He believed in wearing the English down. He had already sent Drouet's corps into Portugal, but with no orders to join Masséna and enable him to bring matters to a decision. All that he undertook to do in addition was to send orders to Soult to move forward on the south bank of the Tagus. Meanwhile, Masséna was to hold fast, to look to his communications on both sides of that river, and to lay siege to the important Portuguese fortress of Abrantes some fifty miles above Santarem.

Wellington grimly waited. He had been longing to attack, even while Masséna was still in front of the Lines. He pursued him the moment he retired. But he found the position of Santarem more powerful even than that of Bussaco. There was no object in running any risk in order prematurely to compel Masséna to do what he would eventually be obliged to do by famine. How delicate the enemy's position was growing was evinced by a curious incident. So active were the Portuguese irregulars that, towards the end of November, General Gardanne, who led a convoy escorted by 2,000 men from the Spanish frontier, suddenly lost his balance when within a day's march of Masséna's army, and retreated precipitately with considerable loss. The Marshal now based his hopes on Drouet's corps of 30,000 men. But he was disappointed. Drouet brought only one division of 6,000 men as escort to a few hundred convalescents and remounts, and even this division was not permitted by the Emperor's orders to join Masséna's army. It remained at Leiria, rather more than half-way from the Mondego to Santarem. However, communications were now re-established with Spain by way of Almeida. But Masséna's attempts to capture Abrantes and to place himself astride of the Tagus were frustrated by Hill's division, which had been sent up the left bank. As the year drew to a close Wellington grew easier in his mind. He still kept a considerable portion of his troops in or near the Lines, and he did not cease to strengthen them. He refused as yet to part with the transports, and was sarcastic about the Government's wish to save their hire. "It is useless to expect more money from England", he wrote to Charles Stuart, the Minister in Lisbon, on the 22nd of December, "as the desire of economy has overcome even the fears of ministers, and they have gone so far as to desire me to send home the transports in order to save money!"

Napoleon had yielded to the temptation of looking, in part at least, to a political solution for a military problem. Disturbances might, he flattered himself, break out in the famishing population of Lisbon. Better still, there were prospects of a change of ministry in England which would lead to the withdrawal of the British army from the Peninsula. It had always been expected as a matter of course that the death of George III, or any recurrence of his insanity, which would put the Prince of Wales in his place as Regent, would bring Grey and Grenville into office. The more tragic of those two events had now occurred.

During the year which had passed since Perceval had become his chief adviser, George had shown several instances of his wonted shrewdness and mental vigour. But now a calamity occurred which proved that neither advancing years nor the distracting cares of kingly office nor the consolations of a numerous family, confer immunity from the shock of domestic affliction. The princess Amelia, his youngest and favourite daughter, fell ill. Parliament met on the 1st of November, the day before her death, but already the King's mind had become deranged. At first the character of the disease was in doubt; and later there were some signs of improvement, which proved illusory. At last on the 19th of December, after some sharp criticism from the Opposition for a delay which he could scarcely have avoided, Perceval, following the precedent set by Pitt on a similar occasion in 1788, introduced resolutions preparatory to an Act of Parliament conferring the powers of the King on the Prince of Wales as Regent, subject to certain restrictions. The House of Commons was still considering them when the year came to an end.

It seemed certain that Perceval's Ministry had only a few more days to run. "We are all, I think, on the *kick and the go*", wrote Palmerston with characteristic jauntiness. The expected change boded little good for the country so far as its most important interest was concerned—the prosecution of the war in the Peninsula. Here the tide had at last turned. And by a strange coincidence, at this moment in the extreme north that rift began at last to show itself which rapidly widened into the breach between Napoleon and Alexander that caused the advance to Moscow, the retreat, and the ruin of the Grand Army.

The French Emperor's hopes were now high. He had already planned for the year 1812, after he should have the Peninsula off his hands, a grand campaign in which over a hundred ships of the line besides two hundred thousand troops were to have their share. But this was merely for a final blow—to take possession of a bankrupt and moribund empire. For Napoleon could claim that the Continental System had at last begun to tell. He put even Goldsmith's failure down to speculators in colonial goods being in want of money and having to sell out, and thus depress, the price of stocks. In very truth his plan to kill England by abundance was not far short of success. Her warehouses were crammed with unsaleable colonial produce, which—in the words of British merchants themselves—was brought in from friendly, neutral and enemy countries in amount beyond all precedent and all calculation. As regards manufacturers, over-exportation to South America had led to a series of failures of shipping houses; manufacturers had followed suit, and had been obliged to work their mills on short time to the grievous distress of their employees, or had also failed; banks had done the same. It was, Napoleon exultantly wrote, only a question of weeks. In October he begged Alexander to confiscate a large flotilla of vessels then cruising in the Baltic under neutral flags. It would be a crushing blow to England. But the Czar refused compliance.

Napoleon's anxiety to tighten the cord of his land blockade further west was another source of coolness between him and his eastern rival. One of the coastal dominions which he had found it necessary to annex in northern Germany was Oldenburg, whose Grand Duke was the Czar's uncle. Alexander refused to be pacified. He replied by a measure which, injurious to France as it was, was strictly justified by Russia's own economic interests. In 1805 a high British authority on all questions connected with the Baltic trade had written these words: "It is from Britain only that Russia receives a balance in cash. Were the trade suspended, the importation of wines, brandies, and foreign produce and manufactures, from other countries, would totally absorb the moneyed capital of Russia." That contingency had now actually arrived. On the very last day of the decade the Czar met it by a customs ukase which imposed heavy duties upon products which came to Russia by land —which were French, and accorded much more favourable treatment to sea-borne merchandise—which was English. It was a declaration of economic war upon France.

CHAPTER VI

INDIA (1807—1810), OTHER POSSESSIONS, SCOTLAND, SOCIAL ENGLAND AT THE CLOSE OF THE DECADE

LORD MINTO's arrival in India as Governor-General in June 1807 introduced a period—for the Company's possessions at any rate—of recuperation and rest. He came, as a descendant of his said at the beginning of his own viceroyalty, to give the horse a rest between his gallops. But not long after his arrival in India he was confronted with an internal problem—one very different from those which arose during the stormy days of Wellesley, but which provoked an even more acute controversy at home. Many persons, those in particular who were affected by the growing evangelical movement, held strongly that it was impossible for anyone to call himself a consistent Christian without a desire to spread his religion wherever possible. The Church Missionary Society had been founded in London in 1799. Long before the end of the century, however, the Baptists had sent a mission to India; and in 1804, when the British and Foreign Bible Society was founded with a former Governor-General, Lord Teignmouth, as President, a Baptist and a member of the Church of England were Joint Secretaries. As regards India the movement had authority from a House of Commons Resolution of 1793, which prescribed the religious and moral improvement of the natives of that country. But it had now reached a stage when it attracted the attention of those who held that every nation has usually the beliefs which suit it best, and that religion is a question of race and climate. Pamphlets were published full of enthusiasm for the virtues of the Hindus, citing such facts as that in India Europeans can safely leave their dwellings open the whole night, and that they are in the habit of sending the poorest messengers on long journeys with large sums of money. But as regards the merits of the Hindu systems of belief they had the worst of the argument. Zachary Macaulay, the editor of the leading evangelical organ, the Christian Observer, had his own supporters too among those who knew the East and could describe what they actually saw. For example, the Reverend Claudius Buchanan, Vice-Provost of Wellesley's Calcutta College, described the death of two persons whom he had seen to throw themselves under the Car of Jagannath at Puri in Orissa, soon after its acquisition by the British. Practices such as this, and the self-immolation of widows on their husbands' funeral pyres, were openly carried out under English rule, and there was very little concealment of the custom of female infanticide. The first step towards putting such things down was to show that the ruling race itself possessed principles opposed to such practices. The Directors had in 1797 issued an order for building churches in Bengal, and Wellesley had been the first Governor-General to stand boldly forward as the head of a Christian Government. But, so far as the churches were concerned, economy hindered advance. The building of them in the interior was one of the many pious aspirations of the Directors which remained unfulfilled for many years. Apprehension of the recurrence of such events as the Vellore mutiny deterred officials in India from interference with any custom even distantly referable to religion.

There remained the possibility of conversion by missionary endeavour. Unfortunately the leading missionary in India, William Carey, the son of a schoolmaster and parish clerk, was a man of little education. He was rough in his methods, countenancing coarse abuse of Hinduism and sending native preachers about Calcutta whose style of attack on that religion endangered the public peace. Minto found it necessary to suspend such preaching there altogether, and it was not easy to carry on work up-country. From this time onward the principle of the Indian Government's neutrality in religious matters became firmly established. No doubt this was furthering the good work of what Sydney Smith called rooting out a nest of consecrated cobblers—a genial reference to Carey's former trade. But however useful a service may have been done to what the Whig divine called rational religion, there was little but pusillanimity in hesitating to proceed further along the course boldly marked out in 1802 by Wellesley when he prohibited the drowning of children from Saugar, the sacred island at the mouth of the Hooghly.

Minto was no less ready than Wellesley had been to do all that appeared from time to time to be necessary to counteract the French menace. Long before his arrival a French agent had been received in Persia, and he had been followed at the end of 1807 by General Gardane's splendid embassy. Accompanied as it was by a number of officers who spread themselves over Persia, there was an apprehension of French influence extending into Afghanistan and even the Punjab, apart from the more remote possibility of Napoleon giving effect to his scheme for despatching a combined force of French, Russians, and Austrians for the invasion of India. In 1809 treaties of friendship were concluded with Shah Shuja-ul-Mulk, Amir of Kabul, by Mountstuart Elphinstone at Peshawar, and with Raja Ranjit Singh by Charles Metcalfe at Amritsar, the sacred city of the Sikhs. The Sutlej was now definitely made the boundary between the two spheres of influence. Minto had already taken up the case of Persia. The Shah had for the time being thrown himself into the arms of France, because it had appeared to him to be the only means of getting aid against the Emperor of Russia, whose troops had invaded his territories. The first article of Malcolm's treaty of 1801 had provided for mutual aid and assistance between the two States. But the only assistance which England was prepared to offer was her mediation with Russia, and even this never materialized. Fortunately by the end of 1808 the Shah discovered that his expectations from France were equally delusive. Gardane withdrew from Tehran by one gate the day before Sir Harford Jones, the envoy sent from England, entered it by another. The King's representative now had no difficulty in concluding a preliminary treaty of defensive alliance. The terms were not satisfactory to the Governor-General, who had from the first insisted upon sending his own negotiator —Malcolm. He even recalled Jones. But he created all this confusion, wasting a considerable sum of public money, and placing himself in almost direct opposition to the Home Government, to no purpose. It was definitely decided that diplomatic relations with Persia should be carried on from London, and Malcolm was not even allowed to conclude the definitive treaty. This was the work of Sir Gore Ouseley, a man who, though sent out from home, was, like Jones, as thoroughly conversant with Eastern conditions as Malcolm himself.

In the interior the pacification effected by Cornwallis and Barlow had not been completely successful. The petty chiefs of Rajputana and Central India, whom Wellesley had endeavoured to secure from Maratha oppression, suffered. In Bundelkhand military operations had to be carried out against refractory chieftains in 1809 and the following years. West of Delhi the policy of allowing no extension of territory broke down for a curious reason. Several chiefs in succession had resigned the charge of Hariana, a turbulent district conquered by Lake from Sindhia, and it had to be annexed to the Company. In Central India Holkar's savage temper, maddened by immoderate indulgence in brandy, had passed the bounds of sanity. He was no longer a power in the land, but this did not restrain his captains; and British troops were called into activity in 1809 to defend the friendly States of Hyderabad and Berar from their attacks. In the extreme south of India, in Travancore, there had been trouble over the payment of the arrears due from the Raja, who was bound by one of those subsidiary treaties which Wellesley had found so unsatisfactory on this very ground. During the dispute the Minister or Diwan, whose resignation had been demanded, made a treacherous attack on the Resident, who escaped on board a British vessel. Early in the following year, 1809, the Government of Madras sent columns to reduce the Raja to submission—an affair of little difficulty. A new Diwan was appointed, but the finances of the State remained unsatisfactory until he was succeeded at the Raja's own request by the new Resident himself. He was Major John Munro, an officer whose financial energies in another sphere had already led to what was perhaps the strangest event which has ever taken place in the armies of the empire.

It is only the effects of a climate singularly exasperating to Europeans which can account, even partially, for the astonishing series of occurrences known as the Madras Mutiny, in which waves of unreasoning irritation beat helplessly against almost equally unreasoning obstinacy. At the end of 1807 Sir George Barlow was consoled for his supersession as Governor-General with the Governorship of the Southern Presidency. He was a typical Indian Civil Servant of the Secretariat stamp, resolute, courageous and hard-working, loyal himself and expecting equally implicit loyalty in others, but ignorant of men—at any rate of those of his own race. In particular he thought that military men, being under discipline, had nothing to do but obey, and could not bring himself to see the necessity for temporizing with them in any circumstances. He was reserved, and did not know how to open himself to people, and he was unpopular with military and civilian alike. He came, moreover, with that most unpopular of tasks in an official community—that of enforcing economy, and when, for the preceding two months—in the words of his immediate predecessor William Petrie, the Acting Governor—a dangerous spirit of insubordination and cabal had shown itself among several officers in the army. Another difficulty was that the Court of Directors had exasperated the new Commander-in-Chief, Lieutenant-General Hay Macdowall, by refusing him the seat on the Governor's Council which was held by his predecessors and which they proved unable to refuse to his successor. But nothing seems to have been done by Barlow to smooth this over.

It is easy to imagine how quietly and how unanswerably Arthur Wellesley, for instance, would have represented the difficulties of such a position. But such was not Macdowall's method. He looked for partisans among factious officers, and he encouraged at his own table talk against the Government which he served. At last the opportunity for which he was waiting seemed to have come. His own predecessor had among other objects of reform in the Madras army taken up the system by which commanding officers had had since 1802 a tent allowance for the equipment of their men, more than enough in time of peace—inadequate in time of war, and had called upon his Quarter-Master-General, John Munro, then holding the rank of Lieutenant-Colonel, for a report. "Six years' experience of the practical effects of the existing system of the camp equipage of the Native Army", it ran, "has afforded means of forming a judgment relative to its advantages and efficiency, which were not possessed by the persons who proposed its introduction; and an attentive examination of its operation during that period of time has suggested the following observations regarding it." One of several objections which he made to it ran as follows: "By granting the same allowances in peace and war for the equipment of Native Corps, while the expences incidental to that charge are unavoidably much greater in war than in peace, it places the interest and duty of officers commanding Native Corps in direct opposition to one another; it makes it their interest that their corps should not be in a state of efficiency fit for field service, and therefore furnishes strong inducements to neglect their most important duties." The difference between peace and active service was the difference between a gain of nearly £400 and a loss of £250 a year by the contract; and the imputation that such a prospect might have a somewhat disheartening effect upon a married gentleman of advanced years was most certainly just and in no way offensive. In the summer of 1808 the abolition of the allowance was ordered It was now the most trying season of the year, when very little was needed to make Europeans discontented. The Adjutant-General, Lieutenant-Colonel Francis Capper, who was at one with his chief in the desire to make mischief, took care to promulgate the remarks justifying the change—remarks which Munro had made in a report intended for office use. The calculated effect was produced. The commanding officers of native corps went so far as to call for a court martial upon Munro for aspersing their characters. But they had not entirely lost all wisdom. On the Judge-Advocate-General reporting this mode of action to be ineffectual and irregular they withdrew their demand; and, in January 1809, substituted a memorial to the Court of Directors. Macdowall forwarded it to Government in spite of the fact that such a memorial was in violation of his own orders. He went even further. He actually took up the charge himself and placed Munro under arrest.

Barlow's course was clear. He at once ordered Munro's release. Macdowall's time was now short. He had already resigned and was on the point of sailing. He could do no more than issue a general order censuring Munro for— among other offences—petitioning Government direct for his release, after he had himself refused to forward his petition. The order was published on the 28th of January, two days before his departure. But Barlow was never at any loss. There was a Madras precedent for an even stronger action than that which he was about to take. In 1776 a military officer had put a Governor of that Presidency in confinement, but six years later it was a Governor who prevailed and placed the same officer, now become Commander-in-Chief, under arrest. Macdowall was already on board ship. But, determined to have the last word, Barlow published an elaborate order censuring him and also removed him from the command, his resignation not having yet been formally accepted.

But Barlow would not stop even here. Disagreeing with Macdowall in everything else, he was ready to imitate him in one piece of folly at all events. The General had taken action against a subordinate for an act done merely in obedience to orders—for giving an opinion which, as Lord Wellington wrote from Badajoz with his usual cogency, he not only ought not to have been brought to a court martial for giving, but which he ought to have been brought to a court martial if he had refrained from giving, when called upon by his Commander-in-Chief to do so. The Governor suspended both Major Boles, the Deputy-Adjutant-General, who had signed the offending order, and his superior, Capper, who avowed his responsibility. He punished them too for merely obeying orders. Macdowall's departing manifesto was not actually outrageous—merely silly, and a staff officer could not refuse to sign an order because it was silly. It was true that both Capper and Boles agreed with its contents, but no man can be punished for his thoughts. The result was what might have been expected. The tone of the Madras or Coast army, as it was called, was already far from good. It had in the past twenty years seen good posts gradually being monopolized by the officers of the King's Army. Its allowances were not so good as those in Bengal, and it chafed under the recent reductions.

It was ready to take up any grievance. Both Capper and Boles were regarded as martyrs. The officers of the King's Army had been very indignant on behalf of the General, who was, as usual, one of their own men, but took little interest in further agitation. It was those of the Native Army, whose fellow feeling on behalf of Boles, a brother officer, condemned for several months to a bare subsistence in India, reached to such a point of exasperation that they not merely got up a subscription to compensate him, but presented him with an address containing gross reflections on the Government.

Three months followed, during which Macdowall's successor, Major-General Francis Gowdie, vainly attempted to improve matters. The strictest of disciplinarians is occasionally deaf or blind to something which it is politic to ignore. But Barlow was of a different stamp. He could not help knowing of the address to Boles, as it was insubordinately brought to his notice by one of the officers who had signed it. But he also set himself to collect all the information he could, both about this document and another, which was never sent, addressed to Lord Minto for his own removal. At the same time there was a tendency to minimize the seriousness of the situation—on Barlow's part because he was interested in denying that he had given any provocation—on that of his opponents because they did not wish to give him any excuse for severity. But private letters disclosed a different state of things. Jonathan Duncan, the Governor of Bombay, had written at the end of March: "What is written from Madras would almost indicate a dissolution of Government, or something tantamount to the height of anarchy." The Senior Member of the Madras Council, Petrie, was in undisguised opposition to his Chief. On the 1st of May Barlow published an order suspending four officers and removing four more from their commands or staff appointments. He professed his belief that the agitation was confined to a few, and that severity to the leaders would bring the whole movement to an end. The maxim, "There is nothing good or bad but thinking makes it so"—so dear to Anglo-Indian statecraft—did not hold in this instance. Quite the contrary proved to be the case. Not merely did his asseveration that sedition where it existed was only the work of a few ringleaders fail to bring about the result for which he had hoped, but another assertion made in the same order brought about its own complete falsification. He had specially exempted the subsidiary force at Hyderabad from any complicity in the agitation. The Company's officers at that place took the Governor's praise as a reproach, and circulated a highly inflammatory letter to the rest of the army in which they disclaimed what they called the unexpected compliment.

The first outbreak took place at Masulipatam, a station almost due east of Hyderabad on the coast. Here the Company's European regiment had grievances of its own. The men in particular objected to service on board ship as marines. The officers drank a mutinous toast at mess. This was reported to Madras, and, as nothing petty was ever overlooked in that quarter, stringent measures were ordered. On the 25th of June the officers met them by placing their colonel under close arrest. Barlow now had the wisdom to send Malcolm to command the station. That officer showed the same diplomatic talent in dealing with unruly and half-drunken European officers as he had with pettish Oriental potentates. He effected the release of the colonel, and gained a few days for peace. On the 22nd of July he left for Madras to confer with the Governor. But Barlow had already committed himself to severer courses in which Malcolm would take no part. This was not the first of such affairs, though he was determined that it should be the last. Barlow had had experience of an officers' mutiny in Bengal of thirteen years before, in which the Government had yielded everything; and there

AT THE CLOSE OF THE DECADE

were men still serving who could recall another of thirty years earlier still, which was put down by the great Clive.

On the 26th of July the Government of Madras issued an order requiring a declaration from every Company's officer to the effect that he would obey the orders of the Governor in Council agreeably to the tenor of his commission. Those who should refuse were to be sent away from their regiments or stations to stations on the coast, receiving their ordinary allowances till re-employed. At the same time a step was taken which showed that Barlow did not shrink from bringing a second mutiny into being if necessary to counteract the existing one. Commanding officers were to explain to the native officers and men that their duty was only to Government, and that the grievances of other officers were merely personal to themselves. The result of the first measure—the imposition of the declaration on the European officers—must have surprised Government. There was some harshness even in the proposal of such a test, and greater harshness in the manner in which some officers commanding stations put it to their subordinates. The widespread character of the refusal to sign the declaration was a revelation in military psychology. Out of thirteen hundred officers not much more than one-tenth would sign, and the majority contained many men of unimpeached loyalty.

Matters came to a head at Hyderabad. Here the officers had, on the 21st of July, given in an ultimatum. To their honour it must be said that, offensive and absurd as this document was, it contained no reference to monetary allowances or any similar grievance. It merely demanded amnesty and reinstatement for those officers who were on their side, and the punishment of those who were against them. The Government determined upon this exceptional effort to bring back this large garrison to its allegiance. It called up Colonel Barry Close from Poona to take command of the subsidiary force. There was no more popular and influential officer in the Presidency. But his efforts were for the moment unavailing; he was refused obedience, and he returned to Poona. Four days later, on the 11th of August, a tragedy occurred more than three hundred miles to the southward. The garrison of Seringapatam, under Lieutenant-Colonel John Bell, had openly raised the standard of revolt, and had called in two regiments to join it from outside. The Mysorean Horse, which was loyal, had orders to prevent their entry if possible, and skirmished with them on the march. The majority, however, reached the fortress in safety. But on the last day a serious attack was made both by the Mysorean Horse and the King's 25th Dragoons, which resulted in the lives of some of the native troops being sacrificed to the misconduct of their officers, and in a hundred and fifty men being wounded.

When matters seemed to be at their worst, the mutiny suddenly collapsed. Barlow had determined to go on to the last calling the recalcitrant officers' bluff. Every effort which he had hitherto made had failed to reduce them. But he had sent for a large reinforcement of King's troops from Bombay and Ceylon. He now showed that he would have no hesitation in calling upon them to crush the insurgents, and there was no doubt that he could safely do so. The Company's officers' game of bluff was over. They were ready to grasp at any excuse to escape from their difficulties. Distant as all these cantonments were from one another—spread over an area of a quarter of a million square miles—communication between them was rapid and incessant. The firm yet moderate attitude of Malcolm and of Close had its due effect, most particularly where the latter had been actually present. As in the days of the mutiny which Clive had suppressed, there was the present menace of a Maratha invasion, which threatened the Nizam's territory first of all. After Close's departure

AT THE CLOSE OF THE DECADE

the sense of the gravity of their position, and the want of a leader, wrought upon the officers of the Hyderabad force so that they decided to accept the test. Minto was at last expected at Madras. They wrote that they had signed the declaration relying upon his justice—not, however, meaning what passionate men almost invariably mean when they speak of justice—a decision in their own favour. Minto had openly supported Barlow from the first, and the surrender to the Governor-General was only an excuse. Hyderabad led in submission, as it had led in revolt, and, amid some complaints of treachery, the other garrisons followed its example. The mutiny was at an end.

Minto did not arrive till the 11th of September, after a passage of thirty-seven days through the Bay of Bengal in the monsoon. He had, indeed, little left to do. Had a public man from England, a parliamentarian or diplomatist, been in Barlow's place, the mutiny would never, in all probability, have reached so dangerous a stage. Timely concessions would have been made. But had the danger not been warded off by these means, the usual type of public man would assuredly not have met it in so dauntless a spirit as Barlow. For this Minto gave him unstinted praise. He was now himself to do the work for which Barlow was not competent—pacification. He declared a general amnesty. He excepted only three ringleaders, whom he sent for trial by court martial, and eighteen others, who received their option between trial and dismissal. Sixteen chose the latter. In the end four officers were cashiered. Minto atoned for his previous neglect by spending fourteen months in Madras. India was now calm. But a wordy warfare of pamphlets in the English Press and minutes at the India House continued for some years. In 1812 the party opposed to Barlow obtained the upper hand in the Court of Directors. Sir George was recalled, and by 1814 all the officers who had been punished were reinstated except Bell and three others.

The latter part of Minto's Governor-Generalship was a period of considerable overseas activity. In 1809 a successful expedition was sent to the Persian Gulf which put an end to piracy in those waters for the time being—one of those services to mankind for which Great Britain has usually been repaid by graceless envy of the influence which she may have obtained in the process, or of her occupation of some miserable rock on which white men cannot live, but which has become necessary for the purpose of the operations. In the previous year an event occurred which certainly lent colour to the usual charges of British greed. When Portugal was occupied by France, the Committee of Super Cargoes had apprehensions that a French force might seize possession of Macao at the mouth of the Canton River. That place was in Portuguese occupation, but there had been no territorial cession. The East India Company authorities both in China and in India failed to realize the importance, even if they knew of the existence, of the distinction. Portugal's Indian possession, Goa, had already been occupied by a British force without friction. Accordingly detachments were sent both from Madras and Bengal, and in September 1808 Rear-Admiral William Drury landed the first party of troops at Macao, in spite of the objections of both the Portuguese and the Chinese. The Committee, with the ignorant insolence characteristic of the type which makes no effort to realize a foreign nation's point of view, ascribed the opposition of the former to intrigue and that of the latter to barbarity. But, barbarian or not, the Chinese Viceroy was in the strongest position, and showed it. He met the British contention—a perfectly just one so far as it went—that the Company had only come to trade, and that trade was to the interest of both parties, by the equally legitimate retort that it was rather a British interest than

AT THE CLOSE OF THE DECADE

a Chinese, else why had the English come so far in their ships? He taunted them with being denizens of a miserable island which could not afford them adequate sustenance, so that they were obliged to gain a livelihood by making watches and carrying them abroad to sell. In fact he successfully upheld the position that the Company's servants were only in Canton by favour of his Emperor. He broke off relations with them. Business was at a standstill, and the commanders of the Company's ships were afraid to move down the river from Canton without pilots. In December, Drury confessed himself beaten and evacuated Macao, and trade was restored.

It was more logical and more effectual, instead of endeavouring to prevent them in all their aggressions, to turn the French—and also their allies the Dutch—out of the Indian and China seas altogether. The official correspondence of the time reveals anxiety for the safety of every port which the British possessed within reach of the enemy—Colombo, Goa, even Bombay itself. In spite of convoys the East Indiamen were in constant danger. In September and October of 1807, 19 British merchant vessels were captured in the Bay of Bengal. The loss to trade from French cruisers and privateers had reached many hundreds of thousands of pounds. But for a long time Castlereagh, a stronger character than Mulgrave, besides being in a stronger position as Secretary of State than the First Lord of the Admiralty, had, exercised as he was by the difficulty of maintaining an army strong enough for its present commitments, strenuously resisted any further tropical expeditions which might, if failures, waste men, and if successful, entail garrisons. Even the support of the President of the Board of Control would have been of little use to the Admiralty, as that Minister had very little influence. But the determination once made, the capture of the French islands in the Indian Ocean presented little difficulty. The smaller island of Bourbon fell in July 1810 to a force of four thousand British and Indian troops. As had been done in the case of Martinique, proclamations were at once published pointing out to the inhabitants of Mauritius, an island principally defended by militia, the superior advantages of British rule; and a naval officer of indomitable heroism, Captain, afterwards Sir Nisbet, Willoughby, landed several times in the course of the following month and distributed them through a considerable part of the island, attacking and destroying the military works which lay in his way. The gallantry of the Navy would not wait for the expedition which was being prepared in India. One of several captured East Indiamen, the Windham, mounting 26 guns and manned by 30 Frenchmen, was cut out from under the enemy's batteries by Lieutenant Watling at the head of ten British sailors armed only with stretchers. An attempt by Willoughby to follow up this success by the capture of four more French ships moored in the harbour of Grand Port led to one of the most serious reverses in British naval history.

Four frigates commanded by Captain Samuel Pym as senior officer made this disastrous attack. Only Willoughby's ship, which led, had a pilot; the rest took the ground, and all four were captured, Willoughby's not until he had himself been terribly wounded and almost four-fifths of the ship's company put out of action. The command of the sea in those waters now passed to the French, but reinforcements arrived in sufficient strength to restore the balance in a few weeks. Not only this, but the time was now ripe for the capture of France's last stronghold in Eastern waters. A force of ten thousand men, of whom two-fifths were sepoys, was collected under Major-General Sir John Abercromby, son of Sir Ralph. The great obstacle to the capture of Mauritius had been the difficulty of finding a safe anchorage for a large fleet of transports off that reef-bound coast. But the Commodore, Josias Rowley, surmounted that difficulty, and the force was disembarked without mishap. More fortunate than his father in Egypt, the General found his landing unopposed; indeed, he met with little resistance in his march on the capital, Port Louis. The proclamations had had their effect, and the French colonial militia could not be trusted, while the regular troops were not much more than a thousand strong. On the 3rd of December the whole island was surrendered, with all the ships in Port Louis harbour, including the captured British frigates and East Indiamen.

Further to the east successful attacks had been made upon the Dutch settlements in the Moluccas, some of them places of great reputation in the seventeenth century—Amboyna and Ternate and Tidore. One is noted for the wonderful feat of Captain Christopher Cole of His Majesty's frigate Caroline, an exploit comparable with, although even more daring than, Brisbane's capture of Curaçoa in 1807. His naval force consisted of two frigates and two brigs, to one of which he added an extra mast one morning to disguise her as a full-rigged ship; his military force of a hundred officers and men of the Madras European regiment. He reached his object, the small island of Banda Neira, the chief of a group of islands among the most southerly of the Moluccas, on the evening of the 8th of August. The night fell dark and squally, and he took advantage of this to attempt a surprise. But this did not help only one side, for the boats with rather more than half of his four hundred men missed their way. Yet with the rest he took first a battery near the shore, then a powerful fortress defended by men who were at their guns and on the ramparts before the British had placed their scaling-ladders against the walls, "the service being performed", as Cole wrote with justifiable pride in his despatch, "with scarcely a hurt or wound". That fortress commanded the town which now surrendered, and by noon of the 9th an island mounting 138 guns and defended by 700 regular troops and militia was in British hands.

South of the equator lay a new British possession with a very different history from that of these productive and populous islands. Those of Australasia had one thing in common with the Dutch islands of the China seas. The British were not the first discoverers. Australia, not known until 1803 to be a single island, and not yet given that name, was called New Holland along its north-west coast, which the Dutch and the English after them had passed by as useless for purposes of trade. The eastern coast was given the special name of New South Wales by its discoverer Captain Cook in 1770. No one supposed that either that country or New Zealand would be of use as a colony. But soon after the establishment at Sydney in 1788 of the penal settlement for criminals sentenced to transportation for life, settlers began to appear. By 1801 a settlement had been made on an area of about 1,500 square miles stretching inland from that part of the coast which had been occupied as far as the as yet untraversable Blue Mountains. It contained, besides aboriginals, 5,515 European inhabitants, of whom rather more than half were supported by the Crown.

Viewed through the medium of subsequent colonial history, there often seems to be very little in the early days of New South Wales which was creditable to any of those concerned — Governors, rough ignorant naval officers, yet not too simple to use their public position for private advantage, military officers constituting themselves a permanent opposition to civil authority, and presenting a model to the trade trusts of a later day by the thoroughness of their monopoly of the necessities of life, a brutal and debauched soldiery, free settlers grasping and idle, and unfavourably compared with the convicts themselves, these last very nearly as bad labourers as any that could be found, even when the reward of good conduct was freedom and the opportunity of rising to independence and even opulence. But the French naturalist François Péron, who visited Sydney in 1802, was struck by what he considered a signal example of British genius for extracting civilized life out of the most unpromising materials. He admired the system by which the settlers had convicts assigned to them, and were rationed from the public store just long enough to give them time to bring their lands under cultivation. He admired, too, the general good behaviour of the settlement. For five months that he had been there he had not heard of a murder or a theft.

In point of fact the constant disputes and even rebellions which chequered the life of the growing colony could not disguise the interest which every class had in uniting to promote its welfare. For many years all were drawn together by a common fear of famine; they depended on store ships from England, the Cape, and India. In 1798 the Governor, Captain John Hunter, wrote home to an official at the Colonial Office: "Suffer me here, my dear sir, to beseach you to recollect that the whole colony are actualy naked; that no cloathing worth mentioning has been received for more than two years." He added that they had not a blanket to wrap themselves up in at night. Had they been determined, the convicts might have risen and murdered every free man in the place, but when they made such attempts they did so only half-heartedly, as, if successful, they had nowhere to go and nothing to do but to starve. All classes depended so much upon the Government—not so much because of the functionaries controlled by the Governor at Sydney as of the ships which brought the necessities of life, and which he controlled in his capacity of Captain-General—that in the first years any serious opposition would have been suicidal. Later on there was a growing divergence of interests in the settlement which reached a climax in

1808. The result turned out greatly to the benefit of the colony, though in a very different way from what the promoters of the movement had expected. The principal part was taken by one who was also the discoverer of Australia's greatest source of material prosperity.

In the New South Wales Corps, which formed the permanent garrison of the colony, one officer, John Macarthur, since known as the Father of New South Wales, had been conspicuous for his success as a colonist. He was the first man to bring an educated wife into the settlement. He won the reward of a second grant of a hundred acres for being the first to clear and cultivate one half of his first grant of a hundred acres. He was the first to use a plough, the settlers for the first six or seven years having been content with large hoes. Dissatisfied with the Indian and Irish strains of sheep which had already been introduced, he procured in 1797 three rams and five ewes from the Cape of Good Hope, and in 1804 five rams and one ewe from the King's flock at Kew, all of the Spanish merino breed, which had proved a success in neither of these places. Another who had brought Spanish rams into the country had been the Reverend Samuel Marsden. His success, and that of Macarthur with his first consignment, both in maintaining a pure stock of rams and in improving the mixed breed which was already in the country, struck the woollen manufacturers throughout the kingdom in 1804; and they urged Government strongly on the subject, pointing out that it was the object of France to cut them off from the trade in Spanish wool, the only material from which fine cloth could at present be made. Macarthur himself, who was then in England, was not backward. He inspired a well-known writer of the same name as himself with the prophecy that there would be millions of sheep in the colony, a prediction since almost literally fulfilled, although it must then have been scarcely possible to read it without a smile. Three years later the number of sheep was still only 25,000. Macarthur's vision of the colony as a great producer of a valuable raw material of manufacture, as well as the support which he received from Lord Camden, the Secretary of State for the Colonies, and Captain Philip Gidley King, the Governor—all this at a time when it was more natural for the colonist to think of the carcase of a sheep than its fleece—was highly creditable to all concerned. It led to the reversal of a land policy hitherto pursued by successive Governors. So long as the object had been to bring land under the spade or the plough, large grants were not made to individuals. Even in 1807 the total grants up to date had amounted only to 142 square miles. But if large flocks of sheep were to be encouraged, it was necessary to grant extensive tracts of land to individuals; and the new policy had already been inaugurated in the case of Macarthur. On his return in 1805 he possessed 8,500 acres and about 6,000 sheep with 90 servants. Of these about 36 were assigned convicts, a class receiving regular annual wages of £10 or £7, according to sex, throughout the colony.

In August 1806 New South Wales received a new Governor in Captain William Bligh, a hard rough-tongued sailor who brought matters to a head with some of the refractory elements in the colony. The curse of the place was spirits. "A Sawyer", wrote Bligh, "will cut one hundred feet of Timber for a Bottle of Spirits—value two shillings and six-pence—which he drinks in a few hours; when for the same labour he would charge two Bushels of Wheat, which would furnish Bread for him for two Months." Apart from the demoralizing effects of drink, the system of barter tended to ruin labourer and farmer alike, and to concentrate the wealth of the colony in the hands of the officers and those with whom they shared their monopoly. Six months after his arrival Bligh decided to prohibit the barter of spirits under severe penalties. He also came into collision with Macarthur—a man equally with himself possessed of the art of making enemies—and ordered his trial on a criminal charge. The Court was rather strangely constituted of the Judge-Advocate as President and six officers. The former, Richard Atkins, had been described by Bligh himself as one who had been the ridicule of the community, and who had been known to pronounce sentences of death while in a state of intoxication. Macarthur was no longer in the army; but he was influential in his old regiment, and he was the greatest settler in the colony. He appeared on the 25th of January, 1808, and protested against being tried by Atkins, alleging substantial grounds of personal enmity. On being appealed to, the Governor took up an equally unassailable position. He was unable to alter the constitution of the Court as enacted by letters patent.

A situation had arisen for which it appeared that there could only be a violent solution. Bligh precipitated it by unwarrantable action. Early next morning Macarthur, who was still on bail until the court had been sworn in, was arrested and lodged in gaol. The six officers met, and despatched a protest to the Governor both against this and against Atkins's continuing to sit as Judge with them. Bligh's reply to this was to order them to appear before him the next morning to answer a charge preferred by Atkins of usurpation of the Government. It was almost impossible to expect that the officers, who had constantly resisted the civil power in various ways almost since the birth of the colony, would endure this. The New South Wales Corps was now commanded by Major George Johnston, as mild a man as ever headed a rebellion or mutiny. But he lost no time in assuming the authority of Lieutenant-Governor, releasing Macarthur, and finally in that same evening marching upon Government House, and making Bligh a prisoner there after seizing his papers. He addressed a despatch to Castlereagh explaining that he had no alternative but to put Governor Bligh in

AT THE CLOSE OF THE DECADE

arrest to prevent an insurrection of the inhabitants. It is at least clear that, had he not done so, only the strongest and most active loyalty on his own part could have prevented grave disorder, once matters had come to the pass which they had reached. A chequered two years of military governorship followed, during a part of which Macarthur as Secretary to the Colony—a post created for him by Johnston—was the virtual Governor of New South Wales.

When, in course of time, the contending parties reached England, Bligh received his regular promotion to flag rank, but was not again employed. Johnston was court-martialled, found guilty of mutiny, and cashiered. He returned to the colony to live upon his estate there. Macarthur also succeeded after several years in getting permission to return to New South Wales. But as soon as the Home Government heard of the mutiny of the 26th of January it had decided upon a change of policy. The Governor should no longer be a naval officer. The permanent garrison should be removed. In December 1809 the new Governor arrived. He was Lieutenant-Colonel Lachlan Macquarie, and he brought with him his own regiment, the 73rd Highlanders, to replace the New South Wales Corps. Under his vigorous rule the colony enjoyed rest and prosperity. By the end of the decade there were not much less than a hundred thousand acres under cultivation or in pasture, and the European population was ten thousand. Other industries besides agriculture were beginning to flourish. The colony had long had its own coal and its own Newcastle.

It had its dependencies also. One was Norfolk Island in the Pacific Ocean, nearly a thousand miles from Sydney. But the settlement had been withdrawn from there in 1807 and the inhabitants removed to Tasmania. Péron's reports had suggested the value of New South Wales as an acquisition to his Imperial Master, and in 1810 Napoleon sent orders to the Governor-General of Mauritius to take it. It was too late. The French possessions in the Indian

Ocean themselves had fallen. But suspicion of French designs had been long at work, and had years before had the effect of directing the attention of British authorities to the Bass Strait dividing Tasmania from South Australia. The mainland was rejected. Settlements were made in 1804 in Port Dalrymple in the north of Tasmania and Hobart in the south. By 1810 they had 8,000 inhabitants.

The remaining important British possession in the Old World, the Cape of Good Hope, was not a new acquisition. The British flag had been hoisted there as early as 1620. It then passed into the hands of the Dutch, was taken from them in 1795, restored by the Treaty of Amiens, and finally conquered in 1806. On each of the two occasions when the Cape came under British rule, a few high posts were created for Englishmen, but the colony remained Dutch. The system of judicature was retained, and the punishment of death by breaking on the wheel—a punishment which, although never inflicted, could not be suffered to remain even upon the Statute Book—abolished. But the institution of slavery continued. A few hundred Government slaves were regularly transferred at a valuation of £30 a head when the colony was handed back to the Dutch. The condition of the slaves had, however, improved. While the arrival of the English had added enormously to the cost of necessaries, it brought wealth to the farmer. In this the slaves shared. The females were seen in the streets of Cape Town wearing silk stockings and fashionable pointed shoes. Although, as a temporary acquisition, the colony did not invite settlers, it was impossible for a government responsible for a population living at times very near the margin of subsistence to neglect the improvement of farming. The Dutch farmers were described by Rear-Admiral Curtis in 1800 as the fat and lazy tyrants of their little monarchies, "enamoured with sloth and wallowing in abundance". Their methods were as clumsy as their appearance. A successful attempt was made at least to demonstrate on

AT THE CLOSE OF THE DECADE 387

a Government farm the superiority of English methods of stacking hay and ploughing with two horses instead of eight oxen.

It was not natural for the strongly conservative Dutch population to feel great attachment to a home country which was divided against itself, and in which the party which had taken up French revolutionary ideas had the upper hand. There was considerable jealousy of French influence, even when supported from Holland. These circumstances, combined with the apathy and the unwarlike character of the Dutch, facilitated Sir David Baird's task in January 1806. By the 18th of the month the whole colony was once more surrendered into British hands. By a census of the year before it contained 25,757 Europeans, exclusive of soldiers, owning nearly 30,000 slaves, who were for the most part from Mozambique and Malay, and having also in their service 20,000 Hottentots, half-breeds and Bushmen, besides those Hottentots and other natives who lived at large in the country. They had become so debauched by the European introduction of brandy and tobacco that they were in a condition little removed from slavery. The six districts forming the colony covered an area estimated at over 150,000 square miles, stretching from the Buffalo river on the west coast round to the Fish river on the south, and from a hundred to two hundred miles inland. Cape Town itself had nearly 17,000 inhabitants, of whom 9,000 were slaves. The 6,000 Europeans formed a heterogeneous population including many Germans, Swiss, French, and British, as well as Dutch. Although the abolition of the slave trade in 1807 brought the influx of slaves to an end, it caused an increase in the coloured population of the colony in a different form. Slave ships brought for condemnation by the Admiralty Court had their negroes discharged, and they were apprenticed to Europeans in the colony. In so hot a climate it was natural to make full use of coloured labour, but the indolence induced by the custom retarded the growth of its prosperity. It was already observed by Robert Wilson, who accompanied Baird in 1806, and who left a lively account of the hospitable graces of the Dutch housewife, that the country produced corn, wine, brandy, tobacco, hides, wool, and—as a whale-fishery centre—whalebone and oil. But the attention of the British authorities was naturally directed in the main to its strategic value. It was obviously essential to keep it out of enemy hands. But as to its positive value opinions were not favourable. Nelson thought it worse than useless from a naval point of view, and Wilson thought it undesirable to use it as a stage on the way to India. The colony was not, however, neglected. An excellent choice was made for the first regular Governor after 1806 in the Earl of Caledon, a young Irish peer. One of his acts was to send an exploring party along the southern bank of the Orange River, which gave his name to a large tributary on the opposite bank. But no fresh annexations were made.

Besides Goree, the island off Senegal, and that colony itself, both wrested from the French during the war, Great Britain had one other foothold in Africa—Sierra Leone. It had an interesting origin. It was founded by a Chartered Company formed by some of those slave-trade abolitionists afterwards known as the Clapham sect, under the chairmanship of Henry Thornton, for the double purpose of finding a place for liberated slaves from Nova Scotia and introducing civilization into that part of Africa from which the slaves came. Zachary Macaulay was its first Governor. But it received a severe shock in its infancy, being raided and plundered by a French squadron in 1794, and the adventure, which would have been a difficult one in any case, did not prosper. In 1807 it became a Crown Colony.

During the first decade of the century the West Indian colonies, notwithstanding frequent representations made to Parliament to the contrary, continued to enjoy prosperity.

During the Peninsula War the trade of the Spanish Main and the West Indies generally came through Kingston in Jamaica. The cost of production of sugar in that island was higher than elsewhere, and there was some over-production, followed by a serious glut, during the prevalence of the continental system. On the other hand, coffee in Jamaica increased sevenfold between 1800 and 1805. The British planter was in several ways benefited by the war, and even by the unfriendly relations with the United States. The completion in 1810 of the capture of the French West Indies had removed a dangerous competitor. The interruption of relations between the States and Europe encouraged the growing of cotton in Guiana. The apprehensions entertained by many West Indians that the abolition of the slave trade would encourage those still in servitude to expect their freedom and become troublesome proved imaginary. A shrewd old planter in a letter to Lord Grenville of January 1807, when the trade had already been restricted preparatory to doing away with it entirely, pointed out that the negroes would say, "Master will for his own interest take the better care of us". Abolition certainly assisted old colonies like Jamaica by checking over-production, and hindering the breaking up of new lands in younger colonies such as Trinidad which competed with them in sugar and its by-product rum. The slave trade had been so far controlled by England that little was to be feared from the competition of foreign colonies employing slave labour. Moreover, the United States had also abolished the trade in 1807.

As relations grew more strained with the United States, the Bermudas rose in importance. The long-projected naval dockyard was finally begun in 1810. Similar apprehensions influenced His Majesty's Government in its arrangements for Canada. In 1807 General Prescott, who had lived in England since his recall in 1799, was still Governor-General. In that year it was decided to send out a soldier to Quebec. The choice fell on Lieutenant-General Sir James Craig, who went as Governor-General. He found that the elements of discord between the Assembly and the other Estates in Lower Canada, which Milnes had described in 1800, had already burst into flame. New taxation had become necessary in 1805 for building gaols, and the English or commercial interest wished to throw the burden on the land. The majority of the Assembly decided in favour of taxing such commodities as tea, wines, and spirits. An attempt was made to get the measure vetoed by the Crown. The French-Canadian leader Pierre Stanislas Bédard drew up an able memorial in its favour, pointing out that the alternative of a land tax, urged by the English merchants, if imposed at the same rate everywhere, would be most inequitable, while, if a method of valuation were to be adopted, the recurring costs would be prohibitive. The law was sanctioned as proposed by the Assembly.

The commercial people were greatly embittered by this rebuff. In the year in which the measure was passed, the Mercury, the organ of that interest, said that the province was too French for a British colony, and that it was time after forty-seven years of possession for it to become English. The challenge was taken up by Le Canadien, established as the French organ at the end of the following year, 1806. It lost no time in defining its position as hostile to what it called the most abominable of all orders, a mercantile aristocracy, on the one hand, and to Yankee interlopers on the other. It published attacks on intruders and strangers, directed against new arrivals from England or the States, who expected to have the best Government posts and grants of land. It stood for the freedom of the Press as the right of an English people, and as secured by the English constitution to all peoples under its protection. The French party, as a whole, embraced a conception of the British Constitution which they desired to see copied on their side of the Atlantic, not very dissimilar from that traditional view of which Bentham made game in his criticism of Blackstone. There were to be three forces in the State each pulling a different way, and the result of this combination was somehow to be that the State itself would proceed steadily forward in the right direction. They did not realize that it was desirable to work towards a harmony between the Governor, the Legislative Council, and the Assembly, as an eventual goal at least. In 1810, when the curious situation arose of a colonial assembly making an offer to relieve the mother country of the charges of its Government, and that offer being rejected on the mother country's behalf, their object was to invade the executive Government's province of the appointment of civil officials.

The new Governor was far from being the mere soldier. He had governed Cape Colony, at the time of its first conquest ten years before, with great consideration for its Dutch inhabitants. In carrying out the curious duty which governors then had of presiding over the Court of Appeal, he showed considerable knowledge of law. He very shrewdly pointed out the inability of the French party to understand the constitutional questions which they had raised. But he suffered terribly in health, he was badly advised and limited in his views, and he mistook the situation. He imagined that Le Canadien and its supporters were heading straight for rebellion. In 1808 he dismissed five militia officers on account of their connection with the newspaper. Among them were the Speaker, Jean Antoine Panet, and Bédard himself. Next year he dissolved the Assembly in order to get one more agreeable to his views. The experiment was a failure. At the general election the number of members of British origin had fallen to thirteen out of forty. In 1810 he seized the press of Le Canadien and threw Bédard and others into prison. He again dissolved the Assembly. He sent his Private Secretary, Herman Ryland, to London to explain his views. One of his objects was the suspension of the Constitution. The impending war with the United States appeared to him to make the continuance of power in the hands of an Assembly in permanent opposition to the executive dangerous. The Home Government refused either to support or to recall him. From the imminence of war it drew precisely the opposite conclusion to Craig. It thought it dangerous to alienate the affections of the overwhelming majority of the inhabitants of a colony whose invasion was likely to be attempted. The event proved the home authorities to be right. On the hints which he had received from home, Craig addressed the new Assembly which met in December 1810, with now no more than nine British members, in a much milder vein. What had with Latin exuberance been given the name of the reign of terror was now at an end.

Although by failing to allay a discontent, the extent of which was bound to be fully appreciated if not exaggerated in the United States, Craig assisted the war party in that country, his policy in other respects deserves praise. He improved communications in the eastern townships to the great benefit of trade. It was in his time too that the lumber trade first rose into importance. The indirect effect of the various retaliatory measures carried out by the United States against Great Britain was that, instead of the former country being to a great extent the means of communication between Canada and the outside world, Americans of the Eastern States carried on a trade with the outside world through Canada. One traveller, indeed, related an instance in which the effect of Jefferson's embargo had been to cause a merchant to leave Boston and settle in Canada with his family. The increase in the British and American population of the Lower Province was, however, inconsiderable. In 1810 Craig did not think that it was as much as one tenth of the whole, which he computed at 250,000. This figure, although an advance of 90,000 on Governor Milnes's estimate of ten years before, is unlikely to have been excessive. Joseph Bouchette, who was Surveyor-General two decades later, believed it to have been already reached in 1806. The population of Upper Canada for that year was estimated by him at 70,000, and that of the remaining five North American Provinces at nearly double the number. It was in Prince Edward Island that took place the most noteworthy of the immigrations of these years of distress for the Scottish Highlands into various parts of North America. In 1803 the Earl of Selkirk led out a colony of 800 Highlanders whom he settled on an uninhabited part of the island for which he had obtained grants of 50 to 100 acres for each family.

Upper Canada received during these years an interesting inflow of Highlanders from Glengarry, which a correspondent of the Morning Chronicle in 1803 was informed had been entirely emptied of its inhabitants. Such men as these, inured to a hard life and kept together by the sentiment of clan, became valuable settlers. The troubles of Upper Canada proceeded from that common source of turbulence in British colonies—Irishmen. It was never a very easy matter to supply judges and officials of the requisite education for the colonies, except perhaps New South Wales, where the ranks of convicts were able to provide for a post similar to that of Attorney-General a penitent attorney who had once stood in the pillory. Even at Quebec it had been necessary to make a mere merchant, Thomas Dunn, a Judge as well as Member of the Legislative Council, in consequence of the scarcity of of professional men. Upper Canada had even greater difficulties, and became indebted to Castlereagh for the services of some of his compatriots. They did not do so well in the public service as Dundas's Scotsmen. Their congenital itch for faction actually drove protégés of such high Tories as Castlereagh and Arthur Wellesley to combine with United Irishmen like Joseph Willcocks, who held the post of Sheriff of the Home District, in a turbulent opposition to the Government. The Lieutenant-Governor, Francis Gore, was so much afraid of his letters being intercepted by what he called "some of our democratic faction", that in 1807 he gave one to an officer to carry to England. Willcocks conducted a paper, printed in New York, called The Upper Canada or Freeman's Journal, full of seditious activity; and the people of that town were informed that the population of Upper Canada was on the verge of rebellion. Ultimately this bundle of firebrands was removed. Willcocks himself, after undergoing a short imprisonment for insulting the Assembly, which was much more exasperated against him than Gore himself, passed to the United States, and was afterwards killed fighting against Canada.

One part of the empire remains—one whose inhabitants so permeated the rest of the British dominions that its history has almost been told already. Scotland did not always keep step with England in prosperity. It had seemed to one of her greatest sons, when he wrote the Wealth of Nations in 1775, that she was advancing less rapidly; and until the nineteenth century was well on its way this was most certainly the case. That part known as the Highlands in particular was, during the time of the French wars, going through one of its recurrent periods of so-called depopulation. The true Highland- or Gaelic-speaking population of 1801 was nearly 300,000. In spite of considerable shipments to North America and elsewhere, that number was being maintained. The census of 1801 was more defective even than in England, and no returns at all were obtained from several parishes. Accepting it, we only find a decrease—and that slight—in two counties in the enumeration of 1811. They were Nairne, and Orkney and Shetland. Emigration took off no more than the natural increase of population. The people were deserting the overcrowded glens for the coast. A minister of the Church, Alexander Irving, knew, he said, of some spots where ten or twelve people lived to the acre—most of them with no trade—apparently by the produce of the place. Already that precarious remedy for overcrowding had begun to appear which had proved so fatal across the Irish Channel. The common food of the three classes which lived on the land—farmer, crofter, and cottager or cottar—had been barley bread and bannocks of peas. They seldom knew the taste of meat except when a sheep had died by accident or by disease. In Cromarty eggs were a luxury even to a farmer. It was the introduction of the potato which had, in the last years of the eighteenth century, frequently saved some of these communities from famine. But they escaped the temptation to rely on it, which would have invited the disaster which befell Ireland in 1846. The Highland proprietors, with what appeared a strange callousness to those who remembered the devotion of the tenants to the heads of their clans a couple of generations earlier, raised the rent of their land, which had been paying less than half its economic value, engrossed farms, and introduced the Cheviot sheep in place of the Highland breeds of sheep and cattle. Much harshness was shown, and the changes were bitterly resented. There were serious disturbances in Ross and Cromarty in 1792. The French traveller Baert noted it to the honour of some of the largest proprietors, such as the Dukes of Argyll, Atholl, and Gordon, that they preferred the affection of their clansmen to an inflated rent-roll. But the gradual conversion of the land to its most economic use was wrong neither in its principle nor its effects. At the same time the people could not remain in their inland glens. There were no industries. Eden found that the Highlander made everything at home except a few tools: he even got his dyes from trees which grew near his door. The only exceptions were the 1s. 6d. which he paid to a tailor for his bonnet, and 1s. for sewing his coat. Sir John Sinclair, himself a large proprietor in Caithness, who was also a leader in the introduction of the Cheviot sheep, had great expectations from the introduction of the cotton-mill to absorb the labour which the sheep had displaced. David Dale, the founder of the New Lanark Mills near Glasgow, had in 1791 diverted a stream of emigrants destined for America to his factory on the Clyde. Encouraged by this, he and others attempted to establish one on the coast of Sutherland, but it proved a failure. It was only possible to turn the Highlander to industrial life when caught young.

An Edinburgh Reviewer unkindly wrote that the zeal professed by such persons as the members of the Highland Society to restrict emigration upon the plea that a great nursery of soldiers was in danger of destruction, was really inspired by an interest in the manufacture of kelp. This was produced from seaweed at a cost of 35s. to 50s. a ton in the Western Highlands, and sold to glass manufacturers in Newcastle and elsewhere at a price which averaged as much as £10 a ton during the French wars. Kelp and fish furnished some employment for Highlanders who remained in their country. Other work was provided by Government, which undertook with this object a survey of a part of the Highlands in 1801, leading to the construction of roads and bridges and harbour works and the Caledonian Canal.

Many customs remained in the Highlands which belonged to a feudal order of things. Cottars, and even the higher class of crofters, had to work for the farmers in return for their own plots of land. Rent was often paid in part in farm produce. Sir James Grant of Rothiemurchus in Inverness-shire regularly had fifty to dinner at Castle Grant; those who in medieval times would have been sitting below the salt had whisky-punch instead of wine. Right up to the death of Charles Edward in 1788, Jacobitism survived as an active force. Even so late as

1803 a former emigrant from France assured Napoleon Bonaparte that there were many Catholic Scots—presumably in those glens where the Reformation had never penetrated—who hated the English and wished to have the Stuarts back, and that thousands would join a handful of men landing in the Moray Firth. But Napoleon would not have been wise had he depended on such assurances. The old Tory proprietors had transferred their devotion from the Stuarts to King George III in the manner in which Sir Arthur Wardour did in Scott's Antiquary. The Highlands had lost almost everything which rendered them formidable for evil. Its inhabitants had much in common with their cousins in Ireland. They possessed courage and hardiness combined with a certain fatalistic helplessness and aversion from continued exertion; an impulsive temperament capable alike of devotion and treachery; on the romantic side the Celtic charm of manner and strain of melancholy; on the ludicrous side a strutting vanity which excited ridicule. They shared even those indirect turns of speech by which a lively imagination parries a direct question. But there were differences due partly to a less genial climate and more rugged country, and partly to the penetration of most of the Highlands by the most severe and uncompromising of the main forms of Protestant Christianity. The Irishman was quicker, and had much less national pride. It is not easy to imagine an Irish landlord—such a man, for instance, as the King Cornie of Maria Edgeworth's Ormond—however racy of the soil, refusing to speak anything but Irish. Yet there was a gentleman living in Perthshire in 1793 of the name of Macdiarmid who disdained to speak a word of the Sassenach tongue, or to wear any dress but the philabeg and belted plaid. Again the Irishman, like the Highlander, developed gifts outside his own country which were unknown in it. But the latter when he left his cabin for another life rose a great deal higher.

There were factors in the Lowlands as well as the Highlands which long caused that delay in the advance to a better condition of which Adam Smith complained. Bracing as the Calvinistic faith was to the moral fibre, its fatalistic side provided that excuse for an inert resistance to all progress which the woman in Elizabeth Hamilton's story found when she set out to reform the Cottagers of Glenburnie. Indeed, her account of this village—its dirt and its pretentiousness—suggested Ireland. "It consisted of about twenty or thirty thatched cottages, which, but for their chimneys, and the smoke that issued from them, might have passed for so many stables or hogsties." She went on to observe that every dwelling had its horse—a fact made obvious by every door having its dunghill as well as a small cart, often broken as well as dirty, ostentatiously displayed in front of it. A tourist late in the eighteenth century observed a great change after he had crossed the border from the neat English cottages to the mud-built sheds and ragged barefoot children of the Scottish lowlands; and found them even dirtier than the Highlanders. Nor, in spite of that national characteristic of deliberateness which hindered advance, had the Lowland country that double portion of common sense which usually goes with it. Mrs. MacClarty in Elizabeth Hamilton's book, although she had not a moment to wash her hands, spent much of her time spinning linen of a quality which the best English farmers' wives might have envied—but not for use. "Na, na, we're no sic fools as put our napery to use! I have a dozen table-claiths in that press thretty years old, that were never laid upon a table." Watt, himself a Scotsman, had a poor opinion of his fellow countrymen so far as doing anything with their hands was concerned, and Telford had an equally poor opinion of his country as a field for energy. "Having acquired", he wrote, "the rudiments of my profession, I considered that my native country afforded few opportunities of exercising it to any extent." Telford was to see the situation almost reversed, but it was not until the new century was well on its way. Feudal survivals, moreover, which acted as a drag upon agricultural progress, were more often to be found in Scotland than in England. Such was the system of thirlage, particularly common in Galloway, by which every farmer had to pay a due to a mill owned by his landlord, and also get his corn ground there.

On the other hand Scotland enjoyed several advantages. The country had developed so strong and elastic a banking system of its own that the financial crisis of 1797 in England, which had its origin not very far south of the Tweed, was very easily met to the north of it. Scotland derived considerable benefit too from low taxation. In 1810 she was accused in parliament of paying only £4,000,000 against England's £59,000,000, and £600,000 income tax against £11,000,000. Francis Horner, on behalf of his countrymen, did not contest the figures; he could only suggest that collection was at fault. The land tax was light, and some other burdens which pressed upon land south of the Tweed almost non-existent. The Scot succeeded in escaping the evils of the Poor Law. He did not allow the law of settlement to become a cause of persecution to the pauper and expense to the parish. The poor were partly supported by the church collections. When these failed there was begging. In an inquisitive country, where everyone knew everyone else's affairs, there was room for the judicious treatment of such a local institution as the Edie Ochiltree of Scott's Antiquary. He was less of a burden to the parish as a sturdy beggar, getting what he could free and occasionally doing an odd job, than he would have been either pensioned off or furnished by the parish with unremunerative work. There was a strong feeling that the toleration of a moderate amount of begging was better than an assessment. Taking advantage of the fact that the Scottish Poor Law recognized no right to work or maintenance, the proprietors had made use of this compulsory means of providing for the poor in only 96 parishes up to 1800. The number of assessments was increasing. But for many years later Edinburgh City, and even parts of Glasgow, had no assessment.

Education was, however, in Scotland, unlike England, a local burden. The proprietors were obliged by law to appoint and pay a village schoolmaster. In 1803 a new Schoolmasters Act was introduced to remedy the deficiencies of the old. The proprietors had now to build houses for them. Charles Hope, the Lord Advocate, who had charge of the Bill, told the advocate Henry afterwards Lord Cockburn, that he had the greatest difficulty in getting a measure passed which ensured that most characteristic member of the Scottish village community being decently lodged. The house was only required to have two rooms. But even then many lairds and Scottish Members of Parliament were indignant at being obliged, as they called it, to erect palaces for dominies. Humble as the schoolmaster so designated was, the result of his efforts was, as Baert wrote, that the Scottish people was better and more generally instructed than any other. Nor did education at the public charge end here. Scotland had an excellent system of burgh council secondary schools maintained from fees and rates. The condition of the two northern universities of St. Andrews and Aberdeen was far from being so creditable. But Edinburgh and Glasgow maintained their traditions of a good general culture suitable to a rather younger and a very much poorer class of student than that at the English Universities.

The other great formative influence, the Established Presbyterian Church, was no burden on agriculture. The Ministers' stipends were paid by the local proprietors, and the amount could only be raised by application to the Court of Teinds or Tithes. So successful was the resistance made to every attempt to increase them in some sort of proportion to the enormous increase in the value of agricultural produce and the cost of living, that the State had to step in. In 1810 an Act was passed setting aside an amount originally fixed at £10,000 for raising the stipends to a minimum of £150 a year.

The Church of Scotland was not at this time the great influence in the nation which she had been in the seventeenth century, nor yet what she became during the nineteenth. Some of the indifference which characterized the Church of England existed also north of the Tweed. There was in consequence a bewildering variety of secessions from the Established Church, and Quakers and Methodists and even evangelical preachers of the Church of England, such as Rowland Hill and Charles Simeon, also entered the field as though Scotland had no religious enthusiasms of its own. How small was the importance which the clergy then attached to their duties was curiously illustrated in the revolution which took place in the ideas of one who became the greatest of them—Thomas Chalmers. In 1805 he became a candidate for a mathematical professorship, and broke a lance with Professor John Playfair on the subject of the Mathematical Pretensions of the Scottish Clergy. In his pamphlet he asserted, on the authority of his own experience, that after the satisfactory discharge of his parish duties a minister might enjoy five days in the week of uninterrupted leisure for scientific pursuits. Twenty years later he was so ashamed of such latitude that he tried to suppress the pamphlet, and when publicly taxed with it admitted frankly that he had been wrong. In Edinburgh itself the clergy had one great leader in the baronet Sir Henry Moncrieff, the head of the Wild or Evangelical party among the clergy. This was the Whig party. The Moderates—or Tory party—were usually stronger. The two parties yearly disputed for several days at the General Assembly in the capital, without being in reality usually separated by any acute differences as to doctrine or administration. In spite of the august proceedings with which the ceremonial of the General Assemblage was yearly held in Saint Giles's Church under the presidency of a great nobleman representing the King as Commissioner, it remained true that, as Cockburn wrote, the clergy had fallen almost entirely out of good lay society. Poorly educated as they were, they had no aspirations after the scientific attainments of Chalmers, and on the other hand were for the same reason in close touch with the country people from whom they were drawn. They kept up the traditions of the seventeenth century in weird—thoroughly national—institutions such as the Scottish sabbath and others which formed a theme for the poetry of Burns— the Cotter's Saturday Night and the Holy Fair of Sacrament Sunday.

In material affairs Scottish pawkishness was gradually asserting itself. There were farmers able to pay a rent of as much as £5 an acre in the East of Scotland. Andrew Meikle of Dunbar had perfected the threshing-machine some years before the end of the century, and through a great part of the country it had superseded the flail; even threshing by steam was known in East Lothian. The steam-engine had been applied to the spinning-mill in the neighbourhood of Glasgow before 1800, and occasionally by 1810 even to the loom, in which respect Scotland was as distinctly before England as she was in the use of the threshing-machine. But it was nearer Edinburgh that industrial advance was most marked. Between Stirling and the capital the country was black with collieries, and it was at Carron, half-way to Edinburgh, that could be seen perhaps the most famous works in the world, those iron works which had furnished ships of war with the guns whose name was a common word in the French and British navies alike.

Of a total population for the whole of Scotland of 1,599,068, according to the incomplete census of 1801, the mass was concentrated about the Forth and the Clyde. Of the northern towns Aberdeen and Dundee had about 27,000 each. The need for water power was unfavourable to the concentration of industries in large towns in Scotland, as in England, though not to the same extent. Glasgow in 1801 numbered 83,769 souls. There was probably not a town in England with one half of its population which was half as barbarous. At the beginning of the century, for example, it is said to have boasted only one carriage. In 1796 it was supposed to have 39 cotton water-mills, and to employ 25,000 persons, most of them under fifteen years of age, out of the 180,000 employed in the cotton industry in Scotland. It had some advantages over the English towns as a centre of industry. The river Clyde offered Glasgow an opportunity enjoyed by no riverine or coastal town of the south of becoming alike a great seaport and a great manufacturing centre. The traditions of the place were mercantile rather than industrial. Men like David Dale, who established great factories, had a fair field. Although Glasgow itself was not free from cumbersome restrictions upon industry, the neighbourhood was. Adam Smith knew no country in Europe where the corporation laws were so little oppressive. The Elizabethan Statute, which, imposing as it did a term of seven years apprenticeship as a condition of the exercise of any trade, had come to be so serious a clog on industry in England, was not felt in the north. Here the term was usually three years.

The masters in the Scottish mills had greater trouble in getting their hands—particularly the children—than those in south Britain, and treated them generally better, though the wages were much below the English rates. There was something in the staid character of the Lowland Scot lacking in the Lancashire or Yorkshire man, which kept him from ill treatment of those whom he employed. Of the Blantyre factory on the Clyde a very full description is given by a visitor in 1805, Mary Berry. Dark as the picture is, there are some touches which compare favourably with what is generally known of the contemporary English factory. Most of the workers were children of from six to fourteen, many being from London parishes. They worked for twelve hours in the day, and got oatmeal for breakfast and supper, and broth and beef for dinner, and their education was not neglected. She noted the forlornness and squalor of their appearance. Most of the adult workers were women, the spinners getting 15s. to 16s. Men got up to £2 a week, but of these there were very few. The whole machinery was moved by a water-wheel 21 feet in diameter.

But, owing first to the obstinate disposition of the Scots themselves, and, later on, to the admixture of an element which had refused to allow industries to exist in its native country, and had begun since the last years of the eighteenth century to be an alien disturbing factor in the industries of other countries—the Irish, labour disputes were almost as bitter in the West of Scotland as elsewhere in the Kingdom. In 1810 there was a combination of the men to compel the masters to receive only those whom they allowed to work in the mills. This was met by a fortnight's lockout, at the end of which the men were compelled individually to sign declarations that they would enter into no association whose object was to interfere with the rights of employers to employ whom they liked, or to intimidate men into joining it. Wages, moreover, ruled substantially lower for almost all trades in Glasgow than in Manchester. Weavers were passing through a similar period of trouble towards the end of the decade as in England, though it was not so intense.

The weekly wages of weaving book-muslin according to the books of Perston, a Glasgow employer, were 12s. 9d. in 1801 and had risen to 17s. 8d. in 1806, to fall four years later to 14s. 9d. One witness before the Select Committee on Hand-loom Weavers' Petitions in 1834 said that he had known 40 or 50 Scottish hand-loom weavers who had risen to be capitalists—two to be Lord Provosts of Glasgow. But the class was rather better known for the accumulation of intellectual and spiritual wealth. The philosophic weaver who subscribed perhaps to a library which gave him the benefit of the works of David Hume and Adam Smith was a known character both here and in that other centre of provincial culture—Perth.

The leading influence in Edinburgh, and hence largely throughout the country, was neither the University nor the Church, but the law. The Old Town, its most characteristic part, clustered around the Parliament House, where the Courts were. Until the middle of the eighteenth century this was the whole of Edinburgh. Placed on the ridge of a hill, the town was thought to admit of only one good street, and the lanes leading into it from north and south were steep, narrow, and dirty. The nobility and gentry of Scotland packed themselves in flat piled upon flat along or close to the High Street. It bred a class of guides who existed till well into the nineteenth century —the Cadies of Auld Reekie—who knew everyone's business even if he was a perfect stranger, and could show the way into every corner of those amazing warrens. The first expansion of the town was towards the south. This was an immense improvement from a sanitary point of view. Scott relates an instance of a gentleman living in the High Street who lost six children there of disease. He moved to George Square, where he had five more, all of whom grew up to be healthy men and women. But this part of the country did not lend itself to town planning, being owned by several proprietors, and in 1757 an Act of Parliament was obtained for Edinburgh which enabled Commissioners, including in their number the Town Council, to purchase from Heriot's Hospital a wide level tract on the north, divided from the Old Town by a loch, which was drained and bridged. Here the New Town arose—the greatest contrast conceivable to the Old in its width and regularity. Such was the increase in half a century that an old gentleman living about 1820 said that there were now more streets in the city to which he was a stranger than there were faces when he was a young man; in 1770 he knew almost everyone in the whole town by sight. But even in 1801 Edinburgh recorded 122,954 inhabitants.

The Old Town was gradually left to the Castle where the garrison was quartered, the Parliament House, the University, and—a prominent feature in a nation which sent its males so freely to seek their fortunes in London and the Indies—those old widows and maids so picturesquely described in 1825 by Robert Chambers as "old ladies of quality, who, during the last century, resided in fourth flats of Old-Town houses, wore *pattens* when they went abroad, had miniatures of the Pretender next their hearts, and gave tea or card parties once regularly every fortnight in the world". One of the most celebrated of Scottish national virtues had much to do with the unwillingness of these ladies to leave a situation in which they could exercise hospitality by merely leaning out of their alley windows and inviting one another to tea or supper, instead of being at the expense of formal dinners or routs. It was said of the first Lord Melville that at his visits to Edinburgh he never failed to call upon every one of his acquaintances among them in their fastnesses. "They all dressed, and spoke, and did exactly as they chose; their language, like their habits, entirely Scotch," wrote Cockburn of them. Melville may have thought them the only women in Edinburgh worth knowing. It is astonishing how small a share women seemed to take in that heavy-drinking, hard-thinking life. There were some attempts at literary coteries. There existed that most terrible of human beings —the Scottish Blue-Stocking, among whose favourite topics was the Resumption of Cash Payments. In their anxiety to follow the male fashion women in ordinary society garnished their conversation with legal phrases. An Italian traveller found Scottish ladies more intelligent than English; but they were not sufficiently so for their own mankind. The Scot did not see himself being civilized by the presence of the opposite sex. He left them alone for good or for evil. One traveller was led to observe on the large numbers of men whom he found, able to support a wife, who yet had the fortitude to resist matrimony. Farington the Diarist noted as peculiar to a great town like Edinburgh that women might pass from street to street singly and required no companion. The Duchess of Gordon was a power on the banks of the Spey—and on those of the Thames; but when she travelled to London she held no court in the Scottish capital on the way. What such describers of Edinburgh life as John Lockhart and Lord Cockburn meant by a brilliant social evening was an almost interminable sitting over the bottle at which Scott spouted antiquities or Jeffrey laid down the law on everything. The existence of women was a subject merely of inference.

This was necessarily so in a place where the lawyer held such undisputed sway. Not that any individual lawyer was so influential in the first years of the century as Dugald Stewart, Professor of Moral Philosophy in the University. He was the greatest disciple of Reid, the founder of the so-called Common Sense school of philosophy. But Stewart's merit was not as a clear expounder of another man's ideas. Nor did it lie in any marked originality. Nor was it in his eloquence. It was a sort of compound of all three, in one who had a lofty view of what was possible for human nature, which made his lectures so attractive. It was this combination which enabled men like himself and Playfair, Professor successively of Mathematics and Natural Philosophy, to whose guidance young John Russell owned much the same debt as his future colleague Palmerston did to Stewart, to draw so many young Englishmen to Edinburgh for their education—sometimes even to make it their home.

The lawyer was, however, generically speaking, a much greater force. His yoke upon the country was not easy. The pleadings were of an elaborateness which a Chancery lawyer might have envied. The subject was brought up in Parliament in 1809 by Horner, who pointed out that £500 to £700 had to be spent when the sum on litigation was not more than £200 or £300. This was very likely to be the case whenever "Endless Willie" was brought into the field—a legal practitioner who was always capable, when the tempest-tossed litigant at length thought he saw port, of devising some new point which set litigation off on a new career. A note was made in the Annual Register of that year to the effect that, had it not been for entails, Scottish lawyers would by this time have got hold of most of the country, and it was regarded as significant that in Scotland solicitors were called writers. A sure indication of the existence of a lawyer-ridden country was to be found in the frequency of the unfortunate lunatic whose delusion is to be seriously engaged in an interminable lawsuit or series of lawsuits. It left its mark on the sane too—in the measured and somewhat pedantic speech characteristic of the nation.

But at all events the Parliament House, the seat of Scottish law, which represented since the Union Scottish nationality, was the centre of life in Edinburgh. Here in the Outer House was retailed Henry Erskine's latest jest, or Walter Scott was to be heard giving a lively imitation of some almost incredible absurdity of Lord Eskgrove, the head of the Criminal Court or Lord-Justice-Clerk; or George Fergusson, afterwards Lord Hermand, might break in—bursting with zeal on behalf of some ill-used client, while between his upper and nether garments his shining linen burst out in sympathetic indignation. But a peep into where the Judges were sitting revealed things stranger still. The principal Court was the Court of Session, a Court both of law and equity, deciding civil cases and even some criminal cases without a jury. Here in the Inner House, encased in venerable dirt, sat the fifteen Judges or Barons—the only Lords in the kingdom whose title was not of a hereditary nature. After all the learning of the Bar had been expended on a case, it was never quite certain which Judges would be sitting, whether principles of law or equity applied, whether a British Statute extended to Scotland, whether a Scottish Statute should be regarded as having gone into desuetude, and so forth.

On one occasion a junior counsel unfortunately allowed words to pass his lips to the effect that he was surprised to hear their lordships say something or other. It fell to his senior, the Honourable Henry Erskine, brother of Lord Erskine, and long the leader of the Scottish Bar, to soothe the indignation of the Court. After apologizing for his junior's thoughtless expression he added: "When my young and inexperienced brother has practised as long at this bar as I have, I can safely say he will be surprised at nothing your lordships may say." But the scandal of the fifteen Judges was not long after removed. Grenville wished to reduce their numbers so as to give them a sense of responsibility, and also to introduce civil juries. But he could not get his Bill passed while he was in power, and Scottish law reform fell into the hands of Eldon. Still, in 1808 the Court of Fifteen was divided into two, and other changes set on foot.

The principal criminal court was the High Court of Justiciary, the members of which were drawn from the Court of Session. It tried cases with a jury of fifteen, the verdict of a bare majority of whom was sufficient. The prisoner was allowed a certain right of challenge. If indigent, counsel were always appointed for him. Here his advantages ended. The Sheriff's list of 45, out of whom the jurymen were taken, might be so carefully framed that his right of challenge was not enough protection. The trials were full of prolix formalities leading to wranglings and irritation which did not benefit the prisoner, and the Lords of Justiciary had a reputation for being unfavourable to the defence. There were certainly instances of summings-up which were anything but impartial.

The Judges went on circuit as in England, and there were also justices of the peace and magistrates who had powers as such in towns in virtue of their office as town dignitaries, but there were several points of difference, in some of which Scotland had distinctly the advantage. Counties had their sheriffs, sheriff-deputes, and sheriff-substitutes, whose courts had powers somewhat similar to those of Quarter Sessions in England. These, as well as the local magistrates, were able to try civil cases, the latter up to the value of £5 only, and that at very small expense to the litigant. A typical Scottish functionary—one whose name and functions suggested those French associations so frequent in the country—was the Procurator-Fiscal, who was to the county or the borough what the Lord-Advocate was to the country as a whole. A man who knew everybody and everybody's business, he was coroner, chief criminal investigator, and public prosecutor.

During the first years of the new century efficient boards of city police were gradually coming into being in the large towns. Edinburgh itself still had, until 1805, as picturesque and useless a police as any part of the kingdom, the City Guard of a couple of hundred or so ancient drunken Highland soldiers armed with muskets and bayonets and the Lochaber axe. "One saw Bannockburn in it," wrote Cockburn. The institution was typical of the old Royal Burghs which comprised the principal towns of Scotland. Medieval in their complexity, their elaborate municipal constitutions offered some show at least of a check on arbitrary authority, but there was no popular election. But the trades were well represented on the councils, and it is not probable that—discreditable as their administration was—they would have been very different or better if they had been chosen by the householders.

Through all these years, except during the Ministry of the Talents, the Tories held the same strong control over Scotland as over the rest of the kingdom. A principal channel of influence was the Lord-Advocate, the head of the legal profession. An English newspaper is supposed once to have given as a piece of personal news: "Arrived at Edinburgh the Lord High Chancellor of Scotland, the Lord Justice General, the Lord Privy Seal, the Privy Council, and the Lord Advocate, all in one post-chaise, containing only a single person." A member of parliament once complained of a short Lord-Advocate. "We Scotch members always vote with him," he said, "and we need therefore to be able to see him." The fact was that, as Grey once said, they generally attached themselves to the party of every Minister in power in turn, as the best way of promoting the interests of their country. It was the Secretary of State for the Home Department who formally carried out the King's commands as to Scotland. Henry Dundas had been both Lord-Advocate and Home Secretary, and, even when he no longer held either of these posts, continued to be the uncrowned king of Scotland. But the Scottish members were not all obsequious. Lord Archibald Hamilton, the member for Lanarkshire, and George Cumming, member for one of the groups of Royal Burghs, appear in the ayes division on Whitbread's motion of censure against Dundas after he had become Lord Melville in 1805.

It was natural that during those years the Tories should reserve to themselves most of the best places, although this was not always the case, for one Whig, Henry Cockburn, had one for a time, and another, Henry Erskine himself, had the offer of the post of Lord-Justice-Clerk from them and refused it. In spite of Scott and of one or two more, the preponderance of ability among the lawyers was on the Whig side, and every honour is due to them for the firmness with which they maintained their principles and remained, with that short interval of 1806–1807, for almost forty years in the wilderness.

In England it is not easy to discover in 1810 many signs of the growth of those enormous changes in the religious, moral, and social outlook of the people apparent when the opening of the century is regarded from the standpoint of fifty years later. The current of spiritual reform had so far run outside the Church, or—if within it—mainly underground. The most remarkable instance of religious eccentricity ever known in England, Joanna Southcote, was at this time in the heyday of her strength, emitting reams of religious doggerel. Her biographer wrote truly that posterity would hardly believe that this wretched female, with mental acquirements that scarcely raised her above idiocy, should have succeeded in making willing dupes of numbers of people respectable, not only for their rank of life, but for their understanding also. The unfortunate incapacity of the Church of England to understand religious enthusiasm and to direct it into proper channels, was responsible for a continuance in the growth of sectaries at a time when there were no longer such masters as Wesley and Whitfield to direct it outside the establishment. The naïve absurdities of some of their unworthy successors disgusted intelligent men, and furnished amusement for reviewers. One of them, who thought the world would be interested in the history of his life, wrote in the course of it: "I lost a most beautiful partner, and married another who was rather plain in her person. These afflicting providences I endeavour to support with resignation." One noted visionary, a rival to Joanna, Richard Brothers, who had been a naval officer, wrote a book of revealed knowledge of the meaning of the Old Testament prophecies, as well as of his own additions to the canon, showing how they applied to himself. A Manchester magistrate in 1810 sent the Home Secretary an extraordinary printed notice circulated in the neighbourhood by some enthusiast, headed "At the Theatre of the Universe". He reported it as being blasphemous, which it certainly was, but it was doubtless intended as an honest reminder of the Judgement Day—an occasion when pageantry and tragic intensity alike were expected vastly to exceed anything which could be put on the boards by whore-mongering players. The Puritan underworld had an especial hatred for the stage. Shaksepeare was believed to be in hell.

Such views were not confined to the hawkers of hedge and barn religions, but extended to the great institution of Wesley himself. Southey wrote of their organ in 1810 that no works in the country were so widely studied as the Evangelical and Methodist Magazine. But the extensive range of its readers did not prevent its views, and the views of those whom it represented, from being extremely narrow. They were a peculiar people. The marriages of Wesleyans were forbidden outside their own community. They had even their own madhouses. They propagated their faith in part by suggesting that their own living saints had the power of working miracles, and by telling stories such as that of the man who took a walk on a Sunday, fell into a lime-kiln, and was consumed under the eyes of his family. It was never certain how they would regard a political question, except that they would be certain to approach it from a point of view peculiarly their own. Napoleon was at one time honoured as having both destroyed the Inquisition and expelled the Pope, at another he was proved to have the mystical number of the Beast.

But the existence of such aberrations was at least not made by the established clergy an excuse for relapsing any further into their latitudinarian indifference. The Church remained much as it was outwardly—neither better nor worse. Many incumbents showed cynical disregard of their duties. About Cambridge it was a joke that, on a rainy day, Doctor Drop took the service—the parson stayed at home. This was the place where Charles Simeon's earnest preaching and personal influence was so great a power. In London chapels—the places where a cleric who was a popular preacher was entertained as a financial speculation—railings were put across the middle aisle to exclude those who were called the lower members of society, showing that the Church had its own exclusiveness like the Wesleyans; and there were places where the fashionable congregation sat as in a drawing-room conversing during the service, except when the preacher was saying something beautiful. There were occasional examples of similar laxity in parish churches even so far off as Falmouth. Neither were lapses from a decent standard among those in holy orders confined to such as indulged secretly in some weakness of the flesh; they were openly blazoned in the newspapers. An advertisement would be read of the next presentation to a valuable benefice, situated in a fine sporting country where a number of young divines hunted. Two parsons shamelessly conspired in 1810 to elope with a heiress.

But the ministers of the Church at least regarded those more earnest than themselves with tolerance. George Eliot placed her Adam Bede in these years, and she has well portrayed in that novel the indulgent attitude of such a pluralist as the Reverend Adolphus Irwine towards travelling preachers, male and female. Higher up in the scale such dignitaries as Bishops Porteus of London and Shute Barrington of Durham worked on the committee of the British and Foreign Bible Society along with ministers of the Church of Scotland and Dissenters. The original object of the formation of this Society had been to supply copies of the Scripture in Welsh, which the older Society

AT THE CLOSE OF THE DECADE

for the Promotion of Christian Knowledge had been unable to do. The great Earl of Shaftesbury, who was three years old when it was founded, related afterwards how he was brought up to regard this new venture in the light of an evil and revolutionary institution; and it was emphatically not one which would have commended itself to the typical bishop of the eighteenth century. The Church was in fact becoming gradually penetrated—to some extent unconsciously—by evangelical influence. The efforts of Perceval, Harrowby, and others to improve the condition of the poorer clergy were animated by the same conception of a Church militant and not merely established. In parliament the small group of members nicknamed the Saints was a growing force.

In social life the stream of change ran equally underground. An incident occurred in London in 1808 where offence and punishment alike suggested that the age was losing none of its coarseness. On a summer's evening before dark a peer's daughter was accosted and treated with gross indecency by a middle-aged man in the Haymarket. He was soused under the pump first for half an hour by some gentlemen, and then for an hour by the mob. In the same year a correspondent of the Monthly Magazine noticed that cases of the sale of wives at Smithfield with halters round their necks appeared to be on the increase. In some respects the old graces had gone out of life. The minuet was now definitely out of fashion, and the waltz had begun to take its place. The habit of all dressing nearly alike, the anxiety of every class to ape the affectations of that next above it, were bringing about their inevitable result. In the first years of the century persons of different social standing associated very freely together in the country. Now this was changing. Down in Devonshire Farington was told in 1810 that all who did not wish to live on terms of complete social equality with those whom they considered the lower orders, found it necessary to keep them at a distance. To mark the distinction further they developed fresh tasteless extravagances in their manner of living. Farington mentions as typical a dinner party given by Lord Lonsdale; the guests did not sit down till 7.20—an hour or more later than would have been the case ten years earlier—and the ladies did not retire till 9.10. Such late hours had several indirect results. The evening debating societies and glee clubs were discouraged. The meetings of the Royal Society began to be poorly attended. The useless English habit of lunching —so far only a light snack at the pastry cook's—was growing up to fill the gap. The fashions in dress did not benefit by the prolonged divorce between London and Paris. Dalton, the discoverer of the atom, not necessarily a judge of taste but a shrewd observer of anything, visited London in 1809. "Some of the ladies", he wrote, "seem to have their dresses as tight round them as a drum, others throw them round them as a blanket." The fashion plates show that it was the blankets which won the day.

But while the highest classes were growing reserved, the others were losing much of what made life agreeable, in obedience to that inexorable law by which an advance in civilization means a decline in natural gaiety. It was already observed in 1807 that the middle classes of the metropolis were deserting the tea-gardens, and that there was less joy in the villages than thirty years before. Such local festivals as that of Bartholomew Fair were becoming unreal survivals, and degenerating into mere occasions for rowdyism.

But the same advance which took away so much at least introduced a growing regard for the decencies of life. In 1809 there was an event which caused great scandal at the time, and affecting as it did the relations between the greatest military commander and the greatest cavalry leader of the day, had its effect upon history. Lord Paget eloped with Lady Charlotte, the wife of Henry Wellesley.

Writing in 1801, Richard Cumberland the dramatist had attacked those who regarded adultery as amiable. He would have found no cause to rebuke either the parties or the public in the present case. In the duel which followed with Lady Charlotte's brother, Paget faced the risk to his own life, but aimed purposely to one side; he said that nothing would have induced him to add to the injuries he had already done to the family. This was unlike the typical military libertine of a generation earlier. Moreover, he was said to have written to his father to say that he had sought his escape from his guilty passion by a death on the field of battle. Both the wronger and the wronged man belonged to prominent Tory families, and there can scarcely be a doubt that a few years earlier such an occasion for coarse merriment would have been welcomed by the Whig Press. But the comments of the Morning Chronicle were irreproachable.

How far this advance towards the characteristic nineteenth-century ideal of respectability was shared by the great mass of the people it is difficult to judge. But there can be no doubt that the great industrial communities which were growing up in Lancashire and elsewhere had become self-conscious, and had shown themselves capable of making sacrifices in a common cause. In the great strike of 1810, which had for its object to compel the master spinners outside Manchester to pay their men at the same rate as those inside, a weekly sum of £1,000 to £1,500 was raised, and the strike pay was 12s. a week. This first exhibition of the new-found sense of unity on a great scale was unfortunately chosen. The strike was met by a general lockout and the men lost. The decade closed in a period of widespread labour unrest due to the success of the Continental System. Prices had reached their maximum. The list framed by Stanley Jevons based upon the variation in the prices of forty commodities shows an advance in the cost of living to 164 in 1810, on the basis of the year

1782 represented by the figure 100. The cost in 1801 had been 153 only, and that had been a year of scarcity. The wages even of the once-pampered Bolton cambric weavers were down to a pound—soon to drop to half that amount.

But setting aside all considerations arising from temporary fluctuations in wages and prices, and the sufferings arising from an unwisely timed strike, the lot of the cotton-spinner, the typical factory worker, was not bad at the end of the decade. He was getting in Manchester 42s. 6d. for fine yarns, 20s. to 28s. for coarse. There was considerable improvement in general conditions in the mills. They were now usually worked by steam, which means more regular hours; they were larger and less unwholesome, and had more iron in their construction, and children were not put to work at so early an age.

During these years the operatives in the textile trades had been struggling to retain or to extend certain limitations on the freedom of trade which belonged to a past age. Such were the legislation against gig mills in the woollen trade, the retention of the seven years rule for apprentices, and the fixing of wages by Justices of the Peace. In all this they failed. The time was steadily approaching when, instead of looking for their salvation back to paternal legislation of Tudor times, they would press for measures of a very different stamp in the hands of a parliament more truly representative of their interests.

REFERENCES

(*Full titles of books and dates of editions are not given where they are in the bibliography—either in the general list or one of the two lists for the chapter concerned.*)

CHAPTER I

Pp. 18–19.—*Blake.*—The memoir of young Malkin is in the Monthly Magazine for 1802, II, 329 ff., and the review of the father's memoirs in that for 1806, II, 633.

Pp. 19–21.—*Crabbe.*—Crabbe's preference for the middle class appears from a quotation from his Common Place Book given in his Life in Poetical Works, 1838, I, 198; his request for money on pp. 162, 163.

Pp. 22–23.—*Other Poets.*—Burney's praise of Rogers is in Clayden's Early Life of Samuel Rogers, pp. 449 ff., the sale of his poem given on pp. 216, 217. The quotation from A Winter in London is from Vol. III, Chap. 3.

Pp. 24–35.—*Wordsworth, Coleridge, and Southey.*—Coleridge's account of Bowyer is in his Biographia Literaria, 1847, p. 7. The notice in the Monthly Review is in Vol. XII for 1793, pp. 216 ff. The quotations from Wordsworth are from the Prelude, XI, 345 ff., 143–145, and VIII, 266, 267. The story of Blake is in Gilchrist's Life of him, pp. 310, 311. Wordsworth's profits from Lyrical Ballads are given in his letter in Knight's Life of him, I, 98. The lines "Yet to this hour", etc., are on p. 253. Fox's greeting to him is in Clayden's Rogers and his Contemporaries, I, 33. Southey's defence of his early republicanism is from his Preface to Wat Tyler. The passage about turning their faces to the East is in his letter to William Smith in Essays, Moral and Political, 1832, Vol. I, p. 21. De Quincey's Collected Writings have his account of Southey's and Wordsworth's conversation, Vol. II, 322, 323. Southey's letters to his brothers on politics and religion are in British Museum ADD. MSS., 30927, ff. 148 and 171. Only the first of these letters has been published in Selections from his letters, II, 106 ff.

Pp. 35–37.—*Scott.*—Scott mentions Charles Leslie in his Introductory Remarks on Popular Poetry, Poetical Works, 1868, I, 85. The remarks made on him by Pitt and the sale of the Lay are given in Lockhart's Life of him, II, 34 ff., the sales of Marmion on p. 158.

P. 40.—*Hogg.*—The General who appropriated Hogg's eulogy is mentioned on p. xvii of the Life prefixed to the latter's Works, 1876.

Pp. 41–44.—*Music.*—The account of the King's concert is in the Annual Register for 1805, p. 368. Fiévée's observation as regards German music is in his Lettres sur l'Angleterre, p. 102. The Cave of Harmony is mentioned in The Newcomes, by W. M. Thackeray, Chap. I. Henry Davey's History of English Music is the authority for "Glorious Apollo", p. 380, and organs being given pedals, p. 395. Baert in his Tableau de la Grande Bretagne, IV, 263, 264, mentions the Scottish songs sung in drawing-rooms. Leigh Hunt details Italian tunes set to English words in his Autobiography, I, 74 f. Ernest Walker, in his History of Music in England, p. 240, notes Wesley's superiority in Roman Catholic Music.

Pp. 44–49.—*The Stage.*—Kemble's purchase of the share in Covent Garden is in Boaden's Life of him, II, 344; the extract from Colman's Epilogue on p. 351; and Betty's financial success on pp. 404, 405. The French visitor who remarked on the behaviour of the audience was Simond, in his Voyage en Angleterre, I, 126, 127, the German was J. H. Campe, Reise durch England und Frankreich, Brunswick, 1803, II, 69. Ferri de St. Constant describes the actor's stiffness in Londres et les Anglais, II, 208, 209. Leigh Hunt's remarks on dearth of character, and on the three Irish dramatists are in his Autobiography, I, pp. 286, 287. Barrymore and Pasquin are mentioned by John Bernard in his Retrospections of the Stage, II, 218. Coleridge's description of himself in the earlier chapters of his Biographia Literaria is that of a character. Kemble's acting is described in Letters from an Irish Student, etc., 1809, p. 255. The reference to Baert is to Tableau de la Grande Bretagne, IV, 236, that to Niebuhr to his Life and Letters by Baron C. C. J. Bunsen, 1852, I, 117, that to Madame de Staël to her Corinne, Livre XVII, Ch. 31. The story of Catherine Gordon is in Dr. Doran's Annals of the English Stage, III, 168, that of Robinson in his Diary, etc., I, 39.

Pp. 49–54.—*Painting.*—Lawrence's prices are mentioned in Williams's Life of him, I, 309. The comparison of Wilkie to the Dutchman is in Cunningham's Life of him, I, 95. The authority for Crome's being the first provincial art club is the Studio publication, The Norwich School, p. 1.

Pp. 54–57.—*Architecture, J. J.*—The panegyric on Fonthill is in the Gentleman's Magazine for 1796, p. 784. The references to Young are to his Farmer's Tour through the East of England, 1771, I, 212 note, and Six Months' Tour through the North of England, 1771, I, 265.

Pp. 57–58.—*Prose.*—Mackintosh's ideas of Kant are in Vol. I, p. 250, of his Life, Robinson's in his Diary, I, 129.

Pp. 58–60.—*Godwin.*—Godwin's unchallenged supremacy at the age of 40 appears from his own Thoughts occasioned by the perusal of Dr. Parr's Spital Sermon, 1801, pp. 9, 10, Coleridge's admiration from his marginal note on p. 8 of his copy of Enquiry concerning Political Justice, in the British Museum. The quotation from that book is from Book I, Chapter I, the ridicule of family affection from Book II, Chapter II, the advocacy of free love, Book VIII, Chapter VIII.

Pp. 60–63.—*Malthus.*—Malthus's views on late marriages of clerks, etc., are in his Essay on the Principle of Population, 1803, p. 301, the quotation about the old maid from pp. 549 ff., on the poor man's early marriage, pp. 507 ff., on the country gentlemen, p. 527, on the distribution of wealth, p. 422.

P. 63.—*Paley.*—Paley's sufferings are mentioned in Sketch of the Professional Life of Dr. Clark by J. R. Fenwick, 1806, p. 27.

Pp. 63–66.—*Bentham.*—Paley's definition of virtue is on p. 38, Vol. II, of his Complete Works, 1825, the other quotation on p. 55. Coleridge's acceptance of the doctrine of utility appears from his marginal note on his copy of Malthus's Essay on the Principle of Population, in the British Museum, p. 11. Bentham's view of Greek philosophy is in his Works, 1843, X, 77, his difficulties over his circular prison, Vol. X, pp. 96 ff. Wilberforce's observation is in his Life by his Sons, III, p. 71.

Pp. 67–69.—*Maria Edgeworth.*—R. L. Edgeworth's prefaces to his daughter's Tales of Fashionable Life, Vol. II, 1809, and Vol. IV, 1812, give their views on adult education.

Pp. 69–70.—*Lighter Prose.*—Lamb's complaint of ignorance of the old dramatists is from the Preface to his Specimens of English Dramatic Poets, 1808.

Pp. 71–75.—*The Reviews.*—Lord Cockburn describes the early meetings of the Edinburgh Reviewers in his Life of Lord Jeffrey, I, 136, and has the quotation from him on education, p. 68, and the arrangements for payment to contributors, pp. 134 ff. The authorship of the Don Cevallos article is discussed in Selections from the Correspondence of Macvey Napier, 1879, pp. 308, 309 note. The article in which the people are accused of blindness is in Vol. IX, for 1807, p. 278. The reason of the Review's circulation reaching 9000 is given by Scott in Lockhart's Life of him, II, 203; the description of John Murray is on p. 209.

Pp. 75–76.—*The Universities.*—The numbers of matriculations at Cambridge and Oxford are taken from the Cambridge Historical Register, 1917, p. 990, and the Oxford do. for 1900, p. 909. The requirements for the Cambridge trips are from Pryme's Autobiographic Recollections, p. 92.

Pp. 76–79.—*Education.*—Colquhoun's estimates are in A new and appropriate System of Education for the labouring people, pp. 72, 73. Dalton's school is described in Sir H. Roscoe's John Dalton, pp. 24 ff. The reference to The Flagellant, 1792, is p. 58; that to Espriella is Vol. II, pp. 261 ff. The Borough Road school is described in the Monthly Magazine, 1808, I, 385 ff., and Lancaster's seal in Pryme's Autobiographic Recollections, pp. 93 ff. The King's encouragement of Andrew Bell appears from the Life of William Allen, 1846, Vol. I, 110, and Mrs. Trimmer's from Bell's Life by R. and C. C. Southey, II, 131, 138, 164.

Pp. 79–80.—*Astronomy.*—George III's encouragement of Herschel appears from the latter's life by E. S. Holden, p. 126.

Pp. 80–81.—*Geology.*—Paris mentions the controversy in Scotland in his Life of Sir Humphry Davy, I, 150.

Pp. 81–86.—*Physics and Chemistry.*—Davy's list of elements is on pp. 31 ff. of his Outlines of a course of lectures, etc. Dalton's remarks on his audience are in W. C. Henry's Memoirs of him, 1854, p. 48. The birth of the Royal Institution is described in Paris's Life of Sir Humphry Davy, I, 192; he also mentions Wollaston's methods, p. 147. The reference to Beaufort is in Ferri de St. Constant's Londres et les Anglais, III, 317. Davy's prediction as to what science would achieve is in his Discourse on Chemistry, p. 22.

Pp. 86–90.—*Biology and Medicine.*—Darwin's anticipations are in his Zoonomia, 1794, pp. 502 ff. Capt. John Dobbs's account of bloodletting is in his Recollections of an old 52nd Man, 1859, p. 10. Sir B. Brodie's account of a doctor's education is in his Autobiography, p. 25. Baillie's income is from the Farington Diary, V, 225, Halford's from p. 42 of his Life by Munk, which has also the case of Lord Grosvenor's son, pp. 50 ff. Moseley's assertion as to ox-faces is from his Review etc., pp. 64 ff.

Pp. 90–92.—*Inventions.*—The passage in Watt's letter is in Muirhead's Origin and Progress of the Mechanical Inventions of James Watt, II, 165; his doubts as to the locomotive in Smiles's Men of Invention, etc., pp. 133 ff. The account of Symington is from Woodcroft's Sketch of Steam Navigation, 1848, pp. 54 ff.

Pp. 92–95.—*Engineering.*—Rennie's inventions of the dredger and improvements of the diving bellare from Smiles's Lives of the Engineers, II, 214 and 219, 220; his receipt of £350 from p. 283 note; Telford's of £237 a year from p. 488; Telford's early work from pp. 312 ff.; his general attitude to life from p. 489.

CHAPTER II

Pp. 96–99.—*The Government of India.*—Pulteney's observation is on p. 282 of Parliamentary History, XXXVI. The section quoted is 33 George III. Cap. 52, sec. 42. Malcolm quotes Cornwallis's letter on pp. 64, 65 of his Political History, Vol. I.

Pp. 99–102.—*Lord Wellesley as Governor General.*—The same volume has the character of the Nizam's army, p. 154. Wellesley's apology to Dundas is in his Despatches, II, 203.

Pp. 102–104.—*Annexations from Oudh.*—Bareilly amusements are described in Chapters VII ff. of War and Sport in India. Lord Valentia describes the road cess in his Voyages, etc., I, 194, and the condition of Oudh on p. 128. Castlereagh's observation is in Vol. III, p. 38 of Wellesley's Despatches; Anstruther's in Vol. II, p. 371.

Pp. 104–106.—*The Indian trade.*—The same book has Wellesley's reply regarding Henry's appointment, III, 57; his view as to the real cause of the Directors' virulence being the question of the private trade, p. 56; and his own attitude towards it, p. 54. Udny's note is in Vol. V, pp. 129 ff. C. J. Hamilton's Trade Relations between England and India (1800-1896), 1919, gives the rates on Indian calicoes, p. 255.

Pp. 106-108.—*The Civil Service.*—Criminal administration in Bengal is described in W. S. Seton-Karr's Cornwallis, pp. 91, 92, and note. The circumstances of Munro's appointment to civilian duties are given in Gleig's Life of him, Vol. I, pp. 142, 154; p. 333 has his dispensing with holidays. The early failure of the permanent settlement is described in the Fifth Report, 1812—p. 214 of F. D. Ascoli's Early Revenue History etc.

Pp. 108-109.—*The Calcutta College.*—Wellesley's objection to the term "writers", etc., is in his Despatches, II, 326, 327; his curriculum for the College, pp. 732 ff.; his presence at the disputations, III, 64, 65. Richard's letter is in Wellesley MSS. 37315, f. 70.

Pp. 109-110.—*Wellesley and Anglo-Indian society.*—Valentia describes the barges in his Travels, I, 60, 65. Wellesley on Anglo-Indian society is in The Wellesley Papers, I, 83, 84, Maria Graham on the same subject in her Journal, p. 28.

Pp. 110-111.—*Wellesley and the Directors.*—Wellesley's support of Clive's resignation is in Historical MSS. Commission, Dartmouth MSS., 1896, III, 278, 279. Bentinck's complaint is in Wellesley's Despatches, III, 299.

Pp. 111-112.—*The Maratha Confederacy.*—The Nizam's acceptance of a Maratha minister is in Wellington's Supplementary Despatches, IV, 546.

Pp. 114-115.—*Arthur Wellesley's early career.*—Vol. II, p. 501 of the same Despatches has Arthur Wellesley's letter to Henry. Lord Teignmouth's Life of his Father has his impressions when Sir John Shore, I, 424, 425.

Pp. 115-118.—*The Army in India.*—The emoluments of the Commander-in-Chief in Madras are from Combermere's Memoirs, I, 73, those of the Governor from The Wellesley Papers, I, 32. War and Sport in India has the account of Pattle, pp. 442 ff., and also Lake's prize-money, p. 211. Arthur Wellesley's is in Hon. Sir John Fortescue's Wellington, 1925, p. 55. The return of troops on the E. I. Station is from Public Records Office, W.O. 17. 1747; the statement that in 1804 the establishment was half as much again in Wellesley's Despatches, IV, 225; the details of the troops actually in India in 1803 are from the Bengal Madras, and Bombay Establishment returns in the India Office. The account of the material of which the Indian armies were composed is from the East India U.S. Journal, Vol. II, 1834, Selections, pp. 60 ff., the experience of a young cadet from Vol. I, 1833-34, pp. 259 ff. The passage in John Shipp's Memoirs about how the officers lived is on p. 283 of Vol. I, the reference to his animals on p. 165. The account of the army on the march is from Major Thorn's Memoirs of the War, pp. 87 ff.

Pp. 118–123.—*Outbreak of the Maratha War.*—The authority for the Peshwa's treachery is Grant Duff's History of the Mahrattas, II, 333. The importance of the Peshwa's Prime Minister being Sindhia's own man is emphasized in Wellington's Supplementary Despatches, IV, 574 and 577, and Raghuji's fear of Holkar on p. 580. Wellington's Dispatches, Vol. I, has the declaration of war, pp. 618, 619, and his letter to Malcolm, pp. 513 ff. Lord Wellesley's letter to the Secret Committee is in his Despatches, III, 6, 7; his knowledge of the weakness of Sindhia's control over Perron appears from pp. 211. Grant Duff gives the Maratha strength on p. 337, Vol. II of his History.

Pp. 123–128.—*Campaigns of 1803.*—Lake's strength is taken from Hon. John Fortescue's History of the British Army, V, 47, 48; it also gives the losses at Delhi, p. 56, and Aligarh, p. 52, and Wellesley's strength at Ahmadnagar and Assaye, pp. 15 note and 24 note. The coming over of Perron's British officers to Lake is mentioned in War and Sport in India, p. 148. The Punjab Historical Society's Journal, IX, 1923, Pt. I, pp. 60 ff., throws light on Bourquien's relations with Perron. Vol. III of Wellesley's Despatches has the loss of two officers from the effects of the sun, p. 309, and the supplementary agreement to the Treaty of Bassein, pp. 377, 378. Sir W. Hunter's Orissa has the mention of the slave trade, II, 62. Grant Duff gives the Maratha strength at Assaye in his History of the Marathas, II, 341, and the reinforcement of Sindhia's northern army, p. 352. Skinner's story is in Fraser's Military Memoir of him, I, 306.

Pp. 128–133.—*Campaigns of 1804–1805.*—Arthur Wellesley's earlier view of the mode of warfare most suited to Marathas is in Wellington's Dispatches, II, 868. Holkar's letter to Lake is in the latter's Life by Col. Pearse, p. 264. Lord Wellesley's moderation after Holkar had put officers to death appears from his Despatches, IV, 11; his desire to postpone a campaign from p. 68; the Treaty with Bharatpur is on p. 636. Grant Duff has Malcolm's estimate of Holkar's strength, History of the Marathas, II, 376. The East India U.S. Journal, Vol. II, 1834, Selections, has the success of the 12th Bengal Infantry, p. 71. Shipp's anecdote is from his Memoirs, I, 199. Lake's losses at Bharatpur are from Sir John Fortescue's History of the British Army, V, 127.

Pp. 133–136.—*Close of Lord Wellesley's Governor-Generalship.*— Castlereagh's letter about the military establishment is in Wellesley's Despatches, IV, 225, his efforts to improve Calcutta as well as agriculture, pp. 672 ff.; Lake's emotion is in Vol. III, p. 397, and Metcalfe's tribute on p. 268 note. Indian revenues in 1801 are taken from Intercepted Despatches, p. 93, and the increase in debt and reduction in rate of interest under Wellesley from Review of the Affairs of India, 1807, p. 117. Arthur Wellesley's speech in Hansard, VII, has the estimate of financial position on settlement of the new districts, pp. 1063 ff. and 1071. Wellington's Supplementary Despatches, IV, has his memorandum, pp. 546 ff.

Pp. 136–137.—*Governor-Generalship of Cornwallis.*—The Cornwallis

REFERENCES

Correspondence has the finanical position as he found it and the expedient which he adopted, III, 536, 537.

Pp. 137–140.—*Barlow's succession as Governor-General.*—The observation of the Agent of the Raja of Jaipur is recorded by Malcolm, Political History of India, I, 373. Lt. Col. W. J. Wilson's History of the Madras Army, Vol. III, has the arrest of the loyal sepoy, p. 175, and the composition of the Special Commission, p. 190. Hon. John Fortescue's History of the British Army gives the casualties on the Vellore outbreak, VI, 46. The Morning Chronicle for April 14, 1803, gives an extract from the Duke of Kent's orders.

Pp. 140–141.—*Other interests of the East India Company.*—The character of the China trade in 1801 is described in H. B. Morse's East India Company trading to China, II, 358. Staunton's unique position is described in Memoirs of Sir George Staunton, privately printed, 1856, pp. 17, 27. The value of a Chinese writership is discussed in Kaye's Life of Lord Metcalfe, I, 15.

Pp. 141–143.—*Ceylon.*—Rev. J. Cordiner's Description of Ceylon gives the conditions there, I, 73 ff., 83, 87, 88; the cinnamon trade, II, 416; the educational system, I, 163 ff. Hon. John Fortescue's History of the British Army, V, 141 ff. is the authority for the Kandian war.

CHAPTER III

Pp. 144–146.—*Opening of Parliament.*—Cobbett's charge against Fox was made in his Political Register for 1802, II, 216 ff.; Windham's view is in the Windham Papers, II, 198. Place's account of his deceiving his customers is in Graham Wallas's Life of him, 1898, pp. 35, 36.

Pp. 146–147.—*Honours paid to Pitt.*—Hansard VI, 63 has Fox's objection to the monument, and pp. 128 ff. show the attitude of the House towards Pitt's debts.

Pp. 147–150.—*The new Ministry,*—George III's reply to Grenville is mentioned in the Annual Register for 1806, p. 21, and the parliamentary position of the new Ministry explained on pp. 22, 23. Canning is given the credit of the phrase "All the Talents", by Tierney in Hansard, IX, 464. Spencer Walpole's Life of Perceval has Ellenborough's refusal of the Great Seal, I, 181, 182, and Perceval's refusal of office, p. 209. Canning's is in Historical MSS. Commission, Fortescue MSS., VIII, 331 and 386 ff.

Pp. 151–152.—*Debate on Ellenborough's position.*—Ellenborough's own description of his position in on p. 127 of Private Papers of William Wilberforce, 1897. The definition of the Cabinet is in Hansard, VI, 291; the arguments regarding the examination of political prisoners, and Blackstone, on pp. 294, 295, Fox's argument on pp. 308 ff., Holland's assertion on p. 278.

Pp. 152–153.—*Budget of 1806.*—The same volume has the Budget speech, 564 ff.; Fox's remarks are on p. 613; Vol. VII has Petty's remarks on families, p. 55; and Birmingham's fear of foreign competition, p. 78. The abatements for small annuitants, etc., and labourers are in sections 173 and 177 of the Act (46 G. III, c. 65).

Pp. 153–154.—*Windham's military reforms.*—Hansard VI has Fox's speech, pp. 707 ff. and Windham's, pp. 652 ff.

Pp. 154–156.—*Hostilities with Prussia.*—The Annual Register for 1807 has the Prussian Proclamation and Declaration, and the British Order in Council, pp. 676, 677, and on p. 161 the description of Prussia's conduct in the words quoted. The rest of Fox's speech is taken from Hansard VII, 887 ff.

Pp. 156–158.—*Naval operations.*—The claim for the Impérial is made in Victoires Conquêtes, etc., XVII, p. 268; the incident of the recovery of the captured troops is in the Annual Register for 1806, p. 232, and in James's Naval History, IV, 274; the Dutchmen's drinking the New Year in at Curaçoa is mentioned by E. P. Brenton, The Naval History of Great Britain, 1837, Vol. II, p. 204.

Pp. 158–161.—*Negotiations with France.*—Sorel mentions Yarmouth's relations with Berthier's mistress, etc., L'Europe et la Révolution Française, VII, 67. Fox's admission of the possibility of asking Ferdinand to accept a compensation for Sicily is mentioned in the chapter contributed by Lord Holland to the Annual Register for 1806, p. 180. That number has also Yarmouth's despatches mentioning the 14-hour conference, p. 732, and his production of his powers, p. 738. His draft treaty is in the Public Records Office, F.O. 27. 74, which has also Napoleon's printed notes. P. Coquelle gives Napoleon's omission to mention this draft treaty, Napoléon et l'Angleterre, p. 119. Whitworth's complaint of Lauderdale is in O. Browning's England and Napoleon in 1803, 1907, pp. 135, 139. Lauderdale's tenacity is described in Holland's Memoirs of the Whig Party, II, 76, 77.

Pp. 161–162.—*Restoration of peace with Prussia.*—The date of raising the blockade of the Prussian rivers appears from the Annual Register for 1806, p. 171; the Prussian manifesto is on pp. 800 ff.

Pp. 162–164.—*Measures for the abolition of the Slave Trade.*—Fox's two favourite causes are mentioned in Holland's Memoirs of the Whig Party, I, 250, and by Howick, Hansard, VIII, 324. Clarkson's view that early success would have been precarious is expressed in his History of the Abolition of the Slave Trade, I, 524 ff.; his exculpation of Pitt from the charge of lukewarmness, II, 504; the importance of the point reached before Pitt's death, p. 501.

Pp. 164–166.—*Impeachment of Melville.*—Whitbread's boast is in Hansard, V, 394. The course of the trial is in the Annual Register, 1806, pp. 113 ff.; the voting on pp. 624 ff.; on p. 127 the absence of Grenville and Spencer is noted, and it is commented upon in Holland's Memoirs of the Whig Party, I, 235.

Pp. 166–169.—*Expedition to South America.*—The Annual Register for 1806 has the despatch giving the strength of British and Spanish troops, p. 597, the eight waggons with treasure, p. 446, the visions of wealth from Potosi, pp. 236, 237; the despatch from Monte Video from which losses are taken for Feb. 3, 1807, is in the 1807 volume, p. 655. The strength of the four expeditionary forces is taken from Hon. J. Fortescue's History of the British Army, Vol. V, pp. 369, 374 note, 389, 377.

Pp. 169–172.—*Battle of Maida.*—Stuart's despatch is in the Annual Register, 1806, pp. 591 ff. Sir Charles Oman gives the totals of his and Reynier's troops on pp. 563, 564, and discusses at length the manner of the French attack, and its British reception on pp. 553 of the Journal of the Royal Artillery, Vol. XXXIV.

Pp. 172–174.—*Rupture of the negotiations with France.*—Lauderdale's instructions are in Coquelle's Napoléon et l'Angleterre, pp. 112 ff. The Annual Register, 1806, has his last note to Talleyrand, pp. 788 ff.

Pp. 174–175.—*Death of Fox.* The early symptoms of Fox's fatal illness are mentioned in Colchester's Diary, II, 48, 50, 53. His idea of handing his office over to Holland is mentioned in the latter's Memoirs of the Whig Party, I, 248; the same volume has the account of his last illness, pp. 244 ff. The Annual Register has the details as to his being tapped, pp. 258 and 432.

Pp. 175–179.—*The year 1806 as a turning point.*—William Napier's observation is from his Life of Sir Charles Napier, I, 59, 60. St. Vincent's complaint is in E. P. Brenton's Life of him, 1838, Vol. II, p. 288. The greeting of the mail-coaches is from the Annual Register, 1806, p. 453, the rejoicing of stockbrokers from Holland's Memoirs of the Whig Party, II, 79.

Pp. 179–180.—*Reconstitution of the Ministry.*—The same writer explains the general election, II, 91.

Pp. 180–181.—*Meeting of a New Parliament.*—Lord Howick's speech in Hansard VIII, 67, 68, explains the failure to help Prussia.

Pp. 181–183.—*The Berlin Decree.*—The shipping tonnages for 1792 and 1800 are given on pp. 261 and 535 of David Macpherson's Annals of Commerce, Vol. IV, 1805. The French Resolution of Nov. 2nd is in the Annual Register for 1796, Chronicle, etc., pp. 256 ff.

Pp. 183–184.—*Parliamentary affairs.*—Petty's scheme is set forth in the Tables in the appendix to Hansard, VIII, which volume has also Whitbread's educational schemes, etc., pp. 865 ff.

Pp. 184–189.—*Fall of the Ministry.*—The Annual Register, 1807, shows Ireland's importance to the ministerial party, p. 143. Holland's Memoirs of the Whig Party describes the nature of the Irish disturbances, and the suggestion made to Bedford, II. 160 ff., the Cabinet meeting of March 15th, pp. 200 ff., and gives in the Appendix the resulting minute, the King's unconstitutional demand, and the reply. Historical MSS. Commission, Fortescue MSS., IX, has Grenville's recruiting plans, p. 7, and the first correspondence with the King, pp. 107 ff. Speeches reported in Hansard, IX, pp. 241 and 397 mention the King's declaration to Grenville of March 11; p. 187 has the passing of the Slave Trade Abolition Act, and p. 347 Petty's admission about the Catholic measure. The Prince's conversation with Croker is in the Croker

Papers, I, 300 ff., which is also the authority for George III's unwillingness to receive the Princess. Portland's letter to the King is in the Diaries of Lord Malmesbury, IV, 360 ff.

Pp. 189–194.—*The Dardanelles Expedition.*—Sebastiani's success in Constantinople is detailed by Arbuthnot in a letter in Barrow's Life of Sir Sidney Smith, II, 211, 212, which has also the instructions to Duckworth, pp. 217 ff., and an account of the stone shot, pp. 228, 229. James's Naval History has the date of issuing orders for reconnoitring the forts, IV, 296, and Duckworth's proceedings from Feb. 10 onwards, pp. 299 ff., it also gives the circumference of the stone shot, p. 309. The loan of French officers is mentioned in the Moniteur for 10th and 15th April, 1807. The condition of affairs in Constantinople is from É. Driault's Napoléon et l'Europe (Tilsit), p. 126. Duckworth's reply to the Turks to the effect that he could cut off their supplies is in his letter No. 75 of 24th February, 5 p.m., in Public Records Office, Admiralty I, 413.

Pp. 194–195.—*The Egyptian Expedition.*—Napoleon's plan against India is given in Sorel's L'Europe et la Révolution Française, VII, 136.

CHAPTER IV

Pp. 196–199.—*Portland's Administration.*—Hansard IX, 212, is the authority for Sheridan's taunt to Perceval, p. 340 for Howick's account of the latter's electioneering methods.

Pp. 199–200.—*General Election.*—The comment of the Annual Register for 1807 is on p. 235.

Pp. 200–203.—*The Egyptian Expedition.*—Sir Henry Bunbury's Narrative of Some Passages in the Great War gives Major Missett's character, p. 285, the information given by him, pp. 290 ff., and remarks on Muhammad Ali's good treatment of his prisoners, pp. 305, 306. Moore's remark is on p. 167, Vol. II of his Diary.

Pp. 203–204.—*The Brazil Expedition.*—Craufurd's belief that Buenos Ayres might have been taken on the 4th is from Rev. A. Craufurd's General Craufurd and his Light Division, p. 19. The staff officer's omission is observed by Capt. Lewis Butler in his series, Minor Expeditions, in U.S. Magazine, Aug. 1805, p. 510. The figures of captures by British are from Whitelocke's despatch in Annual Register, 1807, p. 688. His dislike of street fighting was expressed to Craufurd, vide latter's evidence on p. 39 of S. Tipper's edition of his Trial.

Pp. 204–206.—*Army reorganization.*—The figures as to the army and militia are taken from Vol. VI of Hon. J. Fortescue's History of the British Army, pp. 47 and 39. Castlereagh's account of his Militia Transfer Bill is in Hansard, IX, 866, 867; his criticism of Windham's recruiting methods, pp. 1221, 1222; his remark on Napoleon, p. 872. The figures for volunteers are in Appendix, p. iii, to the same volume, and the remark on their deterioration on p. 1132: that on England's dependence on the navy, p. 1127. Windham's observation on Spain is on p. 479.

Pp. 206–208.—*Parliamentary affairs.*—The reference to the coercive measures for Ireland is Hansard IX, pp. 751*, 752* and 1180: to the tithe question, p. 661: Sheridan's speech on Ireland, p. 1196: the unpopularity of the Parochial Schools Bill (Wilberforce's statement), p. 854; Hawkesbury's admission in favour of education, p. 1174; Perceval's doubts as to vaccination, p. 1009.

Pp. 208–209.—*Treaty of Tilsit.*—Russia's complaints regarding the nature of British assistance are in Hansard, X, 111 ff.; Howick's refusal of a loan on pp. 628 ff. The shortage of tonnage is in Vol. IX, 1222.

Pp. 209–214.—*The Danish Expedition.*—The reference to the object of St. Vincent's mission is Vol. X, 538 ff. Robinson's views are from his Diary, I, 264. Howick's instructions to Garlike are in Hansard, X, 765 ff. Rist's complaint of his position is from Erik Möller's England og Danmark-Norge, Historisk Tidsskrift, 1911, p. 332. Canning's and Garlike's complaints to one another are in Public Records Office, F.O. 22. 52, the former's letters being of 7.6.07, and 14.7.97, the latter's of 27.6.97; the letter of 22.7.07, in which Canning gives the substance of his news from Tilsit is in F.O. 22. 53. The figures of naval strength are taken from James's Naval History, IV, 283. Wellington's Supplementary Despatches, V, 192, 193, has a letter on apprehensions for Ireland. Napoleon's letter to Talleyrand is in his Correspondance (1859–1869), XV, pp. 573, 574; that to Bernadotte, p. 584; the earlier intimation to Portugal, p. 433. The Danish newspaper Nyeste Skilderie for 1807 republished the Frankfort announcement, p. 1415. The authority for the rumours as to intended French coercion of Denmark is Holm, Danmark-Norges Udenrigske Historie, II, 274 note. The Times urged the necessity of a Danish expedition in its numbers for July 16, 1807, p. 3, col. 2, and July 24, p. 3, col. 1.

Pp. 214–216.—*Hostilities with Denmark.*—The account of the Comus action is in James's Naval History, Vol. IV, pp. 287, 288, tested from the Comus's log in Public Records Office, Admiralty 51, 1673. The total strength of the Danish forces and those south of Copenhagen and within it are from Raeder's Danmarks Krigs-og Politiske Historie, I, 83, 196, and 93 respectively. An Authentic Account of the Siege of Copenhagen gives examples of the Danish General's confidence; the Nyeste Skilderie's reassurances are on pp. 1427 ff. for 1807. Niebuhr's views are from pp. 417, 418 of his Nachgelassene Schriften, 1842. Wellesley's preference for a blockade, and the reasons justifying it, are given in the Supplementary Despatches, VI, 9.

Pp. 216–222.—*Results of the Expedition.*—The total losses of the expedition are taken from James's Naval History, IV, 291, and its gain in ships from the same source, p. 295. Jackson's account of his audience of the Crown Prince is in his No. 4 of 9.8.07 in Public Records Office, F.O. 22. 54; the Queen's statement in Danske Samlinger, II, 2, gives the fear of Napoleon's army, and Holm, Danmark-Norges Udenrigske Historie, II, 257, the insufficiency of the guarantees as the grounds of the Prince's refusal. Leveson Gower's despatch regarding his interview at St. Petersburg is in Hansard, X, 199, 200. Malmesbury's remark on Canning is in his Diaries, Vol. IV, p. 367. Canning's letter to Brooke Taylor of 22.7.07 in Public Records Office, F.O. 22. 53 shows that several persons were present at the interview between the Emperors on the raft. Sir John Macpherson's letter in Delavoye's Life of Lord Lynedoch, p. 612, is the authority for Mackenzie having been the one Englishman present. That for the parties in Russia is Erik Möller's article in Historisk Tidsskrift, 1911, p. 420. Samuel Parr's complaint is in Rev. William Field's Memoirs of his Life, 1828, Vol. II, p. 28. The passage quoted from Wellesley's speech is on p. 349 of Vol. X of Hansard. The same volume gives Russia's offer of mediation and reply, pp. 113 ff.; p. 195 has the fact of the latter's request to Leveson Gower for the communication of any secret articles; pp. 197, 198, the latter's report of the conciliatory tone of Russia; p. 211 Alexander's protest of Sept. 23. Sir Robert Adair defines the attitude of Austria in his Mission to the Court of Vienna, p. 309.

Pp. 222–224.—*Relations with Portugal.*—Lord Strangford mentions the Prince Regent's letter to George III in his Observations on Napier's History, p. 11. The Portuguese Ambassador's impression as to the danger to his country is given by Holm, Danmark-Norges Udenrigske Historie, II, 201, 202. The South American plans are from Castlereagh's Memoirs, etc., VIII, 96 ff.

Pp. 224–228.—*The Orders in Council and the Continental System.*—Hansard X gives the inquiry of the U.S. regarding the Berlin Degree and the reply, p. 556; p. 404 (Note to Rist) gives Howick's opinion as to what England would have been justified in doing; and pp 558, 559, and 407 his views as to what he expected from U.S. and Denmark; p. 933 has Erskine's remark as to the merchants of London. Perceval's Cabinet paper is in Walpole's Life of him, I, 264 ff.

Pp. 228–229.—*Relations with the United States.*—That exasperation over the Chesapeake affair was general is clear from Memoirs of Thomas Jefferson, 1829, IV, 100. The reinforcement of Canada appears from Castlereagh's Memoirs, etc., VIII, 106. Randall's Life of Thomas Jefferson, III, 243 note, shows when the general sense of the Orders in Council was known in America. Jefferson's prophecy is in Bristed's Hints on the National Bankruptcy of Britain, p. 349.

Pp. 229–231.—*Effect of the Orders.*—The Whig leadership is discussed by Holland in Memoirs of the Whig Party, II, 236 ff. Erskine's attack on the Order in Council is in Hansard, X, 940 ff.; the details as to insurance rates in Vol. XIII (App. II), pp. xxxviii ff. Other petitions on the Orders are mentioned on pp. 194, 203 of the Commons Journals, 1808.

Pp. 231–232.—*Lancashire unrest.*—The details as to the cotton strike are from Annual Register, 1808, Chronicle, pp. 47, 48, 51, 52, 54, 55, 58, 63.

P. 232.—*Budget of 1808.*—The total yearly expenditure of Great Britain is taken from Hansard XI, App., p. VI, and p. 764. Perceval's oan is explained on p. 765; the Irish budget (malt duties) on pp. 829, 830. The arrangements with the Bank of England are set out in Vol. X, pp. 251, 252. The amounts of the public balances are discussed by David Ricardo, Works, 1846, pp. 412 ff.

Pp. 232-234.—*Parliamentary Affairs.*—The fall in the price of sugar is given in the Appendix to Hansard XI, p. LXXXI, and the export figures of sugar on p. LXXXVI; annual import of grain on p. 429; consumption in distilleries App., p. XCII. The passing of the Act temporarily preventing grants of offices in reversion is given on p. 160; the nature of the opposition to the Clergy Bill appears from pp. 1088, 1089, 1092, 1113, 1114. Cobbett's attack on Whitbread is in his Political Register, XIII, 1808, p. 368. The Militia Bill is explained in Hansard XI, 39 ff.

Pp. 234-237.—*The War on the Continent and in the Mediterranean.*—Napoleon's letter to Alexander of Feb. 2, 1808, is fully discussed in Driault's Napoléon et l'Europe, Tilsit, p. 275; his views on Sicily in A. Vandal's Napoléon et Alexandre I, pp. 254-256.

Pp. 237-240.—*Outbreak of the Peninsula War.*—The Conde de Toreño recounts his journey to London in his Historia, etc., I, 104, and mentions the demonstration at the theatre on p. 475. Hansard, XVI, 888, has Sheridan's sayings. Wellesley's suggestion to send a force to Spain is in his Supplementary Despatches, VI, 80, the Duke of York's objection to his command on p. 171; his Dispatches are the authority for so much of Portugal's food supplies being drawn from abroad, Vol. III, p. 70, and for his low estimate of the enemy's force, pp. 46, 57. Burrard's order to Moore to hold back is from the latter's Diary, II, 253, 254.

Pp. 240-242.—*Battle of Vimeiro.*—Junot's strength is taken from Sir Charles Oman's History of the Peninsular War, I, 246, 247, note. The Humble Petition of H. N. S. Shrapnel, printed at Salisbury, 1868, gives the earliest occasions of the successful use of the shrapnel shell, pp. 6 ff. The description of Ferguson's charge is from Sir George Jackson's Diaries, II, 262, and Wellington's tribute to him from Hansard, XII, 158; the Opposition members' tribute to Wellington being on pp. 149 and 157. His Dispatches, III, 110, 111, has the presentation by the general officers, and his Supplementary Despatches, VI, 138, 139, that by the field officers.

Pp. 242-243.—*Armistice.*—Wellington's complaint of Dalrymple's refusal to repose confidence in him is from his Dispatches, III, 112; his speech in parliament has the calculation of the time necessary to drive the French from Portugal, and his explanation as to its having been his duty to sign, pp. 934 and 936. His refusal to become the head of a party against Dalrymple is in his Supplementary Despatches, VI, 132, and his saying that he would sign any paper he was desired to sign in Dispatches, III, 155.

Pp. 243-245.—*Convention of Cintra.*—Toreño mentions the three generals being caricatured, Historia etc., I, 251. Wordsworth's willingness to address a meeting is mentioned by Southey in a letter on p. 117 of Vol. II of the Selections. The indignation of the three Ministers appears from Castlereagh's Memoirs, etc., VI, 421 ff. Siniavin's refusal to land men is in Foy's Histoire, etc., IV, 302. How far Dalrymple succeeded in preventing Junot's army from carrying off plunder appears from Burghersh's Memoirs of the early campaigns, pp. 40 ff., and from Colonel Wyndham-Quin's Sir Charles Tyler, 1912, p. 171. Moira's statement is in Hansard XII, 25.

Pp. 245–249.—*Military situation in Spain.*—Moore's Diary has Dalrymple's instructions to be ready to move, II, 310, and his own remark on the confusion, p. 261. Delavoye's Life of Lynedoch gives his decision to become a soldier, p. 79, and the insertion in his diary, pp. 291, 292. Bentinck's letter endorsing Graham's opinion is in Hansard, XIII (App.), CCCLXI, and his own earlier views are on p. CCCXLIX.

Pp. 250–254.—*Moore's advance to Sahagun.*—Haugwitz's remark is in Jackson's Diary, II, 372. Napoleon's misapprehension as to Hope's movements appears from Cdt. Balagny's Campagne etc., III, 149, 150, cp. the reports on pp. 150, 160. His instruction regarding publication of an account of Moore being surrounded is in his Correspondance, XIX, 1865, p. 185. Moore's claim of success for his diversion is in Hansard, XIII (App.), CCCLXXXI.

Pp. 254–257.—*Retreat to Coruña.*—Stewart's observation is in his Story of the Peninsula War (written when he was Lord Londonderry), p. 129. Maj. Gen. Sir F. Maurice gives the extract from Capt. J. Stirling's MS. on the grenadiers at Sahagun in Diary of Moore, II, 376. The private soldier's impressions are in Journal of a Soldier of the 71st Regiment, p. 54.

Pp. 257–259.—*Battle of Coruña.*—Sir C. Oman gives the words (suppressed at the time) from Moore's last despatch on the demoralization of the army, History of the Peninsular War, I, 566. Soult's reasons for attacking at Coruña are in Cdt. Balagny's Campagne, etc., IV, 339, his numbers on p. 250, the position of his guns, p. 249, the French effecting a lodgement in Elviña, p. 256.

Pp. 260–261.—*Return of the Army.*—The reference to the landing in Plymouth is the Hampshire Telegraph, Feb. 6, 1809. Some account is given of the typhus outbreak in the Autobiography of Sir James McGrigor, 1861, pp. 216, 220, 221. Grenville's view on war in Spain is reported in Hansard XIV, 915.

Pp. 261–262.—*Inquiry regarding the Duke of York.*—Wilberforce's acquittal of York of corruption is in Hansard, XIII, 587; his unfavourable view upon the whole, p. 580; York's letter to his Darling Love in Vol. XII, p. 583. The observations in the two Houses on Lord Burghersh's promotion are in Vol. XIV, pp. 670, 671, and 694.

Pp. 262–264.—*Other parliamentary inquiries.*—Colchester's Diary, II, 171, has "Duke and Darling". That the offer made to the Prime

Minister came from a chaplain to the Bishop of London appears from the Annual Register for 1809, p. 143, note; the offer to Mrs. Clarke is on p. 144. The findings of the Select Committee as to the price of writerships is in Hansard XIII (App.), CXXVII; Castlereagh's admissions are on pp. 218 ff. of Vol. XIV; the division over the purchase of a seat on p. 527; the debate on the Irish distillery is on pp. 787, 788; the refusal to indemnify the excise officers on p. 966.

Pp. 264–266.—*Parliamentary Reform.*—Cobbett's calculation is in his Political Register for 1809, I, 74 ff. Grenville's complaint is in Hansard, XIV, 913; Tierney on reform on p. 509. Francis Horner mentions the "patriots", Memoirs, I, 462. Windham's argument is in Hansard, XIV, 754, 755; Smith's lapse on p. 377; Canning's observation on p. 523; Whitbread's on p. 956. Curwen's reference to Pitt is on p. 357. Romilly on his purchase of a seat is in his Memoirs, I, 422.

Pp. 266–267.—*Other measures in parliament.*—The proposals regarding Irish tithes are in Wellington's Supplementary Despatches, V, 167 ff. Hansard, XIV, 1029*, 1032, and 1071 has the obstruction to Erskine's bill; p. 958, Perceval's remark on sinecures; p. 534 his terms for the loan.

Pp. 267–279.—*Foreign relations.*—Austria's drafts are mentioned in Hansard, XIV, 825. Sir Robert Adair mentions his efforts to reconcile various pairs of countries in his Mission to the Court of Vienna, pp. 322, 461, and 300 respectively, and gives his views on the Erfurt conversations in Negotiations for the Peace of the Dardanelles, II, 134. Canning's letter opening negotiations with the United States is in Hansard, XVII (App.), CXXIII ff., and Erskine's proceedings on pp. CLIV ff. The wheat and wheat-flour imports are given in Commons Journals, 1812, p. 749.

Pp. 269–272.—*Progress of the War.*—The importance of Martinique is emphasized in Joseph Marryat's speech, Hansard, XIV (App.), LXXIX, and the proclamation is on p. XC. The Naval Chronicle, XXII, 6, gives Cochrane's letter on El Gamo, and his heroism at Rosas, Vol. XXI, 195; Capt. Sir H. Neale's report of his conversation with Mulgrave, p. 424.

Pp. 272–275.—*The War in the Peninsula.*—The strength of Soult's field force is taken from Le Noble's Campagne de 1809, pp. 353, 354, the number of Beresford's troops in the first movement on Oporto from Sir C. Oman's History of the Peninsular War, II, 318, that after reinforcement from Hon. J. Fortescue's History of the British Army, VII, 165. Wellesley's confidence in recapturing Madrid is expressed in his Dispatches, III, 344. The authority for Cuesta's and Victor's strength is Sir C. Oman's History, II, 468 and 436, that for the whole French force at Talavera, p. 500.

Pp. 275–281.—*Battle of Talavera.*—The same work gives the strength of the British and Spanish forces, II, 512. Hon. J. Fortescue's History of the British Army shows the brigades' ignorance of their positions before the battle, II, 230 note. It was Lord Munster (Lt.-Col.

Fitzclarence), who observed the number of militia knapsacks, vide An Account of the British Campaigns of 1809, p. 42. Major Leith Hay relates the bringing up of the four guns to the height in his Narrative of the Peninsular War, I, 149, 155, and the repulse of Victor's troops from it by the same men as before, pp. 151 ff. Victor's relations with Joseph are taken from Marshal Jourdan's Mémoires Militaires, p. 256. Sir C. Oman's History of the Peninsular War gives the number, etc., of Spanish guns on the height, Vol. II, 532, and the strength of the force at Puente de Baños, p. 475. Mackenzie's services and death are described in a letter in the Morning Chronicle for Nov. 9, 1809; Stewart's letter to Castlereagh is quoted by Hon. J. Fortescue in his History, VII, 257; Wellesley's to Richmond is in his Despatches, III, 380.

Pp. 281–284.—*Wellesley's retirement.*—The Memoir of Sir F. Whittingham, p. 84, shows that the direction being taken by the French Corps was known early in July. Wellesley's letter on Soult's strength is given in his Dispatches, III, 391, as also his account of Wilson's performance, p. 438, and his confession that he had been in a bad scrape, p. 401. The soldiers feeding off acorns is in Memoirs of a Sergeant, p. 75, the price of goat's offal in Napier's History of the War in the Peninsula, II, 196, that of bread in a letter in Buckingham's Court and Cabinets of George III, Vol. IV, p. 362. Hay's Narrative of the Peninsular War, I, 186, gives the number in hospital. Wellesley's observations on the undisciplined state of his army are in his Dispatches, III, 266, 304. Whittingham's praise of him is in his Memoir, p. 84.

Pp. 284–285.—*Operations in the Mediterranean.*—Adair's interest in the Seven Islands appears from his Negotiations for the Peace of the Dardanelles, I, 301 ff., and Collingwood's from his Correspondence, pp. 536, 537; the nature of Cerigo appears from the same work, pp. 545, 546.

Pp. 285–288.—*The Walcheren Expedition.*—The recovery of the troops by the end of May was attested by Major Gen. Calvert before Parliament, Hansard, XV (App.), CLIV. The idea of Chatham's commanding the expedition as a step to the premiership appears from Lord Stanhope's Conversations with the Duke of Wellington, 1888, pp. 289, 290. Sir N. Wraxall—Memoirs, 1884, V, 152—describes how Chatham obtained his reputation for wisdom. Temple's story is in Buckingham's Court and Cabinets of George III, Vol. IV, p. 356. Sir William Gomm —Letters, p. 131—describes Strachan's temper. The part taken by the Navy in the bombardment is mentioned in Letters from Flushing, 155 ff., and 242. The evidence that the heavy ordnance could not be sent across S. Beveland is in Hansard XV (App.), 5xcvII.

Pp. 288–289.—Chatham's despatch showing the estimate of the French force collected in Antwerp is in the Annual Register for 1809, p. 560. The casualties are taken from Hon. J. Fortescue's History of the British Army, VII, 80, combined with James's Naval History, V, 138, which gives also on the next page the naval results of the

REFERENCES 435

expedition. Napoleon suggests his return to command against the British, p. 368 of Vol. XIX, 1865, of his Correspondance; the same volume has the Minister of War's report, pp. 586 ff. The anxiety in Paris is described in the Memoirs of A. M. W. Pickering, printed for private circulation, 1902, Vol. II, pp. 341, 342. Gentz's observation is in Historical MSS. Commission, Bathurst MSS., p. 123. Popham's conversation as to the unwholesomeness of Walcheren is recorded in his evidence, Hansard, XV (App.), CLXXIX, CLXXX. Castlereagh's knowledge of it appears from his Correspondence, VI, 247, Napoleon's from Éd. Desbrière's Projets et Tentatives de Débarquement aux Iles Britanniques, 1902, Vol. III, p. 207. The result of opening the dykes is described in Letters from Flushing, pp. 117 and 172; the effect of the fever on the 23rd regiment on p. 119. The total number of sick is taken from the Journal in Appendix to W. Grey's Walcheren, p. 160.

Pp. 289–292.—*Dissolution of the Portland Ministry.*—Canning's views as to the Cabinet's shortcomings are given in Historical MSS. Commission, Bathurst MSS., pp. 83, 84. The struggle in the Cabinet is mentioned by Southey—letter of 6.7.09 in Selections from his Letters, II, 149. That Castlereagh's removal was the King's idea appears from S. Walpole's Life of Perceval, I, 353. Portland's sufferings from the stone are mentioned in the Earl of Malmesbury's Diaries, etc., IV, 104. Phipps's Memoirs of Plumer Ward has Canning's suggestion of Chatham for Premier, Vol. II, p. 215. Perceval's of Harrowby and his refusal is in Walpole's Life of the former, Vol. I, p. 360; Canning's letter of Aug. 31 and Perceval's reply are on pp. 362 ff. Bathurst's account of the crisis in the Bathurst MSS. as above has the King's request to Canning to hold the seals until relieved, p. 118, and Portland's support of the latter, pp. 118, 119. George Rose's Diaries, etc., has Canning's plan of making Perceval President of the Council, Vol. II, p. 379, and Twiss's Life of Eldon that of making him Lord Chancellor, II, 90.

Pp. 292–293.—*Duel between Castlereagh and Canning.*—The genuineness of Castlereagh's belief that the disclosure had been made is proved by his letter printed on p. 93 of Vol. III, No. 1 (for 1929), of the Cambridge Historical Journal; a letter of Edward Cooke's on p. 87 shows how Castlereagh distinguished between the motives of his own friends and Canning's. The latter's vindication is printed in the Annual Register for 1809, pp. 576 ff.

CHAPTER V

Pp. 294–297.—*The new Administration.*—Spencer Walpole's Life of Perceval gives the conversation with the King about a coalition, Vol. II, pp. 24, 25, Eldon's share in what followed, p. 34, Canning's remark about a Minister being indispensable, Vol. I, p. 362, and Perceval's refusal of the Chancellor's salary, Vol. II, p. 51. George Rose's Diaries, etc., Vol. II, is the authority for the offers which would have been made to Grey and Grenville, p. 397, the reasons why Dundas and Yorke refused to come in, p. 418, and his own anxiety for economy, p. 432. Milnes's remark to Palmerston is in Sir R. Lytton Bulwer's Life of the latter, 1870, Vol. I, 105. Palmerston's consultation with Ward is narrated in Phipps's Life of the latter, Vol. I, p. 250. Bathurst's letter to the Tyrolese deputies is in Historical MSS. Commission, Bathurst MSS., pp. 131, 132 (draft); the original is in the Innsbruck Museum.

Pp. 297–298.—*The O.P. riots.*—The Covent Garden Journal contains the solution of indicting Kemble, p. 24, and mentions the fandango, p. 368.

Pp. 298–300.—*Affairs in parliament, 1810.*—*The Walcheren Expedition.*—The date of the decision to abandon Walcheren appears from Hansard, XV (App.), p. LXXVIII, and the circumstances of final withdrawal from pp. LXXXI ff. The number of deaths is given by Hon. J. Fortescue, History of the British Army, VII, 91 note. Whitbread's remarks on Craufurd's speech are on pp. 367, 368 of Vol. XVI of Hansard; the laughter at Popham's speech on p. 321 of Walter Grey's Walcheren.

Pp. 300–301.—*The honour to Wellington.*—Tarleton's remark on Wellington's despatches is in Hansard, XV, 287, the Common Council's petition on pp. 600 ff.

Pp. 301–302.—*Chatham's resignation.*—The part quoted of Adam's speech is in Hansard, XVI, 9ff.

Pp. 302–305.—*Naval affairs.*—Cochrane's outburst is in Hansard, XVI, 1007, 1008. Collingwood's Correspondence has his complaint of being almost worn out, p. 253, his application for leave, p. 447. his claim to have seen all the ships and men out three times, p. 529, his remark on the Consul at Tripoli, p. 340, and his not going on deck, p. 288. That Cotton was available appears from Historical MSS. Commission, Bathurst MSS., p. 78. Comte de Vigny's description is in La Canne de Jonc, chap. VI. The King's views as to Gambier are in Walpole's Life of Perceval, II, 83, Melville's prevention of Robert Dundas becoming First Lord on p. 87.

Pp. 305–306.—*Commitment of Jones to Newgate.*—The words of the placard are taken both from Annual Register for 1810, p. 92, and from Hansard, XV, 481. Burdett's contention is on p. 15****, and Perceval's saying on p. 10****** of the same volume.

Pp. 306–308.—*Commitment of Burdett to the Tower.*—The militia mutiny is described in Annual Register for 1810, pp. 341 ff. Cobbett's article is in his Political Register, Vol. XV, 1809, p. 992. Eldon's views are in Twiss's Life of him, II, 107, 108. Hansard, XVI, 137, has the reading of Burdett's manifesto, and, on p. 515, Adam's reference to Fox.

Pp. 308–313.—*The Burdett riots.*—Hansard, XVI, 142 and 154 has Burdett's emphasis on the illegality of imprisoning a non-member; pp. 551 ff. the movements of the Sergeant at Arms; p. 143 the part of Burdett's manifesto in which Plowden is quoted; XVII, 506 has the Rochester petition. The authority for the anti-military action of

REFERENCES 437

the sheriffs and the barricading of Piccadilly is Historical MSS. Commission, Fortescue MSS., X, 25; that for Place's plan is his life by Graham Wallas, pp. 52, 53, which also gives on pp. 55, 56 his share in the arrangements for the procession. Colchester in his Diary, II, 252, mentions the use of the artillery. The Times has the procession programme in its issue on 19th June, 1810, the Bristol riot on the 21st April, the procession on the 22nd June, the rumour about the mob's intentions as to Burdett on the 25th, and his explanation as, to not joining it on the 23rd. Hansard, XVI, 446, has the phrase. "rabble from Saffron Hill". Romilly mentions his refusal to be present at the dinner to Burdett in his Memoirs, II, 161.

Pp. 313–314.—*Imprisonment of Cobbett.*—The Life of Cobbett by Lewis Melville, 1913, gives his negotiations for his release, II, 44 ff.

Pp. 314–316.—*Position of parliamentary parties.*—The number of the Morning Chronicle quoted is that for Feb. 26, 1810. Salusbury's difficulties are described in the Farington Diary, VI, 51, 52. Hansard, XVI, 11 * has Whitbread's comparison of Perceval with Punch; XVII, 600 Grey's of him with Caligula's horse; p. 707 Whitbread's remark on Sheridan; pp. 715 ff. Canning's Peninsular speech. Grenville exhibits his unwillingness for office in a letter on p. 420 of Vol. IV of Buckingham's Court and Cabinets of George III. Wellesley's anxiety to see the Cabinet strengthened appears from the Wellesley Papers, II, 16. The British and Irish budget debates are in Hansard, XVI, 1043 ff., and XVII, 205* ff. Pellew's Life of Sidmouth, III, 29, has Sidmouth's objections.

Pp. 316–320.—*The Bullion Committee.*—Horner's Memoirs gives the names of the leaders in the Committee, II, 61, its number, p. 30, his admission to Stuart, pp. 59, 60. The report in Hansard, XVII (App.), pp. ccii, cciii, has the price of gold and the foreign exchanges; p. 697 gives Perceval's weakness on the Committee; p. 4 lxxix the number of private banks; pp. ccxli ff. the Committee's views as to the contention of the representatives of the Bank of England. Charles Bosanquet in Practical Observations, etc., pp. 80 ff., shows the Committee's views as to the addition to the circulation to have been an exaggeration. The Annual Register for 1810 mentions the bankruptcies, p. 129, and on pp. 279 and 405 the suicides of Goldsmid and Baring. The Public Record Office has the militia officer's letter under date Feb. 27, 1810, in H.O. 42. 105. O'Connell's assertion is in the Morning Chronicle for Sept. 24, 1810.

Pp. 320–325.—*The Continental System and the War.*—Vol. 67 of Commons Journals has the figures of Great Britain's trade for the years in question, pp. 763 and 766. Sir P. Francis's anecdote is in his Reflections on abundance of Paper in Circulation, etc., 1810, pp. 14, 15. The Annual Register for 1809 has the despatch on the expedition from Cuxhaven on pp. 531, 532, and that for 1810 the notification of the blockade of the Corfu Channel on p. 307. Ross's Memoirs, etc., of Lord de Saumarez has Rosen's declaration, II, 218, the reason for choosing

Bernadotte, p. 213, and the latter's experience in the yacht, pp. 214, 215. A. Espitalier, Napoléon et le Roi Murat, brings out the reason for Murat's failure to throw across his whole force, pp. 77 ff. E. F. Heckscher, The Continental System, gives the effects of the edict of Oct. 19, 1810, with date, pp. 221 ff. and 203 note.

Pp. 325–331.—*Relations with the United States.*—Collingwood's Correspondence, p. 316, has the figures of Americans serving. Sir T. Martin's figures are in his Letters, II, 10. Hansard, XVII, 62 has figures of Catholics—presumed mainly Irishmen—in the Navy, p. 469 has Cochrane's assertion, p. 468 Rose's, and pp. 546, 547 Grey's. The disappearance of the East Indiamen is from Hickey's Memoirs, IV, 476 ff. The shipping figures for 1806, etc., are from Vol. LXVII, p. 767 of Commons Journals. Coquelle, Napoléon et l'Angleterre, has Labouchere's negotiations, pp. 219, and those about the prisoners, pp. 256 ff. Henry Adams's History of the United States, Vol. V, has the remark made by a French Minister to Armstrong, p. 238, and Gallatin's indignation at the perfidy of Aug. 5th, pp. 258, 259. The Annual Register for 1810 has the announcement that the Emperor will persevere in his decrees, Chronicle, p. 510. The passage in Madison's letter to Jefferson is in his Writings, VIII, New York, 1908, p. 102, and his saying about a British faction in W. C. Rivers's Life of him, Boston, 1868, II, 596. Wellington's Supplementary Despatches, VII, 264, gives Wellesley's feeling towards the Order in Council. His weakness in the Cabinet is described in Buckingham's Court and Cabinets of George III, Vol. IV, p. 435.

Pp. 331–339.—*Wellington's difficulties in the Peninsula.*—Vol. III of Wellington's Dispatches has his visit to Lisbon and memorandum for the Lines, pp. 544 ff., his advice to the Spanish, pp. 565, 566, his complaint of the press, p. 603, his letter refusing a leave application, p. 605, his two statements about the men plundering, pp. 488 and 700, his calculation of the strength he required, pp. 587, 588, the delay in paying the debts incurred by Moore's army, p. 699. Vol. IV has his letter to Berkeley, p. 8, and the explanation of the Portuguese deficit, p. 221. The strength of the Cadiz garrison is given by Hon. J. Fortescue, History of the British Army, VII, 394; also the manner in which Liverpool met requests for more men, pp. 438 ff. Napoleon's disapproval of Joseph's neglect of Wellington is in his Correspondance, Vol. XX, 1856, p. 194. William Napier's Life of his brother Charles has Wellington's unpopularity, I, 127, the opinion of his rashness, *ib.* (also vide Letters, etc., of Sir William Gomm, p. 137), and his boast to Charles Napier, R.N., p. 149. The authority given by him to Spencer in 1808 is from his Supplementary Despatches, VI, 101, which has also, pp. 364, 365, the order as to regimental officers having duties to their men outside the parade ground and, p. 531, the letter to Liverpool on the necessity of persevering in the Peninsular War. Darnley's questions and the answer he received are in Hansard, XVI, 11**, and 12**** ff.

Pp. 339–343.—*The Portuguese Army.*—Wellington's tribute to Portuguese gallantry is in his Dispatches, III, 245. The panic in the Light Division is described by Napier, History of the War in the Peninsula, III, 22. Luz Soriano in his Historia da Guerra Civil, gives the institution of the central training depot, Ep. II, Tom. III, p. 44, the strength of the army, p. 25 note, and p. 46, and the training of the militia, *ib.* Wellington's Supplementary Despatches has Beresford's views on training, Vol. VI, pp. 345, 346. D'Urban's remarks are quoted by Sir C. Oman, History of the Peninsular War, III, 173. Lt.-Col. Teixeira Botelho in his Historia Popular da Guerra da Peninsula, gives the number of British officers lent to the Portuguese army, p. 321, describes the rifle of the caçadores, p. 336, and Beresford's disciplinary methods, p. 213. Sir R. Wilson's intimacy with Alexander is mentioned in the Diaries, etc., of Sir George Jackson, 1872, Vol. II, 108.

Pp. 343–344.—*Masséna's invasion of Portugal.*—The totals of the French army in the Peninsula, of those employed in Aragon and Catalonia, and of the Army of Portugal, are taken from Napier's History of the War, etc., II, 469, 380, and 75 ff., respectively.

Pp. 344–347.—*Operations of the Light Division.*—The comparison of the rifle to Brown Bess is from Lt.-Col. Verner's A British Rifle Man (Simmons), XVII, XVIII, as is Coote Manningham's introduction of the company system, p. XXII, and Moore's extension of it, p. XXIII. The indiscipline of the Light Brigade during the retreat from Sahagun is on William Napier's authority in Beamish's History of the King's German Legion, 1832, I, 367. Rifleman Harris describes Craufurd bringing the rum on p. 174 of his Recollections, 1848. George Napier's remark on Craufurd is in his Life, p. 226.

Pp. 347–348.—*Masséna's advance to Bussaco.*—Napier's History of the War has the observations of the enemy's movements by Waters and Hill, Vol. III, pp. 15, 16, and the statement that Masséna chose the worst road in Portugal, p. 16. His other difficulties are described in Foy's report in his Vie Militaire by M. Girod de l'Ain, p. 345, his ignorance of the country in Koch's Mémoires de Masséna, VII, 181.

Pp. 348–352.—*Battle of Bussaco.*—The same work has the conflicting views in his camp before the battle, VII, 193, and the discovery of only a few German Hussars in the pass, p. 201. Foy's opinions as regards Eblé and the British are on pp. 98, 99, 101, of his Vie Militaire by Girod de l'Ain. Sir C. Oman in his History of the Peninsular War gives the French strength when entering Portugal and at Bussaco, Vol. III, pp. 540 ff. The French plan of attack is in Gen. H. Bonnal, La Vie Militaire du Maréchel Ney, III, 388. Wellington's commendation of Wallace is in his Dispatches, IV, 306, his complaint of want of support, p. 274. The inconsistent observation on Trant's delay is on p. 307. His letter of Oct. 4th is on pp. 606, 607 of his Supplementary Despatches, Vol. VI. His complaint of Spencer is in Hon. J. Fortescue's History of the British Army, VII, 499. The King's insistence on the reward for Beresford is from Yonge's Life of Liverpool, I, 338.

440 ENGLAND IN THE NINETEENTH CENTURY

Pp. 352–357.—*The retreat to the Lines.*—Napier's History of the War has the French officer's letter to Trant, Vol. III, pp. 364, 365. Major General Jones in his Sieges of Spain, Vol. III, has the time of beginning the works, p. 18, the advantage of the October rainfall, p. 28, the use to be made of the three divisions at the centre of the line, pp. 28, 46, and that of the seamen, p. 45, the revolution in accepted theory on field fortifications, p. 49, the cost of the lines, p. 92. Wellington's wish to fight within the first line appears from his Dispatches, IV, 332, his mention of the maize harvest is on p. 363, his letter to Berkeley on p. 334, that to Liverpool on a relief fund on p. 363. Foy's report, in his Vie Militaire by Girod de l'Ain, mentions the stores which fell into the hands of the French, p. 345, M. Lemonnier-De La Fosse the dismantling of mills, Campagne de 1810 à 1815, p. 90. Baron Fririon describes the foraging for maize in his Journal Historique de la Campagne de Portugal, pp. 84, 89, and has the number before the Lines, p. 84. Hill's remark is in E. Sidney's Life of him, p. 151. Gell's letter is in the Journal, etc., of Miss Berry, 1865, II, 439, 440. The numbers of the British and Portuguese in the Lines are from Sir C. Oman's History of the Peninsular War, III, 431, 432, the number of Romana's troops is estimated after a comparison of various authorities cited by Luz Soriano, Historia da Guerra Civil, Ep. II, Tom. III, p. 218 note.

Pp. 357–359.—*Masséna's retirement to Santarem.*—Koch's Mémoires de Masséna has Napoleon's orders on Foy's report, Vol. VII, pp. 288, 289. Wellington's anxiety to attack is shown by his Dispatches, IV, 390, the strength of Santarem, p. 425; his complaint to Stuart is on p. 471.

Pp. 359–360.—*Mental derangement of George III.*—The weight attached by Napoleon to his chances from political changes is based on Vie Militaire du Général Foy, by Girod de l'Ain, p. 122. Palmerston's letter is in Sir H. Lytton Bulwer's Life of him, 1870, Vol. I, p. 121.

Pp. 360–362.—*Estrangement between Napoleon and Alexander.*—Sorel, L'Europe et la Révolution Française, has Napoleon's plans for 1812, Vol. VII, p. 518, and his confidence that it was only a question of weeks, p. 459. Vandal, Napoléon et Alexandre, has the former's explanation of Goldsmith's failure, Vol. II, pp. 492, 493. The glut of imports is described in Hansard, XIX, 259. The bank failures are mentioned in Historical MSS. Commission, Fortescue MSS., p. 73. The connection of the annexation of Oldenburg with the Czar's ukase appears from Alexandre I et Napoléon, by Serge Tatischeff, pp. 542 ff. The writer on Russian trade was J. J. Oddy—European Commerce, 1805, p. 209.

CHAPTER VI

Pp. 363–367.—*Minto's Governor-Generalship of India.*—Rev. C. Buchanan's experiences are in his Christian Researches in Asia, pp. 27, 28. Lord Teignmouth's Life mentions the order for building the Churches,

Vol. II, p. 111. Minto's dealings with the missionaries are from Lady Minto's Lord Minto in India, p. 74. Smith's gibe is from p. 40 of Edinburgh Review, Vol. XIV (for 1809). Marshman's Life and Times of Carey Marshman and Ward has Wellesley's prohibition of drowning of children, Vol. I, p. 158. Munro's own evidence in Select Committee of the House of Commons, 1832—India, VI, Political—p. 20, is the authority for the Travancore Raja's desire for him to be Diwan.

Pp. 367-376.—*Madras Mutiny.*—Petrie's remark as to a spirit of insubordination is in Parliamentary Papers, etc. (Madras), 1811, p. 96. Munro's report is in Parliamentary Papers, etc. (Madras Army), 1811, pp. 95, 96. Kaye writes of Capper circulating Munro's remarks in his Life of Malcom, I, 460. Wellington's observations are in his Dispatches, III, 620. The complaint of good posts being monopolized by King's officers is made in Parliamentary Papers, etc. (Madras) 1811, p. 48, and a letter on the subject from the Court of Directors is in Do. (Madras Army and Government), 1812, pp. 3 ff. J. Duncan's letter is in India Office Papers, Miscellaneous, Home Series, 693, p. 82. The Masulipatam troubles are detailed in Malcolm's Observations on the Disturbances, etc., pp. 200 ff. The officers' ultimatum of the 21st July is given on pp. 29, 30 of Parliamentary Papers, etc. (Madras Army), 1810, No. 2C; No. 2B has the arrangements made for reinforcement of the army from Bombay and Ceylon, pp. 8 and 17, their effect appears from Letters of John Orrok, p. 111. The nature of the considerations leading to surrender in the case of the Hyderabad officers appears from pp. 464 ff. of No. 698 of the series of India Office Papers quoted above. The results for the officers punished are tabulated by Sir A. Cardew in his White Mutiny, pp. 142 ff.

P. 377.—*Overseas Expeditions from India—Macao.*—The Super-cargoes' Committees' view of the opposition to the occupation of Macao is in H. B. Morse's East India Company trading to China, III, 88 and 96; the sequel is on pp. 87 ff. The Annual Register for 1808, Chronicle, etc., p. 285, gives the Viceroy's taunts.

Pp. 377-379.—*Mauritius.*—The loss of the 19 vessels is mentioned in a memorial of Calcutta merchants given in Hickey's Memoirs, IV, 414. Details of the proceedings in and off Mauritius are taken from James's Naval History, V, 274. J. Marshall in Royal Naval Biography, Vol. I, 1823, Pt. II, pp. 631 ff., points out that the difficulty of anchorage was the obstacle to an attempt.

Pp. 379-380.—*The Moluccas.*—The same book, Vol. II, 1825, pp. 506 ff., is the authority for the proceedings during the capture of Banda Neira; James's Naval History for Cole's of immediately before, Vol. V, pp. 317 ff.

Pp. 380-383.—*New South Wales.*—The Historical Records of Australia, Series I, Vol. VI, has the area of the settlement in 1807, p. 144, the bad conduct of the convicts, p. 148, and the number of sheep in 1807, p. 161; Series I, Vol. II, 1914, gives Hunter's complaint, p. 235. The 1801 population is given in First Twenty Years of Australia, p. 176, by J. Bonwick, who notes the bad behaviour of the settlers, pp. 78 ff., and wages of assigned convicts, p. 193. F. Péron's commendation is in his Voyage de Découvertes aux Terres Australes, II, pp. 394 ff., his observations as regards theft on p. 400. Macarthur's early distinctions as a settler appear from S. M. Onslow's Some Early Records, etc., pp. 20, 21, and 49 and note; his introduction of sheep, pp. 78, 79, and 98; the action of the English woollen manufacturers, pp. 67, 68, his wealth in 1805, pp. 130, 131, and note. The Memoirs of Joseph Holt, 1838, has the ploughing with large hoes, II, 79 and 141. J. Macarthur the author's prophecy is in his Financial and Political Facts, 1803, LXI.

Pp. 383–386.—*Bligh's Governorship and deposition*.—The Historical Records of Australia, Series I, has Bligh on the sawyer, Vol. VI, p. 124, the steps leading to Macarthur's trial, pp. 307 ff., Bligh's view of Atkins, p. 150, Macarthur's protest against being tried by Atkins, pp. 225 ff., its grounds, pp. 726, 727, Bligh's letter on the protest, p. 222, the officers' protest, p. 224, the charge against them, pp. 225 and 236 ff., Johnston's despatch on Bligh's deposition, pp. 208 ff. Vol. VII has figures for the end of the decade, pp. 422 ff. The influence of Péron's suggestions is brought out in Ernest Scott's Terre Napoléon, pp. 21 and 113 ff. Napoleon's order is on p. 467 in Correspondance, XX, 1866.

Pp. 386–388.—*The Cape of Good Hope*.—The luxurious apparel of female slaves is mentioned in Gleanings from Africa, p. 270; it has also the work of the Government farm, p. 278, the place of origin of Cape slaves, p. 58, the decay of the Hottentots, p. 228. Curtis's description is on p. 233, Vol. IV of the Spencer Papers, printed for the Navy Records Society in 1924. Theal's History of South Africa (1795–1836) has the Dutch jealousy of French influence, pp. 101 ff., the population of the colony, p. 111, its boundaries, p. 103, the population of Cape Town, p. 111. The estimate of the area of the colony is from the Life of Sir R. Wilson, p. 392, his list of its products, p. 394, his idea of its undesirability, p. 397. The miscellaneous character of the Cape Town population is taken from Journal of a Soldier of the 71st Regiment, 1822, p. 19. Nelson's opinion is from his speech in Parliamentary History, XXXVI, 185.

Pp. 388–389.—*The West Indies*.—Michael Scott's Tom Cringle's Log describes Kingston as the entrepôt for Central American trade, Chap. VII. The Edinburgh Review, Vol. X (for 1807) has the sevenfold increase in coffee in Jamaica, p. 166. The planter's observation is in Historical MSS. Commission, Fortescue MSS., IX, 29.

Pp. 389–394.—*Canada*.—Bédard's petition is mentioned in F.-X. Garneau's Histoire de Canada, III, 113, the assembly's desire to get the appointment of civil officials, p. 130, Craig's mildness in 1810, p. 141; the end of the Reign of Terror, pp. 147, 148. The allusions to Le Canadien are—as regards the mercantile aristocracy—to Vol. I, No. 1, and—as regards new arrivals expecting privileged treatment— to Vol. II, Nos. 38, 41. Kingsford's History of Canada, Vol. VIII,

REFERENCES

gives the number of British members in the assembly in 1809, p. 52, and those of 1810, pp. 69, 70. John Lambert mentions the emigrant from Boston in his Travels through Lower Canada, etc., Vol. II, p. 241. Craig's estimate of population is in his letter of May, 1810—Public Records Office, C.O. 42, 141. J. Bouchette gives the estimates generally in his British Dominions in North America, II, 235. Lord Selkirk's account of his settlement is on p. 198 of his Observations on the State of the Highlands. The reference to the Morning Chronicle is to the issue of February 18th, 1803. The penitent attorney is mentioned in Hansard, XVII, 326. A descriptive list of Members of the Legislative Council of Lower Canada is given in British Museum Add. MSS. 37845, ff. 189 ff. Kingsford's book—same volume—has the account of Willcocks, pp. 90 ff. Gore's fear of his correspondence being intercepted is in Canadian Archives, 1892, p. 113.

Pp. 394–396.—*Scotland—The Highlands.*—The reference to the Wealth of Nations is to Book I, Chapter IX. Selkirk analyses the Gaelic population statistics in his Observations, etc., pp. LIX, LX; it has also the raising of the rent, p. 21, the disturbances in Ross and Cromarty, pp. 126, 127, the attempt to establish a cotton mill in Sutherland, p. XXXVIII. A. Irvine's observation is in his Inquiry into Emigration, pp. 7, 8, note. W. Marshall gives the common food of the people, General View of the Central Highlands, p. 21. Baron Baert's mention of the Dukes is in his Tableau de la Grande Bretagne, I, 139. Sir F. Eden's observations are in his State of the Poor, 1797, Vol. I, pp. 558, 559. Sir J. Sinclair in Agriculture of the Northern Counties mentions eggs as a luxury to a farmer, p. 82, and in Appendix p. [42] his expectations from the cotton mill.

Pp. 396–398.—The remark in the Edinburgh Review is on p. 197 of Vol. VII (for 1805). Selkirk's Observations, etc., pp. 135 and XLVI, and the Duke of Argyll's Scotland as it was, II, 103, 104, give the kelp trade. The arrangements for the survey of 1801 are outlined in Hansard II, 334, 335. Marshall's book above cited gives the system of crofters and cottars working in return for their plots, p. 33. R. Heron's Scotland Described mentions rent being paid in farm produce, p. 231. Mrs. Smith in Memoirs of a Highland Lady mentions the Castle Grant entertainments, p. 23, and the success of Highlanders outside their own country, pp. 99 and 238. The report on possibilities of invasion is in the Archives Nationales in Paris, A F, IV. Cart. 1597, Plaq. I 2. Mrs. Eliza Fletcher's Autobiography mentions Macdiarmid, p. 67.

Pp. 398–399.—*The Lowlands.*—The quotations from Elizabeth Hamilton's Cottagers of Glenburnie are from Chapters VI and VII. H. Skrine was the tourist who compared the cottages of the two countries, Tours in the North of England, etc., pp. 34, 35, 71. Telford's rejection of Scotland is in his Life by J. Rickman, 1838, p. 19. R. Heron mentions thirlage as common in Galloway, Observations made in a Journey through the Western Counties of Scotland, Vol. II, pp. 105 ff.

Pp. 399–400.—*The Poor Law.*—The discussion on Scottish finance is in Hansard, XV, 212, 213. Sir G. Nicholls discusses assessments and the toleration of beggars in A History of the Scottish Poor Law, pp. 106 ff. The position in Edinburgh and Glasgow is taken from J. H. Clapham's Economic History of Modern Britain, pp. 367 ff.

P. 400.—*Education.*—Lord Cockburn's Memorials of his Time, has Hope's statement, p. 179. Baert's tribute to Scottish education is in his Tableau de la Grande Bretagne, I, 216, 217.

Pp. 400–402.—*The Church.*—J. Cunningham's Church History of Scotland has the difficulties of the Minister's stipends, Vol. II, pp. 434 ff. Chalmer's controversy with Playfair and subsequent change of view are from Rev. W. Hanna's Memoirs of him, Vols. I, p. 93, and III, 1851, pp. 77, 78. Cockburn on the clergy is on p. 226 of his Memorials.

P. 402.—*Material advance.*—The high rents in the East of Scotland are given in Agricultural State of the Kingdom, 1816, p. 416. Threshing by steam is mentioned as established in R. Somerville's General View of the Agriculture of East Lothian, p. 77; the existence of a large number of steam looms in the West of Scotland in Report on Weavers' Petitions, 1811, p. 6. Skrine in Tours in the North of England, etc., describes the black country between Stirling and Edinburgh, p. 64.

Pp. 402–405.—*Glasgow.*—The single carriage is mentioned in Capt. T. Hamilton's Cyril Thornton, Vol. III, Chap. IV. J. Adolphus in The Political State of the British Empire, 1818, gives figures of mills in Glasgow, Vol. III, pp. 247, 248. J. G. Lockhart describes its traditions as mercantile in Peter's Letters to his Kinsfolk, III, 151, and the philosophic weaver, p. 216. Adam Smith's observation on the corporation laws is in his Wealth of Nations, Book I, Chapter X. The Blantyre factory is described in Extracts of the Journals and Correspondence of Miss Berry, II, 302 ff. The Report from the Select Committee on Artizans, etc., has the lock-out of 1810, p. 476, and—the men's case—pp. 611. The low rate of wages in Glasgow as compared with Manchester is exhibited in Porter's Progress of the Nation, pp. 443 ff. The Report from the Select Committee on Hand-loom Weavers' Petitions has the abstract from Perston's books, p. 157; the statement about the Lord Provost is on p. 12. Rev. J. Hall has the account of Perth culture in his Travels in Scotland, p. 261.

Pp. 405–407.—*Edinburgh.*—Lockhart in Peter's Letters describes the Cadies, Vol. I, 237 ff., Melville's attentions to the old ladies, Vol. II, p. 38, note, the conversation of the blue stockings, Vols. I, p. 312, and II, pp. 5, 6. Scott's story of the man who moved to the south of the city is in his Prose Works, Vol. VII, 229, the enlargement of the city to the north on pp. 232 ff. R. Chambers's account of the old ladies is in his Traditions of Edinburgh, II, 22, 23; of their willingness to leave the Old Town, Vol. I, pp. 52, 53. Cockburn's remark on them is in his Memorials, pp. 52, 53. The Italian traveller's opinion is in Scots Magazine, 1810, p. 575. Hall noted the prevalence of bachelors

REFERENCES 445

in his Travels in Scotland, p. 251. The remark on women in the Farington Diary is in Vol. I, 1922, p. 325.

Pp. 407–411.—*The Scottish Law Courts.*—Lt. Col. A. Fergusson's Henry Erskine, p. 465, has "Endless Willie". Horner on the cost of litigation is in Hansard, XIV, 1017. The comments of the Annual Register for 1809 are on p. 171, note. R. Chambers's Traditions of Edinburgh, 1869, describes the litigation ridden lunatic, pp. 148 ff. Cockburn's Memorials has Scott imitating Eskgrove, p. 109, Hermand's peculiarities, pp. 120 ff., the dirt of the Inner Court, p. 101, and the account of the City Guard, pp. 183 ff. Arnot's History of Edinburgh is followed in the account of the Courts of Sessions and Justiciary, pp. 367 ff. Fergusson's Henry Erskine has his jest at the expense of the Court of Session, pp. 421, 422. The powers of small civil courts are given in W. Chambers's Book of Scotland, pp. 122 and 100 ff.; the nature of a Procurator Fiscal on pp. 55 ff.; the growth of boards of city police, p. 85.

Pp. 411–412.—*Scottish Toryism.*—Cockburn gives the newspaper quotation about the Lord Advocate, Memorials, p. 178, note, and mentions the bestowal of a place on himself, p. 214, and the offer of one to Erskine, pp. 178, 179. The requirement that a Lord Advocate should be tall is in the Arniston Memoirs, p. 219. Grey's observation is in Parliamentary History, XXV, p. 101.

Pp 412–413.—*Close of the Decade in England—Religious movements.*—Evans's Life and Death of Joanna Southcott has the passage quoted, pp. 5, 6. Free and Impartial Thoughts has that about the afflicting second marriage, p. 39. R. Brothers's prophecies and revelations are in A Revealed Knowledge of the Prophecies and Times, 1794. The Manchester Magistrate's report is in Public Records Office, H.O. 42, 105. Southey's article in the Quarterly Review, Vol. IV (for 1810) has the belief in Shakespeare being in hell, p. 507, the statement as to the circulation of the magazines, pp. 507, 508, the exclusiveness of Wesleyans, pp. 505 and 510, the story of the man who fell into a lime-kiln, p. 509, their view of Napoleon, p. 510.

Pp. 413–415.—H. Gunning mentions Doctor Drop in his Reminiscences, II, 149. Free and Impartial Thoughts has the railings across the middle aisle and the clerical advertisement about a sporting country, pp. 60 and 76. Congregations seating themselves as in a drawing-room are mentioned in Considerations on the Present state of Religion, 1801, pp. 47, 48. The Farington Diary VI, 102, has the slackness in Falmouth. The conspiracy to elope is reported in Annual Register, 1810, pp. 254, 255. Lord Teignmouth's Life has the origin of the Bible Society, Vol. II, pp. 67, 68. Lord Shaftesbury's reminiscence is in his Life by E. Hodder, 1886, p. 44.

Pp. 415–417.—*Social movements.*—The Annual Register for 1808 has the affair of the middle-aged man, Chronicle, p. 78. The reference to the Monthly Magazine for 1808 is to Vol. II, p. 231. G. Pryme writes of the minuet going out in his Autobiographic Recollections,

1870, p. 96; for the waltz there is Byron's poem by that name (notes). One example of free association of persons of different social standing is in Combermere's Memoirs, etc., I, 107. Farington mentions the decline of this in his Diary, VI, 148, and Lonsdale's dinner, p. 71. Sir B. Brodie's Autobiography, 1865, has the effect of late dinings on the meetings of the Royal Society, etc., p. 33. Sir H. Roscoe's John Dalton, 1895, has his remark, p. 170. The fashion plates for the end of the decade are in the Lady's Monthly Museum for 1810. The Annual Register for 1807 mentions the decline of gaiety, p. 106. R. Cumberland in A Few Plain Reasons why we should believe etc., 1801, mentions the lenient view then taken of adultery, p. 95. Paget's saying that he would not add to the injuries he had done is in a letter written by the two seconds in the duel to the Times of May 31, 1809; his letter to his father is alluded to in the Morning Chronicle for March 9.

Pp. 417–418.—*Economic movements.*—The growth of the feeling of a common interest among operatives appears from pp. 354, 355 of the Report of the Committee on the Woollen Manufacture. The 1810 strike is described in evidence contained in the Reports from the Select Committee on Artizans, etc., pp. 573, 574; allusion to other unrest is on pp. 81, 166, and 405, 406. W. S. Jevons's scale is in his Investigations in Currency and Finance, 1884, p. 144. The reduced earnings of Boston weavers appears from the replies to QQ, 5337 and 5386 in the evidence in Report on Hand-loom Weavers' Petitions. The wages of cotton spinners are from E. Baines's History of the Cotton Manufacture, p. 437. P. Gaskell describes the improvement in factory conditions in his Artizans and Machinery, pp. 140 ff.

BIBLIOGRAPHY

OF BOOKS, ETC., CHIEFLY CONSULTED, WITH DATES OF EDITIONS USED

The first of the two lists under each chapter gives the more important authorities.

As the lists are long, asterisks have been used to mark books and articles of importance for the subjects of which they treat, or—in the case of biographies—of importance for general history.

A dagger denotes the presence of valuable original authorities.

GENERAL

*†Adams, Henry. History of the United States. Vol. III–VI. 1890.
Alison, Sir Archibald. Lives of Lord Castlereagh and Sir Charles Stewart. Vol. I. 1861.
†Annual Registers.
*Auckland, The Journal and Correspondence of William, First Lord. Vol. IV. 1862.
Brougham, Life and Times of Lord. By himself. Vol. I. 1871.
*†Buckingham, Duke of. Memoirs of the Court and Cabinets of George III. Vol. IV. 1855.
*†Bunbury, Sir Henry. Narrative of some Passages in the Great War with France. 1854.
Cambridge Historical Journal.
*†The Cambridge History of British Foreign Policy. Vol. III. 1922.
*The Cambridge Modern History. Vol. IX. 1906.
*†Castlereagh, Memoirs and Correspondence of Viscount. Vols. VI–VIII. 1851.
*Clowes, W. Laird. The Royal Navy. A History. Vol. V. 1900.
†Cobbett, William. Political Register.
*†Colchester, Diary, etc., of Lord. II. 1861.
*†Collingwood, A Selection from the Public and Private Correspondence of Vice-Admiral Lord. 1829.
Combermere. Memoirs and Correspondence of Viscount Combermere. By Mary Viscountess Combermere and Capt. W. V. Knollys. Vol. I. 1866.
†Commons Journals.
*†Coquelle, P. Napoléon et l'Angleterre. 1904.
Craufurd, Rev. A. General Craufurd and his Light Division. 1891.
Creevy Papers. Vol. I. 1904.
*†Croker, The Correspondence and Diaries of J. W. Vol. I. 1884.
Dictionary of National Biography.
*Dowell, Stephen. History of Taxation and Taxes in England. 1888.

Edinburgh Review.
English Historical Review.
Farington Diary, The. Vols. III–VI. 1924–1926.
*Fortescue, Hon. (Sir) John. The County Lieutenancies of the Army. 1909.
*† A History of the British Army. Vol. V–VII. 1910–1912.
Gower, Lord Granville Leveson. Private Correspondence. 1916.
*Grant, A. J., and Harold Temperley. Europe in the Nineteenth Century. 1927.
*†Hansard's Parliamentary Debates. 1925.
*Heckscher, E. F. The Continental System. 1922.
Hickey, Memoirs of William. Vol. IV. 1925.
*†Historical MSS. Commission. Bathurst MSS. 1923.
*† Fortescue MSS. (Dropmore). Vols. VIII–X. 1912–1927.
*†Holland, Lord. Memoirs of the Whig Party during my Time. 1852.
Holland, The Journal of Elizabeth, Lady. Vol. II. 1909.
Holland, Lady. A Memoir of Sydney Smith. Vol. I. 1855.
Horner, Francis. Memoirs and Correspondence. 1843.
*James, W. Naval History. Vols. IV, V. 1837.
Lindsay, W. S. History of Merchant Shipping. Vol. II. 1874.
Mackintosh, R. J. Memoirs of the Life of Sir James. 1836.
*Mahan, Capt. A. T. The Influence of Sea Power upon the French Revolution and Empire. Vol. II. 1892.
Malmesbury, Letters of the First Earl of. Vol. II. 1870.
Minto, Life and Letters of Sir Gilbert Elliot, First Earl of. Vol. III. 1874.
†Naval Chronicle. 1806 ff.
†Newspapers, as Morning Chronicle, Morning Post: also Moniteur or Gazette Nationale.
*†Pellew, Hon. George. Life of Viscount Sidmouth. Vols. II, III. 1847.
Phipps, Hon. Edmund. Memoirs of the Political and Literary Life of R. Plumer Ward. Vol. I. 1850.
Plowden, Francis. The History of Ireland from 1801 to 1810. Vols. II, III. 1811.
Porter, G. R. The Progress of the Nation. 1851.
Quarterly Review.
*†Romilly, Memoirs of the Life of Sir S. By himself. Vol. II. 1841.
*Rose, The Diaries and Correspondence of the Right Honourable George. Vol. II. 1860.
*†Russell, Earl. Life and Times of Fox. Vol. IV. 1866.
*†Sichel, Walter. Sheridan. Vol. II. 1909.
*Smart, William. Economic Annals of the Nineteenth Century. Vol. I. 1910.
†Smith, G. C. Moore. Life of Lord Seaton. 1903.
†Smith, The Autobiography of Lieut. Gen. Sir Harry. Vol. I. 1901.

BIBLIOGRAPHY

*Sorel, A. L'Europe et la Revolution Française. Vol. VII. Paris. 1904.
Southey, Selections from the Letters of Robert. Vols. I, II. 1856.
Spirit of the Public Journals, The. 1807 ff.
Stapleton, A. G. George Canning and his Times. 1859.
*†Tatischeff, Serge. Alexandre I et Napoléon. 1891.
*Temperley, H. W. V. Life of Canning. 1905.
*Treitschke, Heinrich von. Deutschke Geschichte im 19ten Jahrhundert. Vol. I. Leipzig. 1879.
*Trevelyan, G. M. Lord Grey of the Reform Bill. 1920.
*†Twiss, Horace. The Public and Private Life of Lord Chancellor Eldon. Vol. II. 1844.
*Victoires Conquêtes, etc. Vols. XVI–XXI. Paris. 1819–1820.
*†Walpole, Spencer. The Life of Rt. Hon. Spencer Perceval. 1874.
Wellesley Papers, The. 1914.
*†Wellington, The Dispatches of F. M. the Duke of. Vols. I–IV. 1844.
*† Supplementary Despatches, etc., of F. M. the Duke of. Vols. IV–VII, XIII. 1859–1871.
*†Wilberforce, Life of. By his Sons. Vol. III. 1838.
Wilson, Life of Sir Robert. 1862.
Yonge, C. D. The Life and Administration of the Earl of Liverpool. Vol. I. 1868.

CHAPTER I

The works of men of letters of whom an account is given in this chapter are omitted from the bibliography.

*The Cambridge History of English Literature. Vols. XI, XII. Cambridge. 1922. 1921.

Account of the British Institution for promoting the Fine Arts, An. 1805.
Annals of Botany. Edited by C. Konig and J. Sims. Vol. I. 1805.
Armstrong, Sir Walter. Turner. 1902.
*†Baert, Baron. Tableau de la Grande Bretagne. Paris. 1800.
Bell, Andrew. An Experiment in Education, etc. 1797.
Bell, J. Munro. Chippendale, Sheraton, and Hepplewhite Furniture Designs. 1900.
Bernard, J. Retrospections of the Stage. 1830.
Boaden, J. Memoirs of the Life of J. P. Kemble. 1825.
Brodie, Sir B. Autobiography. 1865.
Brodrick, G. C. A History of the University of Oxford. 1886.

Campbell, Thomas. Life of Mrs. Siddons. 1834.
Chaplin, Arnold. Medicine in England during the reign of George III. 1919.
Clayden, P. W. The Early Life of Samuel Rogers. 1887.
Rogers and his Contemporaries. 1889.
Cockburn, Lord. Life of Lord Jeffrey. Vol. I. 1852.
Coleorton Letters, The. 1881.
Coleridge, Letters of Samuel Taylor. 1895.
Colquhoun, P. A new and appropriate System of Education for the labouring people. 1806.
*Courthope, W. J. A History of English Poetry. Vol. VI. 1920.
(Cundall, H. M. See Studio Publications.)
Cunningham, A. The Life of Sir David Wilkie. 1843.
Dalton, J. A New System of Chemical Philosophy. 1808.
Darwin, E. Zoonomia. 1796.
Davey, Henry. History of English Music. 1924.
*Davy, (Sir) Humphry. A Discourse introductory to a course of lectures on Chemistry. 1802.
A lecture on the plan for improving the Royal Institution. (1810.)
Outlines of a course of Lectures on Chemical Philosophy. 1804.
De Quincey, Thomas. Collected Writings. Vol. II. 1889.
Doran, Dr. Annals of the English Stage. 1888.
Ellis, G. E. Memoir of Count Rumford. Boston. 1871.
†Ferri de St. Constant, J. L. Londres et les Anglais. Paris. 1804.
Fiévée, J. Lettres sur l'Angleterre. Paris. 1802.
Galt, John. The life and studies of B. West. 1816–1820.
Geikie, Sir A. Presidential Address at Centenary of the Geological Society. 1907.
Gilchrist, Alexander. Life of Blake. 1863.
*Halévy, E. Histoire du Peuple Anglais. Vol. I. Paris. 1923.
Harper, George M. William Wordsworth, etc. Vol. I. 1916.
Haydon, B. Autobiography. 1853.
Held, A. Zwei Bücher zur socialen Geschichte Englands. Leipzig. 1881.
Hind, A. M. A History of Engraving and Etching. 1923.
Holden, E. S. Sir William Herschel. His Life and Works. New York. 1881.
Hughes, J. L. and L. R. Klem. Progress of Education in the (Nineteenth) Century. 1907.
Hunt, Leigh. Autobiography. Vols. I, II. 1850.
Legouis, E. La Jeunesse de Wordsworth. Lyons. 1896.
(Lockhart, J. G.) Memoir of Sir Walter Scott. Vols. I, II. 1837.
Lucas, E. V. The Life of Charles Lamb. 1910.
Marshall, T. H. James Watt. 1925.
Mason, William. Essays on English Church Music. 1795.
Minutes of Evidence taken before the Select Committee to whom the Bill (Gas Light and Coke Co.'s) was referred. 1809.

BIBLIOGRAPHY

Monthly Review.
Moseley, Benjamin. Review of the Report of the Royal College of Physicians of London on Vaccination. 1808.
Muirhead, J. P. Origin and Progress of the Mechanical Inventions of James Watt, etc. Vols. I and II. 1854.
Munk, William. The Life of Sir Henry Halford. 1895.
Neale, J. P. Views of the Seats of Noblemen and Gentlemen, etc. 1818.
Neville-Polley, L. J. John Dalton. 1920.
Paris, J. A. The Life of Sir Humphry Davy. 1831.
Pryme, Autobiographic Recollections of George. 1870.
Public Records Office. H.O. 42. 94 (Plan for National Vaccine Establishment.)
Richardson, A. E. Monumental Classic Architecture, etc., in Europe, etc. 1914.
Rickman, J. Life of T. Telford. 1838.
Robinson, Henry Crabb. Diary, etc. 1869.
Roscoe, Sir Henry. John Dalton. 1895.
Royal Institution of Great Britain. Journal. 1802.
Royal Society. Abstract of the Papers. 1800-1830. Vol. I. 1832.
Sandby, William. History of the Royal Academy. 1862.
Simond, L. Voyage en Angleterre. 1817.
*Smiles, Samuel. Lives of the Engineers. Vol. II. 1861.
  Men of Invention and Industry. 1884.
Smith, J. T. Nollekens and his Times. 1829.
Society of Arts. Transactions. 1801-1805.
Southey, C. C. The Life and Correspondence of Robert Southey. Vols. I-III. 1849.
†(Southey, Robert.) Letters from England by Don Manuel Alvarez Espriella. 1807.
Southey, R. and C. C. Life of the Rev. Andrew Bell. 1849.
Southey MSS. British Museum Add. MSS. 30927.
*Stephen, Leslie. The English Utilitarians. Vol. I. 1900.
*Stokoe, F. W. German Influence on the English Romantic Period. 1926.
Stuart, Daniel. Letters from the Lake Poets to Daniel Stuart. Printed for private circulation. 1889.
"Stuart, Robert." Historical and descriptive anecdotes of Steam Engines. 1829.
Studio Publications. The Development of British Landscape Painters in Water-Colours. 1918.
  Graphic Arts, The. Etc. 1917.
  Masters of Water-Colour Painting. 1922-1923.
  * Norwich School, The. H. M. Cundall. 1920.
*Sullivan, J. W. N. The History of Mathematics in Europe, etc. 1925.
  Thomson, Thomas. A System of Chemistry. 1807.

Thornbury (G.) W. Life of Turner. 1862.
*Walker, Ernest. History of Music in England. Oxford. 1924.
Watson, Foster. The old Grammar Schools. 1916.
Williams, D. E. The Life of Sir Thomas Lawrence. Vol. I. 1831.
Woodcroft, B. Sketch of Steam Navigation. 1848.
Wordsworth, Christopher. Bishop of Lincoln. Memoirs of William Wordsworth. Vol. I. 1851.
Wordsworth, Christopher. (Fellow of Peterhouse.) Social Life at the English Universities in the eighteenth century, Cambridge. 1874.
*Wormann, Karl. Geschichte der Kunst, etc. Vol. VI. 1915.
Wyndham, H. S. The Annals of Covent Garden Theatre, etc. Vol. I. 1906.

CHAPTER II

*†Cordiner, Rev. J. Description of Ceylon. 1807.
*Imperial Gazetteer of India. Oxford. 1907-1909.
*†Thorn, Major W. Memoir of the War in India, etc. 1818.
*†Wellesley, The Despatches, etc., of the Marquess. 1836, 1837.

Abu Taleb Khan, Travels of Mirza. Vol. II. 1814.
†Ascoli, F. D. Early Revenue History of Bengal and the Fifth Report, 1812. Oxford. 1917.
Blakiston, J. Twelve Years Military Adventure. Vol. I. 1829.
†Calcutta Gazettes, Selections from. Vols. I–III. Calcutta. 1868.
*Cambridge History of India, The. Vol. III. Cambridge. 1929.
Cornwallis Correspondence, The. Vol. III. 1859.
*†Duff, J. G. Grant. History of the Mahrattas. Vol. II. 1921.
†East India United Service Journal. 1833—
Fraser, J. B. Military Memoir of Lt.-Col. James Skinner. 1851.
*†Gleig, Rev. G. R. Life of Maj.-Gen. Sir Thomas Munro. 1830.
Graham, Maria. Journal of a Residence in India. 1812.
Hunter (Sir), W. W. Orissa. 1872.
†Intercepted Despatches from India. 1805.
*†Kaye, J. W. The Life and Correspondence of Charles Lord Metcalfe. Vol. I. 1858.
*Malcolm, Lt.-Col. John. The Political History of India. Vol. I. 1826.
*Mill, James. The History of British India. Vol. VI. 1840.
†Morse, H. B. East India Company trading to China. Vol. II. 1926.
Pearce, R. R. Memoirs of Wellesley. Vols. I, II. 1846.
Pearse, Col. Hugh. Memoir of the Life, etc., of Viscount Lake. 1908.

BIBLIOGRAPHY

Scott-Waring, Major. Supplement to the Letter to the Edinburgh Review. 1810.
Seton-Karr, W. S. The Marquess Cornwallis. 1893.
†Shipp, Memoirs of John. 1829.
Skinner, Military Memoir of Lt.-Col. James. 1851.
Teignmouth, Lord. Memoir of the Life of John Lord Teignmouth. 1843.
Valentia, Viscount. Voyages and Travels, etc. 1809–1811.
War and Sport in India, 1802–1806. 1913.
Wellesley MSS.—British Museum Add. MSS. 37314, 37315.
Wellesley Papers, The. 1914.
Williams, P. E. India under Wellesley. 1929.
*Wilson, H. H. The History of British India. From 1805 to 1835. Vol. I. 1845.
*Wilson, W. J. History of the Madras Army. Vol. III. 1883.

CHAPTER III

*†Oman (Sir), Charles. Lecture published on pp. 541 ff. of The Journal of the Royal Artillery. Vol. XXXIV. 1908.
*†Public Records Office. F.O. 27, 72–74, relating to negotiations with France in 1806.

Adair, Sir Robert. Historic Memoir of a Mission to the Court of Vienna in 1806. 1844.
Barrow, J. Life of Sir Sidney Smith. Vol. II. 1848.
"Book, The." 1813.
*Clarkson, T. History of the Abolition of Slave Trade. 1808.
Crawford, Capt. A. Reminiscences of a Naval Officer. Vol. I. 1851.
*†Driault, Édouard. Napoléon et l'Europe. Tilsit. 1917.
Hook, Theodore. The Life of General Sir David Baird. Vol. II. 1833.
*†Malmesbury, Diaries of the First Earl of. 1844.
Napier, Gen. Sir William. Life of General Sir Charles Napier. Vol. I. 1857.
Windham Papers, The. Vol. II. 1913.

CHAPTER IV

*†Balagny, Cdt. Campagne de l'Empereur Napoléon en Espagne. Tomes III–V. Paris. 1903, 1907.
*†Holm, P. E. Danmark-Norges Udenrigske Historie. Vol. II. Copenhagen. 1875.

*Moller, Erik. England og Danmark-Norge in 1807. Historisk Tidskrift, 3 Bind 5 und 6 Hefte. Copenhagen. 1911.
*†Moore, Diary of Sir John. Vol. II. 1904.
*†Napier, Gen. Sir William. History of the War in the Peninsula. Vols. I, II, and VI. 1886.
*†Oman (Sir), Charles. History of the Peninsular War. Vol. I. 1902. II. 1903.
*†Public Records Office. F.O. 22. 51–57 (Denmark, 1806, 1807).
†64. 77 (Prussian Consular Reports, 1807).
*† 65. 70 (Russia, 1807).

---

†Adair, Sir Robert. Historical Memoir of a Mission to the Court of Vienna in 1806. 1844.
† Negotiations for the Peace of the Dardanelles in 1808–9. 1845.
An Authentic account of the Siege of Copenhagen. 1807.
Baring, Alexander (Lord Ashburton). An inquiry into the Causes and Consequences of the Order in Council. 1808.
Beamish, N. L. History of the King's German Legion. Vol. I. 1832.
Bristed, J. Hints on the National Bankruptcy of Britain, etc. New York. 1809.
†Brougham. The Speech of Henry Brougham. April 1, 1808. 1808.
†Brown, J. The Mysteries of Naturalization. 1806.
†Burghersh, Lord. Memoir of the Early Campaigns of the Duke of Wellington. 1810.
Butler, Capt. Lewis. Series of articles on "Minor Expeditions." U.S. Magazine. 1905.
*†Butterfield, H. The Peace Tactics of Napoleon, 1806–1808. Cambridge. 1929.
Clinton, Brig.-Gen. H. A few remarks (regarding) the late Campaign in Spain. 1809.
†Dalrymple, Gen. Sir Hew. Memoir of his Proceedings, etc. 1830.
*†Delavoye, A. M. Life of Lord Lynedoch. 1880.
D'Ivernois, Sir F. Effets du blocus continental, etc. 1809.
*†Driault, Édouard. Napoléon et l'Europe. Tilsit. 1917.
*† La Politique orientale de Napoléon, 1806–1808. 1904.
*†Du Casse, P. E. Mémoires de Roi Joseph. Vol. V. Paris. 1854.
*†Dundonald, Earl of. The Autobiography of a Seaman. Vol. I. 1860.
†Edgeworth, A Memoir of Maria. Vol. I, pp. 205–208 (on capture of Copenhagen). "Not published." 1867.
†Exposé par la Reine. Danske Samlinger for Historie. Bind I. 1865.
Fitzclarence, Lt. Col. G. (Earl of Munster). An account of the British Campaign of 1809. (1831.)

BIBLIOGRAPHY 455

*†Foy, Le Général. Histoire des Guerres de la Péninsule. Tome IV. 1828.
*Gomez de Arteche y Moro, J. Guerra de la Independencia. Tomos III–VI. 1878–1886.
Gomm, Sir William. Letters and Journals. 1881.
†Grey, Walter. Walcheren. 1810.
(Hamilton, Capt. Thomas.) Annals of the Peninsular Campaigns. Vol. II. 1829.
*†Harris, Rifleman. Recollections. 1848.
Hay, Major Leith. A Narrative of the Peninsular War. Vol. I. 1831.
Henegan, Sir Richard. Seven Years Campaigning in the Peninsula, etc. Vol. I. 1846.
Hitzigrath, H. Hamburg und die Kontinentalsperre. Hamburg. 1900.
Honiger, Robert. Die Kontinentalsperre und ihre Einwirkungen auf Deutschland. Berlin. 1905.
Hook, Theodore. The Life of General Sir David Baird. Vol. II. 1833.
Interesting Proceedings on the Enquiry into the Armistice and Convention of Cintra, The. 1809.
Itinerario Descriptivo Militar. (Used for road distances.) Madrid, 1867.
Jackson, The Diaries and Letters of Sir George. Vol. II. 1872.
*†Jefferson, Memoirs of Thomas. Vol. IV. 1829.
*†Jones, Maj.-Gen. Sir John. Journal of Sieges . . . in Spain, etc. Vol. II. 1846.
*†Jourdan, Marshal J. B. Mémoires militaires sur la Guerre d'Espagne. Paris. (1899.)
Journal of a Soldier of the 71st Regiment. Edinburgh. 1822.
Kjobenhavnske loerde Efterretninger for Aar 1807.
(Lenoble, M.) Mémoires sur les opérations militaires en 1809. 1821.
†Letters from Flushing. By an Officer of the 81st Regiment. 1809.
Literary panorama. Vols. I–VI. (Commercial summaries.) 1807–1809.
Londonderry, Charles Marquess of. Story of the Peninsular War. 1849.
*Luz Soriano, S. J. de. Historia da Guerra Civil, etc. Ep. 2 Tomos I, II. Lisbon. 1870, 1871.
McGrigor, Autobiography of Sir James. 1861.
*†Malmesbury, Diaries of the First Earl of. 1844.
Marryat, Capt. Frederick Frank Mildmay.
Memoirs of a Sergeant late in the 43rd Light Infantry. 1839.
Milburne, Dr. H. A Narrative of the Retreat of the British Army. 1809.
†Moore, James. A Narrative of the Campaign, etc. 1809.
Munster, Earl of. See Fitzclarence.

Münster, Ernst Friederich Herbert Graf von. Lebensbilder aus dem Befreiungskriege. Pp. 50, 51. 1841.
Napier, Passages in the Early Military Life of Sir George. 1884.
Napier, Life of Gen. Sir William. Vol. I. 1864.
Narrative of the campaigns of the Loyal Lusitanian Legion. 1812.
Nyeste Skilderie af Kjobenhavn. 1807, 1808.
Oddy, J. J. A Sketch for the Improvement of the interests of Britain, etc. 1810.
Ormsby, Rev. J. W. An account of the operations of the British Army, etc. 1809.
Paget, Sir Arthur. The Paget Papers. Vol. II. 1896.
*†Papers presented to Parliament in 1809. 1809.
Public Records Office. Admiralty 413.
† H.O. 42. 94, 95, and 98, relating to industrial unrest.
Raeder, J. T. von. Danmarks Krigs-og Politiske Historie. 1807–1809. Vol. II. Copenhagen. 1845.
*Randall, H. S. The Life of Thomas Jefferson. Vol. III. Philadelphia. 1858.
Real State of the Case respecting the late expedition. 1808.
Robinson, Henry Crabb. Diary, etc. 1869.
Rose, J. Holland. A British Agent in Tilsit. English Historical Review. 1901.
*†Ross, Sir J. Memoirs, etc., of Lord de Saumarez. Vol. II. 1838.
*†Savary, Gen. Notes sur la Cour de Russie en 1807-8. Revue d'Histoire Diplomatique. Paris. 1890.
Schaumann, A. L. F. On the Road with Wellington. The Diary of a war commissary (translation). 1924.
Sidney, Rev. E. The Life of Lord Hill. 1845.
Strangford, Lord. Observations on Napier's History, etc. 1821.
Thiébault, le Général Baron. Mémoires. Tome IV. Paris. 1895.
*†Thiers, M. A. Histoire du Consulat et de l'Empire. Tome XI. Pp. 389 ff. (Talavera papers.) 1884. Paris.
*Toreño, Conde de. Historia del Levantiamento, etc. Tomo I. Paris. 1836.
Touchard-Lafosse. Histoire de Charles XIV. Tome I. Paris. 1838.
Vandal, A. Les instructions données à M. de Caulaincourt. Revue d'Histoire Diplomatique. Paris. 1890.
*†Napoléon et Alexandre. Tomes I, II. Paris. 1893.
Vivian, J. H. Minutes of a conversation with Napoleon Bonaparte. 1839.
Whittingham, A memoir of the services of Lt. Gen. Sir S. F. 1868.
Wilson, Sir Robert. Journal, 1808–1809. British Museum Add. MSS. 30099.

BIBLIOGRAPHY 457

CHAPTER V

*†Napier, Gen. Sir William. History of the War in the Peninsula. Vols. II, III. 1886.
*†Oman (Sir), Charles. History of the Peninsular War. Vol. II. 1903. III. 1908.

---

*†Adams, Writings of John Quincy. Vol. III. New York. 1914.
*†American State Papers. Foreign Relations. Vol. III. Washington. 1832.
Andréades, A. Histoire de la Banque d'Angleterre. Paris. 1904.
*†Bonnal, H. La Vie Militaire du Maréchal Ney. Tome III. 1914.
Bosanquet, C. Practical Observations on the report of the Bullion Committee. 1810.
Bristed, J. The Resources of the British Empire. New York. 1811.
Chaplin, Arnold. Medicine in England during the reign of George III. 1919.
Cockburn, Lt. Gen. Sir George. A Voyage to Cadiz, etc. 1815.
Costello, E. The Adventures of a Soldier. 1852.
Cunningham, A. British Credit in the Last Napoleonic War. Girton College Studies, 2. Cambridge. 1910.
Dickson Manuscripts, The. Woolwich. 1908.
*†Driault, Édouard. Napoléon et l'Europe. La Grande Empire 1808–1812. Paris. 1924.
*†Espitalier, A. Napoléon et le roi Murat, 1808–1815. Paris. 1910.
*†Fririon, Baron. Journal Historique de la Campagne de Portugal. Paris. 1841.
*†Girod de l'Ain, M. Vie Militaire du Général Foy. 1910.
Gomm, Sir William. Letters and Journals. 1881.
Grattan, William. Adventures of the Connaught Rangers. Vol. I. 1847.
*†Guingret, M. Relation Historique et Militaire de la Campagne de Portugal sous le Maréchal Masséna. Paris. 1817.
(Hamilton, Capt. Thomas.) Annals of the Peninsular Campaigns. Vol. II. 1829.
Hartmann, von. Der Königlich-Hannoversche General Sir Julius von Hartmann. Hanover. 1858.
Hay, Major Leith. A Narrative of the Peninsular War. Vol. I. 1831.
Holland, Lord. Further Memoirs of the Whig Party. 1905.
Inquiry into the State of our Commercial Relations, etc. 1811.
*†Jones, Maj. Gen. Sir John. Journal of Sieges ... in Spain, etc. Vol. III. 1846.
†Kincaid, Capt. Sir John. Adventures in the Rifle Brigade. (1838.)
†Random shots from a Rifleman. (1838.)

*†Koch, Gen. Mémoires de Masséna. Tome VII. Paris. 1850.
Lemonnier-Delafosse, M. Campagnes de 1810–1815. Havre. 1850.
Lever, Charles. Charles O'Malley.
Literary Panorama. Vols. VII, VIII. (Commercial summaries.) 1810.
*Luz Soriano, S. J. da. Historia da Guerra Civil, etc. Ep. 2. Tomos II, III. Lisbon. 1871, 1874.
Marbot, Mémoires du Général. Tome II. Paris. 1892.
Martin, Letters of Sir T. B. Navy Records Society. Vols. I, II. 1903, 1898.
Maxwell, W. H. Peninsular Sketches. Vol. I. 1845.
Napier, Passages in the Early Military Life of Sir George. 1884.
Napier, Gen. Sir William. Life of General Sir Charles Napier. Vol. I. 1857.
*†Papers presented to Parliament in 1813. 1813.
†Public Records Office. H.O. 42. 105 relating to industrial unrest.
†Radcliffe, W. Origin of the New System of Manufacture commonly called "Power-Loom Weaving", etc. Stockport. 1828.
Ricardo, David. Reply to Mr. Bosanquet's "Practical Observations," etc. 1811.
Robinson, H. B. Memoirs of Lt. Gen. Sir Thomas Picton.
*†Ross, Sir J. Memoirs, etc., of Lord de Saumarez. Vol. II. 1838.
Sidney, Rev. E. The Life of Lord Hill. 1845.
Simmons. A British Rifle Man. The Journals, etc., of Major George Simmons. 1899.
Teixeira Botelho, J. J. Historia Popular da Guerra da Peninsula. Porto. 1915.
Tomkinson, Lt. Col. W. Diary of a Cavalry Officer, etc., 1894.
*†Vandal, A. Napoléon et Alexandre. Tome II. Paris. 1893.
*Wallas, Graham. Life of Francis Place. 1898.
Wellesley MSS.—British Museum Add. MSS. 37292.
Wrottesley, G. Life, etc., of F. M. Sir John Burgoyne. Vol. I. 1873.

CHAPTER VI

*†Chambers, Robert. Traditions of Edinburgh. Edinburgh. 1825.
*†Clapham, J. H. An Economic History of Great Britain. 1926.
*†Cockburn, Henry. Memorials of his Time. Edinburgh. 1909.
*†Historical Records of Australia. Series I. Vols. VI, VII. Sydney. 1916.
*Kingsford, William. History of Canada. Vols. VII, VIII. 1894, 1895.
*Theal, G. M. History of South Africa 1795–1834. 1891.

Account of the origin of the late Discontents of the Army, etc. 1810.
*Argyll, Duke of. Scotland as it was and as it is. Vol. II. Edinburgh. 1887.

BIBLIOGRAPHY 459

Arniston Memoirs, The. Edinburgh. 1887.
Arnot, H. The History of Edinburgh. Edinburgh. 1816.
Baert, Baron. Tableau de la Grande Bretagne. Tome I. Paris. 1800.
*Baines (Sir), Edward. History of the Cotton Manufacture in Great Britain. 1835.
Bamford, Samuel. Early Days. 1893.
Balfour, Lady Francis. The Life of George Fourth Earl of Aberdeen. 1925.
Berry, Mary. Extracts of the Journals and Correspondence of Miss Berry. Vol. II. 1865.
*Bonwick, James. First Twenty Years of Australia. 1882.
Bouchette, J. The British Dominions in North America. 1831.
Brief Sketch of the Services of Sir G. H. Barlow, A. 1811.
Buchanan, Rev. C. Christian Researches in Asia. 1811.
*†Canadian Archives, Reports on. D. Brymner. For 1892, 1893. Pubd. 1893, 1894.
†Canadien, Le. Quebec. 1806–1808.
*†Cardew, Sir Alexander. The White Mutiny. 1929.
*Chambers, W. The Book of Scotland. Edinburgh. 1830.
Concise Account of the Events of the Rebellion at Madras, A. (1810.)
*Craik, Sir Henry. A Century of Scottish History. Vol. II. 1901.
*Cunningham, J. The Church History of Scotland. Vol. II. 1882.
Dionne, M. M. E. Article on Pierre-Stanislas Bédard in Royal Society of Canada's Proceedings. II Series. Vol. IV. Sect. I. Ottawa. 1898.
Evans, J. and Son. Life and Death of Joanna Southcott. 1815.
Fergusson, Lt. Col. A. Henry Erskine. 1882.
Fletcher, Mrs. Eliza. Autobiography. Edinburgh. 1875.
Free and Impartial Thoughts on the Dangers to be apprehended from the increase of Sectarists, etc. 1808.
Galt, John. Annals of the Parish.
Garneau, F.-X. Histoire de Canada. Montréal. Tome III. 1882.
*Gaskell, P. Artizans and Machinery. 1836.
Gillies, R. P. Memoirs of a Literary Veteran. Vols. I, II. 1851.
Glasgow, Extracts from the Records of the Burgh of. Vol. IX. 1914.
Gleanings from Africa. 1806.
Gunning, H. Reminiscences of Cambridge. Vol. II. 1854.
Hall, Rev. J. Travels in Scotland. 1807.
Hamilton, Elizabeth. The Cottagers of Glenburnie.
(Hamilton, Capt. Thomas). Cyril Thornton.
*†Hammond, J. L. and B. The Skilled Labourer. 1919.
Hanna, Rev. W. Memoirs of Thomas Chalmers. Vol. I. Edinburgh. 1849.
Heron, R. Observations made in a journey through the Western Counties of Scotland, etc. Perth. 1799.
— Scotland described. Edinburgh. 1797.

Hughes, J. L., and L. R. Klenn. Progress of Education in the (Nineteenth) Century. 1907.
*Hutchins, B. L., and A. Harrison. A History of Factory Legislation. 1911.
India Office Papers, Miscellaneous, Home Series, 698.
*†Irvine, A. An inquiry into ... Emigration from the Highlands, etc. 1802.
*†Kaye, J. W. The Life, etc., of Maj.-Gen. Sir John Malcolm. Vol. I. 1856.
Lambert, John. Travels through Lower Canada, etc. Vol. I. 1816.
Letter from a Gentleman high in office at Madras. 1810.
*†Lockhart, J. G. Peter's Letters to his kinsfolk. 1819.
(London, J. C.) An immediate and effectual mode of raising the rental of the Landed Property in England, etc. By a Scotch Farmer. 1808.
*Lucas (Sir), C. P. History of Canada. 1909.
Macdonald, J. Reise durch Schottland u.s.w. (Translation into German.) 1808.
Malcolm, Lt.-Col. John. Observations on the Disturbances in the Madras Army in 1809. 1812.
*Marshall, W. General View of the Agriculture of the Central Highlands of Scotland. 1794.
Marshman, J. C. The Life and Times of Carey Marshman and Ward. Vol. I. 1859.
*†Minto, Lady. Lord Minto in India. 1880.
†Morse, H. B. The Chronicles of the East India Company trading to China. Vol. III. Oxford. 1926.
*Nicholls, Sir George. A History of the Scotch Poor Law. 1856.
Onslow, S. Macarthur. Some Early Records of the Macarthurs of Camden. 1914.
Orrok, Letters of John. Aberdeen. 1927.
*Owen, Robert. Life of himself. Vol. I. 1857.
Parliamentary Papers relating to East India Affairs.
† Madras Army. 1810.
† Madras Army. 1811.
† (Madras). 1811.
† Madras Army and Government. 1812.
Passfield, Lord. See Webb, Sidney.
*†Péron, F. Voyage de Découvertes aux Terres Australes. Paris. 1807.
Petrie, W. Statement of facts delivered to Lord Minto. 1810.
Pillet, M. le Maréchal-de-Camp. L'Angleterre vue à Londres et dans ses Provinces, etc. Paris. 1815.
Public Records Office. C.O. 42. 141.
†Radcliffe, W. Origin of the New System of Manufacture commonly called "Power-Loom Weaving", etc. Stockport. 1828.

BIBLIOGRAPHY

†Report from the Select Committee on Hand-loom Weavers' Petitions. 1834.
†Report of the Committee on the Woollen Manufacture. 1806.
†Report on Weavers' Petitions. 1811.
†Reports from the Select Committee on Artizans and Machinery. 1824.
*Scott, Ernest, Terre Napoléon. 1910.
Scott, Sir Walter. Novels—The Antiquary, Guy Mannering, Redgauntlet.
† General Account of Edinburgh. Prose Works. VII. Pp. 226 ff. 1834.
*†Selkirk, Earl of. Observations on the Present State of the Highands. 1806.
Sidney, Rev. E. The Life of Sir Richard Hill. 1839.
Simond, Louis. Voyage en Angleterre pendant 1810 et 1811. Paris. 1817.
*Sinclair, Sir John. General View of the Northern Counties and Islands of Scotland. 1795.
Skrine, H. Tours in the North of England and ... Scotland. 1795.
*Smith, Adam. An Inquiry into the Nature and Causes of the Wealth of Nations. (Editions from 3rd onwards.)
Smith, Mrs. Elizabeth. Memoirs of a Highland Lady. 1898.
*Somerville, R. General View of the Agriculture of E. Lothian. 1805.
Teignmouth, Lord. Memoir of the Life of John Lord Teignmouth. Vol. II. 1843.
Vindication of the Hindoos. By a Bengal Officer. 1808.
Webb, Sidney and Beatrice. The History of Trade Unionism. 1902.
*Wilson, H. H. The History of British India. From 1805 to 1835. Vol. I. 1845.
*Wilson, W. J. History of the Madras Army. Vol. III. 1883.

INDEX

ABAJI, Maratha General, 127.
ABBOT, Right Hon. CHARLES, Speaker, influences a parliamentary measure, 265; his part in Burdett's case, 308 ff.
ABERCROMBY, Major-Gen. Sir JOHN, conquers Mauritius, 378, 379.
ABERCROMBY, Gen. Sir RALPH, mentioned, 259, 378.
ABERDEEN, harbour works, 94; population, 403.
ABERNETHY, JOHN, medical author, 88.
ABRANTES, Portuguese fortress, 347, 359.
ACADEMY, ROYAL, 49–51, 54, 55.
ACADEMY OF ANCIENT MUSIC, 41.
ADAIR, ROBERT, diplomatist, his conciliatory policy, 267, 268; negotiates peace with Turkey, 1809, 268; mentioned, 284.
ADAM, WILLIAM, M.P., speech on constitutional question, 301, 302; on Burdett, 308.
ADDINGTON, HENRY, correspondence with Wellesley, 111; mentioned, 177, 180. *Also see* SIDMOUTH, Lord.
ADMIRALTY, Palmerston a Lord of the, 198; apprehensions at the, 212, 285. *Also see* FIRST LORD OF THE ADMIRALTY.
ADRIATIC SEA, Napoleon's policy, 285, 323.
ADULTERY, growing disapproval of, 417.
ADVOCATE, in Scotland, *see* LORD ADVOCATE.
AFGHANISTAN, Treaty with, 1809, 365.
AFGHANS, invasion of India by, 1796, 101; Rohillas a tribe of Afghan descent, 103.
AFRICA, British footholds in, 386 ff. For West Coast *also see* SLAVE TRADE.
AGRA, Moghul capital of India, 121; captured from Sindhia, October 18, 1803, 125; annexation of adjoining territory, 137.
AGRICULTURE, Davy's lectures, 83; official ignorance of India agriculture, 107; in New South Wales, 382, 383; in Cape Colony, 386, 387.
AHMADNAGAR, capture of, 126.
AIKIN, Dr., quoted by Malthus, 63.
AIX ROADS, attack on French fleet in, 270 ff.; mentioned, 212.
AKBAR, mentioned, 121.
ALBANIA, mentioned, 323.
ALBANIANS, in Egypt, 201, 202.
ALDBOROUGH, described by Crabbe, 19 ff.
ALEXANDER II, Emperor of Russia, makes peace with Napoleon, 208; exasperation with Great Britain, 209; Napoleon's proposal to, regarding Denmark, 211; mediation proposal, 221; breach with Great Britain, 222; Napoleon's letter of February 1808 to, 235; meeting with Napoleon at Erfurt, 248; peace proposal to Great Britain, 248; designs on Turkey 268; friendship with Wilson, 342; economic breach with Napoleon, 361, 362.
ALEXANDRIA, expedition to, 195, 200 ff.; evacuation, 202.
ALIGARH, capture, September 4, 1803, 124.
ALI PASHA, ruler of Albania, his assistance to Great Britain, 323.
ALLEMAND, Rear-Admiral, French Navy, second escape from Rochefort, 235.

ALL THE TALENTS, name for Grenville's Ministry, its origin, 147.
ALMEIDA, Portuguese frontier fortress, its successful defence by Wilson in 1808, 273; capture by Masséna in 1810, 344; Wellington's failure to relieve, considered, 336, 346, 347, 348; operations about, 344 ff.
ALTONA, interruption of postal communication with, 210.
AMBOYNA, Dutch possession, China Seas, 379.
AMERICA, NORTH, Scottish emigration to, 393. *Also see* CANADA.
AMERICA, SOUTH, plans for exciting Spanish colonies to revolt, 166; false impressions regarding, 167, 179; independence movement, 324; trade with, 324.
AMIENS, TREATY OF, how viewed, 144, 145; effect in India, 120.
AMRITSAR, Indian sacred city, Lake and Holkar at, 138; treaty concluded at, 365.
AMSTERDAM, headquarters of Hope and Co., 328.
ANAND RAO, Gaekwar of Baroda, installed by British, 1802, 112.
ANDALUSIA, French invasion in 1810, 332.
ANDERSON, Col., friend of Moore, 260.
ANGERS, Arthur Wellesley at, 114.
ANIMALS, Erskine's Bill for the Prevention of Cruelty to, 266.
ANNUAL REGISTER, remarks in, 200, 262; poetry in, 24; on Scottish lawyers, 408.
ANSTRUTHER, Sir JOHN, Chief Justice of Calcutta, 104.
ANSTRUTHER, Brig.-Gen. ROBERT, in Peninsular War, 256.
ANTI-JACOBIN, Canning's, 74; its ridicule of German drama, 60.
ANTI-JACOBIN REVIEW, 74.
ANTWERP, its strategic position, 285. *Also see* WALCHEREN.
APPRENTICES, use of the system by shirking militiamen, 320; short term of apprenticeship in Scotland, 403; desire of workers for retention of long term, 418.
ARABIC, taught in Calcutta College, 108.
ARAGON, campaigns in, 343.
ARCHBISHOP, *see* SUTTON, MANNERS.
ARCHITECTURE, general state in England, 54 ff.
ARCOT, Nawab of, 100; cavalry sent from, to Vellore, 139.
ARDEN, Lord, his sinecure, 302, 303.
ARGAON, Battle of, November 29, 1803, 128; its general characteristics, 122, 123.
ARGYLL, Duke of, treatment of his tenants, 395.
ARISTOTLE, as medical authority, 89.
ARMSTRONG, Gen., U.S. Minister in Paris, 328 ff.
ARMY, BRITISH, health and medical treatment, 87, 289, 299; rapid promotion prior to Duke of York's reforms, 114; army of Great Britain and Ireland united in 1800, 185; objections to a standing army, 145, 146, 309; Windham's reforms, 153, 154; prestige restored by Battle of Maida, 178; improvement in, 178; relations of Addington's, Pitt's, and Windham's measures, 180; Irish recruiting, 185, 320; strength in 1807, 205; recruitment, 205; Castlereagh's Militia Transfer Act, 205; system of home defence from 1807 to end of the war, 234; a difficulty as to seniority, 247; disciplinary defects of troops disclosed in Peninsula, 1808–9, 255 ff., 283; Duke of York scandal, 1809, 261, 262; Dundas Commander-in-Chief, 262; character of Peninsular army at Talavera, 277; subsequent attitude towards Wellington, 333; weakness in general officers, 333, 334;

INDEX

poor class of regimental officers, 334, 335; indiscipline of rank and file, 335; reinforcement of Peninsular army, 336, 337; company system in Light Brigade, 345; Scottish Highland recruiting, 396.

ARMY, INDIA, prize money and emoluments, 115, 116; strength and composition, 116 ff.; European officers of Indian troops ignorant of their men, 139; grievances, 367 ff.; Madras Mutiny of 1808, 369 ff.; share in overseas expeditions, 376 ff.

ARMY, PORTUGUESE, 339 ff.; Light Infantry, 346; at Bussaco, 349, 350.

ART, not given government encouragement, 49. *Also see* PAINTING, etc.

ARTILLERY, Royal, shortage of horses, 239; deficiency at Talavera, 278; the Chestnut Troop, R.H.A., 280.

Maratha, 123; British galloper guns in India, 124.

ASIA MINOR, Wilkins's travels in, 56.

ASSAYE, Battle of, September 21, 1803, 126, 127; its general characteristics, 122, 123.

ASTRONOMY, taught in Calcutta College, 109; general state of, in England, 79, 80.

ATHENS, Parthenon sculptures, 56.

ATHOLL, Duke of, treatment of his tenants, 395.

ATKINS, RICHARD, Judge Advocate General in New South Wales, 384.

ATOMIC THEORY, Dalton's, 81, 82.

ATTORNEY, a convict attorney in New South Wales, 393.

ATTORNEY-GENERAL, Pigott, 1806, 150; Gibbs, 1807, 197, 198.

ATTWOOD, THOMAS, composer, 43.

AUCHMUTY, Brig.-Gen. Sir SAMUEL, captures Monte Video, 1807, 168, 169; mentioned, 204.

AUCKLAND, Lord, President of the Board of Trade, 1806, 150.

AUERSTADT, Battle of, October 14, 1806, 181.

AUSTEN, JANE, her Mr. Bennet, 42.

AUSTRALIA, botanical expedition to, 86; discovered in 1803 to be a single island, 380. *Also see* NEW SOUTH WALES.

AUSTRALIA, SOUTH, rejection of, for a settlement, 386.

AUSTRIA, breaks off relations with England, 222; question of her reconciliation with Prussia and Russia, 268; renews relations with England and goes to war with France, 1809, 267, 285 ff.; concludes peace with France, 298.

BACON, the philosopher, mentioned, 58, 81.

BADAJOZ, Wellington's headquarters in autumn of 1809, 283, 331, 336.

BAERT, French traveller, on Mrs. Siddons, 48; on medicine in England, 89: on Scottish Highland landlords, 395.

BAILLIE, JOANNA, dramatist, 45.

BAILLIE, MATTHEW, physician, 88.

BAIRD, Sir DAVID, his expedition to Egypt mentioned, 101, 105, 115; to Cape Colony, 166, 167, 387; as Lieutenant-General with Moore in Spain, 251 ff.; wounded at Coruña, 259; mentioned, 168.

BAJI RAO, Peshwa of Maratha Empire, 112; signs Treaty of Bassein, 113; treachery of, 118; cession of Bundelkhand, 125; his cavalry at Assaye, 126, 127.

BALL, Sir ALEXANDER, his connection with Coleridge, 32.

BALTIC, trade, 321, 322.

466 ENGLAND IN THE NINETEENTH CENTURY

BANDA NEIRA, Dutch island, conquered in 1810, 379, 380.
BANK, NATIONAL SAVINGS; Whitbread's scheme, 184.
BANK OF ENGLAND, loan to Government, 232; balances of, 232; the Bank and the Bullion Committee, 317 ff.; building rebuilt by Soane, 55.
BANKES, HENRY, M.P., financial reformer, 266.
BANKRUPTCIES, in 1810, 318.
BANKS, Sir JOSEPH, President of the Royal Society, 83; his botanical work, 86.
BANKS, COUNTRY, and the Bullion Committee, 317, 318.
BANKS, SCOTTISH, 399.
BAPTISTS, their missions, 363.
BARCLAY, Lt.-Col. ROBERT, with Craufurd in Peninsula, 346.
BAREILLY, its amenities, 103.
BARHAM, Lord, as First Lord of the Admiralty till January 1806, 156.
BARING, ALEXANDER, Banker and M.P., presents petition against Orders in Council, 230; member of Bullion Committee, 317.
BARING, Sir FRANCIS, financier, 318; mentioned, 328.
BARING, FRANCIS, relative of the above, commits suicide, 318, 319.
BARLEY, price in 1808, 233; food of Scottish Highlanders, 395.
BARLOW, Sir GEORGE, Governor-General of India, 1805-1806, 137, 138, 366; Governor of Madras, 367; dispute with Macdowall, 368-370; mutiny against, 370-375; recalled, 375; character, 367.
BARODA, Maratha State, 112.
BARRINGTON, SHUTE, Bishop of Durham, 83; evangelical activities, 414.
BARRY JAMES, painter, 50.
BARTHOLOMEW FAIR, decay of, 416.
BARTOLOZZI, FRANCESCO, R.A., 50.
BASQUE ROADS, action in, 1809, 270, 271; mentioned, 302.
BASSEIN, TREATY OF, December 31, 1802, 113; its effects, 118 ff.; supplementary agreement to, 125.
BASS STRAIT, settlement at, 386.
BAT, Chatham's headquarters in Walcheren expedition, 287, 288.
BATHURST, Earl, offered Governorship of Madras, 115; President of Board of Trade, 1807, 197, 294, 297; temporarily Foreign Secretary, 1809, 297;
BATZ, see BAT.
BAVARIA, Rumford's connection with, 85.
BEACONSFIELD, Lord, quoted, 295, 296. Also see DISRAELI.
BEAUFORT, Duke of, interest in science, 83.
BEAUMARCHAIS, importance of his Figaro, 17.
BEAUMONT, Sir GEORGE, friend of Wordsworth, 57.
BECKFORD, WILLIAM, author of Vathek, 55.
BECKWITH, Lt.-Gen. Sir GEORGE, conquers Martinique, 269, 270; and Guadeloupe, 323.
BECKWITH, Lt.-Col. SYDNEY, with Craufurd in Peninsula, 346.
BÉDARD, PIERRE STANISLAS, French Canadian leader, 390, 391.
BEDFORD, Fifth Duke of, mentioned, 150.
BEDFORD, Sixth Duke of, Viceroy of Ireland, 1806, 150; his villa at Chiswick, 175; proposals for Catholic relief in 1807, 185.
BELL, Dr. ANDREW, his educational system, 78, 79.
BELL, Lt.-Col. JOHN, a leader in Madras Mutiny, 374, 376.
BELL ROCK, lighthouse, 93.
BENAVENTE, combat of, 254.

INDEX

BENCOOLEN, E. I. Company's possession in Sumatra, 141.
BENGAL, its relation to the rest of British India, 97; extent in 1798, 100; administration, 106 ff.; permanent settlement, 107, 108; the Bengal army, 117, 118, 370, 372; acquisition of Orissa, 125; churches in, 364.
BENGALI, language taught in Calcutta College, 108, 109.
BENTHAM, JEREMY, his works, 63 ff.; mentioned, 58, 391.
BENTINCK, Major-Gen. Lord WILLIAM, Governor of Madras, 111; recalled, 140; at Madrid, 246, 247; with Moore, 257.
BERAR, Maratha State, invaded by British in 1803, 128; apprehension of invasion by Holkar's army, 367. *Also see* RAGHUJI BHONSLA.
BERESFORD, Major-Gen. WILLIAM, his expedition to South America, 167, 168, 204; receives command of Portuguese Army, 272; in 1809 campaigns, 273, 274, 281; his training of Portuguese Army, 340 ff.; made K.B., 350.
BERKELEY, Vice-Admiral GEORGE, off Lisbon, 337, 356; mentioned, 355.
BERKSHIRE, petition from, 311.
BERLIN DECREE, Novermber 21, 1806, 183, 225 ff., 230; revocation promised in 1809, 329.
BERMUDAS, growth in importance, 389.
BERNADOTTE, Marshal, at Hamburg, 212; chosen for future King of Sweden in 1810, 322.
BERNARD, THOMAS, philanthropist, 83, 85.
BERRY, Capt., R.N., in Battle of San Domingo, 157.
BERRY, MARY, account of a Scottish spinning mill, 404.
BERTHIER, Marshal, mentioned, 159.
BERZELIUS, Swedish chemist, 82.
BETTY, Master, The Young Roscius, 47, 48.
BEVELAND, SOUTH, taken and evacuated, 287, 288.
BEYS, Mediterranean, 303.
BHARATPUR, Jat State, war with, 131, 132.
BHONSLA RAJA, *see* RAGHUJI BHONSLA.
BILLINGTON, Mrs., singer, 43.
BIRMINGHAM, supremacy in hardware trade threatened, 153; firm of Boulton and Watt, 90 ff.
BLACKSTONE, his commentaries, 64; cited, 151; mentioned, 391.
BLAKE, WILLIAM, poet, 18, 19; painter and engraver, 54, 24; admiration for Flaxman, 54.
BLENHEIM, Battle of, mentioned, 338.
BLENHEIM, H.M.S., loss of, 327.
BLIGH, WILLIAM, Capt., R.N., Governor of New South Wales, 1806, 383 ff.; mutiny against, and deposition of, 384, 385.
BLOCKADE, illegitimacy of an ineffective blockade, 224 ff.
BLOMFIELD, ROBERT, poet, 23.
BLUE MOUNTAINS, New South Wales, 380.
BOARD OF AGRICULTURE, Davy's lectures for the, 86.
BOARD OF CONTROL for India, its President, 96, 377; powers, 96, 97; Lewisham as President, 97; Dundases and Castlereagh, 97; Minto, 1806, 150; Tierney, 180; Robert Dundas, 1807, 197; Harrowby, 1809, 291; Dundas, 297; Wellesley a member, 99.
BOARD OF TRADE, Auckland President, 1806, 150; Bathurst, 1807, 197; Rose Vice-President, 197; Smirke architect to, 55; mentioned, 297.
BOLES, Major, his part in events leading to Madras mutiny, 370, 371.

BOLTON, pay of cambric weavers at, 418.
BOMBAY CITY, Society in, 110; Recorder of, 110.
BOMBAY PRESIDENCY, government, 97; extent, 100.
BONAPARTE, JOSEPH, King of Naples, 1806, 159, 169, 174; King of Spain, 1808, 237; expelled from Madrid, 246; in campaign of 1809, 275 ff.; invades Andalusia, 332; mentioned, 248, 253.
BONAPARTE, LOUIS, King of Holland, 285; abdication, 321.
BONAPARTE, NAPOLEON, *see* NAPOLEON.
BOROUGHS, close parliamentary boroughs, 200. *Also see* SEATS IN PARLIAMENT.
BOSTON, U.S.A., a merchant from, in Canada, 392.
BOTANY in England, 86.
BOULTON, head of the firm of Boulton and Watt, 90.
BOURBON, French island, Wellesley's designs against, 100; its capture, 377, 388.
BOURNE, *see* STURGES-BOURNE.
BOURQUIEN, Gen. LOUIS, 124.
BOWYER, Rev. JAMES, 26.
BRANDY in Cape Colony, 388.
BRAZIL, transfer of Portuguese Court to, 223, 342; trade with, 339.
BREST, blockade of, 156.
BREWING, PRIVATE, taxation attempted, 153; Cobbett's views, 234.
BRISBANE, Capt. CHARLES, R.N., captures Curaçoa, 158; mentioned, 379.
BRITISH AND FOREIGN BIBLE SOCIETY, founded 1804, 363, 414.
BROACH, conquest of, 126; area, 137; cotton in, 137.
BRODIE, Sir BENJAMIN, physician, 88.
BROTHERS, RICHARD, religious maniac, 412, 413.
BROUGHAM, HENRY, speech against Orders in Council, 1808, 230, 231; contributor to Edinburgh Review, 71, 72, 177.
BROWN, ROBERT, botanist, 86.
BUCHANAN, Rev. CLAUDIUS, his India experiences, 364.
BUCKINGHAM, Marquis of, parliamentary position, 148; a letter to, 337.
BUCKINGHAMSHIRE, Earl of, Postmaster-General, 1806, 150; mentioned, 149.
BUDGET of 1806, 152, 153.
    of 1807, 183.
    of 1808, 232.
    of 1809, 267.
    of 1810, 316. Irish budget of 1810, 316.
BUENOS AYRES, expedition in 1806, 166 ff.; in 1807, 168, 169, 203, 204.
BULLION COMMITTEE, 1810, 316 ff.
BUNDELKHAND, cession and conquest of, 125; area annexed, 137; disturbances in, 366.
BURDETT, Sir FRANCIS, M.P., re-elected for Westminster, 1807, 200; proposals for parliamentary reform, 266; takes up Jones's case, 306 ff.; his manifesto, 307, 308; his imprisonment, 309 ff.; Burdett riots, 309 ff.; mentioned, 263.
BÜRGER, his Lenore, 31.
BURGHESH, Lord, his irregular promotion, 262.
BURKE, EDMUND, connection with Crabbe, 19; his influence, 59; connection with India, 97, 134; with Windham, 144, 146.
BURN, Lt.-Col. WILLIAM, defends Delhi, 131.

INDEX 469

BURNEY, FANNY, 45.
BURNS, the poet, mentioned, 40.
BURRARD, Lt.-Gen. Sir HARRY, in Portugal, 239 ff.
BUSHMEN in Cape Colony, 387.
BUSSACO, Battle of, September 27, 1810, 349 ff.
BYRON, Lord, early career, 37 ff.; a romantic, 24, 176; parentage, 49; lines on science quoted, 92.
BYRON, JACK, father of the above, 49.
BYRON, Mrs., see GORDON, CATHERINE.

CABINET, question of Ellenborough's position, 151, 152; attempt at definition, 151; Fox's view, 152; King's right to choose, 152, 199; a Cabinet note, 227; limitation of Cabinet responsibility, 245; election of a Premier by, 292, 295.
CABINETS, Grenville's, 1806–1807, Grenville, Petty, Erskine, Fox, Spencer, Windham, Howick, Moira, Fitzwilliam, Sidmouth, Ellenborough, 149, 150; Fox replaced by Howick, Howick by T. Grenville, Fitzwilliam (remaining in Cabinet) by Sidmouth, and Sidmouth by Holland, 179.
Portland's, 1807–1809, Portland, Perceval, Eldon, Canning, Hawkesbury, Castlereagh, Mulgrave, Chatham, Camden, Westmorland, Bathurst, 197.
Perceval's, 1809, Perceval, Eldon, Wellesley, Ryder, Liverpool, Mulgrave, Chatham, Camden, Westmorland, Bathurst, 294 ff.; Chatham replaced by Mulgrave and Mulgrave by Yorke, 1810, 304, 305.
CADIES OF AULD REEKIE, 405.
CADIZ, Spanish Government's retirement on, 332; occupation by British, 332.
CADORE, Duc de, French Foreign Minister, his declaration to U.S. Minister, 329.
CALCUTTA, College at, 108, 109; society, 110; Supreme Court, 110.
CALEDON, Earl of, Governor of Cape Colony, 388.
CALEDON RIVER, discovered, 388.
CALEDONIAN CANAL, 94, 95, 396.
CALICOES, Indian, 105.
CALVINISM in Scotland, 397, 398.
CAMBRIDGE, clergy at and near, 414.
CAMBRIDGESHIRE MILITIA, mutiny of, 307.
CAMBRIDGE UNIVERSITY, 75, 76; education at, of Wordsworth, 25; of Byron, 37; travelling bachelorship, 56; Downing College built, 56; connection with Malthus, 61.
CAMDEN, Earl, his support of Macarthur when Colonial Secretary, 383; President of the Council, 1807, 197; share in arrangement regarding Castlereagh in 1809, 291 ff.; mentioned, 294.
CAMPBELL, Brig.-Gen. ALEXANDER, at Talavera, 276, 280.
CAMPBELL, THOMAS, poet, 21, 22; mentioned, 19, 38.
CANADA, Lower Canada during the decade, 389 ff.; Upper Canada, 393, 394; population of Canada, 392, 393.
CANADIEN, LE, French Canadian newspaper, 390, 391.
CANALS, construction of, 92 ff., 396; Forth–Clyde Canal mentioned, 91.
CANNING, GEORGE, question of his taking office under Grenville, 149, 196; an Opposition leader, 154; Foreign Secretary, 1807, 197; Danish policy, 210 ff.; Spanish policy, 1808, 237; a "taverner", 265; foreign policy in

1809, 267, 268; attitude to U.S., 330; obtains removal of Castlereagh, 289 ff.; efforts to become Premier, 291, 292; resignation, 292; duel with Castlereagh, 293; supports without joining Perceval, 296, 315, 316; his party, 296, 316; speech on Peninsular affairs, 316; on Bullion question, 316; friendship with Crabbe, 21; poem on Pitt, 21; connection with Anti-Jacobin, 74, 60; and with Quarterly Review, 74; author of phrase "All the Talents", 147; not a popular figure, 200; fondness for mystifying people, 218; ungenerous attitude towards the army, 290.

CANTON, headquarters of E.I. Co. in China, 141; affairs there in 1808, 376, 377.

CAPE OF GOOD HOPE, account of under British rule, 1795–1803 and 1806–1810, 386 ff.; Wellesley's view of its importance, 100; capture of a French frigate at, 157; forces sent from, to South America, 168, 169; supplies of food from, to New South Wales, 381; failure of merino sheep in the Colony, 382; Craig's government mentioned, 391.

CAPE TOWN, 387.

CAPPER, Lt.-Col. FRANCIS, his part in affairs leading to Madras mutiny, 369 ff.

CAPRI, island captured by Murat in 1808, 236.

CAREY, WILLIAM, Baptist missionary in India, 364, 365.

CARLISLE, Earl of, attacked by Byron, 39.

CARNATIC, annexation of, 100, 134.

CAROLINE, Princess of Wales, scandal concerning, 189; her conduct investigated, 189.

CARRON, works, 402.

CARTWRIGHT, Major, addresses meeting on Spanish cause, 237.

CASTES, in Indian Army, 117, 138.

CASTLEREAGH, Viscount, President of Board of Control, 97; correspondence with Wellesley, 104, 133, 134; an Opposition leader in 1806, 153, 154; Secretary for War, 1807, 197; his Militia Transfer Bill, 205, 206; general scheme of military defence in 1808, 234; letter on Convention of Cintra, 245; accused of improper conduct as Minister, 263; attacked by Cobbett, 264; question of his removal, 289 ff.; resignation, 292; duel with Canning, 293; former misdeeds brought up in 1810, 311; refusal to join Perceval, 315, 316; aversion to oversea acquisitions, 377; Canadian appointments, 393; mentioned, 155, 196, 197.

CATALONIA, campaigns in, 343.

CATARINI, singer, 43.

CATHCART, Gen. Lord, sent to Rügen, 209; commands Danish expedition, 213 ff.; made a peer of the U.K., 216.

CATHOLIC, music composed by S. Wesley, 43; Catholics in Ceylon, 142.

CATHOLICS, ENGLISH, emancipation of, 185.

CATHOLICS, IRISH, emancipation mentioned, 177; cause ministerial crisis of 1807, 184 ff.; the question not really a party one, 196; Perceval's opposition to the Catholic claims, 196, 197, 199; their support by Irish M.P.s, 199, 200; the question in 1809, 294.

CATHOLICS, SCOTTISH, 185, 397.

CATTLE, Highland, displaced by sheep, 395.

CAVALRY, in India, 116; in Maratha War, 122, 123, 129; shortage of mounts for British cavalry, 239; Paget's force in 1808, 251, 253, 254; ground scouts not used, 279; Portuguese, 340; superiority of K.G.L. cavalry, 345; Cotton's division, 346, 351, 352.

INDEX

CAVE OF HARMONY, 41.
CAYENNE, French possession, S. America, conquered, 1809, 269.
CENSUS, of 1801, defectiveness in Scotland, 402.
CEPHALLONIA, Ionian island, captured from French in 1809, 285.
CERIGO, Ionian island, captured from French in 1809, 285.
CEYLON, conquered from Dutch, 1796, 141; description, 141, 142; Kandian War, 142, 143.
CHALMERS, THOMAS, Scottish Minister, 401, 402.
CHAMBERS, ROBERT, quoted, 406.
CHANCELLOR, Lord, Erskine, 1806, 149; Eldon, 1807, ignorance of equity a disqualification, 149.
  in Ireland, Ponsonby, 1806, 150; Manners, 1807, 198.
CHANCELLOR OF THE DUCHY OF LANCASTER, Derby, 1806, 150; proposal to give the office to Perceval for life, 292.
CHANCELLOR OF THE EXCHEQUER, Petty, 1806, 149; Perceval, 1807, 197; his unsuccessful attempt to be relieved of the post in 1809, 266.
CHARITIES, subscription for Portuguese relief, 357.
CHARLES, Archduke, of Austria, in War of 1809, 286.
CHARLES IV, King of Spain, 237.
CHARLES EDWARD, Scottish devotion to, 396, 397, 406.
CHARTERED COMPANY, formed for Sierra Leone, 388.
CHATHAM, First Earl of, mentioned, 146, 148, 301.
CHATHAM, Second Earl of, Master General of the Ordnance, 1807, 197, 286; considered for Premier, 286, 291; commands Walcheren expedition, 286 ff., 338; inquiry into it, 299 ff.; his resignation, 302; mentioned, 294.
CHATTERTON, his forgeries mentioned, 31.
CHEMISTRY, in England, 81 ff.; organic, 86.
CHESTNUT TROOP, R.H.A., arrival in Spain, 280.
CHEVIOT SHEEP, introduced into Highlands, 395, 396.
CHIEF JUSTICE, Ellenborough, introduced into Cabinet, 149, 151.
CHIEF SECRETARY TO THE LORD LIEUTENANT OF IRELAND, William Elliot, 1806, 150; Arthur Wellesley, 1807, 198, 238, 246; succeeded by R. Dundas, 1809, 272.
CHILD LABOUR, on the Clyde, 405.
CHINA, E.I. Co.'s relations with, 140, 141; Macartney's mission to, 140; trade with, 141; Anglo-Chinese relations in 1808, 376, 377. For Islands in the China seas *see* MOLUCCAS.
CHRIST'S HOSPITAL, Bowyer's teaching at, 26.
CHURCH OF ENGLAND, tithe-collecting from the pulpit, 20; church music, 43; the clergy and education, 79; cry of Established Church in danger, 198, 199; provision for curates' salaries, 233; attempts to obtain corrupt preferment, 263; condition at end of decade, 414, 415.
CHURCH OF SCOTLAND, 400 ff.
CINNAMON, in Ceylon, 142.
CINTRA, CONVENTION OF, 243 ff.; dissensions in Cabinet over, 289, 290.
CIUDAD RODRIGO, Spanish frontier fortress, 336; taken by Masséna, 344.
CLAPHAM SECT, 388.
CLARENCE, WILLIAM, Duke of, in House of Lords, 148.
CLARKE, MARY ANNE, 261 ff.; mentioned, 305.

CLARKSON, THOMAS, Slave Trade abolitionist, 162; tribute to Pitt, 163; mentioned, 189.
CLASSICISM, in literature: in France, 17; Byron's defence of, 24, 38, 176; Wordsworth's attack, 26.
  in design: Flaxman, 54.
  in architecture: 55, 56.
CLASSICS, Wellesley's interest in, 99.
CLAUDE, influence on Turner, 52.
CLEMENTI, MUZIO, musician, 42.
CLERGY, see CHURCH OF ENGLAND.
CLIVE, First Lord, mentioned, 110, 373.
CLIVE, Second Lord, Governor of Madras, his resignation, 110, 111.
CLOSE, Lt.-Col. BARRY, negotiates Treaty of Bassein, 113; during Madras mutiny, 373, 374.
CLUBS, musical, 41.
COAL, in Australia, 385; in Scotland, 402.
COBBETT, WILLIAM, political views in 1806, 144, 145; defends Perceval, 234; attacks Castlereagh, 264; popularity of his Political Register, 307; flogging article, 307; publishes Burdett's manifesto, 307; sentenced for criminal libel, 313, 314.
  views on beer, 234; dislike of jobbers, 265, 318.
COCHRANE, Capt. Lord, R.N., early career, 270, 271; elected M.P. for Westminster, 200; attack on Aix Roads, 271, 272; speech on naval estimates, 302; in alliance with Burdett, 312; on mortality in E. Indies, 326; mentioned, 263.
COCHRANE, Capt. Hon. ALEXANDER, in action off San Domingo, 157; as Rear-Admiral conducts expedition to Martinique, 269.
COCKBURN, HENRY, afterwards Lord, a saying of Hope to, 400; quoted, 406; mentioned, 407.
COFFEE, trade via Heligoland, 321; W.I. trade generally, 326; in Portugal, 355; in Jamaica, 389.
COIMBRA, capture of French wounded at, 352; mentioned, 347, 348, 350.
COKE OF NORFOLK, defends landed interest in parliament, 233.
COLE, Capt. CHRISTOPHER, R.N., takes Banda Neira, 1810, 379.
COLE, Major-Gen. Hon. LOWRY, in Peninsula, 334; at Bussaco, 348.
COLEMAN, GEORGE, his epilogue, 46.
COLERIDGE, SAMUEL TAYLOR, early career and works, 25, 26, 30 ff.; his Christabel a model for Scott, 37; his admiration for Godwin, 59; on Malthus, 61; utilitarianism, 64; reference to, in Anti-Jacobin, 69; friendship with Davy, 83; change of political opinions, 177, 34; mentioned, 38, 45, 176.
COLLINGWOOD, Vice-Admiral Lord, Commander-in-Chief in Mediterranean, 303; the Dardanelles expedition, 190, 191, 194; eluded by Ganteaume, 236; operations in 1809, 284, 285; his work and death, 303, 304; mentioned, 326.
COLLINS, Lt.-Col., Resident with Sindhia, 119.
COLOMBO, capital of Ceylon, 141, 142; attack upon, threatened, 143; danger to, from French, 377.
COLONIAL ADMINISTRATION, in Ceylon, 141; correspondence of a Governor with the office, 381; its support of Macarthur, 383.
COLONIES, connection with Kew Gardens, 86.
COLQUHOUN, PATRICK, his educational statistics, 76 ff.

INDEX 473

COLUMBINE, Commodore HENRY, conquers Senegal, 270.
COMMISSARIAT, Arthur Wellesley's interest in, in India, 114; difficulties in Spain, 239, 251, 283; dishonesty, 334; Craufurd as Commissionary, 345.
COMMITTEE OF PUBLIC EXPENDITURE, 208.
COMMITTEE OF SUPERCARGOES, SELECT, in China, 141; action in 1808, 376, 377.
COMMITTEE ON HAND-LOOM WEAVERS' PETITIONS, SELECT; a witness, 404, 405.
COMPÈRE, French General at Maida, 171.
CONSTABLE, publisher, 72.
CONSTANTINOPLE, Elgin ambassador at, 56; expedition to, 190 ff.
CONSULS in Mediterranean, 303.
CONTINENTAL SYSTEM, 224 ff., 230; its success in 1810, 360 ff., 417. *Also see* BERLIN DECREE.
CONVICTS, in New South Wales, 380, 381, 66; assigned convicts, 383; employment of educated convicts, 393.
COOK, Capt., discoverer of New South Wales, 380.
COPENHAGEN, opinion in, 213, 215; expedition against, 213 ff.
CORFU, Ionian island, its importance to France, 285; mentioned, 236, 323.
CORN, use in distilleries, 233; in Cape Colony, 388.
CORNWALLIS, Admiral, mentioned, 156.
CORNWALLIS, Marquis, Governor-General of India, 1786-1793, his powers, 98, 99; administration of Malabar, 107; permanent settlement of Bengal, 107, 108; consulted by Castlereagh, 109; succeeds Wellesley as Governor-General, July 1805, 136; pacific policy, 136; death and character, 136, 137.
CORRESPONDING SOCIETY, mentioned, 306.
CORUÑA, landing at, 251; Moore's retreat to, 254 ff.; Battle of, January 16, 1809, 256, 259.
COTMAN, JOHN, painter, 53.
COTTAR, in Scottish Highlands, 395, 396.
COTTON, Vice-Admiral Sir CHARLES, in command off Lisbon, 1807, 239; concludes convention with Siniavin, 243, 244; succeeds Collingwood in Mediterranean, 303.
COTTON, Lt.-Gen. Sir STAPLETON, commanding cavalry division in Peninsula, 346, 351.
COTTON, in India, 105, 137; export from China, 141; cotton goods imported into China from India, 141; Order in Council with reference to, 227; the French trade, 227; distress among weavers, 231; American trade, 325; in Guiana, 389; manufacture in Scotland, 396, 403 ff.
COUNTY MEMBERS OF PARLIAMENT, their views in 1810, 314.
COURIER, ministerial newspaper, 244.
COURT MARTIAL, on Whitelocke, 204; on Gambier, 272.
COURT OF SESSION, in Scotland, 409.
COURT OF TEINDS, in Scotland, 400.
COURTS CIVIL, in Scotland, 408 ff.
COURTS CRIMINAL, in Scotland, 408 ff.
COVENT GARDEN THEATRE riots, 297, 298.
COVENTRY, a petition from, 311.
CRABBE, Rev. GEORGE, poet, 19 ff.; mentioned, 107, 175.
CRADOCK, Gen. Sir JOHN, Commander-in-Chief in Madras, removed from command, 140.

CRAIG, Major-Gen. Sir JAMES, former Governor of Cape, 391; retires from command in Sicily, 169; Governor-Generalship in Canada, 390 ff.; mentioned, 170.
CRAMER, JOHN, musician, 42.
CRAUFURD, Gen. CHARLES, M.P., on Walcheren expedition, 299.
CRAUFURD, Brig.-Gen. Sir ROBERT, sent to S. America, 168, 169; in Buenos Ayres, 203, 204; commands successively Light Brigade and Light Division in Spain from 1809, 280, 344 ff.; action on Coa, 346; at Bussaco, 348, 350.
as Commissary, 344; Wellington's leniency to, 334; as disciplinarian, 335.
CRETE, mentioned, 285.
CREWE, Lord, votes as junior Baron, 165.
CRIMINAL LAW, reform of, 233.
CROFTER, in Highlands, 395, 396.
CROKER, JOHN, M.P., in palliation of corruption, 264.
CROMARTY, disturbance in, 1792, 395.
CROME, JOHN, painter, 53.
CROTCH, WILLIAM, musical composer, 43.
CUESTA, Spanish General in Talavera campaign, 275 ff.
CUMBERLAND, Wordsworth's native county, 25 ff.; Dalton's, 81.
CUMBERLAND, RICHARD, on tolerance of adultery, 417.
CUMMING, GEORGE, Scottish M.P., votes against Melville, 411.
CURAÇOA, West Indies, Dutch possession, captured 1807, 158; mentioned, 379.
CURRENCY, see BULLION COMMITTEE.
CURTIS, Rear-Admiral, on Cape Dutch, 386.
CURWEN, JOHN, M.P., proposal for parliamentary reform, 265, 266.
CUSTOMS in India, 106.
CUXHAVEN, in British occupation in 1809, 321.

DALE, DAVID, his New Lanark Mills, 396; Sutherland Mill, 396; mentioned, 403.
DALRYMPLE, Lt.-Gen. Sir HEW, as Governor of Gibraltar, 242; in Portugal in 1806, 239, 242 ff.
DALTON, JOHN, chemist, 81, 82; his school, 77; on female dress, 416.
DANCING, change of fashion, 415.
DARNLEY, Earl of, his inquiry on national defence, 336.
DARTMOUTH, Earl of, President of Board of Control, 97.
DARWIN, Dr., son of Erasmus Darwin, mention, 87, 88.
DARWIN, Dr. ERASMUS, his poetry, 23; his scientific work, 86, 87; death, 87, 88.
DAULAT RAO SINDHIA, Maratha Chief, 112; defeated by Holkar, 113; war with British, 119 ff.; treachery of his officers, 130; unfriendly relations with, 133, 137; Hariana conquered from, 366.
DAVOUT, Marshal, wins Battle of Auerstadt, 1806, 181.
DEBATING SOCIETIES in London, 305, 416.
DELABORDE, Gen., defeated at Roliça, 240.
DELHI, Moghul capital, 121; Battle of, September 14, 1803, 124, 122, 123; capture, 125; annexation of neighbouring territory, 137.
DELICATE INVESTIGATION (into conduct of Princess of Wales), 189.
DENMARK, resentment at Order in Council of January, 1807, 226, 210, 211; relations with Great Britain, 209 ff.; expedition against, 213 ff.; criticism

INDEX 475

of its policy, 213, 217 ff.; her incapacity to resist France, 218 ff.; effect of the expedition on Anglo-Russian relations, 221, 222; seizure of Heligoland and Danish West Indian islands, 223; intrepidity of Danes in war on commerce, 217.
Danish appreciation of vaccination, 89.
DEPOPULATION of Scottish Highlands, 394 ff.
DE QUINCEY, THOMAS, his admiration for Wordsworth, 30, 33.
DERBY, Earl of, Chancellor of the Duchy, 1806, 150.
DERBY, Countess of, see FARREN.
DERBYSHIRE, Duke of Devonshire's landscape gardening in, 57.
DE ROCCA, quoted, 112.
DESPARD, Col., mentioned, 177.
DEVONSHIRE, as native county of Coleridge, 25; of Turner, 51; manners in, 415, 416.
DEVONSHIRE, Duke of, taste in 1771 (circa), 57.
DEYS, Mediterranean, 305.
DIBDIN, CHARLES, 40, 41; in opera, 43.
DIBDIN, THOMAS, in opera, 43.
DIET, of Highland farmers, 395; of Scottish factory children, 404.
DIG, Battle of and capture, 1804, 131; ceded temporarily, 132.
DINNER PARTIES, 416.
DISRAELI, allusion to one of his novels, 158. *Also see* BEACONSFIELD.
DISTILLERIES, Irish, 232, 263, 264; British, 233.
DIXON, "Admiral" (i.e. Flag Officer) in Baltic, 321.
DOAB, between Ganges and Jumna, 123.
DOBBS, Capt., his mention of surgery, 87.
DOCKS, construction of, 93.
DOLBEN, Sir WILLIAM, M.P., his Slave Trade Bill, 162.
DONKIN, Col., at Talavera, 276, 277.
D'OUBRIL, PIERRE JACOVLEVITCH, Russian Minister in Paris, 159, 160, 173.
DOURO, Wellington's crossing in 1809, 274.
DOWNING COLLEGE, building of, 56.
DRAMA, state in England, 44 ff.; Godwin's Antonio, 59.
DRESS, change in female, 416.
DROUET, French General in Peninsula, 358, 359.
DRURY, Rear-Admiral WILLIAM, at Macao, 376, 377.
DRURY LANE THEATRE, destroyed by fire, 297.
DUBLIN, Repeal movement, 320.
DUCKWORTH, Vice-Admiral Sir JOHN, fights action off San Domingo, 1806, 156; commands expedition to Dardanelles, 1807, 191 ff.
DUELS, Castlereagh and Canning, 293; Paget and Lady C. Wellesley's brother, 417.
DUFF, JAMES GRANT, historian of the Marathas, 122.
DUMONT, ÉTIENNE, translator of Bentham, 65.
DUNCAN, JONATHAN, Governor of Bombay, a letter of, 371.
DUNDAS, Lord, a patron of the steamboat, 91.
DUNDAS, Gen. Sir DAVID, appointed Commander-in-Chief, 1809, 262.
DUNDAS, HENRY, President of Board of Control, 97; attitude towards the Slave Trade, 163; his colonial protégés, 393. *Also see* MELVILLE.
DUNDAS, Hon. ROBERT, President of Board of Control, 1807, 97, 197; Chief Secretary, 1809, 272; refuses Secretaryship for War, 296; returns

to Presidentship of Board of Control, 297; refuses Admiralty, 1810, 304.
DUNDEE, population, 403; harbour works, 94.
DUNN, THOMAS, Canadian, 393.
D'URBAN, BENJAMIN, Beresford's Chief of the Staff, 340.
DUTCH, in French Army, 112; discovery of N.W. Australia, 380.
DUTCH POSSESSIONS; Wellesley's designs on Java, 101. *Also see* CAPE OF GOOD HOPE, CEYLON, CURAÇOA, MOLUCCAS, SUMATRA.
DYSENTERY in army in Spain, 283.

EAST INDIA COMPANY, relations with China, 140, 376, 377; miscellaneous possessions, 141; relations with Ceylon, 141; appointment of cadets, 263. *Also see* EAST INDIES.
EAST INDIES, character of the Company's administration, 96 ff.; Wellesley's Governor-Generalship, 1798–1805, 100 ff.; Cornwallis's, 1805, 136, 137; Barlow's, 1805–1806, 137 ff.; Lauderdale's appointment refused, 179; Minto's 1806, 363 ff.; trade, 105, 141, 326; injury to trade, 157, 377.
ÉBLÉ, French artillery General at Bussaco, 349.
ECONOMY, public, importance attached to, 295, 302.
EDEN, Sir FREDERIC, on Scottish Highlanders, 395.
EDGEWORTH, MARIA, 67 ff.; her view of the Irish, 39, 68; her Tales, 70; allusions to Castle Rackrent, 70, 108; allusion to Ormond, 397.
EDGEWORTH, RICHARD, Father of Maria, 68.
EDINBURGH, 405 ff.; study of German in, 36; connection with Mrs. Siddons, 48; Raeburn, 52; Geology, 80; Rennie, 92; without a Poor Law assessment, 400; collieries near, 402; its police, 410.
EDINBURGH REVIEW, 71 ff.; its views on poetry, 73, 38; Byron on, 38; on restriction of Scottish emigration, 396.
EDINBURGH UNIVERSITY, 400, 407, 408, 75.
EDUCATION, interest of the Edgeworths in, 68, 69; elementary, 77 ff., 184; of engineers, 92; in Ceylon, 142; in Scotland, 400, 404.
EGGS, a luxury in the Scottish Highlands, 395.
EGYPT, allusions to the expedition of 1801, 101, 105, 106, 114, 115; that of 1807, 194, 195, 200 ff.; Napoleon's designs upon, 195, 235.
ELDON, Lord Chancellor, 1806, 197; opposes a church reform, 233; carries the Cabinet letter to the King, 295; anxiety for prosecutions, 307; his weight in the Cabinet, 294; reforms in the Scottish judicature, 409; mentioned, 149, 166, 292.
ELECTIONS, general, of 1806, 180; of 1807, 199, 200.
ELECTRICITY, state of the science in England, 84; Byron on, 92.
ELGIN, Seventh Earl of, obtains Parthenon sculptures, 56.
"ELIOT, GEORGE", clerical study in her Adam Bede, 414.
ELIZABETH, QUEEN, her charter to E.I. Company, 96; a Statute of her reign, 403; mentioned, 167.
ELLENBOROUGH, Lord, Lord Chief Justice, joins Cabinet, 149; debate on his position, 151, 152; views on Catholic question, 187; tries Perry, 307; and Cobbett, 313.
ELLIOT, WILLIAM, Chief Secretary for Ireland, 150; share in emancipation proposals of 1807, 186, 187.
ELPHINSTONE, MOUNTSTUART, concludes Afghan Treaty, 365.

INDEX 477

EMBARGO ACT, American, 1807, 229, 268; its effect, 323, 324.
EMIGRATION, Scottish, to N. America, 393 ff.
ENCYCLOPAEDIA, BRITISH, article on medicine, 87.
ENCYCLOPAEDIA, ENGLISH, 80, 81.
"ENDLESS WILLIE", 408.
ENGINEERING, 90 ff.
ENGINEERS, ROYAL, work on Lines of Torres Vedras, 353, 354.
ENGLAND, EAST OF, art in, 53.
ENGRAVING, 53, 54.
ENTAIL, its advantage in Scotland, 408.
EQUITY, in Scotland, 409.
ERFURT, meeting of Emperors at, 1808, 248.
ERSKINE, Lord, Lord Chancellor, 1806, 149, 150, 189; at impeachment of Melville, 165, 166; on Orders in Council, 230; his Bill for Prevention of Cruelty to Animals, 266.
ERSKINE, Hon. DAVID, son of the above, Minister to the U.S., 268.
ERSKINE, Hon. HENRY, leader of the Scottish Bar, 409; his jests, 408; declines post of Lord Justice Clerk, 411, 412.
ESKGROVE, Lord, Scottish Judge, 408.
ETHICS, subject in Calcutta College, 109.
ETON, education at, of Porson, 76; of Lord Wellesley, 99; of Arthur Wellesley, 114; of Burdett's son, 309; mentioned, 79.
EUROPEAN REGIMENTS, E.I. Company's, 116, 372.
EUROPEANS IN INDIA, 110; deterioration, 115; in Maratha service, 121, 122; irreligion, 138.
EVANGELICAL, name of a party in Scottish Church, 401; evangelical influence in English Church, 414, 415.
EVANGELICAL AND METHODIST MAGAZINE, 413.
EXCISE, in India, 106.

FACTORIES, improvement in factory conditions, 418; Scottish, 403, 404.
FALMOUTH, mentioned, 414.
FARINGTON, on Scottish manners, 407; on English, 416.
FARMS, in the Scottish Highlands, 395, 396; in the Lowlands, 398, 399, 402.
FARREN, Miss, actress becomes Countess of Derby, 44.
FARRUKHABAD, surprise of Holkar at, 131.
FASHIONS in dress, 416.
FERDINAND, King of Naples and Sicily, see SICILY.
FERDINAND, Spanish Prince, resigns throne, 1808, 234.
FERGUSON, Major-Gen., at Battle of Vimeiro, 241.
FERRI DE ST. CONSTANT, Italian traveller, on science in England, 83.
FEVER, Guadiana fever, 283, 333; Walcheren fever, 289, 299.
FIELD, JOHN, musician, 42.
FIÉVÉE, on English want of musical taste, 41.
FINANCE, English, see BUDGET, etc.
    Indian, 106; state in 1805, 133, 134.
    Scottish, 399; grant to Scottish clergy, 401.
FIRST LORD OF THE ADMIRALTY, Howick, 1806, 149; T. Grenville, 179; Mulgrave, 1807, 197; Yorke, 1810, 304; weakness of First Lord's position, 377.
FISHERIES, in Scottish Highlands, 396.

FITZPATRICK, Gen., intimate of Fox, Secretary at War, 1806, **150**; visit to Fox, **175**.
FITZWILLIAM, Earl, President of the Council, 1806, **150**; visit to Fox, **175**; resigns Presidentship, remaining in Cabinet, **179**; sickness of, **187**; recovery of his interest in Yorkshire, **199**.
FLAXMAN, JOHN, sculptor, **54**.
FLETCHER, dramatist, mentioned, **70**.
FLETCHER, Lt.-Col. ROBERT, R.E., engineer of Lines of Torres Vedras, **331, 354**.
FLOGGING, in militia, **307**.
FLUSHING, its importance, **285**; capture, **287**; prolonged retention, **289, 298, 299**.
FORBES, Marshal JOHN, Portuguese Army, **332**.
FOREIGN SECRETARY, Fox, 1806, **149**; Howick, **179**; Canning, 1807, **197**; Bathurst (temporary), 1809, **297**; Wellesley, **297**.
FORJAZ, MIGUEL PEREIRA, plan for training militia officers, **341**.
FORTS, in Indian warfare, **122**.
FOSTER, JOHN, Irish Chancellor of the Exchequer, 1807, **198**; introduces Irish budget, 1808, **232**.
FOX, CAROLINE, relations with Moore, **250**.
FOX, CHARLES JAMES, Bonaparte's relations with, **144**; position at Pitt's death, **144** ff.; Grenville an ally only, **146**; becomes Foreign Secretary, 1806, **149**; his party, **150, 148**; argues in favour of prerogative, **152**; on the difficulties of Government, **153**; tribute to the King, **155**; on war with Prussia, **155**; his policy of conciliation of the U.S. as connected with the blockade of 1806, **182, 224**; opens negotiations for peace, **158** ff., **173, 174**; appointed a Manager in impeachment of Melville, **164**; moves resolution for Abolition of Slave Trade, **164**; his heavy duties in parliament, **174**; his last illness and death, September 15, 1806, **174, 175**; his contribution to the new order of things, **178, 179**.
on impeachment of Wellesley, **134**; his coalition with North mentioned, **148**; his History, **145, 175**; quoted as an authority on parliamentary law, **308**.
friendship with Crabbe, **21**; attitude towards Wordsworth, **30**; love of liberty, **145**; no love for reform, **145**; dislike of a standing army connected with his absorption in the past, **145, 146**; his two "glorious things", **162**; enlightened views on the subject of nationality, **156**; catholic tastes, **174**; industry in office, **174**; high sense of honour, **175**; not a nineteenth-century name, **176**; his honesty, **179**; popularity, **200**.
mentioned, **47, 168**.
FOX, Mrs., wife of the above, **175**.
FOX, Gen. HENRY, commands troops in Mediterranean, **168, 182**; despatches expedition to Alexandria, **194, 195**.
FOY, French General, his knowledge of Portugal, **347**; his opinions quoted, **349**; sent to Paris, **358**.
FRANCE, French influence in India, **113, 100, 121**; in Persia, **235, 365**; apprehensions from, in China, **376**; relations with the Cape of Good Hope, **387**; Goree taken from the French, **388**; associations with Scotland, **397**.
For European relations *see* NAPOLEON and WAR WITH FRANCE.
Also see headings under FRENCH.
FRANCIS II, Emperor of Austria, mentioned, **288**.

INDEX 479

FRANCIS, Sir PHILIP, quoted, 321.
FRASER, Major-Gen. ALEXANDER, commands expedition to Egypt, 1807, 201, 202.
FRASER, Major-Gen. JOHN, wins Battle of Dig, 131.
FREDERICK, Crown Prince of Denmark, reception of Jackson in 1807, 213; reason for his refusal of British proposal, 213, 216, 217.
FREDERICK THE GREAT, mentioned, 123.
FREDERICK WILLIAM, King of Prussia, *see* PRUSSIA.
FRENCH, in Cape Town, 387.
FRENCH CANADIANS, agitation during Craig's Governor-Generalship, 390 ff.
FRENCH EMIGRANTS; an officer in South America, 204.
FRENCH GRAND ARMY, its composition, 112.
FRENCH LANGUAGE, explanatory of Bentham, 65.
FRENCH POSSESSIONS IN E. INDIES, 100, 101; seizure and retention of those in India, 120; conquest of the islands in the Indian Ocean, 377 ff.
FRENCH REVOLUTION, as a movement in human thought, 17; attitude of Lake Poets towards, 33, 34; general English attitude towards, 59, 60; Godwin's attitude, 60.
FRERE, JOHN HOOKHAM, diplomatic representative in Madrid, 246, 248.
FREUND, Cambridge fellow, 34.
FRIEDLAND, Battle of, June 14, 1807, 208.
FUNDHOLDERS, their unclaimed dividends, 232; Curwen's and Cobbett's aversion to, 145, 265.
FURNITURE, 57.
FUSELI, HENRY, painter, 50.

GAIKWAR OF BARODA, Maratha Chief, 112.
GALEN, as medical authority, 89.
GALICIA, evacuated by French, 274.
GALLATIN, ALBERT, on Napoleon's perfidy, 329.
GALLOWAY, thirlage in, 399.
GALVANI, Italian scientist, 84.
GAMBIER, Admiral JAMES, in naval command against Denmark, 1807, 213 ff.; becomes Lord Gambier, 216; action in Aix Roads, 270 ff.; unsuitability for First Lord of the Admiralty, 304.
GANGES, alluvial plain of the, 102.
GANTEAUME, Vice-Admiral French Navy, escape from Toulon, 1808, 236.
GARDANE, French General, mission to Persia, 235, 365.
GARDANNE, French General in Peninsula, 358, 359.
GARDENING, 57.
GARLIKE, BENJAMIN, Minister in Copenhagen, 210, 211.
GAS, its introduction for illuminating purposes, 92.
GAWILGARH, capture of, 128.
GELL, Sir WILLIAM, traveller; his visit to Wellington, 355, 356.
GENTLEMAN'S MAGAZINE, 71; quoted, 55.
GENTZ, FRIEDERICH VON, correspondent of Jackson, 216; of Canning, 288, 289.
GEOLOGICAL SOCIETY, foundation of, 80, 81.
GEOLOGY, state of, 80, 81.

480 ENGLAND IN THE NINETEENTH CENTURY

GEORGE III, audience to Grenville, 1806, **147**; Fox's tribute to, **155**; action in crisis of March, 1807, **185** ff.; Portland's letter to, **189**; attitude towards Princess of Wales, **189**; suggests removal of Castlereagh, **290**; audience to Canning during crisis of 1809, **292**; jubilee of 1809, **298**; interferes in appointment of First Lord of the Admiralty, **304**; an article against, **307**; gives Beresford the K.B., **350**; final mental derangement, **359, 360**.

his taste for music, **41**; drama, **44**; painting, **50**; obstruction of Bentham's proposed prison, **66**; interest in education, **79**; astronomy, **79**; feelings on Catholic question, **294**; interest in sheep, **382**.

GEORGE, PRINCE OF WALES, his party in 1806, **148**; conversation with Moira on crisis of March, 1807, **188**.

his taste for music, **41**.

GERMAN LITERATURE, **31, 36, 67**.

GERMAN MUSIC, **41**.

GERMAN PHILOSOPHY, **57, 58, 32**.

GERMANS, in Cape Town, **387**.

soldiers, in French Army, **112, 280**.

in British Army, *see* KING'S GERMAN LEGION.

GERMANY, keen competitor of Birmingham in hardware, **153**; north-west Germany blockaded, 1806, **182**; expedition to N. Germany, 1807, **209**; revolt against Napoleon in N. Germany in 1809, **285**; trade with, **321, 322**; Craufurd's knowledge of German language and military methods, **346**.

GIBBS, Sir VICARY, Attorney-General, 1807, **197, 198**; prosecutes Cobbett, **313**.

GIFFORD, WILLIAM, journalist, **74**.

GIG-MILLS, agitation against, **199**; legislation, **418**.

GILCHRIST, ALEXANDER, biographer of Blake, **29**.

GILLESPIE, Lt.-Col. ROLLO, suppresses Vellore mutiny, **139**.

GIRTIN, THOMAS, painter, **53**.

GLASGOW, **403** ff.; Poor Law in, **400**; the University, **400**; engineering works, **93**.

GLASS, manufacture at Newcastle, **396**.

GLEES, **41**.

GLENGARRY, emigration from, **393**.

GOA, Portuguese possession in India, occupied by British, **376**; danger to, from French, **377**.

GODWIN, WILLIAM, **58** ff.; influence on Wordsworth, **27**; controversy with Malthus, **60, 61**; utilitarianism, **64**; mentioned, **45, 63**.

GOETHE, Scottish admiration for, **36**; mentioned, **31**.

GOLDSMITH, dramatist, mentioned, **47**.

GOMM, WILLIAM, military officer, impression of Wellington, **335**.

GOOD, Dr. JOHN, **87**.

GORDON, Duke of, treatment of his tenants, **395**.

GORDON, Duchess of, as social leader, **407**.

GORDON, CATHERINE, mother of Lord Byron, **48, 49**.

GORDON RIOTS, an allusion to, **198**.

GORE, FRANCIS, Lieutenant-Governor of Upper Canada in 1807, **394**.

GOREE, an expedition from, **270**.

GOWER, Major-Gen. LEVESON-, *see* LEVESON-GOWER, Major-Gen.

GOWER, Lord GRANVILLE LEVESON, Ambassador in St. Petersburg, **218, 221, 222**.

INDEX

GOWDIE, Major-Gen. FRANCIS, commanding Madras Army, 1809, 371.
GRAHAM, MARIA, traveller in India, 110.
GRAHAM, Major-Gen. THOMAS, his career, 246, 247; advice as to Spanish Army, 247; commanding at Cadiz, 332; mentioned, 334.
GRANBY, Marquis of, Lake's services under, 123.
GRAND PORT, Mauritius, Pym's action off, 1810, 338.
GRANT, Sir JAMES, of Rothiemurchus, 396.
GRATTAN, HENRY, mentioned, 263.
GRAY, poet, criticized by Wordsworth, 26.
GREAT BRITAIN—some foreign opinions of—a vampire, 215; a firebrand, 222, 267, 268; disbelief in her success, 215, 229; "always two months too late", 250.
GREECE, Wilkins's travels in, 56.
GREEK ART, architecture, 55, 56; sculpture, 56.
GREENOCK, engineering works, 93.
GREENWICH OBSERVATORY, 79, 80.
GREGORY, OLINTHUS, writer on mechanics, 92.
GRENVILLE, Lord, position on Pitt's death, 146 ff.; becomes Prime Minister, 1806, 147 ff.; his party, 148, 150; designs expedition to Mexico, 168; refusal of loan to Russia, 209; Catholic emancipation question and plans for Irish recruiting, 185; dissensions in his Cabinet, 187, 188; resignation, 188; policy misrepresented by Tories, 199; indifference to office, 294; prospect of office at end of 1810, 359.
    his zeal for abolition of Slave Trade, 163, 164; views on the Danish expedition, 219; pessimism on the war, 261; on extravagance, 264; a letter of a planter to, 389; efforts towards Scottish judicial reform, 409.
    his gardening interests, 57; never more than an ally of Fox, 146; attachment to Pitt, 146; not a popular character, 200; comparison with his brother Thomas, 179.
    mentioned, 155, 165, 166, 177.
GRENVILLE, THOMAS, succeeds Howick as First Lord, 1806, 179; retirement from public life, 315; comparison with Lord Grenville, 179; mentioned, 187.
GRENVILLES, an eighteenth-century name, 176; Wellington's feelings towards the family, 337.
GREY, first Earl, his death, 230.
GREY, CHARLES, afterwards Earl, becomes Lord Howick, 1806, 149; First Lord of the Admiralty, 1806, 149; appointed a Manager in impeachment of Melville, 164; becomes Foreign Secretary and leader of the House of Commons, 179; relations with Denmark, 210; his part in crisis of 1807, 185 ff.; proposal as to Irish tithes, 207; succeeds his father as Earl Grey, 230; refuses office, 1809, 294; attacks Perceval in House of Lords, 314, 315; observation on rearing an enemy navy, 327; prospect of office at end of 1810, 359.
    observation on Scottish members, 411; views as to continental blockade, 225; friendship with Crabbe, 21; not a popular character, 200.
    mentioned, 177.
GROSVENOR, Lady, vaccination of her son, 90.
GRUNDY, Mrs., character in a play, 46.
GUADELOUPE, French apprehensions for, 270; conquered, 1810, 323.
GUARDS, at Talavera, 279.
GUIANA, cotton in, 389.

GUIANA, FRENCH, conquest of, 1809, 269.
GUNBOATS, on Tagus, 356.
GUSTAVUS, CHARLES, his exploit of 1658 mentioned, 220.
GWALIOR, fort of Sindhia, restored to him, 137.

HABEAS CORPUS, writ of, not sued out by Burdett, 312.
HAILEYBURY COLLEGE, founded for Indian Civil Servants, 109.
HALFORD, Sir HENRY, physician, 88.
HAMBURG, Bernadotte at, 213; reports and a letter from, 213.
HAMILTON, Lord ARCHIBALD, Scottish Whig M.P., 411.
HAMILTON, ELIZABETH, her Cottagers of Glenburnie, 398.
HANDEL, English admiration for, 43.
HANGER, Hon. GEORGE, honours Burdett, 312, 313.
HANOVER, occupation by Prussia declared permanent, 154, 155; Fox on, 155; blockaded by British, 182; France's offer to restore to George III, 161; effect of this on Prussia, 161, 162; jealousy of Hanoverian troops, 307. *Also see* KING'S GERMAN LEGION.
HARBOUR WORKS, construction of Scottish, 93, 94.
HARDWICKE, Earl, influences Yorke against Perceval, 296.
HARIANA, annexation of, 366.
HARRIS, Rifleman, on Craufurd, 345.
HARROWBY, Earl of, President of Board of Control, 1809, 291; considered for Premier, 291; resigns, 297; his efforts on behalf of the poorer clergy, 415.
HARROW SCHOOL, education at, of Byron, 37.
HASTINGS, WARREN, consulted by Castlereagh, 109; mentioned, 103, 134.
HAUGWITZ, Prussian Count, his Treaty of 1805 not ratified, 154; a saying of his, 250.
HAWKESBURY, Lord, refuses Premiership on Pitt's death, 147; Home Secretary, 1807, 197; War Secretary, 1809, 296; becomes Earl of Liverpool, 296; mentioned, 155, 198, 294. *Also see* LIVERPOOL.
HAYDON, BENJAMIN, painter, 56.
HAZLITT, WILLIAM, 70; on Wordsworth, 27; mentioned, 177.
HEAT, theories of, 81, 85, 86.
HELIGOLAND, captured from Danes, 223; its importance for trade, 321.
HEMP, shortage of, 327.
HENRY, WILLIAM, scientist, 82.
HERMAND, Lord, mentioned, 408, 409.
HERSCHEL, WILLIAM, astronomer, 79.
HERTFORD, Marquis of, title to which Yarmouth succeeded, 158.
HIDES, a product of Cape Colony, 388.
HILL, Major-Gen. ROWLAND, at Talavera, 276 ff.; on Tagus in 1810, 332; rejoins Wellington, 347; at Bussaco, 348; on hardiness of the French, 355; his reliability, 334.
HILL, ROWLAND, evangelical preacher, visit to Scotland mentioned, 401.
HINDUS, in Company's Army, 117, 138; military form of Hinduism professed by Sikhs, 121; missions to, 363 ff.
HIPPOCRATES, as medical authority, 89.
HISTORY, 57; subject in Calcutta College, 109; Fox's historical work, 145, 175.
HOBART, Tasmania, founded, 1804, 386.

INDEX

HOGG, JAMES, the Ettrick Shepherd, 40.
HOLKAR, Maratha Chief, *see* JASWANT RAO HOLKAR.
HOLLAND, blockaded, 1806, **182**; strength of hostile fleet in Dutch ports, **211**; inquiry regarding captured Dutch property, **263**; wheat trade, **268, 269**; Louis King of Holland hands over Flushing to Napoleon, **285**; abdication of Louis and annexation of Holland to France, **321**; preference shown to, by U.S. over France, **329**. For hostilities in 1809 *see* WALCHEREN.
HOLLAND, Lord, his view of office as Prime Minister, **152**; idea of his becoming Foreign Secretary, **174**; becomes Lord Privy Seal, **179**; his part in crisis of 1807, **185** ff.; mentioned, **162, 175**.
HOMER; Flaxman's illustrations, **54**; the Grenville edition, **76**.
HOME SECRETARY, Spencer, 1806, **149**; Hawkesbury, 1807, **197**; Ryder 1809, **296, 297**.
    Scotland formally under the Home Secretary, **411**.
HOOGHLY, drowning by Hindus of children in, **365**.
HOPE, CHARLES, Lord Advocate, **400**.
HOPE, Lt.-Gen. JOHN, in Peninsula, **251** ff.; in Walcheren expedition, **287**.
HOPPNER, JOHN, painter, **50**.
HOPE AND COMPANY, international bankers, **329**.
HORNER, FRANCIS, contributor to Edinburgh Review, **71, 177**; Chairman of Bullion Committee, **316** ff.; on Scottish finance, **399**; on Scottish legal expenses, **408**.
HOTTENTOTS, **387**.
HOWICK, *see* GREY, CHARLES.
HUGO, VICTOR, his liberation of the French drama, **23**.
HUGUES, VICTOR, French General in W.I., his surrender, **269**.
HULL, *see* KINGSTON-UPON-HULL.
HUMBER, dock, **93**.
HUME, DAVID, read by weavers, **405**.
HUNT, LEIGH, dramatic critic, **45, 47**.
HUNTER, Capt. JOHN, R.N., Governor of New South Wales, **381**.
HUNTER, Dr. JOHN, **86**.
HUNTS, THE, mentioned, **177**.
HUSKISSON, WILLIAM, Secretary of the Treasury, 1807, **197, 338, 339**; leaves office with Canning, 1809, **296**; on Bullion Committee, **316, 317**; management of war finance, **338**.
HUTTON, geologist, **80**.
HYDERABAD, French influence removed from, **100**; annexation to, from Mysore, **101**; British guarantee obtained by Treaty, **113**; menaced by Sindhia, **119, 126**; by Holkar's forces, **367**; mutiny of the subsidiary force at the capital, **373** ff.
HYTHE, military canal, **93**.

IDEALISM, in literature, Blake's, **17** ff.; Crabbe's involuntary tribute to, **20**; Wordsworth's, **27** ff., **64**; Godwin's and Coleridge's, **64**.
INCOME TAX, raised in 1806 to 10 per cent., **152**; debate on, **152, 153**.
INDIA, French designs on, **100, 111**; plans for overland invasion, **195, 235, 365**; supplies sent from, to New South Wales, **381**; Indian sheep in New South Wales, **382**; Moira's exploits mentioned, **149, 150**. For general references *see* EAST INDIES, etc.
INDIGO, in India, **105**.

INDUSTRIES, Scottish, 402 ff.; Scottish Kelp industry, 396.
INFANTRY, arrangement of, in Peninsula to meet the need for skirmishing troops, 276; improvement in training, 178, 344, 345.
INSURANCE, rates for shipping, 230.
INVERNESS-SHIRE, a chieftain in, 396.
IONIAN ISLANDS, Republic of, becomes French possession, 236; its importance, 284, 285; capture of four of the seven islands, 285; of a fifth, 323.
IRELAND, appointments for, in 1806, 150; disturbances in 1807, 184; Roman Catholic question, 184 ff.; dependence of Whig party upon, 184; appointments for, in 1807, 198; Irish M.P.s, 199, 200; Irish question in 1807, 207; threatened with invasion, 212; strength of volunteers, 234; frauds in, 262; tithe question, 266; Dundas Chief Secretary, 1809, 272; repeal movement, 320; military value, 320; economic conditions, 320.

views of the Irish character, 39, 68; Irish Melodies, 39; the Royal Canal, 92, 93; the Wellesleys, 99, 114; Irish sheep in New South Wales, 382; comparison of Irish with the Scottish Highlanders, 397. *Also see* BUDGET, CHIEF SECRETARY, etc., LOANS.
IRISH, in French Army, 112; recruiting for British Army, 185; in British Navy, 326; in Canada, 393, 394; in Glasgow, 404.
IRVINE, ALEXANDER, quoted, 395.
ISCHIA, island off Naples temporarily captured from French in 1809, 284.
ISLE OF FRANCE, *see* MAURITIUS.
ITALIANS, in electrical science, 84; Italian force employed in conquest of an Ionian Island, 323.
ITALY, completion of French conquest, 1808, 236; question of a diversion in, in aid of Austria, 284.

Wilkins's travels, 56. *Also see* NAPLES, etc.
ITHACA, Ionian island, captured from French in 1809, 285.

JACKSON, FRANCIS, Minister in Berlin, sent in 1807 on special mission to Denmark, 211 ff.; mentioned, 250.
JACOBINISM, Wellesley's hostility to, 99; its disappearance, 177; mentioned, 19.
JACOBITISM, in Scotland, 396, 397, 406.
JAGANNATH, temple of, in Orissa, 125, 364.
JAIPUR, Indian State, invaded by Holkar, 129; sacrificed by British, 138.
JAMAICA, condition of, during decade, 389.
JASWANT RAO HOLKAR, Maratha Chief, 112; defeats Peshwa and Sindhia, 113; retirement, 118; danger to Berar from, 119; war with British, 122, 128 ff., 137, 138; Treaty with, 138; his lunacy, 366; apprehensions from his forces, 366, 374.
JATS, 129, 131.
JAVA, Dutch Island, expedition projected against, 101.
JEFFERSON, THOMAS, President of the United States, policy towards Great Britain, 227 ff., 327; letter to, from Madison, 329, 330
JEFFREY, FRANCIS, Editor of the Edinburgh Review, 71 ff., 177; as conversationalist, 407.
JENA, Battle of, October 14, 1806, 181.
JENKINS, RICHARD, Resident with Sindhia, 136, 137.
JENNER, EDWARD, discoverer of vaccination, 89, 90; rewarded, 208.
JESUIT'S BARK, prohibited from entering enemy ports, 233.

INDEX 485

JEVONS, STANLEY, his cost of living scale, 417, 418.
JOHN, Prince, Regent of Portugal; question of his withdrawal to Brazil, 173; coerced by Napoleon, 222; escape to Brazil, 223, 342.
JOHNSON, Dr. SAMUEL, mentioned, 21, 264.
JOHNSTON, Major GEORGE, deposes Bligh from Governorship of New South Wales, 384; is cashiered, 385.
JOHNSTONE, patron of Telford, 94.
JONES, Sir HARFORD, mission to Persia, 1807, 235, 366.
JONES, JOHN GALE, imprisoned for breach of parliamentary privilege, 306; his case taken up by Burdett, 306 ff.; his release, 312.
JOURDAN, Marshal, Chief of the French staff at Talavera, 275.
JUDGES, compatibility of office of a Judge with a seat in the Cabinet, 151; difficulty over, in Colonies, 393.
    Scottish, 408 ff.
JUMNA, character of the river, 125.
JUNOT, Gen., invades Portugal, 1807, 222, 223; defeated at Vimeiro, 1808, 239 ff.; concludes Convention of Cintra, 242 ff.; commands corps under Masséna, 347, 349; mentioned, 159, 353.
JUNTA, CENTRAL, in Spain, 246; Treaty of Alliance concluded with, 284; escape to Cadiz, 332.
JUNTAS, Spanish and Portuguese provincial, 239, 247, 251.
JURIES, special, Bentham on, 66.
    Scottish, 410.
JUSTICE, administration in Bengal, 106; Supreme Courts in the Presidency Towns of India, 110.
JUSTICES OF THE PEACE, fixing of wages by, 418.
    Scottish, 410.

KABUL, see AFGHANISTAN.
KANDY, war with King of, 142, 143.
KAUFFMANN, ANGELICA, painter, 50.
KEATS, Capt., R.N., in Battle of San Domingo, 156, 157.
KELLERMANN, French General in Portugal, 1808, 242, 243.
KELLY, MICHAEL, theatrical manager and composer, 43, 44; mentioned, 47.
KELP, manufacture in Scotland, 396.
KEMBLE, JOHN, actor and manager, 44, 45, 48; in O.P. riots, 297, 298.
KEMPT, Col., commanding brigade at Battle of Maida, 171.
KENT, Duke of, fourth son of George III; mutiny during his command at Gibraltar, 140.
KEW, gardens, 86; failure of merino sheep at, 382.
KINCAID, JOHN, Rifle officer, mentioned, 299.
KING, Fox's high view of his prerogative, 152.
KING, Capt. PHILIP GIDLEY, Governor of New South Wales, 383.
KING'S FRIENDS, 148, 301, 302.
KING'S GERMAN LEGION, at Talavera, 279; in 1810, 345, 346.
KINGSTON, in Jamaica, trade, 389.
KINGSTON-UPON-HULL, petition from, 311.

LABOUCHÈRE, PIERRE, engaged in peace negotiations, 328.
LABOUR conditions in Glasgow district, 403 ff.; in 1810 generally, 417, 418.

LABOUR AGITATION, in Lancashire cotton industry in 1808, 231, 232; in Glasgow district in 1810, 404; in Lancashire and elsewhere in England in 1810, 417.

LAKE, Lt.-Gen. GERALD, Commander-in-Chief Bengal Army, his campaign in N. India, 1803, 123 ff.; campaigns of 1804–1805, 129 ff.; makes a treaty with Raja of Bharatpur, 132; successful negotiation with Sindhia, 137; pursuit of and treaty with Holkar, 137, 138; resignation, 138; death, 1808, 138.

    prize-money, 116; popularity, 131, 132; peerages, 134, 138; mentioned, 135.

LAMB, CHARLES, 69, 70; his play, 45; mentioned, 42, 47, 177.

LAMB, MARY, collaboration with her brother, 69, 70; mentioned, 47.

LANARKSHIRE, returns Lord A. Hamilton to Parliament, 411.

LANCASHIRE, engineering works, 92; distress in, 231. *Also see* MANCHESTER.

LANCASTER, JOSEPH, educationalist, 78, 79.

LANDOWNERS, in Scottish Highlands, 395, 396.

LANSDOWNE, first Marquis of, friend of Bentham, 64; depositary of Chatham's traditions, 148; death, 148, 176.

LANSDOWNE, Marquis of, title succeeded to by PETTY, q.v., 315.

LAPISSE, French General in Peninsula,273; mortally wounded at Talavera,279.

LASCELLES, Hon. HENRY, M.P. for Yorkshire, proposes honours for Pitt, 146; loses his seat in 1807, 199.

LASWARI, Battle of, November 1, 1803, 127, 128; its general characteristics, 122, 123.

LAUDERDALE, Lord, carries on negotiations for peace in 1806, 160, 161, 173, 174, 179; Fox's attempt to make him Governor-General of India, 179.

LAVOISIER, chemist, mentioned, 81.

LAW, Bentham on, 64 ff.; Muhammadan law in Indian courts, 106; Hindu and Muhammadan law subjects in Calcutta College, 108, 109; Romilly's reforms in criminal law, 233; a question of parliamentary law raised by Jones's case, 307 ff.; inconsistency of common law with it, 310; law how administered at Sydney, 384; its importance in Scotland, 407 ff.

LAW, INTERNATIONAL, Grenville's application to the case of the attack on Denmark in 1807, 219; continental view regarding blockade, 224; illegality of Orders in Council and Berlin Decree, 224 ff.

LAWRENCE, THOMAS, painter, 50.

LEEDS, steam-engines in, 90.

LEISSÈGUES, French Vice-Admiral, his cruise and capture by Duckworth, 1806, 157.

LEITH, the Leith packet, 52; engineering works at, 93.

LEITH, Major-Gen. CHARLES, in Peninsula under Moore, 257; at Bussaco, 348.

LESLIE, CHARLES, last of the Scottish minstrels, 36.

LEVER, novelist, his Charles O'Malley, 334.

LEVESON-GOWER, Major-General, at Buenos Ayres, 203, 204.

LEWIS, MATTHEW, author, 67.

LEWISHAM, Earl of, President of Board of Control, 1801, 97.

LIGHT, theories of, 84, 85.

LIGHT BRIGADE, formation and training, 344, 345, 178; departure for Portugal, 286; arrival at Talavera, 280; merged in Light Division, 346.

LIGHT DIVISION, origin, 346; work on the Coa, 346; a panic in, 339. *Also see* CRAUFURD.

LINCOLNSHIRE, draining of, 92.

INDEX 487

LINEN in Scottish homes, 398.
LINIERS, Gen., Spanish Army, at Buenos Ayres, 204.
LINOIS, French Admiral, cruise and capture by Warren in 1806, 157.
LISBON, British soldiers in, 334.
LITERARY MAGAZINE, quoted, 321.
LITERATURE, revival in England—poetry, 17 ff.; prose, 57 ff.; the change from the eighteenth to the nineteenth century in literature, 176, 177.
LIVERPOOL, opposition of the town to Abolition of Slave Trade, 162; petition against Orders in Council, 230; petition from, in 1810, 311.
LIVERPOOL, succession of Hawkesbury as Earl of, 1809, 296; becomes War Secretary, 296; reinforcement of Wellington's Army, 337, 338; letters from Wellington, 351, 357.
LOANS, GOVERNMENT, for Great Britain, £18,000,000, £8,000,000, £11,000,000, £8,000,000, borrowed in 1806 and 1808–1810 respectively, 152, 232, 267, 316; £3,000,000 borrowed from Bank in 1808, 232.
Petty's proposed plan of borrowing £11,000,000, annually, 183.
for Ireland, £2,000,000 in 1806, 152; about £4,500,000 in 1808, 232; £3,000,000 in 1809, 267; £4,000,000 in 1810, 316.
for Portugal, £600,000 in 1809, 267.
for Russia refused in 1807, 209.
depreciation of loan after flotation, and suicide of contractors in 1810, 318, 319.
LOCKHART, JOHN, describer of Scottish life, 407.
LOISON, French General in Peninsula, 347.
LONDON, popularity of the war in 1806, 179; merchants of, and Orders in Council, 227, 230; O.P. riots, 297, 298; petition of Common Council against Wellington's pension, 300; debating societies in, 305; Burdett riots, 309 ff.; petition of the Liverymen, 312; steam-engines in, 90; engineering works, 93, 94; flooding of East London in event of invasion, 93; chapels, 414.
LONSDALE, Earl of, his dinner party, 416.
LORD ADVOCATE, 411; Hope as, 400.
LORD CHANCELLOR, see CHANCELLOR.
LORD LIEUTENANT, see VICEROY.
LORD PRESIDENT OF THE COUNCIL, Fitzwilliam, 1806, 150; Sidmouth, 179: Camden, 1807, 197; Canning's proposal for Perceval, 292.
LORD PRIVY SEAL, Sidmouth, 1806, 150; succeeded by Holland, 179; Westmorland, 1807, 197.
LOUGHBOROUGH, see ROSSLYN.
LOUIS, Rear-Admiral Sir THOMAS, in Battle of San Domingo, 157; in the Dardanelles, 190, 191, 194.
LOYAL LUSITANIAN LEGION, 273.
LUCCHESINI, Prussian Minister in Paris, 1806, 161.
LUNACY, treatment, 87.
LUNCH, 416.

MACAO, seizure and evacuation, 376, 377.
MACARTHUR, JOHN, his improvements of stock in sheep in New South Wales, 382, 383; quarrel with Bligh, 383, 384; appointed Secretary to the Colony, 384; goes to England and returns, 385.

MACARTNEY, Earl, mission to China, 140.
MACAULAY, ZACHARY, first Governor of Sierra Leone, 388; Editor of Christian Observer, 364.
MACDIARMID, Perthshire gentleman, 397.
MACDONALD, General, Hogg's song applied to, 40.
MACDOWALL, Lt.-Gen. HAY, Commander-in-Chief Madras Army, refused seat in Council, 368; dispute with Barlow and removal from command, 368 ff.
MACKENZIE, Major-Gen. ALEXANDER, at Talavera, 275 ff.; death, 279.
MACKINTOSH, Sir JAMES, Recorder of Bombay, 110; on German philosophy, 58.
MACQUARIE, Lt.-Col. LACHLAN, Governor of New South Wales, 1809, 385.
MADDEN, Brig.-Gen. GEORGE, Portuguese Army, 340.
MADEIRA, British occupation of, 1807, 223.
MADISON, JAMES, President of the U.S., 268; his foreign policy, 327 ff.
MADRAS CITY, Supreme Court in, 110.
MADRAS PRESIDENCY, government, 97; extent, 100; Clive's resignation as Governor, 110, 111; his succession by Bentinck, 1803, 111; troubles in, 111; Vellore Mutiny, 138; effect of the disturbances in England, 204, 205; Barlow's Governorship, 1807–1812, 367 ff.
emoluments of the Commander-in-Chief, 115; the Madras Army, 116, 118; Madras civilians in Ceylon, 141.
MADRID, rising against the French, 1808, 237; expulsion of Joseph Bonaparte, 246; threatened by Wilson, 282.
MAITLAND, Major-Gen. THOMAS, Governor of Ceylon, 143.
MALAY, slaves from, 387.
MANCHESTER, distress in, 231; mentioned, 82, 90, 404.
MANNERS, Lord, Irish Lord Chancellor, 198.
MANNINGHAM, Col. COOTE, raises 95th Regiment, 344, 345; introduces company system, 345; as Brig-General serves in Peninsula and dies, 256.
MARATHAS, origin of the confederacy, 111, 112; war with, *see* WAR IN INDIA; subsequent oppression by, 366; apprehensions from Holkar's force, 366, 367, 374.
MARSDEN, Rev. SAMUEL, sheep-breeder in New South Wales, 382.
MARTIN, Capt. BYAM, R.N., his ship's company, 326.
MARTIN, Rear-Admiral GEORGE, takes over Mediterranean command, 304.
MARTIN, THOMAS, dramatist, 46.
MARTINIQUE, conquest of, 1809, 269; French effort to save, 270.
MASSÉNA, Marshal, conquers South Italy, 1806, 169, 172; appointed to command army of Portugal, 343; takes Ciudad Rodrigo and Almeida, 344; invades Portugal, 347; halts before Lines, 353 ff.; retires to Santarem, 358.
MASSINGER, mentioned, 70.
MASTER-GENERAL OF THE ORDNANCE, Moira, 1806, 149; Chatham, 1807, 197; Mulgrave, 1810, 305.
MASULIPATAM, mutinous outbreak at, 372.
MAURITIUS, French Island, Indian Ocean, expedition against, planned by Wellesley, 100, 101; preparations against, in 1810, 377, 378; disaster in Grand Port, 378; conquest of, 378, 379.
MAXWELL, Major CHARLES, in capture of Senegal, 270.

INDEX

MEDICINE, state of, 86 ff.
MEDITERRANEAN, politics of, 303; trade of, 323, 324.
MEERUT, annexation of the division, 137.
MEIKLE, ANDREW, his threshing machine, 402.
MELVILLE, Lord, his impeachment, 164 ff., 411; thwarts Ministry in 1809, 296, 304; politeness, 406; mentioned, 176, 188. *Also see* DUNDAS, HENRY.
MERCANTILE MARINE, difficulties of, 326, 327.
MERCURY, Canadian newspaper, 390.
METALS, trade in, with China, 141.
METAPHYSICS, 57, 58.
METCALFE, Sir CHARLES, tribute to Wellesley, 135, 136; early service as political officer with Lake, 138; negotiates treaty with Ranjit Singh, 1809, 365.
METHODISTS, in Scotland, 401; in England, 413, 414.
MEXICO, projected expedition to, 168.
MIDDLESEX, an election riot mentioned, 177; meeting of the freeholders, 237; petition from, 311.
MILAN DECREE, 228; revision promised, 329, 330.
MILITIA, strength, 1807, 205; Militia Transfer Act, 205; Local Militia Act, 234; mutiny of Cambridge Militia, 307; difficulties, 320. Portuguese, 341, 342; under Trant, 351, 352; at the Lines, 356; mentioned, 357.
MILTON, Lord, elected M.P. for Yorkshire, 1807, 199.
MINT, built by Smirke, 55.
MINTO, Lord, President of Board of Control, 1806, 150; Governor-General of India, 1807, 179, 180, 363 ff.; Madras affairs under, 367 ff.; foreign expeditions, 376 ff.
MIRANDA, South American revolutionary, 166.
MISSETT, Major, British Agent in Alexandria, 1807, 201, 202.
MISSIONS, in India, 363 ff.
MITFORD, MARY, novelist, mentioned, 107.
MOGHULS, 102; Sivaji's rebellion against, 111; Maratha relations with, 121; British relations, 125.
MOIRA, Earl of, leader of the Prince of Wales's party, becomes Master-General, 1806, 149, 150; his view of the Cabinet's action in crisis of 1807, 188; condemns Convention of Cintra, 245; mentioned, 187.
MOLUCCAS, Dutch islands, expeditions against, 1810, 379.
MONCRIEFF, Sir HENRY, leader of the Evangelical Party in the Scottish Assembly, 401.
MONRO, THOMAS, early life in Malabar, 107.
MONSON, Lt.-Col. Hon. WILLIAM, campaigns in 1804 in India, 130, 131.
MONTBRUN, General commanding Masséna's cavalry, 344, 352.
MONTESQIEU, allusion to, 151.
MONTE VIDEO, expedition against, planned 1806, 166; captured, February 1807, 168, 169; gallantry in the assault, 206.
MONTHLY MAGAZINE, Taylor's version of Lenore, 31; a writer in, on Smithfield, 415; mentioned, 71.
MONTHLY REVIEW, 71; Malkin's article, 18; a notice of Wordsworth, 26.
MOORE, Lt.-Gen. Sir JOHN, his work in training the Light Brigade, 178, 344, 345; in Sicily, 1806, 172; opinion on Fraser's movements in Egypt, 202; expedition to Sweden, 234, 235; his claim to command in Portugal in August, 1808, 239; arrival in Portugal, 240; observation on state of the

army, 246; appointed to the chief command, 246; his difficulties, 247, 248; insulted by Frere, 248; last campaign, 248 ff.; death, 260; comparison of his last campaign with that of Talavera, 280.
 character, 249, 250; opinion of Graham, 247; hampered by instructions, 338; mentioned, 283, 295.
MOORE, THOMAS, poet, 39, 40.
MORALS, in India, 117; Annual Register on moral standards, 262.
MORE, HANNAH, her Coelebs, 67.
MOREA, mentioned, 323.
MORLAND, GEORGE, painter, 53.
MORNING CHRONICLE, on Danish affairs, 213; supports O.P. rioters, 298; rhyme on Walcheren inquiry, 300; prosecution of the Editor, 307; on the country gentleman (in parliament), 314; a letter to, 393; irreproachable attitude of, under temptation, 417.
MORNING POST, Coleridge's leading articles, 32; windows broken, 313.
MORPHINE, 88.
MORTIER, Marshal, in Spain, 281.
MOSELEY, Dr. BENJAMIN, opposition to vaccination, 89, 90.
MOZAMBIQUE, slaves from, 387.
MUHAMMAD ALI, Turkish General in Egypt, 202.
MUHAMMADANS, as rulers in India, 106; in the army, 117; in northern India, 129.
MULGRAVE, Lord, First Lord of the Admiralty, 197; interviews Cochrane, 271; is a failure at the Admiralty, 302; becomes Master-General, 305; his opinion of Graham, 246; mentioned, 155, 294, 377.
MUNRO, JOHN, acting Lt.-Col., Quarter-Master-General, Madras Army: his report on abolition of tent allowance, 368, 369; his arrest and release, 369; sent as Resident to Travancore, 367; becomes Diwan, 367.
MURAT, Marshal, King of Naples, 1808, 236; captures Capri, 236; operations against, in 1809, 284; attempts invasion of Sicily, 323.
MURDOCK, WILLIAM, inventor, 91; his locomotive, 91; a building illuminated with gas by him, 91, 92.
MURRAY, Lt.-Col. JOHN, captures Indore, 1804, 130.
MURRAY, JOHN, publisher, 74, 75.
MUSIC, state of, 41 ff.; Moore's songs, 39, 40; Hogg's, 40; Dibdin's, 40, 41; glee-clubs, 41, 416.
MUTINY, at Vellore, 138 ff.
 of Cambridge Militia, 307.
 of Madras Army; its causes, 370 ff.; its outbreak and suppression, 372 ff.
 of New South Wales Regiment, 384, 385.
MUTINY ACT, mentioned, 146.
MYSORE, conquest of, 100; arrangements for its government, 101, 104; cavalry at Assaye, 126, 127; in Madras Mutiny, 374.

NABOBS, 115.
NAIRNE, decrease of population in, 394.
NAPIER, Gen. CHARLES, trained by Moore, 250; as a young officer captured at Coruña, 336; liberated and in Wellington's camp, 336; on Wellington, 333, 335; on Craufurd, 346.
NAPIER, CHARLES, Naval Officer, remark of Wellington to, 336.
NAPIER, Gen. GEORGE, trained by Moore, 250; on Craufurd, 345.

INDEX 491

NAPIER, Gen. WILLIAM, on the Light Division, 178; trained by Moore, 250; on road chosen by Masséna, 348.
NAPLES, Joseph Bonaparte made King of, 159, 169; Murat King in 1808, 236; his capital threatened, 284; preference shown to Naples by U.S. resented by Napoleon, 329. For Kingdom of Naples *also see* SICILY.
NAPOLEON BONAPARTE, naval plans for 1805–1806, 156; plan for reducing Great Britain by starvation, 178; defeats Prussians, 1806, 181; issues Decree of Berlin, 181 ff.; conduct of war with Russia and Eastern affairs, 1806–1807, 190; letter to Sultan of Turkey, 193; plans against India, 195; defeats and makes peace with Russia, 1807, 208; intimidates Denmark and Portugal and proposes Maritime League against Great Britain, 209 ff., 218, 219; induces Russia, etc., to break with her, 222; relations with Portugal, 222, 223; Berlin Decree met by Orders in Council of 1807, 224, 225; Milan Decree, 228; expected in U.S. to win, 229; letter to Alexander of February, 1808, 235; relations with Persia and menace to Egypt and India, 235, 236; seizure of Spanish throne, 236, 237; meeting with Alexander at Erfurt, 248, 268; peace proposals, 248; invasion of Spain, 248, 249; pursuit of Moore, 253 ff.; last instructions before leaving Spain, 272, 273; policy of direct trade with England, 1809, 269, 327; defeat of Austria, 284, 286, 298; anxiety caused by Walcheren expedition, 288, 289; Continental System in 1809–1810, 320, 324, 360 ff.; annexations of 1810, 324, 325; peace advances, 328; confiscations of American ships, 328, 329; delusive offer to U.S., 329; disapproval of invasion of Andalusia, 332; marriage, 343; appoints Masséna to Army of Portugal, 343; fails to reinforce him, 358; hopes from a change of government in England, 359; prospects of ruining her economically, 361; breach with Alexander, 361, 362.

his encouragement of science, 84; designs on India, 101, 365; apprehensions from Windham, 144; relations with Fox, 144, 145; Castlereagh's observation on, in 1807, 206; success in mobilization of public opinion against England, 215; importance attached to Corfu, 285; to Antwerp, 285; design on New South Wales, 385; reports made to him regarding Scottish Highlands, 397; how regarded by Methodists, 413.
NASMYTH, ALEXANDER, painter, 52.
NATIONAL DEBT, Petty's proposed sinking fund, 183. *Also see* LOANS.
NAVY, harbour works, 93; change in character of the war and deterioration of Navy from 1806, 178; gains from Danish expedition, 217; naval deserters, 228; advantage of Cotton's Convention with Siniavin, 244; inquiry into abuses, 262; Mulgrave's administration, 302, 303; inadequacy of pensions, 302, 303; difficulties over manning, 326; use in defence of the Lines, 356; naval officers as Governors of New South Wales, 380; dockyard at Bermuda, 389.
NELSON, views on safety of Sicily, 221, 323; on Cape of Good Hope, 388; mentioned, 176, 212.
NEWCASTLE, New South Wales, 385.
NEW HOLLAND, name given to the north-west coast of what was afterwards Australia, 380.
NEWPORT, Sir JOHN, conducts Irish affairs in parliament, 150.
NEW SOUTH WALES, discovery and early history, 380 ff.; Bentham on, 66.
NEW SOUTH WALES CORPS, 362.
NEWTON, mentioned, 81.

NEW YORK, seditious Canadian newspaper published in, 394.
NEY, Marshal, ordered to support Soult, 1808, 256, 272; indulgence to Charles Napier, 336; placed under Soult, 1809, 281; under Masséna, 1810, 343; on Coa, 346; at Bussaco, 349, 350.
NIEBUHR, on Mrs. Siddons, 48; his defence of Great Britain, 215.
NOLLEKENS, JOSEPH, sculptor, 54.
NONCONFORMISTS, Coleridge, 25, 34; Godwin, 59; Hazlitt, 70; emancipation proposal for, in 1807, 187; activities generally, 412 ff.; attitude of the Church, 414, 415.
NON-INTERCOURSE ACT, American, 1809, 268; its effects, 323, 324, 328; expiry, 324; renewal, 330.
NORFOLK ISLAND, British settlement in Pacific Ocean, 385.
NORTH, Hon. FREDERICK, Governor of Ceylon, 141 ff.
NORTHAMPTON, bye-election of 1807, 198.
NORWAY, relations with Great Britain, *see* DENMARK.
NORWICH, school of painting, 53.
NOTTINGHAM, allusion to riot of 1802 election, 177; petition from, 311.
NOVA SCOTIA, slaves from, settled in Sierra Leone, 388.
NOVELS, 66 ff.
NYESTE SKILDERIE, Danish newspaper, quoted, 89, 215.

OATS, price in 1808, 233.
OCHTERLONY, Lt.-Col. DAVID, defends Delhi, 130.
O'CONNELL, DANIEL, speech in Dublin on repeal of the Union, 320.
O'KEEFE, dramatist, 47.
OPERAS, 43, 44.
O.P. RIOTS, 1809, 297, 298.
OPHTHALMIA, treatment, 87.
OPORTO, Soult expelled from, 274; mentioned, 239, 272, 273.
OPORTO, Bishop of, mentioned, 342.
OPTICS, theories of, 84, 85.
ORANGE RIVER, exploration of, 388.
ORATORIOS, 43.
ORDENANZA, 341, 342, 356.
ORDERS IN COUNCIL, prohibiting import of slaves into new acquisitions, 1805, 163; blockading Prussia, April 5, 1806, 155; blockading N. Coast of France, Holland, and Germany, May 16, 182; forbidding trade from port to port of France and her allies, January 7, 1807, 183, 225, 226; Danish objections to this last Order, 211; Orders of November 1807, 226 ff.; Stephen's view, 227, 325; negotiations with U.S. respecting revocation of Orders relating to trade, 268; evasion of them, 269; licensing system, 269, 327; substitution for Orders of November, 1807, of Order of April, 1809, 325; U.S. view, 327 ff.; attempt by France and U.S. to obtain revocation, 329 ff.
ORDNANCE, *see* MASTER-GENERAL OF THE ORDNANCE.
ORISSA, conquest of, 1803, 125. *Also see* PURI.
ORKNEY AND SHETLAND, decrease of population in, 394.
OSWALD, Brig.-Gen. JOHN, captures Santa Maura, 323.
OUDH, annexation of part of, 102 ff., 134.
OUSELEY, Sir GORE, concludes Definitive Treaty with Persia, 366.
OXFORD UNIVERSITY, 75; education of Wellesley at, 99.

INDEX 493

PAGET, Lt.-Gen. Lord, Commanding Cavalry in Spain, 1808, 251 ff.; elopement, 416, 417; mentioned, 246.
PAGET, Major-Gen. Hon. EDWARD, with Moore in 1808–1809, 256, 259.
PAINTING, state of, 49 ff.
PALEY, Archdeacon, 63, 64; Shelley on, 58.
PALMERSTON, Viscount, a Lord of the Admiralty, 1807, 198; refuses Exchequer, 1809, 296.
PANET, JEAN ANTOINE, Speaker of Lower Canada Assembly, dismissed from militia, 391.
PARIS, apprehensions in, caused by Walcheren expedition, 288, 289.
PARIS, Dr., biographer of Davy, quoted, 80.
PARLIAMENT, criticism in Session of 1806–1807 of ministerial policy, 180; opening speech of Session of 1808, 229, 235; Act affecting placemen passed, 233; Act of 1813 to compensate Bentham, 66; usual duration of parliaments in George III's reign, 180. *Also see* IRELAND, ARMY, MILITIA.
PARLIAMENT, HOUSE OF COMMONS; before 1806: attack on E.I. Co. in 1801, 96; denunciation of Jacobinism by Wellesley, 99; Dolben's Slave Trade measure of 1788, 162; resolution regarding Abolition carried, 1792, 162, 163; resolution regarding welfare of India, 1793, 363; Scottish Schoolmasters Act, 1803, 400; Act for enlargement of Edinburgh, 1757, 405.
  Session of 1806: position of parties at opening, 144, 145; debate on honours, etc., to Pitt, 146, 147; Ellenborough's position, 151, 152; general character of Opposition, 154; threatened impeachment of Wellesley, 103, 134; hostilities with Prussia, 155; Abolition of Slave Trade, 164; impeachment of Melville, 164 ff.; dissolution, 180.
  Session of 1806–1807: character of the new Parliament, 180; Howick's mention of Fox's views, 174, 175; Petty's financial proposals, 183; Whitbread's proposals for dealing with poverty, 183, 184; Bill for removal of Catholic disabilities, 187; passing of Slave Trade Abolition Bill, 188; change of Ministry, 189; new Ministry meets Parliament and dissolves, 199.
  Session of 1807: character of the new Parliament, 199, 200; growing irresponsibility to public opinion, 200; reward given to Jenner, 208.
  Session of 1808: strength of parties, 229, 230; debate on Danish expedition, 219, 220; petitions against Orders in Council, 230, 231; Minimum Wage Bill, 231; disposal of question of Wellesley's conduct, 134, 135; prohibition of use of grain in distillation, 232, 233; [criminal law reform, 233; prohibition of export of quinine to France, 233, 234; Sheridan on Spain, 237, 238; vote of thanks to Arthur Wellesley, 242; Convention of Cintra, 245, 246.
  Session of 1809, inquiries regarding Duke of York and other matters, 261 ff.; parliamentary reform, 264 ff.; rejection of Prevention of Cruelty to Animals Bill, 266; sinecures, 266, 267; Canning's complaint of Government's weakness in defending its measures, 290.
  Session of 1810: opening, 298; Walcheren Inquiry, 299, 300; discussion on and petition against Wellington, 300; Navy Estimates, 302, 303; enforcement of standing order for exclusion of strangers, 305; committal of Jones to Newgate, 306; debate on Burdett, 307, 308; committal of him to Tower, 308; petitions for reform, etc., 311; strength of Perceval and weakness of Opposition, 314, 315; Canning on the War, 316; Bullion

494   ENGLAND IN THE NINETEENTH CENTURY

Committee, 316 ff.; naval matters, 326; Wellington's remark on the frequent ministerial defeats, 337.
extraordinary meeting of Parliament in November to deal with the Regency question, 360.
view held by some M.P.s that it was not the province of Parliament to question the King's choice of his advisers, 199; Canning's view that the Prime Minister should be in the House of Commons, 291; Scottish Toryism, 411; The Saints, 262, 415. *Also see* ARMY, BUDGETS, IRELAND, MILITIA, SEATS IN PARLIAMENT.

PARLIAMENT, HOUSE OF LORDS: Session of 1806: prominence of Clarence, 148; debate on Ellenborough's position, 151, 152; hostilities with Prussia, 155; resolution regarding Abolition of Slave Trade, 164; impeachment of Melville, 164 ff.
Session of 1806–1807: Abolition Bill passed, 1807, 188.
Session of 1807: Selkirk on national defence, 206; rejection of Parochial Schools Bill, 207, 208.
Session of 1808: Danish expedition, 219, 220; Orders in Council, 230; rejection of Perceval's measure of church reform, 233.
Session of 1809: Burghersh's case, 262; Grenville on extravagance, 264; Prevention of Cruelty to Animals Bill, 266.
Session of 1810: Grey on the State of the Nation, 314, 315; Darnley's question regarding home defence, 336.
Curwen's complaint regarding effect of Pitt's peerages, 265.

PARLIAMENT, IRISH, Wellesley in House of Lords, 99.
PARLIAMENT, LONG, mentioned, 262.
PARLIAMENT HOUSE, 408.
PARLIAMENTARY REFORM, indifference to, until near close of the decade, 145; reform agitation in 1809, 264 ff.; Burdett's proposal in 1809, 266; growing desire for, among textile operators, 418.
PAROCHIAL SCHOOLS BILL, 183, 184, 207, 208.
PARR, SAMUEL, Whig divine, on public opinion, 220.
PASQUIN, 47.
PATRIOTIC FUND, mentioned, 41.
PATTLE, Anglo-Indian family, 115, 116.
PEAS, a food of Scottish Highlanders, 395.
PEERAGE, an alleged effect of Pitt's additions, 265.
PENANG, E.I. Co.'s island in the Straits of Molacca, 141.
PENSIONS, Campbell's, 22; Southey's 33; unpopularity of pensioners, 311.
PERCEVAL, Hon. SPENCER, career and character, 295, 296; refuses post in Grenville's administration, 149; a leader of Opposition, 154; agrees to arrange for passing of Slave Trade Abolition Bill, 1807, 189; espouses cause of Princess of Wales, 189; Chancellor of the Exchequer, 197; his election cry, 198, 199; proposed reward for Jenner, 208; share in Orders in Council, 227; on sufferings of weavers in 1808, 231; budget of 1808, 232; attempt at Church reform, 233; prevents France obtaining quinine, 233, 234; speech on York's case, 1809, 261; suppresses trading in public offices, 263; accused of improper conduct as Minister, 266, 267; obstructive attitude towards reforms, 266, 267; budget of 1809, 267; correspondence with Canning on Premiership, 291; succeeds as Premier, October 4, 1809, 292, 294 ff.; conduct of session of 1810, 299, 302; arrangement for Chatham's vacancy, 304, 305; on Jones's case, 306; petitioned against, 311; persistence of his administration, 314, 315;

INDEX 495

obtains further support, 315, 316; weakness on Bullion Committee, 317; Wellington's caustic remark on his Ministry, 337; his management of war finance, 339; moves resolutions preparatory to a Regency, 360.
   lack of interest in finance, 197; narrow religious views, 199; not a popular figure, 200; interest in the poorer clergy, 415.

PERCY'S RELIQUES, mentioned, 31.
PÉRON, FRANÇOIS, impressions on visit to Sydney in 1802, 381; suggests to Napoleon acquisition of New South Wales, 385.
PERRON, French officer in Sindhia's service, 121 ff.
PERRY, prosecution of, 307.
PERSIA, Treaty with, 1801, 101, 365, 366; British and French missions to, 1807–1808, 365, 366, 235; Russian invasion of Persia, 365; Treaty concluded with, 366; mentioned, 195.
PERSIAN, official language in India, 106; taught in Calcutta College, 108.
PERSIAN GULF, Wellesley's interest in, 101; expedition to suppress piracy, 1809, 376.
PERSTON, Glasgow employer, 404.
PERTH, as a seat of Scottish provincial culture, 405.
PERTHSHIRE VOLUNTEERS, raised by Graham, 246.
PESHWA, Maratha Empire, 112; alliance with in 1789, 113. *Also see* BAJI RAO.
PETITIONS, to House of Commons, 230, 231, 300, 311.
PETRIE, WILLIAM, acting Governor of Madras in 1807, 368; subsequent opposition as Member of Council to Barlow, 371.
PETTY, Lord HENRY, becomes Chancellor of the Exchequer, 1806, 148, 149; budget of 1806, 152, 153; appointed a Manager in impeachment of Melville, 164; budget and financial proposals of 1807, 183; impetus given by him to financial reform, 208; on prosperity of the country, 267; mentioned, 187, 189, 236; becomes Marquis of LANSDOWNE, q.v., 315
PHILIPPINES, Spanish possession, Wellesley's designs on, 100.
PHILOSOPHY, 57, 58; Paley's, 63; Bentham's, 63 ff.; Scottish, 407, 405.
PHYSICIANS, 87, 88.
PHYSICS, state of, 81 ff.
PICHEGRU, Gen., capture of a fleet by, in 1795, 221.
PICTON, Major-Gen. THOMAS, sent to Peninsula, 333, 334; as disciplinarian, 335; at Bussaco, 348, 349.
PIGOTT, Sir ARTHUR, Attorney General, 1806, 150; appointed a Manager in impeachment of Melville, 164.
PINKNEY, WILLIAM, U.S. Minister in London, 330, 331.
PIRATES, in Persian Gulf, 376.
PITT, WILLIAM, promotion of Pye, 23; admiration for Scott, 37; and Master Betty, 48; his E.I. Acts, 96 ff.; relations with Wellesley, 134; alienation of Windham and Cobbett by his war attitude, 144, 145; Grenville's devotion to him, 146; reception of his death, 146; praised for suppression of sedition, 147; honours voted to him, 146, 147; his debts paid, 147; efforts for Slave Trade Abolition, 162, 163; accessibility, 163; work for Third Coalition a failure, 175; unreality of his differences with Fox, 177; Additional Force Act mentioned, 180; failure to remedy national pauperism, 184, 265; pledge against Catholic concessions, 188; popularity, 200; the Pitt tradition, 229; additions to peerage, 265; mentioned, 148, 176.
PITTITES, position in 1806, 154; their Tory character, 177.
PLACE, FRANCIS, reformer, his return to business, 145; supports Burdett, 309, 311.

PLACEMEN, 199; their unpopularity, 311.
PLAYFAIR, Professor JOHN, controversy with Chalmers, 401; influence, 407, 408.
PLOWDEN, lawyer, quoted, 310.
POETRY, revival, 17 ff.; partial divorce from music, 41, 42; Turner's, 51; Telford's love for, 94.
POLAND, French campaign of 1806–1807, 190.
POLES, in French Army, 112.
POLICE, Scottish, 410.
POLITICAL REGISTER, Cobbett's, on Whitbread, 234; its popularity, 307; his flogging article, 307; Burdett's manifesto published in, 307; its continuance from jail, 314.
POMERANIA, SWEDISH, expedition to, 1807, 209.
PONSONBY, GEORGE, Lord Chancellor of Ireland, 1806, 150; recommendation as to Irish disturbances, 184; chosen leader of Opposition, 230; a failure, 315.
POONA, Peshwa's capital, 112; Battle of, 1802, 113.
POOR LAW, Malthus on, 62; Pitt's Poor Law Bill mentioned, 65; one-seventh of the population on relief in 1803, 183; Whitbread's Bill, 184; its rejection, 207.
  Scottish, 399, 400.
POPE, poet, Byron's admiration for, 38, 176; mentioned, 38.
POPERY, cry against, 198, 199; Methodist hostility, 413.
POPHAM, Capt. Sir HOME, R.N., carries troops from Cape to South America, 166; his commercial circular, 167; court-martialled, 167; in Walcheren expedition, 287, 289; in parliament, 299.
POPULATION, Malthus's principle of, 60 ff., 208.
PORT DALRYMPLE, Tasmania, founded 1804, 386.
PORTE, *see* TURKEY.
PORTEUS, BEILBY, Bishop of London, evangelical sympathies, 414.
PORTLAND, Duke of, his party in 1792, 148, 150; position in 1806, 148; offers a form to ministry in March 1807, 189; becomes Premier, 196, 197; view of Convention of Cintra, 244; imminence of his retirement in summer of 1809, 286, 290, 291; delays Castlereagh's removal, 290; resignation, September, 1809, 292; supports Canning's efforts to become Premier, 292; death, 294.
  his taciturnity, 290; mentioned, 293.
PORT LOUIS, Mauritius, capture of, 1810, 379.
PORTUGAL, threatened by Napoleon, 1806, 173; St. Vincent sent to the Tagus, 173, 210; temporary breach with Great Britain, 1807, 222; French invasion, 223; choice of, as a British base, 1808, 238; rising against French, 238; liberation of the country, 239 ff.; French invasion of the north, 1809, 272, 273; their expulsion, 273, 274; apprehension from French in 1809, 283, 332; Masséna's invasion in 1810, 344 ff.
  trade, 238, 321; British loan, 267; subsidy, 338, 339; relations between Wellington and Regency, 348, 351.
  British occupation of Madeira, 223; of Goa and Macao, 376.
PORTUGUESE, in Ceylon, 141, 142; with Masséna, 347.
PORTUGUESE ARMY, Beresford given the command, 272; a regiment sent to Cadiz, 332; advanced age of generals, 333; reorganization, 339 ff.; irregulars, 341, 342.
POST, communication with India, 109.

INDEX

POST OFFICE, proposed utilization for savings banks, 184.
POTATOES, Scottish Highland food, 395.
POUSSIN, painter, influence on Turner, 52.
PRESBYTERIANS, in England, College at Manchester, 82.
   in Scotland, 400 ff.
PRESS, opinions in England and on the Continent regarding intimidation of Denmark by Napoleon in 1807, 213; Danish opinion of England, 215; agitation over Convention of Cintra, 244; freedom of, attacked, 305; poor state of provincial press, 307; prosecutions, 307; publicity given to military movements, 332.
PRICES, rise in 1810, 319, 320; comparison of cost of living in 1792, 1801, and 1810, 417, 418.
PRIME MINISTER, the idea abhorrent to the constitution according to Holland, 152; Canning's view that he must be in the House of Commons, 291; custom that, if he is, he must be Chancellor of the Exchequer, 291.
PRINCE EDWARD ISLAND, Selkirk's settlement, 393.
PRINCE OF WALES ISLAND, *see* PENANG.
PRISONERS OF WAR, negotiations for exchange, 328.
PRISONS, Bentham as reformer, 65, 66.
PRIVATEERS, danger from, in home waters, 94, 95; Danish, 217; in Mediterranean, 285; in West Indies, 323.
PRIVY COUNCIL, constitutional position as regards Cabinet, Judicature, and Crown, 151, 152.
PROCIDA, island off Naples temporarily captured from French in 1809, 284.
PROCURATOR FISCAL, 410.
PROTECTION, of Manchester piece goods, 105.
PRUSSIA, ratification of a treaty in substitution for Haugwitz's, 1806, 154; hostilities with Great Britain, 154 ff.; Fox's opinion of Prussia, 155; blockade of, 155, 184; causes of war with France, 161; singular Prussian mentality, 161, 162; cessation of hostilities with Great Britain and conclusion of formal peace in January, 1807, 161; course of war with France, 181; sacrifice of her interests at Treaty of Tilsit, 208; renewed breach with Great Britain, 222; mentioned, 268.
PUBLIC OPINION, in England as to South America, 167; on Jacobinism, 177; on the war, 179; decline of its influence on Parliament, 200; Convention of Cintra, 244; retreat to Coruña, 260; York's case, 262; reform, 264.
PUBLIC SPEAKING by Ministers, 265.
PULTENEY, Sir WILLIAM, a patron of Rennie, 94; on E.I. Co., 96.
PUMP, as a means of punishment, 415.
PUNJAB, Perron's connections in, 121; pursuit of Holkar into, 137, 138; subsequent relations with, 365.
PURI, Orissa, Jagannath car at, 364.
PYE, HENRY, Poet Laureate, 23.
PYM, Capt., R.N., action off Grand Port, Mauritius, 378.

QUAKERS, Joseph Lancaster, 78, 79.
QUARTERLY REVIEW, origin, 74, 75,; Scottish element in, 176.
QUEENSBERRY, Duke of, "Old Quin", 47.
QUININE, first isolated, 1809, 88. *Also see* JESUIT'S BARK.

RADCLIFFE, Mrs., novelist, 67.
RAEBURN, HENRY, painter, 52.
RAGHUJI BHONSLA, Raja of Berar, 112; war declared upon, 1803, 119; loss of Orissa, 125; defeated by A. Wellesley, 126 ff.
RAIKES, ROBERT, his Sunday schools mentioned, 78.
RAJAS, impoverishment in Bengal, 108.
RAJPUTANA, Maratha oppression of, 366.
RAJPUTS, in Army in India, 117; in Northern India, 129.
RAMSGATE, harbour work at, 93.
RANJIT SINGH, Sikh Raja, relations with, 137; treaty with, 365.
REALISM, Crabbe's, 19 ff.; romantic realism in painting, 50.
REDESDALE, Lord, Irish tithes proposal, 266.
RED SEA, Wellesley's interest in, 101.
REGENCY, arrangement for, in 1810, 360.
    Portuguese, 246.
REGIMENTS—
    cavalry: 10th Hussars, in Peninsula, 254.
      18th Light Dragoons, in Peninsula, 254.
      19th Light Dragoons, 126; at Assaye, 127.
      23rd Light Dragoons, at Talavera, 279.
      25th Dragoons, in Southern India, 374.
      29th Light Dragoons, at Laswari, 128.
    infantry: 29th, at Talavera, 278.
      33rd, Arthur Wellesley's regiment, 114.
      43rd, 344, 345; at Bussaco, 350.
      45th, at Talavera, 275; at Bussaco, 349.
      48th, at Talavera, 278, 279.
      52nd, 344, 345; at Bussaco, 350.
      60th, at Talavera, 276; distribution in 1809, 276.
      73rd Highlanders, in New South Wales, 385.
      74th, 126; at Assaye, 127.
      76th, 123; at Delhi, 124; at Laswari, 128.
      78th, 126.
      88th Connaught Rangers, at Bussaco, 349.
      95th, 344, 345.
REID, founder of the Common Sense school of philosophy, 407.
RELIGION, observance in India by Europeans, 110, 138; religions in Ceylon, 142; religious question in India, 363 ff.
RENNIE, JOHN, engineer, 92 ff.
REPUBLICANISM, Wordsworth's, 25 ff., 33 ff.; Southey's 33, 34.
REVENUE, LAND, in India, 106; permanent settlement in Bengal, 107, 108; intention to extend it to Ceded Districts, 108.
REVIEWS, 71 ff.
REYNIER, French General, defeated at Maida, 170, 171; commands Corps under Masséna, 343, 347, 348; at Bussaco, 349, 350.
REYNOLDS, Sir JOSHUA, painter, 50; influence on Turner, 51; monument to, 54; mentioned, 300.
RICARDO, DAVID, his first work, 316.
RICHMOND, Fourth Duke of, Viceroy of Ireland, 1807, 198; mentioned, 280.
RIFLES, see REGIMENTS.
RIOTS, Malthus on those of 1800 and 1801, 62; Lancashire riots, 1808, 231; Burdett riots, 1810, 309 ff.

INDEX

RIST, Danish Minister in London, 1807, 210, 211.
ROADS, in India, 103, 118; in Scotland, 94.
ROBINSON, HENRY CRABB, anecdote of, 49; appreciation of German philosophy, 57; as Times Correspondent on Danish affairs, 210.
ROCHDALE JAIL, burnt down, 1808, 231.
ROCHESTER, petition from, 310.
ROCKINGHAM, Lord, his grounds, 57.
ROGERS, SAMUEL, poet, 22; friend of Wordsworth, 30; mentioned, 38.
ROHILKHAND, annexation, 1801, 103.
ROLIÇA, engagement at, August 17, 1808, 240.
ROMAÑA, Marquis DE LA, Spanish General, 254; defeated by Soult, 255; his army in danger, 340; reinforces the Lines, 356.
ROMANTICISM, in poetry, 17 ff.; hostility of Byron and the Edinburgh Review, 38, 73, 74, 176; ineffective in music, 41; in painting, 50 ff.; in architecture, 54, 55; in novels, 67.
ROME, Raeburn's visit, 52; Flaxman's, 54; influence of the ideas of ancient Rome on Wellesley, 99; mentioned, 314.
ROMILLY, Sir SAMUEL, Solicitor-General, 1806, 150; appointed a Manager in impeachment of Melville, 164; criminal law reformer, 233; parliamentary reformer, 266; partly supports Burdett, 313; mentioned, 263.
ROMNEY, GEORGE, painter, 50.
ROSE, GEORGE, Vice-President of the Board of Trade and Treasurer of the Navy, 1807, 197; his Minimum Wage Bill, 231; interest in economy, 295; refusal of the Exchequer, 296; on shortage of seamen, 326.
ROSEN, Count, Governor of Gothenburg, his assurances to Saumarez, 322.
ROSETTA, unsuccessful attacks upon, in 1807, 201, 202.
ROSS, disturbances in 1792, 395.
ROSS, Lt.-Col. ROBERT, at Maida, 171, 172.
ROSSLYN, Earl of, his death, 176.
ROWLEY, Commodore JOSIAS, cooperation in conquest of Mauritius, 378, 379.
ROYAL COLLEGE OF PHYSICIANS, on vaccination, 90.
ROYAL INSTITUTION, its inception, 83; Coleridge's lectures, 32; Dalton's 82; Davy's, 82.
ROYAL SOCIETY, 82, 83; decreasing attendance, 416.
RUM, in West Indies, 389.
RUMFORD, Count, 85; connection with Royal Institution, 83.
RUPERT, Prince, his introduction of mezzotinting, 54.
RUSSELL, JOHN, pupil of Dugald Stewart, 407, 408.
RUSSIA, negotiations with France in 1806, 159, 160, 173; refusal of loan to, 1807, 209; French War, 190, 208; Turkish relations, 190, 268; Treaty of Tilsit, 208; Gower's defence of the Danish expedition, 218; Russia's attitude towards neutrals, 219; complicity in divulging the secret articles of Tilsit, 219; declaration of war with Great Britain, 221, 222; Russian fleet off Lisbon, 223; Russian invasion of Persia and fear of a Russian invasion of India through Persia, 1808, 365, 235; surrender of Russian fleet, 243, 244; British moderation towards, 244, 267, 268; alienation from France, 361, 362.
Fox's favourite ally, 168, 175. *Also see* ALEXANDER.
RUTHERFORD, Dr. JOHN, grandfather of Sir Walter Scott, 35.
RUTLAND, Duke of, mentioned, 198.

RYDER, Hon. RICHARD, Home Secretary, 1809, 296, 297; his management of Burdett's arrest, 309, 314.
RYLAND, HERMAN, Craig's Private Secretary in Canada, sent to London, 391, 392.

SAHAGUN, point of commencement of Moore's retreat in 1808, 253 ff.; mentioned, 345.
ST. HELENA, E.I. Co.'s Island, 141.
ST. PAUL'S CATHEDRAL, a monument in, 54.
ST. VINCENT, Admiral Earl, commanding Channel Fleet, 1806, sent to Portugal, 173, 210.
SAINTS, THE, West Indies, capture of, 1809, 270.
"SAINTS, THE," small parliamentary party, 262, 415.
SALUSBURY, Sir ROBERT, M.P., moves for Burdett's committal, 314.
SAN DOMINGO, Battle of, February 6, 1806, 157; reduction of, 269.
SAN JULIAO, Lines of, 354; mentioned, 347.
SANSKRIT language taught in Calcutta College, 108.
SANTA MAURA, captured from French, 323.
SANTAREM, Masséna's retreat upon, 358, 353; mentioned, 240, 355.
SATI, 109, 364.
SAUGAR, island at mouth of Hooghly where children were drowned, 365.
SAUMAREZ, Sir JAMES, commanding Baltic fleet, 322.
SCHELDT, expedition to the, 285 ff.; mentioned, 221.
SCHILLER, mentioned, 36.
SCHOOLS, see EDUCATION.
SCIENCE, state of, 79 ff.; in Edinburgh Review, 72. Also see headings under the special sciences.
SCILLA, captured by French, 1808, 236.
SCOTLAND, general condition, 394 ff.; Scottish portraits, 52; Reviews, 71 ff., 176; geology, 80; engineering, 91 ff., 398, 399; poverty and self-reliance, 183, 184; emigration into North America, 393; the Highlands, 394 ff.; the Lowlands, 398, 399; finance and Poor Law, 399; education, 400, 407, 408, 78; the Church, 400 ff.; agriculture and industries, 402 ff.; population, 402, 403; the great towns, 403 ff.; the law, 407 ff.; Toryism, 411.
SCOTT, WALTER, 35 ff.; connection with the Reviews, 74, 75; his Lay of the Last Minstrel, 176; his Antiquary, 397, 399; on Old Edinburgh, 405; social talents, 407, 408; mentioned, 21, 38.
SCULPTURE, state of, 54.
SEATS IN PARLIAMENT, purchase of, 265, 266.
SEBASTIANI, General, French Army, 190, 193; in Talavera campaign, 275, 282.
SECRETARIES OF STATE, see HOME, FOREIGN, and WAR SECRETARY.
SECRETARY AT WAR, Fitzpatrick, 1806-1807, 150; Palmerston, 1809, 296.
SECRET COMMITTEE (of Directors of the E.I. Co.) constituted, 97.
SEDITION, Pitt's suppression of, 147.
SELKIRK, Earl of, leads colony to Prince Edward's Island, 393; on national defence, 206.
SENEGAL, conquest of, 270, 388.
SERINGAPATAM, capture of, 100; prize-money, 116; collision between troops at, in 1808, 374.
SERMONS, as literature, 58.

INDEX 501

SEVEN ISLANDS, see IONIAN ISLANDS.
SHAFTESBURY, Earl of, a reminiscence, 415.
SHAH, see PERSIA.
SHAKESPEARE, his plays staged, 45; Mrs. Siddons, 49; Lamb's Tales, 69, 70; supposed in hell, 413.
SHEEP, in New South Wales, introduction of Cheviot sheep into Scottish Highlands, 396.
SHEFFIELD, Lord, pamphleteer, 227.
SHELBURNE, see LANSDOWNE.
SHELLEY, quoted, 58.
SHERATON, THOMAS, furniture designer, 57.
SHERBROOKE, Lt.-Gen. JOHN, at Talavera, 276, 279; leaves Peninsula, 333; mentioned, 335.
SHERIDAN, RICHARD, Treasurer of the Navy, 1806, 150; appointed a manager in impeachment of Melville, 164; jest on his own party, 189; on Perceval's want of interest in finance, 197; on Spain in 1808, 237, 238; on a motion for exclusion of strangers, 305; decay of his powers, 315.
  as theatrical manager and dramatist, 44 ff.; interest in India, 134; his Rivals mentioned, 186; unfitness to lead Opposition, 230; mentioned, 174, 176.
SHERIFFS, of City of London, in Burdett riots, 309.
SHETLAND, see ORKNEY AND SHETLAND.
SHIELD, WILLIAM, composer, 43.
SHIP-BUILDING in India, 105.
SHIPP, JOHN, leader in assault on Bharatpur, 132; account of Lake, 132; mentioned, 117.
SHIPPING, difficulties, 326, 327.
SHORE, Sir JOHN, see TEIGNMOUTH.
SHRAPNEL, Major, his shells, 241.
SHUJA-UL-MULK, Amir of Kabul, concludes treaty with British, 1809, 365.
SICILY, negotiations regarding, 1806, 159, 160, 173; British defence of, 169, 170, 221; troops sent to Egypt from, 195, 200, 201; unsuccessful attack upon, by Murat, 1810, 323.
SIDDONS, Mrs. SARAH, 48, 49.
SIDMOUTH, Lord, Lord Privy Seal, 1806, 150; his party, 149; Lord President, 179; his opinion as to Catholic emancipation, 186; abstention from Cabinet, 187; influence unfavourable to Ministry, 1809, 296; supports without joining, 315, 316; financial views, 316. Also see ADDINGTON.
SIERRA LEONE, early history of the colony, 388.
SIKHS, 121, 129; early relations with, 137, 365.
SILKS, INDIAN, 105.
SIMEON, Rev. CHARLES, his work at Cambridge, 414; in Scotland, 401.
SINCLAIR, Sir JOHN, Caithness proprietor, promotes Highland cotton-mill, 396.
SINDHIA, see DAULAT RAO SINDHIA.
SINECURES, proposed abolition, 266, 267; Lord Arden's, 302, 303; unpopularity, 305, 311.
SINIAVIN, Russian Admiral, refuses to help Junot, 244; surrenders fleet off Lisbon, 243.
SINKING FUND, Petty's proposal, 183.
SIVAJI, founder of Maratha Empire, 111.

SJAELLAND, see ZEALAND.
SKINNER, Lt.-Col. JAMES, at Laswari, 128; his crossing of the Sutlej, 137.
SLAVES, in Cape Colony, 386, 387; settlement of liberated slaves in Sierra Leone, 388.
SLAVE TRADE, steps leading to Abolition, 162 ff.; Abolition Bill becomes law, March 25, 1807, 188, 189; Windham's defence of the Trade brought up against his party at an election, 199; effect of Abolition in Cape Colony, 387; in West Indies, 389; Abolition by U.S., mentioned, 389.
SLOUGH, observatory at, 79.
SMALL-POX, 89, 90.
SMEATON, his lighthouse, 93.
SMIRKE, ROBERT, architect, 55.
SMITH, ADAM, on backwardness of Scotland, 394, 398; on the Scottish laws, 403; read by weavers, 405.
SMITH, JOHN RAPHAEL, engraver, 53.
SMITH, Rear-Admiral Sir SIDNEY, commands squadron off Sicily, 1806, 169; made Viceroy of South Italy, 170, 172; aggressive plans, 169 ff.; in the Dardanelles, 191 ff.; off Portugal in 1807, 223; escorts Portuguese Regent to Brazil, 223, 342; mentioned, 357.
SMITH, Rev. SYDNEY, his Peter Plymley, 70, 233; connection with Edinburgh Review, 71, 72; on missionaries, 365.
SMITH, WILLIAM, geologist, 81.
SMITH, WILLIAM, M.P., a "patriot", 265.
SMITHFIELD, sale of wives, 415.
SOANE, JOHN, architect, 55, 56.
SOCIETY FOR BETTERING THE CONDITION OF THE POOR, mentioned, 83.
SOCIETY OF ARTS, 83.
SOULT, Marshal, campaign in Spain, 1808–1809, 252 ff.; in Portugal, 1809, 272 ff.; in Spain, 280 ff.; in 1810, 356.
SOUTHAMPTON, mentioned, 93.
SOUTHCOTE, JOANNA, religious maniac, 412.
SOUTHEY, ROBERT, 32, 33; change in his opinions, 33, 34; on water-colours, 53; prose works, 70; connection with Quarterly, 75; his expulsion from school mentioned, 77; on Yorkshire schools, 77; on the Evangelical Magazine, 413; mentioned, 38.
SPAIN, Collingwood's relations with, during war with her, 303; French occupation, 1808, 236, 237; rising of May 2, 237; deputation to Great Britain, 237; peace proclaimed by Great Britain, 237; British expedition to Peninsula, 1808–1809, 238 ff.; campaign of summer 1809, 272 ff.; Wellesley's mission to Cadiz and Treaty of Alliance with Junta, 284; trade in 1810, 320, 321, 328; unwise conduct of the war, 331 ff., 340; advanced age of generals, 333; loss of Ciudad Rodrigo, 344; reinforcement of the Lines with Spanish troops, 356; interruptions to Masséna's communications, 358.
  Edinburgh Review article, 74; dependence of British wool on Spanish merinos, 382. *Also see* WAR, BRITISH, Peninsula.
SPANISH POSSESSIONS, *see* AMERICA (SOUTH), BUENOS AYRES, PHILIPPINES.
SPEAKER OF THE HOUSE OF COMMONS, Burdett's case, 1810, 308 ff.
SPENCER, Earl, Home Secretary, 1806, 149; signs for Fox during his illness, 173; his own illness, 187; Cabinet meeting at his house, March, 1807, 188; mentioned, 66, 165, 166.

INDEX 503

SPENCER, Major-Gen. BRENT, 238, 240; unfit for Second-in-Command, 334, 351; at Bussaco, 348.
SPIRITS, in New South Wales, 383; taxation of, in Canada, 390.
STAËL, Madame DE, on Mrs. Siddons, 48.
STANHOPE, Earl, "Citizen Stanhope", mentioned, 47.
STANHOPE, Lady HESTER, relations with Moore, 250.
STAUNTON, Sir GEORGE, in China, 141.
STEAM ENGINES, state of the invention in the decade, 90, 91; applied to threshing machines in Scotland, 402; spinning, 402; weaving, 402.
STEPHEN, JAMES, pamphleteer, 227; views on shipping, 325, 327.
STERNE, imitation of, 300.
STEVENS, JOHN SAMUEL, composer, 42.
STEVENSON, Col., under Arthur Wellesley in 1803, 126, 128.
STEWART, Brig.-Gen. Hon. CHARLES, in parliament, 242; at Benavente, 254; quoted, 256, 280.
STEWART, Professor DUGALD, his influence, 407, 408.
STEWART, Brig.-Gen. Hon. WILLIAM, in Egypt, 1807, 202.
STIRLING, collieries near, 402.
STIRLING, Rear-Admiral, commanding in South America, 168.
STRACHAN, Rear-Admiral Sir RICHARD, despatched after French squadron in 1806, 156; in naval command in Walcheren expedition, 287, 288; mentioned, 178, 300.
STRANGFORD, Lord, Minister in Portugal, 1807, 222, 223.
STRIKES, in Lancashire, 1808, 231, 232; in Glasgow, 1810, 404; in Lancashire 1810, 417.
STUART, CHARLES, diplomatic representative in Madrid, 246; Minister in Lisbon, 359.
STUART, Major-Gen. Sir JOHN, commands troops in Mediterranean, 1806, 169, 170; fights Battle of Maida, 170 ff.; returns to England, 172; operations in Mediterranean, 1809, 284; defence of Sicily, 1810, 323.
STUARTS, Scott's family connection with, 35; memories of Charles Edward, 36, 406; Fox's historical studies, 145; effect of Charles Edward's death, 396, 397.
STURGES-BOURNE, WILLIAM, leaves office with Canning, 296.
SUBSIDY, to Sweden, 234, 235; Sicily, 236; Portugal, 339; mentioned, 237.
SUGAR, an Indian export, 105; fall in price, 232; its use for distilleries, 233; trade in, via Heligoland, 321; West Indian trade in, generally, 325, 326, 389; in Portugal, 355.
SUMATRA, former British Island, since Dutch, except Bencoolen, 141.
SUNDAY, observance in India, 110; evangelical view of, 413.
SURR, novelist, 67; quoted, 23.
SUTHERLAND, a cotton-mill in, 396.
SUTLEJ, crossing of, 137; established as boundary, 365.
SUTTON, MANNERS, Archbishop of Canterbury, opposes a Church reform, 233.
SWEDEN, expedition to Swedish Pomerania, 1807, 209; expedition to Sweden, 1808, 234, 235, 338; subsidy to, 235; at war with Russia and Denmark, 235; peace concluded with Russia, 1809, 322; Bernadotte chosen as future King, 1810, 322; war nominally declared on Great Britain, 322; mentioned, 217.
SWISS in French Army, 112; a Swiss regiment in British Army, 116; in Cape Colony, 387.

SYDNEY, penal settlement in 1788, 380. *Also see* NEW SOUTH WALES.
SYMINGTON, WILLIAM, inventor, 91.

TALAVERA, Battle of, July 28, 1809, 275 ff.
TALLEYRAND, correspondence with Fox and negotiations for peace between France and Great Britain, 1806, 158 ff., 173, 174, 179; mentioned, 212.
TARLETON, Gen., M.P., criticizes Wellington, 300.
TASMANIA, first settlements in, 386.
TATE AND BRADY, metrical version of Psalms, 43.
TAXATION, proposed successively on pig-iron and on private breweries and withdrawn: assessed taxes raised, 1806, 153; principle adopted in 1807 of imposing no new taxation for three years, and adhered to till 1810, 183, 232, 267, 316; new taxation imposed on Ireland in that year, 316; complaints regarding high taxation, 264, 311.
    in India, 106.
TAYLOR, WILLIAM, man of letters, 31.
TEA, trade with China, 141; taxation in Canada, 390.
TEIGNMOUTH, Lord; Sir John Shore, Governor-General of India, 1793–1798, created Lord Teignmouth, 99; his treaty with Wazir of Oudh, 102; relations with Hyderabad, 113; appreciation of Arthur Wellesley, 114; First President of Bible Society, 363.
TELFORD, THOMAS, engineer, 92 ff.; on Scotland, 398, 399.
TEMPLE, Earl, son of Lord Buckingham, a Lord of the Treasury, 1806, 150; mentioned, 287.
TERNATE, Dutch possession, China Seas, 379.
THACKERAY, novelist, his Josh Sedley, 107; his presentment of Lord Hertford, 158.
THEATRES, the Haymarket, 43, 44; Covent Garden and Drury Lane, 44, 45; these last burnt down, 297; rebuilding of Covent Garden followed by O.P. riots, 297, 298.
THEMISTOCLES, saying of, 134.
THEOLOGY, state of, 58; Paley's Natural Theology, 63.
THIRLAGE, Scottish custom of, 399.
THOMPSON, BENJAMIN, *see* RUMFORD.
THOMSON, THOMAS, chemist, 81.
THORN, Capt., on the Army in India, 117, 118.
THORNTON, HENRY, member of Bullion Committee, 317.
THRESHER OUTRAGES, disappearance of, 320.
THRESHING MACHINES, in Scotland, 402.
TIDORE, Dutch possession, China seas, 379.
TIERNEY, GEORGE, President of Board of Control, 1806, 180; in parliament, 264; his decay, 315; unfit to lead Opposition, 230.
TILSIT, TREATY OF, 208, 218, 221; secret articles, 209, 218; how probably communicated to British Government, 219; refusal of Russian Government to communicate them, 221; Ionian Islands, 236.
TIMBER, shortage of, 327.
TIMES, THE, Robinson as Correspondent, 210; on Danish affairs, 213; on Wellington, 335.
TIPU, Sultan of Mysore: his defeat and death, 100; his family at Vellore, 138.
TITHES, Crabbe on, 20; in Scotland, 400, 401.

INDEX 505

TOBACCO, American trade, 325; corruption of Hottentots by, 387; a product of Cape Colony, 388.

TOREÑO, Conde de, historian, deputy from Asturias to England, 237.

TORIES, mentioned, 177; the Tory period of power from 1807 to 1830, 198; Scottish, 411, 412.

TORRES VEDRAS, LINES OF, 353 ff.; projected, 331; Wellington's retirement within, 352; mentioned, 347.

TOWER OF LONDON, Burdett's confinement, 310, 311.

TOWNS, administration in Scotland, 410, 411.

TRACTORS, a quack cure derided by Byron, 92.

TRADE, with India, 105; with China, 140, 141; with Ceylon, 142; during revolutionary war, 182; blockade of Prussia and N. coast of France and Holland, 155, 182; Berlin Decree, 183; encouragement of neutral trade, 182; Order in Council of January, 1807, 183, 224 ff.; loss from Danish privateering, 217; later Orders in Council and French Decrees, 224 ff.; restriction in case of quinine, 233, 234; speculative trade with S. America encouraged by Buenos Ayres expedition, 167, 179; slackness of speculative activity in 1809, 267; wheat and aggregate trade, 268, 269; effect of licence system and smuggling, 269; general speculative character at end of decade, 317 ff.; effects of continental system and U.S. embargo, 320 ff.; protection by British Navy of international trade, 330.

the woollen trade, 382; Central American trade, 389; Canadian, 392; Glasgow, 403.

TRAINING ACT, 1806, 154; utilized in 1808, 234.

TRANSPORT, see COMMISSARIAT.

TRANSPORTATION, Bentham on, 66. *Also see* CONVICTS.

TRANSPORTS, insufficiency in 1807, 209.

TRANT, NICHOLAS, Brig.-General in Portuguese service, 341, 351, 352.

TRAVANCORE, S. Indian State, disturbance in 1808–1809, 367.

TRIMMER, SARAH, educationalist, 79.

TRINCOMALEE, mentioned, 142.

TRINIDAD, mentioned, 389.

TRINITY COLLEGE DUBLIN, education of Thomas Moore at, 39.

TRIPOLI, Consul at, 303.

"TRISTRAM SHANDY", an imitation of, 300, 301.

TROUBRIDGE, Rear-Admiral Sir THOMAS, death, 327.

TUCKER, St. GEORGE, in charge of Indian finances, 133.

TURKEY, equivocal position in 1806, 190; invaded by Russian army, 190; declares war on Russia, 190, 191; British fleet enters Dardanelles, 191 ff.; rejects British proposals, 193; hostilities with, 193 ff., 200 ff.; danger to, from arrangements made at Erfurt, 268; treaty negotiated with, in 1809, 268.

Collingwood's relations with, 303; permission given by, to carry off Elgin marbles, 56; allusion to the Turkish question, 235.

TURNER, CHARLES, engraver, 54.

TURNER, JOSEPH, painter, 51, 52; his watercolours, 53; engravings of his works, 54.

"TWIST, OLIVER," mentioned, 28.

TYPHUS, outbreak in the army in Spain, 283.

TYROL, deputation from, 297.

UDNY, GEORGE, Member of Council in Bengal in charge of trade, 105.

UNITED STATES, conciliation of, by Fox's concession in favour of neutral trade in 1806, 182; inquiry as to scope of Berlin Decree, 225; resentment at Orders in Council, 1807, 226 ff.; trade, how affected by the Orders and by continental system, 228; Leopard and Chesapeake affair, 228, 229; Embargo Act, 229; Madison succeeds as President, 1809, 268; Embargo Act replaced by Non-Intercourse Act, 268; negotiations for its withdrawal concurrently with that of the Orders, 268; wheat trade, 268; strained relations with Great Britain, 295; injudicious British policy towards, 325; British commercial competition and trade with, 325 ff., 392; relations with Great Britain and France, 328 ff.

Rumford's connection with, 85; appreciation of vaccination, 89; Americans in British Navy, 326; British protection of U.S. trade, 330; abolition of Slave Trade, 389; relations with Canada, 390, 392.

UNIVERSITIES, English and Scottish compared, 75, 76; Scottish, 400, 407.

UPPER CANADA OR FREEMAN'S JOURNAL, 394.

VACCINATION, 89, 90; Byron on, 92; reward to Jenner, 208.

VANSITTART, NICHOLAS, one of Sidmouth's party, a Lord of the Treasury, 1806, 150.

VAUGHAN, Dr., see HALFORD, Sir HENRY.

VELLORE, mutiny of, 138 ff.; an effect of, 364.

VENEGAS, Spanish General, his campaign, in 1809, 275.

VENEZUELA, independence movement, 324.

VICEROY (Ireland), Bedford, 1806, 150; Richmond, 1807, 198.

VICTOR, Marshal, threatens Portugal in 1809, 273; in Talavera campaign, 274 ff.

VIGNY, Comte ALFRED DE, on Collingwood, 304.

VIMEIRO, Battle of, August 21, 1808, 240 ff.

VIRGIL, influence on Wordsworth, 24; Fox's love for, 175.

VOLTA, scientist, 84.

VOLUNTEERS, strength in 1807, 205; their deterioration, 206; strength in 1808, 234.

WAGES, of weavers: in 1808, 231; in 1810, 418.
 in Glasgow, 404.

WAGRAM, Battle of, July 6, 1809, 286.

WALCHEREN EXPEDITION, projected, 285 ff.; carried out, 287 ff., 298, 299; inquiry, 299, 300; finance, 338; mentioned, 221, 311.

WALES, engineering works, 93; translation of the Scripture into Welsh, 414.

WALL, JOSEPH, mentioned, 177.

WALLACE, Lieut.-Col., commanding 88th Regiment at Bussaco, 349.

WALLACE, ROBERT, author, 61.

WALLACE, Lieut.-Col. WILLIAM, in Maratha War, 130.

WALPOLE, HORACE, his Gothic tastes, 55.

WAR, BRITISH, general: engineering works built in connection with, 93; French War how viewed by statesmen, 144, 337, 338; folly of a mere defensive war, 146; change in its general character from 1806, 178; unity of the country, 179, 196; sketch of the commercial war with France, 1793–1806, 181, 182; a prediction of Castlereagh, 206; Whig

INDEX 507

view, 261; A. Wellesley's, 272; nominal character so far as Sweden was concerned, 322.

in India: the war with Tipu, 1799, 100; maritime expeditions projected or carried out by Wellesley, 100, 101; declaration of war against Maratha Chiefs, 1803, 119; its extent and general character, 122, 123; Lake's and A. Wellesley's campaigns, 123 ff.; conquest of Broach, Bundelkand, and Orissa, 125, 126; war with Holkar, 1804–1805, 129 ff., 137, 138.

limitation of powers of Governor-General, 98, 99; Maratha method of warfare, 129.

naval and expeditionary: capture of Cape Colony from the Dutch, 1806, 386, 387; progress of the naval war with France, 156, 157; Buenos Ayres expedition, 166 ff., 203, 204; operations in Southern Italy, 169 ff.; forcing of the Dardanelles, 1807, 190 ff.; expedition to Alexandria, 194, 195, 201 ff.; Danish expedition, 213 ff.; capture of Heligoland, etc., 223; defence of Rosas, 1808, 271; war in the New World and Africa, 1809, 269, 270; action in Aix Roads, 271, 272; Mediterranean operations, 284, 285; Walcheren expedition, 287 ff., 298, 299; capture of Guadeloupe, 1810, 323; capture of Santa Maura, 323; Murat's attack on Sicily, 323.

suppression of pirates in Persian Gulf, 376; capture of French Islands in Indian Ocean, 377 ff.; expeditions in the China Seas, 379, 380.

Peninsula: origin, 237, 238; Wellesley's campaign, 1808, 239 ff.; Moore's, 1808–1809, 246 ff.; Wellesley's, 1809, 272 ff.; defensive attitude in 1809–1810, 331 ff.; Masséna's invasion of Portugal, 1810, 343 ff.

WAR, FRANCO-AUSTRIAN, 1809, 267, 284, 286.
WAR, FRANCO-PRUSSIAN, 1806, its causes, 161, 162; its course, 181.
WAR, FRANCO-RUSSIAN, 1806–1807, 190, 208.
WAR, RUSSO-TURKISH, 190.
WARD, JAMES, engraver, 53.
WARD, ROBERT PLUMER, Minister in 1809, 296.
WARRE, Lieut.-Gen. Sir WILLIAM, his service in Portuguese army during Peninsular War, 343.
WARREN, Rear-Admiral Sir JOHN, sent after an escaped French squadron, December, 1805, 156; captures Linois, 1806, 157.
WAR SECRETARY, Windham, 1806, 149; Castlereagh, 1807, 197; Hawkesbury, 1809, 296.
WATERS, Col., 347.
WATLING, Lieutenant, R.N., his recapture of an East Indiaman, 378.
WATSON, Dr. RICHARD, Bishop of Llandaff, attacked by Wordsworth, 25.
WATT, JAMES, inventor and partner in Boulton and Watt; his retirement, 90, 91; on Scotsmen, 91, 398; on a bridge of Telford's, 94.
WAUCHOPE, Major-Gen., killed in Egypt, 1807, 201, 202.
WEBBE, SAMUEL, composer, 42.
WEDGWOOD, JOSIAH, friendship with Coleridge, 25.
WEDGWOOD, cameo wares, 54.
WELLESLEY, MARQUIS, early career, 99; Governor-General of India, 99; policy of opposition to French influence, 100 ff.; southern India, 100 ff.; overseas and northern India, 100 ff.; Oudh, 102 ff.; disputes with Directors, 103 ff.; trade, 105; Calcutta College, 106 ff.; life in Calcutta, 109, 110; offers to leave India in 1802, 111; relations with Nizam and Peshwa, 113; begins Maratha War, 1803, 119; refuses to restore French possessions at the peace, 120; exercises military authority as Captain-General, 122; makes peace with Sindhia and Raghuji Bhonsla, 128;

508 ENGLAND IN THE NINETEENTH CENTURY

is driven to war with Holkar, 1804, 129; averse from a hot weather campaign, 129; makes peace with Bharatpur, 132; final ultimatum to Sindhia, 133; his finances, 133, 134; relations with Ministers, 134; hostility to, in England, 134, 135; appreciation of, in India, 135, 136; possible member of Grenville's Cabinet, 196; refuses Foreign Office under Portland, 197; speech on Danish expedition, 219, 220; Ambassador to Spanish Junta, 1809, 284; accepts Foreign Office under Perceval, 297; desire to see Cabinet strengthened, 315, 316; willingness to abandon Orders in Council, 330; want of influence in Cabinet, 331; negotiations with Pinkney, 330, 331.

fondness for classical studies, 99; liberalism, 99; eloquence, 99; megalomania, 109, 110, 134; attitude towards religion and morals, 110, 364; not an imperial adventurer, 120, 133; his lengthy correspondence, 134; popularity and greatness, 135.

WELLESLEY, ARTHUR, birth and early career, 114, 115; negotiations with Sindhia, 1803, 118 ff.; campaign against Marathas, 126 ff.; concludes peace, 128; knighted, 134; designated to command expedition to Mexico, 1806, 168; Chief Secretary, 1807 198; fears for invasion of Ireland, 212; commands brigade in Danish expedition, 214, 215; suggests expedition to Peninsula, 1808, 238; campaign of 1808, 239 ff.; connection with Convention of Cintra, 242 ff.; proposals as regards tithes in Ireland, 266; advice on the War, 272; resigns Chief Secretaryship, 272; campaign of 1809, 272 ff.; raised to peerage under title WELLINGTON, q.v., 284.

a letter of his, 115; fortune made in India, 116; on character of Maratha warfare, 129; memo on Indian affairs, 135.

capacity for command in early years, 114; vitality, 114; diplomatic talent, 114; causes of his general good health, 115; fondness for sweeping statements, 120; popularity, in 1808, 242; conciliatory disposition, 283, 284; linguistic talent, 283.

mentioned, 368.

WELLESLEY, Lady CHARLOTTE, 416, 417; wife of

WELLESLEY, HENRY, 114; work at Bareilly, 103; a letter from Arthur Wellesley, 115; wife's elopement, 416, 417.

WELLESLEY, RICHARD, training of, 109.

WELLESLEYS, the family, 99, 114; unpopularity, 300; income from public money, 301.

WELLINGTON, Viscount, opinion of Munro, 370; criticized in England, 300, 301, 335; his difficulties, 331 ff.; plans the Lines, 331; campaign of 1810, 344 ff.; change of line of attack of his critics, 347; troubles with the Regency of Portugal, 348.

opinion of Moore, 257; patience, 331; change of character and loss of popularity, 333 ff.; readiness to repose confidence, 334; capacity for work, 334; proneness to exaggerate, 335; confidence in himself and aggressive spirit, 335, 336; good humour, 355, 356.

mentioned, 416. *Also see* WELLESLEY, ARTHUR.

WERNER, geologist, 80.

WESLEY, JOHN, his religious movement, 412.

WESLEY, SAMUEL, composer, 43.

WEST, BENJAMIN, President of Royal Academy, 49, 50.

WESTERN, "Squire", champion of agricultural interest, 233.

WEST INDIES, general account of, from 1806, 388, 389; concession regarding military service in, 154; Battle of San Domingo, 156, 157; damage to

INDEX 509

trade from French, 157; capture of Curaçoa, 158; slave trade, 162, 163; capture of Danish Islands, 1807, 223; depression in, 232, 233; inquiry, 262; captures in 1809, 269, 270; conquest in 1810, 323; trade, 323, 324.

WESTMINSTER, Burdett's election for, 200.
WESTMORLAND, the statesmen of, 34.
WESTMORLAND, Earl of, Lord Privy Seal, 197; mentioned, 294.
WHALE OIL, brought to Cape Colony, 388.
WHEAT, price in 1808, 233; in 1809, 268; trade with U.S., France, and Holland, 268.
WHIGS, Malthus a typical Whig, 61; Whig attitude towards republicanism, 164; Fox's Whiggism, 174; dependence of Whigs on Ireland, 184; Whig champions of the agricultural interest, 233; pessimism on the war, 261; Whigs in Scotland, 411, 412; mentioned, 177.
WHITBREAD, SAMUEL, M.P., his resolution against Melville mentioned, 411; in charge of the impeachment, 164; proposals for dealing with poverty, 183, 184, 207; in Walcheren debate, 299; on Perceval, 314; resolutions against Chatham, 301, 302.

his republicanism, 164; relations with the aristocratic Whigs, 164; unfitness for leadership of Opposition, 230; on Sheridan, 315.

mentioned, 234, 263, 265.
WHITELOCKE, Lieut.-Gen. Sir JOHN, commands forces in South America, 169; failure at Buenos Ayres, 203, 204; cashiered, 204.
WHITFIELD, his religious movement, 412.
WHITWORTH, Lord, mentioned, 160.
WILBERFORCE, WILLIAM, M.P., eulogy on Pitt, 147; re-elected for Yorkshire, 1807, 199; on York's case, 263.

Wordsworth's affinity with him, 35; remark on Bentham, 66; interest in Royal Institution, etc., 83, 85; and in Slave Trade Abolition, 162, 189.

WILKES, mentioned, 306.
WILKIE, DAVID, painter, 52; influence on Turner, 52.
WILKINS, WILLIAM, architect, 56.
WILLAUMEZ, Rear-Admiral commanding French cruising squadron, 1806, 157.
WILLCOCKS, JOSEPH, Canadian official and traitor, 394.
WILLOUGHBY, Capt. Sir NISBET, services in and off Mauritius, 378.
WILSON, painter, influence on Turner, 52.
WILSON, JOHN, British officer commanding Portuguese militia, 341.
WILSON, Sir ROBERT, Brig.-General in Peninsular War, 1809, 273, 282, 342; on Cape of Good Hope, 388.
WINDHAM, WILLIAM, relations with Pitt, 144; hatred of the Peace, 144, 145; rejoins Fox, 144 ff.; opposes honours to Pitt, 146, 147; becomes War Secretary, 1806, 149; military measures, 153, 154, 180, 205; system of recruiting, 205; signs for Fox, 173; his part in 1807 crisis, 187; prediction regarding Spaniards, 206; observation on the standard of living, 264, 265; attacks press, 305, 306; his death, 315.

hatred of reform, 145; a defender of slave trade, 199; unfitness for leadership of Opposition, 230; approval of amphibious warfare, 338.

mentioned, 174, 176.
WINE, in Ceylon, 142; in Cape Colony, 388; taxation of, in Canada, 390.
WOLLASTON, WILLIAM, scientist, 84.
WOLLSTONECRAFT, MARY, her Original Stories from Real Life, 24.

WOOL, trade to China in woollens, 141; imported from Spain and New South Wales, 382, 383; a Cape product, 388; legislation against gig mills, 418.
WOOLWICH ACADEMY, mentioned, 92.
WORCESTER, petition from, 311.
WORDSWORTH, DOROTHY, 25, 27; sister of
WORDSWORTH, WILLIAM; early career and works, 24 ff.; classicism, 24; as landscape-gardener, 57; admiration for Godwin, 59; utilitarianism, 64; Jeffrey on, 73; critic of Convention of Cintra, 244; mentioned, 38, 45, 176.
WRITERS, name for young servants of E.I. Company, 108; and for solicitors in Scotland, 408.
WYATT, THOMAS, architect, 55, 56.
WYNN, CHARLES, supporter of Grenvilles and friend of Southey, 33.

YARMOUTH, Lord, son and successor of Marquis of Hertford, 158; carries on peace negotiations with France, 1806, 159, 160; conversation with Lucchesini, 161.
YORK, FREDERICK, Duke of, Commander-in-Chief of the Army; one of his reforms mentioned, 114; an objection as regards Wellesley, 239; and as regards Graham, 247; Mrs. Clarke scandal, 261 ff.; resignation, 262; merits, 262; mentioned, 245.
YORKE, Hon. CHARLES, refuses to join Ministry, 1809, 296; becomes First Lord of the Admiralty, 1810, 304; motion to exclude strangers from House of Commons, 305; motion on privilege, 306.
YORKSHIRE, schools, 77; engineering works, 92, 93; Henry Lascelles, M.P., 146; 1807 election, 199.
YOUNG, ARTHUR, on landscape gardening, 57.
YOUNG, THOMAS, scientist, 84, 85.

ZAMAN SHAH, Afghan ruler, invades India, 101.
ZANTE, Ionian Island, captured from French in 1809, 285.
ZEALAND (Denmark), British expedition to, 1807, 214 ff.; questions as to its reoccupation, 217.
ZOOLOGY, state of, 86.

For Product Safety Concerns and Information please contact our EU representative GPSR@taylorandfrancis.com
Taylor & Francis Verlag GmbH, Kaufingerstraße 24, 80331 München, Germany

www.ingramcontent.com/pod-product-compliance
Lightning Source LLC
Chambersburg PA
CBHW052136300426
44115CB00011B/1402